CALIFORNIA

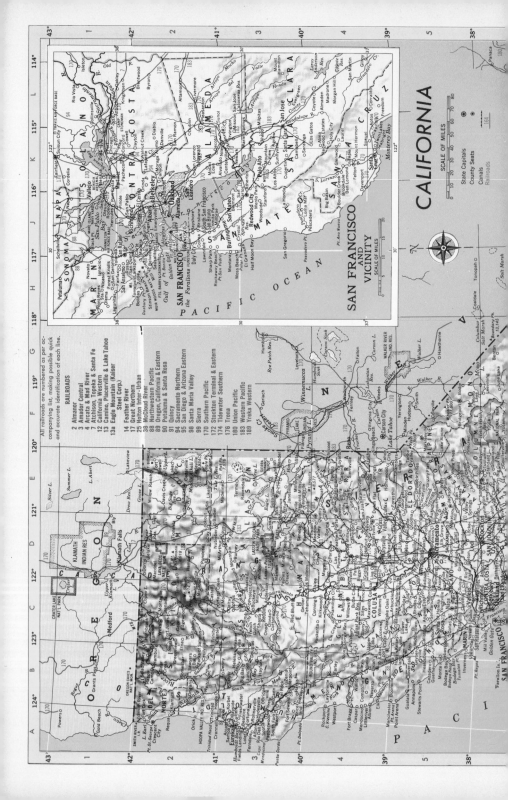

CALIFORNIA

SCALE OF MILES

0 10 20 30 40 50 60 70 80

⊛ State Capitals
◉ County Seats
 Canals
164 Railroads

SAN FRANCISCO AND VICINITY

SCALE OF MILES

RAILROADS

All railroads are numbered as per accompanying list, making possible quick and accurate identification of each line.

2 Almanor
3 Amador Central
4 Arcata & Mad River
7 Atchison, Topeka & Santa Fe
12 California Western
13 Camino, Placerville & Lake Tahoe
13a Eagle Mountain (Kaiser Steel Corp.)
14 Feather River
17 Great Northern
25 Holton Inter-Urban
38 McCloud River
88 Northwestern Pacific
89 Oregon, California & Eastern
90 Petaluma & Santa Rosa
91 Quincy
94 Sacramento Northern
95 San Diego & Arizona Eastern
98 Santa Maria Valley
99 Sierra
170 Southern Pacific
172 Stockton Terminal & Eastern
174 Tidewater Southern
176 Trona
180 Union Pacific
183 Western Pacific
189 Yreka Western

First Printing ....August, 1953
Second Printing ....May, 1954
Third Printing ....June, 1955
Fourth Printing ....June, 1957
Fifth Printing ......December, 1958
Sixth Printing ....January, 1960
Seventh Printing .....January, 1961
Eighth Printing ....September, 1961
Ninth Printing ....April, 1963
Tenth Printing .....September, 1964

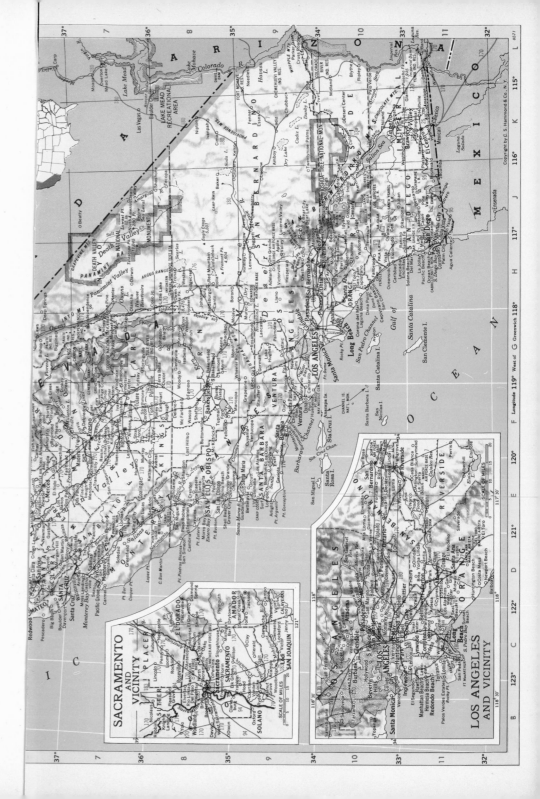

CALIFORNIA

by

John Walton Caughey

Professor of American History
University of California
at Los Angeles

SECOND EDITION

PRENTICE-HALL, INC.

Englewood Cliffs, N. J.

TO
LaRee

PREFACE

CALIFORNIA BEGAN with a static and provincial Indian society. Upon this base, a handful of Spaniards, using a formula worked out on older frontiers, erected an outpost of empire. A short Mexican period, self-consciously transitional, led up to annexation to the United States. Then the forty-niners brought the sleepy province abruptly to life and began a rapid transformation, which their successors continued both by extension and by innovation. Finally, in the modern period, this crescendo reached full fortissimo. Change thus appears to be the dominant note in the state's experience, yet continuities are also strong, as one may observe by comparing the areas of Spanish settlement and of modern population concentration.

I have tried to make this book an accurate reflection of California's past. In allotting space to the several epochs, I have kept in mind proportionate significance, with a consequently more generous treatment of recent decades. Topical balance seemed to me equally important, and social and intellectual elements have been incorporated into the more familiar political and economic narrative. Attention has been accorded to relationships with Spain's empire, the frontier West, the American nation, and the world at large. I also felt under obligation to venture into the rather neglected field of historical bibliography and to offer an extended appraisal of the truly massive array of published materials on this state's history. Throughout, by selection and by forthright statement, I have sought to interpret the processes of California's development and thus make the present understandable. In the process I hope that I have not unduly beclouded the glamor and the human interest with which the original record abounds.

In the course of somewhat less than a lifetime devoted to the study of California I have benefited from the help of a host of persons.

vii

Members of my family have endured impositions. Undergraduate and graduate students have joined me in ferreting and in philosophizing. Collectors of Californiana have assembled the documentation on which my conclusions ultimately rest. Writers by the thousand, from early participants in the making of California history to contemporary zealots in research, have committed to paper their knowledge and their opinions on the myriad phases of my topic. To them all I express indebtedness.

JOHN WALTON CAUGHEY

LOS ANGELES, MAY, 1940

In the interval since the first appearance of this book, California has had tumultuous experiences and another great wave of rapid growth. In new chapters I have taken stock of these developments. In the light of what I have learned since 1940 I have reconsidered the earlier chapters and expanded several of them. The bibliographical essay is revised to take account of works published since 1940, and some of the maps and most of the illustrations are new.

In addition to the institutions credited, I am indebted for pictures or maps to Edward Weston, Ansel Adams, Dave Packwood, John W. Gunter, and W. W. Robinson, and to Houghton Mifflin Company for permission to reproduce two of the Ansel Adams pictures. Dr. John E. Baur gave expert assistance in the making of the index. My wife lent a hand at every stage except the typing and made all the difficult decisions. Any responsibilities not assumed by these good friends devolve upon me.

J. W. C.

LOS ANGELES, JULY, 1953

CONTENTS

MAPS AND ILLUSTRATIONS

MAPS

ILLUSTRATIONS

CALIFORNIA

CALIFORNIA'S RAPID RISE

IN 1849 CALIFORNIA suddenly emerged from comparative obscurity to be the cynosure of world-wide attention. Discovery of gold could not have come at a more opportune time. The news reached the East on the heels of the announcement of American acquisition of the province. It caught the United States on the rebound from the Mexican War and when the American frontier was piling up against the baffling subhumid and treeless Great Plains. Europe also was still in ferment after the revolutions of 1848. Thus it is entirely understandable that gold seekers poured into California from every state in the Union and from practically every foreign nation. Those who could not join the trek took a lively interest in the experiences of the Argonauts, an interest that still persists.

The fashion has been, however, to insist that beyond this golden beginning California's renown rests on the artificial basis of extravagant advertising and publicity-seeking. Boosting California has been an obsession of many, notably José Antonio Carrillo, Lansford W. Hastings, and Charles F. Lummis. The same tendency has been institutionalized by the Chambers of Commerce, the All Year Club, and Californians Incorporated. A few decades ago the railroads were doughty publicists, largely for the sake of increasing sales of railroad lands; and in the drive to create a national market for its Sunkist oranges, the California Fruit Growers Association loosed a similar flood of propaganda. Writers from Mark Twain and Bret Harte to Jack London and Harold Bell Wright have given California literary prominence. Striking individuals such as John C. Frémont, Joaquin Miller, Hiram Johnson, and Will Rogers have lent much of their personal fame to the state. The movies, the radio, the expositions, and

1

the constant stream of tourists spread California's name abroad. Most effective of all has been the spontaneous enthusiasm of visitors and residents, praising, in books, magazine articles, and newspapers, in personal letters and by word of mouth, the climate, the resources, and the opportunities which California affords.

Even the most cursory examination of California's history reveals abundant reason for this widespread interest. In the first place, California has a long history. More than four centuries have passed since the Spaniards, exactly fifty years after the discovery of America, first set foot on California soil. Even earlier the conquistadores had drawn upon one of their favorite romantic novels for the name and had applied it to the coast that beckoned them northwestward. None of the "original thirteen" states on the Atlantic seaboard had yet been christened. For almost a century longer Massachusetts was to remain merely an Indian word, and the Virgin Queen, in whose honor the Old Dominion was to be named, was not yet crowned. In fact, of the forty-eight states Florida is the only one whose name came into accepted usage earlier.

In the second place, California's history features variety and sharp contrast. Until the latter part of the eighteenth century Indians were the unchallenged occupants of the region. The few earlier visits by Spanish explorers left the Indian pattern of life totally unmodified. Moreover, the Indians of California were in many respects as primitive and backward a people as could be found anywhere on the face of the globe. They had no system of writing, knew nothing of metals, and had only the most rudimentary social organization, government, and military methods. Housed in miserable huts, nearly naked, unversed in the arts of planting and cultivating, and only moderately skilled as hunters, they lived in extreme simplicity. An early observer described them as "among the most unhappy people in all the world." Only because they had the human form could he believe that they belonged to mankind.

Such was the scene upon which the Spaniards arrived in 1769, at a time when the English colonists on the Atlantic Coast were on the verge of the Revolutionary War. With their missions the Spaniards introduced many elements of European civilization and brought about a partial transformation of the manner of life along the coastal fringe of the province. They made a slender beginning in gardening and horticulture and a feebler start in field cultivation, but cattle raising came to be the real economy. These fundamental pastoral habits carried over on an even larger scale into the period of the ranchos.

In character the Spanish and Mexican periods are so far removed from the bustling present that they are reminiscent of the very remote past. The Franciscan missions seem to belong to the Middle Ages. The land system was distinctly feudal and the ranchos were essentially medieval manors. In its arcadian simplicity, pastoral California harked back to the very dawn of history, before the intrusion of such disturbing influences as industry, commerce, or militarism. There is an Old World charm about these early days, in retrospect most appealing. It is no less than startling that this leisurely pattern of life in the days of the dons persisted until hardly more than a century ago.

Then ensued American immigration and American acquisition. Discovery of gold set in motion a train of forces which quickly altered the northern part of the state. Southern California continued to be predominantly pastoral for almost a generation longer, but with the building of the transcontinental railroads, the rise of the new agriculture centered around the orange, and the striking of oil, rapid transformation began. Today California is one of the ranking states of the Union in population, finance, agriculture, mining, commerce, industry, and cultural leadership. Practically the entire story of its growth is crowded into the years since 1849, and for southern California in particular the change has come so suddenly that individuals still living have witnessed the development practically in its entirety.

Growth so spectacular strongly suggests uniqueness. Californians have been quick to recognize and to capitalize this uniqueness; witness the fact that "unusual" is the most overworked word in their vocabulary. In large degree the judgment is correct. California's climatic conditions are not duplicated in any other state, nor is the range of her natural flora and fauna. Her agricultural products range from prosaic wheat and cotton to exotic avocados and dates. In industry there are also distinctive elements, notably motion picture production. Los Angeles, to cite another example, is one of the few large cities situated in a subhumid environment. The heroic measures employed to supply this metropolis with water and electric power challenge the imagination. Extraordinary, too, was the manufacture of a harbor at San Pedro.

Comment on the unusual may, however, be carried to such an ex-

treme that the impression is conveyed that California has no kinship
with the rest of the nation or even with her sister states in the West
and that her development has taken place, so to speak, in a vacuum.
Historically, as the subsequent chapters of this volume should make
clear, such an interpretation is most unsound. California was discovered in the course of a broad investigation of New World geography which resulted in contemporaneous exploration of Florida and
New Mexico, the valleys of the Amazon and the Plata, Chile, and the
Philippine Islands. She was colonized in a continent-wide strengthening of Spain's northern frontier in America, and the institutions,
such as the mission system, which the Spaniards installed were characteristic of Spanish America as a whole.

The tie-up with the North Pacific area is more often overlooked.
Yet the name California once applied to the entire coast from the tip
of Lower California to Alaska. It is a familiar fact that Spanish
occupation came in direct response to reports of foreign activities
farther north. California was a base for Spanish voyages to Nootka
and beyond, and in turn, with the establishment of Fort Ross, was
brought within the sphere of Russia's active interest. It is equally
significant that the province's first visitors from the United States were
the Yankee otter hunters sailing in the wake of Cook and Gray and
Kendrick, who had inaugurated international trade rivalry in the
North Pacific. Similarly, the British advance across Canada touched
the northern part of the province and embraced plans for commercial and perhaps political absorption.

In the American period likewise, California development has been
part and parcel of a larger movement. In Texas, Oregon, and Utah,
infiltration of pioneer settlers preceded annexation by the United
States. Gold rushes inaugurated settlement of most of the Rocky
Mountain West. A Spanish-styled cattle industry spread from Texas
as well as from California over the grasslands of the semi-arid West.
Transcontinental railroads to Oregon, Washington, British Columbia,
southern California, and Sonora followed construction of the Union
Pacific-Central Pacific. Nor have more recent phenomena, such as
great increase in population, reclamation of arid and semi-arid lands,
and expansion and diversification of industry, been confined to California.

One is led to conclude, therefore, that California's peculiarities are
overshadowed by likenesses, first to the other provinces of the northern

Spanish borderlands, then to the several Pacific Coast communities that were affected by the international contest for the North Pacific, and finally to all the states carried forward on the flood of the American westward movement.   But in the same breath one must add that ever since 1849 California has been not merely representative but the leading representative of the West.   Statistics of population, wealth, and production reveal the margin by which California has outdistanced the other western states.   They do not reveal, however, the extent to which California's leadership has been dynamic and a stimulant for the entire West.   An example or two will suffice.   Veterans of '49 were the major element in the rush to the Fraser Valley a decade later.   Nevada mining was initiated by California prospectors and was carried on principally by California labor and capital.   The railroads that were built to bind California to the Union led quickly to rapid settlement of the Great Plains and the Rocky Mountain region.   Boulder Dam became a reality because of the active demands of metropolitan southern California, but other southwestern states share in the benefits.

One of the familiar assertions about California—sometimes made in the present tense and sometimes in the past—is that a great deal of history has been made in the state.   In terms of the definition of history as "past politics" or in terms of history as a record of wars and rumors of wars, this assertion has little meaning.   But in terms of the more modern and commonplace definition of history as pertaining to change, not in a restricted compartment of life but in all the spheres of human activity, it becomes obvious that California has indeed had much history.   Changes in status from Indian realm to Spanish colony, Mexican province, and American state, and changes in economy from concentration on cattle raising to production of gold, wheat, oranges, oil, and motion pictures, have been far-reaching in extent and kaleidoscopic in quickness.   The color and glamor that so many see in this history may be attributed largely to the spectacular variety of actors, events, and experiences, and the rapid tempo of change unquestionably helps to capture attention.   But the importance of California history lies not so much in its colorful variety or its feverish pace as in the enduring consequences of these changes as felt by succeeding generations of Californians, by their neighbors in the West, and to an appreciable degree by the world at large.

1

THE LAND AND ITS
INFLUENCE

IN THE STUDY of any region's history the geographical approach is advisable. For California it is a necessity. The successive cultures that have existed in this area have been closely integrated with land and climate. Also, California's geographic conditions are so different from those of the eastern and midwestern parts of the United States that most Americans are at a loss to understand them. Many Californians, schooled in traditional political geography, find their state equally baffling.

Topography

Whereas the East and Midwest are characterized by uniformity of elevation, by uniform, nonseasonal precipitation, and by temperature variation on a strictly latitudinal basis, California has varied relief, including the lowest and highest elevations in the United States, seasonal rains, and temperatures of which latitude is the least determining factor. On one side of the continent the way to escape the rigors of winter is to go south, but in California oranges ripen several weeks earlier at Oroville in the north than at Riverside, 400 miles farther south.

California topography is dominated by its mountains, chief of which is the mighty Sierra Nevada, a continuous rampart over 400 miles long, with more than fifty peaks towering above 13,000 feet, including the loftiest in the United States, Mt. Whitney (14,496). Passes over this eastern bulwark of the state are at elevations of

7,000 to 10,000 feet, and the approaches are tortuous and difficult. The first explorers, pioneer settlers, and forty-niners found the Sierra their most serious barrier. So did the builders of the Central Pacific Railroad, and so do modern highway engineers and even the still more modern air lines.

From a simple relief map it would appear that the Cascades are the northern continuation of the Sierra. But whereas the Sierra was created by the raising of a great block of the earth's crust, with faults or slips at the eastern edge and tilting toward the west, the Cascades were volcanic in origin. Geologically these mountains are more recent than the Sierra and have a very different aspect. Mt. Shasta has built itself up to 14,161 feet and because it is not surrounded by other towering peaks it is more imposing than Mt. Whitney. Mt. Lassen was an active volcano as recently as 1914.

The northwestern corner of the state is a jumble of nonvolcanic mountains known as the Klamath. Like the Cascades, these mountains extend on into Oregon; like the Sierra Nevada, they contain important mineral deposits. Several peaks approach 10,000 feet in elevation.

The Coast Ranges continue southward from the Klamath Mountains. Set at a slight southeastward angle to the coast line, these parallel ranges are interspersed with a series of valleys opening northwestward to the ocean. In the vicinity of San Francisco the Coast Mountains have an altitude of no more than 3,000 to 4,000 feet. But in the Eel River area at the north they reach 7,000 and 8,000 feet. The rugged Santa Lucia Range crowding the coast west of the Salinas Valley attains about the same elevation, and Mt. Pinos farther south is elevated 9,214 feet.

From Mt. Pinos the Tehachapis extend east and northeast to connect with the Sierra Nevada and enclose the southern end of the great Central Valley. Stretching a little south of east from Mt. Pinos is the main mountain axis of southern California, culminating in the San Gabriel and San Bernardino Mountains. A few miles to the south of the San Bernardinos is San Jacinto, northern outpost of the Peninsula Range, which continues down into Lower California. Not so high as the Sierra Nevada, it is very similar in formation. The eastern slope is abrupt, but many small valleys open out to the coast along the more gentle western incline.

These mountain masses occupy a good half of the surface area of the state. The northern ones have important lumbering resources, and the Klamaths and the Sierra Nevada contain rich mineral deposits. But from the standpoint of directly supporting a large population the mountain areas must be written off as a loss. The Volcanic Plateau in the northeastern corner of the state is utilized primarily as grazing land and consequently has but a scanty population. Pressing against the Sierra on the east and extending down the eastern boundary of the state almost to Yuma is a wasteland known as the Mojave Desert. This salient of the Great Basin juts westward in the angle between the Tehachapis and the San Gabriel-San Bernardinos to within fifty miles of the Pacific.

Sprinkled through this desert are irregular mountain clumps which, particularly in the north, attain respectable elevations. Telescope Peak in the Panamints has an elevation of 11,045 feet, and White Mountain farther north, 14,225 feet. Most of the mountains, however, are not high enough to get much more rainfall than the floor of the desert. Consequently, streams are lacking which might be impounded for irrigation purposes. The water of Owens River, which otherwise would permit agriculture in the valley of that name, has been diverted through a 240-mile aqueduct to Los Angeles. The next most promising supply of water is in the Mojave River, which in flood reaches Soda Lake but ordinarily disappears into the sand much earlier in its course. Settlements are scattered through this sagebrush and creosote-bush waste, engaged mostly in mining precious and nonprecious minerals and in serving the transportation lines that crisscross the desert.

From the remaining portions of the state's surface several additional desolate areas might be subtracted. Only a fraction of the Colorado Desert has been brought under irrigation and occupation. The Carrisa Plain, adjacent to the southwestern part of the great Central Valley, is so arid that it is useful only for grazing. The same applies to the upper Salinas and to much of the San Joaquin Valley, while Eel River Valley, second largest along the coast, has too much rainfall for agriculture to flourish.

Perhaps 10 or 15 per cent of the state is left to accommodate and support something like 90 per cent of the population. The arid expanses contribute little, but the mountains have such a profound effect upon the climate that they are an immeasurable asset to the valley-dwelling Californians.

These principal valleys should be enumerated. Most prominent on the map is the great Central Valley of the Sacramento and the San Joaquin. Some 400 miles long and 40 miles wide, it is the largest agricultural area west of the Rockies. Between the Coast Ranges are numerous valleys, most of them longitudinal. Reading from north to south, they are: the Napa-Livermore; the Santa Clara-Santa Rosa, its central portion drowned in San Francisco Bay; the Salinas; the San Luis; the Santa María; the Santa Ynez; and the narrow Santa Clara of the south. Southern California has a broader valley, the Los Angeles Plain, its eastern part known as the San Bernardino Valley, with numerous tributary valleys, such as the San Fernando, the Perris, and the Elsinore. On the other side of the Peninsula Range lie the Imperial and Coachella valleys. Owens Valley, nestled against the eastern base of the Sierra Nevada, was once a potential agricultural site, but, as has been intimated, it is now reverting to sagebrush.

Climate

California's most remarkable geographic feature is unquestionably its climate or, to put it more accurately, its climates. The basic determining factor is the broad Pacific Ocean lying off the 800-mile shore line. Implementing the Pacific in its effect upon climate are the prevailing westerlies, which come in moisture-laden and equable in temperature throughout the year.

Their summer influence is particularly felt along the coast and in the valleys most accessible to the coast. Throughout the summer these areas are bathed almost nightly with what are called velo clouds. These sometimes come in as a low fog, but usually as a high fog which overcasts the sky until dispelled by the sun toward noon. The velo clouds perform a double service, first, by moderating summer heat, and second, by retarding evaporation. They reach farthest inland in southern California but are also characteristic of the lower Salinas Valley, the San Francisco region, and the Sacramento-San Joaquin Delta.

Winter winds come from the same general direction. They are accompanied, however, by a series of cyclonic storms, whirling counterclockwise around low-pressure centers. These storms follow a fairly regular course from the North Pacific to the coast and eastward across the continent. Northern and central California lie more directly in their path than does the southern part of the state. The southerly decrease in storm frequency is reflected in the annual rainfall averages along the coast: forty inches at Eureka, twenty-two and a half at San Francisco, twenty at Monterey, fifteen at Los Angeles, and ten at San Diego. Since the storms are cyclonic, the wind direction at a given point changes as the low-pressure center moves eastward. First the wind blows from the south and southwest, then from the north. It is the south and southwest wind that brings the rain; the north wind that follows is essentially a cold and dry land wind.

Except for differences in storm frequency the winds sweeping in from the Pacific are pretty much the same all up and down California. That their actual effects are so diverse is due primarily to the varied relief. Wherever mountain ranges are lifted high enough they intercept the moisture which these winds bring. The slopes exposed to the wind get heavy rainfall or, at higher elevations, heavy snowfall; on the lee side of the mountains there is hardly any precipitation, vegetation is scantier, there is no phenomenon comparable to the coastal velo cloud, and the parching rays of the sun have full access.

To this general rule there are apparent exceptions, but upon more careful analysis they are understandable. Thus the two largest coastal valleys are protected on the west by mile-high mountain ranges; yet the upper Salinas Valley has very light rainfall, while the Eel River Valley is heavily watered. The explanation is that on its eastern side the latter valley has a still higher mountain rampart that intercepts the rain clouds.

Again it may seem paradoxical that the southern half of the Sierra Nevada, though greater in elevation, has a lighter snowfall than the northern Sierra. It is the northern part, however, which lies more open to the southwest winds of the cyclonic storms, and these are the principal bearers of precipitation. The same factor accounts for the heavy rainfall in the upper Sacramento Valley as contrasted with the inadequate watering of the southern end of the great Central Valley. Through the central gap in the Coast Ranges the rain-bearing south and southwest winds have open access to the northern interior. The same winds reach the upper San Joaquin only after passing over the southern Coast Ranges.

Thus it happens that the Sacramento Valley has a surplus of water, periodically in evidence as a flood menace, while the San Joaquin

Valley has to depend upon irrigation and could use even more water than its eastern mountain reservoirs can supply. The Central Valley project attacks this problem. With power generated at Shasta Dam, some of this surplus northern water is pumped into the lower San Joaquin Valley. Meanwhile, Friant Dam impounds for use on the highly fertile but subhumid lands of the upper part of the San Joaquin Valley most of the water once used in irrigation in the lower valley. With its other ramifications of flood control and prevention of salt water encroachment, the Central Valley project is an engineering undertaking of greater magnitude than any thus far completed in California. The transformation that it will make possible is not so sharp a contrast, however, as that achieved earlier by the comparatively simple feat of diverting water from the Colorado River onto the desert floors of Imperial and Coachella valleys.

Elevation exerts another influence of tremendous significance. It not only plays an essential role in determining precipitation, but it also goes far toward governing the length of the growing season. Thus the Volcanic Plateau in the northeast, elevated 3,000 to 5,000 feet, is ruled out for much else than stock raising, and elevation sets the limit beyond which cultivation of mountain valleys and slopes is not practicable.

A cross-state trip from Monterey to Death Valley would illustrate the wide range of California climates. At Monterey summer and winter are differentiated chiefly in that one presents fog and the other rain. Salinas, a few miles to the east, is the center of a rich garden belt, the so-called Salad Bowl. The Coast Ranges at this latitude are low, Pacheco Pass being at an elevation of only 1,387 feet, but they account for the semi-arid conditions in the San Joaquin Valley, where the summers are very hot and dry and the winters frosty. Through broad grazing lands the highway descends to Fresno in the heart of the grape, raisin, peach, apricot, and melon country. On toward the east one enters the Sierra foothills, where the hardier deciduous fruit trees flourish. As the trail ascends, rainfall increases and temperature drops, until in the vicinity of Mt. Whitney there are perpetual snow and arctic winters.

Across the divide, one drops abruptly into Owens Valley, which despite its elevation of 4,000 feet is a desert landscape. The lofty Inyo-White Mountain Range, next encountered, is shut off from moisture-bearing winds by the still higher Sierra, and aridity increases as one proceeds across Panamint Valley and the Panamint Range. The climax is reached in Death Valley, its lowest point 276 feet below sea level. A temperature of 134 degrees Fahrenheit is on record for the valley, one of the highest officially recorded anywhere in the world.

A shorter journey inland from Los Angeles or San Diego to the Imperial Valley would likewise run the whole gamut of climates from subtropical to arctic and from forty or more inches of rainfall a year to less than two. The wide range of land utilization that these climates make possible is the key to much of California's remarkable agricultural development. In passing, it might be remarked that several of the world's outstanding civilizations—for example, the Egyptian, the Mayan-Aztec, and the Incan—also were cradled in regions where subtropical and temperate conditions existed in close proximity.

Communications

Communications within California are somewhat easier than its mountainous topography would suggest. Although the successive Coast Ranges rise immediately from the ocean, leaving no coastal plain for continuous north-south travel, the long valleys between the ranges provide a fairly open route from Los Angeles to San Francisco. Here ran the Camino Real, and more recently the Southern Pacific Railroad's Coast Route and the so-called Coast Highway. Construction of a highway along the west side of the Santa Lucias proved far more difficult, and such a route was not opened until 1937. The Central Valley affords an open avenue for north-south traffic. A highway, now more heavily traveled than the Coast Route, climbs over Tejón Pass to Los Angeles, and the railroads reach southern California by a more circuitous route across Tehachapi Pass and the Mojave Desert.

In the matter of accessibility from the east, southern California has an advantage over the central part of the state. The Sierra passes are difficult of approach and at elevations of 7,000 to 10,000 feet. From the Los Angeles Plain there are two gateways: Cajón Pass (elevation 3,823 feet) opening northeastward to the Mojave Desert and Needles, and San Gorgonio Pass (2,500 feet) opening southeastward to the Colorado crossings at Yuma and Blythe. San Gorgonio is a broad gap approached by easy gradients, but because its eastern approach was so poorly supplied with water, this pass was almost totally neglected until the day of railroads, automobiles, and trucks.

In her 800-mile shore line California can boast only three good natural harbors. Two of these, Humboldt Bay in the north and San Diego in the south, are so hemmed in that they serve only a very limited hinterland. The third, San Francisco Bay, is one of the most magnificent harbors in the world. It was formed by the subsidence of what was once the lower course of the combined Sacramento and San Joaquin rivers. The result is a sheltered bay almost fifty miles in length, on which are located the thriving ports of San Francisco and Oakland and the Mare Island navy yard at Vallejo. Dredging has opened a deep-water channel that enables large ocean-going vessels to reach Stockton, and plans are afoot to do the same for Sacramento. In terms of railway and automobile traffic the great bay has hampered San Francisco's development, leading at length to the building of the Bay Bridge and the Golden Gate span.

For the southern metropolis, Los Angeles, it was the other shoe that pinched. Her location in the midst of the broad Los Angeles Plain and the convenient passes through the surrounding mountains assured easy communications by land, but the adjacent coast provided no natural harbor, and engineers had to be called in to build one at San Pedro.

Earthquakes and Floods

When flaws are picked in the California environment, first place is usually given to the earthquake hazard. One of the initial entries in the history of the Spanish colony in California is the record of an earthquake. Commemorating the experience, Portolá named the river where he was camped Santa Ana de los Temblores. In usage the name was shortened to Santa Ana, and out of deference to local feelings the appendage has not been revived. Earthquakes, however, have gone right on. Several of considerable severity are on record, for example, one in 1812 which wrecked the Mission San Juan Capistrano, one in Owens Valley in 1870, the San Francisco quake of 1906, one at Santa Barbara in 1925, one at Long Beach in 1933, and one at Tehachapi in 1952.

At the present stage of scientific attainment, earthquakes are not predictable as to exact time, place, or severity. Geological formations do make clear that California will experience additional shocks in the future. The likelihood of a strong disturbance is less than for Japan, Turkey, Chile, or Guatemala but considerably greater than for western Europe, which had a damaging quake in 1938, or for the Mississippi Valley, which was sharply shaken in 1812.

For a time Californians sought to cure this defect in their environment by wishful thinking. Thus it came to be de rigueur to mention the San Francisco disaster as "the Fire." True enough, the flames did the principal damage, but they got out of control because the earthquake had broken the water lines and rendered the fire fighters ineffective. In rebuilding the city, large cisterns were constructed in the business district to guard against another such contingency. Even so, it was something more than the kick of Mrs. O'Leary's cow that had started the conflagration. Similarly it used to be most unpopular to urge the enforcement of stricter building codes that would take into account the earthquake hazard. Recently, a saner attitude has prevailed. Fortunately it is relatively easy to construct earthquake-resistant buildings. Wooden frame buildings, if well constructed and securely anchored to their foundations, stand up very well; so do steel frame structures, such as modern skyscrapers and buildings of reinforced concrete. Ordinary masonry construction is unwise, especially for public buildings with large rooms, but if tied together with steel or even by strong cross walls, masonry buildings withstand a considerable shock.

Earthquakes are spectacular, yet statistics could be introduced to show that they are far less dangerous to life and property than floods, tornadoes, influenza, and automobiles. In proportion to the large number of persons massed in close proximity to the epicenter of the 1933 earthquake, the number of fatalities was exceedingly small. It is estimated, too, that at least five-sixths of the property damage could have been avoided by proper construction of houses and public buildings. Undoubtedly such precautions would also have reduced the toll of lives.

Exposure to flood sounds much more prosaic. Yet it is a factor with which California has to reckon. Sacramento Valley floods have been mentioned. The most famous ones occurred in the days of '49, when Sacramento was a new city; but when heavy rains augment the run-off from melting snow on the mountains, the danger is repeated. Imperial Valley was threatened with complete inundation when the Colorado River broke out of its banks in 1906.   One of the functions of Boulder Dam is to preclude the possibility of another such disaster.

Semi-arid southern California probably has the most serious flood problem.   The mountains which rise abruptly from the Los Angeles Plain have only a chaparral or elfin forest cover.   Consequently, when heavy rains occur, the run-off is very rapid and contains great quantities of rock debris.   If any area has been burned over, the rapidity of the run-off and the amount of debris carried are increased. Watercourses are soon choked with boulders and gravel, and the waters run riot over the adjacent lowlands.   Thus a region which is normally devoid of flowing streams occasionally has flooded streets, washed-out bridges, buildings floated away, and disrupted communications.   Los Angeles County has a good-sized budget for flood control.   Prevention of flood damage, however, has been made needlessly difficult by frequent unwise selection of building sites.   Houses have been set at the mouths of canyons or in the very channels through which flood waters must run off.   As in the matter of builders disregarding the earthquake hazard, it is a case of eastern-minded persons failing to make the proper adjustment to a new environment.

Pseudogeography

Some curious notions have circulated concerning California's geography.   One is the idea that the climate is changing.   Here, of course, California has no monopoly.   It is an idea that arises naturally out of the hazy recollections of old timers and flourishes in the absence of accumulated weather reports—and often in spite of such records.   Suffice it to say that the weather bureau denies that an appreciable change has taken place.

Another curious notion was the theory, of wide acceptance after the 1906 earthquake, that a more violent temblor had opened the Golden Gate shortly before Portolá's arrival in 1769.   It is perplexing that Drake, Cermeño, Vizcaíno, and the Manila galleons came as close to the Gate as they did without discovering that the great bay lay just inside.   Nonmiraculous explanations, however, are not lacking.   And the archaeological evidence in the shell mounds on the bay is conclusive proof that the shore line had been approximately stationary for centuries.

It is also often said that southern California's climate is stultifying to the progress of civilization.   Final proof on this point will not be forthcoming in this generation or the next.   The inclination of a newcomer from a colder clime to loll on the beach is not conclusive evidence.   The material development of the region and the athletic attainments of its youngsters would seem to speak well for the climate. In terms of cultural progress, furthermore, a most hopeful sign is that life and activity are prolonged beyond the normal span.   This is especially encouraging since man's later years seem to be the more productive in creative work and thinking.

Historical Geography

The foregoing description is designed to emphasize the fundamentals of the California scene.   It omits many interesting details that might find place in a volume entirely devoted to the subject.   It also leaves out of consideration certain facts of historical geography that are of profound significance.

One of these facts has to do with California's isolation.   Today this isolation has been effectively broken down by radio and television, telephone and telegraph, by airlines, highways, and railroads, by steamships plying the Pacific and shuttling through the Panama Canal.   Yet California is still remote enough from the centers of world population that getting her wares to market is costly.   For most American tourists, transportation to California is more expensive than to Florida.   Historically, the isolation was much more pronounced.   The Spaniards were a long time in occupying the province because of the headwinds encountered along the coast and because of the desolate and forbidding territory which intervened between their frontier and California.   For Spain and Mexico the chief drawback to development of the province was the difficulty of maintaining regular contact with it by land or sea.

With the transfer of the province to the United States, the problem was changed but made little easier.   Instead of a connection with Mexico City, the aim came to be a maritime link with New York and New Orleans or overland communications with Missouri.   By the combined efforts of government and private initiative the modern transportation systems were created, but only after heroic struggles which constitute the real epic of the West.

Similarly, with regard to California's abundant resources it is necessary to point out that many of them were of little or no value until very recently. Petroleum and hydroelectric power, for example, acquired value only when the necessary technological advances had been made. Other resources were of only local importance until transportation was made available to get them to a wider market. Imperial Valley's crops would be worth little except for the railroads and refrigeration. It is worth noting that in the prerailroad days the Americans in California were producing wheat and beef in the conventional midwestern fashion. The new agriculture had to wait for better transportation.

These considerations remove some of the sting from criticisms of the Spaniards and Mexicans for not achieving a more rapid development of California. In cowhides and tallow they did develop marketable commodities that represented a great improvement over the Indian period, when the acorn was the most prized resource. After the colony was set on its feet the Spaniards derived a comfortable living from it. Since they confined themselves to the coastal fringe of the province, it was their bad luck not to discover the great treasure of gold, which, after all, was the cornerstone of American development of California. From it stemmed the first American agriculture, then the railroads, which in turn led to the new agriculture and the engineering achievements in irrigation, harbor improvements, and industrialization. But take away these elements and one can more readily understand why the Spaniards esteemed the province so lightly and why Portolá was half inclined to leave it to the Russians.

A Versatile Environment

In retrospect, the conspicuous fact about California's environment appears to be its versatility. Since the days of the Pharaohs, Egyptian agriculture has featured the small grains; rice culture in southern China has remained essentially unmodified since long before Confucius; Spain has produced olive oil since time immemorial; and England was exporting wool at the dawn of its history. California, in the short space of two centuries, has evolved from an economy focused on the acorn, through a period of hides and tallow and another of gold and wheat, to the present complex scene with its emphasis on horticulture and industry and urban life. To these widely divergent cultures the environment has proved readily adaptable. Thus does history substantiate current observation that California's ability to produce is constrained only by the limits of man's ingenuity.

2

THE INDIANS

THE POOR CALIFORNIA INDIAN has almost never had a good word said for him. The first Spanish visitors employed no adjectives more complimentary than "peaceful" and "numerous." Later, when the Spanish colony was planted, the governors repeatedly characterized the natives as very sorry specimens, and the Franciscans, despite their compassion, entered practically the same judgment.

In the course of early overland migration from the United States, the uncomplimentary term "Digger Indians" was imported from the region of Great Salt Lake and the Humboldt Valley and applied indiscriminately to the California tribes. In the Great Basin area the name had not been entirely fitting; for the Californians it was a complete misnomer, except that it gave adequate expression to the contempt felt by the majority of Anglo-Americans. Modern anthropologists, while admitting that native attainments were meager, protest the term as inaccurate, for the Californians were root grubbers only incidentally. Nowadays the expression is heard less often, yet it is so euphonious and so picturesque that it will not down. It is used without qualification in certain recent publications on California.

Culture Deficiencies

In all candor it must be admitted that the California Indians were backward. They shared, of course, the material deficiencies of the New World as contrasted with the Old. They knew nothing of gunpowder, iron and steel, the wheel, the plow, domesticated animals other than the dog, wheat, barley, and the other small grains. They had no system of writing, much less a printing press. They had no

18

*The Coast
near
Point Lobos*

Edward Weston

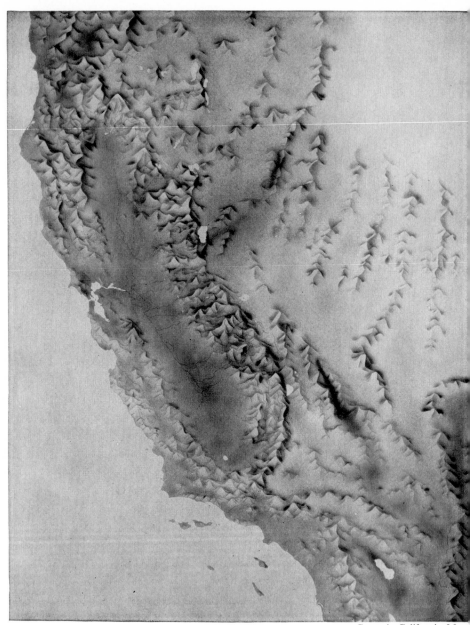

Gunter's California Map

California and Environs

inkling of the Christian religion and were sadly deficient in Christian modesty.   In every part of the Americas, even in such centers of high attainment as the Aztec and Inca empires, whites have reveled in the delights of a superiority complex.   Consequently, it is natural that many who entered California in the Spanish service or in the fur trade or gold rush should have looked down upon these natives as a most benighted race.

Fairer comparison would be with other Indian groups.   The Californians lacked the military cunning and ferocity that inspired respect for the Indians of the Plains and the Eastern Woodlands.   They were not such expert craftsmen in woodworking as their neighbors on the Northwest Coast, nor had they so interesting an art form or so highly developed a social system.   They were obviously inferior to the Pueblo Indians in the Southwest, who had developed multistoried buildings, agriculture and irrigation, excellent textiles and pottery, and a complex social organization.   Between California culture and that of the highly advanced Indians of Mexico and Peru a still greater disparity existed.   Thus, in comparison with most other Indians, the Californians made a poor impression.   More careful analysis reveals, nevertheless, that they had a number of commendable traits and that their solutions of some of the problems of human relationships were not without merit.

Number and Groups

No exact census, of course, was taken in pre-Columbian California. In spite of frequent comment by the Spaniards on the large population, the earliest estimates were set rather low.   Then, in the seventies, an enthusiastic amateur ethnologist, Stephen Powers, boosted the estimate to the astronomical figure of 700,000, which is just a trifle short of today's best guess for the pre-Columbian population of the entire area of the United States.   The most mature judgment for California is that its population was in the neighborhood of 130,000. Such a number, not much in excess of a capacity crowd for one of our football stadiums, is very small as compared to the present population of California or as compared to the several million Indians of Mexico.   It represents, however, three or four times the density to the square mile that would have been found for the United States as a whole.

The total number, in some respects small, in others large, is easier

to comprehend than the great diversity in language and tribal groupings. Indian California was a veritable babel of tongues. A traveler
would have encountered a new language every few miles. There
were some 135 different idioms and on the average only about 1,000
persons to speak each idiom. For many years these dialects defied
reduction to less than twenty-one or twenty-two linguistic families.
Additional relationships have since been worked out, but half a dozen
distinct language groups still remain, indicating that diversity of
speech was of long standing.

Villages, usually designated rancherías as in the Spanish, numbered approximately one thousand. By arithmetic this figure yields
130 as the village population average. Some to be sure were smaller,
others larger, but few communities exceeded twice that size. For
political units, the individual ranchería is about as high as one can
go. A number of tribal groupings, however, are a convenience to
the student and reflect cultural, if not political, actualities. The
habitat of such a group was often coextensive with one of the natural
geographic units mentioned above.

On a map Indian California appears to have been split into very
small linguistic and governmental units. In a sense, however, this is
an optical illusion, for the average number of persons speaking an
idiom or comprising a village or tribal group was not excessively
small. Had the Great Basin Indians, the Plains Indians, or even
the Algonkins been compressed into smaller areas of the same population density, the effect would have been very similar. Viewed thus,
the distinctive feature about the California natives was not the smallness of the units but the smallness of the area occupied by each unit,
or in other words the density of population. The latter rested, of
course, upon the distinctive economy that had grown up in California.

Perhaps the most convenient method of tracing the linguistic and
tribal groupings is to start at San Francisco Bay and move out in
concentric ellipses. Just north of the Golden Gate and up the west
side of the Sacramento Valley from Suisun Bay to Mt. Shasta resided
the Wintun. Across the Sacramento were the Maidu, while in the
Sierra foothills from the Cosumnes to the Merced lived the Miwok.
The southern half of the Central Valley was given over to the Yokuts,
while in the Coast Ranges from Soledad and Carmel to San Francisco were the squalid villages of the Costaño, or coast men. These

tribal groups constituted the Penutian speech family and are estimated to have numbered 57,000.

The second largest linguistic family, the Hokan, was made up of
tribal groups which roughly encircled the Penutian speakers.   In
modern Sonoma, Lake, and Mendocino counties were the Pomo, renowned for their excellent basketry.   Capping the northern end of
the Central Valley were the Chimariko, Karok, Shastan, and Yana.
Of these the Karok were the most advanced in culture and the Yana
the most vindictive.   The Washo, a Nevada group, intruded as far as
Lake Tahoe and flanked the eastern Sierra from the lake northward.
In the southern Coast Ranges and along the Santa Barbara Channel
lived the numerous and prosperous Chumash, followed by the Salinan
and the Esselen.   Fringing the state at the south and southeast were
still other members of the Hokan family: the Diegueño (their name
derived from Mission San Diego), and the Cocopa, Yuma, and
Mojave along the Colorado River.   These tribes were noted for
their warlike disposition.   Because it included the Pomo and the
Chumash, the Hokan family was important out of proportion to its
number, estimated at 37,500.

Some 23,500 Californians used languages belonging to the Sho-
shoean family and are consequently linked to such distant tribes as
the Comanche of the Plains and the Aztec of Mexico.   The Paiutes
in the northeast corner of the state belong to this speech family, but
most of its representatives were in the Great Basin and southern California.   Such were the Mono in the valley that bears their name,
the Tübatulabal of Kern River, the Chemehuevi and others in the
Mojave Desert, the Cahuilla in the Colorado Desert, the Serrano or
mountaineers in the San Bernardino Mountains, and several groups
so effectively missionized by the Spaniards that they are known by
mission names, the Luiseño, the Juaneño, the Gabrielino, and the
Fernandeño.

The remaining groups were comparatively small and confined to
northern California.   North and inland from the Pomo were the
ruder Yuki, who had not only a speech of their own but a distinctive
physical type as well.   On to the north were several groups that,
like the Dene of Alaska and the Apaches of the Southwest, belonged
to the Athabascan family.   Inserted among them in Humboldt
County were the Algonkin-speaking Wiyot and Yurok, whose superior
culture was similar to that of the Hokan-speaking Karok.   Finally,

among the lava beds of the Tule Lake region was a small group of Modocs, having linguistic and cultural connections with the Indians of Oregon. They are widely known because of the embarrassment they caused the United States Army in 1873.

From one standpoint, any attempt to generalize about the culture of the California Indians is futile; instead, they should be observed group by group and village by village, and account should be taken of the endless variety of institutions, customs, methods, and habits. Only thus can one remain adequately aware of the diversity and the provincialism that prevailed. Such a procedure would be tedious and would require us to be anthropologists rather than historians. Then, too, the specialists themselves find that generalizations are a helpful short cut in describing primitive societies. This method has crystalized in their device labeled the culture area, which by definition is a region embracing not identity but rough similarity of customs, habits, and ways of life. Of the fifteen such areas usually indicated for Indian America, one centers in the Sacramento-San Joaquin Valley and includes most of the Great Basin east of the Sierra. California south of the Tehachapi is generally classified as a fringe of the Southwestern culture area, but the margin of decision is slight and most elements of a general description of central California apply to it equally well. With the reservation that the tribes along the northern border really belonged to the culture area of the Northwest Coast and that the Colorado River Yumas had a much stronger affinity with the Southwestern area, there is good anthropological basis for attempting a broad description of the state's aboriginal culture.

Material Culture

Throughout California the fundamental garment was a two-piece apron of buckskin, shredded bark, or other plant fibers, worn with the smaller apron in front. The back piece extended to the thighs and might meet the front apron at the sides. For females this double apron was universal, even girl babies a few days old being so attired. The manly fashion was to go naked. In inclement weather both sexes employed blankets, preferably of otter skins though more often of deerskin. Other items of clothing were localized and incidental in use. The central and northern Californians had moccasins for special occasions but normally went barefoot. Skin leggings and oval snowshoes had a more restricted distribution. South of the Tehachapi sandals replaced moccasins, but again they were not worn constantly. Basketry caps occurred in the north and south but not in central California. Southern women used them as a comfortable pad for the pack straps; in the north they were fashionable as a constant item of female attire.

Buildings varied widely. Some were brush-covered, others were covered with thatch, bark, or earth. The conical and dome shapes were favorites, except in the northwest, where the rectangular pattern of the neighboring woodworking experts made itself felt. Some houses were partly dugout. All were of the one-family type, and except in the northwest, where a non-California idea had penetrated, all were rude huts.

Sweat houses rather than residences were the most characteristic structures. Throughout central California these were small and conical, earth-covered to conserve heat, and reserved for men. After kindling an open fire inside the sweat house (temescal), three or four men would enter and dispose themselves on the floor to escape the smoke. When a free perspiration had been produced, they rushed out and plunged into a near-by stream or lake. For certain disorders, such as rheumatic complaints, this treatment was very beneficial; but not so for new maladies introduced by the whites, such as measles and smallpox. Yet therapeutic use was at most an incident; the sweat house was really a daily masculine social habit. In northwestern California the temescales were larger and served as clubs where the men assembled to discuss affairs of state. Masculine emancipation existed in some villages where it was customary for the men to spend the night at the temescal club and only the women and children slept in the ordinary houses.

Most of California had no better boats than tule balsas or rafts. Reeds were often bundled together hurriedly for ferrying over a river, or a basket might be put to such use. On lakes and bays, balsas were made with greater care and were propelled by poles or paddles, some of which were double-bladed. Dugouts, nicely fashioned from redwood logs, were employed in the northwestern rivers and bays and to a lesser degree on the ocean. The Chumash of the Santa Barbara Channel made seaworthy boats by lashing planks together. They are described as trim, light, and capacious. Here the double-bladed paddle is the only type recorded.

The commonest archaeological specimen in California is the stone grinding bowl or mortar. The Indians had many other implements of stone, bone, shell, and wood, many of them less enduring. A catalog of them would be rather pointless. They included simple bows in the south and sinew-backed bows in the north; arrows, usually with an obsidian point; harpoons and spears; in the south a throwing stick for rabbit hunting; awls and arrow straighteners, rattles and whistles, but almost no drums; here and there bull roarers; and crude flutes and jew's-harps, which, however, had no ceremonial uses. Pottery was poor and limited to the region of strongest Southwestern influence.

Shields and protective armor were practically unknown. For the offensive, bows and arrows, spears, slings, and clubs were available, but in actual fighting the Californians exhibited a still more primitive tendency to let fly any stones that might be lying about. Warfare was uncommon. One village might attack a neighboring one to avenge a visitation of disease supposedly caused by the neighbors, but the fighting was wont to stop before many lives were lost. There was very little discipline or strategy, though Stanislau and Modoc Jack later won recognition as brilliant leaders. Scalping as a means of winning renown and scalp dances to confer public honor upon scalp takers were not California traits. Nevertheless, scalps were sometimes taken and danced over. When taken, they were taken very generously, the ears and most of the facial skin being included, instead of just a neat circle around the scalp lock, and sometimes the whole head was brought home.

Hunting and fishing were largely by nets and traps. Though fish and game were sometimes speared, the Channel Indians did most of their fishing with hook and line. Larger game was generally avoided. Coyotes and eagles had mythological connections that secured them a reverent regard. Bears were looked upon as semi-human, and the flesh of the dog was abhorred as poisonous. Along with the total lack of agriculture, these taboos seriously restricted the food list. Yet an adequate food supply was characteristic rather than exceptional. Acorns were the staple, and herbs and grass seeds were next in importance, followed by fish, shellfish, rabbits, and other small game. Snakes and angleworms, grasshoppers and honey, snails and slugs were relished here and there, but their use was by no means universal.

Oak groves dotted the landscape throughout most of the area and provided large and regular acorn crops. Acorns could readily be stored, and being richly nutritious, were eminently suited for human consumption, provided only that the tannic acid could be removed. The clever extraction process represents one of the greatest California achievements. Taking a few handfuls of acorns from the basketry granary, the squaw would remove the husks and pulverize the nut meats, using a stone pestle on a bedrock mortar or in a bottomless basket on a rock slab or a stone bowl. The flour was then winnowed by tossing it in a shallow basket. Meanwhile, water had been heated by stone boiling in a cooking basket. The meal was spread out on a sand pile and leached with eight or ten doses of water. When the water ran off clear, revealing the meal's freedom from tannic acid, the meal was gathered up and boiled in water. It swelled up like cornstarch, forming a gruel or pudding, which was eaten either plain or flavored with berries, nuts, rabbit meat, grasshoppers, or insects.

Although very ingenious, the acorn process was a most laborious and time-consuming one. Like manna, prepared acorn meal would keep only a short time, and consequently the California women were almost constantly employed in some part of the process. Once developed, the process became firmly established. On the one hand, it was extended to other foods, such as buckeye berries and rabbit meat, which many old people prepared similarly. On the other hand, the process seems to have operated against development of other sources of food, as in the neglect of larger game and the failure to develop agriculture.

Basketry was the one handicraft in which the Californians excelled. They used baskets for all conceivable purposes—for hats, for storage granaries, for containers of all sorts, for cooking vessels. These last were frequently calked with pitch or tar, but some were woven so compactly as to be watertight. Cooking was by stone boiling—that is, by plunging hot stones directly into the concoction in the cooking basket. They had command of several basketry techniques and decorated with geometric designs, usually woven in by the use of different color combinations but sometimes achieved by the application of shell mosaics. Museum collections provide the most vivid exhibit of this skill of the Californians. They enjoyed proving their craftsmanship by fabricating tiny thimble-sized baskets, perfect in every microscopic detail, though of course utterly useless except as jewel-like demonstrations of virtuosity. The basketmaking virtuosos, it should be added, were the women.

Social and Religious Practices

Without ascending to technicalities it is difficult to elaborate on the statement already made that the largest political unit was the ranchería. The Yuma and Mojave were better organized and the Yokuts had a semblance of a tribal system, but in the northwest the essential groups were even smaller than the rancherías. In most villages the chieftainship was hereditary and strictly civil, though if a chief happened to be a distinguished fighter he might be the war leader as well. Some chiefs were women, some had an assistant chief, some had specified assistants to act as messengers, speakers, and so forth, some were accorded a good deal of deference, but all lacked real power.

Social phenomena worthy of note include the following. Most of the tribes south of San Francisco were split into exogamous moieties that were patrilinear and totemic. Marriage was characteristically by purchase, though in the south it was often only a token purchase. Several tribes had kinship taboos, the most famous of which was against conversing with one's mother-in-law. The Yana had separate dialects for men and women. Widows mourned by cropping their hair and by smearing their faces with pitch or by allowing them to go unwashed for a season. Cremation was the standard disposition of the dead in most of California, but in part of the state burial was customary. In the northwest the Indians held slaves and placed great emphasis upon wealth, though they lacked the associated symbolism of the property-minded Kwakiutl and Haida. Other Californians were less mercenary, but most of them set great store by strings of dentalium shells or of clamshell beads and by cylinders of magnesite or shell, which have been called the equivalent of our precious stones.

This acquisitive spirit shows through in the California addiction to gaming. They had a variety of games calling for strength and dexterity. Some of these were roughly similar to shinny, lacrosse, football, double ball, and the hoop and pole game. In them the contesting teams were almost always heavily backed. A more convenient form of gambling was provided by the several guessing games. The favorite bore a close resemblance to our game of Up-Jinks. The Californians by all accounts played this hand game zealously, passionately, and tenaciously. Betting was less reckless than with some eastern tribes, but they played long and hard and often and loud. Songs were a regular accompaniment to the hand game and doubtless helped the hiding players to maintain poker faces. The allusion is in point because psychologically the two games are very similar. What may most surprise modern poker addicts is that no odium was incurred by playing the guessing game; on the contrary, society thoroughly approved.

In California the foremost men of religion were the shamans, or witch doctors. Although some cured simply through songs, the prevailing method was by removing the "disease object," usually by sucking. Contact with the spirits was but slightly relied upon; the guardian spirit idea was also very weak in California. Throughout the central part of the state the shaman's power to cure was believed to rest upon his having within his own body disease objects which would have caused a nonshaman immense pain. Such medical practice may sound primitive, but in addition to general practitioners there were three sort of specialists. Weather shamans in southern California engaged in rain making, and rattlesnake shamans throughout the state handled snakebite cases. Grizzly-bear shamans either changed into bears or masqueraded in bearskins, thereby gaining extraordinary powers, which, it was hoped, they would use for the good of the tribe rather than against their fellow tribesmen.

Outright ceremonials were few, but some were highly developed for a people whose political and material culture was as rudimentary as the Californians'. A girls' adolescence ceremony was universal and was taken as the occasion for liberal preachments on the advisability of good behavior. Southern California and Sierra tribes also had an annual mourning ceremony. Other ceremonies occasionally encountered included the semicouvade, in which a father went into semiconfinement at the time of childbirth, New Year observances, boys' puberty rites, the first salmon rites, the ant ordeal, and numerous others.

More distinctive were the initiation rituals of the Kuksu cult in central California and the toloache or Jimson-weed cult in the south. Simply organized and embracing almost every man in the villages involved, the Kuksu and toloache societies had developed complicated and impressive ceremonies of initiation. The Kuksu rituals were built around impersonated spirits, which called for elaborate costumes, regalia, and disguises, so that the mythical characters could be adequately represented. In the toloache cult, costumes and dances were much simpler. The ceremonial began with the administration of the powerful drug, which produced complete stupefaction for one or more nights and in some instances death. The visions seen during this period of narcosis were of life-long sanctity. Then followed several nights of dancing and a period of fasting. Mingled with it was much instruction, partly by song and partly by means of ground painting.

Theological beliefs, or mythological, if the term be preferred, were choate in a profusion of legendary animal tales. Many of these stories represent high achievement in speculation on fundamental philosophical problems. Explanations of the creation, of the origin of death, and of the problem of good and evil bear some resemblance to the Biblical accounts. Coyote is a ubiquitous character, an arrogant, mischievous trickster, sometimes an unintentional benefactor of humanity, at other times bringing disaster and embarrassment in his wake. Apart from mythology these tales make very good reading, and like the Old Testament of the Hebrews they shed much light on the mundane habits of the people who passed them on to posterity.

Such in brief was the culture of the California Indians when the white man arrived. Their subsequent experiences at mission and rancho, in the gold fields, on the reservation and off, and as town or farm laborers are threads in the general fabric of the state's history since 1769 and are handled in that fashion in the chapters that follow.

Since modern California has moved so rapidly, the question naturally arises why the Indians were so backward. One reason has been discussed in the chapter on geography, namely, that many California resources of today were valueless until released through technological advances. Isolation was also a brake upon progress. California was remote from the actively creative culture centers of the New World. The degree of isolation is illustrated by the fact that, although the Spaniards had been settled in Mexico for 250 years and in New Mexico for 170 years, not a single Spanish culture trait seems to have penetrated to California before the coming of the settlers in 1769. Less is known about the accumulation of resistance to new ideas, but it appears that the Californians were set in the pattern of life that had grown up in the region. Agriculture had been knocking at the door, so to speak, for many generations, but the idea of cultivating could not make headway against the idea of gathering what nature provided. A like statement would hold for pottery making and woodworking. And after all, the old California culture was in many respects commendable. Later, many Indians looked back upon the pre-Spanish period as a happier day of peace, leisure, enough to eat, and lots of fun. Why jeopardize such a nirvana merely to have the new-fangled? This conservative tendency may well be the essence of the explanation. At any rate, the evidence is that for several centuries prior to the arrival of the Spaniards the culture of the California Indians had been practically static.

3

SPANISH FOUNDATIONS

CALIFORNIA, as everyone knows, began as a Spanish colony. In this respect she differs from the northern and eastern two thirds of the United States. Modern Californians cherish this fact of Spanish beginnings, not only as a distinction, but also because it links their land with the southern tier of American states from Florida to New Mexico and Arizona and with the score of nations stretching southward through two continents.

A Marginal Colony

To understand the significance of this Spanish background it is advisable to describe the relationship with greater precision. California was a late addition to the Spanish empire, her occupation taking place some two and a half centuries after the establishment of the Spaniards at Mexico City. She was one of the northern frontier units occupied as a measure of defense against restless Indians and the greater menace of foreign encroachments. Beyond this strategic value the province was esteemed very lightly by the Spaniards, and in view of the small population, the excess of expenditure over income, and the slow progress of the missions, this attitude seems to have been fitting. California, in other words, was not a fair sample of Spanish America, but only a marginal colony.

There are, in addition, good local reasons for observing the earlier development of Spanish America proper, and particularly of the viceroyalty of New Spain, or Mexico. New Spain, rather than Spain itself, was the base for explorations toward, to, and beyond California. It was the base for the sacred expeditions of 1769 and furnished the recruits who colonized the province. Administratively, California was likewise an off-shoot of New Spain, and this relationship held until the United States took control. The essential decisions regarding California were made in Mexico rather than in Spain for, unlike England, Spain developed a unified system of colonial control whereby broad powers were placed in the hands of key officials such as the viceroys.

New Spain and the other older provinces were in many respects a far cry from California. Several sixteenth-century techniques and institutions—for example, the encomienda or trustee system of Indian control and exploitation—were not transplanted to California. On the other hand, practically every device that was employed in California had been previously tested by use in New Spain. Furthermore, the Spaniards of the sixteenth century had developed a philosophy of colonization or at least a set of imperial concepts, and though outward forms changed, this fundamental philosophy carried over to the end of the colonial period. The same rules held as to what constituted a good and desirable colony; the relationship between monarch and colonial was as before; the Indian's place in colonial society was defined as in the original terms; and the church was still the good right arm of the government. This remarkable continuity in Spain's methods, though it is often lost sight of, justifies a careful examination of the early functioning of this imperial system.

Spanish Beginnings

An outstanding characteristic of the sixteenth century was that Spain had America practically to herself. The fact that Columbus sailed under Spanish auspices was of obvious advantage. It was also true that the centuries had imbued Spaniards with a militant crusading and adventurous spirit that fitted them well for heroic ventures in the New World. In the very year of the great discovery, the fall of Granada marked the completion of reconquest of the peninsula from the Moslems and left the Spaniards looking for new worlds to conquer, a wish that found literal fulfillment in Columbus' America. Thanks to the Catholic Kings, Ferdinand and Isabella, Spain was more effectively organized as a nation than any of her neighbors and consequently could launch upon empire building under centralized monarchical direction. The other nations of western Europe lacked one or all of these advantages. Even Portugal, which had been far more maritime-minded than Spain, was preoccupied with sailing down the African coast and shortly after with the round-Africa route to the Spice Islands. To safeguard this route the Portuguese king insisted that the Line of Demarcation be moved westward. On the South American coast that thus fell to his lot, a few struggling settlements were established in the 1530's, the nucleus of modern Brazil, but with this exception no non-Spaniards were able to found permanent settlements in any part of the New World until after the sixteenth century.

The opportunity to colonize on a noncompetitive basis was of incalculable value. One need only compare the experiences of French Acadia or of the Georgia-Florida frontier to get an intimation of how great a boon it was. It meant that the Spaniards could take the cream of the New World. They could skip over lands that were worth little and concentrate on those of more abundant resources. They could attend to the constructive features of colony development without the necessity of military expenditures beyond the minimum requirements for Indian control. In the entire gamut of Occidental history it is hard to find a comparable opportunity; the westward expansion of the United States in the first century of independence, though threatened repeatedly by international rivalries, is perhaps the closest parallel that modern history has to offer.

In the beginning the Spaniards had an unbounded curiosity about the new lands before them and an equal optimism about finding a westward route to the Orient. In consequence, they were indefatigable explorers. They began in the Caribbean area. Columbus' four voyages, together with those of Pinzón, Ojeda, and Bastidas, carried to completion the exploration of the shore line of the Caribbean Sea, which thus became the first portion of the hemisphere to be mapped with a semblance of accuracy. Within twenty-five or thirty years the Atlantic Coast from Maine to the Straits of Magellan was brought into the ken of geographers. John Cabot for England and Cabral and Vespucci for Portugal deserve mention, but Spain is to be credited chiefly. Ocampo circumnavigated Cuba in 1511. Córdova, Grijalva, and Pineda circled the Gulf of Mexico between 1517 and 1519. Ponce de León and Gómez explored from Florida northward, while García, Sebastián Cabot, and Magellan went down to the Plata and the Straits. The first generation of Spaniards in America carried to practical completion the mapping of the eastern coast line of both continents, while the Magellan voyage around the world helped to reveal how distant that coast line was from the Spice Islands of the East.

In actual colonization the men of Columbus' day likewise achieved much. The island of Española, now called Haiti, was occupied first, and for a decade and a half, from 1493 to 1508, it was the sole settlement in the New World. Accordingly, Española has the oldest cities, churches, and schools of the hemisphere. More noteworthy is the fact that it was on this island that Spain's colonial system began to take form. The island was a laboratory or a proving ground where experiments were conducted in governmental, social, and economic methods, and the procedures thus developed—often by modification of methods used in the conflict against the Moslems in Spain—were transferred bodily to the subsequent colonies on the mainland. In this sense, as well as because much of that later expansion was from the island as a base, Española was the Mother of America.

At Española the emphasis was first upon placer gold mining, but the Spaniards soon recognized a superior source of enrichment through the plantation system of subtropical agriculture, which has been the fundamental economy of the West Indies ever since. The Spaniards learned what not to do as well as what should be done. The biggest mistake in the islands was that the natives were subjected to so strenuous an exploitation as to bring about, in conjunction with the ravages of disease, their extermination. Although the Spaniards may not have been very sentimental about this tragedy, they recognized in full the practical disadvantage of having no native labor supply. On the mainland it came to be a major objective not to repeat the mistake of the islands.

Between 1508 and 1511 settlements were planted on the three other larger islands, Jamaica, Cuba, and Puerto Rico, and the first establishment on the mainland was achieved in the isthmus region. These steps were important on their own account, yet they are usually regarded as preludes to more significant achievements. Ponce de León, conqueror of Puerto Rico, is better known for what was really a lesser venture, namely, his search for the Fountain of Youth in Florida. The work of Balboa and Pedrarias at Panama, heroic though it was, is overshadowed by the more brilliant success of Pizarro in Peru. And Velásquez' conquest of Cuba is largely remembered because it led to the outfitting of Cortés' expedition to subdue the mighty Aztecs. This last is the line of expansion of most moment to California.

The epic story of the conquest of Mexico City has been told so often and so brilliantly that it would be supererogation to rehearse it here. Reference is made instead to Cortés' own letters, to the inimitable *True History* by Bernal Díaz del Castillo, and to the classic account by William H. Prescott. Suffice it to say that, although Cortés' force was absurdly small and ill-equipped, his inspiring leadership, his adroit use of dissension among the Indians, the reckless valor of his men, the advantages of horses and sailboats, firearms, crossbows, and chain armor, and a method of warfare that Díaz called "a Christian siege," not to mention a potent ally in the dread disease smallpox—all were factors in accounting for the crushing of the Aztec power. By August of 1521, when most accounts of the conquest terminate, the Spaniards were masters only of the ruined city of Tenochtitlán, or Mexico. Yet as victors over the Aztecs they were in position to spread their conquest rapidly over southern Mexico. This process was accomplished by Cortés and his lieutenants during the course of the next ten or twelve years. This expansion and the completion of the conquest of the vastly greater area of New Spain were but a drab aftermath following the dramatic action of the siege of Mexico City. As such they were long neglected by historians; in fact, it is only very recently that much attention has been given to this larger conquest and to the institutional development that accompanied it.

At the outset, Cortés and his fellows had no very constructive attitude. Their first thought was to seize the gold and silver, the turquoises and emeralds which the Indians had, and this they did as expeditiously as possible. For some years the most profitable pursuit was to plunder the natives. Montezuma's treasure house was raided early, and many a Spaniard drowned on Noche Triste because he was weighted down with gold and silver. But the survivors persisted. Throughout southern Mexico they called upon the Indians to hand over their metals and then, by an easy transition, went on to the next step, grave robbing. Such exactions upon the living and the dead soon exhausted the accumulations of the natives. Mining, meanwhile, was producing very little. The Spaniards, therefore, had strong incentives to look about for other possible sources of wealth.

The one most obviously at hand was agriculture. Next to the Incas of Peru, whose irrigation systems were engineering masterpieces, the Indians of southern Mexico were the most advanced agriculturists of the Americas. In addition to the inevitable maize, beans, and squash, their crop list included chili peppers, cacao or chocolate, cashew nuts, tomatoes, pineapples, guavas, agaves, prickly pears, cotton, and tobacco. Agriculture had long since reached the stage where it was considered man's work, and the social setup was such that in pre-Columbian Mexico labor was well regimented for the benefit of chiefs and caciques. It was relatively simple for the conquering Spaniards to substitute themselves for the native ruling class and to continue the exploitation of native labor. Some West Indian methods were brought over and Spanish wheat, vines, fruits, cattle, horses, and mules were introduced, but the basic Mexican system was continued. As illustrative of the importance of agriculture, it might be remarked that Cortés' personal fortune rested less upon the fruits of conquest than upon the fruits of his Indian-worked plantations in the Valley of Oaxaca.

Establishing Royal Authority

With the conquest of Mexico, with its abundance of wealth and its millions of skillful and hard-working inhabitants, Spain's interest in the New World quickened. Here was something as worth while as Portugal's islands in the East. King and court, therefore, redoubled their efforts to make imperial control effective in this distant land. They worked toward this end with such determination that Mexican political history of the late twenties, thirties, and forties is largely a record of such activity. Obviously, royal authority could be built up only as Cortés' power was reduced. Curtailment of the great conquistador's privileges and power was gradual, because his military leadership was temporarily useful, but it was nonetheless relentless. Like Columbus, Cortés had reason to consider himself ill-rewarded by his monarch. In his last letter to Charles he besought relief from contending with the officers of the crown, "against whom it was more difficult to defend himself than to win the land from the enemy."

As early as 1524 financial control was taken over by royal officers who established the real hacienda in Mexico. Two years later a residencia—that is, a legal hearing as to his conduct in office—was instituted against Cortés, and to defend himself against the actions proposed he had to go back to Spain. An audiencia, an administrative court such as had become the principal governing agency in the islands, was decreed for Mexico in 1527 and purposely timed to go into operation during Cortés' absence from the country. Under the presidency of Nuño de Guzmán, this first audiencia encountered opposition from Cortés and his friends and also from the church, which complained against it so vigorously that the king decided in 1530 to replace it by a new one. Although its members had been bludgeoned into serving in New Spain and were constantly looking forward to release from duty, this second audiencia served the king well. It forced the Spaniards in New Spain to observe the law, it intervened to protect the natives from undue abuses, and it sponsored expansion into Querétaro and Yucatán, but it was not an adequate curb upon Cortés or upon Guzmán, who was acting independently in the conquest of Nueva Galicia.

In 1535, therefore, Charles took the final step to clinch his hold upon the colony by despatching a viceroy to be his personal representative at Mexico City. The man chosen for this responsible post, Antonio de Mendoza, was specially selected on the basis of ability and loyalty to the crown. He was a nobleman with military and diplomatic experience and was to prove an administrator of exceptional competence. Cortés and Guzmán tested his mettle and then gave in to him. Though faced with an Indian uprising of the most serious aspect in the Mixton War, he managed to quell it. He forced the encomenderos to moderate their treatment of the natives but was wise enough not to insist upon enforcement of the New Laws, which would have disrupted the labor supply absolutely. When he left in 1551 to undertake a similar task in Peru, New Spain was an orderly state. Agriculture had grown apace, exploration had been carried far afield, a new mining frontier was in the midst of its initial rush, the church had taken firmer root, schools were operating, royal authority as personified in the viceroy was everywhere acknowledged, and viceregal government had changed from a vague theory to an accomplished fact. Where there was no alternative, Mendoza had used force, but for the most part his methods were the more moderate ones of diplomacy and manipulation.

Mendoza figures directly in California history as the superior official under whom the Coronado and Cabrillo expeditions were made. His indirect contribution, through the later functioning of the viceroyalty, is probably of greater moment. By the late eighteenth century viceregal government had undergone modification, yet in essential structure it was still the first viceroy's handiwork.

Another office that was to have a prominent place in California affairs was utilized in the period of Mendoza. In 1543 the court took cognizance of the charges which Cortés had lodged against the viceroy and sent Tello de Sandoval to conduct a visitation or inspection. The office of visitador was one of long standing in Spain. A visitador was empowered to conduct an inquiry and, unlike our fact-finding commissions, was also empowered to act. This particular visitador was extremely hostile to Mendoza in ill-disguised hope of succeeding him as viceroy. For four years he was a thorn in Mendoza's flesh and a hindrance to good government. Finally he was recalled to Spain, and the Council of the Indies cleared Mendoza of the injudicious charges against him. But though Sandoval's visitation failed of its purpose, later visitadors provided excellent stimulation, and one of them José de Gálvez, contributed much to California.

The Mines of Mexico

In midcentury, after witnessing turbulent beginnings under Cortés and stabilization under Mendoza, New Spain took on a new character through the opening of the rich silver mines of Zacatecas, Guanajuato, and Potosí. Juan de Tolosa discovered the first silver deposits near Zacatecas in 1546. Led to them by Indians whom he had befriended, he brought back samples of ore that proved to be fabulously rich. Before making any public announcement of his find, Tolosa confided it to three of his friends, Diego de Ibarra, Cristóbal de Oñate, and Baltasar de Bañuelos, and with them he formed a partnership for the exploitation of the mines. The partnership has some significance, because these four men had the advantage of a running start in the mining development and reaped so rich a harvest that they became the first millionaires of North America. In later years a dispute arose as to which of the partners had made the original discovery. Each one claimed to have been most instrumental; Diego de Ibarra, for example, said that he was the principal discoverer "after God Himself." Yet there seems to be no doubt that Tolosa was first, after his Indian friends.

A secret like Tolosa's could not be kept long. It was soon common knowledge that Zacatecas abounded in silver, and a rush to the mines ensued.   Southern Nueva Galicia was well-nigh depopulated, while boom towns sprang up on the frontier.   Within two years forty-five reduction plants were in operation.   The excitement and hectic conditions that prevailed were the prototype for the whole series of mining rushes in western North America; indeed, the "days of '48" at Zacatecas, though three centuries removed, are often compared with the "days of '49" in California.

After Zacatecas still richer mines were discovered.   Guanajuato, which began as a way station on the trail to Zacatecas, proved to be even wealthier, and for three centuries its Veta Madre was the richest mine in the world.   Sombrerete, San Martín, Nombre de Díos, Durango, Indé, and Aguas Calientes were the sites for other strikes and other rushes.   Nueva Galicia was enlarged, as well as increased in population and wealth, and as the direct result of this mining activity the new province of Nueva Vizcaya was created.   A nephew of one of Tolosa's partners, young Francisco de Ibarra, was the most active leader on this frontier.   He made numerous entradas (exploring expeditions) as far to the northwest as modern Sonora, which have given him fame as an explorer and Indian fighter.   He was also a protector of the Franciscans, a founder of numerous towns, and a mine developer, though the more notable progress in Nueva Vizcayan mining came after his death.

To the northeast a corresponding advance was made by Luís de Carbajal, a Portuguese Jew who later fell afoul of the Inquisition. His province of Nuevo León was less on the road to California than was Nueva Vizcaya, and it was also less immediately successful.   No comparable mines were discovered, agricultural markets were consequently inferior, and the colonization project rapidly degenerated into a group of slave-hunting raids.   The captured Indians were sold to the western mine operators.

Boom years in the mines were followed by less satisfactory seasons, but these silver deposits were so extensive that they made mining possible as a permanent industry.   Many of the mines are still producing, and total production to date of merely the Zacatecas mines exceeds a billion dollars.

On the basis of mining alone, the provinces of Nueva Galicia and Nueva Vizcaya would have prospered; but without the backlog of agriculture they would have been subjected to wild fluctuation between good times and bad.   As in most mining regions, the number of men catering to the needs of the miners was about as great as that of the actual extractors of silver. There were presidios where soldiers were stationed to protect against Indian danger. There were Franciscans carrying the cross abreast of the mining frontier. Great wheat farms were brought under cultivation and tremendous grazing ranches developed to provide foodstuffs for the thousands of miners. A measure of this development in ranching is the fact that Diego de Ibarra branded 33,000 calves in 1586, while his neighbor Rodrigo del Río branded 42,000. Such calf crops bespeak ranching on a large scale. And to an even greater extent than mining, which had its ups and downs, agriculture was basic to the steady prosperity and growth of these provinces.

In the imperial scheme, it was of course the mines that were particularly valuable. The earlier windfalls of accumulated gold and silver in southern Mexico, Colombia, and Peru had enriched the royal treasury by the fraction of treasure-trove due it, but the first regular and sizeable income that the Spanish crown received from America came from the silver mines of Upper Peru and from those of Mexico's old northwest. The royal quinta (fifth) shrank to a tenth and then to only a twentieth, but the sum total was an astounding figure. It provided an important supplement to the royal revenues and helps explain how Charles I and Philip II could hire the best army in Europe, build the Invincible Armada, and make the Spanish monarchy the foremost in sixteenth-century Europe.

Meanwhile the older settlements were taking on more and more of a civilized aspect—that is, they came to have a Spanish rather than an Indian stamp. Such was the early result at Santo Domingo and Havana and soon thereafter at Bogotá, Lima, Santiago de Chile, and other South American cities. Southern Mexico likewise absorbed much that was European, and before the end of the century Mexico City took rank as the leading metropolis of North America, a position she held throughout the colonial period. By 1600 Spain's success as a colonizer was apparent in the vast area which she controlled; in her eight or ten million colonial subjects, a number somewhat in excess of the population of Spain at the time; in the transmission of her religion and language to these millions; in the spread of many other elements of Spanish civilization; in the wealth displayed at the provincial capital; in the industries that were flourishing; and in the notable attainments of colonial architects, artists, and writers.

Philosophy of Empire

The institutions of the old regime have been alluded to and several have been described. At the risk of repetition, their fundamental and permanent features may be summarized. One distinguishing characteristic was that the Americas were regarded as the property of the crown, not of the Spanish nation, to be governed by and for the crown. The centralization of control inherent in this attitude was observable in such matters as taxation, the hold which the crown had over ecclesiastical appointments, and even in crown-controlled frontier advance.

Another characteristic was the prominent role of the church. The Spanish monarchs were unswervingly orthodox and undertook to make and keep Spanish America so. On other scores too it was natural that great reliance was placed on churchmen for the conduct of educational and charitable institutions, for the spread of the Catholic faith among the natives, and for the transmission to them of the first elements of Spanish civilization.

Spain's Indian policy is especially to be noted. It was simplicity itself; in fact, it was so simple that many outsiders have had great difficulty in comprehending it. It was, in brief, that the Indian be made Spanish. To accomplish this end he was to be taught the Spanish religion, the Spanish language, and the basic Spanish habits. Indians were to be encouraged to be village dwellers, and the Indian and Spanish races were to be fused by intermarriage. The policy was the direct opposite of the English one of extermination, summed up in the phrase "A good Indian is a dead Indian." This habit of thought plus the ingrained Anglo-American habit of frowning upon interracial marriages account for misunderstandings of the Spanish policy.

In the first two or three generations after the discovery Indian population declined by something more than 50 per cent. Disease accounted for most of this appalling loss, but war and harsh treatment were contributory factors. By the latter part of the century the tendency toward decline was counteracted. Thereafter, to the end of the colonial period, Indian population remained roughly constant or, indeed, increased, if we count in some five million mestizos as representative of Indian blood. Their descendants are dominant in numbers in most parts of Spanish America today.

Thus resulted Spain's determination that the Indians should live. The purpose underlying this policy was eminently practical; it was that the Indian should work. Various devices of persuasion and force were utilized: slavery, the encomienda, the repartimiento, mission discipline, and in later years debt peonage. Each entailed coercion, balanced, however, by a measure of benevolent protection against undue exactions.

Other features of Spanish colonial policy might be cited, for example, the pueblo or town as the preferred unit for frontier advance rather than the individual clearing or homestead of the American frontier. The continuous factors are apparent in a careful reading of Spanish American history. On the other hand, the latest colonies are distinguishable from the earlier both through such a reading and through the contrast of the modern survivals of Spanish influences in the respective areas. California stands as a good example of a colony that derived much from sixteenth-century New Spain and had much, though not everything, in common with it.

4

DISCOVERY OF CALIFORNIA

THE GREAT WORK of colonization, which was the substantial achievement of the sixteenth-century Spaniards, was interspersed with spectacular explorations. Such is the fame of these explorers that the Spaniards oftentimes are not thought of as colonizers at all, an attitude which is unfortunately myopic. The explorers, however, should not be blamed, for the magnitude of their work staggers belief.

Exploration on a Grand Scale

After Columbus and his contemporaries had charted the Caribbean Sea and run the eastern coasts of North and South America, a second generation of explorers surpassed even those results. Andagoya went down the coast of the South Sea, followed by Pizarro, Almagro, and Valdivia, who were not only the conquerors of Peru and Chile but also explorers par excellence. Alcazaba mapped the rest of the South American west coast, while other expeditions from Spain overran the Plata basin. Gonzalo Pizarro crossed the Andes to seek a Land of Cinnamon in the jungle of the Amazon, and the deserter Orellana gained fame by descending the great river to its mouth. The story of El Dorado, the Gilded Man, was a magnet drawing treasure seekers from all sides to the plains of Bogotá. Ordaz, von Speyer, von Hutton, Herrera, and others plunged into the Orinoco Valley and explored the northern tributaries of the Amazon. Through the cumulative efforts of such explorers the horizon of geographic knowledge was carried forward from the periphery of the southern continent into practically every major area of the interior.

In North America there was a corresponding advance. Men

whose names are familiar to every schoolboy—Ponce de León, Ayllón, De Soto—crisscrossed the southeastern quarter of present-day United States. Cabeza de Vaca, Marcos, and Coronado complemented their work farther west. North America's west coast was not neglected, with the northernmost landfall probably in the Oregon region, and one long arm of this generation's maritime exploration reached across the Pacific to the Philippine Islands. By 1543 the Spaniards had a good acquaintance with at least the southern half of North America, and the Pacific Coast had been traced from the Straits of Magellan to Cape Mendocino.

The Antilles, Panama, and to a lesser extent Spain itself were the bases for expansion into South America. Penetrations into La Florida emanated mostly from the islands. For the northwestward advance by land and sea Mexico was the base. Only this latter salient pertains to California, but there was an essential unity about all these explorations. Coronado and Cabrillo cannot be understood if absolutely divorced from De Soto, von Speyer, Orellana, Villalobos, and the rest.

There was ample incentive for this explorational activity. The fabulous wealth uncovered by Cortés at Mexico City and by Pizarro in Peru kindled hopes of locating another Mexico or another Peru. The men of this generation still labored under Columbus' delusion that Asia was much closer than in actuality. South America had been reckoned a new continent almost from the outset, but North America was at first identified as Asia, and even after the Magellan voyage the distance to the Orient was greatly minimized. Another persistent and hopeful fallacy was the idea of a Strait of Anian, a water passage through America to the Orient. Spaniards were not alone in entertaining this hope, but whereas they had dismissed the possibility almost completely by the close of the sixteenth century, Englishmen, Frenchmen, and Americans kept up the search into the seventeenth, eighteenth, and even nineteenth centuries. John Smith on the Chickahominy, Verrazano at Chesapeake Bay, Verendrye west of the Great Lakes, and Robert Rogers at Michilimackinac were looking for such a passage, and the Buenaventura River, which American fur trappers sought as an avenue to the Pacific in the middle nineteenth century, was really a rechristened Strait of Anian.

The early explorers were urged onward by a number of fanciful ideas that had enjoyed credence in Europe for generations. The

Fountain of Youth, the Amazon Island, the Seven Cities, the Terrestrial Paradise, and other like wonders had been thought of as more than mere figments of the imagination. They had been regarded as real enough but located far away in the Orient. After the discovery of America it was natural that there should have been expectations of finding these marvels in the New World and that the explorers should have read into the words of their Indian informants suggestions of these Old World wonders. The Land of Bímini in Florida appeared as a probable Terrestrial Paradise, the Pueblo towns were transmuted in prospect into the Seven Cities, and Lower California assumed the aura of the Amazon Island.

American wonder tales were no less entrancing. The Indians often entertained the Spaniards with vivid accounts of the attractions *mas allá*. Frequently these tales had basis in fact. A tribe at Lake Guatavitá in Colombia actually had a ceremony in which their chief was gilded with gold dust and literally became El Dorado. The Carolina region once had a superman on the order of the Giant King Dotha described to the Spaniards. His size and strength may not have been produced by the early greasing and stretching of his joints by his thoughtful mother, but the report was all the more convincing because of the addition of these graphic details. Some Indian yarns were spun in the guileless enthusiasm of the raconteur; others were deliberately fabricated to speed the departure of burdensome Caucasian guests. In most cases the disappointment of the Spaniards was due to the fact that they had higher standards of opulence than the abjectly poor Indians who sang the praises of a somewhat less squalid village, as when the Tampa Indians extolled the wonders of Appalachen.

The early explorers expected to find fabulous wealth; any lesser success was accounted failure. The very meager returns for all investigators of the northern mysteries lent color to the assertion that De Soto, Coronado, and the rest were gullible visionaries engaged in wild-goose chases. As a matter of fact, the evidence upon which they acted was almost as tangible as that which led Cortés to Mexico City, or Quesada to the treasure house of Cundinamarca, or Pizarro to the unbelievable riches of the Incas. The explorers of the north made a substantial contribution to geographical knowledge. They also rendered a real service toward the development of Spanish America by exploding most of the extravagant notions about the great beyond, thereby enabling their compatriots to concentrate on the districts nearer at hand.

Cortés on the West Coast

The first important figure in Pacific Coast exploration was Cortés. Immediately after the fall of Tenochtitlán he was busy building a Spanish city on its ruins and spreading the conquest throughout southern Mexico.   Much of the work was handled by his lieutenants, but the great captain personally led an expedition to Honduras.   Soon, however, his interest was directed to the west coast.   Here seemed to be the best likelihood of finding an Otro Méjico; here signs pointed to the fabled Amazon Island; here appeared a convenient approach to the Strait of Anian.

For a full decade the chronicle of Cortés' efforts at shipbuilding for west coast exploration is one of discouragements and delay.   Shipbuilding materials were hard to get.   The west coast could provide only timber; nails, ropes, and the other requisites had to be brought across from the Gulf of Mexico or from Spain.   Skilled workmen were likewise at a premium.   To these natural difficulties were added fortuitous troubles.   After shipbuilding materials had been laboriously collected, a fire broke out in the warehouse and nullified more than a year's work.   In 1527 four vessels were completed, but, just as they were about to set out, there came a royal communication ordering them to the Moluccas to strengthen Spain's claims in that quarter.   Then, when Cortés had to return to Spain to defend himself against the charges of his enemies, the project was set back at least another two years.

In 1532 two ships were at last ready for use.   They sailed under the command of Diego Hurtado de Mendoza and did not return. Some news of their achievements and their fate trickled in through the Indians, which made it appear that Cortés' inveterate rival, Nuño de Guzmán, was partly responsible for the unfortunate outcome.   Two more ships sailed the next year.   Hernando de Grijalva deserted with one of them and discovered the Revilla Gigedo Islands.   On the other, Fortún Jiménez led a mutiny against the commander, Diego Becerra, in which the latter was killed.   Jiménez proceeded to a bay, which he named La Paz, on what he thought was an island but which was really the peninsula of Baja California.   In an encounter with the Indians on the mainland, Jiménez was subsequently killed, but the survivors got back to Cortés with this first report of California.

When these men reported an abundance of pearls at La Paz, Cortés announced that he himself would go there. So great was his reputation as a treasure finder that this announcement produced a rush of volunteers. Ship space was available for but half the men anxious to go, and when Cortés sailed in 1535, he could only promise to send back for the others. At Santa Cruz, which was his name for the "island" of California, Cortés found few pearls. He also found that the voyage from the mainland was most difficult. Grijalva, who was sent back for more men and supplies, could not make the "island" again, and when Cortés attempted another trip he got back to Santa Cruz only after much trouble. In the meantime, twenty-three men had died of starvation. The barrenness of the land, the backwardness and hostility of the natives, and the adversity of sailing conditions impelled Cortés to abandon these pearl fisheries. The last of his men were taken off in 1536. There is some evidence that the viceroy insisted on the withdrawal.

Flagging interest in the northwest was revived almost at once by the arrival at Culiacán of Cabeza de Vaca, who had a marvelous tale to tell of shipwreck on the Texas coast, of six years as slave, trader, and medicine man among the Indians, and of a transcontinental hike with black Estevanico through western Texas and northern Mexico to the outpost of Spanish settlement. His story was exciting, not merely as a hair-raising adventure, but also because he had heard mention of seven wondrous cities farther north. These, it seemed obvious, must be the Seven Cities.

As the chief protagonist of northwestward exploration, Cortés considered himself the proper person to investigate this new attraction. Viceroy Mendoza, however, thought otherwise. His was an inevitable reaction. One of the main reasons for his being sent to New Spain had been to place adequate restraint upon Cortés. Now to allow the great conquistador to lead in an enterprise which promised to surpass the conquest of the Aztecs would ill comport with such a policy. Without hesitation, therefore, Mendoza excluded Cortés from the land expedition that was to follow up Vaca's report and designated as its leader Francisco Vásquez de Coronado. In March, 1539, Friar Marcos and Estevanico went ahead to reconnoiter. When Marcos returned, affirming that he had actually seen one of the cities from a distant hill, that it was large enough to rank as another

Mexico, and that the buildings were of silver, the viceroy's expectations became so sanguine that he invested heavily in equipping Coronado's force. The Seven Cities henceforth were further identified by name as the Seven Cities of Cíbola, a word of doubtful derivation later applied to the buffalo.

Blocked on land, Cortés was still able to operate by sea. In 1539, as his final gesture toward the northwest, he sent Francisco de Ulloa with three vessels to sail up the coast of the mainland, on the chance that the Seven Cities might be within striking distance of the sea rather than farther inland. Performing his task with great thoroughness, Ulloa sailed to the head of the Gulf of California and turned south again, convinced that the supposed strait was a gulf and that the "island" of California was in reality a peninsula. He rounded the tip of the peninsula and sailed up its outer shore as far as Cedros Island, at about the twenty-eighth parallel. From this point he sent back his larger vessel with a report of the discoveries made, while with the 35-ton vessel he continued the explorations. Except that maps of the time soon showed the coast another degree to the north, quite possibly reflecting discovery by Ulloa, no further record of his work has been preserved, and some historians have written him off as lost. A court record revealing his appearance years later as a witness proves that he survived. He may have seen more of the California coast, but his fame properly rests on his voyage up the gulf and along both sides of the peninsula and on the proof that it was a peninsula.

The Ulloa enterprise marked Cortés' last connection with Pacific Coast exploration. He went to Spain in 1540 to seek redress for the losses for which he blamed Guzmán, Mendoza, and the Audiencia of Mexico, and to insist on his rights to explore. Legal complications engulfed him, and he spent the rest of his days in Spain, for the most part involved in endless litigation.

The Search for the Seven Cities

Coronado, meanwhile, was gathering a most pretentious expedition. He had three hundred Spaniards and several hundred Indians, besides thousands of head of livestock for remounts and provisions. The viceroy traveled to Compostela to review the force, the Spaniards resplendent in polished mail, their horses richly caparisoned, and the Indians decked out in war paint and parrot-plumed headgear. Coronado's own armor was golden. By far the most brilliant review New Spain had yet witnessed, it was a measure of the investment in the undertaking on the part of Mendoza, Coronado, and others.

The sequel was a bitter disappointment. Marcos' silver buildings proved to be whitewashed adobe glistening in the sun. The Seven Cities increased in number but dwindled in splendor to the humble status of the Pueblo towns. Coronado called the region New Mexico, but it lacked a great deal of being another Mexico. Hope revived when an Indian dubbed El Turco (The Turk), "because he looked like one," told of a richer land *mas allá,* Gran Quivira. Coronado plunged into the Great Plains in the spring of 1541, in search of this new wonder, but of course it was not there. It had existed, in fact, only in El Turco's imagination, as he later confessed, and the purpose was to lure the Spaniards onto the trackless Plains, whence it was hoped they would not return. Coronado did get back to the Rio Grande, but not to tarry long. The next spring his tattered followers were on their way to Mexico. Because of the high expectations with which he had set out and because of the lavishness of the original equipment, Coronado's lack of success was regarded as particularly reprehensible. A disgraced and ruined man, he did not long survive the bitter criticism.

Immediate settlement of New Mexico might have changed the course of California history. As it was, occupation of the upper Rio Grande was deferred half a century. Coronado's expedition was rich only in explorations, and these turned northeastward rather than northwestward, away from rather than toward California. From a strictly local standpoint, then, there is some justification for taking more careful note of the sea expeditions of the early forties, though they were intended as subsidiaries to Coronado's main move on the Seven Cities.

In 1540, shortly after Coronado's departure for the north, Alarcón was sent up the coast. He reached the head of the gulf, entered the Colorado River and ascended it, perhaps to the mouth of the Gila. Finding no sign of Coronado, he turned back to Mexico. A detachment of Coronado's men led by Melchor Díaz was sent to meet Alarcón. It arrived too late. Díaz crossed the Colorado and got down into the peninsula but lost his life in the process. Both Alarcón and Díaz were in sight of California, but the record does not indicate that either set foot within the present limits of the state.

The next year, as a by-product of the Mixton War, Viceroy Mendoza came into possession of a larger number of ships. Eleven vessels had been brought from Spain by way of Guatemala and Honduras by Pedro de Alvarado, formerly the ranking officer under Cortés. Alvarado had planned a westward voyage, but the report of the Seven Cities lured him northward. He and Mendoza arranged a partnership, and when the gallant Alvarado was killed in the rebellion at Mixton, the viceroy took over the fleet.

Alvarado and Mendoza had been planning to send part of the fleet to the Spice Islands with Ruy López de Villalobos as commander, while the other ships were to go up the coast to continue Alarcón's efforts to get in touch with Coronado and the Seven Cities. The Mixton War delayed Villalobos' departure, but in September of 1541 a few ships were sent up the coast under the command of Francisco de Bolaños. Before he had made much progress Bolaños encountered a severe storm, his vessels were damaged, and he had to turn back. His explorations were in the vicinity just beyond the tip of Baja California, and a few place names there, for example, that of Cabo de San Lucas, seem to have been applied by him.

California's Name

Bolaños, it should be added, is often given credit for conferring the name California. There is no record, however, of the christening. The earliest use of the name of which record is preserved is in the journal of the Cabrillo expedition of the following year, but there California is used casually as a name already thoroughly established. Cortés had called the "island" Santa Cruz; neither account of the Ulloa voyage employs the name California; and although the Domingo del Castillo map of the Alarcón expedition has the lower end of the peninsula marked California, the authorities insist that this name was not on the map when first drawn. Particularly since other place names of his persisted in the peninsula, it seems probable that Bolaños was responsible for the name California.

Derivation of the name, though once a matter of wildest speculation, is now fixed. It is traced to one of the most popular pieces of early sixteenth-century Spanish fiction, *Las sergas de Esplandián* (The Deeds of Esplandián), by Ordóñez de Montalvo. *Esplandián* was a fantastic thriller, written as a sequel to the more famous *Amadís de Gaula.* Among other wild adventures it relates how the

Christians at Constantinople were opposed by a force of Amazons led by Queen Calafía of the island of California. The island of California was described as being "at the right hand of the Indies" and very close to the Terrestrial Paradise, an Amazon Island abounding in gold and infested with many griffins. Cortés as early as 1524 and Guzmán in 1530 expressed their expectations of finding an Amazon island ten days' sail off the coast. This fact, together with the certain familiarity of Cortés' men with the Montalvo romance, establishes the derivation of the name almost beyond peradventure of doubt.

Cabrillo Reaches Alta California

By the time of Bolaños' return, the viceroy had been disillusioned about the Seven Cities. One of the expeditions in which he utilized the rest of Alvarado's vessels was expected to reach the Spice Islands. With these vessels Villalobos reached the Philippine Islands, which he named in honor of the Spanish prince and claimed for Spain. The other expedition was encharged to a Portuguese pilot, Juan Rodríguez Cabrillo, and sent along the coast toward Cathay, apparently with instructions also to look for the western entrance to the Strait of Anian.

Cabrillo gave the coast only a cursory examination up to Cabo del Engaño, apparently because Ulloa had explored this far. When he landed and took possession for the king, he heard from the Indians of other whites to the east, presumably the men of Coronado. Continuing northward, he passed the subsequent boundary and became the first authenticated visitor to Alta California. On September 28, 1542, he discovered San Diego Bay, which he named San Miguel, and behind Point Loma his two tiny ships lay sheltered during a three-day storm. "They discovered a port, enclosed and very good," reads the relation of this voyage. They were at Santa Catalina and San Clemente Islands on October 7 and 8, named San Pedro Bay the Bay of Smokes, and journeyed on to the Town of Canoes, where possession was again taken in the name of the king. Repeatedly the Indians made mention of other Spaniards to the east. Cabrillo followed the coast very closely as far as Point Concepción, stopping at several places.

Finding it difficult to proceed beyond the point, he returned temporarily to San Miguel Island and there had the misfortune to break an arm, or, as other accounts have it, a leg. Although the break was

*Lake
Tenaya*

Edward Weston

Edward Weston

Juniper at Lake Tenaya

most painful and did not heal properly, Cabrillo shortly took advantage of a southwester to explore more of the coast. Just how far north he got is not clear. He made no landings and much of the time had to stand well out to sea. He did, however, become well acquainted with a Baia de los Pinos, Monterey Bay, and he observed some other parts of the coast both north and south of this bay. Stormy weather finally forced him back to San Miguel Island, where the old injury brought death on January 3, 1543.

On his deathbed Cabrillo enjoined his second in command to persevere in the northward exploration. Bartolomé Ferrelo made a sincere effort, but stormy weather still interfered, and like his master he was unable to land anywhere north of Point Concepción. His northernmost glimpse of the coast was not far from Point Reyes. Either out at sea off the mouth of Rogue River in Oregon or more probably off Eel River or Mad River, at about the forty-first parallel, there were signs that seemed to point to a great river in the locality. This was interpreted to mean the western embouchure of the Strait of Anian, but except for this conjecture Ferrelo got little information about this part of the coast. He gave up the battle against the storms and took the survivors back to Navidad, whence he submitted Cabrillo's reports and his own to the viceroy.

In Alta California they had found no more wealth than had Coronado in New Mexico and Kansas. The Indians of southern California were numerous and friendly but not advanced or wealthy enough to invite Spanish exploitation. The bay at San Diego was admittedly excellent but of little or no practical use until some excuse for occupying Alta California should arise. Even the recognition of southern California as a "land of endless summers" did not suffice to rouse Spanish interest in this distant region. The viceroy, in fact, seems to have found his chief gratification in the evidence that the Strait of Anian, if it existed at all, must strike the Pacific so far north that its discovery by other Europeans would not seriously menace Spain's hold upon Mexico and South America.

5

EXPLORATION RENEWED

For a score of years after the Coronado and Cabrillo ventures, interest in California lagged. The poorness of the far northwest as reported by these explorers was one good reason. Furthermore, Spanish exploration in general was slowing down after the extreme activity of the thirties and early forties. In addition, this was the period of most rapid development of the rich silver mines of Nueva Galicia, in which the Spaniards found, so to speak, a "moral equivalent" of exploration.

Early in the reign of Philip II, who acceded to the throne in 1556, Spanish expansion was renewed on several fronts. In addition to localized causes there was a central impulse, indirectly represented by Philip's "Ordenanzas sobre descubrimiento nuevo é población" of 1563, which specified uniform contracts for those who were to be commissioned to make new discoveries and settlements. In Europe Philip was busy with the French, the Turks, Queen Elizabeth, the Portuguese, and the Dutch. In the colonies his period was signalized by expansion into Florida, Nueva Vizcaya, the Philippines, and New Mexico, and by renewed exploration of the California coast.

Florida is far enough away from California that its occupation can be dismissed hurriedly as not part of our story. Furthermore, the narrative of the intrusion of the French Huguenots and their bloody and treacherous destruction by the Spaniards under Menéndez has been related in masterly fashion by such stylists as Francis Parkman and Woodbury Lowery. For the sake of perspective, however, it should be remarked that the adelantado to whom Philip entrusted this important task was his most competent naval commander and that the expedition numbered 2,646 select men and cost something like $1,800,000. For Menéndez it was a bad investment, but the French settlement was broken up and a Spanish colony established to stand guard over the Florida passage for the Silver Fleet.

Ibarra and Nueva Vizcaya

On the Mexican mainland the reason for expansion had nothing to do with guarding against French freebooters and heretics. Instead, it was a matter of protecting the silver miners against Indian raids, of bringing those wild Indians to a knowledge of God, and of finding perchance still other veins of silver. To this end Viceroy Velasco, on July 24, 1562, commissioned Francisco de Ibarra as governor and captain general to explore, conquer, settle, and govern the region that came to be called Nueva Vizcaya. It was an adelantado contract in all but name.

As early as 1554 Ibarra had made an entrada which resulted in the discovery of the important mines of San Martín and Aviño in northern Nueva Galicia. Four years later he was off in search of Copalá, "another Mexico" of wealthy and highly civilized Indians, and the equally alluring Topia. Among other evidence of his keen anticipation of finding a fabulous wonderland is a letter in which, in the vein of Friar Marcos, he gave a preview of Copalá as he had seen it "with his own eyes," a land of abundant food, of adobe and stone houses; a valley that was the best that he had seen in all of New Spain, "inhabited by a great number of people, with much fuel, and as skilful in the cultivation of their fields and in the irrigation of them as one can find in the world."

A land of exactly this description was not found, but in the period of his governorship Ibarra made half a dozen entradas in search of it which carried him as far afield as Paquimé and the Yaqui Valley. He pacified large numbers of Indians, the Franciscans who accompanied him made many converts, and he opened additional mining areas in modern Durango and Potosí. The province of Nueva Vizcaya is his principal monument, but much of Nueva Galician development was due to him no less directly, and for the later land advance to New Mexico and California his work provided a useful foundation.

The Philippines Added to New Spain

Strangely enough, however, the incentive for renewed interest in California came from the Philippines. Magellan, Loaysa, and Saavedra had touched at these islands; Villalobos had named them and claimed them for Spain, but he died in the Moluccas and his men had no more success than their predecessors in returning to Mexico over the route of the westward voyage. One of Villalobos' ships sailed 750 leagues northeast in an endeavor to get above the adverse trade winds but was driven back by a storm.

Not until 1564 did another expedition leave Mexico for the Philippines. After a three-month voyage this expedition, commanded by Miguel López de Legazpi, reached the islands early in 1565. The Portuguese from the Moluccas had roused the natives by announcing themselves as Spaniards as they snatched up slaves and perpetrated other atrocities. Consequently, Legazpi found the natives suspicious and antagonistic, which complicated the task of dominating more than a million natives with a force of 500 men. Nevertheless, Spanish control was made a reality on the island of Cebú and was gradually extended.

An essential element in Legazpi's task was to "discover the return route to New Spain with all possible speed." Fray Andrés de Urdaneta had been persuaded to accompany Legazpi for the express purpose of discovering such a course. "Besides faith in the Lord," the king had said, "confidence is felt that he will be the principal factor in finding the return route." In the spring of 1565, therefore, the 500-ton *San Pedro* was placed at his disposal. The general plan for accomplishing the return had been clearly understood for many years. It was to sail north far enough to catch the prevailing westerlies, which would carry a vessel across the Pacific and down the California coast to Mexico. Bernardo de la Torre, who had ventured northeast for Villalobos, and Cabrillo, who had found that the winds along the coast favored such a route from beyond the fortieth parallel, laid the groundwork for the scheme. The official test, however, was made under Urdaneta, and he is usually credited with the conception as well as with the execution of the plan.

Leaving Cebú in June Urdaneta followed the great circle course, northeast toward Japan, east toward the California coast, and then southeast to Acapulco. The first land sighted was one of the Santa Barbara Channel Islands, probably San Miguel. The voyage consumed 129 days; sixteen of the crew died before reaching port and four afterward, in addition to four Filipinos. Yet the actual distance sailed was only slightly in excess of the latitudinal course from Mexico, and the Japan Current and the prevailing westerlies made the route still more convenient.

Urdaneta's feat is somewhat eclipsed by the fact that he was preceded across the Pacific by the deserter Alonso de Arellano in the 40-ton patache *San Lucas*. Arellano left Legazpi's fleet, hurried on to the Philippines, and began the return voyage in April. His account bristles with extravagances about pelicans the size of ostriches, porpoises as large as cows, barking sea dogs with hands and feet and foxes' ears. These inaccuracies make it easy to doubt his claim that he reached latitude forty-three, but there seems to be no question that he sailed into Navidad before Urdaneta arrived and that he sought, though unsuccessfully, to get recognition and rewards as the real pioneer of the route from the Orient. The Spanish government continued to regard him as a deserter from the Legazpi-Urdaneta expedition, and his only consolation was that cartographers adopted some of his names for islands in the Pacific.

On strategic grounds the Philippines were considered a worth while part of the Spanish empire, yet the mortality rate in the islands was so high and so many lives were lost on the sailings to and from Mexico that maintenance of the colony was most difficult. Direct contact from Spain had been precluded by a treaty in 1529, whereby, in exchange for a Portuguese loan, Spain agreed not to use the Cape of Good Hope route, and not until 1763 did she open a direct contact with Manila. Since the Straits of Magellan route was too roundabout, the next best connection was across the Pacific with New Spain. Therefore, from the outset the Philippines were administered as a subdivision of the viceroyalty of New Spain and for more than two centuries their connection with the mother country was entirely through that viceroyalty. For the islands the routes to and from Mexico were thus a veritable life line.

Urdaneta's sailing course acquired almost immediate popularity. Trade was at first unrestricted and many merchants were attracted to engage in it. Silks, wax, chinaware, spices, and other eastern staples were the principal items involved. The trade assumed such great proportions that merchants in Spain protested to the court that they were losing the market of New Spain. The king obliged them in 1593 by restricting the Mexican-Philippine trade to a single 500-ton vessel each year, with a cargo not to exceed 250,000 pesos in value and not to include any silks, and with the privilege of exporting reserved to citizens of Manila. The restrictions lessened the volume of the trade, though there were evasions—as by under-valuation of cargoes really worth a million pesos or more—but they enhanced the profits for those who could participate.

Annually, until almost the very end of the Spanish colonial period, the Manila galleon in making its eastward trip skirted the California coast from Cape Mendocino or Monterey to the tip of Baja California. Landings were infrequent, it is true, and usually the shore was not sighted north of Cenizas Island, but for almost two centuries this was the one regular contact of Spaniards with the California region. Some of the galleons were utilized for exploration of the California coast, notably the one of 1595, commanded by Cermeño. The patent advisability of having a port along the coast at which the galleon could inquire for news of pirate activities and perhaps secure an escort for the remainder of the voyage to Acapulco came to be a basis for recurrent suggestions that California ought to be occupied.

A California port of call would also have lessened the ravages of the scurvy that always raged on the galleon. The restrictions upon the trade had operated to make every bit of cargo space exceedingly valuable. Profits were supposedly limited to 100 per cent but usually ran higher, sometimes to 400 per cent. Consequently, it was perfectly natural to ship an additional bale or two of silk instead of an extra barrel of water or foodstuff. Only the bare necessities were provided, and if the voyage was at all prolonged, suffering was certain. Since fresh foods were out of the question for a five- to eight-month trip, the scurvy afflicted every galleon. Those who advocated a California station emphasized, therefore, the salutary service that a cabbage patch would render to crew and passengers aboard the galleons.

Drake at Nova Albion

Throughout the English-speaking world the 200-odd sailings of the Manila galleon have been eclipsed by a single voyage of Sir Francis Drake. His famous voyage did represent several notable achievements. It was the first English circumnavigation of the globe; and by plundering the Spaniards and Portuguese, and above all by capturing the Panama-bound treasure galleon from Peru, he acquired literally tons of silver and gold and ranks as the most successful freebooter save only Piet Heyn, the Dutchman, who managed to capture a whole Silver Fleet.

In the course of his voyage Drake spent a month along the northern California coast, repairing and provisioning the *Golden Hind,* exchanging presents with the Indians, taking possession in the name of his queen, and conferring upon the entire region the name Nova Albion (New England). Undoubtedly these actions had some significance, and yet Californians have been prone to magnify them out of all due proportion. In the nineties there was real need for a book proving that, contrary to the popular supposition, Drake had not discovered San Francisco Bay. Another bay which he perhaps never saw now bears his name, as does one of San Francisco's largest hotels, while regional histories have made much of his alleged dream of founding an English colony on this coast.

Of recent years the magic of Drake's name and the circumstance of his taking possession of California have been shamelessly exploited by confidence men in a game played almost as widely as the "Spanish prisoner" racket. Drake's "heirs," running into the thousands, have been bilked because of their gullibility in believing that through their illustrious ancestor they had valid claim to California and that they might come into possession by merely advancing a little money for legal services. Rather than in such a gold brick these "heirs" might better have invested in a *History of California* in which the temporary nature of Drake's influence and of the English claim to California was made clear.

In 1937 there was much excitement over the discovery of a plate of brass, provisionally identified as the one which Drake had had affixed to a post at the time of taking possession of Nova Albion. Upon this plate the experts have blown hot and cold, but without demonstrating their unanimous expertness by coming to agreement. The discussion reveals the difficulty of dating such a document on the basis of vocabulary, spelling, punctuation, and formation of the letters, or even by metallurgical analysis. At the least, this plate of brass has given California history a cause célèbre comparable to Minnesota's Kensington Stone and has occasioned the issuance by the California Historical Society of a pamphlet in which the essential sources on Drake and California are conveniently assembled.

Drake's voyage seems to have sprung from the same motive that prompted many other English expeditions in the Elizabethan period, namely, the desire to develop new trades. When the Muscovy Company sent vessels northeastward, when the Levant Company penetrated the eastern Mediterranean, when other investing adventurers sent Frobisher to seek the Northwest Passage, the desire was not merely to accomplish exploration but chiefly to open the door for new commercial activity. Similarly, those who invested in equipping Drake's ships were concerned primarily in the trading aspect of the venture, and for the same reason the Moluccas were the predetermined destination.

En route Drake found golden opportunity for freebooting, especially after he had passed through the Straits of Magellan into the Pacific. Until his appearance the Pacific had been a Spanish lake. No other foreign vessels had appeared anywhere along the American west coast, and naturally the Spaniards had not bothered to fortify their ports or to maintain naval patrols. Drake seized the opportunity of this defenseless and unsuspecting state to plunder towns and ships all the way from Chile to Mexico, his biggest haul being the treasure galleon *Cacafuego* on its way from Lima to Panama.

After this capture, the original problem of opening a Moluccan trade became secondary to that of getting the treasure safely to England. The round-the-world route seemed best, particularly after trans-Pacific charts, sailing instructions, and a pilot were found on another Spanish ship. But first it was advisable to go to an out-of-the-way harbor to repair and provision the *Golden Hind,* and to await the favorable season for crossing the Pacific. Thus it was that Drake came to California. Incidentally, he took possession and looked for a Northwest Passage. There is no real evidence, however, to indicate that he had any expectations of finding such a passage or that he looked forward to English colonization of California.

Where Drake anchored has been a much discussed question. The most probable solution is that offered by Henry Raup Wagner, in his detailed discussion of the voyage around the world, to the effect that Drake casually visited several other inlets north of Point Reyes and stopped at Trinidad and Bodega Bays, but that he did not go to Drake's Bay at all.

Spain was tremendously concerned about Drake's freebooting in the Pacific. The galleons henceforth were armed, larger naval forces were maintained, and some of the coastal towns were better garrisoned to prevent a recurrence of the incident. These precautions were partly but not completely effective; Cavendish, Anson, and others followed Drake's example with varying fortunes. The menace to the Manila ships, which Drake and more especially Cavendish represented, was one of the factors inviting renewed attention to the California coast. Establishment of a California station where warnings of pirate danger could be given the Manila ships was the primary motive for the explorations by Gali, Unamuno, Cermeño, and Vizcaíno.

Drake's excursion to the California coast, on the contrary, aroused no Spanish concern. It is difficult to say just when the Spaniards learned that he had been there, but they seem to have estimated correctly that he had found no compelling attraction in California. They did not make the mistake made by some Drake biographers of supposing that an English colony would eventuate from his thirty-six-day stop. The English, the erroneous interpretations of the Fenton expedition of 1582 notwithstanding, made no endeavors to plant a colony here, and subsequent Spanish activity along the coast apparently had absolutely no connection with his visit.

The Manila Galleon Seeks a Port of Call

Quite aside from the English intrusions into the Pacific, individual Spaniards had kept in mind improvements in the Manila-Acapulco trade route. Coincident with the arousal of English interest in a Northwest Passage, the Spaniards, because of their Philippine possessions, took a new interest in discovering a short cut to the Orient, which came now to be denominated the Strait of Anian. Several propositions to utilize a Manila ship in the search for new trade and a strait were made during the 1570's. Financial difficulties precluded action until 1584, but in that year Viceroy Moya of New Spain had his interest aroused by the report of Francisco Gali, captain of a ship coming from Manila by way of Macao. Gali quoted his pilot's description of the Armenian Islands, some distance east of Japan, and claimed that he had "found them not far from the place which the Chinese pilot had indicated." He also reported sailing 700 leagues in a current or strait characterized by a heavy swell and "a great number of whales, tunny, mackerel, and bonitos, fishes which usually haunt straits and currents," and he gave some description of the California coast where first sighted in latitude thirty-seven and a half degrees. Neither of these points, however, was as interesting as the Armenian Islands. A port of call just east of Japan would, in fact, have been ideal for the Manila ships. Their greatest delay was in threading their way through the Philippines and in working up toward the North Pacific. By the time they reached the California coast, only a few days' sail remained.

Upon consulting others with regard to Gali's plan to establish a trading connection with the Armenian Islands, the viceroy received a very graphic description of the islands from Fray Andrés de Aguirre, whose information was "according to Father Fray Andrés de Urdaneta who had a report from a Portuguese captain." His description was honeyed with phrases such as: "many well-dressed and well-mannered people," "displaying much friendliness," "abundant and rich in silver and other things such as silk and cloth," "a great and rich profit," and "they all became very rich and loaded their ship with silver." Thus persuaded, the viceroy sent Gali back to Manila with 10,000 pesos to defray the expenses of another voyage to these islands, now mentioned more elaborately as Rica de Oro and Rica de Plata.

Gali died, his ship proved unserviceable, and there was delay in getting the expedition under way. Further difficulty ensued when Pedro de Unamuno, Gali's successor, sailed to Macao, where he was deprived of his ship. By some means he secured another vessel, in which he set off in July, 1587. He could not find the islands. "Although we searched from east to west, making every possible effort, we could not find the island," he noted concerning Rica de Plata. "Doubtless it does not exist, but somebody on hearsay ordered it drawn on his chart." His conclusion was the same regarding the other islands.

In accordance with his further instructions, Unamuno put in at the first bay he encountered on the California coast, probably at Morro Bay just north of San Luis Obispo. Here he landed and with twelve soldiers and some Filipinos made a short reconnaissance inland. They saw many trails and a few Indians, but these were timid and fled precipitately. Unamuno erected a cross and took possession. The next two days they penetrated farther inland and then when off guard were surprised by an Indian attack. One of the Spaniards who had taken off his coat of mail was killed, as was one of the Filipinos;

several suffered severe wounds.   In view of the number of men
wounded and of the scant supply of powder, Unamuno forewent the
pleasure of punishing the Indians and set sail for Mexico the following day.

Unamuno's disproof of the Armenian Island myth was not as permanently effective as it should have been.   There was to be still another search for them.   His experience with hostile Californians,
however, seems to have impressed the authorities, who enjoined subsequent explorers of the coast to desist from excursions inland.

Viceroy Luís de Velasco sponsored the next survey of the California ports.   He persuaded the king to order another reconnaissance
and selected Sebastián Rodríguez Cermeño for the task.   Cermeño
set out from Manila on July 4, 1595, in the 200-ton *San Agustín*.
The vessel sailed at the king's order, but the expenses were borne
by the owner, by Cermeño, and by others whose profits would derive
from the sale of the 130 tons of cargo.   The *San Agustín* also carried
a knocked-down launch, which was to be assembled when the exploration of the coast began.

Crossing the Pacific in the usual fashion, Cermeño made his first
landfall at what he called Cape Mendocino, apparently somewhat
south of the cape so called today.   Unable to land on the bold and
dangerous coast because of the heavy sea and the boisterous weather,
he sailed slowly southward.   Appreciating the risk to the ship, the
pilot, master, and boatswain presented a written demand to Cermeño
that he abandon the examination of the coast and run forthwith to
Mexico, but the captain, undismayed, persisted in his explorations.
A day or two later he brought the ship to anchor in a great ensenada,
which he named "La Baya de San Francisco" (not the present San
Francisco Bay, but Drake's Bay).

Many Indians appeared on the beach, and one paddled out in a
balsa to be rewarded with some cotton and silk cloth and a red cap.
The next morning four natives came out and received presents, whereupon the captain and twenty-two men went ashore.   They described
the Indians as friendly and hospitable, well built and more robust and
corpulent than the Spaniards.   Cermeño thought their culture roughly
comparable to that of the Chichimecos of northern Mexico.   Farther
inland the Spaniards met a more warlike band, which deployed around
them in a circle and howled loudly.   But the Indians who had al-

ready received gifts reassured these others, and they laid down their bows and arrows and exchanged embraces with Cermeño's men. Taffeta sashes were presented to them.

The Spaniards tarried here a month, assembling the launch whose pieces had taken up much of the cargo space on the galleon.   During the course of this work there was opportunity for a journey or two inland.   The estuary of Drake's Bay was visited, and Cermeño's exact description of it confirms identification of the anchorage. These Spaniards recorded far more accurate descriptions of the topography and of the friendly Indians than Drake had done sixteen years earlier.   The fact that they had no intimation of a previous intrusion of Europeans, either by word from the Indians or by finding material relics, militates strongly against the possibility of this being the bay where Drake refitted the *Golden Hind.*

On November 30 a storm arose and drove the *San Agustín* ashore. She was a total wreck, the cargo and all the provisions were lost, and at least two of the crew lost their lives.   The only thing left for the survivors to do was to complete the open launch, get what supplies they could from the natives, and set sail.   They made another journey inland and acquired a quantity of acorns, though only after a sharp skirmish with the natives.   On December 8 Cermeño and his seventy men sailed across toward the other point of the great bay, passing inside the Farallones.

The men seem to have taken it for granted that, in view of the disaster to the *San Agustín,* their commander would abandon further examination of the coast and proceed with all possible haste to Mexico.   Some stops, of course, were essential so that they might go ashore to seek water and food; but Cermeño had the launch heave to on dark nights and imposed other delays so that the work of exploration might be accomplished.

He acquired a knowledge of the coast from forty-one degrees to about thirty degrees latitude that was surprisingly accurate, considering the difficulties under which he was operating.   As a thorough survey of the coast his compares favorably, in fact, with any other prior to the late eighteenth century.   He crossed Monterey Bay from point to point and ran down the coast to San Luis Obispo.   Much of the time the launch was within a musket shot of the shore.   At San Luis Obispo the natives surprised them with shouts of "Christianos" and "Mexico," evidently echoes of Unamuno's visit in 1587.   In response to signs that the Spaniards were hungry, these natives obliged them with a few acorns and some acorn mush. The Indians here exhibited an avarice such as was later attributed to the Santa Barbara tribes. As Cermeño wrote: "After we gave them pieces of taffeta and satin and woolen blankets, they asked for more." Cermeño's men fished and traded at San Miguel and Santa Rosa Islands. They passed across Santa Monica Bay, continued down the coast, and landed at San Martín Island.

The story of the voyage of these seventy men in their open sailboat is one of incredible hardships and privations. Their one stroke of good fortune was finding a large fish, probably a tuna, stranded in the rocks on San Martín Island. "We went on shore and found many wild onions and prickly pear trees," runs Cermeño's account, "and likewise God willed that we should find a dead fish among the rocks with two mortal wounds, and it was so large that the seventy of us sustained ourselves on it for more than a week, and if it had not been so large we would have perished there of hunger." Finally the men reached such desperate straits that Cermeño gave in to their importunities and abandoned efforts at further discovery. Making no further stops he sailed to Chacala, where his weary, half-starved, and half-sick crew disembarked. A few men took the launch on to Acapulco, while he and the ship's officers journeyed inland to report their achievements and their misfortunes.

Cermeño's remarkable accomplishments in surveying the coast were unfortunately overshadowed by the loss of the galleon with its valuable cargo. Even the explorations that he had made were discounted. After much taking of testimony the viceroy held that there seemed to be "convincing proof, resting on clear inference, that some of the principal bays, where with greater reason it might be expected harbors would be found, they crossed from point to point and by night, while others they entered but a little way. For all this a strong incentive must have existed, because of the hunger and illness they say they experienced, which would cause them to hasten on their voyage." He concluded, therefore, that the king's plans for surveying the California coast had not been entirely carried out. The fact that Cermeño was Portuguese may have contributed to the bitterness of the criticism heaped upon him, but at any rate the wreck of the *San Agustín* stood out as the one noteworthy or notorious feature of his voyage. As the moral of this costly lesson came the decision to conduct future explorations of the coast with smaller unladen vessels sent out from Mexico expressly for that purpose, rather than to subject the rich Manila galleons to so great a risk.

Oñate and Vizcaíno

In the meantime there had been a recrudescence of interest in New Mexico. Francisco de Ibarra and after him Francisco de Urdiñola had carried the frontier of mines and settlements forward in Nueva Vizcaya. Castañeda's belated account of the Coronado expedition once more conjured up the dream of another Mexico in the upper valley of the Río Grande and made men wonder if the region was as poor as it had been pictured at the time of Coronado's return. Slave-hunting raids down the Conchos added to the interest and outlined an approach less roundabout and less infested by hostile tribes than the Coronado route along the Pacific slope.

In the eighties and nineties several preliminary entries were made into New Mexico, most of them in technical violation of the ban on unauthorized expeditions among the northern Indians. Meanwhile, the viceroy received bids for the contract to colonize New Mexico. Many applied, but the choice fell upon the man who best demonstrated his financial competence to outfit and equip the expedition. Appropriately enough, this was Juan de Oñate, son of one of the four discoverers of Zacatecas, and the fortune he now offered to stake on the New Mexico project had been built up in the preceding step of Spanish expansion. The contract was made in 1595, at which time the viceroy was also contracting with Sebastián Vizcaíno, of whom more later, to explore the California coast. Indeed, Oñate and Vizcaíno were regarded as coöperating in the extension and strengthening of the northern frontier.

When Oñate finally set out in 1598, his expedition included 130 soldier-settlers, their families, numerous Indian and Negro slaves, a band of Franciscans, eighty-three carts and wagons loaded with baggage, and 7,000 head of stock. From the Conchos he cut across to the Río Grande, striking it just below modern El Paso. Here he took possession in the name of the king on April 30, and the day was given over to celebration, mass, a sermon, and the presentation of a play written for the occasion. Headquarters were established at San Juan (formerly known as the pueblo of Caypa), and such signs of civilization as a church and an irrigation ditch soon appeared. In the kiva, on September 9, the chiefs from several pueblos gathered to swear fealty to King Philip, whose death was to occur just three days later. The chiefs were blessed by the Franciscan father and received rods symbolic of the Spanish authority now vested in them.

The high lights of the next few years were two trips out onto the buffalo plains, a search for mines that had been reported in western New Mexico, and the siege of the pueblo of Ácoma, the sky city perched on a mesa top. While Oñate was making his second expedition on the plains, most of the settlers deserted the colony, but he sent after them and brought them back from Santa Bárbara with reinforcements. He made one more effort to reach the Pacific. By Bill Williams Fork he went to the Colorado and down to its mouth, looking unsuccessfully for pearl fisheries along the gulf shore. On this trip the weary travelers were entertained by an Indian story teller who dramatized the wonders of the north. Giant Amazons, a tribe whose ears trailed on the ground, a tribe of unipeds, a tribe whose habit was to sleep under water, a tribe which lived on smells—these were some of his yarns. "Since they have been affirmed by so many and different tribes," Father Escobar opined, mindful of God's great power, "they cannot lack foundation."

Along the Río Grande discouragement mounted. Oñate finally asked to be released from his contract. A successor being appointed, possibly to Oñate's surprise, he returned to Mexico to face ten years of prosecution in the courts for asserted mismanagement of the New Mexico enterprise. His rewards were "poverty, enemies, and disappointment," but he had established a settlement in New Mexico, an outpost hundreds of miles beyond the rest of the frontier, a colony that was a constant incentive to the Spaniards to bridge the gap between it and the frontier of continuous settlements. Though New Mexico was somewhat off the trail that the Spaniards were to utilize in the settlement of California, it was nonetheless a contributing factor in the ultimate development of that province.

On the coast, the years of Oñate's work in the Pueblo country witnessed renewed activity. Throughout the seventies and eighties and perhaps earlier there seem to have been several endeavors to continue Cortés' project of pearl fisheries in Baja California. Few documents remain to describe these voyages, but it does appear that a man named Sanctotis was granted special privileges for this purpose by the viceroy in 1584 and by the king in 1587. In Thomas Cavendish's raid on the shipyard at Navidad one of the ships destined for the use of Sanctotis' company was destroyed, and therefore pearl fishing was not prosecuted vigorously. Other men applied for pearl-fishing licenses, among them Sebastián Vizcaíno, who was to be the next important figure after Cermeño in northwestward exploration.

Vizcaíno was neither a mariner nor a military man but a merchant. He had had some experience in the Philippine trade and was anxious to venture pearl fishing in California. His offer was protested by Sanctotis, whose monopoly had a few years yet to run, and the audiencia was called upon to adjudicate the matter. A compromise was effected and Vizcaíno and the viceroy entered into a contract. The former was to have a twenty-year monopoly of pearl fishing in a district measuring ten leagues along the California coast, for which he would deliver to the king one fifth of all pearls, gold, and silver acquired, and one tenth of any salt fish secured.

The first ship sent out in fulfillment of this contract accomplished nothing. Several of the partners became discouraged, and court actions were necessary to prevent their defaulting. In 1596 Vizcaíno sailed in personal command of another expedition, which consisted of 230 men in one 500-ton ship and two smaller craft. They landed at a large bay where the Indian speech sounded "like the bleating of sheep." Many of the men were already discouraged by the sterility of the land. They moved north to La Paz, where they found the remains of Cortés' town, and then went on to another bay where nineteen of their number were drowned. Back at La Paz on October 21, fire destroyed much of their provisions and munitions. Since no food could be had from the natives, Vizcaíno perforce sent most of his men back to the mainland. In one of the smaller boats he made a brief effort to explore more of the gulf, but a succession of storms forced him back to the mainland.

This voyage had proved a complete failure; Vizcaíno had discovered nothing new and had found no great wealth. He spoke in most unflattering terms of the land he had visited; the only hopeful sign he mentioned was that the natives seemed anxious for conversion. Yet he may have confided to the viceroy that he had found some better indications of pearls. At any rate he was still interested in leading another expedition, and the viceroy, though not highly impressed with Vizcaíno's ability, was ready to give him another chance.

This was the more just in view of the expenditures already made by Vizcaíno and his associates.

Arrangements for another expedition went forward slowly. Vizcaíno and Viceroy Monterey could not get together on the terms of a new contract. There was another aspirant for a pearl-fishing license. Intrusions of Dutch pirates into the Pacific distracted Spanish attention, and the death of King Philip interrupted definite action by the Council of the Indies; consequently, the voyage was postponed until 1601 and then again until 1602.

Finally, three vessels were provided, seamen were engaged, and by a special dispensation Vizcaíno was permitted to enlist a limited number of soldiers. The viceroy displayed great interest in the preparations, assigned three experienced soldiers to assist Vizcaíno in an advisory capacity with regard to all matters other than navigation, and took great pains to procure a cosmographer.

In March, Vizcaíno received detailed instructions from the viceroy. He was not to enter the gulf on pain of death, but should proceed at once to the exploration of the outer coast. On the return voyage he might fish for pearls in the gulf. He was to avoid conflict with the natives and attend to the business of exploration, noting landmarks, making soundings, observing his position each day and night, and mapping his discoveries. The most peculiar feature of the instructions was the great authority assigned the councils on navigation and military affairs. They were not merely advisory but had such powers that little discretion was left to Vizcaíno, possibly a reflection of viceregal lack of confidence in him.

Vizcaíno's fleet had an easy voyage to Navidad, the Mazatlán Islands, and across to the tip of the peninsula. On the beach at San Bernabé there were so many pearl oyster shells to catch the rays of the sun that Father Ascensión likened it to a starry heaven. Contrary winds delayed the voyage up the outer coast. Four times the fleet set out, only to be forced back to San Bernabé, and consequently it was more than two months later when the vessels reached Cedros Island. Aside from adverse winds the major difficulty thus far had been in getting an adequate supply of water. Their equipment for carrying water seems to have been unsatisfactory, and search for springs or streams along the arid coast was frequently unavailing. The very slowness of their progress, however, spelled more exact acquaintance with the coast. Beating back and forth along these few hundred miles of shore line, they came to know it intimately. The cosmographer's map took on a wealth of detail, and Father Ascensión's diary was enlivened with snatches of interesting minutiae such as that about the Indians who "fished with dry feet" by tying a pelican with a broken wing and then helping themselves to the fish contributed by his concerned and devoted pelican friends.

Along the peninsula Vizcaíno made free with the geographic names assigned by earlier explorers. His San Bernabé, Magdalena, San Hipólito, San Roque, and San Bartolomé, for example, permanently displaced earlier names. After he reached Upper California the same process continued. He rechristened with their present names San Diego, Santa Catalina, most of the Channel Islands, Buenaventura, Santa Barbara, Point Concepción, Point of Pines, Carmel, and Monterey.

From San Diego to Point Concepción, Vizcaíno's journey was more pleasant. As compared with the barren peninsula, southern California seemed a very rich land. In his enthusiasm, Father Ascensión mentions "golden pyrites . . . , a sure sign that there must be gold in the mountains," and quantities of another substance which the Spaniards called amber. The Indians were numerous and friendly and offered the Spaniards water, fish, and jicama roots. Their worst feature was a proclivity toward petty thievery, which led the good father to insist that "they beat the gypsies in cunning and dexterity."

The Port of Monterey

North of Point Concepción, Vizcaíno ran the coast somewhat more hurriedly. He charted one bay, probably San Luis Obispo, but the next stop was at Monterey. The Port of Monterey was the prize discovery of the voyage. Vizcaíno called it "the best port that could be desired, for besides being sheltered from all the winds, it has many pines for masts and yards, and live oaks and white oaks, and water in great quantity, all near the shore." In another connection he spoke of the land as being thick with Indians and very fertile, the "climate and the quality of the soil resembling Castile," and the port commodious, "sheltered from all winds," and at the ideal latitude to provide "protection and security for the ships coming from the Philippines."

Since Vizcaíno had been sent to explore the California coast very largely with a view to selecting a port for the use of the Manila galleons, his enthusiastic description of Monterey was the feature of his report that made the greatest impression.   In fact, until the time of Portolá, more than a century and a half later, the excellence of Monterey was accepted as the central fact about Alta California and was the chief motivating force attracting Spanish interest in the region.

From Monterey, Vizcaíno sent back one ship bearing the sick and disabled.   With the other two he started north on January 3, 1603. He entered Drake's Bay, which to all these Spaniards was Puerto de San Francisco, and which his chief pilot Bolaños, who had been with Cermeño, recognized.   They planned to go ashore to look for the silk and wax left there after the wreck of the *San Agustín,* but did not do so.   Instead, they rounded Point Reyes—again the name is Vizcaíno's—and bore on up the coast.   They sighted a cape near snowy mountains, which Bolaños opined was Cape Mendocino. Now fog, heavy seas, and stormy weather beset them.   The two boats were already separated.   Vizcaíno's pilot thought his farthest north was forty-one or forty-two degrees, while the other vessel was said to have reached forty-three degrees, but neither gained much actual information about the coast north of Point Reyes.

Vizcaíno's decision to turn back was prompted by the unfavorable weather and the sickness of his men.   "There were only two sailors," he reported, "who could climb the maintopsail."   He had also complied with his instructions to explore as far as Cape Mendocino.   The voyage had stretched out over eight months and supplies had run short.   Finally, off the northern California coast, "the pitching was so violent that it threw both sick and well from their bunks and the general [Vizcaíno] from his.   He struck upon some boxes and broke his ribs."

The voyage south was a rapid one.   Some additional observations of the coast were made, but they did not anchor because they doubted their ability to lift the anchor again.   Another search for pearls in the Gulf of California had been contemplated, but it was obvious that the men were not equal to it.   Vizcaíno hurried to the mainland. With the five men who were still fit he went ashore at Mazatlán to get aid and supplies.   Thus succored, the expedition continued to Acapulco.   The men on the other vessel had equally harrowing experiences.

Viceroy Monterey was highly pleased with what Vizcaíno had done and appointed him to command the next Manila galleon, a posi-

tion highly lucrative as well as honorable. But unfortunately for
Vizcaíno, the Conde de Monterey was promoted to the viceroyalty of
Peru, and his successor at Mexico City reversed many decisions and
appointments. It is not clear just why the new viceroy, Montesclaros,
was so spiteful toward all connected with the Vizcaíno expedition,
but the fact remains that he was. He took the galleon away from
Vizcaíno and had the cosmographer Martínez Palacios tried for for-
gery, condemned, and hanged. Even when the king ordered that
Vizcaíno be suitably rewarded for his efficient survey of the difficult
California coast, Montesclaros found a way to evade the command.

No excuse apears for his vindictiveness, but from one point of view
he was correct in his insistence that a California port of call would
not greatly benefit the galleon. The galleons seldom sighted the
coast north of Cenizas Island, and by the time they were opposite
Monterey, they considered the voyage practically over. The fact that
they hardly ever stopped in California after it was finally settled substantiates Montesclaros' reasoning on the point. His advocacy of
further search for the Armenian Islands was less defensible, even
though a station in that locality would have been worth much more
to the galleons. Unamuno's negative findings were, however, insufficient to counteract all the alluring fabrications about these islands.
Consequently, the expedition which Vizcaíno wanted to lead to occupy Monterey was presently diverted to a useless search for these
phantom islands.

Denied thus the opportunity of fathering the first settlement of Alta
California, Vizcaíno nevertheless deserves full recognition for his
exhaustive survey of the coast from the tip of the peninsula to beyond
Monterey, for his permanent contributions to the nomenclature of
the coast, and for the glamor that he bestowed upon California
through his praise of the Port of Monterey. His work was a fitting
climax to the revival of interest in exploration, which had characterized the latter part of the sixteenth century.

6

THE JESUIT MISSIONS

WITH OÑATE AND VIZCAÍNO an epoch ended. They were the last adventurers of the conquistador-adelantado type, represented earlier by Cortés, Coronado, and Ibarra, which had directed the sixteenth-century aggrandizement of Spanish America. In later years such leadership appeared only occasionally, as, for example, in the Marquis of Aguayo, resplendent hero of the founding of Texas. For the most part, frontier expansion ceased to be the work of ambitious and profit-minded individuals.

The reason was not far to seek. Incidentally the change was due to the government's zeal to centralize control and to eliminate personal exemptions. Adelantados and encomenderos were under fire for this reason; the government was not only refraining from issuing new grants but was also seeking to revoke those made earlier. More fundamentally, abandonment of the adelantado-encomendero system was because the lands lying next ahead were so meager in resources and so infested with wild and backward Indians that they did not attract the investment of private fortunes or endeavors.

The Mission as a Frontier Institution

Happily for Spain, as one agent faltered another was ready to step into the breach. The new device, that of the mission, was not completely untried. In the earlier conquests the cross had been a constant support for the sword; the religious had spread the faith among the many Indians subjected; they had taken great strides in educational advancement, and frequently had been called upon to take over the reins of government. Drawing merely from the age of the

71

conquistadores one could compile a roster of notable churchmen whose achievements were of far-reaching significance. To mention but a few: Bartolomé de las Casas, protagonist of the New Laws; Sebastián Ramírez de Fuenleal, bishop of Santo Domingo and president of the second Audiencia of Mexico; Pedro de Gante, first schoolmaster in Mexico; and Pedro Sánchez, first provincial of the Jesuits in New Spain. Throughout this period, however, the religious had been secondary rather than primary agents in frontier advance. It was a new departure to make the mission the chief reliance for extending Spanish control into new areas.

The mission, though not duplicated or even approximated on the Anglo-American frontier, is doubtless the best-known institution of Spanish America. It was essentially a system whereby Indians were induced to congregate in a pueblo or town, where under clerical discipline they were taught the Catholic religion, the Spanish language, and the rudiments of the white man's way of life. These fundamentals are reminiscent of the encomienda system.

It was these mundane functions of the mission that particularly endeared it to "Their Most Catholic Majesties," the monarchs of Spain. These kings, as loyal and devout sons of the church, had a genuine interest in the conversion of the heathen, yet even churchmen admit that state support of missions was due to the practical services that missions rendered the empire. For these services the government paid. A significant hint is that in the royal bookkeeping expenditures for missions were lumped together with those for presidial upkeep and for the establishment of new pueblos, under the general heading of frontier expense. And appropriately so; for whereas the presidio, as an army post not unlike those which the United States Army maintained in the Indian country of our Trans-Mississippi West, and the pueblo, as an example of control through colonization, represent standard devices for holding a border, the mission came to be the kingpin of the Spanish frontier system.

Theoretically, the mission was temporary. It was to continue in a given locality only long enough to get the Indians started on the road to Christianity and civilization. Then it would be secularized—that is, converted into a parish church. Its neophytes would be released from mission discipline, given their share of the mission property, and launched as full-fledged members of colonial society. Ten years was once designated as the proper duration for a mission.

Seldom, however, was the schedule met. Often the Indians needed a longer period of tutelage, and usually the lay settlers among whom the secularized Indians were supposed to be assimilated had lagged behind. Many missions operated for two or three score years and others passed well beyond the century mark.

To the end of the mission period the fundamental aims and methods were uniform. There was slight variation in procedure, for example, between Jesuit and Franciscan missions, and there were occasional modifications of technique as the conditions of mission operation came to be better understood. One such modification was in the matter of the language of religious instruction. The original program called for use of the native tongue, but when it was discovered how many dialects would have to be employed, sometimes several at a single station, and that most Indian idioms had no words to convey the most essential Christian teachings, the decision was to fall back upon Spanish.

Daily drill in sacred music, prayers, and the catechism was a feature of the mission program. The Indians were also kept busy at a variety of tasks essential to the material success of the mission. Because the neophytes had to toil, misplaced sympathy is sometimes showered upon them, yet there is abundant testimony that they found compensation in the salvation of their souls, in the transfer to the missionary of responsibility for the provision of food, clothing, and shelter, and in the enjoyment of the pageantry of the Catholic religion, the fiestas, the art and music, and the higher standard of living at the mission. There were occasionally a few malcontents who fled from the missions or stirred up rebellions, but the preponderant testimony is that most of the mission Indians preferred their new life. From the standpoint of the missionary, to plan and supervise such a program obviously called for executive talents and also presupposed a considerable amount of competence in such matters as farming, stock raising, carpentry, and the other basic trades.

The disciplinary feature of the mission system is to be emphasized. It was enforced in part through the missionary's personality, in part through the mission guard of from one to half a dozen soldiers, or by the soldiers at the near-by presidio. Great reliance was placed upon native officers who in reality made the control effective. This device was carried over from the encomienda system, but more important, it was consistent with the habits of the Indians in their indigenous state. And discipline, of course, was but a means to the end of domesticating and civilizing these childlike primitives and of training them to be valuable members of colonial society.

The center of the mission was its church. Around it were clustered the missionary's house, quarters for the Indians, granaries and storerooms, and workshops for carpentry, blacksmithing, weaving, and the making of such things as pottery, candles, and soap. Farther out were corrals, irrigated fields, and grazing lands. A new mission would not boast all these things, but as a self-sufficing agricultural community a successful mission needed some such layout.

If a mission prospered, its buildings were enlarged and made more substantial, with special attention devoted to beautification of the church. Many a mission church in plastered adobe or cut stone was as well designed and executed and as richly and tastefully decorated as the parish churches in more settled communities. The partially restored or surviving mission structures in California, beautiful though many of them are, do not adequately represent the achievements of the builders in the older mission areas. And since the outbuildings have so largely disappeared, still less do they impress one as having been the center of the busy, bustling life of a community of hundreds or thousands of persons.

Missions of this generic pattern were still being established at the close of the colonial period; many persisted into the nineteenth century and some into the twentieth. Nevertheless, the later missions were usually considered anachronous by the government and by the colonials, and the tendency was to place them on a more subordinate basis or to eliminate them entirely. The most glorious mission era was in the seventeenth and early eighteenth centuries. Indeed, the mission of this period was so vital an institution that it may appear that none but the missionaries were exhibiting any initiative or vigor for the advancement of Spanish America. Certainly it is true of this century and a half that frontier expansion was almost solely the work of the missions.

The scattered distribution of the mission areas makes statistical measurement difficult. As one writer remarks, only the recording angel knows how many missions were founded or how many converts were made. At the time of their expulsion the Jesuits claimed 717,000 neophytes at their mission stations, while the number under the control of the mendicant orders would easily have brought the

total to more than a million.   Certainly the work was on a magnificent scale.   A mission salient was thrown out on almost every frontier where older colony bordered heathendom: in southern Chile, in
the Paraguay mesopotamia, in the Gran Chaco, among the Chiquitos
and Moxos, in Mainas, in the steaming valley of the Atrato, on the
plains of Casanare, in the jungle along the Meta and the Orinoco, on
the llanos of Venezuela, in the sweltering Guatemalan lowlands and
in southern Mexico, in Florida and Georgia, in Texas and New Mexico, and along the northern frontier of New Spain.

A Jesuit Province

Of these areas one of the most notable was that opening northwestward along the Pacific coast of New Spain.   Here the Jesuits labored

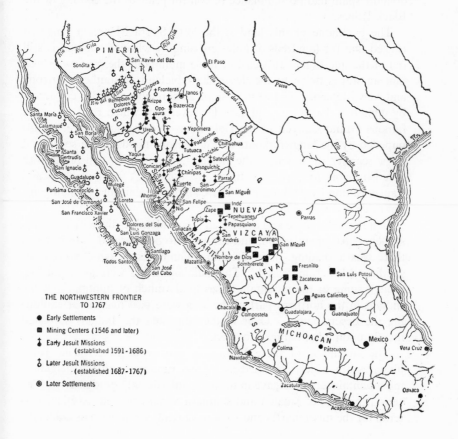

for a century and three quarters (from 1591 to 1767). Chronologically, they bridged the gap between the sixteenth-century conquistadores and explorers and the late eighteenth-century colonizers of Alta California. Geographically, also, they carried the frontier forward from central Mexico until California was but one step removed.

This northwestern province of the Black Robes was as large as Spain itself. It embraced modern Nayarit, Durango, Sinaloa, Sonora, Baja California, most of Chihuahua, and part of Arizona. Coronado's and Ibarra's trails had traversed a portion of this land, the southern part of which was dotted with silver mines and occasional settlements, but the real work of subduing and civilizing its native inhabitants was left for the Jesuits. In the northern part of this domain Spain had no semblance of control prior to the coming of the Black Robes.

The backbone of this land is the lofty Sierra Madre, a range so rugged that for hundreds of miles crossing by wheeled vehicles is still out of the question. Just east of these mountains the monte-covered plateau slopes down to the desertlike tableland of southern Arizona and New Mexico. The western slope is more abrupt and is cut across by numerous barrancas and canyons several of which rival the more famous Grand Canyon of the Colorado. North-south travel is also impeded by the tangled monte and dangerous floods in the south and by a scarcity of water in the north. Terrain thus conspired with Spanish habit to prescribe travel by horseback or muleback and transportation by pack train. The California peninsula is analogous, but drier and more barren.

In a region so large and so broken a considerable diversity in native speech, tribal organization, and culture is to be expected. In general, there was a shading off in cultural attainments as remoteness from southern Mexico increased. The mainland tribes were agriculturists, though some of the mountain tribes made much of hunting, and the Indians in the northern part of the area were past masters at exploiting the desert plants. Over in the peninsula the Indians subsisted merely upon what nature provided.

The sturdiness of these Indians is worthy of note. The Tarahumares are widely heralded as tireless runners; with the neighboring mountaineers they gave in to the Spaniards only grudgingly. The coastal peoples of Sinaloa and southern Sonora proved excellent material for the missionaries and soon were ready for a place as colonials.

Farther up the coast were the Mayo, the Seri, and the Yaqui. The latter have a contemporary reputation as upstanding and courageous fighting men; in the colonial period warriors of the other two tribes were equally respected. The Pimas of northern Sonora were at once amenable to mission life and yet stalwart enough to stave off the attacks of the Apaches. Less can be said for the peninsula tribes, yet the barrenness of their environment is some excuse for lack of attainment.

As early as the 1550's the Franciscans had begun work among the Indians in the southeastern corner of this area. The chroniclers report half a dozen martyrdoms and numerous instances of miraculous assistance for these friars, of fish that jumped from a stream into Friar Cinto's hands when he was starving, and of arrows shot at Friar Cossin that turned back against those who had drawn the bow. Nevertheless, the work of the Franciscans in Nueva Vizcaya was less notable than that of the adelantado Francisco de Ibarra and it was quite overshadowed by subsequent Jesuit achievements.

Meanwhile, the Jesuits had been attempting missions on the Atlantic coast. Father Martínez was martyred in Florida in 1566, and Father Segura and seven companions met a like fate in Virginia five years later. Soon after this tragedy the surviving Black Robes were transferred to New Spain, where they joined a newly-arrived group under the energetic provincial, Father Pedro Sánchez. Assisted by reinforcements from Spain and by generous contributions from the faithful in New Spain and Old, the Jesuit work expanded rapidly. First emphasis was upon teaching. Schools were opened for creole and Indian youths, and under the impetus of Jesuit instruction Mexico City soon took rank as one of the New World's foremost seats of learning.

The Black Robes at Work

Then in 1591, pursuant to a contract of the preceding year between Philip II and the head of the order, the Company of Jesus undertook the spiritual conquest of the northwestern frontier. Gonzalo de Tapia and Martín Pérez were the first Black Robes in the field. Going to San Felipe on the Sinaloa they planted the earliest mission on the northwest coast, one which developed into the Jesuit regional capital. The Indians proved willing converts, some 2,000 being baptized the first year. Six other Jesuits came to aid in the work, which was now expanded into the valley of the Mocorito. Tapia pushed on to the Fuerte and eastward into Topia, scouting for new mission sites. In 1593 he made a trip to Mexico to solicit further support. But the next year an Indian shaman, Nacabeba, smarting under punishment for neglect of Christian duties, cut short Father Tapia's promising career—he was but thirty-three—and made him the first Jesuit martyr in New Spain.

Mission advance came to a temporary standstill. But in 1595 a force of twenty-five soldiers came to fortify San Felipe. Father Tapia's remains were recovered—Nacabeba, we are told, had tried to roast one of the martyr's arms, but fire had had no effect. By 1597 conversions were sharply on the increase, and two years later they were further stimulated by the capture and execution of Nacabeba. By the end of the decade the Jesuit reports tell of sixty temporary structures for religious use, eight modest but well-built churches, and 10,000 baptisms.

In this same decade other Jesuits launched missions east of the Sierra. A gift of 22,000 pesos from Governor del Rio and others provided for a college at Durango. From it, two padres went among the Laguna Indians of modern Coahuila, where they soon had a mission with three visitas and 1,500 converts. Fathers Santarén and Ruiz labored to the accompaniment of noteworthy miracles among the Acaxees of mountainous Topia, while Ramírez and Fonte launched work among the Tepehuanes.

In 1601, in the absence of Santarén, 5,000 Acaxees rose in revolt. Their grievance was against forced labor in the mines rather than against the Jesuits, but they took a solemn oath to kill all the Spaniards in Topia, the padres included. Five Spaniards were killed in the initial outbreak and many buildings in the province were burned. According to the Jesuit chroniclers, Padre Ruiz was the hero of the defense of the church of San Andrés, where forty Spaniards were besieged by 800 rebel Indians. Protected only by his crucifix, the padre led a sortie, but amidst the cloud of arrows not one struck him. The siege was lifted when Governor Urdiñola hurried over from Durango, but the Acaxees were pacified only when Padre Santarén went fearlessly among them to offer pardon and to persuade them to return to the fold. A few of the western Acaxees continued the revolt under a shaman who, in imitation of the Spaniards, set himself up as a bishop and then as God, named two associates St. James and

St. John, and baptized, married, and divorced "by original formulas of his own." Santarén weaned away most of this "bishop's" followers, and his rebellion was brought to an end. Then, partly by force and partly by persuasion, the faith was carried to the cannibal Xiximes in the mountain fastnesses south of the Acaxees. By 1611 some 7,000 of these erstwhile cannibals were living peaceably under Santarén's supervision.

The Laguna missions, meanwhile, met with a series of misfortunes. Smallpox carried off 400 neophytes in 1608, four years later the Nazas River broke its banks to do serious flood damage, and the following year was one of drought and famine. But through thick and thin the Lagunas were steadfast in their attachment to the Black Robes, on whom they counted for protection from their more warlike neighbors.

On the west coast the new century opened even more auspiciously. Ten additional soldiers arrived, increasing the presidial force at San Felipe to thirty-six, and, more important, the command was assigned to the dynamic and resourceful Captain Diego Martínez Hurdaide. For three decades Hurdaide was a prodigious help to Jesuit advance. His picturesque methods endear him to historians, but he was no more loyal to the faith than many another presidial commander and his bravery was drawn from the general Spanish store. His valorous deeds are a good illustration of the militant evangelism characteristic of this golden mission era.

Hurdaide's first duty was a mere preliminary to greater heroic exploits. The Guazaves had burned their church. Hurdaide promptly seized and hanged the leading rebels, but when Don Pablo, the Guazave chief, promised that he and his people would behave, the captain as promptly extended full pardon.

The warlike and unconverted Suaquis were his next objective. He entered their country with twenty-four soldiers, to whom he had distributed shackles, explaining that each man must seize and bind two of the enemy. To the Indians, however, he made out that the expedition was a wild-cattle hunt in which they were invited to join. The Suaquis swarmed into his camp, and then at his suggestion the chiefs sent their men to gather firewood for the great barbecue. Thereupon the Santiago was sounded; Hurdaide and his men fell upon the astonished chiefs and soon had forty-three of them roped and tied. The wood-gathering warriors returned and attacked, but without avail.

The wives of the forty-three chiefs pelted the Spaniards with stones, killing two of the captives. The others were waited upon by Fathers Méndez and Velasco and, after thirty-nine of them professed Christianity, all were hanged on two trees. A certain Luisa, meanwhile, had been sent among the Suaquis to warn them that peaceful submission was the only course that would save them from the fate of their leaders.

Upon the conclusion of his Suaqui campaign in the spring of 1601 Hurdaide set off on a prospecting expedition into the Chinapa country. Silver mines found there were less rich than had been hoped. The Sinaloa guides were blamed for leading the expedition into an ambush in a mountain pass, and though no lives were lost in this battle, Hurdaide took vengeance upon the Sinaloas on his return by ravaging their maize fields and killing fourteen.

Then, at the behest of the friendly Ahomes, Hurdaide set out to chastise the Tehuecos. On the way he found the Suaquis and Sinaloas in arms, and although he personally captured the Sinaloa chief, Taxicora, the Indians continued to resist until he rushed out alone to seize another Indian and hang him to a tree. In Matava Valley he met up with the Tehuecos and captured 200 women and children, who were returned upon promise that the Ahomes would be let alone. Upon his return, the Ahomes clamored for missionaries; the Suaquis laid all the blame on the Sinaloas and, in token of their submission, were shorn of their war locks. Back at San Felipe, the campaign was terminated by the gibbeting of Taxicora, now a good Christian.

Accompanied by a delegation of chiefs, Hurdaide next visited Viceroy Montesclaros in Mexico City, returning with two Jesuits and the promise of more. In the absence of the doughty captain the neo-phytes at the upstream missions had revolted. There were also floods which damaged several of the mission stations, frightened away many Indians, and marooned Padre Méndez in a tree for twenty-four hours. Hearing of these misfortunes Hurdaide hastened his return. He defeated and suitably punished the Bacoburitos; the Tehuecos he forced to give up four culprits, who were promptly executed; and some 400 Ocoronis were driven from their homes.

Among the tribes chastened by these several campaigns mission progress was now rapid. Padre Ribas, subsequently the author of a voluminous history of Jesuit labors in Sinaloa, went to the Ahomes and within a year had baptized the entire tribe. Other neighboring groups soon came under his influence, and the Suaquis, thanks largely to the suasion of Doña Luisa, settled down to the Christian life and built three fine churches in their principal towns. Padre Méndez came down from his tree to labor among the Tehuecos. Baptizing 400 Sinaloas on the first day of his residence among them, Padre Villalta within a year had this entire tribe perfectly reconciled to mission life. By 1607 Padre Velasco and Captain Hurdaide were credited with 6,000 converts in the mountains southeast of San Felipe. The good captain also put to sea on a raft in pursuit of fugitive Toroacas, hanged seven leaders, and distributed the rest at various missions. Baptisms thus far had totaled more than 40,000.

Next ahead lay the Yaquis, some 30,000 of them in eighty villages. Hurdaide had gone to the border of their land in pursuit of the fugitive Ocoronis, but his demands for surrender of these renegades had been unavailing. With forty soldiers and some 2,000 Indian allies, Hurdaide made a second attempt. At dawn 8,000 Yaquis attacked his camp. After an all-day battle, in which many Indians were killed and many of the Spaniards wounded, Hurdaide had to retreat. Raising fifty soldiers and 4,000 Indian allies, he marched north once more. After another drawn-out battle the Spaniards had to retreat, this time with the Yaquis harassing their rear. In a countercharge, the captain and twenty-two men were trapped in an ambush. Though most of them were wounded—Hurdaide by five arrows—they managed to reach a hilltop, whence they escaped by night through a ruse. The Spanish retreat, however, had become a rout.

A part of the Yaqui success is to be attributed to Lautaro, a renegade Ocoroni, who, like his Araucanian namesake in Chile, had seen enough of Spanish warfare to be able to instruct his Indians how to prevail against it. The two Lautaros were not unlike in the methods that they employed; each stressed assault on the mounted Spaniards in terrain where horses could not be maneuvered, and each had Indians of superlative strength and bravery with which to carry out his battle plans.

Thrice vanquished on the field of battle, Hurdaide turned to strategy to overwhelm Lautaro's Yaquis. He began to boast about a still greater expedition which was to be organized against the tribe and saw to it that this word reached them. As a matter of fact, no such preparations were being made; the governor had not even approved of the preceding campaign. Nevertheless, the Yaquis sued

for peace.   They may, as one Jesuit maintains, have been swayed by
admiration for Spanish valor in defeat.   Another theory is that God
haunted them with the noise of battle until in frightened exhaustion
they gave in.   At any rate, they made a treaty, returned the plunder
they had captured, surrendered Lautaro to be executed, and begged
that missionaries be sent among them.

Next on Hurdaide's list were the mountain Tepahues.   In 1613,
when renegade Tehuecos took refuge among them, he marched an
army into their country and sent out word that he was prepared to
stay a year if necessary.   Then he settled down to prove to them that
his supplies would outlast theirs.   Such a mode of warfare was too
much for the Tehuecos.   They begged for mercy.   Hurdaide threatened dire punishment but, upon Padre Ribas' intercession, as prearranged, he let them off.   Bloody fighting with the Tepahues followed, and seven chiefs were seized and executed.   Hurdaide's supplies ran out before the Tepahues could be brought to terms, but he
was hardly back at San Felipe before messengers arrived asking for
peace and padres.   A missionary went out; the Tepahues met him
on the Mayo and for thirty years were orderly Christians.

That same year, 1613, Hurdaide conducted the venerable Padre
Méndez to the Mayos, who in their unchristian state had been his
allies on numerous campaigns.   Méndez' success among them was
"immediate, extraordinary, and permanent."   Seven towns were
founded and 3,100 children were baptized in a fortnight, and ere
long these Mayos were the best of Indians.

East of Sinaloa the Tepehuán Indians, ministered to by eight Black
Robes, seemed to be fully devoted to mission life.   But a messiah
arose among them, working miracles, preaching revolt against the
Spaniards, promising supernatural rewards to those who fought for
him, and prophesying complete victory.   In November, 1616, this
revolt was precipitated.   At Santa Catalina, Padre Tobar was assas-
sinated, and 200 Spaniards were massacred at Atotonilco.   At Santiago Papasquiaro several Spanish families and two padres, after
courageous resistance for three days, surrendered on the promise of
safe conduct to Durango.   Instead, they were brutally murdered as
they filed through the cemetery.   At Zape four padres and nearly a
hundred others were killed.   Padre Santarén, hero of the Acaxee
wars, was also slain as he was traveling toward Zape.   Only one
Jesuit escaped, and Durango itself might have fallen had not the out-

break at Santa Catalina been premature.   Worse luck for the Tepehuán messiah, he got little response from the near-by Acaxees and
Xiximes.

The Spaniards quickly brought up soldiers and, in January of 1617,
invaded the area in force.   The bodies of the martyrs were collected
for Christian burial, the rebels were defeated in several battles, and a
few captives and much plunder from the missions were recovered.
By the end of the year a thousand or more Tepehuanes had been
killed and the survivors were badly scattered.   Early in 1618 these
were ready for peace on the Spaniards' terms.   Although mining and
agriculture in central Durango recovered but slowly—some say not
for a half century—a new spiritual conquest was undertaken at once.
For a decade the Jesuits confined their work to the old sites; then in
the thirties they branched out to the Himes in the adjacent mountains.

In Sinaloa there had been grave fears that the Tepehuán Revolt
would strike a sympathetic chord among the Yaquis.   The reverse
was the case.   In 1617 the Yaquis welcomed Padres Ribas and
Pérez into their country.   Baptizing 4,000 children and 500 adults
on their first circuit, the padres entrenched themselves solidly with
the inland Yaquis, who gathered in eight large pueblos.   Within four
years the number of converts was set at 30,000.

By the 1620's Sinaloa and Durango were standing proof of the
effectiveness of the mission as a frontier agency.   In the space of a
generation the Jesuits, abetted by the military, had established permanent Spanish control over two major provinces.   The spiritual harvest had been great: in 1624 there were more than 100,000 converts
at the west coast missions alone.   Perhaps more remarkable was the
degree to which these Indians had become reconciled to and capable
of civilized life.   The 1620's also mark the passing of the generation
which had achieved this transformation.   Tapia, Santarén, and others
had been martyred earlier.   Ribas retired in 1620 to be provincial
(and historian) at Mexico City.   The year 1626 saw the passing of
Padre Martín Pérez, Tapia's original companion, and also of that
stalwart and zealous soldier, Captain Hurdaide.   At his retirement
in 1636, Padre Méndez was by all odds the oldest pioneer in the
area.

While Ribas settled down in the capital to write his monumental
Triumphs of Our Holy Faith, a new generation carried the frontier
forward.   Padre Castaño began work among the gentle Opatas in the

Valle de Sonora, soon the nucleus for fourteen pueblos with 20,000 converts ministered to by seven Jesuits. Across the Sierra, missions were opened at Parral on the Conchos and among the Tarahumares. The latter missions flourished until 1650, when these mountaineers rose in revolt to massacre the Spanish settlers and martyr their black-robed mentors. Missions were at once reëstablished in the southern district but not until 1673 in Tarahumara Alta. At about the same time the Chínipas missions were reoccupied. As the century drew to a close, the better parts of Chihuahua and Sonora had been thoroughly missionized. The work was as heroic as that of the earlier period. It is dismissed with a paragraph here because it differs only in detail from that which had preceded in Sinaloa and Durango.

Kino's Pimería

Further expansion of the mainland missions was largely the work of Padre Eusebio Francisco Kino, doubtless the best-known Jesuit of New Spain. As a student in the universities of Ingolstadt and Freiburg, the Italian-born Kino so distinguished himself in mathematics and astronomy that he was offered a professorship. He did not accept because he had already determined to follow in the footsteps of San Francisco Xavier, cofounder of the Company of Jesus and pioneer missionary in the Orient. Although his heart was set on the China missions, Kino dutifully came to America in 1681. After two years of teaching and preaching in the vicinity of Mexico City, he was assigned as missionary, astronomer, and cosmographer to accompany the Atondo expedition to Baja California, as described in the chapter that follows. Finally, in 1687, after he had requested to be assigned to the Seris, he was sent beyond them to Pimería Alta, land of the Upper Pimas, where his great work was to be performed.

When Kino came to the frontier, the last mission station was at Cucurpe. Fifteen miles farther north, where the valley of the San Miguel broadened into a rich and irrigable garden spot, was the Indian village of Cosari. On a promontory jutting out from the western mesa and overlooking this mountain-girt valley, Kino built Nuestra Señora de los Dolores (Our Lady of Sorrows), the mother mission of Pimería Alta. Other missions followed to the number of a score or more, strung out along the Magdalena and the Altar, and northward along the Santa Cruz. In addition, there were numerous visitas where the Indians were instructed less regularly. Other Jesuits, of course, labored with Kino in these Pima missions, but Remedios and Cocóspora as well as Dolores he administered in person.

Kino discharged the multifarious duties of mission administrator with great success. The agricultural development that he initiated and particularly the stock ranches he set in operation would earn him an important place in Sonora and Arizona history even had he done no missionary work. He was the original cattle king of Pimería and was responsible also for the planting of garden crops and fruit orchards, for the maintenance of pack trains connecting with the mines and older settlements, for the introduction and improvement of several mission industries, and for leading the Pimas to accept Spanish rule.

In this vast territory athwart the present international boundary between Sonora and Arizona, Kino was also a notable explorer. The land had been traversed by Coronado a century and a half earlier, but it was left for Kino to rediscover it and to explore it in detail. Besides scores of trips through Pimería, he made half a dozen journeys to the Gila, by five different routes, two to the Yumas on the Colorado, and one across into California. Occasionally he had a squad of soldiers as escort; more often he went almost alone or accompanied only by Indian friends and retainers, and this on a frontier by no means thoroughly pacified. Padre Saeta was martyred by his Pima neophytes at Caborca, and Apache inroads were all too common. Hard riding characterized the travels of this "Padre on Horseback." On month-long journeys he averaged twenty-five to thirty miles a day, and his record bristles with day's rides of forty, sixty, and even seventy-five miles.

Like many another Jesuit, Kino was a man of scholarly attainments. On the way to the mission frontier he had engaged Mexico's foremost scholar in a spirited debate concerning the comet of 1680. In Pimería there were few persons with whom such discussions could be carried on, but Kino found other intellectual outlets. His explorations had issue in several excellent maps, one of which continued to be the standard authority for Pimería until after the Mexican War, a century and a half later. He also found time to write an autobiography, which he modestly entitled *Celestial Favors*. As a history of the Spanish beginnings in Pimería Alta it is the fundamental source for the period.

In many other respects Kino exhibited the qualities characteristic of the Jesuits of his day.　Like Tapia, Santarén, and Ribas before him, he subordinated all else to the service of the missions.　He was undaunted by dangers and hardships, including the sore trial of loneliness, cut off as he was from companionship with men of kindred education and culture.　He was buoyed up by the frequent manifestations of divine assistance, as God and the Saints intervened to forward the missionary cause, and cheered by every indication of progress in the faith on the part of his Indian wards.　The fact that he was a learned man and a practical man—among other things, astronomer, historian, and ranchman—should not obscure the fact that above all he was a missionary, the Apostle to the Pimas.　In his own writings and in the various biographies and sketches of his career that have been published one glimpses a man of parts and an excellent representative of the Black Robes who won northwestern Mexico for the church and the Spanish empire.

7

BAJA CALIFORNIA

THE TIME HAD BEEN when the Spaniards were more interested in the California coast than in the mainland of northwestern Mexico. Throughout the seventeenth century, however, no progress was made toward occupying California. The general pace of frontier advance had slowed down, and the Jesuits, now the chief agents of northwestward expansion, had a sufficient field for their labors on the mainland. By advancing the frontier from Durango and San Felipe de Sinaloa to Tubac and the Gila they had made the most notable addition of the century to Spanish North America.

That task completed, it was natural that the Jesuits should look about for new fields of endeavor and, in so doing, that they should turn to Baja California. North of the Pimas lay an uninviting land peopled by wild and roving Apaches. Past experience had made clear the probable difficulty of missionizing these fierce raiders of the Pimas. California was equally at hand. Its praises by sixteenth-century enthusiasts were not entirely forgotten and assisted the rekindling of interest. Furthermore, throughout the seventeenth century there had been intermittent contact with Baja California by pearl fishers.

The Pearl Fishers

The story of their activities has not as yet been told in any satisfactory detail. In fact, so little has been written about them that the impression became widespread that Spanish interest in California died with Vizcaíno in 1603 and was not revived until the very end of the century. As a matter of fact, the procession of commercial ex-

87

peditions to California was well nigh continuous. None of them was outstandingly successful, few returned handsome profits, none resulted in important new exploration, none got beyond the pearl-fishing districts of the peninsula; yet they served to perpetuate interest in California and knowledge of the avenue of sea approach.

In 1611 a certain Tomás de Cardona was granted a monopoly of pearl fishing in the New World. The first expeditions that he sent out were to the West Indies. In 1614 his men crossed New Spain to Acapulco and prepared for pearl fishing on the Pacific. There were delays occasioned by the death of Tomás de Cardona and the transfer of the company to his nephew Nicolás, by the death of the American commander who was succeeded by Juan de Iturbe, and by a pirate scare on the west coast. Dutch pirates, for whom the local name was Pichilingues—that is, chest speakers or guttural-voiced—had been reported. Iturbe and his men were drafted for the defense of Acapulco. But when the pirates did not appear, his three vessels were allowed to sail on March 21, 1615. He had aboard some thirty soldiers and many Negro divers.

Iturbe's most spectacular achievement was to upset the prevailing cartographical theory concerning California. Returning from his voyage up the gulf, in which he claimed to have reached latitude thirty-four degrees, he reported that it was no gulf at all but a strait extending still farther north and that California was an island. The maps fell in line, showing the "Strait of California" opening again into the Pacific usually north of Cape Mendocino. For more than a century the insular theory prevailed, and when the peninsularity of California was eventually demonstrated again, cartographers and Spanish officials were most reluctant to believe.

A second result of the Iturbe expedition was to illustrate the seriousness of the Pichilingue danger. With two of his ships Iturbe tarried on the Sinaloa coast. The third vessel was sent back toward Acapulco, but at Zacatula it was attacked by the dreaded Pichilingues under Spilberg. The captain and a few soldiers escaped by jumping overboard, but most of the crew, the padres, and the accumulated pearls were captured.

Even so, Iturbe's expedition showed a profit. On the Baja California coast his divers had collected a large quantity of pearls. Other pearls, though often damaged by roasting, were acquired from the natives, including one valued at 4,500 pesos. Already one encounters the insinuation that, in order to avoid payment of the royal fifth, the full haul of pearls was not registered.   Whether Nicolás de Cardona sent out more pearl fishers does not appear; certainly he kept on memorializing the court on the subject until as late as 1643, proposing also to make settlements in California.

In the meantime other memorialists applied for pearl-fishing concessions in California.   A son-in-law of Vizcaíno, Martín de Lezama, started construction of a vessel in 1627 in the vicinity of San Blas but was discouraged, it is said, by the swarms of mosquitoes. Another aspirant went to Spain to solicit a royal license, whereupon the viceroy was ordered to collect information about California and its pearls.

Francisco de Ortega made the next known voyages in 1632, 1633–1634, and 1636.   He got many pearls and managed in 1632 to warn the Manila galleon of the presence of Pichilingues.   In 1636 a great hue and cry arose over a projected California voyage by Esteban Carbonel.   He was discovered to be French and was charged with planning to seek a strait to open the Pacific to France.   Very probably he merely planned pearl fishing, and except for the excitement incident to the charges of an international conspiracy his voyage might have been no better recorded than others that seem to have occurred clandestinely during this period.

In the late thirties there were four rival claimants of pearl-fishing privileges in California.   The authorities at length settled in favor of Pedro Porter y Casanate, who, however, was too busy to leave Spain until 1643.   The following year his boat was rushed off to warn the Manila galleon of Pichilingues.   The galleon missed the smoke signals at Cape San Lucas but got into Acapulco safely, and Porter's ship returned with a few pearls.   Porter's plans for further pearl fishing were shattered by a double disaster.   Some of his men absconded with much of his material, and then a fire broke out at his shipbuilding plant on the Rio Santiago, destroying the two vessels which had almost been completed.   Not until 1648 was he able to send ships to California and then apparently without accomplishing much.

Bernardo Bernal de Pynadero is the next entrepreneur on record. Sailing with two ships in 1664, he was guilty of gross cruelty toward the natives but was rewarded with a rich harvest of pearls, so rich in fact that his men quarreled over the division of the spoils and several were killed.   Pynadero was stayed temporarily by the Audiencia of

Guadalajara, but his ships sailed again in 1667 or 1668 without notable incident or result. There are hints of more frequent unlicensed expeditions to these pearl fisheries.

Atondo and Kino

Throughout the seventies the authorities frequently adverted to the question of California colonization and of Pynadero's fitness for the work. Finally, the decision was to contract with the Governor of Sinaloa, Isidro Atondo y Antillón. The contract, drawn in 1678 and approved the following year, differed from the earlier ones with Cardona, Ortega, Porter, and Pynadero in that it provided for the major expense of the expedition to be borne by the royal treasury. This change was at once a recognition of the importance and of the difficulty of colonizing Baja California.

Atondo's preparations were more elaborate than those of the merchant adventurers who had preceded him in California pearl-fishing voyages. Also there was much red tape to be wound and unwound in the assembling of equipment and personnel at Chacala. Finally, on January 17, 1683, he set sail for the Sinaloa River. Winds were contrary, and not until two months later was his little fleet ready to sail across to California. Land was sighted on the twenty-fifth, and on April 1 he anchored at La Paz.

Our most graphic accounts of what happened at La Paz are from the pen of Padre Eusebio Kino, cosmographer of the expedition. As this was his first taste of missionary work among the heathen, Kino saw California through rose-colored glasses. Reading between the lines, however, one can observe that the land was barren and parched, the natives backward and inclined toward treachery, and pearls about the only source of profit for the Spaniards. Abandonment of La Paz was hastened by the incident of June 6, when Atondo ordered a cannon fired on a group of Guaicuros who were eating a largess of pozole, or corn-meal mush. They were suspected of having killed a mulatto drummer boy, who actually had deserted and fled to the mainland. Atondo's purge did no good. The Guaicuro hostility increased, and when the supply ships still failed to appear, abandonment was ordered on July 14.

Atondo spent two hot summer months on the Sinaloa coast gathering supplies and then in October he was back for a fresh start, this time farther north at San Bruno. Here missionary work progressed more rapidly, chiefly through presents of pozole. For similar pay, the Indians helped in the construction of stone and adobe fortifications, storehouses, barracks, and a church. San Bruno began to have an aspect of permanency. Expeditions were made to the north and to the south, as well as several entradas inland, one of which carried clear across to the Pacific. Much geographical and ethnographical information was gathered, but better acquaintance with the land did not make it more inviting. It had been planned, for example, to use the water of the Rio Grande, now called the arroyo of San Bruno, to irrigate fields of maize and frijoles, garbanzos, and melons, but this California river soon dried up. Some land was cleared and planted, but the rainfall was disappointing, frosts did additional damage, and the end result was pathetic. Horses, mules, sheep, and foodstuffs were brought across the gulf from the Yaqui missions, and inland, at a fine water hole and pasture, the station of San Isidro was established. The supply service across the gulf, however, was both laborious and uncertain. Scurvy broke out at San Bruno, due in part to the salty water, and although Kino objected, Atondo ordered abandonment of San Bruno in May, 1685. Sending the sick across to the mainland, he despatched one ship to explore northward for a better site, while he himself turned southward for another fling at pearl fishing. From May until September his men worked industriously, but according to the official report the harvest was no more than a hundred pesos worth of pearls. Not yet ready to give up, Atondo was preparing to sail once more to California when the order came to go out to warn the galleon of Pichilingues, this time the Grogniet freebooters who had raided Panama. Thus ended the Atondo-Kino project of colonizing California, a project which had cost the royal treasury approximately a quarter of a million pesos.

The chief return on this investment was the engendering in Father Kino of an affection and a pity for the California Indians that became one of the ruling passions of his life. Ever afterward he cherished the ambition to go back to California to resume the evangelization and civilization of these simple souls, whom he considered more in need of such ministrations than any people elsewhere. He never returned—his subsequent years, as has been related, were devoted to brilliant labors in Pimería Alta—but still he was able to render momentous services to California.

Many of his explorations were directed toward California, and eventually he demonstrated that California was a peninsula, not an island, and that a land route to it might be opened. In preparation for the Atondo expedition he had studied the latest maps of the west coast, and consequent to Iturbe's erroneous report of 1616, these maps showed California as an attenuated island. Though older maps indicated a peninsula, Kino naturally accepted the most recent testimony. Gradually, in the course of his explorations evidence accumulated to correct this error. From Santa Clara Mountain he saw the head of the gulf, but supposed that farther west the "strait" turned a point and continued. Later he chided himself for this failure to recognize California when it lay before him, just as Joseph's brethren had failed to recognize him in Egypt.

A trivial occurrence crystallized the idea. At Yuma in 1699 the Indians presented to him some peculiar large blue shells. By and by, it flashed into his mind that these were like the shells he had seen on the shores of the South Sea when he and Atondo had crossed California in 1685. He summoned Indians from distant villages to question them concerning the source of these blue shells. Twice more he went to the Yumas, crossed the Colorado in 1702, and descended far enough into Baja California to see "most plainly more than thirty leagues of continuous land to the south." Furthermore, "the sun rose over the head of the Sea of California, proof most evident that we were now in California."

To clinch the matter, Kino drew up a list of "Cogent Reasons and Clear Arguments which Establish the Certainty of the Land Passage to California." Besides the evidence already adduced and the testimony of the older maps, he had detected botanical evidence west of the Colorado and traces of connection in the Indian vocabularies. It was characteristic of Kino the missionary and mystic that scriptural evidence was also introduced: *"Apparuit terra arida, et in Mare Rubro via sine inpedimento,"* and *"Euntes in mundum universum. Predicate Evangelium omni creaturae."* Despite this excellent evidence, some officials were still not convinced of California's peninsularity. Kino corrected his maps, but other cartographers abandoned the error only gradually, and not until Father Fernando Consag's voyage in 1746 was the island theory finally scotched.

The Jesuits Enter

Meanwhile, Kino had been insistent, in season and out, that the missions in California ought to be reëstablished. His first convert was Padre Juan María de Salvatierra, who came in 1690 to inspect the Pimería missions.   As the two went about from station to station, Kino filled the visitador's ears with pleas for California and gained a staunch ally in urging the matter upon Jesuit and government authorities.   Other ears remained deaf until Kino and Salvatierra won the approval of Father Santaella, general of the Jesuit Order, when he visited Mexico in 1696.   Government approval quickly followed.

Having had such ill success in getting California colonized by government expeditions, merchant adventurers, and pearl-fishing companies, the Spanish crown was willing to grant unusual powers and inducements to the Jesuit Order if it would undertake the task.   It is a good illustration of the elasticity of frontier technique that Spain was able to attain.   The Jesuits were to be in full control.   On most missionary frontiers regular army officers controlled the presidios, but for Baja California the Jesuits were to command all soldiers and civilians as well as the missionaries.   Because of the strategic usefulness of having California occupied—the reference was especially to Dutch, English, and French freebooters who might lurk in California waters—the government agreed to subsidize the Jesuit colony. It also departed from the customary procedure by permitting the order to solicit an endowment fund for the support of the missions. The faithful in New Spain, Central America, and elsewhere responded in most generous fashion to this campaign.   The solicitors, of whom Father Juan de Ugarte was one of the most successful, built up the Pious Fund to more than a million pesos, thus creating a handsome if not munificent income for the California missions.

Yet the actual start was humble enough.   Kino could not go and Father Picolo was detained temporarily; consequently Salvatierra went as the lone missionary.   At his command was an army of six soldiers, one swivel gun constituting their artillery.   Salvatierra's boat traversed the gulf in a single day, but the other vessel was more than a month making the voyage.   A tiny fort was built a few miles south of Atondo's San Bruno, and the natives who assisted were rewarded with gifts of maize and porridge.   To stimulate interest in his religious teaching, Salvatierra began to withhold presents from those Indians who failed to attend.   They resented this discrimination, demanded a share in the material benefits of Christianity, and became so obstreperous that actual fighting inevitably ensued.   Salvatierra held his fire as long as seemed prudent and then ordered a shot from the swivel gun.   The result was more of a surprise to the Spaniards than to the Indians.   The gun burst, two soldiers were killed, and the Indians would have wiped out the rest except that the muskets proved far more effective.   The next day the Indians sued for peace.

Before the end of November the second boat arrived and the first returned with Padre Francisco María Picolo, bringing additional men and supplies.   The force now included seven soldiers, five sailors, four Christian Indians from the mainland, and the two padres.   Salvatierra founded Loreto, which was to be the capital and mother mission.   San Javier followed two years later.   In 1701 Padre Juan de Ugarte joined the force and four years later Padre Jayme Bravo. These four—Salvatierra, Picolo, Ugarte, and Bravo—were the principal missionaries until Salvatierra's death in 1717, by which time five other missions had been established.

The narrative of these twenty years abounds in stirring events. More than once Salvatierra showed his fortitude and proved the support of Providence.   Once, when the Indians attacked, he went out to reason with them.   Three arrows were shot at him with mortal intent but lodged harmlessly in the folds of his robe.   On another occasion he and his companions escaped injury when most of the Indian arrows struck the pavilion housing the image of Our Lady of Loreto, sainted patroness of the Baja California missions.   Again, losing his way as he was summoned to baptize a dying Indian, he gave free rein to his mule and was miraculously guided to the ranchería of the stricken Indian.   His official biographer does not record the incident, but tradition has it that Salvatierra saved the pitahaya crop in the peninsula by praying for gulls to come and devour a plague of locusts.

Conversions, however, were few; the natives were more interested in porridge than in religion, and the mission field was by no means self-supporting.   Except for the Pious Fund, the government subventions, and the herculean work of the missionaries, the colony could not have endured.

A major difficulty was the isolation of Baja California.   Kino proved that a land connection existed, but a land route from the mainland was never opened.   Dependence was entirely on navigation across the gulf, and this was notoriously hazardous.   The voyage might take a day or two, but frequently it required more than a month.   Boats were often lost, too; the average seems to have been about one a year.   The barren nature of the land stood in the way of development in farming and stock raising, such as Kino achieved in Pimería Alta, nor did the Indians have the ability demonstrated by Kino's wards. Unlicensed, and for the most part unrecorded, pearl fishers persisted in coming to the peninsula despite the monopoly that had been granted the Jesuits. Their influence upon the Indians was usually bad and served to counteract the work of the Fathers. Salvatierra refused to sell them supplies, but the secular authorities on the mainland did little or nothing to stop their coming. Sometimes the soldiers likewise proved more of a handicap than a protection. On one occasion Salvatierra courageously discharged eighteen of his army of thirty.

In 1717 the gentle Padre Juan María was succeeded by robust Juan de Ugarte, already notable as the prize solicitor for the Pious Fund. Since 1701 he had been in charge of the Mission of San Javier, where, despite a tradition of failure, he had succeeded in raising crops. This first successful farming in the peninsula expanded to include stock raising and spread in limited degree to other sites. Ugarte staved off abandonment once by announcing that he would remain even though all others left. On another occasion he used his great physical strength to quell an Indian uprising by seizing two ringleaders by the hair and cracking their heads together. Largely by personal bravery he and Padre Jayme Bravo overawed the Guaicuros, who had caused Atondo and Kino so much trouble, and forced them to submit to mission discipline. Another of Ugarte's feats was to cajole the Indians to work with him in cutting timber and packing it a hundred miles to the coast, where it was fashioned into a ship, *Triunfo de la Cruz,* for exploration of the gulf. By the time of his death in 1730 the mission staff had been increased and the number of missions doubled.

The Troubled Thirties

The decade that followed was the most troubled in the annals of the peninsula. The southern Indians, always a restless lot, had been further contaminated by infiltration of foreign blood: mulatto, Spanish, and Pichilingue. When the padres attempted to stamp out polygamy, a mulatto named Chicori and a mulatto Indian named Botón stirred up a rebellion. This outburst in 1733 was quickly suppressed, but Chicori and Botón fomented another uprising that broke in the fall of the next year. Three of the six soldiers who garrisoned the southern missions were promptly killed, Padres Carranco and Tamaral were martyred, and Padre Taraval and his guard of three escaped only by a night flight to La Paz and thence to the island of Espíritu Santo. The rebels, however, massacred twenty-seven of Taraval's neophytes.

From Mission Dolores, Captain Estevan Rodíguez Lorenzo launched a retaliatory campaign. With twenty soldiers and a few Indian allies he hastened to La Paz, where much time was wasted trying to enlist the coöperation of the supposedly friendly Callejues. In his journal Taraval vividly depicts the fears and uncertainties that afflicted Lorenzo's little band. Finally the timorous Callejues gave proof of their loyalty, and a tour de force was made through the hostile territory, but without visiting real punishment upon the rebels. Rumors that the rebellion was spreading to the northern area led to the recall of Lorenzo and to the concentration of all the missionaries at Loreto.

Those at Loreto did not know it, but the emboldened savages had attempted the capture of the Manila galleon. Following a practice inaugurated the preceding year, the galleon of 1735 put in at Rio San José near Cabo San Lucas to provision and recruit the sick. Led by a certain Gerónimo, the Indians killed twelve men who had been sent ashore and tried to lure the other Spaniards to land. Finally the captain became suspicious. Seizing Gerónimo and a few others, he beat off the attack of some 600 Indians and sailed away. With a little better luck Gerónimo and his followers might have captured the galleon.

The arrival of 60 Yaquis quelled any potential disorders in the north. Then, belatedly, Governor Manuel Huidobro came over from the mainland with 40 soldiers and 100 more Yaquis. He strutted about the south, contemptuous of all advice proffered by the padres. The hostile savages fought by running away, and after months of marching up and down, Huidobro still had not succeeded in coming to grips with them. At length he condescended to accept Jesuit assistance. The Black Robes are credited with maneuvering the insurgents into two pitched battles, after which they sued for peace, but Huidobro again is berated by the chroniclers for letting the ringleaders off with inadequate punishment. At any rate, the region was not effectively pacified. Mission work was resumed, but other uprisings necessitated a call for more troops and new campaigns. Not until a decade later was the region quieted, and then largely because epidemics had carried off the majority of these turbulent savages.

The End of the Jesuit Epoch

The remaining annals of Jesuit activities are more humdrum. On the northern frontier new stations were established, notably Santa Gertrudis, San Francisco de Borja, and Santa María de Calamajue. But as the population declined, some of the older missions were consolidated. Although the dying out of the Indians was tragic, it was not without an element of comic relief. In the south the women died off more rapidly than the men, and the latter complained loudly about their enforced bachelorhood. Various attempts were made to import wives from the mainland but without avail. Toward the last the Jesuits adopted a less exclusive policy. Pearl fishing was encouraged, the galleons stopped regularly, a few settlers and miners were welcomed in the peninsula, and the southernmost missions were secularized. Yet at best Baja California was barely a self-supporting colony and no very encouraging or promising step in northwestward expansion.

In 1767 the Spanish court decided to follow the lead of Portugal and France in expelling the Jesuits. The reasons for this decision stemmed but slightly from the Jesuit conduct in Baja California or on the Mexican mainland, though there were some complaints and also wild rumors to the effect that the missionaries were hoarding vast treasures from secret mines, pearl fisheries, and exactions from the natives. The expulsion from New Spain was entrusted to the visitador general, José de Gálvez, who in turn delegated Captain Gaspar de Portolá to carry out the task in Baja California. Thus two men who subsequently were heroes in the occupation of Alta California have their names linked to a less praiseworthy enterprise.

Although the Jesuit provincial had offered to give up the missions the preceding year, the order of 1767 came as a surprise. Precautions of secrecy were taken so that the neophytes would not dispute the actions and so that the Black Robes could not sequester their mythical treasures. Portolá, it must be admitted, cushioned the shock in California by the considerateness of his attitude toward the sixteen Jesuits there. The latter, though reluctant to leave, bowed at once to the royal will, and the Indians confined their reaction to demonstrations of grief over the departure of the padres. Whatever justification there may have been for the general action against the order, it certainly was the grossest injustice thus to reward the padres for the vast northwestern province that their valiant labors had added to the empire.

Portolá reached Loreto on December 17, 1767. He wrote to Padre Ducrue, the Jesuit head, that the sixteen Black Robes must leave on January 25. Actually, they sailed on February 3, leaving the Indians with no guardians other than Portolá's soldiers, for Fray Junípero Serra and his brother Franciscans of the College of San Fernando, who had agreed to take charge, did not arrive until April. Meanwhile, Portolá had made a careful inventory of the mission property, which, although respectable, fell far short of his expectations. The missions and the neophytes suffered gross mismanagement in the interim before the arrival of the Franciscans. There were further losses during a transition period in which the Franciscans had merely spiritual authority without control over the temporalities. On August 12, Gálvez ordered that the missionaries be placed in full charge.

Gálvez saw the need of other reforms. He had several missions consolidated, others abandoned, and neophytes transferred to better situated missions. Some of his proposals were too radical, for example, that of transferring northern Indians far to the south. Father Lasuén, of later Alta California fame, adroitly frustrated this scheme. Gálvez showed a keen interest in mining, which he undertook to foment along with the secular settlement of the peninsula. It was soon apparent, however, that regeneration of the missions was the real hope of the colony, and to this end he bent his efforts. The difficulty of the problem is well illustrated by the fact that in their five-year regime in the peninsula the Franciscans were able to establish but one new mission, San Fernando de Velicatá, important chiefly as a way station to Alta California.

Jesuit occupation of Baja California was the one northwestward frontier advance in the fifty-year interval between Kino and Serra. On the mainland there had been some retrogression from the limits achieved by Kino. The penury of the Spanish government is the principal explanation; draining every possible peso from the colonies, Spain actually spent less in strengthening and protecting the northern frontier provinces than she received in revenue there. Seri, Yaqui, and Apache disturbances militated against frontier development, while in the 1760's such remote occurrences as the forming of the Family Compact and the acquisition of Louisiana removed the French menace as a motive for northward expansion of buffer settlements.

From 1700 to 1768 various delaying circumstances of this nature outweighed such temporal inducements as the Bolas de Plata mining flurry, which produced a rush to Arizonac, the brilliant Indian fighting of Juan Bautista de Anza, Sr. and Bernardo de Gálvez, and the Fernando Sánchez memorials of 1751, reviving the bogey of French discovery of the Strait of Anian and urging Spanish occupation of Alta California as a measure of forestalling such a disaster.

Interest in the occupation of California was not dead; there was still much talk about it. But the Baja California missions were the only positive step in the direction of Vizcaíno's Port of Monterey, and except on a purely religious basis, they were not successful enough to stimulate a further advance.

8

PLANTING THE COLONY

FOR MORE THAN TWO CENTURIES Spain had contemplated the occupation of Alta California, but had been busy elsewhere with more important affairs. Other regions had offered superior attractions, the royal treasury had begrudged the money, and the agents of frontier advance had experienced numerous difficulties in the approaches to California. Suddenly in the 1760's the Russian Bear threatened in the north, the British began to evince a lively interest in the North Pacific, and Spain roused herself to send out five expeditions.

Here we have the story in general terms. Nations, however, act through individuals rather than as personified entities, and in this case one of Spain's agents was of supreme significance. The Russian menace was actually rather remote, for Russian fur hunters had not yet passed the Aleutian Islands to the Alaskan mainland. Certainly the menace was no more serious than previous English and French threats. Alarming rumors transmitted by the minister at St. Petersburg exaggerated the menace to New Spain, anticipating it by at least a generation. Even so, the Spanish court was not so alarmed as is usually intimated. An order was sent the Viceroy of New Spain to investigate the Russian danger, but he was not told to colonize California. He transmitted this order to the visitador-general, José de Gálvez, and it was this officer who really determined that Alta California should be settled.

José de Gálvez, Visitador

José de Gálvez was an Andalusian of humble birth who had risen to some prominence in the Spanish foreign office. His rapid rise is partially explained by his knowledge of French acquired from his second wife, a Frenchwoman. After serving well as a legal councilor and in a secretarial capacity, he was suddenly elevated to the office of visitador-general. He conducted the visitation of the viceroyalty of New Spain with such signal success that his political future was assured. Made a member of the Council of the Indies, he advanced to its head and became Minister of the Indies, next in power over the colonies to the king himself, and most trusted adviser of Charles III.

Gálvez was not without shortcomings. Excessive pride, cruelty and hypocrisy, a predilection toward methods of indirection and deceit, an indiscriminate practice of nepotism, and occasional attacks of insanity were some of the particulars in which he fell short of perfection. Yet he was loyal and efficient in the exercise of his commission and vigorous and compelling in his dealings with colonial officers and subjects. These qualities earned his success.

For the office that he filled no exact counterpart can be found in the United States. In Spain, however, the device was a common one, and antecedents can be cited in the visiting bishops in church government, in Charlemagne's "Missi Dominici," and in the Persian "King's Eye." In essence, it was the sending out of an inspector vested with power to examine and investigate and also to act. A visitador's authority was theoretically superior to that of other officials in the area, but in New Spain the viceroy was not entirely superseded and could not be completely disregarded.

Gálvez' visitation had as its primary purpose the increasing of royal revenues from New Spain. To this end he established the tobacco monopoly, a step long contemplated but postponed because of the fear that it would encounter violent opposition. Spain had hesitated to offend the tobacco interests, and there had been fear that the step would lead to rebellion. But because of the expenses of the Seven Years' War, Charles III determined upon inauguration of the monopoly. There was no revolt, yet Gálvez succeeded in putting through this part of his program only when the old viceroy was recalled and another sent with instructions to coöperate.

Reform of the customs house at Veracruz was a second achievement. Officers had been so lackadaisical and peculation so rampant that a house cleaning comparable to that of Hercules in the Augean stables was in order. For example, the exemption from the alcabala (sales tax) for goods consumed in Veracruz had been so abused that the records indicated that ten times as much brandy was drunk there as in all the rest of the viceroyalty. The customs officers obstructed Gálvez' investigation and reforms, but the king upheld him in discharging the most flagrant offenders, with the result that there was a marked increase in the revenues.

A third task pertained less directly to fiscal reforms, namely, the expulsion of the Jesuits. As has been remarked, grounds for expulsion were not found in the work of Tapia, Kino, Salvatierra, Ugarte, and their brother Black Robes of the northwestern frontier. But the company had great wealth, as well as absolute control in several areas and great influence elsewhere. It was a potent political organization, and its members took an oath of loyalty to the order which seemed to preclude any other sort of patriotism. As concerns the local story, these European-born motives matter but slightly. The task was regarded as most delicate, and its execution was entrusted to the visitador rather than to the viceroy. Working primarily through the officials who were assisting in his visitation, Gálvez made secret preparations to carry out the royal order. His men were distributed throughout the Jesuit area and then, as prearranged, bundled the Black Robes off toward Veracruz to be exiled from New Spain.

Throughout the viceroyalty the expulsion was carried out smoothly. In Guanajuato and Vallodolid, however, it was followed by an Indian revolt. The Indians were protesting more against the new tributes that Gálvez sought to make them pay than against the removal of the Jesuits, but Gálvez chose to attribute the rebellion to this latter cause and induced the viceroy to place him in charge of its suppression. As he advanced into Guanajuato the Indians laid down their arms. Although they had taken no lives and submitted without any fighting, Gálvez meted out bloody punishment for this bloodless revolt. In one town he executed four men; in another, eleven, cutting off the hands of the secretary who had written a declaration of the aims of the revolt; in another, four; in another, twelve; and in another, one; and so forth. The totals were 85 put to death, 73 lashed, 117 banished, and 674 imprisoned.

Gálvez' method of passing sentence was even more reprehensible than the actual punishments. Ordinarily he listened to the evidence and then went into the church to pray. After an hour or two he would rise from his knees, announce that the judgment had been revealed to him, and sentence certain ones to be hanged and others to be whipped, banished, or imprisoned. His taste was also questioned when he climbed the scaffold at Vallodolid to "harangue the populace, to the accompaniment of tears, a white handkerchief, and exquisite expressions." Yet he insisted that he had not been cruel. "But I assure you before God," he wrote, "that I have not upon my conscience the slightest scruple of having exceeded the limits of justice, for I mitigated my sentences always with clemency and mercy." These poor Indians are too long dead to profit by a post mortem. Gálvez' methods, too, should be judged by the standards of his day. The episode reveals his ruthlessness and cruelty but also his energy and determination. That such a man was committed to the occupation of California promised much.

Immediately upon his arrival in Mexico, Gálvez had displayed interest in the northwest, where the Seris and Pimas were in unsubdued rebellion. He took time out from his financial reforming to draw up a plan for the pacification of this frontier. The viceroy and other officials could not understand why a legal and financial luminary should devote so much attention to a minor military problem. The most convincing explanation is that Gálvez was ambitious for military honors and for the prestige of adding a new colony to Charles' empire. His plan called for the raising of funds by popular subscription, a campaign by volunteer troops, and permanent control through the establishment of new settlements drawn from the pauper and criminal classes. The plan was approved only grudgingly, but in March, 1768, Colonel Domingo Elizondo launched the campaign at the head of 350 men.

This Sonora campaign was part of a larger program, the details of which were unfolded by Gálvez as early as January, 1768. He proposed to set up a commandant-general (virtually a viceroy) over the provinces of Nueva Vizcaya, Sonora, and the Californias. Such an officer would restore peace to the frontier, and his commandancy would serve as a buffer to protect New Spain against Indian or English attack. Because of English, Dutch, and Russian projects in the Pacific, Monterey ought to be occupied by a sea expedition and later supported by land from Sonora. Occupation of Alta California, in fact, was an essential element in the scheme. The capital of the commandancy would be at Caborca or, better still, at the confluence of the Gila and Colorado. The plan envisioned increased revenue as well as improvement of frontier defense and was brought forward in connection with the proposal to set up intendancies, offices for the improvement of the revenues through fomenting economic development.

Viceroy and junta approved the plan, designating Gálvez to carry it into operation as soon as Elizondo's army should have pacified Sonora. Meanwhile, the visitador went to San Blas, where he inspected the work being done toward making that place a base for west coast operations. On the way he laid his northwestern program before the Audiencia of Guadalajara and got that body's endorsement. Beyond Guadalajara he was overtaken by a message from the viceroy with the famous communication warning of the Russian menace to Monterey and ordering an investigation.

In his reply some two weeks later, Gálvez adroitly magnified the letter into an order for the occupation of California, while at the same time he made it appear that Viceroy Croix was the one responsible for the step. In reality, the Russian danger was the excuse, and the reason for the occupation was José de Gálvez.

The Sacred Expeditions

From San Blas, Gálvez sailed to Baja California, intent on sending a force to occupy Monterey. He instituted various reforms in the peninsula, but organizing the expeditions for the north was his outstanding achievement.

Everyone had been complaining about the poverty of Baja California, but Gálvez did not hesitate to draw upon its meager resources. He drafted Fernandinos for missionaries in the new field; he requisitioned altar furniture, vestments, implements, foodstuffs, and livestock from the peninsula missions. Despite a few complaints, it was generally agreed that it was proper to call on older missions for assistance in starting new ones. Gálvez commandeered the *San Carlos* and the *San Antonio,* which had been built to assist in Elizondo's Sonora war. From the mainland he called over additional officers and soldiers to join the expeditions. Things hummed, because the visitador had both authority and enthusiasm.

When the *San Carlos* arrived, it was in unseaworthy condition and had to be unloaded, careened, and reloaded. Gálvez directed the work in person, frequently lending a hand, and by January 9, 1769, this 200-ton ship was ready to sail. Lieutenant Pedro Fages and twenty-five Catalan soldiers brought over from Sonora were on board, besides the cosmographer Miguel Costansó, Commander Vicente Vila and his sailors, a baker, two blacksmiths, seed, agricultural implements, altar furniture, and other materials for the new settlements. Gálvez "went a piece" with the *San Carlos,* sailing down from La Paz to see it round the cape at San Lucas. The *San Antonio* was in somewhat better shape, but, to take no unnecessary chances, Gálvez had it thoroughly overhauled before sending it out under Juan Pérez on February 15. Less is known about the personnel and cargo aboard the *San Antonio,* but Pérez came to be the ranking mariner along the California coast.

Captain Fernando de Rivera y Moncada was put in charge of the first division of the land party. He had twenty-five "leather-jacket soldiers," so called because of their sleeveless jackets of tough leather, proof against most Indian missiles. They also carried bullhide shields and wore heavy leather chaps fastened to the pommels of their saddles. They were as much cowboys as soldiers, and Fray Juan Crespi called them "the finest horsemen in the world." This party included three muleteers and forty mission Indians from Baja California with tools for roadwork, who were counted on to help pacify the Indians farther north. Crespi was chaplain and diarist. Encountering difficulty in finding pasturage for his 400 animals, Rivera moved up to Velicatá, the limit at that time of Spanish control, whence he set out for San Diego on March 24.

The second land expedition consisted of Captain Gaspar de Portolá as officer in charge of the entire project, Fray Junípero Serra as head of the missionaries, Sergeant José Francisco de Ortega, ten or twelve soldiers and servants, and forty-four Christian Indians. Starting from Loreto on March 9, they proceeded to Velicatá, where on May 14, with due formalities, the mission of San Fernando de Velicatá was founded. It was designed to be a way station between Baja and Alta California. On May 15, Portolá and his men took the trail for San Diego, the appointed rendezvous. Gálvez equipped a third vessel, the *San José,* which sailed on June 16, but it was lost with all on board.

Having dispatched the expeditions, Gálvez went to Sonora to lay another foundation for Spain's hold on Alta California. Because of the Indian unrest in Sonora he used the peninsula approach to Monterey, but he was aware that a line of communication from Sonora was indispensable if the new colony was to flourish. And Sonora, of course, was important in its own right. When order prevailed, that province yielded an excellent income to the crown. Furthermore, Sonora was to be the keystone of the reorganized frontier as Gálvez planned it.

Unfortunately, the pacification of Sonora proved a thornier problem than the visitador had anticipated. Notwithstanding the 1,100 men under his command, Elizondo had made but slight progress in subduing the rebel Seris and Pimas. The savages eluded the troops and took refuge in the mountain fastnesses of the Cerro Prieto, from which Elizondo's men could not dislodge them. Campaigns against the Indians were made in March, June, October, and November of 1768, and in January and February of 1769, but all six resulted in the capture of less than half a dozen warriors. Gálvez came to Sonora imbued with fanatical vigor, determined to wage a war of extermination against the insurgents, but discovering how futile Elizondo's efforts had been, he turned to amnesty offers. Several were made in the summer of 1769, but very few Indians took avail of them. In October, Gálvez made another general attack upon the Cerro Prieto, which proved as useless as Elizondo's. Thereafter, the strategy shifted to guerrilla operations, which, together with gifts and cajolery, brought many small groups to terms. By May of 1771 all the rebels had submitted.

In the meantime, however, Gálvez had suffered a serious illness. The frustration of his Indian policy preyed on his mind, and he was afflicted with chills and fevers, so that in late August of 1769 he wrote Croix that he was about to die. Though he improved temporarily, illness again set in, unbalancing his mind. He claimed to have revelations from St. Francis; he announced plans to end the insurrection by importing 600 Guatemalan apes; he claimed to be the King of Prussia, the King of Sweden, protector of the house of Bourbon, the venerable Palafox, and "even the Eternal Father." His secretaries had trouble restraining him from foolish acts. Only when he returned to Mexico did he recover his reason.

Gálvez' insanity, together with the stout resistance of the Indians, prevented the consummation of his plan for Sonora. The frontier commandancy-general was not created; nor was the Gila-Colorado district colonized or the land route to Monterey opened. Yet Gálvez had improved conditions in Sonora by secularizing certain missions,

by defining Franciscan powers, and by encouraging mining. Just
after he left, a gold rush to Cieneguilla and Huerta brought thousands of miners to the frontier.   This addition to the civilized population did more than all the military campaigns to stabilize control of
the province.   A safe and sure land route to California was that
much more probable.

While Gálvez and Elizondo were wrestling with the Sonora problem, the sacred expeditions advanced to San Diego.   Because the
latitude of the bay had not been taken accurately by previous explorers, Pérez sailed too far north.   He first took the *San Antonio* to
the Santa Barbara Channel and then dropped down to San Diego,
where he anchored after 54 days' sail.   The *San Carlos,* which had
started a month earlier, was 110 days on the way and did not arrive
until April 29.   Her crew was so wracked by scurvy that Pérez' men
had to come to their assistance to lower the boats, and for a fortnight
the chief work was that of caring for the sick and burying the dead.

The land parties fared much better.   Rivera's men had to make
a number of dry camps along the arid peninsula, and the water they
found for their skin-bag bottles or canteens was not always agree-
able.   By contrast, they were thoroughly drenched in a couple of
rainstorms.   For most of the distance they were breaking a new
trail over rough and mountainous terrain, which inevitably slowed
their progress.   The savages along the way gave numerous demonstrations of hostility, frightening some of the Christian Indians into
deserting and running back to their homes, but Rivera's men had no
fighting to do.   And any self-pity they may have felt over the rigors
of this journey vanished on May 14 with their arrival at San Diego
and the sight of the sad plight of the sea parties.   Portolá and Serra
had fewer cattle to bring over the trail.   They traveled at a better
season of the year and much of the way they followed the route Rivera
had tested.   Consequently, six weeks sufficed for their journey to
San Diego.

By July 1 these four divisions were united.   Possession was formally taken in a ceremony in which Father Serra said Mass, all joined
in singing the *Te Deum,* and salutes were fired.   Shortly thereafter
the presidio was founded, and on July 16 Serra founded the mission
of San Diego de Alcalá.

Of perhaps 300 men who had set out from La Paz and Velicatá,
only 126 now remained.   In addition to those lost on the *San José*

93 had perished on the other two vessels. Only a score of the Indian auxiliaries were left; a few had died en route, the rest had deserted. Almost half of the 126 survivors were unfit for service. Such was the physical toll upon this first band of California pioneers.

Portolá Seeks the Port of Monterey

But since the Port of Monterey, the real objective, was still to be attained, Portolá prepared to march north. He sent Pérez and eight men in the *San Antonio* to get supplies and reinforcements from San Blas. The *San Carlos* was left at anchor in the bay for want of a crew, and Father Serra and a few others were left to care for the half hundred invalids. As Portolá worded it, he then "went on by land to Monterey with that small company of persons, or rather say skeletons, who had been spared by scurvy, hunger, and thirst."

Sergeant Ortega and the scouts constituted the vanguard. Next rode Portolá, Fages, the six Catalans who were fit for service, Costansó, Fathers Crespi and Gómez, and the Indian auxiliaries. The 100-mule pack train followed, while Rivera and the remaining soldier-cowboys, driving the "caballada," brought up the rear. Through southern California, travel was easy and pleasant. The numerous natives encountered were friendly, though often embarrassingly inquisitive and acquisitive. Pasture was abundant and water easily obtained. A sharp earthquake at the Santa Ana River crossing gave rise to the name Río de los Temblores. According to Crespi: "It lasted about half as long as an Ave María, and about ten minutes later it was repeated, though not violently." Other shocks were noticed until the Los Angeles River was crossed.

Along the coast, past San Luis Obispo, they traveled with little difficulty, but a real obstacle confronted them in the Sierra de Santa Lucía. For a week they tarried at its base while Ortega and the scouts sought a pass. "The mountains," wrote Crespi, "are inaccessible not only for men but also for goats and deer." Finally, a way was found, and men and mules scrambled up, only to be greeted at the summit by the sad spectacle of mountainous country in prospect as far as the eye could reach. Through this rough terrain they threaded their way laboriously. The fatigue of the long journey was particularly felt at this stage of the route, and scurvy also broke out. Yet they worked cheerfully, says Father Crespi, "for the greater glory of God through the conversion of souls, and for the service of the king, whose dominions were being enlarged by this expedition."

After the mountains the Salinas Valley proved a real relief. They descended this valley for six days and approached Monterey with breathless anticipation. Ever since Vizcaíno had sung its praises, the Port of Monterey had been California's chief attraction. Portolá recognized Vizcaíno's landmarks—the Point of Pines, the Carmel River, the magnificent sweep of the bay shore—but he was bewildered not to see the fine harbor. Apparently he expected the whole bay to be landlocked. Actually its mouth is more than twenty miles wide. As Robert Louis Stevenson described it, the bay is like a giant fish-hook, curving down from the north, with the Point of Pines as the barb, and the port is the small area behind this barb. When later put to use this anchorage proved safe and reliable. Reconnoitering it on horseback, Portolá could not see its full merits; in fact he did not recognize it. Nonplussed, he concluded that the real Monterey must be farther on and that this spot merely happened to coincide as to landmarks.

Portolá resumed the northward march and consequently achieved the honor of discovering the giant redwoods, to which he gave the name palo colorado. From Half Moon Bay, a few days later, he could see the Farallones, Point Reyes, and Drake's Bay (to the Span-iards, Bahía del San Francisco or Cermeño's Bay). These places he recognized unmistakably, for they had been often and well described. Obviously he had passed Monterey, but before turning back to con-firm its identification, Portolá determined to explore a little farther. Gálvez had ordered that the third Alta California mission, that in St. Francis' honor, should be established at the Bay of San Francisco (Drake's Bay). Since they were only a few miles from the spot, Portolá decided to visit it before facing about.

Ortega was sent off to blaze a trail to Point Reyes. Meanwhile, hunters climbed the hills east of Half Moon Bay. These hunters were the first white men to see San Francisco Bay. They returned to camp to describe the great quiet harbor just over the hills. Hot upon their heels came Ortega, with word that the trail to Point Reyes was blocked by the Golden Gate. Crespi wrote in his diary: "It is a very large and fine harbor, such that not only all the navy of our most Catholic Majesty but those of all Europe could take shelter in it."

Portolá, however, entered in his journal on the day of the discovery that "they had found nothing," and his attitude was really that the bay was an obstacle to further advance northward.

Being advised by the Indians that a large ship, perhaps the *San José* or *San Antonio,* was anchored two days' march to the north, Portolá endeavored to get around the arms of the bay. His farthest north, however, was in the neighborhood of Hayward. On the way south, Monterey was definitely identified and Vizcaíno's Port branded a hallucination. Portolá's band plodded wearily to San Diego, during the final twelve days butchering and roasting one of the weak old mules each evening, and at last entered Serra's camp, "smelling frightfully of mules."

Talk of Abandonment

The outlook for California was now most discouraging. The "Estuary of San Francisco Bay" (what is now known as San Francisco Bay) blocked the way to the site for St. Francis' mission. Monterey apparently had no harbor. The San Diego Indians, repulsing the overtures of the missionaries, had attacked the camp and had stripped garments from some of the invalids. More men had succumbed to the scurvy. Portolá's men returned exhausted from their journey. Supplies were very low; for several months, in fact, the colony subsisted chiefly on geese, fish, and such food as the Indians would trade for the soldiers' clothing. So acute was the crisis that on February 10, 1770, Portolá sent Rivera and forty men back to Baja California. They were to get all the supplies that the peninsula missions could spare, besides driving up the cattle that had been left at Velicatá. In the meantime their absence would be an asset, since it would reduce the number to be fed at San Diego.

For another six weeks, privations were severe and abandonment of the colony hung in the balance. Contemporary records do not mention it, but in his *Life of Serra,* published just seventeen years later, Fray Francisco Palóu states that despite Serra's intercessions Portolá set March 20 as the date for leaving unless a supply ship should appear sooner. Serra and Crespi announced that they would stay and hold out to the last breath. Serra also got Captain Vila to agree to sail the *San Carlos* to Monterey if Portolá should order abandonment. The friars sought heavenly assistance through a novena (a nine-day season of prayer), and their prayers were an-

swered by the appearance of the *San Antonio* one day before the
fateful twentieth.   The critical situation is not exaggerated; San
Diego could not have been held much longer except for the supplies
on the *San Antonio*.   Portolá's men "got very particular consolation out of the corn, flour, and rice which it brought."

No one could accuse Palou of praising Serra beyond his deserts.
It does appear, however, that in eulogizing his brother Franciscan,
whose place as California's hero par excellence is secure for all time,
Paloú cast unwarranted reflections upon Portolá.   The captain doubtless was less entranced with California than was Fray Junípero, but
he had not given up.   To his wise and courageous leadership in this
initial crisis is due much of the credit for preserving the Spanish hold
on Alta California.

Over Pérez' protests Portolá sent the *San Antonio* on to Monterey,
while he marched north again with the sixteen able soldiers who remained.   He repeated the ceremony of taking possession and on
June 3, 1770, formally established a presidio and the mission of San
Carlos.   Then, in accordance with his instructions, he invested Fages
with the government of Alta California and sailed with Costansó and
Pérez for Mexico.

News of the occupation of Monterey was hurried to Viceroy Croix,
who, in special compliment to José de Gálvez, ordered the church
bells rung and flags flown to signalize the 300-league advance of the
frontier to the famed Monterey.   Moreover, he ordered the celebration of a special High Mass of thanksgiving, which he attended with
his viceregal court.

9

THE FORMATIVE YEARS

In CALIFORNIA, celebration of victory seemed premature. The arrival of the *San Antonio* and a few months later of Rivera's pack train removed the immediate crisis, but it gave the colony only a temporary lease on life.

A Precarious Start

For several years the infant settlements continued to be on a most precarious footing. The fewness of the Spaniards made Indian hostility all the more alarming. The store of supplies sufficed only for the time being, and since slight success had attended the efforts to develop local sources for foodstuffs, the supply service from Mexico was a prime necessity. Nothing further could be expected, however, from the missions of Baja California. Gálvez had drawn upon their resources without stint, and Rivera's pack train and cattle represented their last possible contribution. The sea route from San Blas remained, but its difficulties and uncertainties had been manifest in the voyages of the *San Carlos* and *San José*. A better supply service was an imperative need.

Other indications of weakness appeared. The military and religious failed to coöperate in cordial fashion; indeed, there was virtually a feud between the governor and the father-president. Fages insisted that it was for him to decide when and where to establish new missions. Serra interpreted the governor's caution as indifference toward the mission program. In the quarrel that ensued, Serra displayed the more contentious spirit; he even went so far as to urge the displacement of Fages. But when this step was finally taken, Serra found the new governor equally adamant, and the two were soon at loggerheads.

Misconduct of the soldiers, especially toward the Indian women, retarded the development of Spanish influence and control. This phenomenon, of course, was common to practically all frontier provinces. The soldiers were rough half-breeds, none of them accompanied by the sobering influence of wife and family. Salvatierra had faced the problem with his soldiers; but, whereas he could discharge any men who proved a nuisance, Serra could have such offenders restrained only if the military governor would act. An Indian outbreak at San Gabriel in 1771 was the direct outgrowth of the lassoing and mistreatment of the wife of the chief; elsewhere Indian resistance was invited similarly.

Missionary work, meanwhile, progressed at a snail's pace. The San Diego mission operated more than a year before a single conversion was accomplished, and the first baptism at San Carlos had to compensate for six months' labor. By the end of 1773 not quite 500 Indians had been baptized, no very large number in comparison with other missionary fields; and of these 500, almost all were women, children, and old people. Very few men had embraced the new faith. The record was so uninspiring that Rafael Verger, Father-Superior of the Fernandinos, under whose auspices the work was being done, called attention to his prediction that this plan of Gálvez would not bear fruit. In his unenthusiasm he recommended that the mission funds be placed to better use elsewhere. Only gradually did he come to share at all in Serra's buoyant enthusiasm about the Alta California field. Lack of presents for the Indians appears to have been the major difficulty. The missionaries demonstrated no deficiency in zeal, but quite the reverse; yet there was a deplorable shortage of the toothsome morsels and gaudy baubles affording the surest and quickest medium for the winning of souls.

Two presidios and five missions by the end of 1773: the figures have an impressive ring until one steps backstage and sees that the structures were only of logs and tules with wooden stockades, that the entire force for presidial garrison and mission guard numbered but sixty-one soldiers, and that there were practically no Indian men to count on for mission protection. Alta California was but a fragile Spanish outpost.

Already crises had arisen in the matter of supplies. When the supply ships were late in 1772, a starvation period was averted only by a famous bear hunt organized by Fages near San Luis Obispo. Soldiers, padres, and neophytes lived on bear meat and little else for more than a month. Agricultural experiments were made, but the first crops were almost all failures. Not until later, when wheat and citrus trees were introduced, did farming prove worth while. This fact may help to excuse the Indians' failure to cultivate the California soil. It added to the dependence on the uncertain supply ships.

Furthermore, the new colony was proving a great expense. In the five years ending with 1773 the government had expended more than half a million pesos upon California. This figure includes the cost of opening a port at San Blas, which was primarily for California's sake, but not the expenditures under the Pious Fund or the value of requisitions and confiscations from the Baja California missions. At a time when economy and financial reform were the royal watchwords, such expenditures could not go unchallenged. The argument of cost was added to that of missionary failure as calling for withdrawal from the colony. Abandonment was an imminent possibility.

Two other circumstances militated against California's chances for success and permanence. One was that, through Gálvez' illness and his subsequent departure for Europe, she had lost her most ardent supporter in New Spain's officialdom. The viceregal officials were at first only lukewarm in their interest in Gálvez' colony. A second handicap was that until 1773 the Fernandinos had to devote part of their resources of men and money to the older missions in the peninsula.

When the Jesuits were expelled, the Dominicans had applied for a share in the California field. Both Gálvez and the Franciscans opposed the idea at first, but the Dominican spokesman, Fray Juan Pedro de Iriarte y Laurnage, was persistent in arguing that it was not right that one order should occupy a region so large as California. Gálvez and the viceroy gave in, and the king ordered a division of California between the two orders.

In the negotiations that followed, Iriarte found, probably to his surprise, that the Fernandinos were willing to relinquish a good deal. Their experience in the seven southernmost missions had convinced them that this part of Baja California was not promising. Interfer-

ence by secular authorities, as well as the barrenness of the land and
the fewness of the Indians, had led the Franciscans to seek release
from these missions in December, 1771.   They wanted to retain the
stronger missions between Loreto and Velicatá, but finally were persuaded to relinquish them as well as the virgin territory between Velicatá and San Diego.   By the terms of the concordat between Iriarte
and Verger, the Dominican-Franciscan boundary was set just beyond
the arroyo of San Juan Bautista, the northernmost of the potential
mission sites on the trail to San Diego.

In peninsula history this transfer was highly important.   It introduced the third mission period, during which seven northern missions were added to the older Jesuit-Franciscan chain.   These missions of the Dominican frontier bridged the gap between Velicatá and
San Diego.   In Alta California history the significance of the transfer
is apparent in the band of eight Gray Robes who in 1773 reinforced
Serra, Crespi, and the other Alta California pioneers.   Among the
members of this group were Francisco Paloú, Serra's particular friend
and biographer, and Fermín Francisco de Lasuén, later to have charge
of the California missions.

Bucareli Adopts California

At about the same time, Viceroy Antonio María de Bucareli y
Ursúa began to take an active interest in California.   Because of his
contributions to the faltering colony, Bucareli has been acclaimed
"the greatest hero who has ever appeared in the field of California history."   His reputation was great even before he came to Mexico City
to serve throughout the 1770's as viceroy.   As a soldier and engineer
in the Italian campaigns, and then as governor and captain-general at
Havana, Bucareli had so distinguished himself that the king granted
several special privileges in connection with his promotion to the
viceroyalty.   He increased the salary to $80,000, permitted Bucareli
to appoint a dozen friends to lucrative offices, and excused him from
the customary residencia.   Bucareli proved one of the most popular
viceroys.   Mexican historians, for example, have been chary of praise
for Spanish officials, but Manuel Rivera, after praising Bucareli for
his integrity and his intelligence, asserted that he was "one of those
men whose memory will never be erased from the hearts of Mexicans."

Bucareli had taken over the reins of viceregal government in September, 1771. For two years he was largely occupied with the central and routine tasks of that office. He continued some of the Gálvez reforms but blocked the operation of others, such as the setting up of intendancies. Thus far his attitude was that Alta California was a very incidental part of New Spain. The oftenest quoted of his early references to the colony appears in a letter to one of the king's ministers, Julián de Arriaga, in February, 1773, in which he gave warning that Alta California might have to be abandoned.

Then came a change, a change so striking that Bucareli later could reflect that it seemed as though his whole attention turned to the Californias and the opening of a supply route from Sonora to California. Several circumstances explain this change. Fray Junípero journeyed to Mexico City in 1773 to voice California's needs. He had several audiences with the viceroy. The particulars of their conversations have not been reported, but, at Bucareli's request, Serra embodied his suggestions in two papers dated March 13 and April 22 and totaling thirty-three paragraphs. In these representations he subordinated complaints against Fages and gave Bucareli information and constructive suggestions. From the Sonora frontier, at about the same time, came proposals from Captain Juan Bautista de Anza, seconded by Fray Francisco Garcés, that an expedition be authorized for opening a land route from Sonora to Monterey. The viceregal archives contained many briefs supporting this plea, some of which may have come to Bucareli's attention, but perhaps most influential was his increasing realization of the strategic value of the Spanish outpost in California.

Alta California, though apparently on an open frontier, was essentially a borderland colony. It had not been occupied for its own resources, as were Mexico, Peru, Colombia, and the other colonies of the early conquistadores. Rather, it resembled the subsequent buffer provinces: Florida, wrested from the French and garrisoned to guard the passage of the Silver Fleets; Texas, planted in the early eighteenth century because of French activities in the Alabama and Mississippi basins; Montevideo and the Banda Oriental, another early eighteenth-century settlement, whose function was to block the Portuguese drive southwestward; Louisiana, accepted from France after the Seven Years' War to shield New Spain from England's expanding empire. As Gálvez had emphasized, the danger on the northwest coast was partially Russian, but in Europe, particularly after the Seven Years' War, Spain's most formidable adversary was England. In North America, too, England had become the power principally to be feared. Not only had she inflicted humiliation through the easy capture of Havana in 1762, but she had emerged from the war in possession of the Floridas, the eastern half of the Mississippi Valley, and Canada from the St. Lawrence to the Rockies. Thus she was obviously Spain's principal concern, not only in Europe but also in the Caribbean and the Gulf of Mexico and along the Mississippi frontier. The English had already sent out explorers from the Hudson Bay posts. Now they threatened to make this expansion transcontinental and to unite with it voyages to the North Pacific.

In his capacity as captain-general at Havana, just before the Seven Years' War, Bucareli had been face to face with the English menace. It is natural, therefore, that considerations such as the above should have occurred to him. He came to think of Alta California not merely as a field for missionary undertakings, or as a step toward straightening out the Indian frontier, or as a barrier to Russian expansion. Its purpose was also to serve as a check upon the growing English power in North America.

Even a bare enumeration of Bucareli's services to California must be an extended one. His Reglamento, or plan of government and administration, served virtually as the constitution under which the province was ruled to the end of the Spanish period. Issued in July, 1773, it was amplified on August 17 of that year in forty-two paragraphs of instructions issued to the new governor, Rivera y Moncada. Among other matters, Rivera was admonished to promote the conversion of the natives and their civilization at the missions. These missions, Bucareli predicted, would become great cities; Rivera should plan accordingly in selecting sites, laying out streets, and parceling the land. Other paragraphs dealt with the keeping of records, reporting to Loreto and Mexico City, Indian policy, supply ships from San Blas, and the eventual secularization of the missions. Demonstrating his awareness of the strategic importance of San Francisco Bay, the viceroy ordered careful examination of that region with a view to its early occupation. Three years later, in instructions to the next governor, Felipe de Neve, Bucareli restated his general orders for Alta California. Somewhat modified, these orders were promulgated locally over Neve's signature. The document is generally referred to as the Neve Reglamento, but it was essentially what Bucareli had formulated.

In connection with the change in governors Bucareli was able to make a slight reinforcement of California. Though not ready to accept Serra's nomination of the pathfinder Ortega as the new governor, he advanced the latter to the rank of lieutenant and designated him to command the new presidio at San Diego. And since Fages would bring his Catalan troops back to Baja California, the new governor was instructed to enlist married recruits in Sinaloa and to take them and their families to the new province. Rivera collected a party of fifty-one persons, whom he transported across to Loreto. Thence, by way of Velicatá, they reached their destination. Earlier in 1774 Serra had sailed for California, accompanied by a new missionary, Fray Pablo Mugártegui, a new commissary, three blacksmiths and three carpenters, not to mention four reams of fine paper, five bales of cloth for Indian presents, sixteen boxes of panocha and six of chocolate, four boxes of beads, and sundry other articles to be used in converting the heathen. These reinforcements were perhaps more encouraging than reassuring. They were not enough to put the province securely on its feet, but they were valuable because California was in such a state that every little bit helped.

Bucareli also wrought great improvement in the service of the supply ships. Notwithstanding optimistic reports from California, he sent out an extra vessel in 1774, which arrived just in time to avert a serious famine. Every year he was careful to see that the supplies were in good conditions and that the ships left San Blas promptly. Merely to keep the service in operation was no mean feat. The harbor at San Blas silted in, and work on the port was necessary almost constantly. Because of the climate, most supplies could not be stored at San Blas but had to be shipped at once, and consequently, perfect timing was necessary in the arrival and loading of the stores and the sailing of the ships. Ships were scarce. The voyage was always long and arduous and bore such an evil reputation that sailors commonly had to be shanghaied into service. Yet Bucareli not only maintained but improved the supply service by sea.

Further exploration of the coast was a companion task. Pérez got as far north as fifty-five degrees latitude in 1773–1774. Three vessels were sent out in 1775. The one commanded by Ayala was the first vessel to sail through the Golden Gate into San Francisco Bay. In another, Hezeta discovered the Columbia River. Bodega took the third as far as fifty-eight degrees latitude. In 1779 he again went to Alaskan waters but saw nothing of the Russians. These voyages were the sort of investigation the court had ordered Gálvez to make in 1769. They were motivated, however, by concern about English as well as Russian activities in the North Pacific; in fact, renewed interest on the part of the English in discovering the Northwest Passage, as represented by Cook's voyage, must be regarded as Bucareli's primary reason for sending out these ships. Because he did so, Spain could claim priority in the exploration of most of the coast from the Columbia to Alaska.

To facilitate the supplying of California, Bucareli undertook to develop a route across the Isthmus of Tehuantepec. He sent Colonel Agustín Crame to find out whether it would be feasible to move heavy equipment, such as cannon, across to the Pacific. Crame reported an excellent and easy route and even said that a canal could be constructed with little effort. No immediate development followed this recommendation, but in recent years the route has been important and there has been talk of a canal.

The Anza Expeditions

Experience with the sea and peninsula routes to Alta California had fully corroborated Gálvez' original opinion that the province could not flourish unless a land route was opened from Sonora. The supply ships faced so long and so uncertain a voyage that they could not be utilized to carry families of settlers or herds of livestock to California. The first missionaries, soldiers, mules, and cattle came up the peninsula trails; yet Serra estimated that to supply the province by this route would require the constant services of a train of 1,500 mules, many times more than could be fed and watered along the trail. Bucareli's greatest contribution to California unquestionably was in bringing about the opening of the land route from Sonora. Over it came the reinforcements that made Spanish California self-perpetuating and measurably self-supporting. The land route also made possible the founding of San Francisco as the northernmost outpost of Spain's empire. So significant were these achievements that they must be described in greater detail.

In choosing leaders to open the trail to California the viceroy made

a most happy selection. His principal agent in the land advance was
Captain Juan Bautista de Anza, whose father and grandfather before
him had served the king as frontier captains on the rim of civilization
at Frónteras and Janos. For two decades Anza had seen similar
service at Frónteras and Tubac. Though only thirty-seven, he was
ripe in experience in Indian control, seasoned through Apache fighting, and expert in campaigning in a half-desert land. At Bucareli's
behest Anza led two expeditions to California. One was to explore
the trail; the other, to bring supplies and livestock and families of
settlers, the lifeblood of Spanish Alta California. He did his work
brilliantly, getting his parties through expeditiously and almost without loss of life. In length and in difficulties of terrain and hostile
natives, Anza's first expedition has been compared to that of Lewis
and Clark. His second journey corresponds to the conduct of the
first pioneer settlers to Oregon.

Father Francisco Garcés, a young Franciscan sent to San Xavier
del Bac in 1768, when the Jesuits were expelled, shared honors with
Anza in advancing land exploration. He became the idol of the Pimas.
He made three journeys inland, traveling, as Governor Sastre wrote,
"with no other provisions than a little pinole, a little chocolate, and a
few strips of jerked beef, and with no other escort than his guardian
angel." Twice he traveled El Camino del Diablo to the Pimas on
the Gila, and once he crossed the Colorado, going as far as Signal
Mountain near Calexico. Intrepid, dynamic, fearless, and trusted by
the Indians, Garcés was another Kino, though even more of a wan-
derer.

Opinion may differ as to what other individual should be mentioned
in connection with the opening of the land route. Serra's trip to
Mexico in 1773 seems to have gone far toward awakening Bucareli's
interest and thus to have set in motion the advance beyond Sonora.
Lieutenant José Moraga, as Anza's second in command, did signal
service along the way and was in personal charge of the settlers at the
actual founding of San Francisco. To the historically inclined, however, the work of Father Pedro Font must take precedence. Not an
explorer in his own right as was Garcés, and not a member of the
first expedition, Font is nevertheless memorable as the diarist of the
colonist group. His book-length journal of the day-by-day experience of this party is unsurpassed by any other description of western
travel. It is so accurate a record of distances and landmarks that

its modern translator could make positive identification of every camping place and almost every footstep along the way. At the same time, the diary presents such a wealth of intimate detail that it recreates for every reader a vivid picture of the experiences of these pioneers.

Take, for example, Font's description of Garcés' missionary method, of how he assembled a mob of Indians at Santa Olaya, won their attention by distributing a few beads and a little tobacco, and then drew forth from his pack a banner depicting the Child Jesus in the Virgin Mary's arms. The natives were pleased and gladly offered themselves to be baptized. Then Garcés turned his picture around. The reverse side showed a lost soul suffering eternal punishment, at the sight of which the Indians raised a great outcry. The Gileños, the Opas, and the Yumas, as Font remarks, "all replied in the same way, without manifesting any repugnance to Christianity." In Font's opinion, Garcés was ideally suited to missionary work among these Indians. Like them he was phlegmatic, content to sit musing by a fire for hours at a time. Nor had he any repugnance against eating the Indian foods, which Font considered "nasty and dirty." "In short," the latter opined, "God has created him, as I see it, solely for the purpose of seeking out these unhappy, ignorant, and rustic people."

The project of opening a land route to Monterey had a long but futile history up to 1773. It went back clearly to Kino and rather vaguely to Oñate. Anza's father and others had urged it vigorously during the middle eighteenth century, and Anza had suggested it as early as 1756. The plan also was more than implicit in Gálvez' labors for the pacification of Sonora. The immediate inspiration, however, was that in 1769 Anza's Pima neighbors learned through the Yumas of white men going up and down the west coast. The prompt arrival of this news of Portolá argued the existence of a convenient land route; consequently Anza sent an offer to Gálvez to seek it out. Encouraged still further by Garcés' report of his journey across the Colorado and of his sight of a great blue sierra not far to the northwest, Anza renewed and expanded the offer.

Bucareli's careful pondering of Anza's proposal is a worthy example of Spanish thoroughness in colonial administration. He gathered all possible data and consulted whoever might possess pertinent information. Costansó, Portolá's cosmographer, gave his expert approval of the plan and lauded it because it would release the Cali-

fornia soldiers from the "perpetual and involuntary celibacy" to which
they thus far stood condemned.   A junta at Mexico City called on
Anza and Garcés for more information.   Delay ensued which might
have been a permanent obstruction except that Father Serra, then in
Mexico City, added his hearty approval.   Bucareli made his decision,
and a junta voted its approval unanimously.   In addition to the regular mail carriers, a veteran of the Portolá expedition, Juan Bautista
Valdés, carried the news to Anza.

The captain commenced preparations forthwith, but in early December he suffered a serious setback as the result of an Apache raid
on the horses he had collected for the expedition.   So many of the
best animals were run off that he had to change his intended route.
Instead of going toward the Gila, he took a more roundabout course
by way of the Altar Valley settlements and Caborca, where a lesser
number of inferior mounts was secured. "Stacks of bones," Anza
called them.   Yet some consolation was afforded by the enlistment
of Sebastián Tarabal as guide.   Tarabal was a runaway from the San
Gabriel mission who had just come over the course that Anza wished
to follow.   Anza entertained high hopes concerning his usefulness,
but they were to prove too sanguine; his actual assistance was very
slight.

As far as Caborca, Anza traveled through a settled country, passing
presidios, settlements, and several of Kino's missions.   Beyond
Caborca there were no settlements, but as far as Yuma he was following a well-known path, so that the problem was not of trail breaking
but of leading his twenty-odd men and 200 animals over this leg of
the journey with the least possible inconvenience and exhaustion.
The season was propitious; it was January, and rains had just fallen
to fill the tanks along the way.   Yet Anza had to make three dry
camps between Caborca and Sonóita.   To allow water holes to refill
along the Camino del Diablo, the 200-mile stretch just east of Yuma,
he divided his train.   Here the expedition depended entirely on water
holes or tanks, chief of which were the Tinajas de Purificación, now
called the Cabeza Prieta Tanks, on both sides of which dry camps
were unavoidable.

Anza realized that the Colorado crossing was the crucial point
along the trail to California and that it behooved him to make sure
of the friendship and support of the Yuma Indians.   He sent an invitation to Chief Salvador Palma to come out and meet him, but the

conference did not take place until Anza reached the river junction. In an eloquent speech Palma assured the Spaniards of Yuma friendship. He had cautioned his braves not to molest the Spaniards or steal from them. His warriors were children, however, and would like to gratify their curiosity about the Spaniards and all their belongings. He protested that there was no need for the Spanish soldiers to maintain such vigilance while guests of their Yuma friends.

Adroitly explaining that the soldiers' vigilance was a routine requirement in their military discipline, Anza congratulated the Yumas on their promise of friendship and welcomed them into the great host of subjects of Charles III, whose power and majesty he outlined. Around Palma's neck he hung a red ribbon on which was suspended a medal bearing a likeness of Charles, in token that Palma was now a ruler obedient to the king and commissioned by him. Capitalizing the favorable impression he had made, Anza went on to preach a sermon. He expounded the greatness of God, made much of the brotherhood of Spaniards and Indians, and ended by exhorting the Yumas to have done with intertribal warfare. Palma was a full hour haranguing his people in embellishment of Anza's speech. And all night the inquisitive Indians hung around the camp, "making sleep impossible, and life generally miserable."

In the morning Anza forded the Gila, the tall Yumas carrying his baggage across on their heads. The next day they assisted again in the crossing of the Colorado, which was celebrated by a salute of musketry that startled and pleased the Indians. All crossed in orthodox fashion save Father Garcés, who could not swim and did not trust his horse. He crossed on the shoulders of his newly found Indian friends.

Beyond the Colorado, Anza's problem was really that of trail breaking. Garcés had been somewhat farther and Tarabal had wandered across the sand dunes from the California side, but neither proved a reliable guide. Indian advice was more to the point. The Yumas warned against a northwest or west course, which would have led more directly toward Monterey. Pursuant to their advice, Anza descended the Colorado to Santa Olaya, intending to strike westward from there toward the blue sierra. This three-day journey was as picturesque and bizarre as can be imagined. Some 600 Yumas of all sizes, ages, and descriptions made a holiday outing of this jaunt down the river. They swarmed around the soldiers and cattle and

performed a number of small services for the white men, pestering
them meanwhile with their prying curiosity and even with the theft
of an axe. The mob was expectant of another largess such as had
followed the crossing of the Gila, when Anza stood 600 Yumas in
line and gave each a "little gift of beads and tobacco." They were
not disappointed.

From the Cajuenche village at Santa Olaya, Anza struck out west
into the sand dunes. Over a hard trail he made twenty miles the
first day, camping near some pools of water at Arroyo del Carrizal.
His guides would go only three or four miles farther. On the third
day the going got worse. Drifting sand obliterated the trail; saddle
and pack animals plodded wearily through the soft sand, and the head
muleteer reported that his mules were giving out.

In this crisis Anza proposed to go on with half the force, sending
the more weary animals and men back to the Yumas to recuperate.
But Garcés dissuaded the captain, and after further struggle westward
toward the Cerro, he proposed instead that they turn south toward
Cerro Prieto, where he had found water and a Cajuenche village three
years earlier. This they did, the horsemen pushing on ahead to
locate water and pasturage; but though Garcés sought half the night
for his old camp, he failed to locate it, and all the animals had to
spend the night without water or pasturage. Since retreat to the
Colorado was obviously the only means of saving the horses and
mules, Anza reluctantly turned back. A dozen or more head were
lost, but the rest straggled back to the oasis at Santa Olaya.

The ten-day battle with the sand dunes had taken such toll of the
animals that Anza despaired of packing all his supplies to California. He summoned Palma, convinced himself of the chief's
loyalty, and told him he had decided to leave most of the baggage,
the cattle, and the worn-out saddle and pack animals in his keeping.
Palma welcomed the responsibility, but the head muleteer volun-
teered to remain with two soldiers to watch over this property, an
arrangement that Anza approved.

While the animals recuperated, the soldiers relaxed by dancing with
the Cajuenches to the tune of a soldier's violin. "They seemed so
attached to it," wrote Anza, "that they gave up their own pastimes,
and in their stead learned the customs of our men, particularly the
women, who constantly wished to be dancing the seguidillas which
the soldiers taught them, and in whose steps they became proficient."

At the same time more serious preparations were in progress, and by March 2 Anza was ready to set out again, this time with only ten pack mules and with his twenty-five soldiers, friars, and helpers mounted on the "least bad" horses.

To get around the sand dunes he traveled down the Colorado River meadows, around Volcano Lake, and to a lagoon where Garcés met old Cajuenche friends, who explained that the San Jacome village had been abandoned for lack of water. A half day's journey to a dry camp, followed by a forty-mile march, brought them to a well of fresh water near the head of Laguna Salada. The well turned salt before half the animals had been watered, but the next day they found good water and some pasturage three leagues farther on at Santo Tomás in Pinto Canyon. The worst desert stretch was now passed. There was good pasturage just across the present international boundary, and Tarabal soon heartened them all by beginning to recognize signs of the gap in the Sierra. After a dry camp at Arroyo del Coyote, they pushed on seven difficult leagues to a camp which Tarabal at last could identify and which was named in his honor San Sebastián or, more familiarly, El Peregrino. Beyond this camp Tarabal proved a competent guide.

There were still hardships. Two horses were lost at a marshy bog, and most of the men were now on foot. After passing through Borrego Valley, they laid over a day at San Gregorio to take advantage of the best forage found thus far. Then, by Coyote Canyon they ascended to the Royal Pass of San Carlos, where the Cahuilla Valley greeted them, "most beautiful green and flower-strewn prairies, and snow-covered mountains with pines, oaks, and other trees which grow in cold countries." Along the San Jacinto Valley they hurried, then west through Alessandro Valley, past the site of Riverside, and across the Santa Ana on a hastily constructed log bridge. Another two days brought them to civilization again at San Gabriel, and the trail was complete from Sonora to California.

No more positive evidence of the weakness of Spanish Alta California could exist than in the problems Anza faced at San Gabriel in the spring of 1774. He sent to San Diego for supplies and mounts so that he could go on to Monterey, from where he intended to return by another trail farther northeast. But neither sort of help was forthcoming, and consequently he had no alternative but to send Garcés and most of the soldiers back to the Yumas to await him there. By their hands he forwarded to Bucareli a copy of his diary and a letter in which he congratulated the viceroy that his land route had been opened. "From it," he wrote, "I expect great advantage to the service of both Majesties and the glory of your Excellency."

Instead of going around the sand dunes Garcés cut across through the middle of present Imperial Valley. It was a terrifically hot ride but it saved nineteen leagues. At Monterey, meanwhile, Anza and Palóu were laying plans for a chain of missions along the Anza trail and for mail service over it from Mexico to Monterey. Returning to San Gabriel in a nine-day ride, Anza picked up Father Díaz with a newly acquired astrolabe from San Diego and set out for the Colorado. He made a further improvement on Garcés' trail and time, covering the eighty or ninety miles between San Sebastián and Santa Olaya in twenty-five hours.

Palma's Yumas rafted Anza across the Colorado as they had done for Garcés. He journeyed up the Gila and home to Tubac, whence he hoped to set out for Mexico City to report in person to Bucareli. He was detained by Inspector Bonilla on the frontier, but by November the viceroy put through an order bringing him to the capitol to make a full report on the expedition.

Bucareli was thoroughly pleased. He recommended that Anza be promoted to the rank of lieutenant colonel and that his followers receive substantial rewards. Like Palóu and Anza, he saw the possibilities of the route and he ordered that Anza utilize it at once to take settlers into California. Having received Pérez' report about the northwest coast at about the same time, Bucareli was also thinking about sea expeditions. The Hezeta-Ayala-Bodega voyages of 1775 were, in fact, intimately related to Anza's second expedition, conducted that same year. Morever, apart from the sea activities it would be hard to understand why San Francisco Bay became the real objective of the second expedition.

Four days after the viceroy asked for advice concerning the procedure to be followed, Anza submitted detailed and practical recommendations. Settlers should be recruited from the Sinaloa district, where almost all families were "submerged in poverty." Ten regular soldiers from Tubac who had gone on the first journey should be relieved by five recruits and five regulars from Terrenate, so that they could accompany this group. If satisfactory horses and mules were to be had, the Sinaloan hacendados must be required to sell their choicest animals for the use of the expedition. There should be a supply of Indian presents, including "something special" for Palma. The soldier-settlers should be paid in clothing and equipment, not in cash.

His advice prevailed on all essential points. Bucareli authorized him to recruit twenty families and to select ten veteran soldiers. He appointed a lieutenant, a sergeant, and a cosmographer upon Anza's nominations. Once more a junta "rubber-stamped" the viceregal decision. A list of the necessary equipment was drawn up. The colonists were to be provided everything from shoes to hair ribbons; each man's outfit was to cost forty-two pesos one real, each woman's six reales less. Besides complete clothing outfits the men were to have carbines, cartridge belts, "cueras" (leather jackets), saddles, bridles, pack saddles, blankets, and all the necessary provisions for the journey.

Recruiting went forward rather slowly, yet the start from Horcasitas might have been made as scheduled, early in September of 1775, except that an Apache raid again interfered. Swooping down on Tubac, the Indians ran off the entire horse herd of more than 500 animals. Once again, Anza had to outfit his expedition with inferior animals. On September 28, however, the soldiers were reviewed, and the next day, after Mass and a sermon by Father Font, the company set off. It numbered 177 persons, and there were 140 pack mules, 450 saddle animals, 100 beeves to be slaughtered along the way, and 200 cattle for the California colony.

On the road to Tubac the journey was enlivened by Apache scares and the tribulations of the inexperienced muleteers, who were busied with much refastening of the packs. Sixty-three persons joined the expedition at Tubac, making 240 altogether. The stock was increased also to 695 horses and mules and 355 cattle. This was really a ranch on the move, and the number of people was so great that every night the camp looked like a town.

At the first camp beyond Tubac one of the women gave birth to a fine boy, but in spite of all the care given her, she died before morning. Hers was the only life lost all along the 1,500-mile journey; even the infant reached California in good shape.

Instead of following his former route by Caborca and Camino del Diablo, Anza moved north toward the Gila, where he was welcomed by a group of Pima headmen, who presented him with two fresh

Apache scalps.   In the Gileño towns Anza had several ceremonious
meetings with the natives, shaking hands with 1,100 at Uturituc and
distributing presents to 400 at Sutaquison.   The king's birthday next
broke the monotony of the journey.   Garcés said Mass, and Anza
issued a pint of aguardiente to each soldier, in consequence of which
Font reported "more than moderate drunkenness."

After three days' delay, occasioned by the illness of several of the
women, they left the river to cut across Gila Bend to the country
of the Opas and Cocomaricopas.   The horses, as well as many of
the people, showed the ill effects of the bad water at Laguna del Hospital.   By short marches they moved forward to Agua Caliente, and
then to San Pasqual, where the party was increased to 241 by the
birth of another "fine boy."   Near the Yuma junction, Palma came
out to meet them.   He embraced Anza and every member of the
expedition, inquired about the health of the king and the viceroy, and
reminded Anza how faithfully he had adhered to his instructions,
especially with regard to keeping peace with his neighbors.   He renewed his request for a missionary establishment among his people
and expressed regret that this party was going on to California.   But
he was consoled by the gorgeous raiment Bucareli had sent him,
comprised of shirt and trousers, jacket with yellow front, blue cape
with gold braid, and black velvet cap.   At the Yuma village abundant
hospitality was extended, including a present of 3,000 watermelons,
preserved since the harvest season by burial in the sand.

Crossing the Colorado promised to be an arduous task.   The old
ford was no longer passable, and it was too cold for swimmers to
guide rafts across expeditiously.   Rather than delay, Anza explored
for a ford and found one that seemed satisfactory.   The width was
three or four hundred yards and the water three to six feet deep, but
the entire train got across by midday.   There was one near accident
when a rider deviated from the proper course and a child riding in
front of him was swept off.   But Anza had stationed men below the
ford for just such emergencies, and the little girl was rescued, none
the worse for the ducking.   Font, still dizzy from the ague, crossed
with a Yuma on each side holding him on his horse.   Garcés put his
trust in Indians rather than horses, crossing on the shoulders of three
braves, "two at his head and one at his feet, he lying stretched out face
up as though he were dead."

A cabin was prepared and supplies set aside for Fathers Garcés and Eixarch and the seven Indian servants who were to tarry with the Yumas. As four months' supply for these nine persons Anza left an arroba (twenty-five pounds) each of chocolate, sugar, and tallow, five beeves, three tierces of dried meat, a packload of beans, one of flour, an almud (a little over a bushel) of chick peas, a box of biscuits, three hams, and six cheeses. For presents and barter there was a bale of tobacco and two boxes of beads; for holy services, twelve wax candles and a bottle of wine, though the latter proved to be spurious; and for more mundane uses, a frying pan, a griddle, an axe, and two cakes of soap.

At Santa Olaya, just before attempting the desert crossing, Anza's men were treated to more watermelons, a fish fry, and a few days of relaxation. Again, an issue of aguardiente resulted in "great carousing," and the next morning Font reproached the commander for contributing to the drunkenness of the rabble but could not detect "any signs of repentance."

In three divisions traveling at twenty-four-hour intervals, they now set out across the desert. The weather was unusual, with snow and cold instead of desert heat. Much discomfort, consequently, was in store for them all, in addition to the anticipated difficulties of sand dunes, poor pasturage, and shortage of water. The third day was a particularly gruelling one for the advance division—a thirty-five-mile ride in the bitter cold to Santa Rosa, where they had to camp with very poor fires. The men labored all night deepening the wells and drawing water for the animals. The third division really had the worst experiences; its commander, Moraga, so exposed himself to the cold that for some time he was unable to hear.

Beyond San Sebastián, Anza's first party had found the trail fairly easy, but because of the snow and cold this second expedition encountered its worst hardships between San Sebastián and the Royal Pass of San Carlos. They camped without water in Borrego Valley, and the next night, at San Gregorio, they found but little water. From this camp part of the cattle stampeded, and more than fifty head ran clear to San Sebastián, where most of them mired and died. The loss was the more distressing because the end of the journey was so near. The cumulative exhaustion of the animals slowed the party's progress; horses and cattle died every day.

Yet they celebrated Christmas Eve in cheerful fashion, and again Font protested potations of aguardiente. That night Anza was once more called upon in his capacity as doctor and midwife, and again it was a boy that was born. While they waited a day for this boy and his mother to get ready to ride on to California, Font preached a Christmas sermon that was at once a rebuke for the fandangos and drunkenness of the night before and a happy Christmas wish for all.

Through rain and sleet they journeyed up Coyote Canyon, camped just below the pass, and the next morning crossed the divide and began the descent toward the Pacific. On New Year's Day they crossed the turbulent Santa Ana, losing a cow and a horse in the process. A relay of fresh mounts met them from San Gabriel, making travel easier. After a night on San Antonio Creek near present Ontario, they pushed on to San Gabriel, where they found an enthusiastic welcome. Though they were 500 miles from San Francisco, the well-traveled Camino Real lay ahead of them, and they counted their journey practically completed.

But they could not go forward immediately. The mission Indians at San Diego had just risen in rebellion, killing Father Jayme and two soldiers. Anza and Font and seventeen soldiers joined Governor Rivera in a journey to San Diego to punish the offenders. Another cause of delay was the desertion of five muleteers who started back for Sonora with the twenty-five best horses. Lieutenant Moraga went after them in hot pursuit, overtook them just short of Santa Olaya, and brought them back to the San Gabriel calabozo. His exploit was the more brilliant because he returned with most of the horses and recovered several of the cattle that had stampeded from San Gregorio. Still another obstacle was Governor Rivera's disapproval of San Francisco as a site for the colony and his unwillingness to coöperate. Rivera used the San Diego uprising as an excuse not to obey Bucareli's instructions to assist Anza in establishing the new settlement.

Shortage of supplies at San Gabriel made action imperative, and on February 21, 1776, Anza started for Monterey with about half the party, the others to follow with the cattle. Four weeks later they reached Monterey, and there was another day of great rejoicing, signalized by a sermon by Font in which the experiences of the expedition were used to illustrate the text: "The kingdom of heaven is like unto . . . ."

San Francisco Founded

Meanwhile, the San Francisco region had been explored. Fages went there in 1772. Rivera and Palóu planted a cross on Point Lobos above Seal Rocks two years later. In 1775 Ayala entered the Golden Gate and spent a month exploring the various arms of the bay and eleven days trying to sail out the Boca, or Golden Gate. Ayala made a good map of the bay, which he described as the best anywhere along the west coast and as "not one port, but many, with a single entrance." A land party was supposed to coöperate with Ayala, but Rivera found excuse to delay its sending, and when Bruno Hezeta and Palóu finally arrived, Ayala had departed. Consequently, when Anza's settlers reached Monterey, no sites for the San Francisco mission, presidio, and settlement had been selected, notwithstanding the several visits to the bay region.

Encouraged by the California padres, who were anxious to start work in the new mission, but discouraged by Rivera, who maintained that the peninsula did not afford any suitable site for mission or settlement, Anza went north from Monterey to reconnoiter. He and Font waxed most enthusiastic about the setting for the new colony. "The port of San Francisco," wrote Font, "is a marvel of nature, and might well be called the harbor of harbors." In all his travels he had seen no site that pleased him as much as this. Anza chose Fort Point as the site for the presidio and Arroyo de los Dolores for the mission.

Having chosen the site for San Francisco's beginnings, Anza marched around the southern arm of the bay. In the Contra Costa region he looked in vain for the white and bearded Indians that Crespi had reported in 1772. None was found, and Font set down the account as a charitable mistake on Crespi's part. Unable to detect any current at Carquínez Straits or at Antioch, they concluded that this must be an inland fresh-water sea. The guides spoke of rivers farther inland, but Font insisted that what was actually before them was "not a river, but much water in a pond." Marshes blocked further progress eastward, and so Anza returned to Monterey, cutting across by way of Livermore Valley, tick-infested San Antonio Valley, Coyote Canyon, and Gilroy Valley.

Anza had hoped to conduct the colonists personally to San Francisco, but Rivera's dilatory and obstructionist policies precluded. In mid-April he turned the settlers over to Moraga's command and started for Sonora, carrying with him two pairs of cats to combat the mouse nuisance at San Gabriel and San Diego.   Below Monterey he met the governor, half-crazed with anger that the San Francisco project was moving forward despite his disapproval.   Rivera had ridden all the way from San Diego to confer with Anza, but he was in such a rage that he rode on to Monterey, after only the most perfunctory salutations.   Almost immediately he was riding south again to overtake Anza at San Luis Obispo, but the captain declined to have any discussion with him except in writing.   In a smouldering rage Rivera waited for an hour and then posted off to San Gabriel, where it was his turn to deny Anza an audience.

Anza camped hard by the mission for three days.   Some letters passed back and forth, but no spoken words, and after three days he departed for Mexico without having come to any agreement with the governor about the actual move to San Francisco.   An order from the viceroy, however, reached California soon after Anza left, and Rivera had no alternative but to comply.   Lieutenant Moraga and Fathers Palóu and Cambón led the settlers to the chosen site, founded the presidio on September 17, 1776, and dedicated the mission on October 9.   But this outpost of empire was essentially the work of Bucareli, who had sponsored the entire project, and of Anza, who had opened the trail and conducted the colonists to California.   These two men were the real founders.

The Yuma Massacre

Anza's departure in 1776 marked the end of his California career, except as his governorship of New Mexico had an indirect bearing on the development of the entire northern frontier.   His departure also represented the practical termination of Bucareli's direction of the province.   The viceroy continued to administer the supply service by sea, but in 1777 all other phases of frontier control passed into the hands of the newly appointed Commandant-General of the Provincias Internas.   Gálvez had contemplated this reorganization at the time of his Sonora sojourn, but the delay in pacifying the Indians had interfered.   When he became Minister of the Indies, he promptly put through the reform.

Generally speaking, the reorganization was a sagacious step.   It enabled Spain to achieve a more unified policy in the frontier provinces and strengthened these borderlands.   Teodoro de Croix, the first commandant-general, was appointed primarily because of his friendship with Gálvez; yet he had other recommendations, particularly his experience in combating the Apaches in Texas, Coahuila, and Chihuahua. His intimate acquaintance with the Apache problem naturally inclined him to attack it first. In concert with Bernardo de Gálvez of Louisiana he laid plans for a general campaign. Plans went awry because Spain entered the war against England, and the Louisiana governor was busy defending his province and capturing the Floridas. But they were very good plans and helped to win Croix his promotion to the viceroyalty of Peru.

From the standpoint of Spanish California, on the other hand, Croix's appointment appears most regrettable. He had slight comprehension of the California problems, he made no visit to the northwestern frontier, and he failed to carry out the minister's explicit orders to develop the Anza route and the California settlements. It is upon the basis of this California failure that local historians have characterized Croix as well-meaning and industrious, but inexperienced, unwise, and even stupid. For Spanish California, Anza or Hugo Oconor would have been a better appointee, or, better still, Bucareli might have been left in charge.

Having gone to so much trouble to have the Anza route opened, Bucareli had fully appreciated it and planned to secure it by establishing settlements at the crucial points, chief of which was the Colorado crossing. He had begun preparations for a presidio and mission there, and he urged the matter upon Croix when jurisdiction was shifted. The Yumas, whose friendship Anza and Garcés had enjoyed so completely, were equally desirous of a mission—or perhaps more accurately, for the presents which missionaries would bring.

Preoccupied with his Apache plans, Croix postponed the Yuma missions. Father Garcés and others urged action, but not until 1780 did the commandant-general authorize the advance; and then it was a "mongrel" colony that resulted, part presidio, part mission, part settlement. This peculiar and experimental type of colony was excused on the plea of economy. The soldiers were less expensive than a full presidial guard; another saving was effected by paring the budget for Indian presents.

Two of these modified missions were started on the California side of the river. It was obvious almost immediately that the Yuma zest for conversion had waned, the Indians being disappointed by the niggardly allowance for presents. The few settlers and soldiers worked at cross purposes with the friars and disregarded the Indian right to land, firewood, and mesquite beans. The necessity of sending to San Gabriel for cattle illustrates the inadequacy of the colony, which neither attracted nor impressed the Yumas.

Discontent came to a head in 1781 when Rivera conducted an emigrant party over the Anza trail. He appears to have been a careless disciplinarian, who did not restrain his soldiers or settlers from antagonizing the Yumas. Furthermore, the presents he distributed were insignificant. Determined upon retaliation, the Indians plotted in secret. Waiting until the emigrants and part of the soldiers had gone on, they attacked the two missions on July 17, enslaving the women and children and killing all the men save Fathers Garcés and Barreneche, who were spared until two days later. Rivera and his soldiers, encamped across the river to recruit their stock, were unaware that anything unusual had occurred. On July 18 the Yumas fell upon them too and killed them all.

This massacre of four friars and more than thirty soldiers ranks with the worst disasters of the Spanish frontier. Governor Neve refused to permit Limón to avenge it. Croix sent Fages with two expeditions from Sonora, but all that was accomplished was the recovery of the bodies of the priests and the ransom of such prisoners as desired it. No punishment was meted out.

The temptation is to blame Rivera for the tragedy. Croix and Neve chose rather to inculpate Garcés and Anza. They convinced Gálvez that Anza had minimized the danger at Yuma. Croix, however, was chiefly to blame. His delay in establishing the settlements and his boasted economy in Indian presents and presidial guard were fatal.

Anza's route, consequently, was broken. Yuma hostility would preclude further migration over it to California; California's connection with Mexico would be only by the unsatisfactory sea route, and her prosperity, her growth and development, and the tenuosity of her political attachment to Mexico were seriously impaired. The result was not an undoing of all that Gálvez and Bucareli and Anza had accomplished, nor did it bring to a halt all California development, because the simple roots for mission and pueblo prosperity had already been planted. But a period was put to the rapid development of the province that had characterized the preceding half dozen years. Subsequent growth had to come from within.

10

LOCAL ANNALS

THROUGH THE REMAINING two score years of its Spanish
period California followed a blissfully placid and unprogressive
course. The rustic calm is in sharp contrast to the preceding twelve
years, when momentous events had followed one another in rapid succession: the sacred expeditions of 1769, the discovery of San Francisco Bay, the narrowly averted abandonment of San Diego, Bucareli's
energetic measures of relief and supply, the North Pacific voyages,
Anza's expeditions, the founding of San Francisco, the establishment
of the San José and Los Angeles pueblos, the Yuma Massacre. Excitement, adventure, glory were implicit in the meeting of these crises,
while such elements as starvation, shipwreck, Indian danger, and
imminent failure made the times harrowing and portentous. Thereafter, crises arose but seldom and opportunities for spectacular hero-
ism were far less numerous. So untroubled was the province that
the good old days have come to be regarded as California's romantic
and idyllic period. In many respects, though not in all, the two
decades under Mexico were a continuation of this Arcadian age.

A Tranquil Period

Quiet and untroubled as were these final decades under Spain, the
period was far from uneventful. Some of the most colorful figures
in the whole realm of local history flourished in these years. California's most famous romance had an appropriate setting in this
romantic epoch, which abounded with other episodes, perhaps not
pregnant with great consequence, yet of considerable intrinsic interest. The provincial annals record no catastrophes and no revolutionary advances, but besides being rich in highly human entries, they

135

do reveal a satisfactory gradual development of the colony, achieved primarily by the provincials themselves, working through the institutions that had been introduced in the more dramatic epoch of Gálvez and Bucareli.

The basic institutions, of course, were the same three that had dominated the frontier of New Spain since the end of the sixteenth century, namely, the presidio, an army post in the Indian country; the pueblo, a village of agriculturists transplanted from an older frontier to the new one; and the mission, where neophytes, placed under the tutelage and discipline of the regular clergy, were shepherded along the road toward Christianity and civilization. As has been remarked, the Spanish frontier system was quite elastic. In one locality, such as Louisiana, the mission might be entirely omitted; in another such as Baja California, it might be permitted to dominate all other agencies. Alta California was nearer the norm. Here the three agencies functioned together in a relationship that, despite occasional friction, was symbiotic.

As regards political theory, it appeared that the presidio was dominant. The military commander held the title of governor. He had unquestioned jurisdiction over the pueblo settlers. His was the responsibility of safeguarding the missions, and although the missionaries through repeated protests were able to win and to hold a degree of autonomy, the governor's right to apportion the troops under his command enabled him to determine when and where new missions should be established.

On the other hand, the missions were obviously the most flourishing centers. The presidios were only four in number, and except for Monterey, which was the social as well as the political capital of the province, they were miserable establishments, unprosperous, poorly kept, and unable to support the manner of life that existed at the missions. The three pueblos fared somewhat better, but since their chief basis of growth was through the natural increase of population, the census gains loomed more impressive than the actual economic advance. Mission establishments were far more numerous. They had the best locations, for they had been placed where the Indians had already congregated in recognition of geographic advantages. They had the best labor supply in the neophytes, whose training was agricultural and manual as well as religious. They also had the best management. The Franciscan friars were more interested in economic increase than were the presidial officers and more enlightened and ambitious than the pueblo settlers. The civilians and the military envied the missionaries their prosperity and possible comforts, but they do not seem to have deserved comparable success.

Throughout the Spanish period a systematic but gradual process of occupying California is in evidence. Step by step, the progress seemed excruciatingly slow, but viewed in retrospect, the effectiveness of the process can be discerned. Utilizing a minimum of manpower, Spain gained control of the coastal margin of the province from San Diego Bay past San Francisco Bay and was in position to dominate a much larger inland area.

The steps of actual occupation had been gradual. When Portolá left the province, only the mission of San Diego de Alcalá (founded on July 16, 1769) and that of San Carlos and the presidio at Monterey (both founded on June 3, 1770) had been established. A year later the San Carlos mission was moved from Monterey to the Carmel River, and shortly thereafter three new missions were added: San Antonio de Padua (July 14, 1771), San Gabriel Arcángel (September 8, 1771), and San Luís Obispo de Tolosa (September 1, 1772). With the average distance between these stations approximately 125 miles, it is obviously misleading to speak yet of a chain of missions. In no case did the control stretch that far; moreover, in these early years these missions would have been very weak links in any chain.

With the arrival of additional Franciscans released from duty in Baja California, Serra became increasingly insistent that more missions be established. But mindful of the small force at his command, Governor Fages refused to authorize guards for new missions; and when Rivera succeeded Fages in 1774, his attitude was the same. In that year there was some measure of expansion at San Diego. The presidio took over all the buildings at the old site, and the mission was relocated about six miles inland. Except for this step, the reinforcements that Rivera brought up in 1774 were used merely to strengthen the existent posts. Even with the arrival of the Anza emigrants in 1776, Rivera was not anxious to see new establishments attempted, and his role was a grudging one in the founding of the San Francisco presidio (September 17, 1776) and of the mission San Francisco de Asís (October 9, 1776). Two other missions were set in operation at about this time. San Juan Capistrano, which had been founded on October 30, 1775, only to be abandoned eight days later because of the revolt at San Diego, was reëstablished on November 1, 1776. In the San Francisco Bay region Anza's soldiers and settlers made possible a second mission, Santa Clara de Asís (January 12, 1777).

Growth under Neve

In February, 1777, Felipe de Neve came up from Loreto to take direct charge of Alta California. With his coming, a new policy is in evidence. The change was partly a matter of personalities, for Neve was a much more positive executive than Rivera, but it was also forecast in the instructions issued to the new governor. Bucareli had ordered him to reduce the drain on the royal treasury by distributing lands to colonists. Accordingly, in the fall of 1777 Neve had Lieutenant Moraga select five of Anza's soldiers and nine others from the presidios of Monterey and San Francisco to be the first citizens of the pueblo of San José. These men and their families—sixty-six persons in all—moved down to the valley of the Guadalupe, just south of the Santa Clara mission, where they began construction of their dwellings on building sites around a plaza and dammed the Guadalupe to provide irrigation water for their suertes, or planting lots. On November 29 the pueblo was declared officially founded, but in accordance with the established custom, individual titles to town lots and suertes were not confirmed until after the expiration of a five-year probationary period. Moraga made formal confirmation in May, 1783.

Neve's next contribution was to revise and amplify the fundamental laws of the colony as laid down in the Bucareli Reglamento of 1773. Neve's Reglamento was promulgated on June 1, 1779, and after being duly approved by Commandant-General Croix and the king, it continued as the code of law for California to the end of the Spanish period.

Meanwhile, Neve had been making preparations for a second pueblo, to be located near San Gabriel on the river Nuestra Señora la Reina de los Ángeles de Porciúncula, and for a presidio and three missions, so long wanted, among the superior Indians of the Santa Barbara Channel. Neve looked to Sinaloa and Sonora for the recruits needed for these steps. At his suggestion, Rivera was ordered across from Loreto to do the recruiting. Inasmuch as Rivera had led expeditions to California in 1769 and 1770, had raised a party of fifty-one persons in 1774, and had been Governor of California at the time of the Anza expeditions, his task was not entirely novel.

By the terms of his instructions Rivera was authorized to enlist twenty-four married settlers and their families; thirty-four married soldiers, whose families were to be brought with them to California; and twenty-five unmarried soldiers, to take the place in Sonora of a like number of Anza's veterans, who would thus be released for California service. Rivera could hold out liberal inducements. The settlers would not only be granted lands in California but could count on ten pesos a month for three years, plus a daily allowance for rations. Complete outfits, including everything from saddles and shoes to hair ribbons, would be issued to them in advance. Pack and riding animals would be provided, and at the new pueblo each colonist would be started off with two cows, two oxen, two horses, three mares, one mule, two ewes, and two she-goats, in addition to the requisite tools and implements. Repayment for this advance was to be made out of future production. Rivera was cautioned not to exaggerate the attractions of California, but he was authorized to go all the way to Guadalajara if the quota could not be filled in Sonora and Sinaloa.

Despite the generous subsidy offered, recruiting proved difficult. Rivera began his canvassing in February, 1780. Not till May 30 did he enlist the first poblador, or settler, and by August 1 he had but seven. Soldiers were easier to persuade, forty-five having enlisted on the latter date. By the end of the year the full quota of fifty-nine soldiers had been reached, but only fourteen settlers were enrolled, and they not of the best. With this number Rivera decided to stop.

Throughout these months of recruiting, Rivera had been contracting for horses, mules, and cattle to the number of some 960 head, and for the other necessary supplies. Early in 1781 the start was made from Los Alamos. Escorted by seventeen soldiers, the pobladores—now only twelve, because two had deserted—set out for Guaymas, thence to be ferried across to Loreto. In the peninsula, smallpox eliminated another poblador, so that only eleven families, totaling forty-four persons, actually arrived.

With the other forty-two soldiers, some thirty of whom were accompanied by their families, Rivera set out for the Yuma crossing. The details are lacking, because no diary of this march has been preserved. But apparently Rivera reached the Colorado without untoward experience, found there Croix's two settlements in none too favorable condition, and was met by Sergeant Juan José Robles and five or six soldiers of the Monterey company. Rivera sent on his married contingent and a few other men under the command of Alferez Cayetano Limón, and this party was at San Gabriel on July 14. Rivera, meanwhile, was recruiting his animals at Yuma, where, on July 18, he fell a victim in the Yuma massacre, a disaster for which he had a measure of personal responsibility.

This inglorious end beclouds the reputation to which Rivera's earlier attainments in California would otherwise entitle him. The colony had lost a man who had done much for it. The significance of the closing of the Anza route has been discussed elsewhere. Of the animals destined for California, the documents are not clear as to how many were lost, but one gathers that less than half had been sent ahead with Limón.

Since May, Governor Neve had been at San Gabriel awaiting the newcomers. Because of the condition of Limón's pack animals, he decided that those destined for the Santa Barbara Channel could not proceed until after the rainy season. The Los Angeles settlers reached San Gabriel on August 18, where, because of smallpox, they were detained for a time in quarantine. Early in September (the 4th is the most probable date), with the pueblo guard of four soldiers, they went to the site selected and began the foundation of the pueblo of Los Angeles. Although modern writers have panoplied the founding with the pomp and ceremony befitting the start of the largest city in western America, the basis for their assertions is neither documentary nor rational. The beginnings were apparently as informal as at San José, and the first ceremony was held five years later, on September 4, 1786, when Sergeant José Darío Argüello came over from the neighboring presidio of Santa Barbara to confirm titles to solares (house lots) and suertes (planting lots) and to record each poblador's branding iron.

Judging from the comments made about them, these pueblos were not an immediate or an unmixed blessing to the colony. The Los Angeles pobladores had been recruited from the most poverty-stricken classes in Sinaloa. Only two could claim to be Spaniards, the rest being of Indian, Negro, and mixed blood. None was literate. Presidial society looked down upon these rustic villagers, and the missionaries regarded them askance, as being likely to corrupt the neophytes.

Two decades later one of the missionaries could complain that the townsfolk were a set of idlers, addicted to cards, song, and seduction of the Indian women, and that all labor at the pueblos was performed by Indians. By 1800, however, Los Angeles was second only to the mission San Gabriel in agricultural production.

Neve is also to be credited with the actual occupation of the Santa Barbara Channel region. The importance of controlling the numerous and superior Chumash of this district had long been recognized. Gálvez had planned a mission here as one of the first, but various obstacles had arisen, the most serious being the lack of soldiers and funds. Early in Neve's administration the project was brought up again, and a tentative agreement was drawn up between the viceroy and the College of San Fernando, calling for a presidio and three missions of the conventional type, each to be staffed by two Fernandinos. The necessary soldiers were recruited by Rivera and brought to San Gabriel by Limón.

In the spring of 1782 Neve sent this force on to the Channel. Serra and Lieutenant Ortega founded Mission San Buenaventura on March 31, and three weeks later the Santa Barbara presidio was established. Then it was learned that the viceroy and the college had disagreed about whether the missionaries should have the customary control of the temporalities or should operate on Croix's Colorado pattern. News of this deadlock did not reach California in time to prevent the establishment of San Buenaventura and the presidio, but the other two missions were not added until four and five years later, respectively, Santa Barbara on December 4, 1786, and La Purísima Concepción on December 8, 1787.

In California, likewise, contentions between the representatives of church and state had been a persistent factor in provincial affairs. Several of the early altercations have been alluded to; in most of them Serra managed to have his way. But in Neve's administration (from 1777 to 1782) secular authority was more effectively championed. Founding pueblos was, of course, a step in the direction of increasing the importance of secular authority. Under consideration also was a plan to substitute the custodia for the mission system. This plan, in essence, would have relieved the Franciscans of all temporal control over the Indians and would have made them mere religious workers. The Bishop of Sonora espoused the plan and, in accordance with the royal cédula of May 20, 1782, put it into actual operation in Sonora. The Franciscans, although they first assented to extension of the custodia to California, soon took a firm stand against it and were able to stave it off until 1792, when the king decreed in favor of the mission system. Neve, of course, took no steps toward instituting the custodia, but to know that the court favored suppression of the temporal power of the missionaries must have encouraged him in his efforts to add to his authority.

One such step concerned Serra's right to confirm. In 1777 Fray Junípero's college had delegated this power to him and he had proceeded to exercise it. Two years later, Neve notified him that he must cease confirming and surrender his patent to Croix for inspection. Though "pretending obedience"—the phrase is Neve's—Serra went right on confirming. Only after prolonged correspondence with his college and the viceroy did he submit his patent to Croix, who, finding it in regular form, authorized the father-president to continue.

Mention should also be made of several miscellaneous regulations whereby Neve sought to make the missionaries subordinate. He insisted that the friars should have the neophytes elect alcaldes and regidores at each mission, pueblo, or village. He reduced the friars' privilege of franking letters, insisted that they must apply for a government permit before retiring from California, curbed their practice of using Indians as messengers and vaqueros, and, most serious, forbade the use of military escorts by the friars except when they were called from their stations to hear confessions. Neve also urged single-friar missions and establishments such as Croix had set up on the Colorado. The friars resisted strenuously, and in Fages' second administration (from 1782 to 1791) many of these restrictions were moderated. The trend, however, was toward concentration of temporal authority in the hands of the governor.

Serra and Lasuén

At this stage in the annals many entries record the departure of men who had been conspicuous figures in the early development of the colony. Several, of course, were already gone. Portolá had left in 1770. Gálvez' direct connection with California was terminated early. Juan Pérez, dean of the ship captains, died in 1775. Anza left the California scene in 1777. Bucareli died two years later. Garcés and Rivera fell in the Yuma massacre. Juan Crespi, diarist of so many of the early expeditions, died at San Carlos on January 1,

1782. Later in that year Governor Neve was promoted to a more important post in the Provincias Internas, where he died on November 3, 1784. A few months earlier, on August 28, death had overtaken the first father-president of the California missions, Fray Junípero Serra. His closest companion, Fray Francisco Palóu, had already applied for retirement because of his infirmities. Temporarily, Palóu assumed charge of the mission work, but in 1785 he left for the College of San Fernando, where two years later he issued the first great California biography, *Relación histórica de la vida . . . del venerable Padre Fray Junípero Serra.*

To the illustrious group, of which these men are the best known, goes the major credit for pulling California through its initial crises. As the first heroes their fame is secure. Serra, in particular, seems assured of perpetual recognition as preëminent, for, in addition to the dramatic appeal of his brave and unselfish career, he found a most excellent biographer. Palóu's *Life of Serra* is from the pen of a confessedly enthusiastic admirer. Its imputations of miracles and its appropriation for Serra of credit that was partly due Portolá and others may be reckoned as defects, but out of Palóu's love, zeal, and artistry there emerged a portrayal of the first father-president which has beatified Fray Junípero in the hearts of Californians, if not in the official list of the church.

Like Palóu a native of Mallorca, Serra was born on November 24, 1713. At sixteen he entered the Franciscan order, in which, after a period of schooling, he gained a reputation as an effective preacher. Not until 1749, when he was in his thirty-sixth year, was he sent to America. Throughout the fifties he and Palóu labored in the Sierra Gorda missions of what is now Tamaulipas. In 1758 Serra was ordered to San Sabá in Texas, but before he could go, the Indians revolted, broke up this mission, and martyred their Franciscan mentor. Just a slight change in schedule and Serra would have shared this fate.

From 1759 to 1767 Serra was attached to the College of San Fernando, at Mexico City, where he had frequent opportunity for preaching engagements in the capital and its vicinity. Then followed a year as father-president of the missions of Baja California, after which the last fifteen years of his life were devoted to Alta California.

For all that has been written about him Serra is often misunderstood. Many have so magnified his role as to picture him in full charge of Alta California, as Salvatierra had been in the peninsula. In fact, Serra's authority was only over the missionaries. In personal matters he was as humble, as meek, and as self-effacing as the founder of his order, the gentle St. Francis of Assisi. Witness his depreciation of his ability as a preacher. Yet when mission welfare was at stake, he exhibited so firm and intransigent a spirit that those who encountered his opposition did him honor as a doughty and stubborn adversary. When controversies arose, viceroy and court usually ended by upholding Serra rather than the governor, yet many historians assert that Serra was a more tempestuous and pugnacious champion of the missions than was necessary.

Even among his fellow Franciscans, Serra's devoutness was outstanding. He was never content with his success as an evangelist. He was most constant in his devotions; for example, when in Mexico in 1773, in spite of grave illness he insisted upon spending hours on his knees in the cold chapels.

In the twentieth century his extreme asceticism may seem less understandable. Like many of his contemporaries, however, Serra believed that mortification of the flesh was essential for the purification of the spirit. Eschewing many of the comforts of life was a phase of this asceticism, the use of a hair shirt another, and self-torture with a lighted candle during the course of sermonizing still another. While journeying from Veracruz to Mexico City at the outset of his missionary career, he deliberately exposed himself to insects and mosquitoes, with the result that he was lame forever after. On the journey up the peninsula with Portolá, Serra's sore leg plagued him, at length so seriously as to threaten holding up the expedition. Serra had steadfastly refused to submit to any treatments, but finally he relented to the extent of allowing one of the muleteers to apply a mixture of herbs and tallow designed for use on the animals. His insistence upon going about his regular tasks, notwithstanding illness and despite the solicitude of his brother missionaries, expressed the same attitude. His poor health and his advanced age—it was during his late fifties and sixties that he labored in California—make his achievements all the more creditable.

Serra's most distinguished successor, Fray Fermín Francisco de Lasuén, is by comparison most obscure. Yet in solid achievement his presidency compares favorably. During his eighteen years of control, from 1785 to 1803, the number of missions doubled and the number of Christian Indians more than doubled. Father Lasuén's missions included some of California's most famous, such as Purísima Concepción, Santa Cruz, San José, and Santa Barbara. And what was more significant than the numerical growth, Lasuén brought about an economic transformation. In Serra's time a rather slender beginning had been made in stock raising and farming. Under Lasuén these activities were furthered, and the introduction of a number of mission "industries" made the missions diversified establishments rather than mere agricultural centers. Lasuén brought in a score of artisans from Mexico and set them to work at their trades; he also instructed the Indians to be carpenters, masons, smiths, and the like. The new style in mission architecture exemplifies the change; whereas hitherto the buildings had been unpretentious thatch-covered structures, now tile and stone came into general use along with timber and adobe. New missions were constructed, and Serra's nine were rebuilt in what is now known as "the mission style."

Like his predecessor, Lasuén had difficulties with the secular authorities. When it was proposed that new missions be established with but a single missionary, Lasuén, who had had five years of such experience at Borja in Baja California, was adamant that no such unsatisfactory stations should be opened. Nor would he agree to the governor's proposal that the missionaries relinquish all temporal control over the neophytes, allow them to live in their own villages, and have them come to the missions merely for religious instruction. Lasuén was as firm in his stand as Serra had been, but he never gave way to wrath, and he conducted his disputes amiably.

Although an older man, Lasuén was more robust and enjoyed the vigorous longevity for which Californians are noted. He traveled widely and frequently from his headquarters at San Carlos. The most notable instance was in 1797, in his seventy-seventh year, when he presided over the inauguration of four new missions and visited all the others in the province. Governor Borica complimented him for his achievement as well-nigh miraculous.

Later Governors

Of the later governors, Pedro Fages was the most colorful. The central feature of his second administration was the continuation of the contest with the Fernandinos. In 1785 he entered a formal protest with the viceroy who, through the Audiencia of Mexico City, laid it before the College of San Fernando. The Guardian of the College, none other than Francisco Paloú, responded with an elaborate defense of the actions of the friars and preferred countercharges against Fages. The case was then laid before the Commandant-General of the Provincias Internas, Jacobo Ugarte y Loyola. The latter asked for and got from Lasuén a detailed opinion on the issues involved, but because the Provincias Internas had again been placed under the direct supervision of the viceroy, Ugarte contented himself with ordering the agents of state and church in California each to observe the proper limits of his jurisdiction and to work in harmony. In view of the earlier acrid disputes this may call to mind Canute's command to the waves. The tempest between the two authorities, however, soon calmed, not to break out again until after the end of the Spanish period.

Fages' second administration was enlivened by the presence of his spirited wife, Doña Eulalia de Callis. Only by enlisting the aid of Neve and José Antonio Roméu did Fages persuade Doña Eulalia to join him in California, but finally she came to Loreto, where her husband met her and escorted her to Monterey. The journey has been likened to a royal progress because of the enthusiastic receptions en route by friars, soldiers, settlers, and Indians for the first lady of California. Doña Eulalia reciprocated with generous philanthropy, making presents from her own and her husband's wardrobe, especially to the naked Indians, until Don Pedro made it clear that there would be no opportunity to purchase such things in Alta California.

After a short residence at Monterey, Doña Eulalia had had enough of California. She tried to persuade her husband to send her and their two children back to Mexico. When he refused she exerted pressure, first by excluding him from her rooms, and then by denouncing him for infidelity and broadcasting threats that she would sue for divorce. After a sojourn at Mission San Carlos, during which the friars had come almost to the point of flogging her because of her scandalous tantrums, Doña Eulalia began divorce proceedings, which were heard before the acting commandant-general at Chihuahua and then transferred to the Bishop of Sonora. Before a decision could be handed down, Don Pedro and Doña Eulalia effected a reconciliation. A month later, in October, 1785, Don Pedro had the embarrassing task of trying to intercept a letter in which his wife had petitioned the audiencia to remove her husband from office because of

José María Narváez Map of Alta California in 1830

ill-health.   In 1790 Doña Eulalia won her point by less direct action.
She persuaded her husband to ask to be retired, and when a favorable
answer was received late in the year, she and the children sailed at
once for San Blas.

In 1786 California was visited by the first non-Spanish ship since
Drake's *Golden Hind* more than two centuries earlier.   The next
several decades were to witness an increasing international interest in
the North Pacific, one consequence of which was to be a whole series
of English, American, Russian, and French contacts with California.
Of these nations the French gained the least advantage in the North
Pacific, but it was a Frenchman, Comte de la Pérouse, who first visited
Spanish California.   In the course of a round-the-world reconnaissance for his government he stopped for ten days (from September
14 to September 24, 1786) at Monterey, where he was entertained
by Fages, Lasuén, and the provincials as lavishly as circumstances
permitted.   Pérouse's observations on California, as printed in his
posthumous *Voyage autour du monde* (four volumes, Paris, 1797),
were perspicacious and, for the most part, sympathetic.   The Spaniards, he thought, would not develop the province rapidly; and indeed,
except for furs, he did not detect any promising source of wealth.
The persons whom Pérouse met, Lasuén in particular, fare well in
his book, but not the mission system.   His verdict was that the missions were making but slight progress toward converting the savages
into civilized, industrious, and profit-minded persons.

Five years later a Spanish round-the-world expedition, commanded
by Alejandro Malaspina, put in at Monterey for a twelve-day stay
(from September 13 to September 25, 1791).   Fages and Lasuén
again did the honors, but since Malaspina was not a foreigner and
not the first world navigator to visit Monterey, his visit was not as
exciting an event as that of Pérouse.   Nor did Malaspina publish
so graphic a description of the province.

A crisis was now impending on the North Pacific coast.   Consequent to Cook's famous voyage of 1778–1779 and to his still more
famous book, in which he elaborated upon the profit possibilities of
trade in Nootka furs, many adventurers sailed to this region.   Spain,
alert to protect her northwestern claims, sent a naval officer in 1789
to check on the activities of English, Russians, and Americans in this
northern extension of California.   This officer acted with what may
have been an excess of zeal.   While not interfering with American

ships, he did take possession of an English trading post or fort at Nootka (Vancouver Island), seized two English vessels, and held one ship's captain prisoner.   These acts had repercussions in Europe. England demanded satisfaction for these insults to her flag and compensation for the damages to her traders.   Spain perforce acceded, and in 1790 the first Nootka Treaty took shape.

To see that the treaty was carried into effect, England sent George Vancouver to the Pacific.   At Nootka he and the Spanish commander could not agree upon an interpretation of the treaty, which they referred back to Europe for clarification.   Vancouver proceeded to engage in extensive exploration and mapmaking, adequately represented in the three-volume narrative, *A Voyage of Discovery,* which he published in London in 1798.   In the course of his work Vancouver made three visits to California.   He was the first foreign visitor to San Francisco Bay, in November, 1792.   Then followed a fifty-day sojourn at Monterey.   After a trip to Hawaii, he returned to San Francisco on October 19, 1793.   Governor Arrillaga, in the meantime, had ordered that the regulations with regard to foreign visitors should be strictly enforced, and Vancouver got what he considered a very cool reception at San Francisco and Monterey.   At Santa Barbara and San Diego the regulations were more hospitably disregarded.   Vancouver's final visit to Monterey, in November, 1794, was just at the time of the arrival of the new governor, Diego Borica.   He was welcomed into the festivities.   Vancouver had even greater opportunity than Pérouse to observe California.   His comments are prolix.   Except toward Arrillaga he was generous in praise of the personalities he had encountered, but he agreed with Pérouse's judgment that the province did not hold promise of rapid development under Spain.

Apart from the Vancouver visits the governorship of José Antonio Roméu (April 16, 1791, to April 9, 1792) and of José Joaquín de Arrillaga (April 9, 1792, to November, 1794) were relatively uneventful.   Two missions, Santa Cruz (founded on September 25, 1791) and Nuestra Señora de la Soledad (founded on October 9, 1791), were established during Roméu's administration.   Under Arrillaga an abortive attempt was made to fortify and occupy Bodega Bay, but failing because of difficulty of access, the Spaniards contented themselves with erecting a battery at Fort Point, San Francisco.

In November, 1794, the government of Ca▓
by an urbane, convivial, and witty Basque, Diego ▓
becoming enamored of California, Borica liberally▓
ters with tributes to its pleasant and healthful climate,▓
vender that was available at Monterey, the good spirit▓
the province seemed to engender, and the "astounding fec▓
Spaniards and natives. California, he asserted, "is the most p▓
and quiet country in the world; one lives better here than in the ▓
cultured court of Europe."

His governorship was marked by an immediate attention to the
defenses of the province, a natural step in view of the recent Nootka
controversies and the flurry of voyages to the North Pacific and California coast. By this time Spain had foresworn claim to exclusive
control of the northern coast; in her subsequent policy California was
considered the northernmost entrenchment on the west coast. The
state of war between Spain and France called attention to California's
defenseless condition, and Borica was called upon to make improvements. He had the presidios repaired, mounted additional guns at
San Diego and San Francisco, and in 1797 rejoiced over the arrival
of ninety-odd soldiers to reinforce the slender garrisons. Rumors
of an imminent English attack followed the French scare, and Borica
issued elaborate instructions as to how the Californians should flee
inland. In 1800 rumor of a forthcoming Russian attack occasioned
the usual precautionary orders, but the provincials refused to be
alarmed. "An invasion from Kamchatka," Bancroft observes, "seems
to have had no terrors for the Californians after their success in
escaping from the fleets of Great Britain."

California was strengthened in 1798 and again in 1800 by the
arrival of twenty-two convict colonists and nineteen foundlings.
Though not entirely responsible for this immigration, Borica was
responsible for the surveillance and supervision of immigrants. These
convicts and others who followed them, it should be pointed out,
were of various grades of criminality, more improvident than vicious.
Their contribution to California trades and artisanry was considerable. Borica figured personally in the development of irrigation, in
the encouragement of hemp and flax culture, in a rather futile effort
to stimulate sheep raising, and in the launching of the "mission
industries." Thanks to his active interest, schools were opened for
the children of the soldiers and settlers. Borica not only arranged

CALIFORNIA

e public granary at San José,
d that reports and copybooks

.h hold on the province was
five additional missions in the
.ie, 1797. Lasuén is credited as the
a strong helping hand. These missions
/7), San Juan Bautista (June 24, 1797),
July 25, 1797), San Fernando Rey de España
,, and San Luís Rey de Francia (June 13, 1798)
.i as to close the gaps along the Camino Real. They
.of the most famous of the entire California chain.
.t even nearer Borica's heart was the establishment of the
Branciforte. In 1794 Miguel Costansó, quondam engineer
for Portolá, had supplied Viceroy Branciforte with an opinion that
the fortification of Alta California would be most effectively achieved
by enlarging the Spanish settlements at San Diego, Monterey, and
San Francisco. To attract more settlers, commerce would have to
be fomented. Borica adopted the idea enthusiastically. Mindful
of the glaring defects of the San José and Los Angeles pueblos, he
chose instead the device of the villa, a town in which military discipline would be much more emphasized. In 1797 Branciforte was
launched with nine soldier-colonists and a total population of seventeen. By 1800 the number had been brought up to sixty-six, but the
villa was not a success. Even the name did not survive, being
eclipsed by that of the near-by mission, Santa Cruz.

The Coming of the Russians

Throughout Borica's administration and on to the end of the
Spanish regime an increasing number of foreign ships came to California. The majority of these visits can be discussed later, but that
of Nikolai Rezanof must be mentioned here. Rezanof came to Sitka
in 1805 as plenipotentiary for the Russian American Fur Company,
empowered like José de Gálvez to make investigations and to institute reforms. He found Sitka threatened with starvation because one
of the supply ships from Siberia had not arrived. Scurvy had broken
out, causing several deaths, and there was no prospect of securing
supplies. Rezanof gave temporary respite by purchasing the American ship *Juno* with its cargo, but to develop a permanent source

of supplies for Russian Alaska he decided to make a voyage to Spanish California. The Hawaiian Islands might have been a more logical place had supplies been the only objective, but Rezanof was also interested in investigating the fur-trade possibilities along the California coast.

He sailed from Sitka on March 8, 1806, and reached San Francisco on April 5. At first the Russians and Spaniards had great difficulty in communicating with one another; the first conversations were between the engineer Langsdorff and Father Uría, in Latin. Later a priest who could speak French came up from Santa Clara.

Rezanof soon discovered that Spanish law forbade any traffic with foreigners and that the California officials were not inclined to countenance trade with him. A battle of wits ensued, in which he endeavored to conceal the dire straits at Sitka, apparently on the assumption that the Californians would be more apt to permit a non-essential commerce than one which would be the salvation of Russian America and the guaranty of its permanence. Both Argüello, the commander at San Francisco, and Governor Arrillaga came to realize, however, that the Russians were in a critical situation, which only served to strengthen their conviction that they ought not to permit trade.

The Russian officer did not prevail on them until he enlisted the aid of Concepción Argüello, the fair daughter of the San Francisco commander. Their romance is one of the most famous and most touching in all of California's history. She was the acknowledged belle of the province, he as dashing and polished a gentleman as had ever visited California. Rezanof laid siege to Concepción's heart. "I imperceptibly," he says, "created in her an impatience to hear something serious from me on the subject." She quickly accepted his proposal; her father and the padres were more obdurate because Rezanof was of the Greek Orthodox faith, but finally they gave in.

The genuineness of Rezanof's love has been questioned because of his obvious ulterior motives. His fiancée's influence upon her father and through him upon the governor really won permission for the desired trade. From the missions Rezanof secured a full cargo of foodstuffs and on May 21 he sailed to relieve Sitka. The trade permit, however, was merely for this one occasion.

From Sitka, Rezanof returned to Kamchatka and started across Siberia to report to the czar and presumably to seek his permission

to marry his California love.   But at Yakutsk he was stricken with
what proved to be a fatal illness, and consequently did not have the
opportunity to prove that his intentions were ancient and honorable.
Of Doña Concepción's sincerity there is not the slightest doubt.   Year
upon year she remained true to her lover, at first confidently anticipating his return, then assuaging her disappointment through a life of
charity in the robes of a nun.   Not until thirty-five years later, when
Sir George Simpson visited California, did she learn of her lover's
fate.   Her faithfulness has been extolled in poem, novel, and story.
To the Californians of her day the tragic sadness of her blighted
romance was somewhat eclipsed by her kindliness and her charities,
and it may be that she herself found consolation in the cherished
memory of that spring when she was sixteen.

Penetrations Inland

Inland exploration was another high light of the final two decades
of the Spanish regime.   Pursuit of runaway Indians had led a few
Spaniards across the coast range and into the San Joaquin Valley, but
the principal penetrations were between 1804 and 1823.   Apprehension of back-sliding neophytes, recovery of run-off cattle and horses,
for which the eastern gentiles developed a great yen, punishment of
Indian marauders, and investigation of possible mission sites in the
interior were the prime motives.   After 1812 certain expeditions
north of San Francisco Bay were in response to the Russian intrusion.

Father Juan Martín of San Miguel made an unlicensed visit to the
Tulare region, where he longed to establish a mission.   Sergeant Luís
Peralta, Lieutenant Francisco Ruiz, Sergeant Juan Ortega, Father
Luís Martínez, and Lieutenant Luís Argüello led other parties.
Gabriel Moraga, however, was unquestionably the foremost Indian
fighter and explorer.   His achievements are only partially recorded,
but participation in forty-six expeditions is attested by his service sheet
of 1820.   He named, among others, the San Joaquin, the Mariposa,
the Merced, and the Sacramento rivers.   He ranged north to the
Feather River Valley and east toward the Sierra Nevada by way
of several of the tributaries of the San Joaquin.   He traversed the
Tulare district, Antelope Valley, and the Mojave Desert, going possibly as far as modern Nevada.

Moraga's explorations would have been epochal, had anything
come of them, but the results were largely negative.   The inland re-

gion was reported barren and alkaline; a favorable picture of the Merced Valley was contradicted by a second report.   When the possibility of mission expansion disappeared, there remained only the punitive features of these forays.   They doubtless added something to the security of the Spanish tenure of the coastal strip, but exact calculation of this salutary influence is manifestly impracticable.   Settlements remained coastal until John A. Sutter and other aliens began to occupy the great valleys in the 1840's, and consequently the revelation of California's gold was delayed until the American period.

11

A MEXICAN PROVINCE

IN THE SPANISH AMERICAN Wars of Independence, which raged from about 1808 into the 1820's, California played the role of innocent bystander. Such an attitude might have been predicted. The newest English colonies in North America—Canada and East and West Florida—had not joined in the American Revolution. California was not only the youngest of Spain's colonies; she was in addition so effectively isolated from Mexico as to have little opportunity of knowing what was brewing there. Hidalgo's Grito de Dolores, which reverberated through most of Mexico, did not find an echo in California. Isolation is a partial explanation. Also, missionaries, officials, and soldiers had an obvious practical reason for supporting the established government. The pueblo settlers had likewise profited from Spain's paternalism. Furthermore, the potential Indian menace that California always faced was a soberizing influence against any disturbance of the existing social order. Californians, though inactive, were loyalists throughout the struggle.

During the Wars of Independence

Nevertheless, the province was made aware that a war was being waged. The supply ships from San Blas practically abandoned sailings after 1810. In Bucareli's day such a stoppage would have meant starvation for California; now it merely meant inconvenience. Missions and pueblos had large enough herds and crops to supply the entire population adequately. Only the presidial soldiers were threatened with dire want, and to meet their needs the missions were induced to enter upon the highly unprofitable business of cashing the presidial requisitions.   Even so, the lot of the soldier and his family was miserable in contrast to the comparative plenty at the missions. Thus were sown the seeds of later bitterness against the missions.

Except to the soldiers the deprivation was chiefly in luxury goods, and several expedients minimized even this distress.   Two Peruvian vessels, the *Flora* and the *Tagle,* arrived in 1813 with cloth and other goods, which were bartered for tallow and hides.   The captain of the *Flora* was still more the hero because he seized an American smuggler, the *Mercury,* whose cargo was confiscated for the royal treasury. Included was $16,000 in coin, which was retained in the provincial coffers, while a draft on the royal treasury was forwarded to Mexico. Another trade possibility was with the new Russian establishment, Fort Ross, which Kuskoff had established north of San Francisco in 1812.   Governor Arrillaga was meticulous not to give official approval to trade with the Russians, but Luís Argüello admitted $14,000 worth of Russian goods at San Francisco in 1813, and laden vessels continued to come thereafter.

The main relief, however, was provided by American ships.   Boston fur ships, as we shall see in greater detail, were the most frequent visitors to the province and became the principal substitute for the supply ships from San Blas.   They offered no facilities for the transmission of reports and orders to and from New Spain, and consequently a degree of autonomy was thrust upon Californians.   Officials had to make decisions that once would have been referred to Mexico City.

Trade with Fort Ross was interrupted in 1815 when Pablo Vicente de Solá became governor.   Solá's first act was to rebuke Argüello for permitting trade with the Russians.   He had Eliot de Castro and Boris Tarakánof arrested and sent them off to Mexico on the very ship that had brought him north.   It did not take him long, however, to see that California must have some sort of foreign trade, and in the following month he authorized barter for $7,000 worth of goods from an English vessel.   In subsequent years trade was resumed with the Russians, though Solá scrupulously withheld official countenance, and English and American ship captains continued to ply their trade. The provincial records contain many sharp protests from the missionaries against Solá's requisitions for tallow for trading purposes.

In 1818 the war was brought home to the Californians by a seaborne attack. Hippolyte de Bouchard, a Frenchman, commanded a Buenos Aires privateer, the *Argentina,* which apparently was one of the many Baltimore contributions to the cause of Hispanic American independence. At the Hawaiian Islands he recovered another privateer, the *Santa Rosa,* whose operations had been interrupted by mutinies. On his return toward South America, after accomplishing this principal task of his voyage, Bouchard visited Monterey. An American ship had brought a few weeks' warning, and Solá took energetic though none too effective measures to stiffen the defenses. On November 20 the two privateers appeared in Monterey Bay.

The account of the next day's battle is quite confused. It is clear, however, that Corporal José Vallejo, in charge of an improvised shore battery, greatly embarrassed the *Santa Rosa* and prevented a direct landing at Monterey. Bouchard landed a force at Point Pinos, before which Solá prudently retreated as far as present-day Salinas, carrying with him the provincial archives. About a week later, the arrival of reinforcements from San Francisco enabled Solá to advance upon Monterey, which he found evacuated but in flames.

Bouchard's men, who apparently were under the loosest sort of discipline, had spent a busy week provisioning their ships and plundering the town. They ranged the streets, breaking into dwellings as well as storehouses in search of money or other personal effects that could be carried off. In their looting they did malicious damage, wantonly destroying much that they found, laying waste gardens and orchards, and firing the town.

Their next stop was at Refugio, where they burned Ortega's ranch buildings. But the Californians, under Sergeant Carlos Antonio Carrillo, lassoed three of Bouchard's men and carried them off to Santa Barbara. Possession of the prisoners saved that town, because Bouchard agreed not to harm it if the men were given up. Anticipating a descent upon the mission, the San Buenaventurans retreated inland, while the Angeleños for once rejoiced that their pueblo was twenty miles from the coast. San Juan Capistrano bore the brunt for southern California, partly because the commander defied the pirate-patriots. Bouchard's men came ashore, pillaged and burned and got drunk, and the next morning sailed away. San Diego polished its defenses and packed its women and children off to Pala, but Bouchard passed on by, and the War of Independence had been fought as far as California was concerned.

When news of Bouchard's attack reached Mexico, the viceroy was much alarmed. He immediately ordered that two transports be sent to California with reinforcements, and even after receiving Solá's report of the departure of the insurgents, he allowed the order to stand. In the late summer of 1819 these men arrived: 100 good cavalrymen from Mazatlán under Captain Pablo de Portilla, and an equal number of infantrymen from San Blas under Captain José Antonio de Navarrete. These latter were vicious, quarrelsome vagabonds, without discipline and without religion, drunkards, gamblers, thieves, léperos—in short, to sum it all up in a vigorous California phrase, cholos. Solá complained very bitterly that they only augmented his troubles. Yet each of the presidios had a larger garrison by approximately fifty men.

Introducing the Mexican Period

Early in 1822 California was notified of the success of the Mexican revolutionists under Agustín Iturbide. Governor Solá convoked a junta to advise him in this unexpected emergency. Its counsel, inevitably, was that California accept the accomplished fact, declare itself a part of the Mexican empire, and pledge obedience to the regency. Solá, the members of the junta, and the troops at Monterey swore allegiance on April 11, 1822. Throughout the province an oath of allegiance to the new government was required. It seems to have been given with no more hesitation, even on the part of the missionaries, than had been the case two years earlier when the Californians had been called upon to acknowledge Spain's liberal Constitution of 1812. The junta defined the procedure for electing California's deputy to the Mexican Cortes. Electors were chosen in the four presidial districts and at Los Angeles, with the mission Indians apparently having some voice in the matter. The five electors sat at Monterey with Solá and three army officers and chose Solá as delegate and Luís Argüello as alternate.

Before Solá could set out for Mexico City, an American ship arrived from San Blas with a pattern of the new Mexican flag and with news of Iturbide's accession as emperor and of an impending mission to California by an agent of the new government, Don Agustín Fernández de San Vicente, canon of the cathedral at Durango. Solá waited to welcome this distinguished commissioner. Upon Fernández' arrival at Monterey in September, 1822, the banner of Spain was lowered and the Mexican imperial flag unfurled. The Indians, it is said, exulted over the change from lion to eagle. No record indicates requirement of new oaths of allegiance to Iturbide as Agustín I.

Commissioner Fernández got down to business quickly, calling on the missionaries for full reports and summoning the governor and his staff to a conference. At this meeting, Fernández insisted that the governor's commissioners be recalled from the pueblos and the ayuntamientos placed in full control, and that a diputación, or provincial legislature, be organized. Later in the fall, when he saw that Solá was about to surrender the governorship to a Spaniard, José de Guerra, Fernández insisted that the choice must be by the diputación and the army officers. Exerting his utmost influence, he was able to gain a bare majority for Luís Argüello, who as an American-born Spaniard was thought more acceptable to the central government. Argüello took office as jefe político on the departure of Solá and Fernández at the close of the year.

The most controversial issue during Argüello's first year in office had to do with the proposed removal of mission San Francisco to a more salubrious and promising location in the Sonoma Valley. The success of San Rafael, founded in 1817, gave encouragement to the idea of a transfer. Commissioner Fernández having approved, Argüello encouraged Fray José Altimira to petition the diputación to order the move. The diputación voted in favor of it. Altimira reconnoitered the north bay shore, selected a site, and began construction of New San Francisco. His Franciscan superior now objected. Altimira responded with considerable heat and Governor Argüello took a hand, but eventually a compromise was effected whereby Altimira was allowed to found a new mission, San Francisco Solano, the final link in the chain, but without abandonment of the old mission San Francisco de Asís. The scant attention paid to the wishes of the father-president illustrates how far California had moved since the founding of the first missions.

Mention should also be made of a revolt of the mission Indians at Santa Inés, Santa Barbara, and Purísima Concepción in the spring of 1824. The Santa Inés disturbance was quickly suppressed, although the mission buildings were damaged by fire. At Santa Barbara a force from the presidio came to quell the uprising. The Indians fought back for several hours, wounding a number of the Span-

iards, and then decamped to the hills.   Purísima was in
for almost a month.   It was invested by an army of 1(
the Monterey presidio; sixteen of the Indians were killed ᵢ
were forced to surrender.   There followed a number of exp
pursuit of the fugitives from Santa Barbara, and most of tₗ
rounded up and brought back.

In November, 1823, California heard of Iturbide's abdication and
banishment, which had taken place half a year earlier.   Argüello
immediately gave notice of California's adherence to the new national
government and her abhorrence of all that pertained to the old imperial regime.   The overthrow of Iturbide had repercussions at an
Indian village near San Diego, where the natives followed the Mexican example, as they understood it, by killing their old chief and
installing a new one, whom they warned to expect the same fate if
he did not please them.   By the California gente de razón, the change
to republic seems to have been accepted with placid indifference, and
there is no record of an oath of allegiance to the new government.
In the January following, a local plan of government, sometimes called
California's first constitution, was drafted and put into operation, only
to be discarded a year later when governmental instructions were received from Mexico.   The final break with the old order came in the
spring of 1825, when the Mexican constitution of 1824, with its provisions for a federal republic, was received and ratified at the presidios
and pueblos.   The conservatives, in particular the friars, were none
too pleased at the change; but since it had come by gradual transition
through the regency, Iturbide's empire, the Congress, and finally the
federal republic, the opportunity to resist was much diminished.

Enough detail has been offered to illustrate the uncertainties with
which California's Mexican period began.   To the very end, Mexico's
grip on the province was insecure and her voice in its affairs slight.
Separation became something of an ambition and even more of a
fact.   American trade and immigration, foreshadowing acquisition
by the United States, may appear as the most momentous development of the quarter century, yet other changes of genuine significance
were also taking place.

Government by Revolution

In the introduction of the Mexican period an uncertain fumbling
with political problems is discerned.   Turbulent politics continued as

a characteristic throughout the Mexican period. In all parts of Spanish America the first years of national independence were troublous times for which the colonial experience had been inadequate preparation. Spain had allowed such slight leeway for self-government on the part of her colonial subjects that they were left rank novices in the political arts. But what the Spanish Americans lacked in experience they made up in the enthusiasm with which they seized upon the opportunity to enjoy public office. Aspiration to office agitated every ambitious spirit, and although there was much loose talk about such abstractions as democracy, class equality, and constitutionality, the dominating factors were particularism, personalism, and militarism.

California was no exception, save that, thanks to her situation outside the theater of combat during the struggle for independence, militarism had a more rudimentary development. But revolutionary unrest of two sorts was present. One concerned the rivalries of individuals for political preference and of southern California for part of the privileges hitherto monopolized by the north. The other had to do with the emerging conviction that the empty gain of independence from Spain should be followed by some measure, at least, of independence from Mexico.

The Californians of this epoch have been held up to no end of ridicule because their revolutions consisted of much more parading, military maneuvering, and bombastic proclaiming and fulminating than of actual fighting and bloodshed. Certainly there is room to question whether more carnage and fiercer fratricidal intent would have made this turmoil more commendable. It was, after all, a political method rather than an endeavor to exterminate, and the comic-opera atmosphere had elements of appropriateness. The technique was admittedly more dangerous than the electoral method. Occasionally a fire-eater overstepped the customary limits, as in the Battle of Cahuenga in 1831, when José María Ávila accepted the probably unintentional challenge of Governor Victoria and his henchman Romualdo Pacheco to personal combat. Pacheco and Ávila paid with their lives, and the wounded Victoria was sufficiently chastened to agree to turn the province over to the Californians and retire to Mexico. Enlistment of more literal-minded Americans likewise complicated matters, but generally the procedure was political rather than martial.

Whether one starts with Solá, the holdover from the Spanish regime, Argüello, the provisional executive, or José María Echeandía, the first Mexican appointee, the Mexican governors are generally admitted to have been men of lesser caliber than their Spanish predecessors. Echeandía, for example, arbitrarily moved the capital to San Diego so that his fragile health would not be endangered by the fogs of Monterey. He mismanaged the mission problem, and his measures were half-hearted, though ultimately effective, against the revolt engineered by Commissioner Herrera and the ex-convict Joaquín Solís. In 1831 Echeandía accepted the leadership of a southern revolt against his successor, Manuel Victoria, and though this revolt succeeded because of the exciting victory at Cahuenga, little credit redounds to Echeandía. Against him a new rebellion was raised in the name of Agustín Zamorano, better known as California's first printer, and the end result was a temporary division of California, with Echeandía ruling from San Diego to San Gabriel and Zamorano from Santa Barbara north.

For two and a half years beginning in January, 1833, California was blessed with a governor far above the Mexican average. This was José Figueroa, a swarthy Aztecan mestizo, a veteran of the Sonora frontier, and a competent executive. After granting amnesty to all concerned in the Zamorano revolt, Figueroa took up the problem of California's northern defenses. Mariano Guadalupe Vallejo was sent to the north bay region to locate sites for settlements that would serve as buffers against the Russians of Fort Ross and the English on the Columbia. With a handful of colonists Vallejo established settlements at Petaluma and Santa Rosa.

In Mexico, meanwhile, a protective colony against the Russians had been urged by California's congressman, Juan Bandini. In 1833 he interested José María Padrés and José María Híjar in the project and helped them get appointments, Padrés as military commander for California and Híjar as jefe político and director of colonization. Figueroa, it should be explained, had been requesting retirement from office. At government expense Padrés and Híjar recruited 204 colonists for California and sailed from San Blas in July, 1834. Their plan, as now further unfolded, was to take possession of the mission property. But prior to their arrival, a change of government occurred in Mexico. Santa Anna, the new president, sent a courier to Figueroa notifying him that the Padrés and Híjar commissions had been rescinded, and these worthies were foiled in their land-grabbing scheme. The colonists, of much better quality than most of California's recent accessions, were settled by Vallejo in the Sonoma Valley, where they served their original purpose of holding the fort against possible Russian encroachments. Padrés and Híjar participated in a rebellion against Figueroa and were arrested and bundled off to Mexico.

Secularization

During Figueroa's administration occurred the secularization of the missions—that is, their conversion into ordinary parish churches, the release of the neophytes from complete supervision by the friars, and the release of much of the mission lands for other utilization. Secularization had long been contemplated. Spain's original plan had been to secularize after a decade of mission operation, but because of the lagging behind of the settlers who were to assist in the second stage of civilizing and assimilating the natives, the mission period was prolonged. When a secularization law passed by the liberal Spanish Cortes on September 13, 1813, was promulgated in Mexico eight years later, the guardian of the College of San Fernando expressed complete willingness that the Franciscans should be relieved immediately of their responsibilities in California, though with no expectation that the step would be taken. Talk of secularization was stimulated during the struggle for independence, especially when it seemed that the friars were less inconvenienced during the transition than were the laity.

Independent Mexico promptly approved secularization in theory, and a gradual process began in California. No one asserted that the California Indians were ready for secularization. But pressure was brought to bear on the authorities because of a desire on the part of certain individuals for the mission lands, admittedly the best in the province. As white population increased and the number of neophytes declined, the argument strengthened that the friars should not be left in control of such large tracts. Nor was the mission system, with its land monopoly and its virtual enslavement of the Indians, in tune with Mexican republicanism.

The first actual steps were taken by Governor Echeandía. He had come to California with the reputation of being an anticleric. Then he had become embroiled in a dispute with the friars over the question of an oath of allegiance. The friars were willing to take an oath of fidelity but balked at a more far-reaching pledge, and since there were no priests to take their places, they could afford to defy the governor. This controversy inclined Echeandía the more toward secularization. On July 25, 1826, he issued the first California decree on the subject, authorizing married Indians of long standing in Christianity to leave the missions. Only a very few took advantage of the offer, and they gave quick proof of incompetence to manage their own affairs. An English visitor reports that many of these ex-neophytes, "having gambled away their clothing, implements, and even their land, were compelled to beg or to plunder in order to support life," and that they became so obnoxious that the friars were requested to take them back.

In the summer of 1829 Echeandía published a Mexican law calling for the expulsion of all Spaniards, but he made no attempt to enforce it. Several friars seized the excuse to demand passports, which of course were not granted. A year later Echeandía formulated a more drastic secularization measure, which he sent to Mexico for approval. No answer was forthcoming, but on January 6, 1831, he nevertheless promulgated it, a step which Bancroft characterized as "wholly illegal, uncalled for, and unwise." About all that this law accomplished was to stimulate the Indians to roseate hopes of luxurious freedom and to reduce their obedience to the Franciscans.

When Figueroa arrived, the intention apparently was to continue the missions. Indeed, he brought ten Franciscans of the College of Zacatecas to reinforce the Fernandinos. Figueroa outlined a method whereby capable Indians might be released (or graduated) from the missions, but again only a negligible number took advantage of the opportunity. Having observed conditions in California, Figueroa wrote to Mexico advising against any acceleration of secularization and citing the opinions of Friars Durán and García Diego. By the time his protest arrived, the Padrés-Híjar plan had already been adumbrated, with provision for financing secularization by means of the Pious Fund. Shortly thereafter, the Mexican Congress ordered immediate secularization.

Figueroa did not approve, but he had no choice in the matter. By a proclamation dated August 9, 1834, he ordered ten missions secularized. Half the property was to be distributed to the Indians, but they were not empowered to dispose of it. They would still be

ꞁork on essential community enterprises. Secular admin-
e to take charge of the rest of the property. Cattle were
only as necessary. Since curates were not available, the
to continue their religious functions. The process was
ꞁ six other missions in 1835 and to the remaining five in
1836.

Unfortunately, Figueroa died before the work was well begun, and at the same time revolutionary disorder removed another possible restraint upon the administrators. Only a very few of these men were both conscientious and capable, and none was as sympathetic as Figueroa; through their fingers the mission property slithered rapidly into private hands. Notwithstanding the law, the Indians were still more prompt in disposing of their individual shares. Having lost their property, a few returned to the secularized missions, and another few found employment on the ranchos, but the majority relapsed to barbarism among the inland peoples or sank to a degradation still worse.

As for the missions, the final blow came in 1844, when Governor Micheltorena found in the threatened war with the United States an excuse to order the disposal of the remaining mission properties. Only two years elapsed before control of the province passed to the United States, but in that period the Franciscans lost all the missions but Santa Barbara. The properties were subsequently recovered through the American courts, but their operation as missions was a thing of the past. The passing of Father Narciso Durán on June 1, 1846, was another indication of the end of the missions. In his forty years of service in California Durán had proved himself "perhaps the ablest of the Franciscan prelates," yet it was a service of staving off decline rather than of striding progress, such as that under Serra and Lasuén.

Further Political Turmoil

Political annals for the province after the death of Figueroa are a compound of vacillation between home rule and government from Mexico and of neighborly quarreling among the Californians, mingled with general resentment against the governors sent up from Mexico. Figueroa's ad interim successor was José de Castro, followed shortly by Nicolás Gutiérrez, by whom a Mexican decree was proclaimed elevating Los Angeles to the rank of city and designating it officially as the capital of Alta California. Gutiérrez, in turn, was replaced by Mariano Chico, a Mexican appointee who was thus rewarded for his support of the reactionary movement labeled "Centralism." By his arbitrary actions Chico made himself despised by the Californians. He quarreled with Abel Stearns and ordered him from the province. At Los Angeles he arrested several respected citizens on the ground that they had taken part in a lynching. Still less excuse is to be found for his bedevilment of Father-President Durán for refusing to swear to the "Bases," the political credo preliminary to the reactionary constitution of 1836. Within three months California was rid of Chico. At a social function he made the mistake of forcing his mistress and another woman of ill-repute upon Monterey's four hundred. Popular protest was so vehement that Chico took ship for Mexico.

Against the provisional government of Gutiérrez, whom Chico left in charge, a revolt was raised by a dashing young Californian, Juan Bautista Alvarado. A native of Monterey, a protégé of Solá, a product of California's schooling, and a friend or relative of every prominent paisano of northern California, Alvarado had no dearth of followers. He also enlisted the help of Isaac Graham and his rifleros Americanos. Gutiérrez' surrender was easily secured. Southern California's recognition of the new government proved a more difficult prize, but through show of force, skillful maneuvering, and judicious compromise, Alvarado at last got the nominal adhesion of the southerners.

At the outset of his administration Alvarado had the diputación declare California "a free and sovereign state," so to remain until Mexico should return to the liberal federal constitution of 1824. The capital was also restored to Monterey, though in deference to the feelings of the southern Californians the south was to be organized as a canton under a local jefe político, virtually a subgovernor. As governor, Alvarado also promised, if not open toleration, at least noninterference with private religious practices. In the maneuvering for state-wide support of his government, these plans were much modified. The assertion of independence became merely a claim for self-government, and the absolute orthodoxy of the province was reaffirmed.

The clashes between Alvarado and his local adversaries provide the basis for many an entertaining tale. The charges and counter-charges were more often vocal than physical, and one Los Angeles wit threatened to take his barber to the next battle so that there would be some bloodletting. The personal ambitions of the several opposition leaders—Juan Bandini, Pablo de Portilla, Andrés Castillero, Carlos Antonio Carrillo, Juan Castañeda, and Agustín V. Zamorano—have but slight significance except to their biographers. Greater importance attaches to the manifestation of sectionalism within the province, but most illuminating was the proof of California's detachment from Mexico. On the one hand, this detachment was evident in the unconcern with which Alvarado stood first for federalism and then for centralism; on the other, it is borne out by Mexico's complete inability to suppress the provincial uprising and her eventual recognition of the Alvarado government.

By 1842 Alvarado had tired of politics. His earlier troubles with the southern Californians had been followed by a difference of opinion with his uncle Mariano Guadalupe Vallejo, the military commandant. Consequently Alvarado welcomed the arrival of a Mexican appointee, Manuel Micheltorena, who was to take over the reins of government, both political and military. Micheltorena's stay was brief. The 300 cholos who had come with him were an insufferable nuisance, and though Sutter and some other foreigners rallied to his support, a revolution engineered by Alvarado and Castro culminated in the famous "Battle" of Cahuenga Pass, on February 20 and 21, 1845, in which a horse was killed on one side and a mule wounded on the other. The battle, however, proved decisive; Micheltorena agreed to take his cholos out of the province, and political and military government devolved upon the Californians Pío Pico and José Castro. Thereafter, Mexico's hold on California was most nebulous.

Pastoral California

In the economic and social realm the period of this political turmoil witnessed not only the decline of the missions but also the rise of the ranchos. In the earliest years Spain had preferred that new settlers reside in the pueblos or near the presidios, but she was ready shortly to make generous grants to prospective ranchers. Two features of these land grants may appall Anglo-Saxons; first, that they conveyed a usufructuary right rather than an absolute title, and second, that they involved such extensive acreage. Both features, however, were in accord with Spanish custom, and the second represented a far better understanding of a cattleman's needs in a semi-arid land than the United States government has yet achieved. A homestead comprising a quarter section or even a full section makes a ridiculous ranch holding. Less than thirty applications for land grants were received during the entire Spanish period, and not all these applicants bothered to have their titles confirmed by the Mexican authorities.

Although a few of these grants are still important, the great majority of "Spanish grants" date from the Mexican period. A score or so were made during the first decade of independence; from 1830 to 1846 the practice was so accelerated as to bring some eight million acres into the possession of eight hundred grantees. It is significant that the ranchos increased most rapidly just when the missions were crumbling fastest. Many ranchos consisted largely of lands once under the padres' control and were stocked, likewise, with cattle drawn from the mission herds. It goes without saying that scant attention was paid to boundary limits, which is another way of observing that until the American period land itself was not at a premium and had no particular value apart from the improvements upon it and the use made of it.

The entire matter of land titles was thrown into confusion by the American land act of 1851, which declared all claims forfeit unless the grantees appeared before the Board of Land Commissioners with documents and witnesses to prove ownership. Nevertheless, a substantial fraction of present land titles in California rests upon the "Spanish land grants," most of which were really Mexican.

With the rise of the ranchos, pastoral California reached its romantic zenith. Cattle roamed over a thousand hills. Horses became so numerous that they were hunted down to save pasturage for the cattle. Hides and tallow could be bartered to English and Yankee traders for all the attractive gewgaws of a more sophisticated civilization. And the outlanders—English and Yankee traders, Russian fur hunters, Hawaiian hide droghers, Rocky Mountain trappers, and American settlers—though they presaged the end of Mexican control, lent a cosmopolitan touch. Even those two inescapables, death and taxes, seemed to have been stayed, the latter being indirect and therefore unnoticed, while the former at least was long postponed.

The bizarre amusements are an index to the spirit of the times. Grizzly-bear hunting, with lasso and mustang, was a royal sport, demanded, prosaically enough, by the necessity of protecting the cattle herds against these marauders. Similarly, wild-horse hunting was both a diversion and a requisite task, especially in seasons of drought, when the grass had to be preserved for the cattle and sheep. Likewise, the rodeo, in addition to being a gala occasion when the men of an entire district convened, was essential to the adjustment of individual ownership of livestock and the unfenced and communal range. Bull and bear fights, with the odds approximately even, had less of utilitarian value but were natural in view of the frequency with which the vaqueros had to measure the mettle of these ferocious beasts.

Vaqueros escaped much of the drudgery in the lot of the cowboys of the American West. They had no fences to ride. Cattle were raised chiefly for their hides and tallow, and consequently there was less concern about their condition. Because California cattle were turned loose and received practically no attention, save at branding and butchering time, the vaqueros were spared most of the doctoring and the veterinary work of the cowboy's routine. Even the butchering (matanzas) was done from horseback by means of dexterous thrusts of the knife. Removal of the hides and rendering of the tallow remained about the only unadulterated toil.

The ranchero's resplendent attire gives a clue to the desultory nature of his labor. Gold or silver embroidered deerskin shoes; velvet or satin breeches, slashed at the knee, gold-braided and silver-buttoned; velvet or silk vest, with wide sash of red satin; dark cloth jacket embroidered in gold and silver; wide, flat-topped sombrero, with cord of silver or gold. The ordinary vaquero was less gaudily befurbished, but this was his pattern. The women not only dressed in more sedate fashion but are accredited with being more industrious than the men. Since large families were the rule, cooking and housework were substantial tasks, in addition to which these matrons indulged in a prodigious amount of lace making and embroidery. Many women rode and hunted, but picnics and dances were the favorite diversions. Dances celebrated every event—weddings, births, political changes, and religious festivals. The elders were privileged to open the festivities; later on the younger people had their turn at the contradanza, jarrabe, and fandango.

These romantic Californians are also renowned for their openhandedness, especially in the matter of meals, lodgings, and provision of riding animals. These three were available without stint to any wayfarer. The mission fathers, as Robinson relates, might permit a contribution to the saints; rancheros were above accepting remuneration for their hospitality, and some of them even placed a supply of money in their guest rooms into which visitors might dip as they needed.

Spanish and Mexican Heritage

Although to the casual observer it may appear that the brusk Americans wiped the slate clean and supplanted the older manner of life with a civilization in which Spanish, Mexican, and California elements found no place, this judgment is superficial.   Land titles are merely one factor resting on an older base.   Place names by the hundreds have survived; highways such as El Camino Real follow the old trails; the modern vocabulary is enriched by scores of words carried over from the Spanish; numerous celebrations, fiestas, rodeos, and the like hark back to the days of romance.   Certain modern trends in architecture and furniture, in southern California especially, modify and embellish but also perpetuate features of the Mexican period.   Descendants of the old families have been outnumbered by sons of the gold rush, and they in turn by the more recent avalanche of midwesterners, yet these scions of the Arcadian age have attained a position of respect far out of proportion to their small number.

Not the least important part of this heritage has been in history, folklore, and appeal to the imagination.   The historical record is rich in nondocumentary materials, of which the chain of missions is the best known but by no means the sole example.   Besides the still unpublished treasures with which the archives of Spain, Mexico, and California abound, there is a vast literature, of which the Cabrillo and Vizcaíno diaries, the Costansó and Font journals, the Venegas, Ortega, and Palóu histories, and the descriptions by Dana, Robinson, and Colton are merely the outstanding examples.   Authoritative historical studies have followed; and a legion of more popular interpreters, including Bret Harte, Lummis, Atherton, Jackson, James, and White, have found themes and settings for medleys of fact and fiction in the glamorous pre-American period.   Their writings, along with the Mission Play and the Serra legend, have gone far to interpret the spirit and recall the charm of the days of the dons.

Nevertheless, the significance of the Mexican period often goes unnoticed.   Certain writers dismiss it as nothing more than an interregnum between the Spanish and American regimes.   The old Californians are partly responsible, for out of their dislike for the Mexican governors and their cholo troops sprang a tendency to shun the very word Mexican. Without elaborating the case, it may suffice to remark that without any transitional period the change from Spanish colony to American state would have been uncomfortably abrupt. It was most fortunate that the work of secularization, the introduction of such concepts as republicanism, constitutionalism, and representation, and the initial contacts with non-Spaniards could take place while California was a Mexican province.

12

THE COMING OF THE
TRADERS

IMPINGEMENT OF FOREIGNERS upon California began in the days of the Spaniards. The earliest visitors, Pérouse and Vancouver, have already been introduced, and something has been said of the general circumstances that led to their voyages. In the years that followed, there was a quickening of world interest in the North Pacific and incidentally in California. The number of non-Spanish visitors increased, a California commerce developed, and Russians, English, Americans, Aleuts, and Kanakas helped to make the province cosmopolitan.

Otter and Seal Hunters

The approaches of these several nationals might be presented in extended narration. The Russians first entered Siberia in the 1580's, practically contemporary with the first regular sailings of the Manila galleon and the launching of the Jesuit missions. Within a century they had pushed all the way across to the Pacific, and early in the eighteenth century Vitus Bering had carried the czar's flag out into that ocean. His second voyage, across to Alaska and along the chain of Aleutian Islands, led to otter hunting among these islands, and at the end of the century to Russian occupation of Alaska. Thence it was but a short step to California. English and American approaches were at first intertwined. They can be traced through such steps as the founding of Jamestown, shortly after Vizcaíno's trip to Monterey; the chartering of the Hudson's Bay Company, a decade before Kino sailed for America; and expansion into central Canada and to the Mississippi, just before the Spanish occupation of Alta California. The tracing of these earlier steps may safely be left to historians of the Russian and British empires and of the American westward movement, while we notice the immediate background for California contacts in the revival of interest in the North Pacific in the 1770's and 1780's.

At midcentury the Hudson's Bay Company had been prodded into a more active search for the Northwest Passage in the hope, of course, of gaining access to the Pacific. Then, in 1776, Captain James Cook, already famous for his voyages to the South Pacific, was sent to explore the northern reaches of the western ocean and particularly to seek the western entrance to the long-sought strait. Though he failed in this purpose, his voyage did reveal an attractive trade possibility in the North Pacific. On the northwest coast his men purchased otter pelts from the Nootkas, which sold for fabulous prices in China. Cook's men almost mutinied, in order to make another voyage to Nootka expressly for fur gathering, but they were persuaded to continue the trip around the world.

Through several channels the news of this transaction in furs was broadcast. Cook's men said something of it. An American member of his expedition, John Ledyard, carried the exciting word to such distinguished persons as John Paul Jones, Robert Morris, and Thomas Jefferson, besides publishing in 1783 a journal of the voyage. Jefferson was sufficiently interested to start Ledyard off for Nootka by way of Russia and Siberia, but the Russian authorities took an adverse stand and turned Ledyard back. It was Cook's book that gave widest currency to the idea of a Nootka-Canton trade. Published in 1784 in four handsome volumes, it circulated quickly and widely, attracting particular attention to the potentialities of this fur trade. The Pérouse voyage was one consequence; others more direct were the voyages of Hanna, Meares, Strange, Portlock, Dixon, Barklay, Duncan, Douglas, and Colnett for England, and of Gray and Kendrick for the United States. These were traders all, and primarily in search of otter pelts.

In 1784, year of the publication of Cook's memorable book, the first American venture in the China trade had occurred. Since this commerce, as well as the northwest fur trade, was foundational to the subsequent traffic with California, it is appropriate to mention it.

A Boston vessel, the *Empress of China,* pioneered in this trade.   Its excellent success led other New Englanders to venture similarly, and the China trade that resulted came to be a major element in the new nation's initial prosperity.

Not all the China ships touched the northwest coast of America. Many supplemented their New England cargoes merely with Hawaiian sandalwood, Chilean copper, and the commodities of the South Sea Islands and the East Indies.   Nevertheless, furs stood high on the list of goods wanted, and vessels swarmed to the North American coast. The earliest fur trading was to the north, but it was soon discovered that the hunting was even better on the coasts of Alta and Baja California.   The sea otter's habitat extended from the Aleutian Islands to about the twenty-eighth parallel, with the largest numbers available at the Santa Barbara Channel Islands.   The fur seal also abounded and, though a single pelt was worth less, the aggregate return from fur sealing considerably exceeded that of otter hunting.

Russians had plied the fur business in the Aleutian Islands for a decade prior to Cook's voyage, and the British from India, China, and England itself were at first the most active in following up that mariner's disclosures.   But the Russians had the utmost difficulty in procuring ships and maintaining them in North Pacific service, while the English surrendered a possible advantage when they accepted the self-denying provisions of the second Nootka Convention and were further handicapped by the Napoleonic Wars, which broke out at the close of the century.   New Englanders consequently had a golden opportunity, and they seized upon it.   The Russian American Fur Company extended its hunting down the coast but came to depend upon American ships for transportation to China.   While British ships did not disappear entirely, Americans came to dominate the trade, in consequence of which they had most frequent contact with Spanish California.   Yankee seamanship and trading acumen, the latter especially useful in dealings with the Chinese, were additional factors redounding to the American advantage.

The first American ship to visit California, though its name was the *Otter,* did not come for furs.   It put in at Monterey in 1796 to take wood and water, and Captain Ebenezer Dorr surreptitiously took advantage of the opportunity to disembark ten men and a woman, fugitives from Botany Bay.   Governor Borica was much incensed at Dorr's chicanery, and although these ex-Australians proved good workmen, they were, as the law required, forwarded to New Spain. Three years later Captain James Rowan brought the *Eliza* into San Francisco and was permitted to take on supplies. In 1800 still another American vessel, the *Betsey,* under Captain Charles Winship, stopped at San Diego for wood and water. Other ships, both English and American, were engaging in seal and otter hunting along the coast but without visiting any of the Spanish ports.

In the next few years California's usefulness to the Boston fur hunters was increased. They began to utilize some of its unoccupied bays as places to careen their ships before starting on the long voyage to Canton and Boston. Avalon Bay, at Catalina Island, was especially favored for this barnacle scraping. They also opened a small scale trade with the Californians, bartering a wide variety of manufactured goods for beef, grain, scurvy-combatting vegetables, and furs. Since Spanish law forbade such trade, California officialdom had to take a stand against it, but it was such a boon to the isolated province that many officials closed their eyes or even connived at the trade. To the Yankees, it should be emphasized, this traffic was incidental to their hunting and their trade in China.

Occasionally a Yankee captain fell afoul of the California authorities. In 1803, several hundred otter skins and a part of her cargo were confiscated from the *Alexander* by the commandant at San Diego. A few days later the *Lelia Byrd* entered port. Its mate, Richard Cleveland, recorded an opinion that the commandant would have liked to sell his stock of a thousand otter skins, but having just penalized the captain of the *Alexander,* he could not risk doing so. Instead, he put a guard on the *Lelia Byrd* and then captured the second mate and two men when they came ashore for a nocturnal transaction in furs. William Shaler, master of the vessel, promptly sent Cleveland ashore with drawn pistols to rescue these men. He then raised sail, unlimbered his full complement of six three-pounders on the starboard side, and sailed out within musket shot of the defending battery of eight nine-pounders at the entrance to the bay. For three-quarters of an hour the engagement was brisk, but with no serious damage on either side.

Less fortunate was George Washington Eayrs of the *Mercury.* In 1813 Eayrs was near Point Concepción, taking on water and getting oak timbers for repairs, when an armed longboat from the *Flora,* one of the Peruvian ships that had come to California in that year, demanded his surrender and took the *Mercury* to Santa Barbara. There its cargo was confiscated, and for the next two years Eayrs was detained at Santa Barbara and San Diego. His protests, models of forceful rhetoric and irregular spelling, availed him little. It is significant that he was put out of business by a Peruvian competitor rather than by a California official, for most of the latter were sympathetic toward commerce with the fur ships.

In the period of the Wars of Independence, with the suspension of regular shipments from San Blas, trade with the Boston ships found a new excuse. It increased in volume and in openness and came to be of high convenience to the Californians, though remaining a side line as far as the Bostonians were concerned.

To calculate the volume of this trade is not much easier than to compile figures for the number of otter and seal pelts taken. Some estimates of the latter are available. Eighteen thousand otter furs are said to have been marketed in China in 1801. Within half a dozen years the annual average was nearer 15,000, and at the end of the decade it had dropped to about 10,000. Of course many of these furs came from the northwest coast. Otter hunting was pursued so relentlessly that after 1820 not enough of these remarkable animals were left to justify further voyages. A few pelts were occasionally obtained in the next two or three decades, but that was all. Since then, the sea otter has become practically extinct.

The fur seal, as intimated, was present in much larger numbers. Furs of this animal bulked largest in the cargoes carried to China. The islands of the southern Chilean coast yielded millions of these furs, and California was not far behind. Particularly at the Farallones the sealing was excellent. This business was likewise carried on without any thought of conservation, with the result that by about 1820 the fur seal was almost exterminated from southern waters. Thus a period was put to the voyages of the Boston fur ships to California. Their epoch was brief, but it had given to the Californians their first taste of foreign commerce and to the Americans their first contact with the inviting land of California.

Fort Ross

The fur seal and the sea otter had also been largely instrumental in attracting the Russians to California. When Alexander Baránof came out in 1799 as manager for the newly chartered Russian American Fur Company, he found that the Aleutian Islands had been practically exhausted as a fur-hunting region and that removal to Alaska proper was essential. As early as 1803, through a New England ship captain, his agents were introduced to fur hunting on the California coast. Then, in 1806, the czar's inspector Rezánof made his famous voyage to San Francisco with the twofold purpose of extending the Russian fur business and arranging a trade for California foodstuffs.

On his return to Sitka, Rezánof urged the immediate establishment of two posts, one at the mouth of the Columbia River and one in northern California. In 1808 Baránof sent two ships to carry out this plan. One was lost at the mouth of the Columbia. In the other Kuskoff came to Bodega Bay, where he remained eight months trading and fur hunting. Three years later he returned to poach 1,200 otter skins from San Francisco Bay and to purchase from the natives enough land for a post. The price was "three blankets, two axes, three hoes, and a miscellaneous assortment of beads."

Kuskoff came again in 1812 with 100 Russians and 80 Aleuts and established Fort Ross a short distance north of Bodega Bay. Severe hardships marked the first years, many of them due to the unwillingness of the California officials to countenance trade. Cloth and iron were exchanged for cattle and horses, wheat, beans, dried beef, and tallow. Trade often attained a fairly large volume—for example, in 1813, when cargoes valued at $14,000 were exchanged—but the Russians were never able to count on a continuation of the trade with Spanish California, and in the Mexican period there was occasional official interference. In the early years furs were gathered in gratifying quantity, but by the middle twenties there had been such a decline that this justification for the colony was rapidly disappearing.

Agriculture and stock raising had been introduced by Kuskoff in the hope that Ross would become a granary for Sitka. Some vegetables and fruit were produced, but only for local consumption. Grain was planted, but only once did the yield exceed five to one. Even for stock raising the land around Ross was inferior. Eventually 200 cows were milked, and butter and cheese could be sent to Sitka, but otherwise, Ross was not a flourishing agricultural center.

Finally, international pressure was brought to bear against Russian California. The Spanish welcome had not been entirely cordial. Mexico also looked askance at the colony, as a threat to California.

Although there was an irregular trade and amenities were often exchanged by Russian and Mexican officials, there were other instances of friction. A particularly heated dispute occurred in 1840 between the Russian governor and the commandant at Sonoma, Mariano Guadalupe Vallejo. Vallejo took the credit for the withdrawal of the Russians in 1841, though it appears that the decision had been reached many months before the incident in question. Another bit of external pressure against the presence of the Russians in California was the Monroe Doctrine. Monroe's pronouncement was not to the effect that Russia must relinquish her holdings, but it did declare against expansion. Although the actual diplomatic interchanges with Russia may seem to have been principally effective in saving the coast up to fifty-four forty for British Columbia's eventual possession, indirectly the Doctrine thwarted Russian plans in California. In 1841, the fur business having declined, agriculture being only moderately successful, and expansion from Fort Ross being blocked, the Russian American Fur Company was ready to dispose of the fort and its furnishings to John A. Sutter, thus ending Russian control south of Alaska.

Visits of the Whalers

Carrying on where the Boston fur ships left off, American whalers and hide and tallow ships gave Mexican California a foreign trade. Whalers began to appear during the epoch of the fur ships. Inasmuch as the voyages from New England were ordinarily three-year ventures, the whalers needed some Pacific port where their vessels could be refitted and reprovisioned before setting out on the long homeward voyage around the Horn. Hawaii came to be the favorite resort, as many as 400 whaling vessels visiting the islands in a single year. California was next in popularity. A few whalers utilized Monterey and a larger number went to San Francisco Bay. There are reports of as many as forty whalers at a time on the latter bay. Upon payment of a nominal duty, the whalers were permitted to barter manufactured goods for food supplies sufficient for their needs. Evasion of duty payment was not uncommon, but even so, the whalers were stocked for only a small trade. Moreover, the chief significance of their visits was doubtless that information about California was carried back to New England, thus stimulating interest in the Pacific coast. In the latter part of the nineteenth century, offshore whaling became an important California industry and San Francisco dispatched large fleets for Arctic whaling. The narrative of these activities, however, belongs elsewhere.

Traders for Hides and Tallow

In many respects the hide and tallow trade resembled the fur trade of the earlier period and the visits of the New England whalers, but by contrast it centered in California and only incidentally affected other Pacific areas. Throughout the Mexican period it constituted California's chief contact with the outside world. It was a natural outgrowth of the earlier traffic with the Boston fur ships, natural because of the commercial connections already made and because the New England boot and shoe factories offered the best market for California's most abundant export commodity, cowhides.

Cattle raising, favored by Spanish proclivity for the business and by the ideal conditions which California afforded, had flourished mightily in the half century since Rivera and Anza introduced the first herds. These were typical Mexican range cattle, wide-horned, long-legged, small-bodied, wild, and well able to forage and fend for themselves. The tough beef they afforded was the staple food in the province. It was often given the credit for the longevity of the provincials and nowadays would at least be cited as the explanation for their excellent teeth. At the end of the Spanish period Californians could not begin to consume all the beef that was produced; they used only the choicest cuts. At the missions and at a few ranchos a small amount of leather was tanned. A large number of hides were worked up into rawhide, which had manifold local uses. Tallow was also tried out from the carcasses for candle and soap making, but here as with the hides, supply far exceeded demand.

Small quantities of tallow had gone to San Blas before 1810. The Lima ships, beginning with the *Flora* and the *Tagle* in 1813, had taken larger amounts, as well as soap and a few hides. But the real start of the hide and tallow trade was at the opening of the Mexican period. First to arrive were two representatives of the English house of John Begg and Company. These men, Hugh McCulloch and William E. P. Hartnell, operated subsequently as a California partnership, which, in Spanish transliteration as "Macala and Arnel," is often mentioned in the early annals. Bringing a small stock of goods from Lima, they opened negotiations for a long-term monopoly

Mariposa Grove of Big Trees

of California trade. Father Payeras, prefect of the missions, which, of course, would supply the bulk of provincial products, proved a canny bargainer. He warned in advance that "the day was long past when hides and tallow could be had for nothing." By the contract as finally drafted, the English firm agreed for three years to take all hides offered at $1.00 each, and at least 25,000 arrobas of tallow at $2.00 an arroba (25 pounds). Prices of suet, lard, and soap were set at $3.00, $4.00, and $16.00 a hundred, pickled beef at $4.00, and wheat at $3.00 a fanega (1.6 bushels). Horns, wine, furs, and other products were listed, but without a fixed price. The English thus got an early advantage in the conduct of California trade. Hartnell remained as resident agent and became a California patriarch.

Within a month after the coming of McCulloch and Hartnell, the first American hide trader appeared. This was William A. Gale, a veteran dealer in seal and otter furs, who had persuaded a number of Boston merchants to join him in sending the *Sachem* to California with a cargo of goods. Gale came on the vessel as supercargo. The McCulloch-Hartnell contract made it impossible to get a full cargo of hides, yet some of the missions evaded the contract, or perhaps had not signed it, so that the voyage was moderately successful. The *Sachem* returned, other vessels were sent out, and Gale was soon, to all intents and purposes, resident agent for the Boston firm of Bryant and Sturgis. At the expiration of the Hartnell contract, the English advantage disappeared, and thereafter somewhat more than half of the trade was carried on by New Englanders.

From the early twenties until the gold rush the trading methods were the same, the most important exception being that, when the missions were secularized, most though not all of the business was transferred to the ranchos. The trade has been often and brilliantly described. The ships came stocked with every conceivable commodity that the Californians might want, from toothbrushes to millstones. They were, as Dana described them, floating department stores. Mexican law regularized the trade. Upon payment of port duties at Monterey, ranging usually from 5,000 to 15,000 pesos, depending on the amount of cargo, a ship was authorized to trade anywhere in California until its cargo of hides and tallow was completed. Some captains carried on their trade entirely within the law. Others resorted to bribery of port officials and still others to transshipment of goods from a non-duty-paying vessel or to caching part

cargo at one of the islands before putting the ship through the
jms at Monterey. Just how much smuggling went on is not
iy determined, but though there were frequently twenty or thirty
ships engaged in the trade, the annual revenue from port duties seldom exceeded $75,000.

Ship agents went ashore and visited missions and ranchos to arrange
for the purchase of hides and tallow. As the sole purveyors of "civilized" articles, they were welcome visitors and received a special
measure of the hospitality for which friar and ranchero were famous.
There was a strong element of incongruity, however, in the picture of
these enterprising Yankees transacting the business of the Californians. Creaking carretas dumped the hides at the beach or sometimes on the mesa above the beach. It was up to the hide droghers
(the sailors and their Kanaka helpers) to get them aboard. Unfortunately for the sailors, where the hides were the most abundant the
harbor was the worst; the ships frequently anchored three miles
offshore at San Pedro, and the sailors had a long row, in addition to
the customary work of wading through the surf with hides balanced
on their heads.

Thanks to the twin advantages that subsequently found expression
in the nickname "Baynclimate," San Diego became the principal
depot for the hide business. It had the one good port in southern
California, and the weather was ideal for the curing that the hides
required prior to the long voyage around the Horn. Some of the
sailors, together with the ubiquitous Kanakas, were detailed to complete the cleaning of the hides (the Californians were none too meticu-
lous in scraping off all of the flesh). Salt and sunshine had their
roles in the process, after which the hides were stored in warehouses
until the time came to load a ship for the return voyage. Usually
captains were two or three years in making up their cargoes.

Some of the hide and tallow men remained in California. Alfred
Robinson, for example, came in the course of an ordinary voyage,
stayed an extra year to act as resident agent for his company, then
married into the Noriega de la Guerra family and became a permanent resident of Santa Barbara. A few of the sailors did likewise. A
far more significant consequence lay in the dissemination of information about California throughout the United States. Ship captains,
supercargoes, and sailors brought back reports of the life in California
and of the resources of the province. Robinson's *Life in California*

holds leading rank among the descriptions of ι.
the times, and the trade; but it was far surpassed
Dana's *Two Years Before the Mast,* which gained rec
overnight as a literary classic, an outstanding travel t
first sea tale written from the viewpoint of the ordina
a vivid description of Mexican California. It is still the most
read book pertaining to California.

Any account which mentioned merely the immediate satisfaction
of California wants, the revenue to the provincial treasury, the marketing of tallow in Mexico, Peru, and Chile, the supplying of leather
for the New England boot and shoe industry, and the foreign market
for New England manufactures would underestimate the significance
of the hide and tallow trade. Not least of its important features was
the fact that it familiarized New Englanders with California and made
them aware of some of its potentialities. Here in large degree is the
explanation of why New Englanders helped to swell the American
colony in this Mexican province, why they were ready to endorse
the annexation program of the Tennessean James K. Polk, and why
they participated in such numbers in the gold rush. The hide and
tallow trade had made California an outpost of New England.

Entrance of the Hudson's Bay Company

Mexican California enjoyed two other trade outlets. One was supplied by the Hudson's Bay Company, which established a trading
post at San Francisco in the early forties. Carried westward in the
British advance across Canada, the company centered its interests
on the Pacific slope to the north of California in the princely domain
of Old Oregon. But from Fort Vancouver, on the Columbia,
brigades of beaver trappers set out in all directions, and one of these,
the Umpqua brigade, came regularly into the California hinterland,
the Sacramento-San Joaquin Valley. When Sir George Simpson
visited California in 1841, he saw in the turbulence and disorder of
the Mexican province a possibility of advantage for his company.
He was just too late to buy Fort Ross, but he did arrange to purchase
a store at Yerba Buena (San Francisco) from an American merchant,
Jacob Leese. To this station there was dispatched a certain Glen
Rae, son-in-law of the majestic Dr. John McLoughlin, chief factor
at Fort Vancouver and King of Old Oregon. Rae was to conduct
trade and also an intrigue looking toward the possible acquisition of

a for the British company and empire. In the intrigue he The prosaic explanation is that he backed the wrong revolu- ary faction, one that did not even come out second best. A more romantic explanation is that he fell in love with a certain Carmencita and squandered the company's money on her. At any rate, the funds were lost, and rather than return to Oregon to face his implacable father-in-law, Rae shot himself. Though thwarted in this intrigue, the company continued its fur trapping and its San Francisco commerce. The latter, however, was not large in volume.

The Santa Fé-Los Angeles Caravans

The other trade route likewise involved a transcontinental approach. It was an extension of the Sante Fé Trail from Missouri and ran by a circuitous route north of the Grand Canyon, through southern Utah and Nevada, across the Mojave Desert and Cajón Pass, and thus to Los Angeles. A California-New Mexico connection had been advocated in the time of Anza, and long stretches of the eventual route had been explored in the 1770's by Garcés in his travels from Yuma and by Escalante in his expeditions from New Mexico. It remained, however, for polyglot traders in 1829 and 1830 to piece these old routes together into what came to be called the Old Spanish Trail. Over this route from Santa Fé to Los Angeles a regular caravan trade developed. Westward the pack trains brought silver, blankets, and American goods that had reached New Mexico over the more famous Santa Fé Trail from Missouri. Horses and mules for use on that route were the principal California products taken eastward, but China silks were also important.

All too frequently the Americans and New Mexicans who utilized this route collected horses for the return trip by wholesale theft rather than by honest trade. In this practice they were only emulating the example of the valley and desert Indians, who had developed a passionate liking for horse meat. The white horse thieves were better organized and more ruthless. They scourged the ranchos from Los Angeles to San José and made off with hundreds of animals, thus casting a shadow of obloquy upon the only trade of importance between California and her sister provinces in the Mexican republic.

13

MOUNTAIN MEN

THE EARLIEST AMERICAN voyages to California were called forth by the sea otter. The earliest American overland expeditions, complementing the approach by fur ships, whalers, and hide and tallow traders, were due to another very remarkable animal, the beaver. Though long extolled as a model of industry and recently praised as an engineer of no mean value in flood prevention and erosion control, the beaver has not had full recognition for his role in North American history. Beaver pelts were the first marketable product of the French, Dutch, and English colonies. Exploration of the northern half or two-thirds of the interior of the continent was carried on primarily by beaver trappers, who were the vanguard of the westward movement in both Canada and the United States.

The Quest for Beaver Pelts

Samuel de Champlain, at the opening of the seventeenth century, was one of the first notable fur traders. After introducing the traffic along the coast of Acadia and New England, he carried it into the St. Lawrence Valley, where his colony of New France developed, with the trade in beaver pelts as its fundamental economy. In the Hudson Valley the Dutch built up a comparable trade, utilizing not merely local pelts but also those from the west, which the Iroquois brought in by way of the Mohawk Valley. Late in the century French traders, of whom La Salle is the shining example, overran the Great Lakes area and spilled over into the Mississippi Valley. The English, meanwhile, were taking over the Hudson Valley from the Dutch and were establishing new bases for fur trade at Hudson Bay and at Charleston in South Carolina.

Then for sixty-odd years the French and English contested for the heart of North America, the Mississippi Valley and central Canada, and for its prime resource, beaver pelts. From the Hudson's Bay Company posts in the north, through agents such as William Johnson among the Mohawks, and through southern dealers in deerskins and bear oil such as the author James Adair and his contemporary Lachlan McGillivray, the English nibbled at the edges of the vast American reservoir of beaver pelts and lesser furs. Until the end of the Seven Years' War in 1763, however, the French were in possession of the lion's share of the American fur trade. They controlled the St. Lawrence, the Great Lakes, and the Mississippi. Their traders had pushed beyond the Mississippi to the foot of the Rockies, and the quixotic Sieur de Verendrye, in his quest for the Western Sea, had carried French beaver trapping to the Canadian Rockies.

Dissolution of the French empire led to a scramble for control of the trade in furs. The Hudson's Bay Company attempted to expand into the interior. The Montreal trade was taken over and reorganized by a group of Scotch businessmen, first in fierce competition among themselves and then collectively in the North West Company. Under the Spanish flag, local merchants at St. Louis endeavored to engross the Missouri Valley trade. Following the Revolutionary War, Americans made an unsuccessful bid for the trade in the Old Northwest, and the new United States government even undertook to go into the fur business itself through a chain of government factories, or trading posts. In the Floridas and Louisiana after 1783 Spain embarked upon a policy of Indian control through a British-supplied fur trade.

For the first two decades of the nineteenth century the high lights of fur-trade history were the internecine strife of the Hudson's Bay Company and the North West Company and the grandiose schemes of the New York entrepreneur, John Jacob Astor. Hudson's Bay Company men and Nor'westers asked and gave no quarter as they fought for the virgin beaver streams of the Canadian West. Their rivalry involved stimulation of Indian hostilities, bloodshed, and, worst of all, cutthroat competition and reduced profits. It was ended only by the protests of Lord Selkirk and the intervention of Parliament. Meanwhile it had resulted in a race westward, the very rapid opening up of the Canadian West, and the first expeditions down the Mackenzie to the Arctic and across the Canadian Rockies to the Pacific. The Nor'westers were the more active in this push to the west, but in the merger of 1821 their company was absorbed into the older, more conservative, and more influential Hudson's Bay Company.

John Jacob Astor, an immigrant from Germany and a self-made man, had the temerity to challenge these British titans of the fur trade. He began as a middleman dealing in furs from the Montreal market. Then he tried to get furs at their source in the Great Lakes region. From that area it was but a short step to St. Louis and the Missouri Valley, which, as a part of the Louisiana Purchase, was under the flag of the United States. Astor's view also embraced the Columbia Valley, which was claimed by his nation because of Gray's alleged discovery and was in the forefront of popular attention thanks to the Lewis and Clark expedition. By means of ships sent round the Horn and a party sent overland from St. Louis, Astor attempted to occupy Oregon. His plans also called for an arrangement with the Russians whereby his ships would carry most of their furs to China. It was a grand and, for the most part, a well-conceived program, but on every score Astor was dogged by misfortune. His men were outdone by the Nor'westers near the Great Lakes. In the Missouri Valley he fell afoul of a national law which he himself had sponsored to bar foreigners from the fur business. The law was invoked against him because most of his employees were French-Canadian or Scotch-Canadian. His overlanders to Oregon had a most difficult crossing and arrived on the Columbia destitute. His first round-the-Horn ship, the *Tonquin*, was ravaged by the Vancouver Island Indians at Clayoquot Bay and then was blown up by one of the few survivors. On the heels of these reverses came the War of 1812, and Astor's Oregon agent, Duncan McDougal, had no practical alternative but to sell out to John George McTavish of the North West Company. The Treaty of Ghent held out some encouragement, but Astor was never able to rehabilitate his trade.

In Oregon, Astor's plan was taken up by the Nor'westers and brought to fruition by the Hudson's Bay Company. Under Chief Factor John McLoughlin, and with the able support of the American governor of the company, Sir George Simpson, the headquarters were moved from Astoria to Fort Vancouver, across the river from modern Portland, and brigades were sent out in all directions. Penetration of the Umpqua brigade into California has already been mentioned. Others went eastward as far as Great Salt Lake and northward through New Caledonia, which in present terminology is British Columbia. This fur-trading empire of Old Oregon, embracing the territory of half a dozen northwestern states and provinces, was California's neighbor on the north for a quarter of a century.

In these same years St. Louis came into its own as an entrepôt for the fur trade, as American trappers moved into the Rocky Mountain area and the great Southwest. Though they sometimes grouped themselves in organized companies, these Americans were rugged individualists. Their method was the antithesis of the old Hudson's Bay habit of sitting down in a factory and waiting for the Indians to come in and trade. It resembled more the French technique of going out among the Indians. Much of their vocabulary and many of their number were French. But whereas the French had gone out to trade, the American mountain men emphasized trapping. Their dealings with the Indians were at times on a friendly basis, and many a fur trapper was a squaw man, yet perhaps more frequently their attitude was that the Indian was a "varmint" and, as such, worthy of no trust or consideration. These beaver trappers were equally unimpressed by Mexico's claims to the Southwest. By the Treaty of 1819 the United States had accepted a southwestern limit along Texas' eastern and northern boundary, thence by the Red and the Arkansas rivers to the Rockies, and north along their crest to the forty-second parallel. The fur men crossed this boundary with lordly disdain. A large fraction of their trapping was outside the limits of the United States. From Taos in New Mexico, which became one of their favorite haunts, they trapped in the Great Basin, the Gila Valley, and Sonora. Nor did they have any compunction about entering Mexican California.

In this opening of the transcontinental routes to California the mountain men were carrying on the tradition established by Champlain, La Salle, Verendrye, Mackenzie, and a host of others that fur men should be the vanguard in the opening of the West. These particular trappers broke trails later to be followed by pioneer settlers, government explorers, and gold seekers. For many of these later parties, mountain men were available to serve as guides. They were the true pathfinders.

Jedediah Smith, Pathfinder

First of the mountain men to reach California was Jedediah Strong Smith. In 1822, at the age of twenty-three, he had entered upon fur trapping as a member of the expedition of 100 men which William

Ashley and Andrew Henry recruited at St. Louis. After spending the winter with Henry on the upper Missouri in what is now Montana, Smith hurried south to meet the new party that Ashley was bringing up. He was on hand at the famous battle with the Aricaras and was chosen to carry the news of this reverse to Henry and bring his men to Ashley's assistance. This exploit was followed by many others in the course of the next few years. His feats of daring and bravery in conflict with Indian and grizzly bear won him a reputation for the traits dearest to the mountain men.

In these years the fur business was changing rapidly. Smith's own explorations were largely responsible for shifting the center of activities southwestward into the Rockies and into the vicinity of Great Salt Lake. This transfer made necessary a local base, the rendezvous, at which the trappers could make delivery of a season's catch of furs without the necessity of going all the way to St. Louis. It became increasingly common for men to remain in the beaver country for three or four years. Another change came in 1826, when Ashley sold the Rocky Mountain Fur Company to Smith, David Jackson, and William Sublette. At the Jackson's Hole rendezous that same year these men determined to attempt a further expansion southwestward in search of virgin beaver streams and perchance to open a new marketing outlet through California. Smith, then twenty-seven, was the logical choice for leader. The territory into which he was about to plunge was very nearly the least known part of North America. Exploration had swirled all around it— the Spaniards far to the south and on the California coast; Zebulon Pike on the eastern flank of the southern Rockies; Lewis and Clark, the Astorians, the Nor'westers, and Ashley's men in the Northwest— but from Great Salt Lake west and southwest to the Sierra Nevada no one had traveled. Such exploration was prerequisite to the opening of the most convenient land routes from the United States to California.

Accompanied by seventeen men, Smith left Salt Lake in August, 1826. His route was southward past Utah Lake and up the east side of Sevier River, to which he gave the name Ashley. From it he turned southwestward into a range of mountains which he called the Adams in honor of President John Quincy, then south again across the Beaver to the lower course of the Virgin River, in his terminology also the Adams. Smith's whereabouts are not absolutely identifiable for this portion of his trip. One writer is of the opinion that he reached the Virgin by way of the Escalante Desert, Meadow Valley Wash, and the Muddy.

Smith's course down the Virgin is clear enough, though for his little party it was difficult terrain. Arriving at the Colorado or, as he called it, the Seedskeeder, he crossed over and followed it down to the Mojave villages. Here he remained fifteen days recruiting his men and horses. Then, with two Indian guides and fresh horses obtained from the Mojaves, he crossed the river and traversed the desert to the Mojave River, for which he had a more appropriate name, the Inconstant. Following this stream into the San Bernardino Mountains, he crossed the latter, presumably by Cajón Pass, and in November arrived at the mission of San Gabriel.

The friars extended a generous welcome, supplying the Americans with beef, cornmeal, and wine, and with sixty-four yards of cloth with which to replace their tattered shirts. In 1774 the arrival of Anza's party had taxed the province's food supply so severely that half the soldiers had to be sent back forthwith to the Yumas. A half-century later there was no such shortage of foodstuffs. A single mission could set an abundant table for a score of unexpected guests even though they tarried six weeks.

Harrison G. Rogers, Smith's lieutenant and the principal chronicler of the expedition, paid his respects to the prosperity of the mission. It had more than 1,000 Indians employed in a variety of tasks. Some 30,000 head of cattle bore the mission brand, with horses, sheep, and swine in corresponding numbers. There were grain fields, vineyards, and orchards of apples, peaches, oranges, and figs. In workshops lining two sides of the quadrangle skilled workers produced cloth, blankets, and soap, while a water-driven grist mill and a distillery were also in operation. Rogers mentioned all this and more; he was captivated, too, by the favorable location and the attractive appearance of this mission community. His words of highest praise, however, were reserved for the jovial, friendly friars who were gracious and generous hosts to the Smith party. He was particularly drawn to Fray José Bernardo Sánchez. "Old Father Sanchus," in fact, he was prepared to list as his "greatest friend" and in every respect "worthy of being called a Christian."

Six weeks was a long time for these mountain men to remain inactive. The first week sufficed to make them forget the difficult

three months' journey to California. A wedding, the Epiphany celebration at the mission, the setting of a bear trap among the priest's
orange trees "to catch the Ind[ian]s in when they came up at night
to rob his orchard"—these were divertisements. Several of the
Americans were employed to cut wood for the charcoal pit, and a
few others found temporary employment with a hide and tallow
ship at San Pedro. But restlessness increased, and overindulgence
in the wine and aguardiente so bounteously provided by the padres
led to a disturbance that might easily have terminated with bad consequences had it not been for Rogers' restraining influence and the
friars' tolerant attitude.

Smith's plans for a trade outlet in California were balked by the
Mexican restrictions upon foreigners. Following the advice of Father
Sánchez, Smith wrote to Governor Echeandía petitioning permission
to institute this commerce. When ten days passed without a reply,
he went to San Diego to intercede in person. The governor was not
inclined to set aside law and custom, but finally he acceded partially
to the joint persuasions of Smith and the captain of one of the hide
and tallow ships and issued passports permitting the Americans to
leave California by the route over which they had come. Despite a
present of eight fine beaver skins Smith could not secure permission
to traverse California to the Russian post at Bodega.

Having purchased the necessary horses and supplies, Smith left
San Gabriel on January 18, 1827, in apparent compliance with the
governor's conditions. But after crossing Cajón Pass, he turned
northward instead of eastward and by Tejón Pass or the Tehachapi
entered the southern part of the San Joaquin Valley. The journal
describing his next activities is too sketchy to make possible exact
identification of the places visited. Smith apparently traveled
leisurely down the valley and turned up that of one of the eastern
tributaries, perhaps the Stanislaus.

An attempt to take his whole party across "Mount Joseph," apparently his name for the entire Sierra, failed because there was no
pasturage in the deep snow at the higher levels. After five horses
had died, Smith retreated to the valley, where he left most of his
men to trap beaver. On May 20, in company with Robert Evans
and Silas Gobel, he tackled the Sierra crossing again, this time with
seven horses and two mules loaded with hay, as well as with provisions
for the men. They encountered snowfields packed four to eight feet

deep, but within eight days managed to struggle across. Theirs is the first recorded crossing of the Sierra Nevada.

Beyond the Sierra the three men struggled for twenty days across a parched and barren desert. At approximately the Nevada-Utah line Smith's journal resumes. Finding water was the major problem. They saw many antelope, but except for two rabbits that Smith killed they subsisted chiefly on the flesh of the played-out horses. A little farther on, Smith climbed a hill to scout the course ahead, but the prospect was so discouraging that he dared not tell the whole truth to his followers. They lurched on through the soft sand, halting occasionally to search fruitlessly for water, and that night made a dry camp. The next morning at ten o'clock Evans gave out. Smith and Gobel luckily found good water some three miles farther on and rushed back to Evans with a kettleful. And Evans, so Smith reports, downed four or five quarts and asked for more. Their hunger was alleviated the next day by a present of antelope meat from some friendly Indians, but two days later it seemed a real tragedy when a deer that Smith shot got away. Fortunately, Smith was able to track the animal down and hamstring it. No time was lost in building a fire and starting to cook some of this venison. In his journal Smith records that they then employed themselves "most pleasantly" in eating for about two hours and for the time being forgot that they "were not the happiest people in the world."

To their further relief, they had sighted Great Salt Lake, "a most cheering view," and from a band of Snake Indians they soon learned that their fellow trappers were in camp on Bear Lake. Hiring a horse and an Indian guide, Smith hurried on to the rendezvous, which he reached on July 3. His arrival, he says, caused considerable bustle, for his party had been given up for lost. A small cannon was loaded and fired in salute.

Ten days later Smith was off for California again with eighteen companions. His route was approximately that of the preceding year, though somewhat improved by going over to the Santa Clara and Beaver Dam Wash instead of trying to follow the lower course of the Virgin. In this region and from the Mojaves he learned of another party of whites that had come up from the Gila Valley and moved northeastward along the Colorado toward the Sevier. This probably was the party described later in the account of the career of James Ohio Pattie.

As far as the Mojave villages Smith's course was uneventful. Again he traded with these Indians for horses and supplies. But after three days of friendly trade, as the Americans were rafting their goods across the Colorado, the Mojaves suddenly fell upon them, killing ten of their number. Smith and the eight survivors threw their heavier goods into the river and left most of their trappings on a sand bar, in hopes of distracting the Mojaves from pursuit. This ruse gave Smith time enough to get his men to the west bank, where they made a crude breastwork of cottonwood saplings. Four or five hundred Mojaves threatened them there, but when two braves were killed at a long distance by the American marksmen, the rest ran off. Traveling by night, Smith managed to get his party of eight across the desert to the California settlements.

This time his reception was less cordial. He obtained some supplies at San Gabriel, left the injured Thomas Virgin and the free trapper Isaac Galbraith, who preferred to remain, and hurriedly rejoined the men of his first expedition in the San Joaquin Valley. At Mission San José, where he went in search of assistance, Smith was lodged in a most uncomfortable jail by Father Durán, whose displeasure was occasioned by the belief that the trappers had enticed away some of his neophytes. After a time Smith got to Monterey, where he found Governor Echeandía incensed over the breach of the January promise. The governor talked of sending him to Mexico to stand trial, but hide and tallow men again came to the rescue and persuaded Echeandía to allow the trappers to depart.

Early in 1828 they were on their way into the valley of the "Bonadventure" (Sacramento), seeking unsuccessfully a pass through the Sierra. In April they gave up this endeavor, and turning northwestward toward the coast, struggled through very rough and broken country to the mouth of the Klamath, whence they traveled along the coast and sometimes on the beach itself to the Umpqua River. Game was scarce and travel difficult, but beaver hunting and trade proved excellent.

After breakfast on July 14 Smith left camp to blaze a trail for the day's march. The Umpqua Indians, hitherto friendly, attacked the camp during his absence and killed most of the men. John Turner and Arthur Black fought their way out and, together with Smith, were the only ones who managed to reach Fort Vancouver. Dr. John McLoughlin offered Smith men with whom to recover his lost prop-

erty, and when the American shrugged his shoulders over the useless-
ness of the effort, he sent his stepson, Tom Mackay, to put the
Umpquas in their place. The party returned shortly with nearly all
the furs. Charging Smith four dollars a head for horses lost on the
journey and at the rate of five dollars a month for his men's services,
McLoughlin gave him a draft on London for the balance of the value
of the peltries, about $3,200. Furthermore, he assisted Smith to
rejoin his partners in the Rockies. His subsequent experiences did
not concern California directly. After trapping for a while in the
Rockies, he returned to St. Louis, and in 1831 started west over the
Santa Fé Trail. Traveling with a large party on such a well-beaten
trail, an experienced man like Smith might be considered perfectly
safe. Carelessness, however, led him into an Indian ambush near the
Cimarron River, and as he knelt down to drink he was shot in the
back by Comanche arrows and was killed.

Jedediah Smith's contact with California was brief. It was marked
by imprisonment at San Diego, Mission San José, and Monterey. But
it was he who opened the route from Great Salt Lake to southern
California; it was he who first crossed the Sierra and first traveled
between the Sierra and Salt Lake; it was he who opened a trail to
Oregon, a route improved by the Hudson's Bay Company brigades
and utilized thereafter as an Oregon-California link. On all these
routes he was the forerunner of the American pioneers.

James Ohio Pattie

Smith was one of the Rocky Mountain group of American fur men.
Another group fully as influential in California's development operated from Taos and Santa Fé in New Mexico. Of these James Ohio
Pattie deserves chief mention. With his father he had come out over
the Santa Fé Trail to try his hand at silver mining or trade or whatever might offer in the Mexican province beyond the southwestern
frontier. Mining was the first venture, but trapping proved more
attractive, and in 1825 Pattie set out with a group of Americans to
trap in the Gila Valley, the Helay in his orthography.

Since the Gila Valley was virgin territory for trapping, these men
found beaver very plentiful and accumulated a good quantity of
furs. An Indian attack, however, resulted in the loss of most of
the pelts, and they returned to Santa Fé almost empty-handed.

Pattie returned with another group of trappers the next year. The

Pápagos attacked again, killing many of the fur men, but the survivors continued down the Gila Valley, trapping as they went. The Yumas proved friendly, and a brisk trade went on with them, after which the Americans moved north into the land of the Mojaves. One night at about eleven o'clock these Indians surprised the trapper camp with a shower of arrows which killed two men and wounded two others. Pattie's bed-fellow was one of those killed; two arrows struck his own hunting shirt, and sixteen pinned his blanket to the ground. The most provoking thing about the attack, to judge from Pattie's laconic account, was that the Mojaves fled before the trappers could fire a shot in return, but he concluded, "We extinguished our fires and slept no more that night."

Shaking off the dust of the Mojave country, the trappers moved eastward along the Colorado. They skirted the Grand Canyon, whose magnificence evoked no exclamations from Pattie's pen. Instead, he complained about the foot of snow through which they had to struggle. East of the canyon they veered northward again, going as far as the Yellowstone, where they crossed over east of the Rockies and returned to Santa Fé by way of the upper branches of the Platte and the Arkansas. At Santa Fé the Mexican governor welcomed them rudely by confiscating their furs, on the excuse that they had been trapping in Mexican territory without possessing the proper passports and official permission. The ruling was harsh, considering all the hardships and dangers these men had endured; but it was legitimate enough—practically all their trapping had been on Mexican soil.

Quite undaunted, Pattie joined a third party in September, 1827, which was also headed for the Gila. This time the Pápagos were circumspect and the beaver abundant, and trouble was not encountered until the Yumas ran off all their horses. Left stranded on the bank of the Colorado with more beaver pelts than they could carry back to Santa Fé, they decided to fashion cottonwood dugouts in which to carry them down the Colorado to the Mexican town at the head of the gulf. As they approached the mouth of the river, their geographical notions were roughly corrected. They had gone far enough, also, to find that navigation was most hazardous, though they did not experience one of the bore tides for which the locality used to be famous.

Turning about, they made their way laboriously upstream for a short distance. Then, because the current was too strong an adversary and because many of them knew how long, if not how impossible, a voyage it would be to Santa Fé, they decided to cache their furs in the bank of the river and go overland to California.

The desert crossing was reminiscent of Anza's battle with the sand dunes a half century earlier. Their route lay somewhat farther south, but they were miserably equipped, having no animals and not much to eat except dried beaver meat. In desperate straits, they emerged from the desert at an Indian village on the San Quentin River, near the mission of Santa Catalina in Lower California. The Dominican fathers gave some relief but sent them under guard to San Diego, where Governor Echeandía, scarcely recovered from the alarm occasioned by the recent intrusion of Jedediah Smith, lodged them in the calabozo.

What Pattie recorded of his experiences here substantiates the usual impression of Mexican gaols and gaolers. So harsh was the treatment and so poor the fare that Pattie's father, Sylvester, pined away and lapsed into a fatal illness. The fatigue and sufferings of the desert crossing were partially responsible, but the jail life was the final cause. As a particular refinement of cruelty, Pattie was not allowed to be with his father during this last illness.

Thereafter, some improvement in the treatment of the Americans came about. Pattie was even employed occasionally by the governor in the capacity of interpreter. But the hide and tallow men were not as successful in securing release for this group as they had been in the case of Smith a few months earlier. Permission finally was granted for the trappers to go to the Colorado cache and bring in the furs, Pattie remaining in jail to insure their return. Unfortunately, the Colorado overflow had ruined the pelts. Two of the trappers went on toward Santa Fé; the others returned to San Diego and further imprisonment.

Release came finally in most novel fashion. A smallpox epidemic struck northern California. Pattie let it be known that he had a supply of vaccine, and the governor soon contracted with him to vaccinate the Californians—officials, soldiers, settlers, padres, and mission Indians. He toured California in this capacity of "Surgeon Extraordinary to his Excellency, the Governor of California," inoculating 1,000 at San Diego, 4,000 at San Juan Capistrano, 2,500 at Los Angeles, and lesser numbers elsewhere, to make a grand total of 22,000.   The Russians at Fort Ross paid him one hundred dollars for similar medical services.

Besides the liberation of his party, Dr. Pattie expected additional payment for his professional services.   Echeandía offered the remuneration in land and cattle but added the condition that Pattie profess Catholicism.   Though willing to assume Mexican citizenship, Pattie categorically refused to meet the religious requirement.   Even after he had assisted in the suppression of the Solís revolt, he still could not get payment from the governor.   Consequently, he decided to go to Mexico to press his claim.   President Bustamente inclined a sympathetic ear but gave him no tangible satisfaction.   Discouraged and impoverished, Pattie went back to his native Tennessee, there to remain until 1849.   He is said to have come to California again during the gold rush, but history has no record of his experiences then.   Pattie's fame rests on his fur trapping, his opening of the Gila route, his incarceration, and his prophylactic peregrination.

The California visits of Smith and Pattie have an intrinsic interest; their significance expands as one takes into account the numerous similar journeys to California in the subsequent decade and a half by other overland fur men, which in turn led to the coming of the pioneer settlers in 1841.   These immediate successors of Smith and Pattie left only fragmentary records of their doings, but the generic description of Anglo-American fur trade is applicable.   The type had diverged from that exemplified by the Nor'westers and the Hudson's Bay employees in western Canada.   The canoe was now largely supplanted by the Indian pony, French voyageurs became less numerous than men from Kentucky and Tennessee, and company engagés less characteristic than free trappers.   Beaver continued, however, as the central and dominating factor.

Ewing Young

Trappers working out of Taos and Santa Fé improved upon Pattie's route to California.   For several years they had been trapping the various streams in present-day New Mexico, Arizona, and southeastern Utah.   Finally, in 1829 a party of forty men led by Ewing Young set out northwest from Taos.   A short distance out he cut back to the southwest to the headwaters of the Salt River.   In a skirmish with the Indians the trappers were completely victorious. They proceeded to trap the Salt River and the San Francisco, after

which some of the men turned back to New Mexico. Young and
the others continued westward through a most arid country. By this
route south of the Grand Canyon they reached the Mojave villages
on the Colorado. Here they tarried three days and then pushed
across to the Mojave River, which led them to Cajón Pass, the gateway to San Gabriel. After one day of trading for supplies they
went on to San Fernando and by Tejón Pass into the San Joaquin
Valley, where in the spring of 1830 they trapped beaver in company
with a Hudson's Bay Company brigade of sixty men under Peter
Skeene Ogden.

In the fall Young turned southward. At Los Angeles the pueblo
authorities threatened to arrest these interlopers who had neglected
the formality of procuring passports. They began to ply the trappers
with liquor, apparently in order to simplify the problem of making
the arrests. But Young, with the able assistance of one of his
younger men, the subsequently famous Kit Carson, managed to get
his men out of town. A measure of credit should go to a certain
James Higgins, who, though in his cups, resented the bullying of a
fellow trapper and shot him dead. This summary violence and its
casual reception by the rest of the party seem to have given pause
to the Californians. The return to Taos, where they arrived in April,
1831, was without comparable incident.

Meanwhile, two other parties had ventured from New Mexico to
California. One, consisting of Mexican traders and led by Antonio
Armijo, had left New Mexico in November, 1829, by way of the
San Juan Valley. Crossing the Colorado, they had moved on to the
Sevier, whence their route to Los Angeles was not unlike Smith's.
The following year a party of American trappers under William
Wolfskill struck out northwestward from Taos, crossing the Grand
and the Green. From the Sevier they went westward into mountainous country, where they suffered severely in a heavy snowstorm, which
forced them south toward the regular route. In the development
of this "great circle" course, Armijo and Wolfskill had a part, not
to mention Garcés, Escalante and Domínguez, and our good friend
Smith. It came to be called the Old Spanish Trail. Utilized almost
every year thereafter by trading caravans, it was for a decade the most
important land route to California and was still popular at the time
of the gold rush.

In 1831 Young entered into partnership with David Jackson,

former associate of Jedediah Smith. While Young trapped along the
Gila and the Colorado, Jackson was to go to Los Angeles with five
packloads of silver pesos to buy 2,000 mules and horses for the Santa
Fé Trail caravans. The plans went awry. Young got very few
beaver pelts, and Jackson could purchase only 700 animals. It was
agreed, therefore, that Jackson should take the mule herd back to
Santa Fé while Young continued trapping. Just beyond the Colorado
a Mojave attack relieved Jackson of more than half of his animals,
and he reached Santa Fé with only about 200 head.

Meanwhile, Young went on to Los Angeles, and throughout the
summer of 1832 his men hunted sea otter along the coast. In the
fall he crossed Tejón Pass into the San Joaquin Valley and advanced
slowly toward the north until he met a Hudson's Bay Company
party on the Sacramento. Then he swung in a wide circle to the
coast, the Umpqua Valley, Klamath Lake, the Rogue and Pit rivers,
and back to the upper Sacramento. His route next lay southward,
through the San Joaquin Valley, across Tejón and Cajón passes, by
Temecula to the Colorado, and over into the Gila Valley. Early in
1834 he was back at Los Angeles, where he secured a herd of
horses. Accompanied by the self-appointed advocate of Oregon,
Hall J. Kelley, he drove these horses north to the Columbia. Mc-
Loughlin received these Americans with less than his customary
hospitality, because Governor Figueroa had sent a warning that there
were horse thieves in the party. Although Kelley never forgave Mc-
Loughlin, Young adopted Oregon as his home. He returned to California in 1837, but for the express purpose of purchasing five or six
hundred head of California cattle to drive to the Willamette Valley.
Four years later he died in Oregon, a well-to-do and respected settler.
Before forsaking the Southwest, he had gone far toward perfecting
the route between New Mexico and California. After Smith, he
was the pioneer of the Oregon-California trail, and he was considerably more instrumental than Smith in bringing that trail into practical
use.

Joseph Reddeford Walker

Fur trappers blazed still another trail to California, namely, the
central route down the Humboldt Valley and across the Sierra into
California. The prime agent in this work was Joseph Reddeford
Walker, whom Washington Irving characterized as "one of the brav-

est and most skillful of the mountain men." In the summer of 1833 Captain Benjamin Bonneville placed Walker in charge of about sixty trappers and instructed him to reconnoiter west of Great Salt Lake. Walker put a very liberal construction upon this order. Beyond the lake he traveled to a river which he called the Barren, and which was successively christened the Mary's, the Ogden, and the Humboldt. In expressive accuracy, the first name was very much the best. But barren though the Humboldt Valley was, it proved a godsend to California-bound travelers. Walker followed the river to its sink, crossed the forty miles of desert that lay beyond, came to the lake which bears his name, and made his way with great difficulty across the Sierra and into the San Joaquin Valley. It was the first entrance into California by surmounting the Sierra. Irving and subsequent writers have been in some doubt as to the exact route followed. The best surmise is that from the headwaters of the East Walker he crossed over to those of the Tuolumne. It is clear that Walker's men looked down upon Yosemite Valley from the precipitous heights surrounding it, the first white men to gaze upon its majestic grandeur. In their writings these fur men gave but slight indication that they were affected by the beauty of this wonderland. They were more concerned about finding a place to get down with their horses to the game-filled San Joaquin Valley that lay ahead of them. As a wonder of nature, the giant sequoias of the Tuolumne or Merced grove elicited more of a response. Zenas Leonard commented on them as "incredibly large," sixteen to eighteen fathoms around at the height of a man's head.

Walker proceeded to San Francisco Bay and on to Mission San Juan Bautista, where he left most of his men. He went on to Monterey and got permission to winter in California. Half a dozen of his men preferred to stay in California, including George Nidever, of subsequent fame as a grizzly-bear hunter, a crack shot, and a long-time resident of Santa Barbara. With the remaining fifty-two, Walker started up the San Joaquin Valley in the spring of 1834. Crossing the Sierra by the wide and easy pass that has carried his name ever since, he came out upon Owens Valley, which he followed northward practically its entire length. Then the route lay northeastward into the Nevada desert, where the worst suffering of the entire journey was encountered, north to the Humboldt, across that shallow rivulet, and on to join Bonneville once more on the Snake. Of Walker's numerous discoveries on this expedition, including the Yosemite, the sequoias, Walker Pass, and Owens Valley, the greatest historical significance attaches to the route to California, which he had pioneered by way of the Humboldt Valley and a central Sierra crossing. With certain modifications, this trail was to prove the most popular for the pioneer settlers, the forty-niners, and the first railroad builders.

No pretense has been made of calling the entire roll of the mountain men who penetrated to California. Many a name has slipped from remembrance, and men who comprised the rank and file of most expeditions are lost in anonymity. Again, the fur trapping of many of the ordinary members of these parties is so overshadowed by their later activities that they are seldom thought of as trappers. J. J. Warner and Isaac Williams, for example, are better known as California ranchers, Thomas Fitzpatrick and James Clyman as guides for the pioneer settlers, Fitzpatrick and Kit Carson as guides for Frémont and for the United States Army in the War with Mexico and in the Indian campaigns that followed. Other mountain men, such as Jim Bridger, were of great assistance to the overland forty-niners, while Antoine Robidoux is an often quoted advertiser of California.

These functions may seem diverse, but upon analysis they are seen to rest upon the superior knowledge of the West that the mountain men had acquired. In the search for beaver they had penetrated every park and valley in the Rocky Mountain area, every potential trapping spot in the Great Basin, and all the beaver streams in the California mountains and foothills. In so doing they had blazed and mastered the major transcontinental routes to California; they became the experts on the Rocky Mountain and Intermountain West, the most competent guides for all others who wished to venture into this vast area, and the disseminators of information about it and about the Mexican province of California, which lay beyond. Thus they were stimulators of interest as well as invaluable guides for the westward migrations which followed.

14

PIONEERS

THE YEAR 1841 is memorable in California chronology because of the arrival of the first parties of pioneer settlers. By local definition, the term "pioneer settlers" is applied to the overland emigrants from the United States who, prior to the gold rush, set out for California with the avowed intention of making it their home. Most of them were agriculturists, and a goodly number were accompanied by their families. The coming of such persons was indeed significant. In retrospect we can see that it represented a more intense and perhaps a more acquisitive American interest than had functioned in the earlier day of commercial contacts. It led to a more rapid influx of Americans and it presaged annexation to the United States.

The Pre-pioneer Settlers

Yet the Californians were not immediately aware of the portentousness of the new migration. Like the general run of mankind, they did not sense a new direction in the course of events until considerably after the corner was turned. The emigrants of 1841 were not numerous or imposing. They came over trails which mountain men and Santa Fé traders had been using for ten or fifteen years. Throughout the thirty years preceding their arrival the trade of the province had been almost entirely in the hands of English-speaking aliens, and for a round half-century California had been visited first occasionally and then frequently by foreigners. The novelty attaching to the coming of the pioneer settlers was further reduced by the fact that many visitors and traders of the earlier day had taken up

200

permanent residence among the Californians. These foreign residents, the real old timers or, if you please, the "pre-pioneer settlers," deserve an attention that has seldom been accorded them.

Thanks to the prodigies performed by Hubert Howe Bancroft in accumulating information about the early Californians, it is possible to compile trustworthy statistics on the number of foreign residents year by year throughout this period, to identify a surprisingly large number by name, and to trace the career of practically every individual who figured at all prominently in the affairs of the province. Bancroft's disclosures are supplemented here and there by other writers on early California.

The first entry in the record is more macabre than significant. A certain Bostonian, John Groem or Graham, a gunner on Malaspina's ship, died as the expedition reached California, and on September 13, 1791, his body was landed for interment at Monterey. To list him as the first foreign resident is unrealistic. That distinction belongs to John Gilroy, Scotch by birth, English by residence, and a sailor by profession. In 1814, as a lad of twenty, Gilroy was set ashore from an English vessel because of sickness. Baptized in 1814, seven years later he married a daughter of Ignacio Ortega, and in 1833 was naturalized and became a ranchero. A town on the ranch site still bears his name, but Gilroy lost out to the land lawyers, as did so many of the natives, early in the American period. Gilroy had something of a reputation as a happy-go-lucky fellow and a hard drinker. As to the latter, however, he must yield the palm to an Irishman, John Mulligan or Milligan, who came about the same time and perhaps on the same vessel. Mulligan taught weaving to the neophytes at several missions and drank himself to death in 1834.

In 1816 two Americans arrived. From the *Albatross* a twenty-seven year old Bostonian named Thomas Doak landed at Monterey, while Daniel Call, aged seventeen, came on the *Atala* to Santa Barbara. Both married in California and settled down to ply their trade as carpenters, but neither was prominent in subsequent affairs. A more conspicuous figure who arrived two years later, Joseph Chapman, is often mentioned as the first American. Chapman came with the Bouchard expedition and was one of those captured at Monterey. He quickly adapted himself to California and proved his usefulness by building grist mills at several of the missions and even a schooner. He was married and baptized in 1822 and naturalized in 1831. He was a great favorite in the province, particularly with Father Sánchez of San Gabriel, and a most resourceful craftsman. Other foreigners to the number of perhaps a score took up their residence in California before the end of the Spanish period. Their coming, as in the case of Gilroy and Chapman, was usually accidental and unintentional, and the part that they played in provincial affairs was a very minor one indeed.

With the start of the Mexican period and the simultaneous launching of the hide and tallow trade and the visits of the whalers, the entrance of foreign residents was greatly accelerated. The appearance of William E. P. Hartnell and William A. Gale as resident agents for the hide and tallow trade has been noted in connection with the rise of that commerce. Bancroft lists fifteen other new arrivals, including William Anthony Richardson, mate on the whaler *Orion* and renowned as the father of Yerba Buena, from which the city of San Francisco evolved. Robert Livermore, subsequently a noted ranchero in the beautiful valley that bears his name, was another Britisher of the class of '22.

For 1823 only eight additions are noted, the most notable being Captain John R. Cooper of the *Rover,* who sold this schooner to Luís Argüello but continued as its master. Thereafter new foreign residents were added at the rate of fifteen or twenty in 1824, a half dozen in 1825, and twenty-five, twelve, eighteen, seventeen, and twenty-four in the remaining years of the decade. For the early thirties Bancroft's figures are twenty-seven, forty-five, thirty-seven, thirty-six, and sixteen; and for 1836 to 1840 they are thirty-one, twenty-five, twenty, twenty-five, and forty-six.

Obviously space does not permit the introduction of each of these men. Many of them were not of sufficient importance to justify such attention, and the rest exhibit certain similarities which make possible classification and generalization. For many of these men the remarks made in connection with Gilroy and Chapman are apposite; that is, because of sickness or other circumstances beyond their control, they left ship and took up residence in California.

Beginning with Hartnell and Gale in 1822 and continuing with Cooper in 1823, David Spence the following year, William G. Dana and Henry Delano Fitch in 1826, and Alfred Robinson and Abel Stearns in 1829, we meet a different type. These men came with their eyes open, alert to the commercial advantage that might be

gained. They quickly engrossed the trade of the province and, with
a few later recruits—notably Thomas O. Larkin, who arrived in 1832
—they transacted most of California's business to the end of the
Mexican period. The majority of these men found it advantageous
and pleasanter to become Californians. With few exceptions they
professed the Catholic faith, took California wives, learned and used
the Spanish language, adopted California dress, Hispanicized their
names, applied for naturalization as Mexican citizens, and conformed
to the mores of their adopted land. Many of them retained a certain
quality, a superior energy or a more astute business sense, which
made them outstanding among the native residents, but as a class
these were the men who became most thoroughly naturalized, altogether Californians.

Representative Californians

Hartnell is a good example of thorough adaptation to California,
a process made easier by his previous residence on the west coast of
South America. Two years after his arrival he was baptized and a
year later he married María Teresa de la Guerra, who, in the course
of the years, presented him with twenty sons and five daughters.
After a trip to South America to terminate his partnership, he returned and was naturalized in 1830 as a Mexican citizen. The next
year he became a ranchero and in 1834 received patent to Rancho
Patrocinio del Alisal, about twenty miles inland from Monterey. As
a ranchero he had average success. By 1849 he had some 8,000
head of cattle and several thousand horses and sheep. His cultivated
fields, or milpas, were tilled but indifferently, and the vineyard was
also the victim of neglect, but the vegetable garden, with a year-round
production of vegetables and berries of numerous varieties, left nothing to be desired.

Hartnell held various governmental posts: regidor, collector of
taxes and customs, court clerk, interpreter (for he used Spanish,
French, and German as freely as his native English), surveyor, and
county assessor. From 1833 to 1836 he was agent for the Russian
American Fur Company. At about the same time he opened a school
known as the Seminario de San José in which his own children
were often in the majority. His most important commission was as
visitador-general of the secularized missions in 1839–1840. On this
hopeless task he worked faithfully and heroically, only to find that

the forces of spoliation and disintegration were inexorable. Notwithstanding his several official capacities, Hartnell is best remembered
as a genial, liberal, hospitable ranchero, honest and loyal, too easy-
going to prosper greatly in business, but a boon companion and
a most estimable friend and neighbor.

Another of California's adopted sons blessed with a large family
was William Goodwin Dana. Almost immediately upon his arrival
from Boston in 1826 he fell in love with Josefa Carrillo, daughter of
the prominent Santa Barbaran, Don Carlos. To Dana's great
disgust, he was not allowed to contract the marriage until the preliminaries of his baptism and naturalization were fulfilled, processes
which wasted the better part of two years and delayed the wedding
until his intended bride's sixteenth year. Besides his twenty-one
children, Dana's achievements included service as appraiser, captain
of the port, and alcalde of Santa Barbara, and in the American period
as prefect and county treasurer. He is listed as a trader, soapmaker,
physician, and architect, and for a time as the holder of a special
license for sea-otter hunting, but his livelihood was drawn principally
from Rancho Nipomo, near San Luís Obispo, which was granted
him in 1837.

Don Abel Stearns, though childless, became the patriarch of southern California. After three years of residence in Mexico he came
to Monterey in 1829 and played with the idea of a rancho in the
great central valley. Instead, he moved to Los Angeles, where he
became the leading trader, distinguished also by the frequency with
which he fell afoul of the authorities. Smuggling was the usual
charge, but in 1836 Governor Chico added that of being implicated
in a lynching. Stearns quarreled also with a certain William Day
and in the broil that ensued suffered a facial wound which enhanced
the ugliness with which nature had endowed him, so that his nickname Cara de Caballo, or Horseface, was most apt. In matrimony
and in business he was conspicuously successful. He won the hand
of the beauteous Doña Arcadia Bandini, and from modest beginnings in hides and wines at Los Angeles and San Pedro he became
the wealthiest man in southern California. He acquired several
ranchos, including the Laguna and the Alamitos, and despite a setback in the drought of 1863–1864, he left holdings of more than 200
square miles of land to his widow in 1871. In the forties he held
a number of minor offices and in 1849 was a member of the constitu-

tional convention, but his reputation is properly that of a hard-headed businessman.

Thomas O. Larkin, who began in 1832 to make himself the foremost merchant at Monterey, was in many respects unlike his fellows. Instead of marrying a Californian he chose as his bride an American widow who had come to California on the ship that brought him. He mastered Spanish and gained the confidence of the provincial officials, but he did not become a ranchero and he was far from simpático with the Mexican regime. Aside from the rapid increase in his wealth, to which his close-fistedness was a contributing factor, Larkin is best known as the first United States consul, as Polk's secret agent looking toward American acquisition of the province, as a check upon Frémont, and as a prisoner of Castro's during the war. Except for his membership in the constitutional convention in 1849, the remaining decade of his life was spent in the management of his extensive property holdings.

After 1826 the annual increments included beaver trappers from the overland trails. Few if any of these men had set out with the express intention of settling in California. That they did so was as accidental as in the earlier years when sailors had begun to drop off the visiting ships. There was not much of uniformity about the way in which the mountain men fitted into California society. Some of them preferred the back country where trapping could be carried on, others shifted to otter hunting along the coast. Isaac Graham, though best known as a fighting man and a revolutionist, ran a distillery in the Pájaro Valley, near Monterey. J. J. Warner served an apprenticeship in Stearns' store and then went into business for himself before turning to ranching. On the whole, ranch life, rather than commercial activities in the coastal towns, seemed to be the preference of the mountain men. Consequently, they were a trifle less exposed to assimilating influences, yet many married daughters of the country and became dons in habit as well as in name.

Because of their expertness with rifle and knife the mountain men had greater military potentialities for good or ill than their compatriots who had come by ship. The Americanos who were sometimes enlisted on one or both sides of a revolution were mostly former fur trappers, and the most celebrated instance of friction between the provincial authorities and resident foreigners also centered around a group of former mountain men. In his successful revolution of

1836, Juan Bautista Alvarado had been supported by a group of Mexicans, Indians, ex-sailors, and trappers under the celebrated rifleman Isaac Graham. Four years later, Alvarado found this "foreign legion" more dangerous than useful. He brought about the arrest of Graham and some thirty-eight of his followers and shipped them off to Mexico. Through the intervention of British diplomacy they were released and permitted to return to California, Graham and about half the number actually doing so. The incident illustrates a tendency toward apprehension of the wild and reckless Americans whom the fur trade had contributed to California. On the other hand, by no means every mountain man was suspect. The majority had fitted very smoothly into provincial society.

Mention must also be made of one or two individuals who had come to California prior to 1841 but who do not fit into any of the classifications suggested above, of ex-sailors, commercial agents and businessmen, and ex-beaver trappers. John Marsh, for example, came in 1836 with the intention of settling, a purpose that perhaps should not be taken very seriously, since he had gone to Missouri and then to New Mexico with like intent. With his Harvard Bachelor of Arts diploma as a certificate, he practiced medicine at Los Angeles. Subsequently he moved to northern California and a rancho near Mt. Diablo, where he availed himself of Indian labor at a mere pittance, continued his practice of medicine for fees paid in cattle and produce, and spent his spare time urging acquaintances in the States to come to California. Far better educated than most Californians, Marsh was notoriously disagreeable and parsimonious. Yet at times he was an important influence in local politics, and his biographer gives him much of the credit for the Americanization of the province.

John A. Sutter was another who came with the intention of staying and of building up a fortune by pursuits more agricultural than commercial. Swiss by birth and American by adoption, Sutter came to California by way of Indiana, St. Louis, the Santa Fé Trail, the Rocky Mountains (where he joined a trapping party), the Columbia, the Sandwich Islands, and Alaska. From Oregon on, his travels had been motivated by the ambition to develop a feudal colony in California. He secured the necessary permission from Governor Alvarado in 1840 and selected a site in the unoccupied Sacramento Valley. His establishment began as a rancho, differing from other California ranchos only in that Sutter employed Kanakas and for-

eigners as well as Indians and Californians.   In 1841, however, he
bought out the Russians at Fort Ross, securing among other things
horses, cattle, a launch, and forty-odd assorted cannon.

With this artillery he was able to fortify his New Helvetia.   An
adobe fortress was erected, twelve guns were mounted, an armed
garrison was maintained, and sentries were posted.   Sutter was secure
not only against Indian attack but also against any interference by
the Mexican authorities in California, yet for the most part he was on
the best of terms with the provincial officials.

Multifarious economic pursuits characterized New Helvetia.   In
addition to the cattle ranch, Sutter engaged in extensive fur trade
and trapping, planted a large acreage in wheat, constructed an irrigation system, built a mill, a distillery, and a tannery, set some of his
Indian employees to blanket weaving, and ran his launch regularly
to San Francisco Bay.   The debt to the Russian American Fur Company was one incentive for this feverish activity; another was his
feeling of obligation to find or make work for any foreigners who
came and asked it.   "Hospitable, visionary, improvident land baron
of the Sacramento," Sutter has been well called.   The unbounded
hospitality that he extended to American immigrants is the real key
to his greatness.   It made his fort the mecca of the overland pilgrim-
ages.   He set weary travelers on their feet as McLoughlin did in
Oregon.   He sent relief parties as far east as Reno to assist the faltering steps of the less sturdy pioneers.   The military accouterments
and strategic location of his fort made impossible any Mexican exclusion of American immigrants.

By 1840 the number of foreign residents in California had grown,
according to Bancroft's estimates, to something like 380.   Of these
about fifty had come by the overland routes; the rest, in connection
with the various forms of sea-borne commerce.   By reason of old
age, infirmities, indifference, or inertness, a number of these 380 were
inconspicuous; but others constituted "an influential and highly respected element of the population, largely controlling the commercial
industry of the country."   The more thoughtful of these men expected
to see the day when California would cease to be Mexican, but few
were ready to take active steps to turn the province over to Great
Britain or the United States.   In fact, the majority of these foreign
residents, while more aggressive in business, were as conservative in
politics as the native Californians, and except in the Graham incident

(and there the fear was largely feigned), they were not a cause of apprehension to Mexico's California officials. In the stirring events of the next decade the attitude of these old timers continued to be conservative.

The Migration of 1841

The pioneer settlers of 1841 and thereafter are distinguished from these earlier residents by virtue of their greater utilization of the overland trails; their coming almost unanimously from the Midwest; their preference for the inland, unsettled, and agricultural portions of California; and their lesser mingling with the native Californians. Relatively few took California wives, and cultural assimilation did not progress rapidly. In view of what had happened in Texas, the presence of such an alien group was disquieting; and even without looking ahead to American annexation, it is obvious that these pioneers were a jarring note in the California scene. The pioneer settlers, furthermore, were competitors of the Californians in land ownership and crop production, without performing a useful economic service such as that of the resident foreign merchants along the coast.

Their coming was a predictable extension of the American westward movement. By 1841 the frontier of settlement had been pushed to the edge of the treeless and poorly watered plains area, a land regarded as unsuitable for white habitation and therefore called the Great American Desert. The panic of 1837 was a propulsive force, while beckoning to the Far West were the trails which the mountain men had broken, the trade route southwest to Santa Fé, and the path of fur men and missionaries to Oregon. Because the government laid claim to Oregon, the interest aroused by explorers, fur men, and missionaries was fanned by flag-waving editors and Congressional debates. California could not compete with Oregon in its hold on the attention of the United States—the migration figures for the early forties are in the ratio of eight or ten to one—but she did gain a secondary advantage from the Oregon publicity.

California was also the beneficiary of direct advertizing. The overland fur men, in particular, supplemented the reports of the Boston ship captains, and it was what they had to say of California's climate, wild game, fertility, resources, accessibility, and openness that led most directly to the coming of the pioneer settlers. Pattie, for example, after praising the province as "beautiful and sublime in scenery," added that it was "no less remarkable for uniting the advantage of healthfulness, a good soil, temperate climate and yet one of exceeding mildness, a happy mixture of level and elevated ground and vicinity to the sea." Dana, Kelley, and Thomas Jefferson Farnham were even more fulsome in their praise. And more seductive than the written word were the dulcet voices of some of these men who had tasted the wonders of California. The trapper Robidoux, for example, who addressed a meeting in Platte County, Missouri, in the fall of 1840, climaxed his rhapsody on California by extolling the salubrious climate. In answer to an ague-racked inquirer he asserted that the chills were unknown in California except for one fellow who had carried the disease in his system from Missouri. His shaking, Robidoux affirmed, was such a curiosity that "the people of Monterey went eighteen miles into the country to see him."

Consequent to Robidoux's speech and to his roseate answers to all the questions asked him, the Western Emigration Society was organized, and more than 500 persons signed a pledge to meet the next spring at Sapling Grove, just beyond Independence on the Missouri, prepared to journey to California. During the winter the Platte County merchants, fearful of losing so many of their customers, circulated discouraging reports about California. They made particularly good use of a clipping from the New York press in which Thomas Jefferson Farnham recanted all the praise of California that had gone into his volume on western travels. His first impression had been good, but when he visited Monterey a second time and without cause was lodged in jail, he had a complete reversal. Sabotaged thus, the Western Emigration Society dwindled from 500 would-be emigrants to a single person, young John Bidwell, erstwhile schoolmaster. At Sapling Grove he was soon joined, however, by sixty-eight others who had not promised but now proposed to go.

The group organized and selected as captain John Bartleson, perhaps the least qualified member of the entire party. He is remembered chiefly for his blunders, his selfishness, and his ineffectual leadership, especially over the latter part of the journey. Bidwell looms far more important, partly because he was the one member who had signed the original agreement, partly because he subsequently became one of California's leading men, partly because the best contemporary description of the journey is from his pen, but largely because of his informal assumption of command when the real diffi-

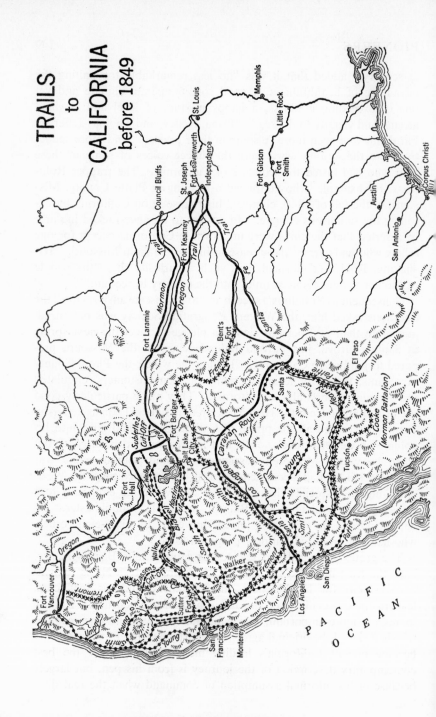

culties were encountered. Historians speak of the Bidwell-Bartleson party or, more simply, of the Bidwell party.

Although many of the group had resided near the frontier of settlement in Missouri and though all had heard a great deal about California, none had an accurate understanding of the intervening country through which they proposed to pass. Bidwell tells how "an intelligent man" with whom he had boarded showed him a standard map on which was shown a large lake in the vicinity of Great Salt Lake, but with two outlets, each appearing as large as the Mississippi and emptying into the Pacific. Bidwell's friend advised him to take along tools for canoe making, so that if the country proved too rough for their wagons they could reach California by water. In view of the fact that this was a fair example of the Bidwell party's advance knowledge of the West, their great good fortune is apparent in falling in with a small band of fur trappers and missionaries who were bound for Oregon. Father De Smet, of the latter group, was a regular globe trotter and particularly versed in northwestern travel. Thomas Fitzpatrick, leader of the trappers, was one of the best of the mountain men. From Sapling Grove to Soda Springs in the southern part of present Idaho, these expert guides smoothed the way for the California-bound emigrants. The route followed was the one that was soon to crystallize as the Oregon Trail. From Sapling Grove it led northwestward across a rolling prairie to the Platte, along this stream to the Forks, past Fort Laramie on the North Platte to Independence Rock and the Sweetwater, through South Pass to the Sandy and the Green, and across a divide to Bear Valley with its Steamboat and Soda Springs.

Thus far the pioneers had smooth sailing, though enlivened with many a stirring incident. Young Nicholas Dawson got himself the nickname "Cheyenne" by venturing out to hunt and shortly rejoining the train "without mule, gun or pistol and lacking most of his clothes," and reporting that thousands of Indians had despoiled him and were about to attack the train. Forty or fifty Cheyennes returned Dawson's belongings, professed friendship, and explained that they had disarmed the frightened hunter to prevent his shooting at them in his excitement. Another member of the party died of an accidentally self-inflicted gunshot wound. Four others turned back. But there was nothing particularly hazardous or difficult in this much of the

journey. Subsequent parties likewise found it comparatively easy
to negotiate this first half of the trail to Oregon or California.

Beyond Soda Springs the Bidwell party faced an unknown trail.
Half the group decided to forego the joys of California and continue
with their guides to Oregon. The other thirty-two struck out southwestward to open their own trail to California. They had asked
directions from the Hudson's Bay Company men at Fort Hall, but
none of these had traveled the route; and all that they could learn
was not to go too far to the north lest they get into rough terrain
where many fur men had died and not to go too far to the south
lest they get into a very arid country where they probably would die.
Sound advice but not very illuminating—yet, nothing daunted, the
thirty-two pioneers moved out.

Soon after leaving Bear Valley they found themselves under the
necessity of abandoning their wagons and much of their baggage and
of packing the bare essentials on their horses, mules, and oxen. At
making and fastening packs they were, of course, inexpert. The
result was great confusion, though soon they and their animals came
to a working understanding. Eventually they got across to the
south branch of the Humboldt. Over alkaline flats, and finding little
grass or game, they went on to Humboldt Sink. Bartleson and eight
of the best mounted men deserted the rest and pushed on ahead
toward California. Bidwell and the others struggled across the
desert to Carson River and the Balm, which was their grateful name
for the Walker. Here the Bartleson deserters straggled into camp,
none the better off for having gone ahead so selfishly.

After the last oxen had been killed and the meat jerked, the men
began the ascent of the Sierra. They were three weeks in finding a
pass and making their way across by the Walker and Stanislaus.
Fortunately for them the winter set in late, and though they did
not get over the divide until the very last of October, they escaped
being snowed in. Their supplies, however, were virtually exhausted,
and the grass and game of the San Joaquin Valley were most welcome.
Bidwell wrote with great feeling about their first California feast, a
fat coyote, of which his own share was only "the lights and the
windpipe." Unappetizing as this may sound, Bidwell thought it a
welcome change from mule meat. He threw the morsel on the coals
and "greedily devoured it."

A little farther on they came to better hunting, "elk tracks by the

thousands" and "hundreds of antelope in view." Many of the party
despondently reckoned 500 miles still to go and another mountain
range (the Coast Ranges loomed to westward) to cross before California would be reached. But the end of their six-month journey
was at hand. They soon reached the rancho of Dr. John Marsh
near Mt. Diablo and had their California geography set straight.

In the reminiscences of his mellower years "Cheyenne" Dawson
wrote very warmly of Marsh and the hospitality he extended to these
wayfarers. Bidwell concurred in the more general opinion that their
host was a skinflint. He charged what Bidwell considered an exorbitant price for a bullock and a small hog, the emigrants paying in
lead, powder, and knives. To this was added a fee of three dollars
apiece for getting them passports from the provincial authorities.
Worst of all, Marsh complained bitterly about the heavy expense
these emigrants were occasioning him, whereupon Bidwell was convinced that they had fallen in with "the meanest man in California."

Yet in fairness it should be pointed out that the emigrants had
made the mistake of butchering a bullock that had been broken to
the yoke. In view of the fact that the California authorities had
repeatedly taken a stand against the entrance of Americans by the
overland route and more recently had shown an anti-American spirit
in the Graham affair, it was not an easy task for Marsh to persuade
Vallejo to issue passports for the party. Furthermore, it was merely
by oversight that a passport was not secured for Bidwell. His three
days without food in the flea-infested jail at San José undoubtedly
sharpened his pen against Marsh.

Nevertheless, the significance of the Bidwell party does not lie in
these personal issues or even in the trying difficulties encountered
along the way. It lies rather in the fact that the party was the
entering wedge for the new type of migration to California. The
group soon scattered. A number of the men went to work for Sutter
at New Helvetia; most of the others—including Benjamin Kelsey's
wife and daughter, the first American woman and child to come
overland—settled in the northern part of the province. Flood tide
in the flow of Americans into California was not to come until the
gold rush and the boom of the eighties, but the arrival of these
pioneers marked the setting in of a steady current of migration.

A second party, twenty-five in number, reached southern California that same season. Included were Isaac Given and Albert

Toomes, who, having missed connections with the Bidwell party near Sapling Grove, had elected to follow the Santa Fé Trail with one of the trading caravans. New Mexico, when they arrived, was in a state of alarm because of an expected invasion from Texas, and consequently a number of American residents decided that the prudent thing for them to do was to move on to California. Given and Toomes attached themselves to this party under the leadership of William Workman and John Rowland. They left Abiquiu in September, followed the usual trade route, the Old Spanish Trail, across the Colorado, through southern Utah and Nevada, and over the Mojave Desert and Cajón Pass to Los Angeles, where they arrived some two months later. The party drove along a flock of sheep for food and traveled much of the distance in company with the annual band of traders from New Mexico. A dozen of these Americans intended to settle in California, and a few others actually did so, including Benjamin D. Wilson, who wanted to go on to China but could not make connections with a ship. Workman, Rowland, and Wilson became rancheros and prominent figures in southern California.

From Oregon a few other Americans moved to California in 1841. Among them was Joel P. Walker, brother of the famous fur trapper, Joseph Reddeford. Joel came with the land party of Wilkes' United States exploring expedition. He brought with him his wife and five children. Two other Oregonians brought their families. Their coming, though less spectacular than that of the Bidwell and Workman-Rowland parties, was not necessarily less significant.

Other Pioneers

In 1842 there was a temporary backwash in the tide of American migration to California. No parties came westward; instead, nine or ten men of the Bidwell party, led by Joseph B. Chiles and Charles Hopper, ascended the San Joaquin Valley, crossed Walker Pass, and by way of the Old Spanish Trail went on to Santa Fé and Missouri. Nevertheless, these men contributed to the advertisement of California as a land highly suitable for American settlement. Many others joined in the same work. John Marsh's correspondence included a nineteen-page letter to Commodore Jones expounding "some of the most interesting facts relative to California." Captain Henry A. Peirce despatched a similar letter to Honolulu, and eastern papers printed his comments on Hudson's Bay Company designs on California. John Rowland went back to New Mexico to fetch his family, while Bidwell forwarded to a printer friend in Missouri copy for a thirty-two page pamphlet on his journey to California. Publicity of this sort, coupled with increasing volume of migration to Oregon and with continued hard times in the Midwest, brought forth a larger migration in succeeding years.

The first additions of 1843 were recruited by Lansford W. Hastings, mostly from a party of 160 persons which he had led to Oregon the year before. Late in May he started south with some twenty-five armed men and their families to the number of fifty-three persons. Beyond Rogue River they met a band of cattle drivers, together with a few disillusioned California settlers. A third of Hastings' party turned back; the remaining thirty-five proceeded by way of Shasta River to California. On the way they had much unnecessary trouble with Indians. According to one informant, two or three of the party were continually taking pot shots at Indians. Hastings tells of one occasion when he did the same thing. Between Stony Creek and Colusa, on the upper Sacramento, a pitched battle took place, and twenty or thirty or forty redskins were killed. In the lower Sacramento Valley and the north bay region these Indian fighters settled down, but first two of the party, George Davis and a certain Miss Sumner, crossed over to New Helvetia and had Sutter marry them.

Joseph B. Chiles, veteran of the Bidwell expedition, organized the second party of 1843. In Missouri he gathered about fifty persons and led them over the standard trail to Fort Hall. There because of shortness of provisions it was decided that Chiles should go on with about ten men to Fort Boise and strike directly for California. He did so, getting in safely by a new route along the Malheur and Pit rivers, though there are intimations of fighting with the Indians and of one of his men having to be extricated from a bear trap.

The rest of Chiles' party was conducted by Joseph Reddeford Walker over the route he had explored a decade earlier. With comparatively little difficulty they took their wagons down the Humboldt Valley, across the desert to Walker Lake, and then "with infinite hardships" across the divide to Owens Valley. There they buried some of their impedimenta, burned the wagons, and packed on into the California settlements by way of Walker Pass. Chiles had been expected to come to their relief in the upper San Joaquin Valley. He did not come, or at least did not meet them, and they encountered their worst hardships in getting across the valley and over the next range of mountains to the Salinas Valley and Gilroy's rancho.

In 1844 a party of thirty-six persons put in its appearance from Oregon. Included were several members of the Kelsey family who had been shuttling back and forth between California and Oregon. More notable was the Stevens-Murphy party from Missouri by the regular route along the Platte and the Humboldt. At the foot of the Sierra this party split. The Murphys and a few others crossed by way of Lake Tahoe and the headwaters of the American River. Three men attempted to winter at Donner Lake, and one, Moses Schallenberger, seems to have stayed there till spring. The main body of the party pushed on into California by Truckee River and Pass, the first to utilize this subsequently favorite route and the first to get their wagons into California.

At least 250 persons came over the trails in 1845, the movement to California having been stimulated by reports carried back by the earlier settlers, by the showmanship of the government explorer John Charles Frémont, and by the strenuous efforts of Lansford W. Hastings, who returned to the States in 1844 to foment American migration to California. A detailed narrative of the experiences of the six or seven parties can be summarily excluded. Green Mc-Mahon and James Clyman brought in a party of forty-three persons from Oregon, among them James Marshall, who was to be the discoverer of California's gold. The Swasey-Todd train came by the Truckee route. One of the Sublettes, presumably Solomon, brought fifteen men from St. Louis described as the best equipped of any who had made the journey. The Grigsby-Ide party, also by Truckee, numbered more than 100 members, and Hastings conducted a much smaller party across the Sierra just before the winter snows closed the passes. There may have been still another party not recorded.

The Donner Tragedy

California-bound pioneers in 1846 were approximately twice as numerous as in the preceding year. After the customary toil and hardships the majority reached California safely, but despite such excellent trail records as Edwin Bryant's *What I Saw in California* and J. Q. Thornton's *Oregon and California in 1848*, these parties are usually lost sight of in the stark tragedy that overtook the Donner party.

In the vicinity of Fort Bridger, Lansford W. Hastings met the westward caravan in 1846 and tried to induce those California-bound to take a cutoff south of Great Salt Lake. Guided by James M. Hudspeth, Bryant's pack-train party followed this route without accident. Hastings personally guided a wagon party which reached the Humboldt after considerable difficulty. The Donner party, coming a trifle later, attempted the cutoff, got lost, and wasted valuable time and strength in clearing a road for their wagons. Loss of oxen here and in crossing the Great Salt Desert necessitated abandonment of essential supplies, and when finally they reached the Humboldt, they were both destitute and belated. William McCutcheon and Charles Stanton were sent ahead for supplies, and Stanton returned with two California Indians and five muleloads of beef and flour sent by Sutter.

An unusually early snow plunged the distraught group into panic. No leader rose in this crisis to insist on energetic coöperation to get over the divide or on careful preparations for a winter in camp. Instead, the party strung out along the trail and was thoroughly snowed in early in November by ten feet of snow. Shelter was inadequate, firewood had not been gathered, and most of the cattle had been lost in the storm. Inevitable tragedy ensued. There was starvation and cold and death at Donner Lake. The "forlorn-hope" party sought to escape on makeshift snowshoes to Sutter's Fort, but only seven of the fifteen got through, and they had subsisted upon the flesh of their dead companions and had shot their two Indian guides for the same purpose. Four rescue parties were necessary to extricate the others. Only forty-five of the seventy-nine who had been snowed in escaped, and their sufferings beggar description, even though some of the worst things said about their experiences are probably untrue. It was the worst western tragedy since the Yuma Massacre.

Smaller parties came over the trails in 1847 and 1848, while in 1846 there had arrived by the sea route from New York a party of 200 Mormons under the leadership of Elder Sam Brannan. Though the pioneers of these three years shared many of the experiences of those who had come earlier, in one respect they belong in a different category. They found the American flag waving over California, for the outbreak of the War with Mexico had afforded the opportunity to terminate the Mexican regime and to claim the province for the

United States. The military completed this step, yet the pioneer settlers of the early forties had laid the foundation for it, and there is good reason to believe that, without any assistance from the military, the infiltration of settlers—the process whereby Texas and Oregon had been acquired—would soon have achieved the same result in California. Viewed in this light the pioneers of 1841 through 1845 appear not as mere curiosities, objects of interest because of their early appearance in California, but as effective agents in the epic of American expansion.

At the risk of anticlimax, however, it should be observed that the vast majority of the pioneer settlers came to California because they envisioned an opportunity for a better livelihood and not for the sake of acquiring the province for the United States. The majority did not scruple about professing the Catholic religion or applying for Mexican citizenship. Paradoxically, a large number of the pioneer settlers did not settle but drifted on to Oregon or returned to the States, and consequently the "foreign colony" in the province was only increased from 380 in 1840 to about 680 at the end of 1845, a fact which would imply that much significance still attached to the older settlers who antedated the covered wagon. To the pioneers, however, goes the credit for setting in motion the first conscious migration to California and for bringing the province within the scope of the westward-moving American frontier.

15

AMERICAN ACQUISITION

A HALF CENTURY of contact with California preceded its annexation to the United States. The flag followed trade, as represented by otter hunters, hide and tallow men, whalers, and beaver trappers. It came only after Americans to the number of several hundred had moved into California as chance settlers, resident traders, or members of the first covered wagon trains. Annexation was also preceded by several preliminary moves on the part of United States officials which foreshadowed the eventual result.

The United States Looks toward California

Official interest is traceable to many of the same factors which had attracted individuals. California's climate, fertile soil, and open spaces, her proven resources in furs, hides, and tallow, and the utility of her ports for China ships and whalers were considerations which the government could not overlook. In addition, the increasing body of Americans resident in California was conducive to official concern, and the idea of Manifest Destiny had obvious implications of particular interest to the men in charge of national policy. The inadequacy of Mexican control, furthermore, was significant because it presaged some change in sovereignty. In view of the policy enunciated in the Monroe Doctrine, the national leaders were vitally concerned as to the outcome. British or French control of California, of which there seemed some possibility, would be viewed with alarm. The strategic value of San Francisco Bay was again something of peculiar significance to the government.

Andrew Jackson made the first overt attempt at acquisition when in 1835 he authorized his diplomatic agent in Mexico to offer half a million dollars for San Francisco Bay and the northern part of the province. His interest had been aroused by the representations of his minister to Mexico, the headstrong and unprincipled Anthony Butler, who later was branded "a national disgrace" and by Jackson himself "a cantankerous, incompetent rascal." Early in the course of his residence in Mexico, Butler concluded that every Mexican official had his price; he advocated "bribery and corruption," or "presents if the term is more appropriate," as the open sesame to advantage in Mexico. His analysis may have been sound, though probably not when he estimated that $500,000 judiciously applied would secure any desired portions of the Mexican domain, but he erred grievously in making this unflattering opinion openly known in Mexico City. The Mexicans were naturally insulted, Butler's usefulness in Mexico was at an end, and the prospect of a successful purchase was shattered.

Although foiled in this effort, Jackson did not give up. Butler had amplified his original interest in Texas to comprehend "the whole of that tract or territory known as New Mexico, and higher and lower California, an empire in itself, a paradise in climate, . . . rich in minerals and affording a water route to the Pacific through the Arkansas and Colorado rivers." Butler's rosy geographical fallacies were supplemented by the sober praise of San Francisco Bay by Lieutenant William A. Slacum, whom Jackson sent to Oregon and California in 1836 to obtain all such information as might prove "interesting or useful to the United States." Slacum's observations were mostly of the Northwest, but he was no more enthusiastic about the Willamette Valley than insistent that the United States must obtain Puget Sound and San Francisco Bay. Jackson was already moving in that direction. Early in 1837, when Santa Anna came to Washington following his defeat at the hands of Sam Houston, Jackson proposed American mediation between Mexico and Texas on the basis of annexation of Texas with a boundary along the Rio Grande and the thirty-eighth parallel (on the erroneous assumption that this would include San Francisco Bay). Mexico would be indemnified with $3,500,000. He also urged the Texans to lay claim to California, as a means of paralyzing the opposition of the North and East to annexation, by giving a harbor on the Pacific. Yet neither through Butler, Santa Anna, nor Texas was Jackson able to acquire California.

During Van Buren's presidency (1837 to 1841) there were no direct attempts to acquire California, but the question was kept open by several reports concerning the province. Alvarado's pronouncement for California independence in November, 1836, was viewed with alarm by the United States consul at the Hawaiian Islands. A Russian protectorate was rumored, he reported, in which case the United States' designs on California would be thwarted. Slacum's report was laid before Congress in December, 1837, where its Oregon proposals were taken up by Senator Linn of Missouri and elaborated in his famous bill and report. Both to the Senate and to the nation it was the Oregon cause which Linn pleaded, yet California got a measure of attention as the tail to the Oregon kite. Again in 1839, when Hall J. Kelley, archproponent of the Americanization of Oregon, laid a long memorial before Congress, he devoted half his space to California, particularly the northern part. He explained this attention to California not merely on the score of the negotiations between the United States and Mexico with regard to the province, but more because he regarded its future addition to the United States as "most unquestionably a matter to be desired."

Later in Van Buren's administration the Graham affair elicited further official interest. The British consul and viceconsul at Tepic were primarily responsible for the release of the prisoners, and the United States is sometimes attributed a Machiavellian cleverness in delaying interference in order to build up a claim against Mexico which might eventually lead to the cession of California. Certainly our successive agents in Mexico, Powhatan Ellis, Waddy Thompson, and Duff Green, endeavored to make the most of the incident as a bargaining point. It led also to a petition from American merchants in California that the Navy station a ship permanently in California waters to protect them against arbitrary miscarriage of justice. The Secretary of the Navy responded by enlarging the Pacific squadron and instructing the commander to explore and chart the Gulf of California, to protect American whalers, and to guard the interests of Americans in California.

With the arrival of Waddy Thompson as Tyler's minister to Mexico in 1842, the proposal of ceding California to the United States was again brought forward. Though he had never seen the land of which he wrote, Thompson was a California enthusiast of the first water. In his first letter from Mexico he lauded the province as "the richest, the most beautiful, and the healthiest country in the world." He mentioned the commercial ascendancy that would accrue to the United States through possession of the ports of San Francisco, San Diego, and Monterey, coupled with internal communications by way of the Arkansas River. He dwelt on the advantage to American whalers and praised California as potentially "the granary of the Pacific." He was highly hopeful that both California and Texas might be secured through cancellation of American claims on the impoverished Mexican treasury, but of the two he considered California incomparably the more valuable.

Secretary of State Daniel Webster professed interest in Thompson's plan and gave him canny counsel about how to approach the Mexican officials. It would be better, he wrote, to profess interest only in the port of San Francisco and if possible to maneuver the Mexicans into offering the cession as a means of settling American claims. Webster also sought to arrange the cession of California by means of a three-party arrangement between the United States, Great Britain, and Mexico. By the terms of this Tripartite Agreement the United States would have contented itself with the Columbia as the northern boundary, would have received Texas and Upper California, and would have paid off American and English creditors and bondholders of Mexico. Although high hopes were held for this plan, and although Webster was once on the point of sailing to England to conclude negotiations, it came to nought. American expansionists balked at surrendering so much of Oregon, and the English did not warm to the plan. A more fundamental defect was that Mexican benefits would have been so indirect; she was to receive no cash, but merely to have her indebtedness somewhat reduced. Finally, a circumstance beyond Webster's control, the famous Jones incident, rendered his scheme completely unworkable.

Commodore Thomas ap Catesby Jones was then in command of the American naval forces in the Pacific with general instructions which took cognizance of the supposed British designs on California. When a despatch delivered to him at Callao, Peru, gave him the impression that the United States and Mexico were at war, he naturally concluded that it was his duty to hasten to California and take possession before Mexico could hand the province over to England for safekeeping. Arriving at Monterey on October 19, 1842, Jones seized the town. Because Californians were unaware of any war and the defenses were in their usual state of disrepair, no fighting was necessary. The next day Jones decided that it was all a mistake, that there was no war. He apologized, restored Monterey undamaged to the proper authorities, and sailed south to San Pedro. There a carriage was provided for his conveyance to Abel Stearns' house in Los Angeles, where Jones and his staff were wined and dined by Governor Micheltorena—and presented with a well-padded bill for the damages done. The Californians had let the Monterey incident pass as a joke, though a rather humiliating one. Micheltorena had fussed and fumed, proclaimed the measures he was about to take to expel the invader, and "advanced" from San Fernando to Los Angeles. In Mexico there was deeper indignation, which was fanned still higher upon receipt of reports of bitter denunciation of Jones' action by anti-administration Americans. Thereupon, Thompson was forced to admit that it was "wholly out of the question to do anything as to California."

Jones' seizure of Monterey, though based on misinformation, illustrates the prevalance of apprehension that the British harbored designs upon California. Thompson had adverted to such designs. "I have information upon which I can rely," he reported in one of his letters, "that an agent of this government is now in England negotiating for the sale, or what is precisely the same thing, the mortgage of Upper California for the loan of fifteen millions." Later he reported certain knowledge that the treaty had been made and that within ten years the province would be English.

But Thompson did not originate the bogey of British designs. As early as 1839 the proposal to write off Mexican debts through the transfer of California had cropped out in a published book; a book, furthermore, written by a British official, Alexander Forbes, vice-consul at Tepic. His *History of California* was the first book in English devoted specifically to California. Although containing much historical material, it was frankly intended as propaganda to bring about British colonization. Forbes outlined a detailed plan whereby British creditors would write off $50,000,000 of Mexican bonds, take over California, and recover their investment through operations modeled after those of the Hudson's Bay Company or the British East India Company. Many American journalists jumped to the conclusion that Forbes' proposal was actually in operation. Of the same opinion was Sir George Simpson of the Hudson's Bay Company, who visited San Francisco in 1841. After commenting on the natural advantages of the province, Simpson affirmed his belief that the Californians would "require very little encouragement" to declare their independence of Mexico and place themselves under the protection of Great Britain.

Actually, the British government was not at this time ready to take aggressive measures toward securing California, but in view of semiofficial statements such as the above, in view of England's established reputation for imperial ambitions, and in view of the Anglo-American rivalry in progress over Texas and Oregon, it was natural for American officials to conclude that England was moving to acquire California. And however uninterested the home government was, British officials in California and Mexico and on naval vessels in the Pacific were thoroughly determined to snatch the province out of the grasp of the United States and to turn it over, if possible, to Great Britain.

Warnings of British designs on California were reiterated. Duff Green in 1844 and Wilson Shannon in 1845 reported from Mexico that "the mortgage on the Californias" was about to be foreclosed. The amount now became $26,000,000. The American press took up the refrain. Santa Anna's opponents in Mexico added to the furor by disclosing that he had been negotiating with Britain for the alienation of Mexican territory, and the Americans seized upon this as more positive proof of British machinations.

Polk's Aggressive Program

Anglophobia took a further upward turn with the inauguration of James K. Polk as president. A son of Tennessee, nurtured in Jacksonian democracy, and elected on a platform stressing a firm stand against Britain in Oregon and in Texas, Polk was ready to believe the worst about British designs upon California. In addition to the data which he found in the files of the Department of State, Polk's own agents furnished evidence of Britain's aggressive attitude. William S. Parrott, his confidential agent in Mexico, sounded the old alarm in a new guise. "Great Britain," he wrote, "has greatly increased her Naval Forces in the Pacific, the object of which as stated is to take possession of and hold Upper California, in case of war between the United States and Mexico."

In a subsequent letter Parrott reported still another British device for obtaining California. A young Irish priest named Eugene McNamara had asked for a grant of land in the province. His aims, he said, were to serve Catholicism and his countrymen and "to put an obstacle in the way of further usurpations on the part of an irreligious and anti-Catholic nation." Father McNamara's plan of bringing 10,000 Irish colonists to a California grant of 3,000 square leagues was not immediately approved, but early in 1846 he was encouraged to go to the province to make selection of suitable lands. In June he chose a location embracing most of the eastern half of the San Joaquin Valley. The provincial assembly at Los Angeles approved his request on July 6, and Governor Pío Pico made the grant at Santa Barbara a week or so later. Because of the raising of the American flag on July 7, Pico seems to have predated the grant as of July 4, thus making it illegal, in that it was made prior to the action of the assembly. Furthermore, the grant considerably exceeded the legal maximum of eleven square leagues. McNamara made no effort to get the United States to confirm his title, but the scheme was potentially alarming to Americans in California and in Washington, and it was later adduced by Frémont and his friends in their rationalization of the Bear Flag revolt.

Of greater influence upon Polk's policy was a Larkin letter of July 10, 1845. In it he reported the rumor that British merchants were financing the impending Mexican reinforcement of California and that the appointment of British and French salaried consuls to California was particularly suspicious. Neither nation had sufficient commercial contact with the province to justify such an appointment, and the British appointee, James Alexander Forbes (not Alexander, author of the *History of California*), was undoubtedly a secret agent for his government and a servant of Larkin's "Colossus of the North," the Hudson's Bay Company.

Communications such as these confirmed Polk in his distrust of Britain and determined several features of his presidential program. Fighting fire with fire, he commissioned Larkin as secret agent in California to "exert the greatest vigilance in discovering and defeating any attempts which may be made to acquire a control" over California. Larkin was to persuade the Californians to resist any endeavors to transfer the province to Great Britain or France, and the United States, it was promised, would sustain them in such resistance. Likewise, the instructions to John Slidell, who was authorized to offer Mexico as much as $40,000,000 for California, harp upon the necessity of counteracting "the influence of foreign Powers exerted against the United States in Mexico" and particularly upon the necessity of preventing the cession of California to any European power. In his first message to Congress, Polk reasserted the Monroe Doctrine in clearer and more vigorous language. California was obviously in his thoughts when he asserted that "the people of this continent alone have the right to decide their own destiny. Should any portion of them, constituting an independent state, propose to unite themselves with our confederacy, this will be a question for them and for us to determine without any foreign interference." And it was equally so when he stated that "no future European colony or dominion, shall with our consent, be planted or established on any part of the North American continent." Finally, the genuineness of his apprehension of Great Britain is revealed in a remark of his after the ultimate acquisition of California. "The fact that it has become a part of the Union and cannot be subject to a European power," he reflected at the close of the war, "constitute ample indemnity for the past."

Nevertheless, it would be misleading to suggest that Polk's interest in California was entirely a consequence of his anti-British proclivities. He had drunk deep of other parts of Jacksonian philosophy, he was a "Manifest Destinarian," and he was not unmindful of direct benefits which would accrue to the United States through possession of the province. Prior to his inauguration he had determined upon annexation as one of the four major aims of his administration. He confided it to George Bancroft and recorded it for posterity in his diary. On September 16 he announced his purpose to the Cabinet, and within a fortnight Washington correspondents were predicting the peaceful acquisition of California. This purpose of Polk's is particularly worth noting, since he, more than any other President in the nation's history, carried out the positive program which he set for himself at the time of his inauguration.

First, Polk attempted to purchase California. In Mexico, however, the cardinal political principle was still the same one reported by Duff Green in 1844, namely, that it was regarded as "treason to sell any part of the public domain to the United States." That this was the situation Polk soon discovered. Having been given to understand that an emissary would be received, he sent Slidell with authorization to pay $40,000,000 for California. Unfortunately, Slidell was preceded by a rumor that he had a million dollars with which to bribe the Mexican government. In a bid for popular favor, President

Herrera refused to receive Slidell, but this did not suffice to prevent the success of the Paredes revolution. The new government, perhaps encouraged by Britain and France, was even more opposed to treating with Slidell, who shortly abandoned all hopes of effecting a purchase.

Meanwhile, Polk had set in motion another procedure for acquiring California. He had commissioned Larkin as his secret agent and had ordered him to undertake, though discreetly, peaceful persuasion of the Californians to break away from Mexico and seek the protection of the United States. This was not the "Texas game," to be played by American settlers insinuating themselves into the province. Rather, as Larkin understood it, it was to be played by the Californians. To them he turned with discretion at least equal to Polk's. Abel Stearns at Los Angeles, Jacob Leese at Sonoma, and J. J. Warner in the extreme south were made privy to the scheme and threw in their support. Native Californians were also enlisted; Mariano G. Vallejo was an advocate of annexation to the United States, and General Castro gave Larkin private endorsement of a written plan for liberating California from Mexico as soon as the number of foreign settlers was sufficiently increased. Before relating how this second plan of Polk's went awry, it is necessary to introduce another manifestation of United States interest in California, namely, the government explorer.

Slacum was the first official investigator. Then in 1841 Lieutenant Charles Wilkes arrived on the coast with the Pacific Exploring Expedition, which had been sent out in the interests of the American whaling industry. After extended observations in the Northwest, Wilkes sent a detachment overland to California and sailed south to join forces at San Francisco Bay. He developed no personal enthusiasm for the province, though after a thorough examination of San Francisco Bay he admitted that it was "one of the finest, if not the very best harbor in the world." An abbreviated account of Wilkes' expedition was published, but his full report was held confidential and then embalmed in a very limited edition.

Frémont's Adventures

Not so with the findings of John Charles Frémont, a natural-born showman and his own best publicity agent. His overland journeys abounded in electrifying experiences, such as the winter crossing of the Sierra, which exerted a tremendous popular appeal.   As the son-in-law of Senator Benton he was in line for special attention from the government, and his *Reports* benefited from his membership in that choice circle of writers who acquire by marriage a very attractive literary style.   It is easy to understand how Frémont became the best known westerner, how he was chosen by the Republican party as its first nominee for President, and how enthusiastic biographers came to do him excessive homage as "A Man Unafraid," "The Pathfinder," and "The West's Greatest Adventurer."

Of Frémont's five expeditions, the second and third were most significant.   The first, in 1842, reached no farther west than South Pass and the Rockies.   On the second, in 1843 and 1844, he came west by Bent's Fort, South Pass, and the Oregon Trail to The Dalles; then south along the eastern side of the Cascades and the Sierra Nevada, and across the Sierra by way of Carson Pass in the dead of winter.   After recuperating his men for a month at Sutter's Fort and having purchased fresh horses and supplies, he ascended the San Joaquin Valley, crossed Tehachapi Pass, followed the Old Spanish Trail into southern Utah, and returned to the States by way of Sevier River, Utah Lake, the headwaters of the Grand and the Arkansas, and Bent's Fort.

This was a notable journey, even though most of it was over beaten trails, except as Frémont turned aside to examine wonders of nature. And it was a personal achievement, even though Frémont relied heavily on his fur-trapping guides, Thomas Fitzpatrick, Kit Carson, and Joseph Walker.   This journey illustrates the enigmatic nature of Frémont's career; riddles persist despite the efforts of eminent historians, from Bancroft and Royce to Nevins and Goodwin, to solve them.   Why, for example, did Frémont include a howitzer in the equipment of this supposedly purely scientific expedition?   Did he really believe that the Buenaventura River existed?   Was the wretched condition of his animals at the site of present-day Carson City sufficient explanation for his decision to cross the Sierra into California?

These and other questions may always baffle, but there exists no doubt that the principal importance of the journey was in fanning eastern interest in the West.   From November, 1843, until the next July, while Frémont traveled from the Columbia to the Kansas, no word of his whereabouts reached the States.   There were allusions to the "lost expedition," and national concern was felt for its safety comparable to contemporary anxiety over some unreported flier or polar expedition. The circumstance awakened interest; appearance of his volume clinched it. Thousands of copies were struck off by government and private presses, and it became the principal popular source of information about the West.

In the spring of 1845 Frémont was on the trail again with a party of sixty-two men. His route was over the regular trail to Salt Lake, thence by the Humboldt Valley to Walker Lake. There, since winter was fast approaching, he decided to take fifteen men across to Sutter's Fort, while Joseph Walker led the main party across the Sierra by way of Walker Pass. A rendezvous was appointed at the "River of the Lake," just west of Walker Pass; but failing to find the place, Frémont proceeded to Yerba Buena and Monterey, and eventually was joined by his men in the Santa Clara Valley. Through Consul Larkin he obtained permission for his "scientific" party to spend the rest of the winter in California, but on condition that they remain back from the coast. The appearance of the entire party at Salinas convinced the provincial authorities that the American leader was acting in bad faith. A blustering correspondence passed back and forth, which reached a climax in Castro's order that Frémont depart forthwith. For three days Frémont remained in his fortified camp atop Hawk's Peak; then he retired toward Oregon "slowly and growlingly."

In the Klamath Lake region he was overtaken by Lieutenant Archibald Gillespie, who, in the guise of a convalescent merchant, had hurried to California by way of Veracruz, Mazatlán, and Hawaii as a special messenger for President Polk. The despatch that he delivered verbally to Larkin was the one described above. Its contents have long been known to historians. What message he delivered to Frémont has been the subject of much controversy. Presumably he vouchsafed the substance of the despatch to Larkin, though Frémont later expressed doubt and disbelief that Larkin had been commissioned as Polk's confidential agent. Gillespie delivered a packet of letters from Senator Benton, but their significance is minimized because of the Senator's slight connection with the Polk administration and because it was only an afterthought of the Department of State to send them by Gillespie. The special messenger was decided upon perhaps ten days after the Larkin instructions were formulated. He was privately instructed by Polk and Secretary of the Navy Bancroft, and again privately by the President. It is possible, therefore, as some writers suggest, that Gillespie brought Frémont a message that went considerably beyond the Larkin instructions. If, on the other hand, there were no secret instructions, the fact that Gillespie had traveled a dangerous 500 miles to overtake him was ample justification for Frémont's turning back to California. He had no hesitation about this being the thing he should do, but there was another duty to discharge first, namely, to retaliate upon the Klamaths for the killing of two or three of his men. Vengeance was swift and ample, and apparently sweet.

By the latter part of May, Frémont was encamped at Marysville Buttes, on the Sacramento. His purposes were not transparent. To his wife and his father-in-law he wrote that he was on the point of returning to Missouri. The same intention was announced to Captain Montgomery of the U. S. S. *Portsmouth,* though qualified by the remark that emergencies might rise to detain him.

The emergency arose almost immediately, and so we cannot be absolutely sure of the genuineness of his intention. Opinions of his subsequent conduct vary. One suggestion is that he was fulfilling Polk's guarded orders to bring on hostilities in California which would perhaps lead to war with Mexico and certainly to the annexation of California. Yet his actions seem to indicate that his first endeavor was to avoid any hostilities which would jeopardize Polk's reiterated plan of acquiring California through the peaceful persuasion of the Californians.

Excited American settlers began to come to Frémont's camp. For some months they had been kept on edge by rumors of war. The Graham incident, the Hawk's Peak affair, and Castro's recommendation that the Mexican government buy out Captain Sutter, presumably as a preliminary to forbidding further American immigration, contributed to make these frontiersmen uneasy. It was also rumored that the Californians were inciting the Indians to attack the Americans, and Frémont's experience with the Klamaths was thought of as a case in point. The presence of his armed force served as a rallying point for these alarmed and disaffected settlers, yet Frémont at first would not concert with them against the California officials. He even dissuaded Carson and others of his men from resigning from the service to join with the settlers. Forty-five years later Frémont

claimed that he "knew the hour had come" before he turned back
from the Klamath region, but his actions at Marysville indicate that
he was not yet ready to join in the violence and thereby ruin all
chances of conciliating the native population and winning them over
to the United States. He was not above suggesting lines of procedure to the settlers and thus had a measure of direct responsibility
for what unfolded.

A band of settlers "who had nothing to lose" launched the revolt
on June 10 by seizing a herd of horses belonging to Castro. The
Californians supposed this to be an act of robbery rather than rebellion. Four days later a similar group descended upon Sonoma and
surrounded the house of Mariano Vallejo. "Almost the whole
party," according to one of its members, "was dressed in leather
hunting-shirts, many of them very greasy; taking the whole party
together, they were about as rough a looking set of men as one could
well imagine." Vallejo's wife urged that he flee out the back door,
but instead he opened the front door and asked the business of the
intruders. He soon discovered that he was to consider himself a
prisoner; and then, through his son-in-law, Jacob Leese, negotiations
proceeded, but in ludicrous fashion.

Ezekiel Merritt, Robert Semple, and William Knight entered as
commissioners to arrange with Vallejo, Salvador Vallejo, and Victor Prudon the terms of surrender. After a long wait the Bear
Flaggers sent John Grigsby to expedite the procedure, and after
another long pause they sent in William B. Ide. The latter found
the preceding emissaries befuddled by Vallejo's aguardiente. Ide declined Vallejo's "potent hospitality," and the negotiations were speed-
ily finished. There was a written guaranty of protection for non-
combatants. There was talk of paroling the prisoners, but instead,
the Vallejos, Prudon, and Leese were sent to Frémont's camp and
thence to Sutter's Fort. The violence to Vallejo was an unfortunate
misdirection of effort on the part of the Bear Flaggers, both in the
way that it was mismanaged and because Vallejo had been a firm
advocate of American acquisition.

The Bear Flaggers went on to construct their flag, a grizzily bear
passant and a lone star on a field of white, bordered at the bottom
by a broad red stripe, and beneath the bear the caption "California
Republic." William B. Ide proclaimed that the aim of the movement was to set up a "Republican Government" in place of the

"Military Despotism" which had seized the mission property, oppressed the people, and made enormous exactions on imports. He promised that the new government would guarantee civil and religious liberty, would detect and punish crime, would encourage industry, virtue, and literature, and would leave unshackled "Commerce, Agriculture, and Mechanism." In peroration he summed up his political credo, saying "that a Government to be prosperous and happifying in its tendency must originate with its people . . . that its Citizens are its Guardians, its officers are its Servants, and its Glory their reward." In style and in ideology Ide's proclamation is at variance with the usual picture of the Bear Flaggers as uncouth ruffians.

Near San Rafael the Bear Flaggers fought their one battle, the practically bloodless "Battle of Olompali," in which one or two Californians were killed and a number of horses captured. Soon thereafter, moved by the capture and execution (and some add mutilation) of two Americans on their way to the Fitch rancho on Russian River for a barrel of powder, Frémont announced his adhesion to the movement. His sixty men joined, as did the other settlers of the vicinity. There was maneuvering back and forth in the north bay region, and Castro cleverly extricated his small force from the Marin peninsula; but a few days later official tidings of the Mexican War arrived, and the Bear Flag movement had no further necessity. The charge is made, in fact, that it never had any excuse; that it occasioned unnecessary violence, engendered ill-will, ended all hopes of peaceful annexation, and neither saved the province from British seizure nor hastened American acquisition. We are observing, however, an interrupted movement, one that did not run its full course. Had the Mexican War postponed its intrusion, the Bear Flaggers might easily have extended their sway over northern California at least in a Texas-like preliminary to annexation to the United States.

The War with Mexico

The causes of the Mexican War, of course, pertain largely to Texas and to the question of title to all of Texas, not merely to the strip between the Nueces and Rio Grande. Another factor was Polk's ambition to add California and other southwestern territory to the national domain. His efforts to purchase this area had failed. The method of peaceful persuasion upon the Californians through the confidential agency of Larkin was not given time enough to operate;

nor was the Bear Flag Revolt, which Polk did not start but probably would have approved. The method of conquest remained. The war was really fought and won south of the Rio Grande and in the Valley of Mexico, but Polk was careful to see that the coveted territories were occupied. The ap Jones drama was reënacted, this time by a less impetuous hero. Commodore John D. Sloat, commander of the Pacific fleet, had standing instructions that virtually duplicated Jones'. As soon as he was assured that war had broken out, he sailed to Monterey in order to forestall any possible intervention by Admiral Seymour of the British Navy. Although Sloat entered port on July 2, he delayed announcing the war or taking possession until the seventh. Just why he held off is not clear, though his instructions were to preserve if possible the good will of the inhabitants. It required a combination of Larkin's persuasion, the urging of his officers, the apprehension of British intervention, and the realization that the Bear Flaggers must be forestalled in acquiring control over the province to spur Sloat to action. On the ninth there were flag raisings at San Francisco and Sonoma, and two days later at Sutter's Fort.

Sloat's proclamation may be criticized as a partisan document casting the entire blame for the war upon Mexico and exaggerating Taylor's initial success against General Arista. It is interesting, however, for the conciliatory tone in which Sloat maintained, "Altho' I come in arms with a powerful force, I do not come among them as enemy to California; but on the contrary I come as their best friend," and for its point-blank assertion, "henceforward California will be a portion of the United States." Sloat went on to promise the Californians full privileges of citizenship, freedom "to worship the creator in a way most congenial to each ones sense of duty," freedom from revolution, and the right to import from the United States free of duty and all foreign goods at one quarter of the duty Mexico imposed. He predicted that under the American flag the province was bound to "improve more rapidly than any other on the continent of America."

On July 15 Sloat resigned his command to Commodore Robert F. Stockton, and a more vigorous policy ensued. The Bear Flag men were enlisted as volunteers in the United States Army with Frémont as major and Gillespie as captain. Stockton determined to extend the conquest into southern California. He also issued a bombastic and inflammatory proclamation full of threats against the California leaders and devoid of Sloat's assurances to the people of the province. On August 13 he entered Los Angeles and on the seventeenth proclaimed: "The Flag of the United States is now flying from every commanding position in the Territory, and California is entirely free from Mexican dominion." So far, so good; but again with unnecessary harshness he went on to decree martial law, to forbid the carrying of arms, and to establish a strict ten o'clock curfew.

Revolt and Reconquest

In southern California, as in the north, the Californians had offered no resistance to the forces of the United States, and the change had been altogether peaceful. But Stockton had erred in the tone of his proclamation; he also made the mistake of leaving Gillespie in command of Los Angeles with an inadequate garrison, and Gillespie unwisely issued tactless regulations further restraining the Angeleños from certain harmless and accustomed enjoyments. On September 23 Gillepie was made aware of the extent of American unpopularity. Sérbulo Varela and other semi-outlaws, filled "with patriotism and perhaps with wine," made a disturbing though innocuous attack on the American barracks, and when Gillespie sought to arrest these disturbers, he found most of the populace arrayed against him.

The first major engagement was at Isaac Williams' Chino Rancho, where B. D. Wilson and a score of Americans were forced to surrender to the Californians. Heartened by this victory, the Californians tightened their siege upon Gillespie's force, which had taken refuge on Fort Hill back of the plaza. Gillespie managed to get a messenger, Juan Flaco (Lean John) Brown, off to Stockton. After a narrow escape from the Angeleños, Brown rode madly to Monterey and on to San Francisco. He covered the 500 miles in five days, but Gillespie could not hold out even this long and had surrendered. He was allowed to take his men to San Pedro on condition that they embark immediately.

Before this ship sailed, the relief party from San Francisco appeared, and Gillespie's men landed again to assist in the recapture of Los Angeles. The ensuing Battle of the Old Woman's Gun, sometimes called the Battle of Domínguez Rancho, was a decisive California victory. On October 8 the Americans marched inland fifteen miles to Domínguez Rancho. California horsemen hovered about, but the principal obstacles were the heat, dust, and thirst. The next day José Carillo's men resisted further advance. They were indifferently armed with carbines and homemade willow lances, but they were excellently mounted and had a four-pound swivel gun that they used with telling effect. A Mexican woman had secreted the gun at the time of Stockton's entrance into Los Angeles; now it was lashed to the front half of a wagon's running gear. Ignacio Aguilar fired it with a lighted cigarette, and reatas whipped it out of the Americans' grasp and back into position. The Americans wore themselves out in futile efforts to capture the gun; the Californians were "content to let the gun do the fighting," which it did so well that the invaders fell back to San Pedro. It was a victory for California horsemen, powder made at San Gabriel, and a salute-firing cannon from the plaza.

Two other forces were converging on the Angeleños. Frémont, with more than 300 men, was marching south from Monterey, and General Stephen W. Kearny was headed west from Fort Leavenworth. Kearny's march was part of Polk's general plan of occupying the Mexican areas whose cession was desired. New Mexico was the first objective; over this province Kearny gained control without serious difficulty. Leaving the greater part of his command as a garrison at Santa Fé, with 300 dragoons he set out by the Gila route for California. On the Rio Grande below Socorro he met Kit Carson on his way to Washington with dispatches from Stockton. When Carson, who had left the settlements prior to the Los Angeles outburst, showed him Stockton's official statement that American control was already established, Kearny decided to send most of his men back to Santa Fé, but he induced Carson to guide him to the coast.

The desert crossing involved frightful hardships. Then, before his men or animals had recovered their strength, Kearny found himself opposed by a large force of Californians under Andrés Pico. At San Pascual the Californians retreated before an American attack, but as soon as the pursuers were strung out and disunited, Pico's men turned and attacked. Sixteen or eighteen Americans were killed and as many wounded, while the Californians had only a few minor wounds. The survivors were still at bay before the California horsemen. Kit Carson and Lieutenant Edward F. Beale slipped through to San Diego; Stockton sent out 200 marines and soldiers, and with their help Kearny got in to San Diego on December 12.

To the War Department Kearny reported San Pascual as an American victory. He had come off in possession of the battlefield, though with practically all the casualties. He could find, however, feeble excuse for bringing on the battle. Even had he won a decisive victory, the California revolt would have remained virtually as strong. He must answer for sending his men into battle on worn-out mules and half-broken horses, with their powder wet and with no weapons but clubbed guns and rusted swords, against skilled and well-mounted lancers. The conclusion must be that the Californians were underrated. Yet Pico appears to have planned the battle and the tactics most vaguely, and when reinforcements arrived, he disappeared entirely.

Weeks passed before Kearny and Stockton were ready to move on to Los Angeles. January 8 found their force at the upper ford of the San Gabriel, with a California force under José María Flores commanding the opposite bank. The Californians were advantageously posted, but dissensions and bickerings within their ranks had dissipated most of the enthusiasm evidenced at Chino, Los Angeles, and San Pascual. Their powder also was poor, and consequently their artillery fire, which otherwise would have been withering, did not hinder the Americans from crossing the river. At Los Angeles River the next day the performance was repeated, again with almost no casualties on either side.

Los Angeles surrendered to Kearny and Stockton on January 10, and Flores turned his authority over to Andrés Pico and left for Sonora. Rather than surrender to Kearny and Stockton, Pico preferred to capitulate to Frémont, who had got as far south as San Fernando. Frémont's pardon of Jesús Pico, another leader in the revolt and a parole violator, doubtless had much to do with Andrés Pico's choice. Vindicating Pico's hopes, the Cahuenga Capitulation on January 13, 1847, ended the revolt without the least semblance of vindictiveness. No punishments were threatened or provided; conciliation was its pervading spirit.

Like the Bear Flag Revolt, this southern California uprising may appear a fruitless and unnecessary outburst. But its causation is clear if not sufficient, and it at least demonstrated the gallantry, the dash, and the valor of the Californians.

The War in Baja California

After this spirited action in Alta California, American attention was directed to the peninsula. On March 29, 1847, Captain Montgomery of the *Portsmouth* raised the American flag at San José del Cabo, and on April 13 he did the same at La Paz. In each instance he exacted a pledge of neutrality and invited all who wished to become American citizens. The American officers were as emphatic as they had been in Alta California that the province would be retained permanently by the United States, yet Commodore Shubrick was more intent upon blockading the mainland ports than upon ensuring the complete submission of the peninsulares. In July, Colonel Burton and 115 men of the New York volunteers arrived from Santa Barbara to garrison La Paz, and in November, Shubrick left Lieutenant Heywood and twenty-four men to hold San José.

Several weeks earlier Captain Manuel Pineda had crossed the gulf from Guaymas to Mulege and had begun preparations to oust the invaders. Waiting prudently until the American naval vessels had left, he launched attacks on the American barracks at La Paz on November 16 and on San José on the nineteenth. At La Paz the investment continued until the arrival of the *Cyane* on December 8, with the sharpest fighting occurring on November 17, 27, and 28. San José was temporarily relieved by two American whalers on November 21, and additional marines and sailors brought Heywood's force up to forty-six men. In January, Pineda renewed the attack. By February 10 he had possession of the town, and two days later Heywood was in distress for lack of food and water, but on the fourteenth the *Cyane* came to the rescue and the siege was lifted. In March, reinforced from Alta California, Burton took the offensive and captured Pineda and several other opposition leaders.

The fighting in Baja California had been many times bloodier than in the northern province, but of course the war was decided not in either California but by the victories of Taylor and Scott at Buena Vista and Chapultepec. The Treaty of Guadalupe Hidalgo, in February, 1848, disregarding the American victories in Baja California and the pronouncements of American officers there, restored that province to Mexico. In the American Southwest and in Alta California, however, the treaty confirmed the American hold and transmuted provisional control into permanent possession.

16

GOLD

IT IS ONE OF THE IRONIES of history that the Spaniards, for all their reputation as miners and treasure finders, did not discover California's gold. Some of the forty-niners rationalized an explanation on the basis of the depravity of the natives and the Catholic religion of the Spaniards. The latter, according to this theory, would have used the California gold "to keep the world in darkness and to extend the dominions of popery," whereas the prevailingly Protestant Americans would put it to a better use. This argument was not entirely convincing, not even to the forty-niners; for as one of them, after speculating on the point, went on to say of his fellows: "But still the majority perhaps nine-tenths are seeking it for wicked purposes," an observation which many witnesses of the gold rush heartily endorsed.

Yet without invoking the intervention of a divine and Protestant Providence, it is understandable that the Spaniards did not make the discovery. Those who came to the province were first of all soldiers and missionaries. In Mexico, as in most of Spanish America, their mining had been for silver more than for gold, and placer mining had been of but slight importance since the days when Columbus and his companions washed the gravels of Española. It is also pointed out that the Spanish mineral discoveries were usually of deposits which the Indians were already working, and the California Indians, of course, had not taken this preliminary step. Finally, and most significant, the Spaniards occupied only the coastal strip. Even when ranchos were extended farther inland, contact with the mother lode area was infrequent and superficial.

To be sure, California had yielded small amounts of gold prior to 1848, the most famous and most important find being that by Francisco López in San Feliciano Cañon in 1842. Several score prospectors followed López into the mountains back of Mission San Fernando and took out varying amounts of gold. From these placers came the first California gold presented to the United States mint, some twenty ounces forwarded by Alfred Robinson for Abel Stearns. It was these placers also which influenced Deputy Manuel Castañares to report to the Mexican government in 1844 that mining promised to be one of the most profitable industries of the province. These southern deposits, however, did not live up to expectations; interest in them was local and short-lived, and it remained for James Wilson Marshall to make effective discovery of California's fabulous wealth in gold.

The Discovery

On January 24, 1848, in the course of constructing a sawmill at Coloma on the American River, Marshall chanced to notice flecks of yellow along the tailrace. The tailrace had cut across a bend in the river and was to all intents and purposes a rough sluice through a bar, such as the Argonauts subsequently learned to look for. Marshall gathered samples of this "color," the next day enough to make three ounces. On the fourth day, despite the incredulity of his companions, he posted off to Sutter's Fort to confer with his employer, the potentate of the Sacramento Valley. Behind locked doors the two men examined the contents of Marshall's pouch and applied every test that their ingenuity or the *American Encyclopaedia* could suggest. By all accounts Marshall, a peculiar and excitable young man, was quite worked up over the discovery, doubtless in large degree because some of the men at the mill had insinuated that he was crazy. Sutter records that his own sleep was disturbed that night by thoughts of the disruption of his ventures which a flurry of excitement about gold might cause. Yet many accounts read entirely too much drama and portentousness into the conference of Marshall and Sutter in the latter's office. The magnitude of the discovery was not yet discernible.

Sutter, still with an eye to the retention of his labor supply, went up to Coloma and persuaded the men there to promise to continue at their task for six weeks. Gold prospects in the vicinity, nevertheless, were sufficiently bright to suggest the advisability of acquiring title to the district. Accordingly, Sutter called together the Coloma Indians and dickered with them for a three-year lease of the ten or twelve leagues of land surrounding the mill. The consideration was some shirts, hats, handkerchiefs, and flour, "and other articles of no great value." Next he dispatched Charles Bennett, one of the mill hands, to Monterey to get Colonel R. B. Mason to validate his title to the land.

Throughout these first weeks Sutter's course was inconsistent. He sought to minimize the importance of the discovery yet rushed to get title to the land. He enjoined Bennett to secrecy yet sent with him six ounces of gold. He made Marshall's men promise to work for six weeks yet allowed them to prospect on Sundays. He attempted to isolate Coloma from New Helvetia yet permitted a returned Swiss teamster to offer gold for whisky at Smith and Brannan's store. He was noncommunicative to his employees but as early as February 10 was writing to Vallejo at near-by Sonoma: "I have made a discovery of a gold mine, which, according to experiments we have made, is extraordinarily rich."

To keep such a secret was manifestly impossible; it escaped through numerous leaks. At Benicia, on his way to Monterey, Bennett could not resist trumping a rumor of coal near Mount Diablo by displaying his sample of a mineral "that will beat coal." At San Francisco and at Monterey he again showed the gold. At Coloma one of the Wimmer boys babbled of gold to a teamster, and his mother, to prove him not a liar, brought forth some of the metal. The teamster, in turn, ordering a bottle of whisky at Smith and Brannan's store at Sutter's Fort, proffered gold dust in payment. In February, Henry Bigler imparted the secret to three of his Mormon friends, who, as Bancroft put it, "united with them three others to help them keep it." So it went, and ere long word of the discovery had permeated much of northern California.

But though the secret escaped, California was not immediately gripped with a furor for mining. The first newspaper mention of the discovery was a perfunctory notice tucked away on the second page of the San Francisco *Californian* for March 15. Three days later the *California Star* made an equally noncommittal statement, while on March 25 it reported that enough gold had been mined to make it "an article of traffic" at New Helvetia. In its next issue, on April 1, the *Star* ran a long installment of V. J. Fourgeaud's "The Prospects of California." He mentioned gold but bracketed the American River diggings with the old *placero* "a few miles from the Ciudad de los Angeles" and dwelt primarily on agricultural and commercial resources. On May 6 Editor E. C. Kemble, after a jaunt through the interior, made only this staccato report:

> Great country, fine climate; visit this great valley, we would advise all who have not yet done so. See it now. Full-flowing streams, mighty timber, large crops, luxuriant clover, fragrant flowers, gold and silver.

A few venturesome individuals stole off to Coloma, but not until the latter part of May did the gold fever really become virulent. Then it was Sam Brannan's quinine bottle full of the precious dust and his infectious shout: "Gold! Gold! Gold from the American River!" that started the rush. Alcalde Walter Colton described the excitement at Monterey on June 20. Everyone, except one old codger who insisted they were "some Yankee invention, got up to reconcile the people to the change of flag," admitted that the specimens of gold were genuine. Monterey was quickly depopulated; even the tapster left his bottle. An American woman who had opened a boarding house rushed off before her lodgers had a chance to pay their bills, and Colton was left to govern "a community of women," a gang of prisoners, and here and there a soldier. By July, for lack of a servant he and Governor Mason and Lieutenant Lanman of the *Warren* were their own cooks.

Other parts of California soon felt the effect of the gold excitement. San Jose was largely deserted; places as far south as Santa Barbara and Los Angeles contributed their quota of prospectors; rancheros and farmers hustled off to the diggings; Army pay of seven dollars a month did not suffice to keep men in the ranks; and ships which put in at San Francisco were quickly stripped of their crews and often of their officers as well. The immediate consequences were frequently grotesque. San Francisco and Monterey bade fair to become ghost towns. Business, except in picks, pans, shovels, and mining outfits, was at a standstill; labor was not to be had, construction stopped, and real estate tumbled to give-away prices. A San Jose stablekeeper was urged by his brothers, already in the mines, to burn his barn if he could not otherwise dispose of it. On the other hand, mining equipment rose to fantastic prices and transportation to the mines was at a premium. Horses could still be had for about fifteen dollars, but every small vessel on the bay was eagerly sought out, and Semple's ferry at Benicia did a tremendous business.

The Season of '48

Meanwhile, the field of mining operations spread rapidly from the initial point at Coloma. Henry Bigler and other employees at the mill discovered better diggings downstream, and friends of theirs dug the first gold at Mormon Bar. Upstream, Marshall discovered Live Oak Bar, where Indians were soon set to work at mining. On March 8, Isaac Humphrey, an experienced Georgia miner, began prospecting at Coloma and the next day had a rocker in operation. Later in the month John Bidwell visited Coloma, observed the alluvial deposits in which the gold was found, and was reminded of similar formations near his rancho at Chico. He soon had his Indian retainers at work at Bidwell Bar on the Feather River. Likewise, P. B. Reading was inspired to put Indians to work far to the north at placers along Clear Creek and the Trinity. Soon, other placers were being worked along Feather River. Here it was that seven men from Monterey, assisted by fifty Indians, took out 273 pounds of gold in seven weeks. On the Yuba, principal tributary of the Feather, gold was still more abundant. The first five prospectors there made $75,000 in three months, and other miners are said to have averaged $60 to $100 a day. Prospecting was extended also to the tributaries of the American River. John Sinclair was the pioneer at its forks, a Mormon group began work at Spanish Diggings on the middle tributary, an Irishman opened the Yankee Jim, and a party sent out by Charles M. Weber, after visiting the Stanislaus and the Mokelumne, mined the first gold at Weberville on the south branch of the American. One of the best strikes in this vicinity was at Dry Diggings, subsequently rechristened Hangtown and still later Placerville. Here the daily yield in the summer of 1848 was from three ounces to five pounds to the man, and that summer, as Bancroft aptly observes, "The 300 Hangtown men were the happiest in the universe."

Such were the northern diggings. Except for Reading's placers far to the north, it was a fairly compact district on the American and the Feather rivers and on their several tributaries, such as the Yuba, Bear, and Weber. The mining was principally by Americans

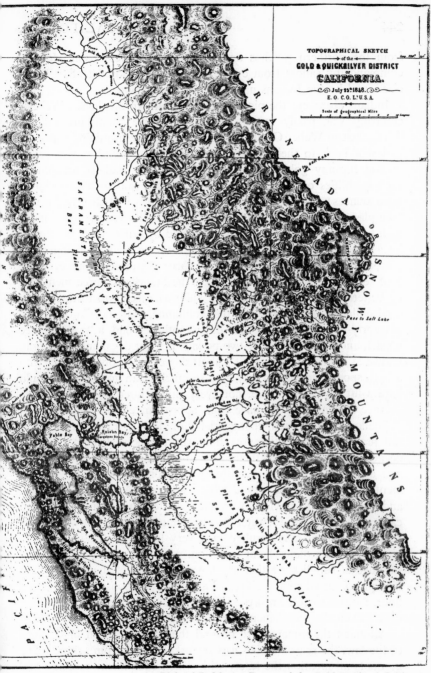

Richard B. Mason, *Report of the Gold Fields of California*
H. Ex. Doc. 17, 31 Cong., 1 sess., Washington, 1849.

E. O. C. Ord's Map of the Mining District, 1848

from the northern ranchos and towns, by deserters from Mason's command, by sailors from every vessel that anchored at San Francisco, and by the Indians native to the gold region.

Indians also were the pioneers in the southern diggings. Weber's company was partly responsible. Twenty-five Stanislaus Indians were taken to Weber Creek, given a short course in mining methods, and sent back to their native haunts with the promise of a ready market for any gold they might gather. The Indians brought in such quantities of coarse gold (one nugget is said to have weighed 80½ ounces) as to convince their white friends that they had found "the place where all the gold came from." The Weber group led a rush to the Stanislaus and was soon joined by others from the north, by a large contingent of southern Californians, and by many prospectors from Sonora. Phenomenal success greeted some of these gold seekers. At Knight's Ferry, on the Stanislaus, three men with no better equipment than pick and knife averaged two to three hundred dollars a day each. On the Tuolumne, Antonio Coronel took out forty-five ounces the first day, another found a twelve-ounce nugget, another secured fifty-two pounds in eight days, and a Sonoran known as Chino Tirador spent a short day cleaning out a pocket with a horn spoon and piled a tray with so much clean gold that he could hardly lift it. To be sure, not every miner fared so well, but the average return seems to have been approximately an ounce a day.

Shallow mining was characteristic of 1848. Prospectors overran practically the entire area that was to be worked in the next decade, but they confined themselves to scratching the surface. With pan and rocker they washed the gravel convenient to the streams mentioned above. At dry diggings, such as Auburn, Hangtown, and Sonora, they creviced with pick, knife, and horn spoon, and carried the pay dirt to water or else winnowed it by dry washing. Scarcity of silver coin resulted in a very low price for gold, six to eight dollars an ounce being common, while abundance of gold and shortage of supplies, particularly toward the end of the season, bred high prices for all commodities. Fantastic quotations could be cited: flour, $800 a barrel; whisky, $100 a gallon; hire of a rocker, $150 a day. Even the forty-niners were less prodigal.

Although the miners were beyond the effective reach of the arm of the law, the season of '48 was remarkably free from crime. The accounts all mention the safety with which equipment, supplies, and gold were left lying around unguarded. One reason was that the forty-eighters, drawn largely from California, continued as friends and neighbors. Another was that honest toil was yielding such high returns; still another, that the mining region was not yet crowded. The fact that claim jumping very seldom occurred is one proof of this obvious proposition: the few thousand miners of '48 were spread over the same area occupied by several times that number in the following years. Probably a measure of credit should go to Mason for his action invalidating the Mexican system of denouncing mining claims. Had a few individuals attempted to file on the best diggings, much friction would have developed. Already the miners were showing themselves capable of working out their own code of mining regulations and of punishing such crimes as were committed. Only two hangings are on record for 1848. The fact that one victim was French and the other Spanish indicates that race prejudice was already in evidence.

The mining population for 1848 has been grossly overestimated by some writers. In May there were only a few hundred at work, by July 3,000 or 4,000, and Colton's estimate of 50,000 at the end of the season must be scaled down to 8,000 or 10,000. California contributed the majority, but the contagion spread rapidly over the Pacific area; Oregon sent some 1,500 prospectors, and Hawaii and Mexico perhaps 2,500, not to mention China's trio.

The Trek of the Forty-Niners

Gradually the excitement spread to the eastern United States and to Europe. By August and September, California letters telling of the gold discovery had been printed in various eastern papers. But as had been the case in California, the first reports were met with polite or raucous incredulity, and months passed before the nation began to believe. Finally attention was riveted by the arrival of official messengers from California. The Navy sent E. F. Beale by way of Hawaii, Peru, Panama, and Jamaica, while Governor Mason sent Lt. Lucien Loeser by way of Mazatlán, Veracruz, and New Orleans with his report and a tea caddy containing $3,000 worth of gold. In his message to Congress on December 5, Polk took official cognizance of the discovery, and his words became the signal for a stampede.

The news came opportunely in the midst of the period of postwar adjustment. The War with Mexico, to be sure, was not a great international upheaval, but thousands of soldiers had been mustered out recently, many had not found themselves again in peacetime employment, and others were dissatisfied with a humdrum existence and longed for new adventures. For them California gold mining had a compelling appeal. Yet the "yellow fever" did not confine itself to the ex-soldiers. Farmers, shopkeepers, clerks, physicians, and politicians caught it too, not to mention "the briefless lawyer, the starving student, the quack, the idler, the harlot, the gambler, the hen-pecked husband, the disgraced."

California could be reached by three principal routes, Cape Horn, Panama, or overland. For New Englanders the sea route was the natural one, both from habit and for convenience. Ships were numerous, seafaring men even more so, and thanks to the otter trade, the hide trade, and whaling, there were many men expert in the voyage to California. Astute shipowners withdrew their vessels from other commerce; some seventy-one from whaling, for example. They fitted these vessels to carry Argonauts to California, and then, after the crews had deserted at San Francisco, wondered how to get their ships home. Other New Englanders formed joint-stock companies, bought vessels, provisioned them, selected ship officers, and sailed to California. Such a group was the Boston and California Mining Company, whose members were exhorted by President Edward Everett of Harvard to go to California "with the Bible in one hand and your New England civilization in the other and make your mark on the people and country." In nine months 549 vessels arrived at San Francisco, many of course from Europe, South America, Mexico, and Hawaii, but about half from the Atlantic seaboard.

Although travelers by sea vied with Panama men and overlanders in stigmatizing their particular path as the worst, the Cape Horn route probably offered the easiest journey. It may, indeed, have been too easy, for many passengers were so softened by four to eight months of inaction as to be unequal to the hard labor in the diggings. It was something of a white-collar route, favored by gamblers, politicians, saloonkeepers, and prostitutes, as well as by Bible-bearing Yankees. Every forty-niner by sea visited San Francisco before proceeding to the mines, and a goodly number went no farther. The sea route also made a material contribution in bulky machinery, furniture, and foodstuffs, which could not have come overland. Included in the cargoes was a choice assortment of patent mining machinery destined for un-Christian burial on the flats below San Francisco. By accident, some shovels and picks were likewise included, along with pianos, printing presses, and other practical appliances.

Potentially, the Panama route was the quickest way to California. The Pacific Mail Steamship Company was just beginning regular service from New York to Chagres and from Panama to San Francisco. From the tentative schedule it appeared that the journey might be accomplished in thirty days. But the forty-niners found Panama a snare and a delusion. To get across the isthmus one had to depend on the caprice and satisfy the avarice of native boatmen and mule drivers, and on the Pacific side ships were woefully lacking. On its initial Pacific Mail voyage the *California* picked up 365 passengers, some of whom paid as much as $1,000 for steerage accommodations. Other vessels were pressed into service, but an impatient horde was left stranded. Some set out in tiny sailboats; others are said to have resorted to dugout canoes for the 5,000-mile journey; the majority had to wait.

While they waited, insects, tropical storms and heat, poor food, and bad drinking water harassed them. Yellow fever brought death. Yet some of the more enterprising Americans, notably Collis P. Huntington, recognizing the opportunity that the situation afforded, prospered through catering to the wants of these thwarted emigrants. With the Panama route we may lump several variations attempted by smaller numbers. But whether one crossed Nicaragua, Tehuantepec, or central Mexico, the problem still remained of finding passage up the Pacific. Congestion was less than at Panama, but delay undiminished.

Almost 40,000 forty-niners followed these water and land-and-water routes. For most residents of the Mississippi Valley, however, the overland trails were nearer at hand and less forbidding. Editors in Texas, Arkansas, and Missouri vied in praising the routes from Corpus Christi through Mexico, across Texas to El Paso, from Fort Smith to El Paso, or down the Santa Fe Trail and on by the Gila or the Old Spanish Trail. These southern trails had the advantage of passing through a number of settled points in Mexico, on the Rio Grande, and in southern California, where it would be possible to rest and reprovision. They were not subject to closure by winter

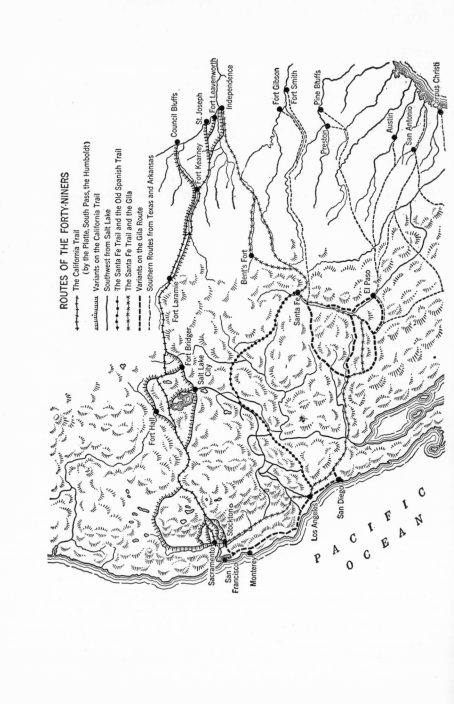

ROUTES OF THE FORTY-NINERS

- +++++ The California Trail
  (by the Platte, South Pass, the Humboldt)
- ↔↔↔↔ Variants on the California Trail
- ⊔⊔⊔⊔⊔ Southwest from Salt Lake
- ——— The Santa Fe Trail and the Old Spanish Trail
- ×××× The Santa Fe Trail and the Gila
- ✕✕✕✕ Variants on the Gila Route
- – – – Southern Routes from Texas and Arkansas

Council Bluffs
St. Joseph
Fort Leavenworth
Independence
Fort Gibson
Fort Smith
Pine Bluffs
Preston
Austin
San Antonio
Corpus Christi
Fort Kearney
Fort Laramie
Bent's Fort
Santa Fe
El Paso
Fort Bridger
Salt Lake City
Fort Hall
San Diego
Los Angeles
Sacramento
San Francisco
Stockton
Monterey

PACIFIC OCEAN

snows; in fact, winter was probably the ideal season for crossing the southern desert into California. Opened by Spanish explorers and by restless beaver trappers, these southern trails had been broadened and perfected by the caravans of the Santa Fé traders and by American military forces during the recent war. They attracted some 10,000 or 15,000 forty-niners, most of whom got through safely, however much they may have grumbled at delays and difficulties.

From Missouri north the consensus of opinion recommended the Platte-South Pass-Humboldt itinerary, which had been broken by the fur men, favored by the pioneer settlers, used in part by the Oregon missionaries and settlers and by the Mormons in their hegira to Salt Lake, and advertised by Frémont. Twenty-five or thirty thousand persons swarmed over this most direct route and made it known as the California Trail.

Though the major overland trails had been well worked out before 1849, there were few competent guides available at the starting points along the Missouri; nor was reliable information available in print. Guidebooks were shortly produced to point the way and advise as to methods, yet it is a curious commentary that the best one, that by Joseph E. Ware, was produced by a St. Louis newspaper writer who had never been west of Missouri. Most of the forty-niners, lacking even such a guide, had to learn by experience the procedure of crossing the plains, the desert, and the mountains. According to a typical gold seeker, "There were few, if any, who possessed a definite knowledge of the road and, as a consequence, there was great suffering."

In outward appearance the migration of 1849 duplicated those of earlier years. The same prairie schooners were used; and the same sorts of teams; the proportion of families to single men was only slightly less than in the earlier migration of agriculturists; and in 1849, for that matter, many of the gold seekers carried the fundamental farming equipment with them. By reason of its very magnitude, however, this movement was basically different. In an earlier period the chief dangers had been from Indian attacks or from losing the way. Gold seekers on their way to California found the Indians harmless, except for depredations on livestock along the Humboldt; and, as for getting lost, the only ones to go astray did so voluntarily.

Short cuts, to be sure, lured the emigrants repeatedly, usually with unfortunate results. The Donner party of 1846, with its delay on the Hastings' Cut-off, is the extreme example. The forty-niners who got off the Salt Lake-Los Angeles trail into Death Valley fared almost as badly and have won very general notice, but they were by no means the only ones who came to grief by turning off from the established routes. Although some trail improvements were achieved by similar experiments, Sublette's Cut-off, for example, the usual result was that voiced by Delano concerning the Lassen Cut-off:

Instead of avoiding the desert, instead of the promised water, grass, and a better road, we were in fact upon a more dreary and wider waste, without either grass or water, and with a harder road before us. . . . We had been inveigled there by false reports and misrepresentations.

Diaries and journals abound with mention of the great concourse of people on the trail, of how each night's camp was made within sight of other campfires, of how the migration resembled a large city on the move. Delano gives this picture of the great trek:

For miles, to the extent of vision, an animated mass of beings broke upon our view. Long trains of wagons with their white covers were moving slowly along, a multitude of horsemen were prancing on the road, companies of men were traveling on foot, and although the scene was not a gorgeous one, yet the display of banners from many wagons, and the multitude of armed men, looked as if a mighty army was on its march.

In such a concourse the trail was unmistakable.

Exhaustion of the grass supply and ravages of cholera, the two most serious problems facing the forty-niners, were products of the crowded trail, the grass shortage obviously, and the cholera just as surely. At many camping sites where former caravans had found luxuriant pasturage, the grass was cropped clean by the cattle of the earlier forty-niners, and subsequent parties found none. Then there were certain mendacious individuals who fired the grass as a deliberate hindrance to those who followed, apparently on the theory that they were thereby reducing competition in the diggings. Nightly detours or side trips of two or three or four miles became the rule for the hindmost parties. From the Missouri to the Rockies the ravages of cholera were frightful. Men were struck suddenly. Some died after two or three hours of violent chills and fever; others lingered between life and death for days or weeks. Medical attention was seldom to be had, and relatives were not always on hand to care for the afflicted. Supposed friends occasionally abandoned their companions, but in as many instances utter strangers went out of their way to minister to those in distress.

Fortunately the cholera did not cross the Continental Divide; mountain fever took its place as the principal ailment, and then it likewise was left behind. But the road became worse. The Platte Crossing, the alkaline lakes, Sublette's Cut-off with its thirty-five miles without water, the Green River Crossing—these earlier crises paled before the Humboldt. In its valley the forty-niners, excepting those who had circled south of Great Salt Lake, got their first real taste of desert travel. It was hot and dusty. The landscape was cheerless and devoid of vegetation except for a little grass and a few small willows at the immediate margin of the river. As the grass along the south bank was exhausted, many of the later travelers had to cross the stream nightly to gather grass for their cattle, and these discomforts and annoyances made the Humboldt the butt of their grumbling, as numerous diaries attest. Argonaut John Steele opined that this was "the neighborhood of the rich man's hell"; versifying his salute, Horace Belknap started off in this vein,

> Meanest and muddiest, filthiest stream
> most cordially I hate you;

and the average Argonaut would have been ready to endorse Horace Greeley's subsequent observation, "Here famine sits enthroned, and waves his sceptre over a dominion expressly made for him."

The Humboldt Valley had its shortcomings, yet as an attenuated oasis stretching most of the way across the Nevada desert it made possible the use of this overland route. Unfortunately, the river terminated in the "Sink," beyond which lay forty miles of unrelieved desert before one reached the Carson River or the Truckee. Because men and animals were weakened and worn out by the rigors of the long trail, the desert crossing was the more difficult. Milus Gay, one of the more restrained diarists, described it in these terms:

Continuing across the Desert got across to Carsonville on Carson River about 4 p.m. 12 or 15 miles of the latter part of the Journey being sandy was very hard on our cattle the distance across is perhaps about 40 miles—Such destruction of property as I saw across the Desert I have never seen I should think I passed the carcases of 1200 head of cattle and horses and a great many waggons—Harneses—cooking utensils—tools water casks &c. &c. at a moderate estimate the amount I would

think the property cost in the U. S. $50,000.   We also see many men
on the point of starvation beging for bread.   We stopped an hour in this
wagon and tented ville.   bought 2 lb Beef for which we paid $1—and
eat it all for supper.   went up some 3 or 4 miles and encamped.   Grass
scarce ☞ (N. B. Water 8 miles from C[arson] R[iver] sold for $1
gallon.)

After tarrying briefly to recruit their cattle on the luxuriant grasses
at the eastern base of the Sierra, the emigrants hurried on.   Several
routes were available, but there was not much to choose.   The
route by the Truckee and Donner Pass was in some respects the
easiest, but it was in ill-repute because of the Donner tragedy.   The
Truckee could be followed to Henness Pass and the Yuba, or one
could ascend the Carson to either Johnson's Pass or Carson Pass and
Placerville on the American, or one could go up the Walker to
Sonora Pass and the Stanislaus.   By any route the rocky fords and
steep ascent made it hard pulling for man and beast.   Some wagons
and much baggage were taken no farther.   To add to the difficulty,
winter set in earlier than usual; but thanks to the energetic measures
of relief directed by Major Rucker of the United States Army, dupli-
cation of the Donner tragedy was averted.

The migration of 1850 was a repetition differing only in detail.
The number was as great, the cholera was worse, ferry service was
now available at a dozen rivers along the way, and the regular trail
along the Humboldt was under water as the result of most unusual
rains.   The desert took its accustomed toll, and again California
relief agencies—this time managed by William Waldo of Sacramento
—saved thousands from impending disaster in the Sierra.

In the Diggings

These overlanders plunged immediately into mining.   They imi-
tated the old timers' use of pick and shovel, pan and cradle.   Even
when the more efficient long tom and sluice were introduced, they
found that gold mining was back-breaking business.   One moved
as much dirt as a ditch digger, frequently standing in icy water and
under a broiling sun.   There was excitement, of course, and any
day might bring a rich prize; but the excitement was a temptation to
overwork and to neglect such prosaic tasks as cooking.   The miner's
home was an uncomfortable tent or shanty, his clothing nondescript
and often inadequate to protect against the elements.

The rewards, furthermore, were not only uncertain but on the average unsatisfactory. The "pound diggings" of 1848 were succeeded by the "ounce diggings" of 1849 and 1850, and thereafter there was a further decline. The statistics are incomplete and conflicting, but it has been calculated that the mean return after 1850 was about two dollars a day a man. Apart from the few who struck it tremendously rich, it seems obvious that the wisest forty-niners were those who turned to saloonkeeping or merchandising or hauling or farming or dishwashing, where the compensation was not only surer but higher.

A glance at the miner's amusements reveals that the favorites were drinking, gambling, and dancing, with certain men delegated for the ladies' parts. Dissipation and roistering, however, were less prevalent than is sometimes represented. Horse racing, cock fights, and practical jokes were frequent. Evenings were devoted to conversation and song, some of the ballads being only less distinctive than those in the cowboy's repertory. Sundays were largely given over to frolic (and washing and baking), but many of the miners set an example of rectitude with debating societies or even religious services. The theater also came to the mines. There was a regular circuit from Rabbit Creek to Mariposa, played by such celebrities as Lotta Crabtree, Lola Montez, Katherine Sinclair, and Edwin Booth.

Frank Marryat offers this eye-witness description of an active camp:

A turn of the road presented a scene of mining life, as perfect in its details as it was novel in its features. Immediately beneath us the swift river glided tranquilly, though foaming still from the great battle which a few yards higher up, it had fought with a mass of black obstructing rocks. On the banks was a village of canvas that the winter rains had bleached to perfection, and round it the miners were at work at every point. Many were waist deep in the water, toiling in bands to construct a race and dam to turn the river's course; others were entrenched in holes, like grave diggers, working down to the "bedrock." Some were on the brink of the stream washing out "prospects" from tin pans or wooden "batteaus"; and others worked in company with the long tom, by means of water sluices artfully conveyed from the river. Many were coyote-ing in subterranean holes, from which from time to time their heads popped out, like those of squirrels to take a look at the world; and a few with drills, dissatisfied with nature's work, were preparing to remove large rocks with gunpowder. All was life, merriment, vigour and determination, as this part of the earth was being turned inside out to see what it was made of. . . .

Small patches of garden surrounded the village which bore so palpably the stamp of cheerfulness and happy industry, that I was disappointed on learning that its name was "Murderers' Bar."

It is elementary to observe that the effects of the gold rush were not confined to gold mining. As on most mining frontiers, many who came to prospect never washed a pan of gravel, and others experimented only briefly in the diggings before turning to farming, merchandising, transportation, and other familiar work. Some were not physically equal to the hard life in the mines; some became disgusted with their luck and threw up the work. Enough miners were deserting the diggings to afford William Harlan a profitable business buying their implements for a song and reselling them to greenhorns at California prices. Some of these disappointed ones returned to the States, but vast numbers remained in the West, the majority in California and particularly at San Francisco. The urban forty-niner developed as great a significance as his red-shirted brother of the placers.

When gold was discovered, San Francisco was a village boasting two hotels, two wharves nearly completed, and 812 persons. Early in the summer of 1848, the population shrank almost to zero; everyone had gone to the mines, and the town was dead. It revived rapidly under the impetus of hundreds of thousands of dollars in gold pouring in from the diggings. The miners wanted supplies, and San Franciscans assumed the twin responsibilities of providing supplies and an outlet for the miners' gold. Business flourished during the last months of 1848, but the next year saw the real boom, with 40,000 Argonauts avalanching upon the town.

No amount of stretching and crowding would make facilities planned for the accommodation of 800 commodious for the sudden throng. Hotels and lodging houses put ten or twenty men in a room and charged exorbitant prices. Rents skyrocketed to $40,000 a year for the El Dorado gambling saloon tent and $3,000 a month for a small store. Other prices jumped correspondingly. A meal cost three dollars or more, drinks twenty-five and fifty cents, and coppers and small coins were virtually unknown. Wages went up in proportion. Unskilled labor commanded ten or twelve dollars a day.

Excitement surcharged the entire atmosphere. Everyone was in a hurry. Loans were for a month rather than a year. An abnormal fraction of the population was to be found in the streets or the gambling saloons, adding to the bustle. Gambling itself was rapid-fire, for the tables were crowded and others were anxious to make their bets. The regal splendor of the fifties was not yet attained, but plate-glass mirrors, prism chandeliers, ornate bars, and the appropriate paintings had already arrived.

Whereas San Francisco had at least a municipal existence prior to the gold rush, several other communities owed their origin to it. Such were Grass Valley, Auburn, Placerville, Columbia, and Sonora, which flourished mightily and then with the eclipse of mining went into as sudden a decline. Sacramento and Stockton likewise came suddenly into existence on the flood of gold, but demonstrated commercial, industrial, and political reasons for continued existence after the passing of the mining era.

The rise of San Francisco and these satellite cities was but one consequence of the gold rush. Others included the drastic alteration of the price structure in California and, to a lesser extent, in the world at large produced by the sudden outpouring of gold. Commerce, agriculture, lumbering, and countless other pursuits were greatly stimulated in northern California and up and down the Pacific Coast. New arguments and incentives were created for transportation development. California's population was multiplied many times over. The additional foreign strains that came in intensified its cosmopolitan character, while the predominance of Argonauts from the States greatly accelerated the change from Mexican to American society. The world-wide interest in California, so suddenly created, brought to an end the intellectual as well as physical isolation of the province. Most important, perhaps, were the psychological consequences, entailed in such matters as the unrestrained and masculine society of gold rush California, a willingness to believe that the fabulous could be realized, and a fortification of the historical heritage as a unifying factor for all Californians. Gold, without question, has influenced the state's history more than any other single factor.

17

A NEW ECONOMY

MOST OF THE ARGONAUTS harbored no intention of becoming Californians. They came to make their pile and then to return to civilization in the States, Europe, Sonora, or from wherever they had come. Many adhered to this purpose. The earliest instance was in July, 1848, when a party of two score Mormons, including several of Marshall's associates at Coloma, turned their backs on the gold area and set out over the Sierra and across the desert to join their brethren at Great Salt Lake. The overland forty-niners met a few parties headed eastward. When the onset of winter closed down most of the diggings, the departures by ship and by southern trails mounted. In the fifties the number leaving was much greater; the Panama route was the favorite, and passage from San Francisco was frequently at a premium. The magnitude of this backwash of the gold rush is attested by the records of the transportation companies and by the large number of forty-niner diaries that have come to light in the East. Its significance lay first of all in the attitude of many of the gold seekers toward California, and secondly in the wide dissemination of information about the state.

Yet, numerous as were the miners who came and went, a larger number came and stayed. By the end of 1849 population exceeded 100,000; in 1852 the state counted 224,435, and in 1860 the official census showed 380,015. This sudden increase, in a province that for generations had lain practically dormant, was at once symptomatic of and conducive to far-reaching change. The state shortly acquired among other things a new political setup, a new social structure, and a new economy.

Mining Techniques

Fundamental to the latter was, naturally enough, gold mining itself. For a while almost every Californian was a gold miner, and as late as 1863 it was still true that mining employed more of the state's workers than any other pursuit. Production also held up well. The peak was attained in the early fifties, followed by a gradual tapering off. In the first decade and a half, however, the average annual output was $50,000,000. After 1865 gold production displayed remarkable stability at approximately one third of this amount annually. In recent years other minerals, particularly petroleum, have far overshadowed gold; yet to the end of the century gold was the unchallenged leader in the state's mining.

In the first hectic years placer mining predominated. Techniques improved rapidly. The pan and cradle were superseded by the long tom and it in turn by the sluices, which became the essential apparatus in all gold washing. A standard form developed, each section of open trough twelve feet long, a foot and a half or two feet in depth, and sixteen or eighteen inches wide (though sometimes wider). Sections or boxes of this pattern were fitted together to make a sluice 200, 300, or even 1,000 feet long, with a drop of from eight to twenty inches per section. Riffle bars or cleats were wedged in transversely or diagonally to catch the heavy gold, and mercury was thrown in to amalgamate with the smaller particles of floating gold. A two-inch stream of water coursed down the sluice. Every six to ten days the run was stopped so that the riffle bars could be removed and the accumulated gold cleaned up.

In the more elementary form of sluice mining, the gold-bearing clay, sand, or gravel was shoveled into the upper sections of the sluice from adjacent bars of river-bank deposits. Often it was brought more laboriously from a greater distance, from a deposit from which the top soil had first to be stripped off, or from a stream bed exposed by damming and diverting the water. The hydraulic method, feasible only in hill country, represented the easiest method of delivering gold-bearing dirt to the sluice. With a nozzled canvas hose or iron pipe delivering fifty or more feet of water pressure, half a dozen men could wash more dirt than a couple of hundred wielding pick and shovel. The method was so cheap that it could be employed profitably on dirt yielding as little as one cent to the cubic foot, which would have been considerably beneath the attention of the non-hydraulic miners. Popularity of the hydraulic method is revealed by statistics of 1854, which indicate 4,493 miles of ditches delivering water for mining operations.

Almost from the beginning, the placer miners displayed an eagerness to work back to the source of the gold. An early and pseudo-scientific theory was that a volcanic eruption had spattered gold over the area of the diggings. Most of the miners, however, inclined to the belief that it had washed down from veins or from a single vein and that sooner or later this mother lode would be brought to light. The vein theory was ridiculed by Dr. Philip T. Tyson, the first geologist of reputation to report on the gold region, but before the end of 1849 quartz mining had been started on Frémont's Mariposa grant, and many reckoned it the branch of mining most likely to endure.

The first step in quartz mining was that of quarrying. At Mariposa and the other early mines the deposits were surface or shallow; later, auriferous quartz was to be pursued a mile or more beneath the surface. The next step was to crush the quartz to a powder. Various devices were employed, ranging from the Mexican arrastra, in which mules pulled a heavy stone drag, and the Chilean mill, in which heavy wheels rotated around a pivot, to batteries of square and rotary stamps. These latter, run by steam or water power, operated on the pile-driver principle with a straight fall or a twirling motion. The final step was to mix the powdered ore with water and mercury, and then by gravity process to separate the amalgamated metal. Although the early quartz mills were so inefficient as to bring the method into disrepute, improvements were soon made. By 1863 one third and by the end of the decade more than half of the gold mined was from quartz.

Much of the mercury required in California gold mining was produced within the state. The New Almaden mine near San Jose had been opened in the Mexican period and named after the famous quicksilver mine in southwestern Spain. Under the impetus of increased demand and price, the working of this mine was accelerated until production reached 220,000 pounds a month. Both the mining and the reduction of the ore were fairly simple processes. The ore occurred in large and irregular masses rather than in veins. For reduction, it was placed in a furnace. When heated the mercury was driven off in gaseous form and recovered by passing through a series of condensing chambers opening into each other alternately at top and bottom. In the period here under discussion California's other mineral resources were almost entirely neglected.

Trade and Freighting

Of the three quarters of a billion dollars worth of gold, which is a conservative estimate of what was produced in California up to 1865, an indeterminate fraction was carried out of the state by the miners returning eastward. A much larger quantity changed hands at least once in California. The effects of this tremendous increase in purchasing power and of the concomitant spurt in the number of customers and consumers challenge the imagination. The first consequence was that stores sprang up throughout the diggings to cater to the miners' wants. At the outset many stores stocked only the basic commodities, salt pork and beef, flour, and whisky. As quickly as circumstances permitted, however, the list was extended. The storekeepers, it was generally agreed, were surer to profit than the diggers of gold. Perhaps on that account there was a tendency to look down upon them as a class. Although John Bidwell, Charles M. Weber, and Alonzo Delano, and certain other storekeepers were highly respected, the majority were not held in such high esteem; in fact, the Yankee merchant was reckoned not much above the professional gambler, another familiar figure in the diggings.

Closely associated with the storekeepers were the freighters who replenished their stocks. By wagon or pack train over abominable roads and the roughest of trails, they moved a varied cargo from Sacramento and Stockton to the most remote mining camps. They took the first consignments of gold away from the diggings and by easy transition became the pioneers in mail, express, and banking services. Though now superseded by railroads, buses, and trucks, the freighters were less transitory than those who made their living by hunting game for the miners or by driving up cattle and sheep to be butchered at the diggings.

San Francisco and Sacramento soon boasted wholesale and retail merchants who became the commercial czars of California. The fortunes of the "Big Four" of Central Pacific fame were laid on foundations of this sort of commerce, and the well-known stories of Collis P. Huntington's warehouse, his dealings with ship captains, and his corner on shovels amply illustrate the complexities, the uncertainties, and the ethics of this first big business in California. At first there was no such thing as ordering goods from the East; merchants merely dealt in whatever commodities New England, New York, or foreign shippers had seen fit to send to San Francisco. The result was an unpredictable schedule of prices. Of some goods there was an oversupply, hence the San Francisco sidewalks paved with tierces of tobacco, with sacks of flour, and in another case with cook stoves. Again, there was a dearth of some other commodity, resulting in a price that seemed exorbitant even to Californians. A frequent comment was that the spread between wholesale and retail prices was out of all proportion.

Beside the round-the-Horn shipments, the movement of goods to gold-rush California involved many other avenues. The wagon trains on the overland trails brought household goods, tools, and implements that in the aggregate were important. These trains and more formal drives brought horses, cattle, and sheep. Ships from Puget Sound and the Columbia delivered lumber, while the agricultural settlements in the Willamette Valley sent eggs, garden produce, and grain. Dried beef—charqui, or jerky—came from Chile, and diversified cargoes were sent from Hawaii and the Orient. In 1849 California was producing few of the things that her new population required. It is said, for example, that San Francisco's soiled linen was sometimes sent to Hawaii or China for laundering. Soon, however, local producers and enterprisers came to the rescue. Existing branches of agriculture and industry were stimulated, and new branches were started to supply the gold seekers. In many instances it was found that a much broader market existed or that it could be developed.

Agriculture

Cattle raising was the branch of agriculture that could most readily be expanded to meet the new opportunity. Cattle which had found no market at $5.00 and $6.00 a head brought as much as $500 at the mining camps. The price did not long remain at this fantastic figure, but in the fifties beeves often brought from $50 to $100 a head.   With its Mexican ranchos California was well grounded in the cattle business.   Additional herds were driven in from Texas and the Midwest, several hundred head in 1850 and as many as 40,000 a year in the middle fifties.   It was a "long drive" antedating the more famous one from Texas to the northern plains, and as beef cattle the California breed was somewhat improved.   Southern California rancheros suddenly became prosperous, though the easily acquired wealth was in most instances as rapidly dissipated.   In the San Joaquin Valley, Henry Miller began to build up the more enduring Miller and Lux ranches and fortune.   From less than 300,000 head of cattle in the state in 1848, there was an increase to 3,000,000 in 1860.   In the great drought of 1863–1864 cattle died by the tens of thousands.   The distress of the cattle men was aggravated by the extremely high interest rates that then obtained.   In 1870 the official inventory showed only 630,000 head of cattle in the state.

At the missions, sheep had been almost as numerous as cattle, but after secularization they fell into disfavor, and in 1849 there were less than 20,000 in the state.   With the miners providing a market for mutton, the industry revived.   There were drives from Chihuahua, from New Mexico by way of the Old Spanish Trail, and from the American Midwest by way of the Salt Lake-Los Angeles route, with Kit Carson, Wilson Flint, and the Bixbys as some of the better-known participants.   The peak years seem to have been 1853, when 135,000 head were brought in, and 1856, with 200,000.   By 1860 the state had 1,000,000 head, yielding, however, only 2,000,000 pounds of wool.   Importation of blooded stock brought an improvement, and by 1870 the number of animals had increased to 2,750,000 and the wool clip to 11,000,000 pounds.

Another mission activity which was revived and expanded in the golden era was that of cultivation of the small grains.   The rancheros of the postsecularization period, being less abundantly supplied with laborers than the friars had been, allowed grain cultivation to lapse. Sutter was sowing large fields of wheat in the Sacramento Valley on the eve of the gold discovery, but he also found the labor supply inadequate.   The farming of the fifties was more directly an outgrowth of Sutter's agriculture than of the earlier cultivation at the southern California missions.   The local market created by the hungry gold diggers suggested a "back-to-the-farm" movement.   The lower San Joaquin and Sacramento valleys and northern California provided the lands first brought under cultivation, though subsequently the San Joaquin Valley became the center of California's wheat belt. California soil and climate proved most congenial for wheat production. The yield per acre surpassed the midwestern average, and the dry summers prolonged the harvest season and made the wheat very dry and hard. It was unimpaired by shipment to distant markets, and flour milled from it was preferred in tropical markets. Another advantage was that ships which had been sailing from San Francisco in ballast could now take on cargoes of wheat. Fundamentally, however, the great expansion of California wheat raising was made possible by the invention of the McCormick reaper, which on the other side of the Rockies was enabling Nebraska and Dakota pioneers to start prairie farming. Without such labor-saving devices California farmers could not have boosted wheat production from 17,000 bushels in 1850 to 5,900,000 in 1860, 16,000,000 in 1870, and 40,000,000 in 1890. Barley was a close second, with 4,500,000 bushels in 1860, 8,700,000 in 1870, 17,500,000 in 1890, and 25,000,000 in 1900, a year in which wheat was down to 36,000,000.

California's suitability for a wide variety of other crops was thoroughly proven in the fifties and sixties. In 1854, for example, B. D. Wilson wrote to his brother in Mississippi that Los Angeles County produced "every species of grain and fruits in the greatest abundance." To prove his point he listed the different fruits growing on a farm he had just purchased: grapes, oranges, pears, apricots, peaches, apples, almonds, English walnuts, cherries, figs, olives, quinces, and plums, all growing so luxuriantly that he did not know which grew best.

In his *Resources of California,* a few years later, John S. Hittell catalogued the state's subordinate agricultural products: oats, maize, hay, potatoes, kitchen vegetables in great variety, berries of all sorts, and fruits of the several kinds listed above. The potatoes he described as half again as large as those in the States, and he vouched for a 10-pound carrot, a 26-pound turnip, a 53-pound cabbage, a 118-pound beet, and a 260-pound squash. At the time of his writing in 1863 half the state's 2,500 orange trees were in the grove of William Wolfskill at Los Angeles. Much of this horticulture was carried over from the mission period, but Johnny Appleseeds were not lacking, bringing in additional stock and new varieties from the East. In California, fruit trees were more precocious, practically every vegetable was in season twice as long as in the East, and San Francisco had a year-round supply of strawberries from the Santa Clara Valley; yet in the fifties and sixties all these foodstuffs, though grown commercially, were limited to the California market. Consequently, they did not rival the big four in the state's agriculture: beef cattle, sheep, wheat, and barley.

Through its associated industry of wine making, grape culture offered better possibilities. As a heritage from the Franciscans, California possessed a number of plantings of "mission grapes," hardy vines and good bearers, though not extraordinary in quality. This was the stock on which the earliest commercial vintners depended, notably Luis Vignes of Los Angeles. By 1842 he was doing a thriving business in supplying northern California and the coastal trade with wine and brandy. After the gold rush created an enlarged market, others entered the business. It was profitable because vines could be brought into production more rapidly than fruit trees of any kind. There was good demand for table grapes, and the derivatives, wine and brandy, had the great advantages of being compact for shipment and relatively imperishable. The assessment records indicate 1,000,000 bearing vines by 1855, 8,000,000 by 1860, and nearly 28,000,000, by 1870. In 1870 production approached 2,000,000 gallons of wine. A fourth, mostly in sweet wines, was from Los Angeles County; a sixth, mostly in dry wines, came from Sonoma County.

Meanwhile, sanguine hopes arose that the ideal industry for California would be silk raising. In 1864 the legislature offered a bounty of $250 for every planting of 500 two-year-old mulberry trees and $300 for every 100,000 salable cocoons. Under this impetus some ten million trees were set out by 1869. The leading individual enthusiast was Louis Prévost. He organized the California Silk Center Association, which bought some 8,500 acres in the Jurupa district (later to be called Riverside) and went in for sericulture on a grand scale. Predictions were freely made that silk would become the state's most valuable product. Silk-worm eggs sold for a time at ten dollars an ounce, and a few men profited greatly. When Prévost died and the legislature, somewhat alarmed over the drain on the state treasury, withdrew the bounty offer, agriculturists turned unanimously from this glamorous fad.

Cotton likewise was in style for a brief season. In Civil War days William Workman and others made a few plantings. In 1876

Matthew Keller planted sixty acres in a field just north of what is now the University of Southern California campus. He got a good crop but found no satisfactory market, which was the experience of other cotton planters. The ambitiousness of their plans, however, was reflected in the formation of the California Cotton Growers and Manufacturers Association, which had 10,000 acres at Bakersfield and a colony of Negro cotton pickers imported from the South. These Negroes, however, preferred other work, and since white labor was expensive and marketing difficult, California cotton growing was postponed for another half-century.

Notwithstanding these failures, California agriculture was shifting from the pastoral economy of the ranchos to a stress on cultivation of the soil. The droughts of the early sixties dealt a body blow to the cattle industry and the positive success with grain and grapes confirmed the shift. By 1872 the trend had advanced to the point where there was overpowering sentiment in favor of the "no-fence law," an act which placed the responsibility for the restraint of live-stock upon their owners rather than upon the planters, who formerly had had to fence other people's stock out of their fruit groves, vine-yards, and grain fields. Characteristic of the shift from stock ranch-ing was the experience of B. D. Wilson. In the fifties he had run thousands of head of cattle and sheep, but in 1873 he considered a herd of 100 cattle overlarge. The new agriculture included cattle and sheep but centered on grain and grapes and other fruits.

Expanding Industry

Hand in hand with the development in mining, commerce, and agriculture, manufacturing began to flourish in the northern towns. The discovery of gold, it will be recalled, had come about as a by-product of lumber manufacture as sponsored by Sutter. The gold rush, though it wrought havoc with Sutter's affairs, returned the compliment to lumbering by creating a great demand for sawmill products. The placer miners required quantities of planks for their sluices, flumes, and wing dams. A special twelve-foot plank, two inches thick, fourteen inches at one end and eighteen at the other, was turned out for sluice bottoms, so that the sections could be fitted together without nails. Quartz miners also required timbers and planks for bracings in their shafts and tunnels. For building pur-poses likewise, lumber was the favored material, at least after San

Francisco got past the canvas and paper stage. Railroad construction provided another important market for lumber, and since barbed wire had not yet appeared on the scene, fencing called for many rails and planks as well as posts.

Mendocino and Humboldt counties boasted the largest mills and produced the most lumber, thirty-five and thirty million feet respectively in 1860. Most of it was redwood, sawed from logs averaging four and a half feet in diameter. Schooners of from 150 to 300 tons' burden transported the lumber to San Francisco. Santa Cruz County was next with ten million feet a year, all redwood, and much of it shipped to southern California. Santa Cruz lumber was distinguished also by the fact that much of it was split rather than sawed. For a skilled workman, redwood splits straight and smooth; consequently this technique was efficient for getting out fence posts, rails, rough planks, joists, beams, and shingles. More than one Argonaut found that he could make his pile more quickly and surely by splitting shingles in the Santa Cruz Mountains than by wielding pick and shovel in the diggings. Other sawmills, many of which were portable, operated in the Sierra forests, turning out lumber for the miners.

For the milling of flour the forty-niners provided an excellent market, but it was not until three or four years later that the raw material was available in adequate quantities. The first two mills in the state, in fact, were largely engaged in remilling spoiled imported flour. But as wheat raising boomed, flour milling followed suit. The flinty character of the California wheat made the local flour excellent for shipment, even through the tropics, and when the Crimean War and the Civil War handicapped older areas of flour production, the California industry was greatly stimulated. In the late sixties California flour was exported not only to the mining camps throughout the Rocky Mountain West but also to Japan and China, to the British Isles, and to continental Europe. By the end of the decade the state had over 200 mills, several capable of milling 1,000 barrels a day.

Of even wider distribution throughout the state was the business of wagon and carriage making. As a Spanish and Mexican province California had gotten along without such establishments, but with the coming of the Americans the wheeled-vehicle complex was introduced. The first wagon shops were crude, because the state lacked hardwoods and foundries. Soon, however, wagon and carriage making was as universal as the automobile repair shop is today. The most famous names connected with the business were those of John Studebaker of Placerville, of subsequent fame as an Indiana manufacturer of wagons and automobiles; George P. Kimball of Oakland, who built a quarter-million-dollar factory in 1868; and Phineas Banning of Wilmington, whose specialty was coaches of the Concord type.

The abundant supply of cowhides, coupled with the great demand for heavy boots in the mines, for harness and pack saddles in the freighting business, for thoroughbraces on the Concord stages, and for belting in all sorts of machine operations, suggested the erection of tanneries and leather-working establishments. The first large tanneries were on the San Lorenzo River, in Santa Cruz County. San Francisco soon took first place, and tanneries appeared at Sacramento, Benicia, and several other northern towns. The output was mostly in heavy leather goods until Civil War days, when an additional impetus was given the manufacture of shoes. In spite of the relatively high wage scale in California, this industry flourished until the advent of hard times in the nineties.

Quartz mining in California, silver mining in Nevada, and excavation and tunneling for railroad construction set up a heavy demand for explosives. When the Civil War made the continued importation of powder both dangerous and expensive, its manufacture was begun. The California Powder Works put up a $150,000 plant on the San Lorenzo River. The Pacific Powder Works in Marin County was even larger. In 1868 these two mills manufactured 1,000,000 kegs of blasting powder, while Contra Costa County boasted half a dozen smaller plants.

Textile mills were introduced at about the same time and under similar provocation. Those designed for cotton, such as the one William H. Rector built at Oakland in 1864, did not succeed, chiefly because cotton raising did not flourish as expected. Manufacture of grain sacks out of jute from the Orient was temporarily more profitable, but the largest and most thriving mills were those turning out woolens. Of these the best known was the Mission Woolen Mills of San Francisco. Other plants were located at Marysville, Santa Rosa, and Sacramento.

Among industries of incidental importance in the fifties and sixties mention should be made of sugar refining and cigar making. The former industry utilized raw cane sugar from the islands of the Pacific and China, though a number of unsuccessful efforts were made to promote sugar-cane cultivation in southern California. In the early American period William T. Coleman and Claus Spreckels were the leading refiners. San Francisco was also the cigar-making center, with Chinese labor predominant.

Of broader importance was iron working. California did not furnish the raw material, but it was brought in at low cost as ballast on the wheat ships. The state and the adjacent West, through the several industries mentioned above, but especially through mining and railroad building, furnished a large market for cables, pipe, wire, pulleys, and machinery of various sorts. The Union, the Neptune, and the Vulcan Iron Works of San Francisco were the earliest large plants. Besides smaller products they turned out locomotives and iron river boats.

Banking and the Comstock

While the foregoing does not purport to be a complete catalog of the industrial expansion of California in the early American period, sufficient detail has been offered, it is hoped, to demonstrate that, although the gold seekers colored and stimulated and perhaps dominated the scene, they were by no means the only factor in the state's new economy. Closely correlated with these various forms of production was the rise of banking. Prior to 1848 California had had only rudimentary banking as carried on by the government account keepers, the prefects of the missions, the hide and tallow traders, who extended credits, and the Army and Navy quartermasters in the period of the conquest. As gold came into production, facilities for storing and transmitting it were called for; and as commerce and industry sprang up, some means of handling financial transactions was required. Merchants and saloonkeepers provided the first banking service, that of safekeeping the miners' sacks of gold. Then, by easy transition, were added the buying and selling of gold, arrangement for its transmission to the East, and the making of loans. The earliest banking was but a side line to other businesses; soon, however, it became a business in itself. A number of Californians entered it, and eastern firms such as Adams and Company, Palmer, Cook and Company, and Page, Bacon and Company opened branches in the state.

The first banking was largely in the hands of inexperienced men and was entirely unregulated by the state. Remoteness from the financial centers of the world made the matter of remittance and exchange difficult and expensive. Nor were the unsettled conditions in California conducive to the most conservative banking practices. In consequence, the early record is full of irregularities. For half a decade most banks prospered; interest rates were from two to five per cent a month, and the miners did not object to a substantial charge on drafts on eastern banks. In 1855, however, a panic gripped San Francisco, which several banks could not weather. Most spectacular was the closing of Page, Bacon and Company. News of the failure of its St. Louis branch precipitated a run on the San Francisco house. For a week the bank met every demand, but on February 23 it was forced to close its doors. Other banks were affected, notably Adams and Company, whose crash was rendered all the more disquieting by reason of the eleventh-hour transfer of its remaining assets to Palmer, Cook and Company. Not until the sixties did California banking fully recover from the shock of 1855. Then its recovery was greatly assisted by the upsurge of local industry and agriculture and by the outpourings of the Nevada silver mines.

These early banks helped much less than might have been expected in the provision of a circulating medium of exchange. Out-of-state exchange was managed fairly well, though it was so expensive that California exporters often resorted to conversion of their receipts into commodities for shipment to San Francisco. Locally, the banks were not privileged to issue bank notes, and Californians had such an addiction to gold that it is probable such paper money would not have circulated anyhow. Throughout '48 and '49 most payments were in gold dust, weighed or guessed at, a pinch passing for a dollar. Then slugs of approximately three ounces passed for fifty dollars. Even after a government mint was established in San Francisco in 1854 much Mexican silver remained in use. In the sixties, when the rest of the nation was doing business chiefly in greenbacks, California scorned them and stuck to hard money, the favorite being the double eagle, the twenty-dollar gold piece.

California's financial history in this period was profoundly affected by the opening of the silver mines of Washoe, now called Nevada. For the better part of a decade after Marshall's discovery in 1848 mining had been confined to the California diggings, but in the late fifties prospectors began to turn up mineral wealth all over the mountainous West. There were strikes in Colorado and eastern Oregon, in Idaho and along the Fraser, in Arizona and Nevada, and eventually in Alaska and the Klondike. In many of these rushes Californians predominated, and for the majority of the new fields San Francisco stood as the logical entrepôt. Most intimate were the relations with Washoe and its Comstock Lode. California contributed most of the miners, supplied food, machinery, whisky, and even water, and in turn felt a Nevada influence upon its literature, commerce, and transportation, and particularly upon its banking and finance.

To Nevada history belongs the detailed story of the discovery of the Comstock, of the working of the mines, of the experiments conducted in milling the ore, of the problems of mine drainage, cooling, and ventilation, and of life in Virginia City. In brief, it may be remarked that the discovery in 1859 followed several years of desultory gold panning, that the eastward rush across the Sierra in the late fall of that year sorely overtaxed the accommodations of Virginia City and the other mining camps in the vicinity of Mt. Davidson, but that nothing could daunt these men in the staking out of claims, the organization of companies, and the floating of stock. In the first season some thirty-seven companies were organized with a stock issue exceeding $30,000,000, and in 1861 an additional forty-nine companies incorporated, all clustered on the slopes of Mt. Davidson, though some had no footage on the Comstock Lode.

Silver mining, the erstwhile gold seekers soon discovered, was a business entirely different from the operation of gold placers. It had a closer affinity to quartz mining, but required even more elaborate machinery and heavier capital investment. Financing by sale of shares was thus the most obvious procedure and San Francisco the most convenient money mart. Mining stocks have a reputation for speculative character and sudden fluctuation. Under the most favorable circumstances those for the Comstock would have surged up and down, because the vein unpredictably widened or pinched out, the miners worked in bonanza and then in borrasca, and there were floods, cave-ins, and fires to reduce still further the regularity of output. Other factors made the Washoe shares plummet wildly. Neither Washoe nor California had seen fit to provide any restrictions on stock issuance or exchange, or any regulation on banking. The door was open for the most unscrupulous rigging of the market.

When mining first began on the Comstock, San Francisco bankers and investors had their fingers burned. They bought shares indiscriminately and then found to their chagrin that many of the properties were nowhere near the real lode. Other mines, however, were pouring out ore assaying from $50 to $2,000 a ton, such solid encouragement that investors could not be scared away permanently. For several years the strategically located mines all paid well. The ore was rich and was located near the surface; mechanical difficulties encountered were surmounted successfully; and those who could raise the money did not hesitate to put millions into a mine's excavation, timbering, hoists, and pumps, hundreds of thousands into a mill, or tens of thousands into a Virginia City saloon. Capital investment on the Comstock mounted rapidly; much of it in mining profits plowed back into the enterprise, but another large fraction derived from California.

Until about 1864 all went well. Then several of the mines ran into borrasca and at the end of the year only the Gould and Curry, with a nine-million-dollar gross, was producing satisfactorily. Seasoned operators, engineers, and geologists believed that still richer ores were to be had for the digging. Whether they actually knew of these may be a different question. In the meantime most of the mines had to levy stock assessments in order to proceed, and the mill owners had to borrow money to tide them over until quantity production was resumed. For their loans they turned almost without exception to William C. Ralston's Bank of California.

Launched in the summer of 1864 with a paid-up capital of two million dollars, this bank promptly established branches in Nevada. Its Nevada manager, William Sharon, adopted a liberal lending policy. He established an interest rate of two per cent a month in place of the prevailing three to five per cent, and he seldom refused a prospective borrower. When he had lent two million dollars on mills and mines and Ralston came over to reason with him about such plunging, Sharon was able to persuade his employer that the risk was good, that sooner or later the mines would strike another bonanza and the bank would recover its money and more. Without a bonanza the bank would be ruined, because the mills and mining machinery to which it held mortgages or title were of value only where they were. No mean plunger himself, Ralston gave the order to proceed.

Shortly the bank was involved to the extent of three and a half millions and had foreclosed on most of the mills. Through 1865 and into the next year the outlook continued very dark. Sharon and Ralston, however, hit on a device to keep their heads above water. With D. O. Mills and one or two other bank officers they organized the Union Mill and Mining Company to operate the mills which the bank had possessed, and through the bank they exerted pressure on the mines to deliver their richest ore to these mills. The scheme worked, though to the distress of the private mill owners. It also appealed to Sharon and Ralston because, when a bonanza was struck, the profits would go to this small group rather than be dissipated among all the stockholders of the bank.

While matters stood thus, the Ralston-Sharon forces were threatened from another quarter, for Adolph Sutro, a young mill owner who was subsequently to be Mayor of San Francisco and a generous benefactor of that city, was proposing a plan which would divert most of the business from the bank's mills. His proposal was for a tunnel tapping the lode at the 2,000-foot level, which would ventilate the mines, carry off the excess water by gravity flow, and save correspondingly on ore-hoisting expense. Though sound from an engineering viewpoint, Sutro's tunnel would have made the bank's mills and hoisting machinery obsolete. The bank, therefore, refused to coöperate; it opposed Sutro on every turn and delayed for more than a decade the completion of the tunnel.

Throughout the late sixties and into the next decade Sharon, as the bank's manager, was unquestionably King of the Comstock. He controlled the railroad built up from Carson City, his lumber company had a virtual monopoly on supplying the mines and mills with timber and fuel, and in other departments of business the bank's power was equally felt. All these years the mines were in borrasca more often than in rich ore, but the bank's monopolies continued to show a profit. Yet a few straws in the wind intimated that Sharon's hold might be broken. A disastrous fire in the Yellow Jacket enabled Sutro to rouse the miners to support his tunnel. Two members of the bank ring, John P. Jones and Alvinza Hayward, went off very profitably on their own. Finding new ore bodies in the Crown Point, they quietly bought up its stock and, by organizing the Nevada Mill and Mining Company, excluded the bank from any direct share in the Crown Point bonanza. Another syndicate comprising two

mining men, John W. Mackay and James Fair, and two San Francisco saloonkeepers, James C. Flood and William S. O'Brien, acquired control of four mines: the Bullion, the Kentuck, the Hale and
Norcross, and the Savage. On the Hale and Norcross they struck a
small bonanza, the profits from which were promptly reinvested in
exploration digging and in buying up the stock of the Virginia and
the California, two mines which had yielded little, though located
between the rich Ophir and the Best and Belcher.

With $212,000 raised by assessment on the Virginia and California
stock, Fair began a search for pay ore. There were discouragements,
which enabled the partners to buy up still more of the outstanding
shares, but in March, 1873, Fair came to a rich vein fifty-four feet
in width. Having gained control of practically all the Virginia and
California stock, the partners neglected no opportunities to publicize
their good fortune. Dan De Quille, the most reputable mining re-
porter in Nevada, was invited to appraise the ore in sight. He
published a figure of $116,748,000, while the director of the mint
estimated the value at $300,000,000 and practical miners were ready
to multiply the figure by five.

With this bonanza pouring out an unprecedented treasure, with
Jones' Crown Point continuing to do well, with the bank's mines
and mills taking a new lease on life, and with English money at last
available for the Sutro Tunnel, Virginia City prospered as never
before. Speculative investment in Comstock shares also touched
a new high, with San Francisco the scene of the most hectic trading.
Because of the great advance of the most interesting stocks, trading
was now principally upon margins and thus subjected to a new hazard. A rumor that the bonanza was exhausted produced a panic in
which, within a single week, the market value of Consolidated Virginia
and California dropped $24,000,000. The bonanza kings professed
to be undisturbed. Their profits, they said, were in ore and not in
stocks; and when the price went low enough, they bought a few more
shares. Among the players of the market, however, the distress was
great. As increasing bullion output disproved the rumor of exhaustion, the market recovered with another wave of margin purchases,
only to crash again in the sumer of 1875. This time the book loss
was over sixty million dollars, and this time the Bank of California
was carried down in the crash.

Sharon, Mills, and some others of the bank ring were able to salvage their personal fortunes, but Ralston was not. Ousted as cashier, he walked to North Beach for his customary swim and, by accident or design, drowned. An audit of his books showed unsecured liabilities in excess of $4,500,000. The temptation is to condemn Ralston as a predatory economic royalist. He had taken the lead, however, in many enterprises of great civic importance. The Palace Hotel, his estate at Belmont, and the Bank of California had been his principal monuments, but steamship lines, the Spring Valley Water Company, the Lone Mountain Cemetery, the University of California, and so many other projects had benefited from his promotion as to suggest to a biographer the title "The Man Who Built San Francisco."

On the ruins of Ralston's bank the bonanza kings erected the Nevada Bank of San Francisco and assembled a Comstock monopoly more complete than its predecessor's. In another few years, however, the bonanza was exhausted, and Virginia City soon dwindled to ghostlike proportions. Fortunes based on the Comstock, such as those of Mackay, Fair, Flood, O'Brien, Sharon, Mills, Jones, Sutro, and Hearst, were prominent in subsequent chapters of the nation's and particularly of California's history. To San Franciscans, however, the Comstock is above all memorable for the two decades of great excitement and the glorious opportunity for speculative investment that it afforded. In popular fancy it dwarfed such enterprises as wheat ranching, flour milling, carriage making, or lumbering.

So much for the survey of California's new economy. While similar adumbration of the social structure that accompanied it and issued from it must be left to the sociologist or even to the student of abnormal psychology, some notice of the new society is indispensable. At first, and for some years to come, the population was predominantly masculine, a condition which had its ridiculous consequences—as when men with patched trouser seats took the feminine parts in a square dance—but which also affected more important standards of social usage and intercourse throughout northern California. The sudden flood of gold prompted extravagance and recklessness, symbolized by the prevalence of gambling, while the flush times enabled northern California to command superior theatrical talent, the best transportation equipment that money could buy, and a periodical press attuned to the local taste. Paradoxically, prosperity did not produce a demand for good government; instead, men became so engrossed in their private affairs as to have time only occasionally to ponder on the conduct of state and local officers.   Southern California, meanwhile, was passing through a more gradual transition, was discarding less rapidly the Spanish and Mexican traditions, and was affected only indirectly by the social metallurgy of '49.

18

POLITICAL EXPERIMENT

WHEN HE RAISED the American flag at Monterey in 1846, Commodore Sloat had proclaimed that California was to be a permanent possession of the United States. "Its peaceable inhabitants," he continued, "will enjoy the same rights and privileges as the citizens of any other portion of that nation. . . . They will also enjoy a permanent Government, under which life, property, and the constitutional right and lawful security to worship the creator in a way most congenial to each ones sense of duty, will be secure." Under such a regime, he predicted, "the country cannot but improve more rapidly than any other on the continent of America." Stockton was even more explicit in promising that territorial government would be provided.

Military Government Protested

For the time being, however, in accordance with the precedents set in other newly acquired American territories, military government was put into operation. This action had further justification after the southern California revolt had necessitated reconquest by force; yet even in this district the military governors tempered martial rule by encouraging the alcaldes and other local officials of the Mexican regime to continue functioning. From the native Californians, despite the childish wrangling of Stockton, Kearny, and Frémont over precedence and authority, there appears to have been no objection to the type of government that prevailed.

Not so with the Americans in California. They protested bitterly

275

against government by the military, asserting that the Constitution accompanied the flag, and demanding immediate provision of civil government. Curiously enough, the one feature of civil government that did exist, namely, alcalde rule, struck them as particularly un-American and was the target of their sharpest shafts. Alcaldes were orthodox Spanish American local officials, unhampered by the Anglo-Saxon fetish of separation of powers. Anglo-Americans looked aghast at the wide range of their authority, which, it must be admitted, was occasionally misused. A writer in the *California Star* complained that alcaldes exercised "authority far greater than any officer in our republic—the president not excepted. . . . The grand autocrat of the Russians . . . is the only man in Christendom I know of who equals him."

Whether the constitutional guaranties of civil government entered California with Sloat's proclamation, with the Cahuenga Capitulation, or with the Treaty of Guadalupe Hidalgo is a question on which the jurists have engaged in inconclusive hairsplitting. Certainly the Californians did not delay their criticisms of the military regime until after the signing of the treaty. Exactly one month after Cahuenga the *California Star* urged the formation of a constitutional convention, and a year later, on January 22, 1848, "Pacific" complained in the same paper that California, "since the United States flag was hoisted over it, has been in a sad state of disorganization . . . , we have had no government at all during the period, unless the inefficient mongrel military rule exercised over us be termed such." Other journals called on the military governors to take the necessary steps or advised the people to assume the initiative.

With the end of the war and the definitive cession of California to the United States, the arguments against military government gained added weight. Washington recognized that civil government was in order for California but saw also a number of complicating circumstances. For one thing, the Mexican Cession possessed populations that eastern Americans distrusted. Congress granted Oregon territorial government in the spring of 1848, but an amendment to broaden the act so as to provide the same sort of governmental machinery for California and New Mexico was voted down on the ground that "native-born" Oregon should not be unequally yoked with territories "peopled by Mexicans and half-Indian Californians." A worse drawback involved the question of slavery extension. President Taylor advocated procrastination because he feared the flare-up that would inevitably attend Congressional attempts to provide civil government. Delay lasted two and a half years after the Treaty of Guadalupe Hidalgo. To the Californians this seemed unconscionable; as a matter of fact it was not extraordinary, for Oregon had waited two years for territorial government and New Mexico was to wait sixty years for statehood.

In California the impatience with military government was mounting. Colonel Mason, in announcing on August 7, 1848, the formal cession to the United States, attempted to mollify the Californians by predicting that Congress would provide civil government within a few months. He also issued a code of *Laws for the Better Government of California* (published by S. Brannan, San Francisco, 1848), but the rarity of this volume and its infrequent contemporary mention indicate that the reform was not entirely effective. Throughout the summer and fall of 1848 Californians were so preoccupied with the search for gold that they gave little thought to things political, but with the onset of the winter rains and the consequent interruption of mining many of the gold seekers had time either at their camps or in the settlements to reflect upon the injustice of Washington's delay. On February 12, 1849, some four or five hundred assembled San Franciscans resolved that a better-defined government was absolutely necessary. They proceeded to organize a town government along American lines, but Mason's successor, General (and Governor) Persifer F. Smith, refused his support.

The inrushing forty-niners shortly thereafter changed the whole complexion of the province. Although politics was not their major interest, they were not in a mood to accept complacently the disenfranchisement symbolized by military government. Whatever the jurists might opine, they were absolutely certain that they had brought their constitutional prerogatives with them across the plains, across Panama, or around the Horn. They quickly fell in line with the proposals for direct action, such as that mentioned at San Francisco, and with the plan for a constituent assembly. Mass meetings at San Jose, Sacramento, Santa Cruz, and Monterey endorsed this plan and set the date for its convening on the first Monday in August.

Organizing a State

Facing this situation upon his assumption of the governorship in April, General Bennett Riley concluded that it would be more seemly for a convention to gather at his invitation. Accordingly, as soon as he learned that Congress had adjourned without acting for California, he issued a call for a convention to meet at Monterey on September 1. San Franciscans particularly resented his "interference," but in the end they concluded that more might be gained by coöperating than by resisting. The elections were held, and early in September the delegates gathered.

Riley's proclamation had designated ten districts: San Diego, Santa Barbara, and San Luis Obispo to send two delegates each; Los Angeles, Sonoma, Sacramento, and San Joaquin, four each; and Monterey, San Jose, and San Francisco, five each. There was an optional clause, however, authorizing any district that considered itself entitled to a larger representation to elect additional delegates. The southern districts sent only the ten delegates specified, but the northern districts increased Riley's allotment by eleven, which enlarged the convention's membership to forty-eight.

That the convention proceeded to frame a state rather than a territorial government was because of the gold rush. California had received such a great influx of population that it could skip the territorial stage. Forty-niners, however, did not dominate the convention. Not more than a dozen of the forty-eight members had come in the rush. The others were "old timers": a few native Californians, such as Vallejo, Carrillo, and De la Guerra; some Americans of long residence, such as Stearns and Larkin; others like Semple, who had come with the overland immigrants in the forties; and Mexican War veterans, of whom Halleck is representative. These old timers who were to be California's Founding Fathers were not old in years; only four had passed fifty, thirty were not yet forty, and nine were still in their twenties.

The most debated question before the convention was where to locate the eastern boundary. The large-state faction urged the Rockies; the small-state faction, the Sierra. Six or eight compromise lines were proposed, and the convention repeatedly switched its approval from one to another. From the debates it was evident that the territory west of the Sierra and that fronting on the Colorado was what really mattered. For the rest, the prime consideration was to get a line that Congress would approve promptly. Exclusion of the Mormon district around Salt Lake seemed advisable, because the Mormons were not represented in the convention and preferred to remain apart. Another argument of the small-state advocates was that the national government should be left responsible for protecting and relieving emigrant parties in the intermountain desert basin. The present line was the eventual compromise.

The work of the convention was much simplified because of the availability of other state constitutions. Chief reliance was on that of Iowa, the most recent constitution in the West, and on New York's newly revised frame of government, but the influence of six or eight others can be detected.

Several circumstances tend to impair the reputation of this first California constitution. It was suspect because it had been drawn up in the wild and boisterous West and by a body irregularly convened. The disgracefully low standards of political conduct in California in the following decade also reacted unfavorably upon the constitution's standing. Furthermore, within thirty years the state discarded it in favor of a new one. On the other hand, it is worth noting that the work of the Monterey convention was approved almost without dissent when submitted to popular vote. Congress criticized the procedure followed with regard to California but made no complaint about the constitution. Moreover, political scientists agree that this first constitution was a superior document. It was a simple statement of fundamental principles and procedures, not cluttered with a multitude of technical provisions really legislative in character.

A most striking tribute to the excellence of this constitution of '49 is that it was a principal inspiration and model for the Argentinian constitution of 1853. Comparison of the two documents reveals their similarities. We have also the testimony of Juan Bautista Alberdi, father of the constitution of 1853. Acknowledging his indebtedness, Alberdi had this to say of the California document:

Without universities, without academies or law colleges, the newly-organized people of California have drawn up a constitution full of foresight, of common sense and of opportunity.

California statehood was not approved by Congress until almost a year later. The constitution, some Congressmen charged, had been "concocted" by President Taylor through Governor Riley. Others objected that the Californians were heterogeneous adventurers who could not be trusted to operate a state government; furthermore, they were ill-mannered upstarts who had not waited for an enabling act as the signal to draw up a frame of government. Such a dangerous manifestation of disregard for Congress should be rebuked as an example to the rest of the West.   Yet the real reasons for the delay were eastern rather than western.   They concerned the overlapping claims of Texas, New Mexico, Deseret, and California in the Mexican Cession; they had to do with party jealousies and with factional disputes between the President and Congress; above all, they were inherent in the disagreement between the North and the slave-holding South.   Only through the exercise of Henry Clay's suave peacemaking could these several issues be compromised.   In the end the national government approved what the West had done, and on September 9, 1850, California took her place in the family of states.

This admission to statehood is widely heralded and celebrated. It is not so well known that the impatient Californians had not waited for formal admission to start operating their state government.   After approval of the constitution at the election in November, 1849, the first legislature assembled in December, and on the twentieth of that month Peter H. Burnett was sworn in as the first civil governor of the state.   The wheels of government creaked, not so much because they were new as because money raising was practically impossible so long as ultimate recognition of the state government was uncertain. In this intermediate stage, of course, California had no representation in Congress.   Consequently, admission to the Union meant much to the state.   It dispelled the specter of military government, it regularized the state government which was already operating, it seated California's Senators and Congressmen at Washington, and it set a seal of approval upon a state constitution which was a lasting monument to the good sense and wise decision of the Californians of '49.

Whereas the constitution of 1849 demonstrated the political capacity of the Californians, their day-to-day citizenship was more nearly of the caliber predicted by the Congressional pessimists who had hesitated to entrust state government to these gold-mad westerners.   Inexperience was one obstacle to good government.   A contributing factor was inattention induced by the absorbing and highly profitable nature of private enterprise.   In the conduct of state government, the result of this crass neglect was a record of the grossest abuses.   The legislature of 1849, as has been intimated, faced a peculiar handicap in that the delay of admission left all its acts in a position of dubious legality.   This first legislature enacted a code of laws and chose the first United States Senators, but it is better known as the "Legislature of a Thousand Drinks," in remembrance of Senator Thomas J. Green's constant advocacy of adjournment for liquid refreshment. The legislature of 1851, it pleased a San Francisco journalist to observe, was "an infamous, ignorant, drunken, rowdy, perjured and traitorous body of men."

In the Mexican period the capital had been shifted from Monterey to San Diego, Santa Barbara, or Los Angeles at the caprice of the governor. As the American period began, one of the major issues was to decide where to bring the capital to rest. The military governors had stationed themselves at Monterey. There likewise the constitutional convention assembled, but the sudden importance of the mining area seemed to dictate removal to some point nearer the center of population. Local aspirations influenced the decision. For the first legislative session San Jose was designated. Then arose the question whether to continue at San Jose, return to Monterey, go to New York of the Pacific, a budding metropolis on Carquinez Straits, or cross the straits to a site tendered by Mariano Guadalupe Vallejo. By offering 156 acres of land and a contribution of $370,000 to the building fund, Vallejo prevailed.

In 1852, however, when the legislature convened at Vallejo, it found none of the conveniences which the general had promised. The decision was shortly to take ship for Sacramento, and the merchants of that town having thoughtfully chartered a river boat for the purpose, the legislature moved, lock, stock, and gavel. The next year it tried Benicia, but in 1854 it returned permanently to Sacramento. While gold mining dominated the economy this site had the recommendation of convenience, but with the shift of population to southern California the argument lost weight. Certainly the removal from Monterey meant the abandonment of a distinctive geographical environment, rich in historical associations, for one with climatic handicaps reminiscent of the midwestern states.

Gwin versus Broderick

Throughout the fifties California was emphatically Democratic. Only once did the governorship fall to the opposition, and the United States Senate seats, which were regarded as much higher political prizes, were reserved exclusively for Democrats. Within the party, however, a most bitter rivalry developed. Leadership was in the hands of two most astute politicians, each of whom had come to California with a determination to dominate the politics of this new commonwealth.   Their spirited contest, fortunately, has seldom been surpassed in bitterness in the subsequent political experience of the state.

First on the scene was William M. Gwin of Tennessee and subsequently of Mississippi, a well-educated man, a physician, a magnetic personality, a veteran of Jacksonian politics, and a protégé of the Polk regime.   His leadership was particularly acceptable to the southerners in California, and his faction of the party was often spoken of as the Chivalry or Chiv Democrats.   Gwin assumed leadership at the constitutional convention at Monterey and immediately impressed himself upon the Californians as a most capable and experienced political leader.   He encountered little opposition in his candidacy for the first full-term seat in the United States Senate, Frémont being chosen for the other place.

David C. Broderick, who was to enter the lists against Gwin, had gained his political experience in a very different environment, but perhaps the ideal place for one who was to oppose Jacksonian demagoguery.   He was a Tammany Democrat, schooled there in all the tricks of political chicanery and the approved methods of building a political machine.   Not so well educated as Gwin, Broderick was a likeable young Irishman with considerable genius for leadership.

Although the federal patronage was beyond his grasp, Broderick quickly built up a personal following through the state patronage, the municipal machines at San Francisco and Sacramento, and control of the party conventions.   By 1854 his control of the legislature had reached the point where he thought it safe to call for the choice of a successor to Gwin in the Senate, though normally the vote would not have been taken until the following year.   By a narrow margin the Gwin forces managed to defeat this proposal, but only after both sides had resorted to every conceivable device to sway the legislature. The breach widened, and in 1856 the Know Nothings or Native Americans, who in California were more antiforeign than anti-Catholic, were able to take advantage of it to elect J. Neely Johnson governor.

In 1857, when the Senatorial question was finally brought to a vote, Broderick was able to dictate the terms.   He got himself elected to succeed John B. Weller, whose term was to expire that year.   The other place went to Gwin, but only after he had agreed to place the federal patronage in Broderick's hands.   Gwin gave evidence of a sincere intention of going through with his part of this hard bargain, but President Buchanan would have nothing to do with Broderick, who had vigorously opposed the President's policy regarding Kansas. His colleagues in the Senate likewise failed to warm to him, with the result that Broderick returned to California in 1859 very much embittered and, because of his noncontrol of the patronage, with fewer supporters in the state than when he had left.

Broderick plunged immediately into a strenuous and bitter campaign against the Gwin forces. Neither side refrained in the least from mud slinging and the bitterest invectives, which led at length to Broderick's being challenged by Judge David S. Terry of the State Supreme Court, who had been a testy member of the Law and Order faction at the time of the Second San Francisco Vigilance Committee and in state politics was a firm adherent of Gwin. Broderick promptly accepted the challenge, and on September 13, 1859, the two met on the field of honor in a valley near Lake Merced, just across the line into San Mateo County. Broderick's shot struck the ground near his feet, but Terry's carefully aimed shot went true to its mark. Public opinion turned devastatingly against Terry and reacted also against Gwin. The Democrats held the governorship in 1859, but the Broderick faction swung toward the Republican ranks, and in 1860 the state's votes in the electoral college went to Lincoln.

Movements for State Division and for a Pacific Republic

Throughout the fifties there was a strong undercurrent of feeling in favor of a division of the state. The southern delegates had raised the question at the constitutional convention in 1849 because they thought territorial government more suited to the needs of their section, and as state government went into operation, the worst expectations of the southerners were realized. The southern counties were given less than their due share of representation in the legislature, legislation was selfishly or thoughtlessly directed for the exclusive benefit of the mining counties, and taxation was visited most heavily upon the nonmining cow counties. In 1852 Governor McDougal admitted that the six cow counties with a population of 6,000 paid $42,000 in property taxes and $4,000 in poll taxes, while the north with 120,000 population paid only $21,000 and $3,500, respectively. Los Angeles newspapers protested in similar vein and fumed over the inadequate representation of the south. Even the San Francisco

Daily Alta protested that the majority of representatives from the
mining counties acted as though "no bond of connection or sympathy existed between their interests and those of the commercial
cities and other sources of wealth of our infant state."

Skeptical about producing any change of heart upon the part of
the established politicans, southern Californians began to advocate
state division. In 1851 a "Convention to Divide the State of California" was called to meet at Los Angeles. The men who summoned this convention asserted that state government had proved a
"splendid failure," that Los Angeles in particular was tasting its bitter
fruits in political neglect, paralyzed commerce, insupportable taxation, and the complete lack of protection against Indian depredations.
Separation, "friendly and peaceful but still complete," they asserted
to be an imperative necessity. Other efforts followed, and in 1859
Andrés Pico secured legislative approval for the incorporation of the
counties from San Luis Obispo south as the Territory of Colorado.
A two-thirds vote of approval in the counties affected was assured,
but before Congressional approval could be gained, the Civil War
broke out to block the step completely.

Without disparagement of the values of unity, it may be remarked
that discrimination against southern California continued. There
have been damages to its pride in the bestowal of adjectives such as
non-American, backward, rustic, and disloyal, and in the permanent
appropriation of the expression "the City." Taxation, bearing more
heavily upon real estate than upon industry, has not applied evenly.
Appropriations, such as those for state highway construction and
maintenance, have favored the north. Finally, although the census of
1920 revealed that the population majority had passed to the south,
reapportionment of representation at Washington and Sacramento did
not begin to take effect until 1933.

Of the remaining political issues of the fifties the one of broadest
potentialities was doubtless the recurrent suggestion of a Pacific Republic. Back in the Mexican period there had been something of a
tendency toward independence, which the Revolution of 1836 put
largely into effect. Certain of the early Americans in the province,
Lansford W. Hastings in particular, also dreamed of a western independence. The Bear Flag movement, had it been allowed to run its
full course, might have led to such a consequence. For a decade and
a half thereafter the scheme was proposed as often as California had

a real or fancied grievance. When military government was prolonged and statehood denied, the idea came to the fore. Again,
during the days of the Second Vigilance Committee, when there
seemed to be a possibility of federal interference, a "strong undercurrent of secession" animated the vigilantes. They made no public
announcement to that effect, because such a statement would have
justified the interposition of national arms, but later several of the
leaders admitted that it had been so. Whenever the Californians
felt that they deserved better mail service, more protection against
the Indians, a transcontinental railroad, or additional ports of entry,
their dissatisfaction with Washington was apt to inspire visions of a
Pacific Republic.

Lincoln's election raised the question in earnest. Although a free
state, California had been consistently Democratic and in 1858 had
endorsed Buchanan's Kansas policy. The state was isolated. Its
population was drawn mostly from the North, but a substantial minority was of southern extraction. Should any Californian be called
upon to fight against the "land of his nativity"? Governor Weller
had advised escape from the dilemma of choosing between the North
and South by founding on the shores of the Pacific "a mighty republic,
which may in the end prove the greatest of all." Other officials
agreed, particularly Congressman John C. Burch, who became the
leading advocate.

California's gold and her population, comprised of "the most enter-
prizing and energetic men of the country," were counted upon to
secure the new nation favorable reception into the family of nations.
Advantages were also foreseen in the rivalry of North and South for
California's trade. On the other hand, western population was small,
Oregon and Utah could not be counted on for financial support, the
bulk of trade had been with northern states, and the national government had been spending millions for California's benefit. Consequently, sober second thought discouraged westward secession.

The Civil War

The choice of supporting North or South remained. The legislature passed loyal resolutions, while the governor repudiated Lincoln's
policy. "I do not believe," he said, "that an aggressive war should
be waged on any section of the Confederacy, nor do I believe that
this Union can be preserved by a coercive policy." Loyalty demon-

strations answered pro-South appeals, and men rallied to both sides. The plain truth was that California was a border state, fairly evenly divided between Union and secession sentiment.

Although a divided Democratic vote in 1860 had allowed the Republicans to carry the state for Lincoln, they had polled only three votes out of every eight; loyalty was not absolutely proved, and the state election of 1861 was looked upon as a significant test. The "Secesh" faction redoubled its efforts; Union sympathizers organized the Home Guard and made a systematic effort to swing the state to Leland Stanford, the Republican candidate. Helped by the firing on Fort Sumter and by the death of Douglas, and especially by the oratory of a Unitarian divine, Thomas Starr King, the Republican and Union ticket carried.

Far from being silenced, the "Secesh" faction continued its protests in press and pulpit, in poem and harangue. Sometimes the criticism was direct, with the Union Army assailed as "a whining running army, that has disgraced our flag, lowered our cause and dishonored Republican chivalry," or with Lincoln called an "unprincipled demagogue," an "illiterate backwoodsman," and a "narrow minded bigot." At other times there was more subtle reference to "Mr. Lincoln" and "President Davis." The Visalia *Equal Rights Expositor* "prayed" on Thanksgiving Day, 1862:

O Lord we thank thee for letting the rebels wallop us at the battle of Pittsburg Landing—for letting them smite us hip and thigh, even unto the destruction of 9,600 of our good loyal soldiers, and 463 of our officers; and for giving speed to their legs through the awful swamps of Chicahominy; and, O Lord, most especially do we thank thee for the licking they gave us at Bull Run the second, and assisting our flight from that fatal field; and, O Lord, never while we live will we forget Antietam, where we had 200,000 and they only 70,000—if they, O Lord, had a happened to a had as many men as we, we'd a been a done gone in— and that friendly creek between us, the mountains that kept our men from running. . . .

General George Wright responded to the most vicious of these attacks by excluding half a dozen papers from the mails. When this and other forms of persuasion failed to moderate the editors of the *Expositor,* some thirty soldiers, without consulting their officers, broke into the newspaper office, broke the press, and pitched type, paper, and ink into the street. The Reverend Mr. Scott, a clergyman in San Francisco, had the temerity to insist before presbytery that

Jefferson Davis was no more a traitor than George Washington had been. Berated by the press and threatened by a mob, Scott was forced to resign his pulpit and leave the state, though he later returned to his pastorate.

Southern sympathizers in California made one effort to strike for the Confederacy. Under the pretext of a commercial venture to Manzanillo, they loaded a quantity of ammunition and arms on the schooner *Chapman,* intending to intercept a Pacific Mail steamer, convert it into a privateer, and ravage Union shipping in the Pacific. Federal authorities got wind of the plot, seized the *Chapman* before she passed the Golden Gate, and interned the men involved.

Since Confederate sentiment was so strong, the government hesitated to draw many loyal volunteers out of California. Of some 16,000 who were enlisted, a few did garrison duty along western trails, but the majority remained in the state. The "California Hundred" and the "California Battalion" were attached to the Second Massachusetts Cavalry and participated in more than fifty engagements. The next nearest approach to active service was when the California Column under General Carleton marched through Yuma and Tucson to the Rio Grande to repel the Confederate invasion of New Mexico. The invaders had already fallen back, and the principal consequence of the march was that a number of deserters started a mining rush to Bill Williams Fork. Gold shipments rather than fighting men were California's greatest contribution to the northern cause.

Although California was not in the heat of the conflict, several of her citizens gained great fame for their war work. There was, for example, Leland Stanford, the war governor. A more popular figure was Colonel E. D. Baker, a great orator and one of the most prominent members of the California bar. Shortly before the war he had gone to Oregon, where he was promptly elected to the United States Senate. His speeches did much to strengthen the Republican cause in California and to bring about the election of Stanford, and in the Senate he was one of Lincoln's most valued supporters. Upon the outbreak of hostilities he resigned his place in the Senate to serve brilliantly in the northern army and to die at Ball's Bluff. The Reverend Myron C. Briggs of the Methodists was another favorite patriotic orator, only less famous than his Unitarian colleague, Thomas Starr King. King had been a very popular lecturer on nature topics. He spoke for Lincoln in 1860 and for Stanford in 1861, but his greater fame rests upon his eloquent solicitation for the Sanitary Commission, the Civil War precursor of the Red Cross. Largely through his efforts California contributed $1,233,831.31, which was more than one fourth of the entire amount received by the Commission. For humanitarian as well as patriotic reasons, therefore, Thomas Starr King is considered second only to Father Serra among California's heroes.

For a decade after the end of the war Californians were more alive to national issues and the problems of Reconstruction than to local politics. No arresting questions arose comparable to the contest between Gwin and Broderick or the crucial election of 1861. The war had laid to rest several of the issues of the fifties, such as the questions of state division and of a western secession. Others, such as the location of the capital, had died a natural death or had gone into protracted hibernation. The problem of governmental inefficiency and corruption held over, but was not considered particularly pressing. Attack upon it was delayed until the late seventies, when it was caught up in a wave of more general unrest and discontent.

19

VIGILANTES AND FILIBUSTERS

THE BOLD, IMPETUOUS, and swashbuckling temper of the Californians of the golden era is apparent in their approach to the problems of economic development and state politics. It is observable also in their attack upon the problems of law.

Law and Justice in the Diggings

In the diggings a peculiar situation existed. Gold seekers poured in so rapidly that the regular agencies of lawmaking and law enforcement could not keep pace. The miners, therefore, took matters into their own hands, devised a mining code to regulate their relationship with one another, improvised courts for the adjudication of disputes and for the trial of criminal suspects, and inflicted forthright punishments upon those found guilty. Political scientists often refer to these achievements of the forty-niners as an illustration of government created by compact. It should be noted, however, that it was by no means creation de novo. The ideas utilized were drawn from the system current in the States and descended from older English and Teutonic practices.

The miners' preference seemed to be for the simplest procedures possible. Their fundamental premise was that every person should be free to do as he pleased so long as he did not harm his neighbor, and that anyone who violated this code should be put where he could not repeat the violation. The first necessity was a set of claim regulations. In detail these varied from camp to camp, but their essentials were that a claim must be reasonable in size and that the only way to perpetuate title was to work the claim. Absentee landowners

289

had no place in the miners' society; nor was anyone allowed to enclose natural resources or place them out of the reach of labor, which was recognized as the prime agency in wealth production. The concept was more redolent of the frontier than of common law. State and national authorities eventually recognized the soundness of the code as the ideal foundation upon which to build the official system of mining laws. "And the beginning," as Branch observes, "was a signboard on a California gravel bar: CLAIME NOTISE, —Jim Brown of Missoury takes this ground; jumpers will be shot."

The civil code was an everyday necessity in the diggings; need for criminal law arose only occasionally, but the extralegal democracy of the forty-niners also met these emergencies. Dry Diggings, near Coloma, provided the first instance. In January, 1849, five men were caught red-handed in an attempt to rob a Mexican gambler. Courts, jails, and authorities being far away, the alternatives seemed to be to turn them loose or to set up a local substitute for court machinery. The miners chose the latter alternative. A jury of twelve was formed and its verdict of thirty-nine lashes duly executed. Then new charges were made against three of the culprits for crimes of the preceding fall on the Stanislaus. Hanging was the popular verdict. E. Gould Buffum entered a vigorous protest, but the mob was not to be dissuaded. Three corpses soon dangled from a convenient oak, and Dry Diggings was ready for its new name, Hangtown.

As occasion arose, other mining communities followed the Hangtown example until, as Bancroft put it, the quiet oaks were "tasselled with the carcasses of the wicked." Again, procedure varied from camp to camp, but in general, suspected thieves or murderers were haled before a miners' meeting, testimony was heard, a jury returned the verdict, or in smaller camps the decision was reached by an open vote of all assembled, and the group promptly executed the sentence. Since imprisonment was out of the question, hanging, banishment from the camp, ear cropping, and whipping were the customary penalties. A typical account of miners' justice is recorded in Gay's diary:

I was called up last night 11 or 12 o'clock to assist in taking and trying a man for stealing money—George Gillin late of Ioway—Took him up to Dry Town—went into the "Southern House" I was appointed Judge —selected 12 men for Jury tryed him—found him guilty—sentenced him to 39 lashes on the bare back—blind folded. Tryal occupied the night—Jury rendered their verdict about sun up—took him out—tied him up and applyed the lash—required him to leave by 3 p.m.

Some writers insist that the miners' justice was no justice at all, with the innocent suffering as often as the guilty and with only the most haphazard correlation between crime and punishment. Bret Harte, for example, tells the apocryphal tale of the jury that was told its verdict had better be right because the defendant had already been hanged. Yet the consensus of opinion is that the miners administered justice admirably in civil cases and remarkably well in criminal cases. The happy result is attributed to the Anglo-Saxon genius for spontaneous self-government, a genius balanced at the time only by the gross corruption in the municipal government of San Francisco. The miners' justice savored of lynch law, yet Hangtown was thought an opprobrious name long before the residents transmuted it to Placerville, and the most famous case, the execution of Juanita at Downieville in 1851, was one of the very few examples of sadism. Barstow characterized this meeting as "the hungriest, craziest, wildest mob" he had ever seen and insisted that "the hanging of the woman was murder." "Since that time," he continued, "I have had no sympathy with or confidence in mobs; I prefer the law for redress of grievances." At the time, of course, there was no law, and the only valid comparison must be with the anarchy that would have prevailed except for the functioning of extralegal democracy.

This justification of lynch law decreased in validity as regular courts and sheriffs appeared on the scene. Oftentimes, however, there was a preference for direct action even after the orthodox machinery was available. Many of the forty-niners, it must be admitted, enjoyed the excitement of taking the law into their own hands. On other occasions local chauvinism entered in, as in 1857, when the prospectors at Grass Valley preferred to try their own culprits rather than turn them over to the county authorities at the rival town of Marysville. Politics also figured, as in the case of the hanging of Hamilton McCauley at Napa in 1851. He had been convicted in regular court for the murder of the municipal judge, but fellow Chivalry Democrats brought persuasion to bear upon Governor McDougal and procured a reprieve, which was to be delivered by the sheriff from the rival town, Benicia. The Napans got wind of the sheriff's coming and delayed him on the road just long enough so that the prisoner could be properly hanged, thus serving the ends both of party politics and of town pride.

The San Francisco Committees

Related and yet distinct from these rustic manifestations were the famous popular tribunals of San Francisco. As early as 1849 the ineffectiveness of police, prosecutors, and courts had led to the appearance of the Hounds, or Regulators. Ostensibly a volunteer police organization, this group of young men was actually a gang preying chiefly upon the weak and the inoffensive. Few Americans suffered, but the various groups of foreigners were victimized in turn. Not until the Hounds perpetrated a particularly atrocious raid upon Little Chile were the San Franciscans sufficiently aroused. Led by Sam Brannan, the citizens then took a day off, gathered at the Plaza, contributed money for the rehabilitation of the Chileños, and ordered the arrest of the leading Regulators. Banishment and other penalties were decreed for several of these "Sydney Ducks"; others fled before the wrath of the citizens, and the gang was entirely shattered and demolished. In embryo, this was a foretaste of what the Bay City citizenry would do when a municipal house cleaning should become absolutely imperative.

Ordeal by fire resulted in another civic improvement. In eighteen months San Francisco was devastated by six fires that did at least twelve million dollars worth of damage. Rebuilding on a grander but no less combustible scale had followed each fire. Volunteer fire companies were organized, but their service was more social and political than protective. The fire houses became clubs and later powerful political organizations. A fire alarm started a race to the conflagration. The hook-and-ladder companies had a glorious time ripping off the side of the building to give the hose companies a chance to stop the fire's spread. The engine companies, meanwhile, were pumping water from one engine to another and eventually to the fire. They jerked the hand rails up and down at frantic speed, far less anxious to extinguish the flames than to "wash" the next crew—that is, to produce an overflow by pumping water in faster than it could be pumped out.

Since the fires were commonly attributed to incendiaries, San Francisco at length recognized the need for striking at the cause as well as the effect. Immediately after the great fire of 1851 the Vigilance

Committee was formally organized, with Sam Brannan as a leading figure. In an earlier endeavor to get the notorious James Stuart convicted of crime the committee had failed because its own jury divided; now the equally infamous John Jenkins was apprehended robbing a safe and brought before the Committee for trial. Jenkins fully expected that the criminal element would come to his rescue. The Committee did display some hesitancy about proceeding to his execution, but the leaders gained in resoluteness and sentence was passed. Sam Brannan, in the meantime, harangued the unruly crowd that had gathered and won its acquiescence if not its unanimous support. Jenkins was marched to the Plaza and hanged, and when the coroner's jury listed nine of the men implicated the Committee promptly published its entire roster of 180 names. Ninety others suspected of murder, robbery, and incendiarism were haled before this extralegal tribunal. Three of them were hanged, one was whipped, twenty-eight were deported, fifteen were delivered to the authorities for trial, and forty-one were released.

It was summary action which is said to have given the criminal element more pause than fifty regular hangings. Danger is inherent, of course, when men take the law into their own hands; yet even the severest critics of the First Vigilance Committee grant that the provocation was great, that the regular courts were supine or helpless, and that the Committee acted without undue passion or severity.

Thereafter, robbery and incendiarism were less flagrant, but within a few years new abuses developed. Municipal offices fell into the hands of unprincipled persons. There were scandals in connection with public-works contracts, local government expenses shot up, and elections were brazenly manipulated. The courts also were notoriously corrupt. They tolerated and connived at the sharp practices of criminal lawyers to such an extent that it was practically impossible to get a conviction for murder, no matter how clear the evidence. The Chivalry Democrats reaped political profit from this sad state of affairs, but it was the apathy of businessmen and of the people generally that made its existence possible.

When the panic of 1855 redirected attention to governmental problems, the editor of the *Bulletin,* the dynamic James King of William, launched a vigorous campaign for better government. Conceiving of himself as "a moral gadfly" and "the conscience of San Francisco," he was in vituperation and invective another John Randolph of Roanoke. In fearlessly outspoken fashion he set about a systematic exposure of the iniquities of Palmer, Cook and Company, one of the leading financial concerns of the city, and went on to analyze the workings of the courts, the practices of leading lawyers, and the operations of the sheriff's office. He mentioned men by name, specified their misdeeds, and called upon the citizens to demand legal steps toward reform. Among others he antagonized James P. Casey, a county supervisor. Because King had broadcast that he was a former inmate of Sing Sing and had refused to give any space in the *Bulletin* to a denial or rebuttal, Casey challenged the editor to a duel, and when the latter declined, threatened to shoot him on sight. At least a score of like threats had been made by others pilloried in the *Bulletin,* and King apparently took this one no more seriously. But fired up by his cronies, Casey intercepted King as he left his office and shot him down.

King had not been in all respects admirable. One of the most reputable attorneys then practicing in the San Francisco bar insists that he was a notorious, broken-down money dealer, that his paper was small and scurrilous, and that its leading columns were devoted to daily abuse, without much regard to facts. This attorney further asserts that King refused to publish evidence disproving his charge against Casey, that he declined the latter's challenge to a duel, that he provoked a street fight, and that he was warned to draw and defend himself and had his cocked pistol half drawn when Casey fired. Had the latter withheld his fire one second longer, according to this informant, the fracas would have been called a fair fight rather than an assassination. As it was, Casey lifted the somewhat unworthy James King of William to martyrdom.

Public indignation welled high, and Casey was put in the county jail for safekeeping. He had abundant confidence in the courts, and well he might, for Charles E. Cora had just escaped conviction for the murder of a United States marshal. For like reason the people had no confidence that the courts would administer justice upon Casey. A mob swarmed around the jail, but the mayor, the police, and the militia succeeded in quieting it. Mass meetings followed, but the matter might have been dropped except for an advertisement in the morning papers calling a meeting of the Vigilance Committee.

Fundamentally the Committee faced the same problem as in 1851, but whereas then the legal government had been marked principally by inefficiency and weakness, it was now characterized by corruption and abuse of authority. City and county officials, the forces of the police and the sheriff, the powerful political machine, the leading newspapers, a majority of the bar, and a substantial number of sober citizens stood for "Law and Order" and opposed illegal action by the vigilantes. Furthermore, since the corrupt officials might be able to get state or national troops to suppress the insurrection, it behooved the Second Vigilance Committee to move cautiously. Throughout, the leadership of such wise and determined men as William T. Coleman and Clancy Dempster proved of inestimable value.

Solemnity, secrecy, and deliberateness marked the Committee's policy. Advisable because of the psychological effect upon the entire populace as well as upon the vigilantes, this policy was necessary because of the strong forces arrayed in opposition. The Committee could not afford to take an overt step until its membership had risen to several thousand trustworthy men, until its military equipment and discipline had been brought to a satisfactory stage, and until a definite plan of action had matured. To many the delay seemed interminable, but actually only three days were required for the preparations.

On Sunday, May 18, 3,000 armed men surrounded the jail, a cannon was brought to bear upon the door, and a mounted horseman rapped on the window and handed the jailer a note demanding Casey's surrender. Thereupon two carriages drove up, and Casey was brought out and carried off to the vigilante headquarters. On a second trip Cora was taken. The trials of these men were not hedged about by legal technicalities, but otherwise they were fair. Just before sentence was passed, word came that James King of William had died, but the outcome was already certain. Both men were condemned to die. On Thursday, at the first stroke of the bell signaling the start of King's funeral procession, the platforms under the two murderers dropped.

Casey and Cora were, of course, only the symbols of what the vigilantes were striking at. The Committee worked on down through its black list, banishing from the city thugs, robbers, murderers, and other criminals, and turning certain offenders over to the regular courts, which, significantly enough, promptly sentenced them, although previously convictions had been exceedingly rare. Besides these obvious criminals, the Committee banished a dozen hitherto respected characters, such as Judge Edward McGowan, who had no police records but were regarded as undesirable citizens.

Opponents of the Committee rallied under the slogan "Law and Order." Included were practically all the local officials, most of the attorneys of the San Francisco bar, and many prominent persons throughout the state. Governor J. Neely Johnson vacillated, as he did on every vital question, but his sympathies were chiefly with the Law and Order faction. William Tecumseh Sherman served as military commander against the vigilantes and subsequently slandered them in the forgetfulness of his *Memoirs*. Judge David S. Terry left the bench in Sacramento to rush to the assistance of the so-called Chivalry. Other men, less famous but more substantial, cast their lot with the opponents of the vigilantes. Their stand was that, even if conditions in San Francisco were as bad as represented, the proper remedy was to bring the pressure of public opinion to bear on the officials then in office or to wait less than two years until the next regular election provided an opportunity for legal reform. In theory and in practice there is much to be said for the Law and Order distrust of extralegal procedures.

The Second Vigilance Committee, however, avoided the worst pitfalls besetting its path and rapidly gained strength. The vigorous but dignified punishment of Casey and Cora lent confidence; revelations of the iniquities of the political machine helped, as did blunders by the opposition. Terry ended whatever chances the Law and Order party may have had when he plunged a knife into one of the vigilantes, thereby exemplifying the illegal tendencies of the Law and Order faction. He was taken prisoner and indicted before the Committee on a number of counts, including four other attacks upon citizens. The Committee was convinced that Terry deserved punishment, but it was a ticklish problem to attempt to impose a sentence upon a Supreme Court Justice. After twenty-five days' deliberation —his victim in the meantime having recovered—it was decided to acquit. Though Terry was not punished, the incident had discredited the opposition to the Committee. State interference had shown its impotence before Fort Gunnybags, the vigilante headquarters, and the federal authorities, especially General Wool, in command of the military department of California, had declined to provide men or arms to suppress the Committee. Its work done, the Committee displayed its strength in a mammoth parade of 6,000 armed men, held a public reception at Fort Gunnybags, and adjourned sine die.

Admittedly, it is dangerous to flout the regular avenues of justice and turn to extralegal means. Wise and high-minded leadership kept the Second Vigilance Committee from extremes, and its work was well done in the face of great opposition. Nor can anyone deny the iniquities that called forth the Committee. It would be a mistake, however, to attribute them all to the official class. Throughout the citizenry of San Francisco the sense of civic responsibility had sunk virtually to the point of disappearance, and all were responsible for the development of the malignant growth of venality that the vigilantes had arisen to remove. Back of this lapse in civic duty the gold rush is plainly discernible. The mushroom growth of the city and the fabulous profits of private business made men forget the necessity of control of government.

Rustic Vigilance

Influenced perhaps by the fact that the city's business leaders were strong supporters of the Vigilance Committees, most of the San Francisco papers espoused the cause. Certain eastern journals agreed. The New York *Courier and Enquirer,* for example, said in 1856: "Our admiration is commanded no more by the promptness and decision of their action than by the dignity and decorum which seems to have accompanied it"; the New Orleans *Delta* affirmed that "the people of San Francisco acted well"; and the Boston *Journal* and the New York *Sunday Times* endorsed the summary proceedings and the peremptory justice which the venality of the courts had made necessary. The majority of eastern editors, however, while granting that the provocation had been great, refused to admit that popular tribunals had been justified, branding them as pregnant with lamentable and disastrous consequences.

As far as San Francisco was concerned these fears were unnecessary. Upon the disbanding of the Second Committee there was a prompt and lasting restoration of judicial functions to the regularly constituted authorities. On the other hand the rest of the state, not to mention other parts of the West, was profoundly influenced by the example of the metropolis. Vigilante action became so common that it was the accepted order of the day. Often it was kept at the same high plane of dignity and dispassion characteristic of the San

Francisco committees, but in other instances it sank to the lowest level of mob vengeance and lynch law. The excuse given, as in San Francisco, was that the regular courts were totally ineffective; or it was that the cleansing of San Francisco had shunted habitual criminals to the provinces; or it was that horse stealing and cattle stealing must be stopped. Again, judgments differ as to the adequacy of these excuses, yet it is patent that the arm of the law was of much more rudimentary development in most parts of the back country than in urban San Francisco.

In 1851 there seemed to be good reason to believe that a state-wide criminal ring existed. The burning of Stockton on May 6, just two days after the great San Francisco fire, was an incendiary attempt at jail delivery. Sacramento, Marysville, Nevada City, and other communities seemed to be caught in the same toils. Accordingly, there were proposals for a state-wide organization under the sponsorship of the San Francisco Committee. Some correspondence was exchanged, both in 1851 and in 1856, chiefly warnings as to the whereabouts and past records of known criminals. The Sacramento Committee used the constitution of its Bay City counterpart. This spirit of coöperation strengthened the position of local committees—it helped forestall any effective state interference in San Francisco in 1856—but the metropolitan leaders wisely refused to assume any responsibility for possible excesses by local bodies beyond the limits of their control.

Their fears proved well founded, for in the smaller communities the vigilante movement ran the entire gamut from fair and temperate trial to the most degenerate and revolting forms of mob violence. A few random illustrations will suffice. At Weaverville in the early fall of 1852 a certain Michael Grant was charged with murdering a Missourian named Holt. Arrested by the sheriff, he was taken in hand by the miners, who appointed judge and jury and attorneys for prosecution and defense. Fairly tried and convicted, Grant was allowed a ten-day stay of execution and the ministrations of a clergyman, after which he was solemnly hanged. At Visalia in 1858 vigilantes brought pressure to bear upon a certain William C. Deputy in an attempt to force him to restore properties fraudulently taken from his nephew. The pressure was in the form of marching the old man out to a tree, adjusting a rope around his neck, and swinging him. After three or four trips skyward he agreed to the demands of the vigilantes and was returned to the jail. In the morning a lawyer and a notary called and took the necessary depositions, after which the sheriff turned his prisoner loose. Sonora had one of the most active committees. In the summer of 1851 it disposed of a case almost every day, usually by laying on 50, 75, or even 150 lashes, but sometimes by branding horse thieves with the appropriate initials.

In Los Angeles, lynch law frequently supplanted regular justice. In rationalization it is asserted that Los Angeles was one of those proverbially tough cow towns, with cowboys often on hand to shoot it up, with teamsters from the Salt Lake freighting line, with desperadoes expelled by the San Francisco vigilantes, with Latin bad men like Joaquín Murieta and Juan Flores, and with Indians crazed with the poisonous potations dispensed in "Nigger Alley." The press inveighed against the mounting crime wave—forty-four homicides in fifteen months and not a conviction was the figure in 1851; by 1854, though doubtless with appropriate exaggeration, the rate was quoted at a murder a day. Licensed automobile drivers today do not quite treble that figure. The courts proving inadequate, lynch law was invoked.

Though responsible persons usually decried the resort to lynch law, on July 13, 1851, a vigilance committee was called into being by formal action of the mayor and city council of Los Angeles. Among its more famous actions were the hanging of two Mexican murderers in August, 1852, and a few months later, the hanging of three others charged with the murder of Major General J. H. Bean. Five years later proof came to light that one of these young men had been innocent. In January, 1855, Mayor Stephen C. Foster resigned his high office so that he might take active part in lynching a certain Dave Brown. The good work done, he was promptly reëlected mayor. This particular lynching, besides being personally directed by the mayor, was outstanding because a full report of it was printed in the *Southern Californian* some hours before the actual hanging. This anachronism occurred because the enterprising editor of this sheet wanted to feature the story in his issue for the 10 o'clock San Francisco steamer. At three, when the hanging actually occurred, the vigilantes had, so to speak, a full, printed script for their performance, complete even to a last-minute confession by the murderer. The chief divergence from the printed program was that Brown objected to being hanged by "a lot of Greasers," and in deference to his wishes the Spanish American volunteers stepped aside and let an all-American crew haul on the rope.

Thus was justice served at Los Angeles. The ranger company, in other words the vigilantes, in 1854 and 1855 brought about twenty-two executions "in accordance with the law or without the law, whichever was most convenient." Two years later some 200 men turned out to avenge the slaying of Sheriff James R. Barton by the Flores gang. Not counting those killed in the process of apprehension, eleven members of this gang were hanged at the jail. As late as 1863 a single month witnessed seven lynchings.

These popular tribunals of town and country have but a fraction of the fame enjoyed by the two great committees of San Francisco. In nicety of organization and in dramatics they were far inferior. Few of them would be held up as high examples of good citizenship triumphing over difficulties occasioned by corrupt and venal officials. They were, nevertheless, close kin to the vigilance of San Francisco, and they belong in every general picture of extralegal justice in California. In fact, they perhaps should have the principal attention, for in number of hangings these rural tribunals exceeded San Francisco's two committees by at least twenty to one. In the year 1855 alone, there were nineteen vigilante hangings for murder, twenty-four for theft, and four for minor crimes—a total of forty-seven, not one of which took place in San Francisco.

Southward the Course of Empire

Californians of the fifties expressed their lofty disdain for the due process of criminal law through the vigilance movement. Their corresponding disregard for international law was revealed in numerous filibustering expeditions. California was merely the starting point for these expeditions directed toward Sonora, Baja California, Hawaii, or Central America. The main operations lay outside the state, and none of these forays succeeded; yet the work of these filibusters sheds considerable light upon the state of mind of many Californians of the day.

The United States, it should be recalled, had just taken long strides westward with the annexation of Texas in 1845, the Oregon treaty in 1846, and the Mexican Cession of 1848. Manifest Destiny, as we are well informed, had ordained all this. Many Americans and particularly many Californians of the fifties were reluctant to believe that this much expansion was all that had been ordained. These surely were not the final limits of the nation but merely marked a pause before the advance should be resumed. Many filibusters of the fifties considered themselves as the logical successors of Pike, Austin, Houston, Jed Smith, Bidwell, Frémont, and their comrades, who by venturing across into foreign soil had prepared the way for American acquisition.

Furthermore, several other provinces seemed to be as eligible for American picking in the fifties as Texas and California had been in the preceding decade. Baja California and Sonora were remote from Mexico's central government and were neglected by it. Sonora lay open to Apache inroads, from which no force short of that of the United States promised surcease. Hawaii's native government was decrepit, her commercial ties were with the United States, and her foreign colony was largely American. Even Central America, by virtue of the faltering of its national governments and because of the popularity of the Panama and Nicaragua routes to California, came within the purview of American interest. California's proximity and its volatile and adventurous population made it the inevitable rallying point for the filibusters, and, as in most other matters, San Francisco led.

California's first filibuster was Joseph C. Morehead. He seems to have had invitations of a sort to bring a force into Sonora and Baja California to assist in Indian control and doubtless in a revolution. Recruits were not lacking, and inasmuch as he was Quartermaster-General of California it was easy for him to outfit his followers. Drawing on the funds and supplies left over from the Yuma campaign of 1850, he purchased what was necessary, including the bark *Josephine*. In the spring of 1851 his men left for the lands which they expected to seize for the United States. Some 200 arrived at La Paz in June. They professed to be interested merely in trade and soon dispersed. Meanwhile, a larger party was moving through Los Angeles toward the Gila River and the Sonora frontier. It likewise broke up. Morehead in person was to lead a third detachment to Mazatlán. At San Diego most of his men deserted and he narrowly escaped arrest. Warned of his approach, the Mazatlán authorities were ready for him, but to their surprise they found no arms or ammunition or other warlike manifestations on board the *Josephine*. Morehead's filibusters proved entirely innocuous.

To the Mexican government, however, it did suggest the advisability of strengthening Indian defenses on the Sonora frontier. Various expedients were considered, but the decision was to recruit colonists from the French of California. Of the foreigners contributed by the gold rush, the French were second only to the Chinese in clannishness and picturesqueness. English and Irish were soon assimilated; Germans were temporarily conspicuous because of their penchant for large watches and heavy watch chains; Sydney Ducks created a special problem for the vigilantes; and Chileños were numerous enough to give their name to a section of San Francisco. The French outranked all these in numbers. Individual migration was supplemented by several companies devoted to exporting Frenchmen to the land of gold. Most famous of these was La Société de l'Ingot d'Or, which by 1853 was credited with sending 3,046 Frenchmen to California. In the mines these immigrants encountered miscellaneous persecution, plus the discriminatory foreign miners' tax. Many of them, therefore, turned back to San Francisco, where some of their number became prominent as merchants and importers, hotel and restaurant keepers, gamblers and bankers. Others turned to more menial employment as barbers, bootblacks, waiters, scullions, woodcutters, or hunters. It was from this latter class that the recruits for Mexican ventures were chiefly drawn.

Such were the eighty-eight Frenchmen who sailed with Charles Pindray for Guaymas in November, 1851. Augmented by later arrivals to about 150 men, Pindray's party moved inland to an assigned tract near one of Kino's old missions, Cocóspera. There they set about developing an agricultural colony as an outpost against the Apaches and, they hoped, as a base for mining operations. The colony did not flourish. The Apaches ran off their stock and the Mexican authorities did not furnish the promised support. Pindray went to Ures to protest and on the return journey was shot, by himself, by another Frenchman, by a Mexican, or by a tool of the Mexican government—just which does not clearly appear. His colony soon dissolved. Near Tucson, in the Santa Cruz Valley, a smaller group under Lepine de Sigondis and T. P. Sainte-Marie was equally unsuccessful.

Despite these discouragements the California French rallied almost immediately to send new expeditions to Sonora. A new leader took charge, Count Gaston de Raousset-Boulbon, an imperious, reckless, and magnetic scion of France's decayed nobility. At the invitation of certain Mexican officials, and with some indications of support from the imperial agents of Louis Napoleon, Raousset led expeditions from San Francisco to the promised land of Sonora in 1852 and again in 1854. On the first occasion his following was ostensibly a mining organization known as La Compañía Restauradora de la Mina de la Arizona. From Guaymas it proceeded to the frontier, though not without considerable friction with the local authorities of Sonora. This eventually led to outright hostilities, culminating in a brilliant exploit for Raousset, the capture of Hermosillo and its 1,000 defenders by his 240 followers. As the hero of Hermosillo, Raousset was in a fair way to make himself the "Sultan of Sonora," an intention once imputed to him. On the other hand, the Sonorans had no enthusiasm for the victors. Raousset was laid up with dysentery, and his lieutenants ordered a retreat to Guaymas to await expected reënforcements from San Francisco. En route they were opposed by General Blanco and 1,200 troops, to whom in discouragement they capitulated.

Back in San Francisco the next spring, Raousset began recruiting a force of 1,000 men. Enlistment proceeded satisfactorily, but the promised financial support for the expedition did not materialize, and the principal result was to stimulate the Sonora authorities to strengthen their defenses. Hopes revived when Raousset was invited to Mexico City to confer with President Santa Anna about bringing 500 Frenchmen to defend the Sonora frontier. These two worthies failed to agree, and the Count returned to San Francisco still further discredited. Shortly thereafter, a confederate of his at Mazatlán exposed proposals for a grandiose west coast revolution, to be supported by 5,000 California Frenchmen.

Meanwhile, the "grey-eyed man of destiny," the famous William Walker, was openly recruiting filibusters in California. After his offer of "assistance" to Sonora had been rebuffed, Walker sailed from San Francisco with forty-five men in the brig *Caroline*. At La Paz he seized the Governor of Baja California and issued a bombastic proclamation as President of the Republic of Baja California. The hostility of the countryside led him to retreat to Ensenada, just below San Diego, but in his proclamations he became more pompous and annexed Sonora to his republic. His project ended ignominiously in May, 1854, when he scurried back into the United States after a farcical attempt to march around the head of the gulf to conquer Sonora. His filibustering had embarrassed the negotiation of the Gadsden Treaty and had prevented the inclusion of Baja California in that purchase.

The incident also led to renewed Mexican overtures to Raousset to establish a French outpost on the Sonora frontier. The Mexican and French consuls at San Francisco were haled into court on charges of violating the United States law against filibustering. There were other obstacles, but in the spring of 1854 Raousset was able to despatch 400 men. The Count followed most uncomfortably and hazardously on an overloaded schooner. Arriving at Guaymas, he and his men were looked at askance by the local officials. Misunderstandings led to conflict, culminating in the Battle of Guaymas, on July 13, 1854, in which the French were completely defeated. Raousset's execution thirty days later was the coup de grace to French filibustering from California.

The following year Walker embarked with some fifty-eight Californians for Nicaragua. After much adventure and some good fortune he became the master of this Central American republic. But incurring the wrath of the Vanderbilt transportation interests, Walker lost prestige as rapidly as he had gained it, and after a series of disappointments and humiliations he faced a firing squad at Truxillo, Honduras, in 1860.

Less deserved and consequently more tragic was the fate of the Stockton lawyer and California State Senator, Henry A. Crabb. Interested in Sonora because of his wife's property holdings there, Crabb was led to take some fifty colonists to the province in 1856. By a local revolutionist, Ignacio Pesquiera, he was urged to recruit a still larger force of Californians to assist in the revolution and to prepare the way for annexation to the United States. Crabb raised 100 men, most of whom he marched by the Los Angeles-Yuma route to Sonora. At the frontier the filibusters encountered unexpected opposition, offered by the very man who had urged their coming. Pesquiera had gained his end without the necessity of armed revolt, and now was utterly opposed to the entrance of filibusters. Crabb pushed on as far as Caborca, where, partly by superior force and partly by treachery, he was induced to surrender. The next morning the fifty-nine prisoners were taken out in batches and butchered.

The senseless savagery of this holocaust was protested in only perfunctory fashion by the United States government, and this supineness contributed to the impression that Crabb's fate was fully deserved. On the contrary, it appears that his expedition was more colonizing than filibustering in character, that his followers were high in reputability, that his coming to Sonora was by semi-official invitation, and that the opposition to him was motivated by a desire on Pesquiera's part to cover up his own misdeeds.

Others might talk about further southwestward expansion of the United States, but Crabb was the last of the California filibusters. The actual expeditions, from Morehead to Crabb, are perhaps less significant than the restless, adventurous, and imperialistic attitude of the Californians, which made them ready to enlist in such enterprises, made them ready to condone actions which violated the statutes of the United States, and made them as jurymen unwilling to convict leaders like Walker who were brought to trial for violation of the anti-filibustering law. One may deduce that the West was a law unto itself, and also that it did not yet realize that Manifest Destiny had run its complete course.

20

LAND TITLES

THE FOREGOING NARRATIVE of vigilance and filibustering illustrates the unsettled condition of California in the early American period. This unrest is further illustrated and in part explained by the awkward, faltering, and unjust procedure whereby the United States government dealt with the land titles carried over from the Mexican period.

The Problem and the Policy

Sloat's proclamations, not to mention other official statements in the course of the conquest, had assured the Californians that they would not be disturbed in their property ownership. The Treaty of Guadalupe Hidalgo also clearly obligated the United States to confirm titles to lands held, and the military governors gave repeated assurance that the national government would act in good faith. Instead, a policy was followed which placed an unreasonable burden of proof upon the grant holders, involved them all in court action, kept most of their cases in litigation for a decade and a half and some for much longer, piled up legal expenses which cost most of the grant holders the bulk of their property, and throughout this period deprived California of any security or certainty in land titles.

On the surface the issue would seem to have been very simple. By all the evidence available it appears that it would have been no superhuman task to distinguish between valid and invalid grants. Documents in the provincial archives, supplemented by sworn testimony that could have been taken from former officials, would have enabled any competent investigator, familiar with the land system which had functioned in the province, to determine which titles would have continued valid had the Mexican regime continued. These grants, probably nine tenths of all that were claimed, should have been duly surveyed and their titles confirmed. The task might reasonably have been completed within two or three years at the most.

Yet numerous hindrances arose. For one thing, the previous experience of Americans had not prepared them to understand the propriety of such large grants as were customary in California. For cattle raising as it had been conducted in the province and as it was later to be conducted on the Great Plains, holdings of from one to eleven square leagues (that is, up to 50,000 acres) were not excessive. Land was abundant; it required several acres to graze a cow, and one could own many head of cattle and still not be rich. Few Americans, however, could comprehend this situation. Furthermore, most of the Mexican grants were vague as to boundaries or seemed irregular in other particulars. It was argued that they should be reduced to the American norm before confirmation. Another argument was that confirmation of all these titles would leave none of California for the Americans, whereas Manifest Destiny was usually expected to confer individual advantage as well as national aggrandizement.

Before any decision was reached, the entire issue was complicated by the great gold rush. In the eyes of eastern Americans the broad holdings of the Mexican grantees now appeared fabulously and inexcusably rich. The inrushing tide of Americans increased the pressure upon California's land supply, thus jeopardizing the older titles, while at the same time these newcomers as a group were more strongly afflicted with race prejudice against all things Mexican than had been the earlier arrivals from the States. The most forcible mass expression of this attitude was in the Sacramento squatter riots, a bold attempt to eradicate all preconquest titles without so much as the formality of legal action. The scheme was defeated "by the good sense of the community," but squatterism remained a potent force, its influence constantly directed toward breaking down the old and the large holdings and throwing them open to the "conquering" Americans.

The authorities at Washington, meanwhile, were moving toward a policy. They soon had the benefit of two reports on land titles in California, one by Captain H. W. Halleck and the other by William

Carey Jones. Halleck intimated that there were imperfections in most of the Mexican titles which would give the United States an entering wedge for breaking them. Jones, after a careful examination of the California archives and consultation with Mexican and American officials in the province, reported that most of the titles were valid and that the few which were fraudulent could easily be detected. An official survey, he said, would be a sufficient preliminary to confirmation of most of the grants. The chief flaw in Jones' report was that it provided a more sensible basis for action than was desired by the majority at Washington or in California.

Jones' proposals were echoed in the Senate by Benton and Frémont. Benton stoutly opposed the creation of a special tribunal to pass on land titles. Such a step, he insisted, would be a violation of the recent treaty. He would have had confirmation made very simple, with the district court's findings final for values not exceeding $5,000. Frémont proposed a commission, from which the claimant only could take an appeal. Senator Gwin countered with a substitute bill eliminating the restrictions on appeal by the United States. He argued very plausibly that there was precedent in the Louisiana claims and that the courts could be counted on to decide justly, but neither he nor anyone else answered Benton's protest that the prolonging of litigation would spell confiscation rather than confirmation. Reading between the lines of the debates, it is clear that the Senators were more in sympathy with the squatters than with the grantees, that they suspected many of the grants to be fraudulent and most of them excessive in size, that they were alarmed by rumors concerning the McNamara colony, and that they pictured every California rancho as a prospective gold mine. Gwin's bill was enacted by the Senate with but a few negative votes on February 6, 1851, and by the House without debate on March 3.

The Course of Litigation

In accordance with this act a board of three commissioners was installed at San Francisco in January, 1852. Every claimant of land was required to appear before it within two years to present proof of title. The commission is probably the least denunciated feature of American land policy in California. It is admitted that the several commissioners were honest and conscientious men, though totally unfamiliar with local usage and with the Spanish and Mexican land system. They went as far as legal-minded persons might have been expected to go in simplifying the hearings and the taking of testimony from the non-legal-minded Californians. Even so, it was no easy matter for many of the Mexican grant holders to marshal the necessary proof for presentation; their expenses were much increased, because the commission, except for a short session at Los Angeles in the fall of 1852, held all its meetings at San Francisco. The commission acted fairly expeditiously on the 813 claims presented; by the date of its final adjournment on March 1, 1856, it had confirmed 521, rejected 273, and discontinued 19. The worst feature was one prescribed by the law, namely, that claimants were considered guilty until they had proved their innocence—their claims were reckoned faulty or fraudulent until positive proof to the contrary was brought forward.

The decisions of the commission, as already stated, were subject to appeal by either party for retrial in the district court. Some 132 claimants availed themselves of this privilege, and through the introduction of new testimony to strengthen their cases, some 98 won reversal of judgment. The government attorneys were much more persistent in appealing. Their infinitesimal ratio of success—5 out of 417 cases—is proof positive of excess of zeal. Following a consistent "make-work" policy, these lawyers laid great emphasis on petty technicalities and refused to content themselves with test cases. This needless persecution of the grant holders was applauded by the squatters. It was also a great boon to the legal gentry retained by the claimants. This group waxed fat on the additional fees, most of which could be raised only by sacrificing land or cattle or by mortgaging at ruinous interest rates. In many cases the cost of fighting an appeal was out of all proportion to the risk involved. Some ninety-odd cases were carried on further appeal to the United States Supreme Court. Here again the majority of decisions favored the claimants. The latter, however, were put to heavy expense, the most vexatious being that of paying for transcripts of the records of the lower courts, even though the government had lodged the appeals. The Supreme Court heard no new testimony, but certain cases in which fraud was suspected were remanded to the lower courts for retrial. Even without retrial the process was long drawn out and costly.

The long-suffering claimants soon found that the end was not yet.

Confirmation of title did not lead automatically to the issuance of a patent. In the first few instances a deputy of the Surveyor-General made a survey of the grant, which he forwarded to Washington, where the commissioner of the land office, if he found everything in order, issued the final patent. By a law of 1859, however, this procedure was changed. It was required that the survey be submitted to the district court, whose decision as before was subject to appeal to the Supreme Court. Thus the unfortunate claimants were subjected to another long round of ruinous litigation, with its full complement of delay, expense, and uncertainty. It meant that every claim might have to be defended six times against the United States: before the board of land commissioners, in the district court, and in the Supreme Court; then before the Surveyor-General and the land office, again in the district court, and again in the Supreme Court. It may be appalling that such an unjust course was followed, but it certainly is not surprising that the government's unrelenting opposition should have kept most of the titles unsettled for a full fifteen years.

Many of the claimants, needless to say, found that the confirmation and patent of their titles afforded only an empty victory. For some it was a matter of their property having been eaten up by the heavy expenses of the protracted litigation. For others the real difficulty was that squatters refused to get off, even though the land case had been decided in favor of the grant holder. The squatter spirit is in evidence in a proposal of Gwin's in 1852 to allow squatters to "homestead" eighty acres on Mexican grants, the grantees to be allowed a like number of acres from the public land. A state law four years later required grant holders to pay for improvements which squatters might have made or to sell at the appraised value of the land. This law was declared unconstitutional in 1857.

Barbecues to celebrate the defeat of Pico's Moquelumne claim in 1876 and of Berreyesa's Milpitas claim in 1877 may be considered proper manifestations of squatter feeling, though not so the six-month imprisonment of Domingo Peralta by militant squatters in the East Bay area, or the defiance of the sheriff who had come to evict them by 1,000 armed squatters near Santa Clara in 1861. Other examples might be cited of obstruction of justice and defiance of the authorities by squatters who had been worsted in the regular courts.

Even where such tactics did not succeed they added to the expenses and the difficulties of the grant holders.

It is not easy in short compass to indicate the methods followed by commission and courts, the principles developed, and the points of law established. Obviously, the prime requisite was to prove that the grant had actually been made by an authorized agent of the Spanish or Mexican government. In support of such a grant the archival record was the preferred evidence. If archival evidence no longer existed the testimony of witnesses was considered, but the court insisted that such testimony be full and conclusive. In the absence of archival evidence the Cambuston claim for eleven leagues in Butte County was confirmed by the commission and the district court largely because the United States did not contest the point. The Supreme Court, however, remanded the case, and upon retrial the district court decided that the original grant was not proved.

One point on which the courts were insistent was that no grant would be considered legal if dated after July 7, 1846, the date of Sloat's taking possession at Monterey. Though Governor Pico and the diputación had been still at large and still functioning, it became a fiction agreed upon that the Mexican regime had ended then. Incentive was thus offered for claimants of later grants to see that they were antedated, and this was the fraud most frequently alleged. The government attorneys, on the other hand, cited the statement of Mexico's treaty commissioner that no grants had been made after May 13 and urged invalidation of all grants made subsequent to the outbreak of the "war of conquest." The courts ruled, however, that July 7 was the magic date. The Palmer claim to Point Lobos, for example, was rejected upon proof that Governor Pico had not been at Los Angeles on the date when the grant was claimed to have been signed.

To many claimants it was equally vital to have determined the date of perfection of title to the grant. Under a Spanish grant of 1820 Luís Peralta claimed the San Antonio, comprising the sites of present-day Berkeley, Oakland, and Alameda. In 1842 he had divided this rancho among his four sons, a step confirmed also by his will nine years later. The courts upheld the titles thus created, excluding the sisters' claim, which would have been valid had the title of 1820 been considered perfect. Another example was provided by the descendants of Manuel Nieto. Occupation dated back to a grant from Governor Fages in 1784. Fifty years later Figueroa approved a division between two sons and the widows of two others. One of the widows, Josefa Cota de Nieto, sold her portion. Confirmation having been made by the United States courts on the basis of the grants of 1834, the California state courts decided that Josefa's sale was valid. Had the title derived from the grant of 1784, her sale would have been held illegal, and her children, as heirs of Don Manuel, would have been placed in possession.

Practically all the Mexican grants were conditioned upon occupancy and improvement within a year from the date of the grant. The district court was at first inclined to insist upon literal fulfillment of such conditions. But in the first case decided by the Supreme Court a rejection on these grounds was overruled, and thereafter reasonable excuses were accepted for the failure to meet the conditions. The line was usually drawn to bar claims to lands completely neglected or abandoned until the rise in value in the American period led to occupancy—for example, Noé's claim to an island in the Sacramento. Confirmation of Frémont's Mariposa claim represented perhaps the ultimate stretching of excuses for nonfulfillment of conditions; grantee Juan Bautista Alvarado had never set foot on the land and there was no attempt to improve it until after the Mexican period had ended. In the same case it was judicially determined, although the Spanish-Mexican grants had not covered mineral rights, that mineral title accompanied land ownership.

The government attorneys attempted to invoke the Mexican statute prohibiting any grant within ten leagues of the coast, but the courts wisely declined to give sudden effectiveness to a law which had been so frequently honored in the breach. The limitation to eleven leagues in grants to any individual was scrupulously upheld. William E. P. Hartnell, for example, presented adequate proofs for a five-league grant to the Todos Santos at Santa Barbara and to eleven leagues at the Cosumnes. The latter was arbitrarily reduced to six leagues so that his total would not exceed eleven. Other grants were for so many leagues, poco más ó menas, which came to be interpreted to mean plus not more than one additional league.

Floating grants were a problem in themselves. These were grants usually within a specified area but with undefined boundaries. Needless to say, many such claims overlapped. In the second case that came before it the land commission adopted the procedure of permitting rival claimants to appear and contest the confirmation of conflicting claims. The method apparently was necessary, but the government attorneys abused it by encouraging opposition to claims that otherwise would have been incontrovertible. Where a floating grant, such as the Cajón at San Diego, was not impinged upon by others, no particular difficulty arose. But where there was conflict, decision was more difficult, particularly if priority in grant, occupancy, and confirmation was distributed rather than concentrated. Generally the earliest perfect title held, though with the proviso that in making out his boundaries the grantee must start with the land he had actually occupied. In a number of instances, confirmed and patented grants left no room for other claims confirmed slightly later. For the Butano near Santa Cruz, for example, the surveyor could find only half a league of unpatented land left; worthless mountain land was thrown in to complete the amount allotted.

Sutter's claim to eleven leagues in the Sacramento Valley was confirmed as valid even though the original document had been burned in 1851. Location of the grant, however, proved a most difficult problem, which was not in the least simplified by Sutter's sales of parcels of land all up and down the valley. These land parcels are said to have been scattered over 100 leagues. On the basis of an error in the statement of the latitude of the southern boundary, the Sacramento squatters sought a ruling that their city and Sutter's Fort were not included in the New Helvetia grant, but the courts ruled otherwise. The first survey approved a two-league tract embracing the fort and Sacramento City and a nine-league tract on the Feather including the site of Marysville. The district court preferred a gerrymandered survey which attempted to weave in all the lands the General had sold, but the Supreme Court returned to the first and simpler survey. Sutter claimed an additional twenty-two leagues under supplementary grant from Micheltorena in 1845, but the Supreme Court ruled adversely. Nor would it countenance the "general title" grants, claimed on certificates from Sutter, which had been issued on the basis of a permit from Micheltorena dated December 22, 1844. The court ruled that the document from Micheltorena was nothing more than a bid for support against the Castro-Pico revolutionists, and that it was irregular and illegal. Bidwell's was the only "general title" claim upheld. The charge was made that he was favored because of his prominence, but in theory confirmation was on the basis of an earlier permission to occupy.

Particularly conducive to resentment was the tendency of the courts to decide land cases on what appeared to the laymen to be trivial technicalities. Thus one judge was ready to rule that P. B. Reading's grant was invalid on the ground that Mexico would have revoked it because of his participation in the Bear Flag movement. Vallejo's claim to the Soscol was rejected, though the documentary evidence was admittedly excellent. The grant had been made by Micheltorena in partial satisfaction of bills for supplying the provincial garrisons. Rejection was on the fantastic ground that the Mexican governor had been empowered to give away land but not to sell it. Another unpopular decision was that against Serrano for the Temescal near San Diego. Serrano had occupied the land in question ever since 1819. Such long and uncontested occupancy based on some sort of initial permit would probably have sufficed to establish title, but the document which Serrano submitted in support of his claim was a temporary permit of 1819. The court ruled that it ruined his claim to permanent title, though without the document title would presumably have been confirmed. The logic of such a decision was baffling.

Another apparent injustice was in the New Almaden case. In 1845, with the sanction of the Mexican authorities, Andrés Castillero had denounced the quicksilver mine a few miles south of San Jose. The surrounding land had previously been granted in two ranchos. In the American courts the New Almaden mining claim and the New Almaden land claim were purposely confuted by the government attorneys with these rancho claims. The Castillero land claim had not a leg to stand on. The mineral claim, having passed into the hands of a British company, was upheld by the land commission and the district court after prolonged hearings whose record ran to 3,584 printed pages, but the Supreme Court, by a four-to-three decision, reversed the verdict. The mining company strove mightily to get the survey modified to include the mine in the rancho it had acquired. Here again the result was failure. For the mine the company received only nominal compensation to the amount of $1,750,000, whereas the new syndicate which acquired it extracted $12,000,000 worth of mercury within fifteen years. The British mining company sought redress through the "Alabama" claims commission at Geneva

in 1873, but without success. The impression is inescapable that
this particular claimant was the victim of sharp practice on the part
of the United States government.

Of outright fraudulent claims the most famous was that of Limantour. In February, 1853, this intrepid Gaul astounded the residents
of San Francisco by laying claim to a four-league grant including
the better part of their fair city. The decade-old grant had never
been announced, yet the documents and the testimony of witnesses
seemed to be in order and the land commission approved the claim
early in 1856. San Francisco was immediately in turmoil, and excited lot holders rushed to pay tribute to the Frenchman's gall by
paying handsomely for quitclaims. William Carey Jones denounced
the claim as fraudulent. Henry W. Halleck insisted that the grant
would be invalidated because it included practically all the pueblo
lands. John S. Hittell, on the other hand, gave his opinion that the
claim was valid and that the squatters' only recourse was to deal
with Limantour. Two years later, in Judge Hoffman's court, the
fraud was laid bare. Documents, it was proved, had been antedated, signatures had been forged, witnesses had committed perjury,
and finally the seals on the Limantour grants were demonstrated to
be counterfeit. Limantour not only abandoned his claim but prudently fled the country. Several other fraudulent claims were exposed, though none so grandiose as this one. A smaller number
escaped detection until after the titles had been patented. The policy
of the courts then was not to permit the reopening of the case by the
government, certainly a tempering of justice with practical wisdom.
A patent, however, did not protect against third parties. In 1870,
for example, a litigant named Majors was awarded one third of the
Rancho Refugio near Santa Cruz, though it had previously been
patented to a certain Bolcof. Majors proved that the original grant
had been to the Castro sisters, one of whom he had married, but
that in the earlier trials the document had been presented with Bolcof's name fraudulently substituted for theirs.

Mission and Pueblo Lands

A special set of claims concerned the mission lands. In their
original status under Spain and Mexico the missions had been granted
no lands. The system was merely that the government refrained
from granting to anyone else such lands as were needed by the neo-

phytes. After secularization, parts of the mission tracts had been granted to individuals, both Indian and white, and these grants were handled by the land commission exactly as any other Mexican grants to individuals. In a special category, however, fell some seventeen claims based on sales by Governor Pico in 1845 and 1846. Differing from the regular colonization grants to which conditions of residence and improvements were normally attached, these sales were regarded as emergency measures partially necessitated by the crisis in provincial affairs. The validity of these titles was at least doubtful: sales had been private rather than at auction; a communication from Mexico City, dated November, 1845, had ordered suspension of such sales; and a subsequent order giving Pico and Castro "ample powers" for the defense of the province had not arrived until after most of these sales had been consummated. Eight of these titles were confirmed. The rest, including those of greatest intrinsic value, at San Francisco, San Gabriel, and Santa Barbara, were finally blocked by a Supreme Court ruling. Through its archbishop, the Catholic Church entered a claim for a league of land at each mission, but since no semblance of a grant could be produced, these titles were refused. The courts did confirm title to the actual mission sites, the cemeteries and gardens attached thereto, the Santa Inés College tract, and La Laguna at San Luis Obispo.

The Act of 1851 gave due recognition to the Spanish-Mexican practice whereby a town was entitled to four leagues of land. San Jose and Los Angeles as pueblos and Branciforte as a villa were obviously eligible; the pueblos subjoined to the presidios at San Diego, Santa Barbara, Monterey, and San Francisco could present a strong case for inclusion; and a number of Indian villages located at secularized missions were also qualified. Branciforte and several villages of the third class, including Las Flores, San Dieguito, San Pasqual, San Juan de Argüello, and San Juan de Castro, presented no claims. The post-Mexican towns of Sonora and Sacramento presented claims which were promptly thrown out, and the commission and courts were left with eight or ten claims of respectable antiquity. Several of these had complicating factors. Los Angeles asked for a tract four leagues square instead of four square leagues. At San Jose the tract claimed was interspersed with parts of ranchos and other private grants, a condition that prevailed elsewhere as well.

Litigation delayed confirmation of most of these titles until the sixties and the issuance of patents until the seventies or eighties.

The great contest, meanwhile, involved San Francisco. Government attorneys, in fighting the claim, charged that San Francisco had never been a pueblo. They insisted that Kearny had had no authority to relinquish the United States' claim to beach and water lots or even to ordinary town lots. They pointed out irregularities in the sale of lots by the town council and by a justice of the peace. Further complications included such matters as the sheriff's sale at nominal prices of many lots to satisfy Stephen Smith's claims against the city, and a variety of delineations of the town limits. Uncertainty was at its height in the late fifties when Limantour's claim was still pending, when parts of the city were being claimed as parts of other similar grants, and when a claim under Pico's sale of the mission lands had not yet been invalidated. San Franciscans could not be sure whether their title to lots should derive from the pueblo, from Limantour or some other "ranchero," from the purchase of the mission lands, or directly from the United States. Under such circumstances the difficulty of conveying title to town lots can well be imagined.

Various attempts to cut the Gordian knot were made. In 1851 the state legislature ceded water lots to the city. In 1855, by the Van Ness Ordinance, the city legalized lot holdings as of 1851. The legislature approved in 1858, and in a test case two years later the State Supreme Court upheld the pueblo title. Congress made the ordinance effective against any possible federal title, and in 1867 the pueblo title was finally confirmed. The matter of survey remained, and not until 1884 were attendant difficulties sufficiently ironed out so that the patent could be issued.

In summary, it might suffice to quote Bancroft's opinion that the United States' system of dealing with the California land claims "was thoroughly bad in almost every respect" and "merits only condemnation," or Josiah Royce's stigmatizing of it as "legalized meanness," or John S. Hittell's verdict that it was outright "persecution." That the grant holders were unjustly treated is a patent fact. The damage, however, was by no means confined to them. All Californians suffered, the squatters included. For throughout the long period of this litigation, lasting until after the Civil War, no land title in the state was secure. It was impossible for a settler, whether business-man or agriculturist, to get certain title to any real property. All enterprise was thus subjected to an extra hazard. Since real estate was a doubtful collateral, interest rates were kept abnormally high, successful forty-niners hesitated to send for their families, and many of the most substantial men who had come in the gold rush reluctantly left the state. In 1863 Hittell estimated that California's population was one million persons less than it would have been had the question of land titles been settled promptly, fairly, and generously. The fig-ure may be too large, but excepting the land lawyers, it does appear that every class in California would have been much better off.

Mineral Rights

A companion evil, and one for which the Californians were largely responsible, was the delay in providing for private ownership of mines. In the first years of gold washing it was simpler that the entire mother lode country should be reckoned public domain and the individual ownership of a mining claim be purely usufructuary. By the middle fifties the drawbacks came to outweigh the advan-tages. Because of the impossibility of acquiring permanent title, miners were discouraged from installing expensive and efficient equip-ment. Like the ranch owners with clouded titles, they found it im-possible to borrow money at reasonable rates. Consequently, they had no incentive to build adequate or respectable houses, and they wasted inordinate time and energy in moving about from one digging to another. But the roving habit was strong, and since the system seemed to embody freedom, it was praised, though perhaps inaccu-rately, as a safeguard against monopoly. It did render the miners largely untaxable, which, despite the hardship on the tax-ridden cow counties, may have seemed a boon to the miners. As an unsettling factor, however, the practice was subject to most of the criticism leveled against the delay in providing sound titles to the state's urban and agricultural lands.

21

LIQUIDATING THE INDIANS

THE FIRST INDIAN POLICY in California, of course, was that which the Spaniards had introduced in 1769. Its underlying principles were that the Indian should be preserved, civilized and improved, and utilized as the basic element in the permanent population. In coastal and southern California, mission, presidio, and pueblo had carried this process well along toward realization, at least to the degree that most of the labor at mission, town, and rancho was performed by "domesticated" Indians. The earliest arrivals from the United States accepted this status quo and soon came to regard the California native as a useful and acceptable element in the local population. Sutter, Bidwell, and others even extended the practice into the Sacramento Valley, and the mining season of 1848 witnessed something of the sort in the gold area, where the two races worked side by side and for the most part without friction in the extraction of the precious metal.

"Wars" and Massacres

After the secularization of the missions, however, the Indian policy derived from Spain had lost its vital features. The Indians already civilized or "domesticated" might continue so, though many reverted to their ancestral customs; no effective agency was at work for the training of additional Indians. Besides the decline on the positive side, grave abuses developed in the treatment of many of the former mission Indians. Walter Colton tells of the problems created by the ex-neophytes at Monterey. The annals of Los Angeles for the late forties and fifties abound with mention of the Indians reduced to starvation, beggary, and petty crime, of their hopeless addiction to

319

drink, of Indians caught like cattle for the work season, and of the Monday slave mart at which their services for the week were auctioned off to cover the fines for their inevitable drunkenness. It is not a pretty picture; still less so was the callous indifference to the killing of an Indian. The prevailing attitude seemed to be that such an act was by no means a crime.

In retrospect this misuse of derelict humanity may seem the darkest phase of local Indian history, but most southern Californians of the day were more alarmed by the depredations by Indians from the mountainous and desert interior. Such things had occurred during the Spanish and Mexican periods. Now the tendency was accelerated by renegades from the missions and by a growing taste for horse meat and beef, while at the same time the greatly improved market for ranch products served to magnify the value of the losses. To the local military and to the federal and state authorities southern rancheros clamored loudly for protection and for punitive expeditions against these marauders. What these forays accomplished may best be related in connection with the operations in the state at large.

With the gold rush, the great central valley, the Sierra foothills, and northern California were suddenly overrun by headstrong Argonauts, engulfing whole tribes and dispossessing others of their hunting and food-gathering lands. These gold seekers had had no opportunity to absorb the Spanish philosophy of race relationships. Most of them had been nurtured on the contrary Anglo-American principle that the Indian should be made to give way before the advancing tide of white settlement, a principle alternately practiced through wars of extermination and treaties for Indian removal. On the overland routes to California, difficulties with the Pawnees and the Humboldt Valley Diggers had augmented hatred of Indians, and many miners visited this feeling upon the California natives. The whites are charged with the first violence, though the mere entrance of miners into certain districts roused the Indians to resistance. Thereafter retaliation flowed in both directions, oftentimes without any discrimination between the original sinners and the innocent.

For the operations that followed, the name "wars" is sometimes employed. Bancroft more sagely observes:

> The California valley cannot grace her annals with a single Indian war bordering on respectability. It can boast, however, a hundred or two of as brutal butcherings, on the part of our honest miners and brave pioneers, as any area of equal extent in our republic.

It is a sordid and disgraceful chapter, never stressed in local histories. The first of the so-called wars occurred in the spring of 1848. Outrages attributed to former members of the New York Volunteers led to retaliation by the natives of the Coloma district, whereupon the miners organized parties for Indian hunting. McKay's party is credited with killing thirty at one ranchería and capturing seven men and forty women, while Greenwood's party at another village killed twenty and captured a number, of whom six were sentenced to run before a firing squad. Only one escaped. For the rest of the year hostilities were avoided, but in 1849 they broke out anew, particularly on the Yuba and in the Kings River region, where the natives perpetrated a number of atrocities, such as flaying intruders alive. The Yumas also inflicted sundry insults and damages upon immigrants passing through their territory. In the Clear Lake country two settlers met a well-deserved death at the hands of the Indians. They were promptly avenged by a force under Captain Nathaniel Lyon which killed 175 Indians.

Indian depredations continued, often provoked by inconsiderate whites, and had cumulative effect in a series of campaigns in 1850. Regulars and militia, after several pitched battles, brought the Yubas to terms in May. Yet opportunities for friction were numerous, so that the peace did not last; and when hostilities spread up and down the valley, the governor authorized Sheriff Rogers of El Dorado County to lead 200 volunteers into action. This time most of the Indians managed to elude Rogers. Those who put up a fight gave good account of themselves with their arrows; all the damage the posse could do was limited to the destruction of huts, acorn stores, and the like, and its exploits were reckoned far from brilliant. Subsequent campaigns in the San Joaquin foothills had similar results.

From Los Angeles, meanwhile, a company was raised to chastise the Yumas for killing eleven Americans who had operated a Colorado River ferry. The campaign won little popular support, the general opinion being that the ferrymen were murderers and robbers who had deserved such a fate. By conscripting from emigrant trains, Joseph C. Morehead got together 125 men. He found the Indians quiet, but prodded them into a fight in which a score of Indians were killed. The principal achievement of this campaign was an expense account of $76,588.

In 1851 the Yumas and the Luiseños gave southern California a more serious scare. The Luiseño chief claimed that 3,000 warriors would take the field. But regulars and volunteers were gathered at Los Angeles and San Diego, and the obstreperous Luiseño chief was seized by the Cahuillas and handed over for execution. Major H. P. Heintzelman made war on the Yumas and at length captured and executed their chief, and southern California returned to normal.

The most famous campaign of 1851 was that of the Mariposa Battalion under James D. Savage. After strenuous efforts the people of several hostile and semihostile rancherías were rounded up, but by a clever ruse Chief Tenieya and 350 Yosemites and Chowchillas gave their captors the slip, and a second campaign was necessary. To recapture the chief the whites resorted to perfidious trickery. Exciting though the campaign was, the Mariposa Battalion's greatest achievement was the effective discovery of Yosemite Valley. Walker's fur men had looked down on the valley seventeen years earlier, but not until these Indian hunters of 1851 came along was the majestic beauty hailed and appreciated. Yosemite soon became one of the show places of the state.

The northern fringe of the state was the next scene of conflict. Oregon was then in the throes of a bloodier war than any this state has witnessed. The Klamaths showed a disposition to follow the example of their northern neighbors, but were held fairly well in check by army posts established at Humboldt, Reading Valley, and Scott Valley. Then, in 1852, the Shastas went on the warpath, and the contagion spread to the Pit River Indians and the Modocs. The latter were held responsible for a midnight onslaught on an immigrant train on its way to California. Nearby miners organized to strike back. Negotiations were opened. Both sides suspected treachery, but the whites struck first, slaughtering some forty Modocs in what is known as Ben Wright's Massacre.

To continue the melancholy narrative: Oregon's Rogue River War kept on disturbing the northern California tribes. The Shastas were on a rampage in 1853, and other tribes committed depredations. Regulars and volunteers retaliated upon the lower Klamaths in 1854 and 1855, forcing them to accept reservation life. The fighting in Siskiyou County was longer drawn out. Even the mission Indians of southern California provided a war scare in 1857, but they were placated by the appointment of agents, supposedly to provide for them. The same year witnessed hostilities in the San Joaquin Valley. General Kibbe responded in 1858–1859 by campaigning in the Coast

Ranges along its western edge, where he killed more than 100 natives and rounded up several times that many for the reservations.

Similarly, on Mad River and Eel River in the north, cattle stealing was the excuse for campaigns in which more than 200 Indians were massacred. The grand jury entered a courageous protest against these atrocities, but the prevailing sentiment is clearly indicated by the fact that Francis Bret Harte was practically run out of Humboldt County for sharply criticizing the massacre in his paper, the Union *Northern Californian.* The Hoopas held out obstinately for five years and were rewarded with an excellent reservation in the lower Trinity Valley.

Owens Valley supplied the next massacre. As advancing settlements cut down on their forage grounds, the natives were forced into cattle stealing. To abate this nuisance the settlers took the field in 1862 and again in 1865. In January of the latter year more than forty Indians were massacred at one ranchería. The next month 100 or more were driven into the brackish waters of Owens Lake, where, to put it with graphic bruskness, the whites "saw to it that they perished." This was the last major engagement in southern California, though there was occasional sniping back and forth. In 1866, for example, the owner of Rancho San Pascual, at present-day Pasadena, was killed by Indian arrows. In 1867 the scene shifted to Pit River, where there occurred the usual sequence of depredations by the Indians, which were answered by a punitive campaign directed by General Crook.

The Modoc War

Nearby the stage was already being set for the dramatic climax of California Indian fighting, the Modoc War. In 1864 the Modocs had been forced to agree to move to a reservation in Oregon. They reckoned their lot doubly unsatisfactory because they were thrown in with a larger number of Klamaths, who made their life miserable. After a short taste of reservation life Captain Jack (Chief Kientepoos) led his people back to their old haunts on Lost River. In 1869 he was persuaded to give the reservation another chance, but in the spring the 200 Modocs decamped once more in favor of their home land. Again overtures were made to persuade them to return to the reservation, but the Indians proving adamant, the army was called on to round up Captain Jack's band.

Warned of the advancing column, the Modocs took refuge in the impenetrable lava beds near Tule Lake. Captain Jack had only fifty fighting men, equipped with muzzle-loading rifles and a few revolvers and encumbered with at least 150 women and children. Arrayed against them were 400 well-armed soldiers, 225 of them regulars, supported by a battery of howitzers. Colonel Frank Wheaton came to the natural conclusion that the quickest way to end the war was by an immediate attack in force. The attack was made on January 17, 1873. The Americans advanced bravely enough. They saw no Modocs, but from howitzers and rifles they poured a heavy fire into the lava beds. The Modocs answered with careful shots from their places of concealment, killing nine and wounding thirty before the Americans fell back. Wheaton sent for four more howitzers and 410 more men. Other attempts to dislodge the Modocs were no more successful; in fact, by means of captured rifles and ammunition the Indians were probably stronger than at the outset.

In such circumstances the Americans turned to a renewal of negotiations. Late in March, Captain Jack was persuaded to come out to a peace conference. He soon found that the only terms his antagonists would consider were those of absolute submission, and this in spite of the fact that the Modocs had by no means been vanquished. His moderate proposals, such as a mutual surrender of thieves and murderers, were brushed aside as naïve, as perhaps they were. The American commander, General E. R. S. Canby, would not concede the Modocs a reservation anywhere except among the overbearing Oregon Klamaths. Captain Jack seems to have had no illusions of success, but he agreed to consult with his tribesmen. They opposed his plan of working for peace, and by taunting him as a "fish-hearted woman" won him over to a plot to kill the American leaders at the next peace conference. The commissioners were warned by a Modoc woman, Winema or Tobey, but they proceeded with the conference on April 11. At Captain Jack's signal the Modocs whipped out revolvers and knives and even rifles. Canby and the missionary, Rev. Eleazer Thomas, were killed, and Indian agent A. B. Mecham was wounded.

The Modoc leaders got off to the lava beds. More soldiers were brought up and battle was joined again. Another attempt to storm the Modoc position was as disastrous as had been the assault in

January. But the Indian supplies were running low, and the Indians had given up hope of attaining any favorable terms from their opponents. Split into smaller groups, they fled from their haven in the lava beds. One such band was captured, and its leader, Hooker Jim, offered to help take his former chief. At length, accompanied by three forlorn followers, Captain Jack came out and surrendered. With the loss of five men, two of whom were killed while trying to open an unexploded howitzer shell, Captain Jack had held off a far superior force for over three months. The Americans, meanwhile, had lost eight officers, thirty-nine privates, sixteen volunteers, two Indian scouts, and eighteen civilians, besides numerous wounded. The expenses of the war were a round half million, whereas the Modocs would have been satisfied with a 2,000-acre reservation worth at the most $20,000, or even with the worthless lava bed area. Besides having the best of the fighting, Captain Jack seems to have advanced the more reasonable arguments and proposals in the conferences that were held. His captors, however, were not swayed by any sentimental admiration. They tried him for his violation of the code of the whites, and in company with Black Jim and Boston Charley he was hanged at Fort Klamath.

Introducing the Reservation System

Throughout these years of warfare the United States government had employed its customary peaceful devices to solve the Indian problem in California. The first agents, Sutter, Vallejo, and J. D. Hunter, were named as adjuncts of the military by Kearny in 1847. Two years later they were followed by Subagent Adam Johnston, whose responsibility was to the newly created Department of the Interior. That same year California Indian affairs were given cursory examination by an emissary extraordinary of the Department of State, the cavalier Thomas Butler King. Far more important was the arrival in January, 1851, of three commissioner agents, Redick McKee, G. W. Barbour, and O. M. Wozencraft. These men found that the militia had just been called out for an Indian campaign in Mariposa County and that the legislature had just set up a "war chest" of $500,000.

The three commissioners plunged immediately into negotiations with the Central Valley and Sierra foothill tribes. Their basic theory was that the tribes whose lands had been taken over by the miners should be assigned tracts on the floor of the valley and suitably indemnified with beef, blankets, and other supplies. More prosaically stated, the theory was that to feed the Indians for a year would be cheaper than to fight them for a week. Eighteen treaties were negotiated, calling for the settling of some 139 tribes or villages on reservations adding up to about one fourteenth of the total area of the state. The program was endorsed by Edward F. Beale, newly appointed superintendent of the California Indians, but the Senate promptly rejected all eighteen treaties. The Senate may have been aghast that the three commissioners with $50,000 appropriated for their expenses had laid out more than $700,000; it certainly was moved by the vehement protest lodged by California's representatives that the treaties deeded to the red men some of the best land in the state.

The summary rejection of the treaties encouraged further encroachment upon the Indian lands and necessitated resort to new expedients by the Indian superintendent. This officer, the spirited young lieutenant who had made the perilous trip to San Diego to get relief for Kearny after the battle of San Pascual, was equal to the occasion. He arrived on the scene in mid-September, 1852. Six weeks later he submitted a detailed proposal for a new program, calling for a system of military posts "for the convenience and protection of the Indians." At each post there should be a resident agent vested with disciplinary authority and responsible for instruction of the natives. The reservations thus created should have exactly defined limits. The Indians should be required to stay on the reservation and should be taught civilized pursuits, such as farming and the simpler trades, which would enable them to be self-supporting. To the historian this plan sounds very much like a revival of the Spanish mission, shorn only of its religious aspects. It sounds very little like the old-style "reservation" system through which the United States had been shunting the Indians out of the way of the juggernaut of white settlement. On the basis of the blueprint drafted by Beale and his southern California subagent, B. D. Wilson, the new-style reservation system was inaugurated in California. Thence, with slight modifications, it was taken to Oregon, to Kansas and Nebraska, and to New Mexico, and became the kingpin of the United States' Indian policy. It became so much the standard that few persons would guess that its first use was as recent as the 1850's or that its place of origin was Beale's California.

Beale and Wilson are to be credited with devising and introducing the policy which the nation adopted, yet immediate results in California were far from brilliant. In the fall of 1853 they launched the first reservation at Tejon. The neighboring Indians were not easily persauded to come in and experiment with the new life, but the superintendent's boundless energy and optimism, together with the loyal support of Wilson and other assistants, overcame the initial obstacles. The next June, Beale could report 2,500 Indians on this reservation and a first harvest of 42,000 bushels of wheat and 10,000 bushels of barley. Already, however, Beale was in disfavor at Washington. Political opponents had been after his scalp. They found a talking point in the irregularity of his financial accounts, and although subsequent investigation absolved him of all blame, this scurrilous attack led to his dismissal.

The next superintendent, Thomas J. Henley, expressed himself as fully in sympathy with Beale's program. He established four more reservations: at Fresno, at Nome Lackee near Tehama in the northwestern extremity of the Sacramento Valley, at Klamath River, and at Cape Mendocino. He even found a way of circumventing the legal limitation of the reservations to five by setting up "farms" that were reservations in disguise. Unfortunately, however, the increase in reservations seems to have appealed to Henley primarily because of the multiplication of the lucrative positions at his disposal. Most of his appointees were not of the high caliber of Beale's, and they were soon joined by their chief in mulcting the government and the Indians. An official investigation in 1858 by J. Ross Browne disclosed the grossest mismanagement; for example, Indian supplies had been issued to laborers at a private sawmill, and other supplies had been bought at inflated prices through a store in which Henley had an interest. Consequently, there was a new superintendent in 1859, a sharp reduction in the appropriation, discharge of many of the persons who had in theory been working for the Indians, and abandonment of most of the farms and reservations.

The subsequent vicissitudes need not be followed in detail. Tejon was abandoned in 1863. At the end of the decade only three stations were left, Hoopa and Round Valley in the north and Tule farm in the

San Joaquin Valley. In 1870 these were transferred from army to Methodist supervision, a change that seemed to be for the better. Not so the relocation of Tule farm in 1873; the new site could support only about one fourth of the agency population. In 1870 there was a half-hearted attempt to provide a reservation for the mission Indians of the south. The Pala and San Pascual valleys were set aside for their occupancy, but white settlers of the vicinity took the announcement as an invitation to rush in and occupy this land. A resolute agent might have prevailed against these squatters, and a tribe like the Klamath probably would not have given in without a fight. These mission Indians, however, had repeatedly been imposed upon. They seemed aware of the futility of resistance. Their resignation in the face of injustice was at length rewarded with sturdy championing of their cause by Helen Hunt Jackson, Charles F. Lummis, and others, but not until much later was their lot ameliorated.

Decline in Number

Early census figures are not particularly illuminating concerning the number of "wild" Indians in California, yet it is clear that in the third quarter of the nineteenth century the number of "wild" and of "domesticated" Indians was alarmingly and shamefully reduced. Wars and massacres contributed, as did the expansion of white settlements and industries, which diminished the food resources of the natives. The reservation system or its abuses bore heavily on many tribes. Also, the government played fast and loose with the natives, keeping only those promises that suited its convenience. And finally disease, respiratory and venereal, took a heavy toll. By 1875 not more than one fourth as many natives remained as had occupied the state a quarter of a century earlier.

The crushing of the natives in numbers and in spirit was certainly no glorious achievement. It is sometimes given the credit for the state's freedom from Indian "troubles" in the years thereafter, yet this happy result seems due primarily to the still more rapid augmentation of the white population. Reduced to so insignificant a minority, the Indians had no alternative but to accept the white man's rules and regulations.

For us of the present generation the natural tendency is to take the side of the Indian. For a long span of years—in fact, the mind of man now runneth not to the contrary—we have been in perfect safety from Indian attack or depredation.   Anthropological studies have played up the aboriginal virtues and attainments.   The Indian was the underdog, and the land, we freely admit, was originally his.   In the early American period, however, even this justice was denied the California native.   The Treaty of Guadalupe Hidalgo, it was held, had transferred full title to the land from Mexico to the United States government, and consequently no further formalities or compensations were necessary for extinguishment of the Indian title.   This legalistic argument is a clue to the attitude then current.   Rather than idealized as at present, the redskin was feared, hated, and despised.   Awareness of this state of mind and of the conditions that produced it renders understandable, though not excusable, the heartless liquidation of the California Indians.

22

CULTURAL AWAKENING

FROM THE SORDID ANNALS of land cheats and Indian slaughter it is a pleasure to turn to more creditable manifestations of gold-rush influence, the stimulation of a cultural awakening. This awakening found expression in the establishment of schools and churches, in a flourishing theater, a lush growth of journalism, and a sudden outpouring of creative and entertaining writing.

Church and School

Long before the coming of the Americans the Spaniards had made California a Christian land. To them, of course, Christian meant Roman Catholic. By contrast, the American pioneers and most of the gold seekers came from an environment where Protestantism prevailed. Their impingement on the province included holding Protestant services and organizing Methodist, Baptist, and other churches. Several of the faiths sent missionaries to California, the American armed forces brought chaplains, and the forty-niners included a goodly number of clergymen. One observer, doubtless exaggerating, put the preachers at one in ten. San Francisco, as in all else, took the lead. In November, 1848, a conclave of its citizens invited Rev. Timothy Dwight Hunt to be city chaplain on a non-denominational basis. Thirteen months later there were twelve bona fide ministers established in their work. By the mid-fifties San Francisco could boast thirty-two churches, ranging from the African Methodist to Welsh Presbyterian.

The pioneer period is better represented by William Taylor's street preaching in San Francisco or by the circuit rider in the diggings who persuaded a saloonkeeper to clear a space before the bar for a Sunday morning discourse. Except in the suddenness with which organized churches took shape, California's experience was that of the West in general. Many of her pioneers had no interest in churches. Others, out of homesickness or conviction, wanted the solace of religion. They tried to achieve as close a reproduction as possible of their accustomed church.

How well they succeeded is another matter. Sarah Royce, perhaps with excess of charity, remarks on the "fixed attention," the "intense earnestness," and the "reverence, devotion, and glow of intelligence" characterizing the congregation she observed in San Francisco. Visiting that city in 1859, Richard Henry Dana, author of *Two Years Before the Mast,* met a Harvard man, a regular churchgoer in New England, who could not even direct him to Bishop Kip's church. Once he found it, Dana observed that the congregation was "precisely like one you would meet in New York, Philadelphia, or Boston." In mundane terms this was exactly what those who brought Protestant Christianity to the Pacific Coast wanted to accomplish.

In one respect the results were far inferior to the Spanish achievement. Despite some lapses, as at San Luis Rey, the massive architecture of the missions was well suited to the land. The church buildings of the early American period were of all shapes and styles or of no style at all. They disfigured the scene more often than adorned it, although they did symbolize the cosmopolitan character of gold rush California. To all concerned, what went on within them was the thing that mattered.

The story of formal education in California begins with the Franciscan missions. For pupils other than Indians Bancroft lists fifty-five schools of the Spanish and Mexican periods. Except for W. E. P. Hartnell's Colegio de San José, all were elementary, and most of them functioned only briefly. It is understandable that, when it could be afforded, boys were sent away to Honolulu, Valparaiso, or even to Paris for their elementary schooling. In 1847 several American-type schools were opened, the first at Santa Clara. On April 3, 1848, San Francisco pioneered with a public school taught by Thomas Douglas, formerly of the Young Chief's School in Honolulu. By the end of May, when four of the five trustees and all but eight of the pupils had been carried away by the gold fever, schoolmaster Douglas closed his classroom and took himself off to the mines.

The upsurge of population, wealth, and, more gradually, of stability which the gold rush contributed gave momentum to the demand for schools. Organized religion lent its support. Several of the missionary pastors engaged in teaching as well as preaching. Other schools were opened under private auspices. This development was all very well, but in the American culture pattern being transfixed upon the state a cardinal feature was recognition of the public responsibility to provide for instruction. The state constitution obligated the legislature to provide for a school, operating at least three months every year, in each district in the state. The legislature in 1851 passed an implementing act, which was later improved and broadened. On the basis of the school law of 1866, State Superintendent John C. Swett could rejoice that California had completed the transition to an American free school system. Three years earlier, just twenty-six years after its introduction in Europe, California's first kindergarten opened in San Francisco. Meanwhile, a number of academies and seminaries, approximately of high school level, had been started, and in 1856 San Francisco pioneered with the first public high school.

Just when college and university work actually began is more difficult to determine. The University of Santa Clara traces its origins back to the College of Santa Clara and beyond that to classes conducted in 1851.

The College of the Pacific likewise counts back to 1851, and the University of California, through the private College of California, which it later absorbed, to 1855. In 1868, encouraged by the federal subsidy offered through the Morrill Land Grant Act, the legislature chartered the University of California as a state institution. It enrolled its first students at Oakland in 1869, and the next year it took the radical step of admitting women students. In 1872 it gained distinction through the appointment of Daniel Coit Gilman as president, and the following year it shifted to its campus designate at Berkeley. From the start the university had some excellent men on its faculty, including the LeConte brothers and Ezra S. Carr, professor of agriculture and horticulture. It was not, however, a university in today's sense, associating several collegiate programs or offering advanced work. In 1874 a controversy came to a head over whether the stress should be on agriculture and mechanic arts, with instruction in carpentry, blacksmithing, and other practical fields, or whether it should be on a more comprehensive and liberal program of instruction.

The general education advocates prevailed, but before the year was out President Gilman decided that he would find a more congenial climate of opinion in the East and resigned to go to Johns Hopkins, there to develop the first genuine graduate school in the United States. Nevertheless, gold rush California was doing well to have made available educational facilities at the college level.

The Theater

The theater was a culture form that could respond buoyantly to the stimulation of gold. Although there had been amateur performances such as those by the men of Stevenson's regiment, bored by garrison duty at Monterey, the first professional to take a turn apparently was Stephen Massett from England. In June, 1849, he put on a one-man show at San Francisco. In a rich baritone, he sang several of his own compositions. In falsetto he mimicked an operatic diva. Next came a series of monologues in Yankee dialect, and as a climax a seven-voice rendition of a New England town meeting.

Massett was followed by a minstrel show at the Bella Union, its run cut short when one of the "bones" was killed. Later in 1849, in a large tent at Clay and Kearney, Joseph Rowe presided over a circus featuring nine acrobats and equestrians and a posing horse.

At Sacramento, meanwhile, the Eagle Theater company opened with "The Bandit Chief; or, The Forest Spectre." Plays such as "The Wife," "Dead Shot," "Othello," "Batchelor Buttons," "William Tell," "Rent Day," and "Charles II," were also in their repertoire. In January, 1850, this company brought legitimate theater to San Francisco. Although the manager of the troupe lost the first week's receipts at monte, the popular response encouraged other impresarios to provide similar entertainment. Rowe built a platform across one end of his tent and substituted actors for acrobats. As an annex to the Parker House saloon and gambling hall, Tom Maguire opened a theater which he called the Jenny Lind. When this theater burned he built a second Jenny Lind; when it burned, a third, which the city fathers bought for a city hall. With $50,000 raised by popular subscription Dr. David Robinson built the Adelphi. He was responsible also for the American Theater and had a share in Bryant Minstrels, later converted into San Francisco Hall and still later into Maguire's Opera House.

The ebullience of the audience often made playing the San Francisco stage an exciting experience. Making the circuit of the mining camps was even more of a test. Traveling by stagecoach or on horseback, putting up at primitive hotels, living on rough fare, and performing in makeshift theaters, the troupers had to rise above circumstances. A play, often sharply curtailed, was the feature of each performance. To it the artists added solos, dances, readings, impersonations, and skits, so that the evening's entertainment combined legitimate theater and vaudeville.

Although their critical faculties may have been dulled by long absence from the theater, the mining camp playgoers were exacting. As in San Francisco, when lines were cut, forgotten, or muffed, they stamped and hooted. On the other hand, if a performance caught their fancy they showered the stage with coins, nuggets, and bags of gold dust.

The theater faced competition from cockfights, bull-and-bear fights, and other bizarre amusements. The saloon and the gambling hall were more potent counter attractions. Borrowing from the theater, the larger of these establishments added musicians, dancers, variety acts, and minstrel acts. That the theater did compete successfully was in part due to the headline talent that came to the Gold Coast. Representing the minstrels were Ed Christy, end man Eph Horn, soft-shoe dancer Dan Bryant, and banjo virtuoso Thomas F. Briggs. Singers Elisa Biscaccianti and Kate Hayes joined the trek. So did a host of noble actors, including the Booths, the Chapmans, Edwin Forrest, Catherine Sinclair, and such personalities as Lola Montez, Adah Isaacs Menken, and Mathilda Heron.

Above all others, the paragon of the gold-rush theater was Lotta Crabtree. Her debut was at a tiny log theater in Rabbit Creek. In long-tailed green coat, knee breeches, and tall hat, she bounced on stage and danced a vigorous Irish jig and reel. After many encores she reappeared in a white dress with round neck and puffed sleeves and sang a plaintive ballad. The hardened miners went wild, showering the stage with coins, nuggets, and a fifty-dollar slug. Black-eyed, red-haired Lotta, all of eight years old, but looking no more than six, was their darling.

Tutored by her ambitious mother, Mart Taylor, and other willing helpers, Lotta made a rapid tour of the camps. She learned new songs and steps. A Negro minstrel taught her to do a soft-shoe breakdown. Lola Montez introduced her to Spanish dancing, and

Jake Wallace taught her how to make a banjo ring. From others she picked up buck and wing and new bits of pantomime. Thus equipped, she could put on a whole show in the style of Stephen Massett. By the midfifties, however, talent was so abundant that the real problem was to get a chance to perform. Lotta's mother was a persistent agent. With barrel-top numbers at auctions, variety billings in the mines and at San Francisco, bits in the regular plays, and specialties between acts, Lotta had a busy childhood. In one little vibrant bundle of energy she represented the things the Californians of this generation most prized: humor and pathos, high skill and lower buffoonery, mastery of the traditional forms and indulgence in pyrotechnics.

The theatrical pageantry that Lotta represents rested on the gold rush. Without the rewards so manifestly present, none of the name talent would have come all the way to California. Probably, had it not been for the confidence lent by the gold, the provincial audiences would not have been so free about molding actors and vehicles to suit the California taste.

Less spectacularly, the gold rush encouraged the pictorial arts. In illustrated books, in canvases hung on widely scattered walls, and in illustrated letterheads issued by California stationers, this record is partly preserved. Delano's drawings, Charles Nahl's group scenes, J. W. Audubon's travel sketches, J. Goldsborough Bruff's sketches, the paintings of W. S. Jewett and Thomas Hill, and Edward Vischer's lithograph prints are examples of this work. Realism is in conflict with romanticism, and usually it is realism that prevails.

Journalism

California writing began long before the golden era. The classics include Palóu's *Life of Serra,* Font's *Complete Diary,* Shaler's *Description,* Pattie's *Personal Narrative,* Robinson's *Life in California,* Bryant's *What I Saw in California,* and Frémont's *Report.* Most of these books are distinguished for content more than for style, yet they are usually pronounced readable, and one of their company, Dana's *Two Years Before the Mast,* besides being widely circulated, is frequently used in academic courses as a model of style in English composition.

Palóu's and Font's writings were works of Christian duty, but these writers, like the others, were inspired by a conviction that the exciting

California experiences of which they had acquired direct knowledge were eminently worth recording and would be read with interest in Mexico and Spain or in the States. The same is true of the trail journals, ocean logs, and miners' diaries of '49. Like their predecessors, these chroniclers were writing for the effete East rather than for local consumption. The first book printed in the province, Figueroa's sixteen-page code of laws (1834), though intended for local use, was hardly literature; nor was the arithmetic book *Tablas por los niños que empiezen a contar,* printed two years later. The same charge may be safely leveled at Mason and Brannan's *Laws for the Better Government of California,* printed in 1848.

The outset of the American period was marked by an improved demand for reading matter, a demand that was met after a fashion by the shinplaster journals started by Semple and Colton at Monterey and by Brannan and Kemble at San Francisco. With the gold rush, this demand was greatly increased. It was evidenced by the long queues at the San Francisco post office, by the special fees readily collectible for delivery of letters at the mines, by the popular excitement whenever a steamer entered the Golden Gate, and by the high prices current for eastern newspapers which were part of the incidental baggage of the Argonauts. Fifteen hundred copies of Greeley's *Tribune,* brought by a fellow passenger of Bayard Taylor, sold within two hours for a dollar apiece.

The first repercussion of the gold excitement in the summer of 1848, drawing away editors and compositors as well as subscribers and advertisers, was the suspension of publication of the pioneer weeklies, the *Californian* and the *California Star.* The secondary effect was the creation of a much larger field for journalism. Reviving their moribund sheets, the editors decided on January 4, 1849, to pool their resources in a new venture, the subsequently famous *Alta California.* In May the *Placer Times* blossomed at Sacramento, to be followed shortly by a motley assortment of papers scattered through the bay region and the mining towns. Included for a short time in the fall of 1850 was the *Illustrated Times,* which lived up to its name by featuring woodcuts. Likewise of short duration was the allegedly humorous *Hombre* of 1851, a pioneer in its field. Reflecting California's cosmopolitan character, the press quickly became multilingual. In 1850 there appeared the first French paper, in 1852 a German organ, two years later the first Spanish journals, and shortly thereafter one in Chinese, until eventually there were publications in practically all languages, including the Scandinavian.

Quantitatively, California journalism scaled heights that, without the gold rush, would not have been attained for decades. For many years the state could boast a per capita circulation exceeding even that of New York. As to quality, praise must be more niggardly. The presses, type, and paper available were uniformly inferior, composition and presswork were but indifferent, and proofreading was an undeveloped art. Most of the sheets were grossly partisan and reflected the malodorous state of local politics. News coverage was haphazard, editors depended largely on their shears, and much that was printed seemed to have no other justification than that it filled space. Perhaps the most hopeful sign was a tendency to escape some of the current inhibitions of eastern journalists.

San Francisco, naturally enough, had the lion's share of these early newspapers, yet some of the most influential journals were not of the city. Two examples stand out, the Sacramento *Union* and the Virginia City *Territorial Enterprise*. In the fifties the Sacramento *Union* was of moderate significance. It had the advantage, however, of propinquity to the seat of state government, and the greater advantage of honest, patriotic, and high-minded management. Its proprietors, James Anthony, Paul Morrill, and H. W. Larkin, aimed to be fearless champions of the common people, and to the best of their ability they adhered to that policy. The most momentous example was doubtless in the early sixties, when the paper was one of the staunchest supporters of the Union cause and was credited with greater effectiveness than an army corps. Most dramatic was the refusal of the three partners to move their paper to San Francisco, even though it was clear that in no other fashion could it be maintained as a dominant journal. They elected to stand by their guns, with the result that the *Union* declined in importance and in 1875 was purchased and absorbed by its rival, the *Record*.

Betimes, the *Union*'s proprietors had wielded a remarkable influence and had employed and subsidized a notable staff of writers, among whom Henry Clay Watson and Samuel Seabough were the most notable examples and Mark Twain was the most famous. It was a "travel grant" from the *Union* that had made possible Mark's jaunt to the Sandwich Islands, which in turn led to his career as a platform lecturer, his subsequent world tour, and the travel book *Innocents Abroad.*

The *Territorial Enterprise* emanated from Washoe, later to be labeled Nevada, but the society which it vocalized was part and parcel of the California culture area, and it is no violence to the facts to include it in a discussion of the state's early journalism.   In addition, the *Enterprise* had special ties with California.   Joseph T. Goodman, its editor and guiding genius, was a graduate of California's *Golden Era,* as was also Rollin M. Daggett, whose principal fame is as cofounder of that magazine.   Mark Twain heads the list of those who reached California publishers by way of the Nevada paper, which he immortalized so satisfactorily in *Roughing It.*   The journal flourished in the lush environment of sagebrush and alkali, nurtured on the white gold of the fabulous Comstock.   The Washoe community was, if possible, more masculine and more unrestrained than had been the camps of the forty-niners, and journalism in this unreal setting was free to follow any path of hyperbole or to perpetrate any outlandish hoax, and was under no obligation to print a story just because it was news.   With what gusto the "sagebrush school" embraced this opportunity is to be seen in the books of Mark Twain and Dan De Quille (William Wright) or, better still, in the broken files of the *Territorial Enterprise.*

From Golden Era to Overland Monthly

Most of the early California newspapers contained a modicum of literary pieces, which had been received with sufficient favor to suggest in 1852 the issuance of a weekly paper largely devoted to such materials.   This journal, the *Golden Era,* did not disdain ordinary news, but its distinction is for priority in laying the emphasis upon literature.   Its popularity was both immediate and sustained; it flourished for almost half a century and was read more widely than any of its competitors.   This very popularity rendered the journal suspect.   Superior and condescending critics have often remarked that the *Era* catered to low tastes, specifically to those of California's rustics and miners.   The accusation may be true; attired in miner's boots and flannel shirt, Co-editor Daggett did tour the diggings soliciting subscriptions.   The editors furthermore chose to emphasize California themes.   To start the paper off, Daggett had written up an episode experienced on the overland trail from the States, while his partner, J. Macdonough Foard, had drawn similarly on his recollections of Cape Horn. To the end the *Era* dealt largely with matters within the comprehension or even the experience of a majority of Californians. Only in dramatic criticism did it take on airs; for years it constituted itself the mentor of the San Francisco stage.

For all its popularity, or perhaps because of it, the *Era* did not garner the best writing. Contributors, having acquired a reputation through its columns, were quick to desert to more pretentious journals. Thus surprisingly little of the prose and poetry that appeared in the *Era* was judged worthy of inclusion in the collected works of Mark Twain, Bret Harte, and the rest. Yet with one or two exceptions the entire galaxy of early California writers found their initial opportunity in the *Era*. Alonzo Delano's pen name, Old Block, was a frequent signature during the fifties, as were also Caxton (William A. Rhodes) and Yellow Bird (John R. Ridge). In the sixties the new editor, Colonel Joe Lawrence, was even more indefatigable in casting the net for local writers. Mark Twain, fresh from his triumphs with the *Territorial Enterprise,* contributed enough sketches to make a small volume. Bret Harte entered "by the backdoor" as compositor and ere long contributed "M'liss," archtype of the California short story. Ina Coolbrith, Joaquin Miller, Charles Warren Stoddard, and Charles Henry Webb, better known to his readers as Inigo, are representative of others who got their start with the miners' favorite. So notable a roster is ample justification, if any be needed, for the *Era's* policy of being popular and unpretentious.

Competitors were numerous but for the most part short-lived. Such, for example, was the *Pioneer,* launched as a monthly in January, 1854, and kept afloat only two years. Its editor, Ferdinand C. Ewer, is better known for his fervent espousal of one ism after another. He was in turn a Unitarian, an Episcopalian, an atheist, a Trinitarian, a spiritualist, and finally an Episcopalian again. His excursion into mysticism, entitled "The Eventful Nights of August 20th and 21st," was the toast of the spiritualists—until he announced that it was a hoax. The *Pioneer* was of too short duration to exemplify his theological mutations. It was, furthermore, but slightly philosophical.

In the first issue, probably to emphasize the contrast to the *Golden Era,* Ewer announced that the new magazine would be devoted to literature, politics, science, belles lettres, poetry, and "the more flowery paths of Literature." The contributions of California writers, he predicted, would make the magazine a credit to "the noble State in which it had its origin." The promise was in fair degree realized. Descriptive pieces and semihistorical reminiscences outbulked fiction, and space was devoted in each number to a commentary on the contemporary scene—music and the stage, books and magazines, recent law decisions, and "Gossip with Readers and Correspondents." The poetry was often notable. Edward Pollock contributed some of his best, including "Evening" and "The Chandos Picture," while among the lesser luminaries were Charles Havens, J. P. Anthony, Frank Soulé, and John Swett, the last better known as the father of education in San Francisco.

Nevertheless, the fame of the *Pioneer* really rests on certain of the prose contributions. Early issues contained a serial, "California in 1851," now known as the *Shirley Letters* and hailed as one of the most accurate, penetrating, and charming descriptions of life in the diggings. Another outstanding contributor was Stephen Massett. His column, signed James Pipes of Pipesville, contained many a sparkling gem. Ewer's greatest triumph was to entice George Derby to contribute. Beginning in June, 1854, nine successive issues contained humorous sketches representative of the best achievements of his alter ego, John Phoenix, the more remarkable because they were composed in the somnolent desuetude of San Diego. Eastern journals hailed the *Pioneer* as "a capital periodical . . . freighted with good things," and, said the Boston *Post,* "we prize it like a nugget of gold for its many excellencies." These journals paid the *Pioneer* the more obvious compliment of copying its material wholesale, especially the John Phoenix sketches. Yet despite such wide and favorable notice, and notwithstanding its fine roster of writers, the *Pioneer* could not continue beyond its second year.

Next in the field was *Hutchings' California Magazine,* begun in 1856. Two years later the number of woodcuts was increased, though without corresponding improvement in quality, and for the remaining three years of its existence the word "illustrated" was added to the title. Though it contained nothing so uproarious as the Phoenix sketches, the new magazine was on the whole in a lighter vein. The most quoted example was Editor James H. Hutchings' "The Miner's Ten Commandments." Hutchings' favorite theme is illustrated by his "In the Heart of the Sierra," an impassioned tribute to the beauty and grandeur of the Yosemite Valley. He is often regarded as the first of the California nature enthusiasts, a company shortly joined by Charles Warren Stoddard, Thomas Starr King, Clarence King, John Muir, and a host of others.

The *Hesperian,* begun in 1858, gained distinction by falling into the hands of Mrs. F. H. Day. She improved the quality of illustrations, introduced a juvenile department, and gave the magazine something of a homey tone, yet managed to retain a measure of masculine interest. "The contents," it is asserted, "vary from sublime thoughts upon Milton to the best method of making muffins and embroidering flannel skirts." In 1863 the *Hesperian* got a new editor and a new name, *Pacific Monthly,* but it did not long survive. Minor ventures included the *San Francisco Pictorial Magazine,* the *Sunday Mercury,* the *Golden Gate,* and, emanating from Tuolumne, the *California Mountaineer.*

The *Californian,* established in 1864, ran for only three years, but its quality was so high and its contributors so distinguished as to make it of more than passing interest. Editor Charles Henry Webb had left the *Era* with the avowed intention of producing a more "high-toned" magazine. Assisted by such literati as Stoddard, Coolbrith, and Twain, he succeeded in this laudable purpose, only to find that the market was entirely inadequate.

One other magazine of importance was to grace the field of early western publishing, and in it California's first literary tradition reached its culmination. The reference, of course, is to the *Overland Monthly,* launched in July, 1868, and terminating its first series in 1875. Revived in 1883, the *Overland* survived various vicissitudes, but without duplicating the achievements of the initial series. Origin of the magazine is to be credited to the publisher Anton Roman, and to him goes a further plaudit for vesting absolute editorial control in Francis Bret Harte. It was Bret Harte's editorial genius, and often his pen, that gave the *Overland* its high repute. This fact is illustrated by the steady decline of the magazine after he relinquished the editorship and also by the rueful remark of Roman's successor, John H. Carmany, that in pocketing the loss on the *Overland* he had "spent thirty thousand dollars to make Bret Harte famous."

As the vehicle in which the best of his stories and poems appeared, the *Overland* was an important chapter in Bret Harte's personal development, yet no more so than in the literary evolution of the West.

In its heyday this journal garnered in the writings of practically every promising local author, and by its high standards challenged them to improve. Significant also was the stress it laid on the potentialities of the West. Its subtitle proclaimed that the *Overland* was "devoted to the development of the country." This pledge was redeemed in a number of ways. Besides a quota of enthusiastic descriptive pieces, the early numbers contained items such as "High Noon of the Empire," "The Tropical Fruits of California," "Art Beginnings on the Pacific Slope," and "Farming Facts for California Immigrants," all of which were frankly promotional.

Even more noteworthy was the determined effort to give the *Overland* an unmistakably western flavor. The *Atlantic Monthly* is often cited as its model and inspiration; the *Overland,* however, was not a mere imitation of the Boston monthly but rather its Pacific counterpart, differing from it as West from East. A glance at the contents of the first volume reveals a few contributions, such as the Reverend E. C. Bissell's "Egotizing" or T. H. Rearden's "Favoring Female Conventualism," which were environmentally detached. A much larger number would have seemed outlandish in the *Atlantic*. They are by no means confined to California but range broadly over the American West and the Pacific area, illustrating the expansive outlook of the *Overland* and of Californians. Random examples are: "Portland-on-Wallamett," "The Apache Race," "A Ride on the Texas Frontier," "The French in Mexico," "Carthagena," "Lima," "Hawaiian Civilization," "Japanese Holy Places," and "In Nankin." Yet to catalog the subjects tells only half the story. Much of this writing had about it a vibrancy, a freshness, a western aroma, difficult of analysis but unmistakably recognizable. It was this quality which won the *Overland* so warm a reception on the Atlantic coast as well as on the Pacific.

Books along with magazines made their appearance. Included were such compendia as *The Annals of San Francisco,* by Soulé, Gihon, and Nisbet (1855); *The Resources of California,* by John S. Hittell (1863); *The Natural Wealth of California,* by Titus Fey Cronise (1868), and two anthologies of western poetry. Two thrillers were far more widely read: John R. Ridge's *The Life and Adventures of Joaquín Murieta* and Royal B. Stratton's *Captivity of the Oatman Girls.* Treatises on philosophy and political economy are conspicuously absent, and history has no better representatives than

Frost, Dwinelle, and Tinkham. Thus, nonfiction was at the level of simple reporting and narration rather than of contemplative inquiry.

The Galaxy of Writers

By posterity, if not by their contemporaries, many of the writers of this early period have been judged worthy of no more than passing attention. The majority of the poets, in particular, may be dismissed with the remark that their outpourings to the muse were indifferent in quality and contributed little to the store of American letters. Quantity was not lacking. The wares of these poets may be sampled in the files of the early magazines and newspapers, and in anthologies like *Poetry of the Pacific,* assembled in 1865 by May Wentworth, and *Outcroppings,* sponsored the following year by Bret Harte. The modern reader is apt to close these volumes with little reluctance. As to early acclaim, Bret Harte and Joaquin Miller were the leaders, together with Ina Coolbrith, Charles W. Stoddard, and Edward Pollock.

In the field of prose the percentage of distinction was somewhat higher. In the fifties, for example, there was the miners' particular favorite, Alonzo Delano, who wrote under the name of Old Block, contributing to sundry papers and journals and illustrating many of his pieces with appropriate caricatures. It was inevitable that Delano's fame should decline with the passing of the forty-niner generation, for much of his writing was dated and presupposed familiarity with the diggings. Furthermore, Delano's readers in the fifties were under the spell of his personal magnetism: his nose, California's largest, and his integrity, demonstrated so forcefully in the panic of 1855. Posterity, less acutely aware of these admirable qualities, has a lesser appreciation for his *Pen Knife Sketches* (1853) and the play *Live Woman in the Mines* (1857). Today readers are much more apt to turn to his narrative of '49, *Life on the Plains and Among the Diggings.*

Of greater fame and doubtless of greater stature was George H. Derby of the Topographical Engineers. He came to California in 1849 with an excellent military record and left half a dozen years later with the reputation of being the nation's favorite humorist. This rocketing to popularity was in part the consequence of his penchant for practical jokes, a vice to which Californians of the fifties were particularly addicted. An unconscionable number of pranks are attributed to him, many of them no doubt incorrectly. Tastes having changed, most of these jokes seem to be mere encrustations on the portly lieutenant's real humor, but in the fifties they were an effective stepping stone to fame.   The more important stepping stones were of course the sketches that he published in the *Alta California* under the name Squibob and then in the *Pioneer* under the name John Phoenix. Immediately the vogue, these hilarious sketches were reproduced in journals far and near.   In 1856 a hastily assembled collection was brought out as a book, *Phoenixiana,* which soon ran through thirty-five editions.   Some of his choicest bits can be appreciated today only by antiquarians immersed in the nicer details of post-gold-rush California, yet even the most modern reader will find that the wit has not lost all its savor.

Derby's place in American letters is something on which the pretenders to authority cannot agree.   The tendency to call him a crude and ill-mannered buffoon seems to be waning, and some critics, veering to the other extreme, rank him as a polished and skillful workman and the founder of a new school of American humor.   He was one of the first to demonstrate that one could evoke laughter without resorting to illiteracy and bad grammar.   His salty burlesques were also diametrically opposed to the artificial romanticism whose stronghold was then New England.   With all his horseplay, Derby was still an exponent of realism, and much of his popularity was due to the conviction of his readers that his finger was on the fundamental verities.

Whatever the effect on national letters through the wide circulation of his *Phoenixiana* and through his subsequent contributions to the *Knickerbocker,* it is obvious that Derby's influence upon western writing would be more marked.   Punsters like "Inigo" Webb, pranksters such as the members of the sagebrush school, and, above all, Mark Twain profited greatly from the exploits and the tradition of this earlier artist in fun making.

Mark Twain and Bret Harte need no introduction.   Their place in California letters is only exceeded by their indebtedness to it.   It was in the West that Mark Twain found himself; it was there that he got his first practice in writing and as a platform lecturer.   Western themes were his first stock in trade, and western readers were his first, his most loyal, and his most consistent supporters.   The Derbyesque realism which he attained was a quality which Californians were best prepared to commend.   Bret Harte's debt to California was even greater. Not only were California journals his first medium of publication, but in gold rush California he found the setting for all that was meritorious in his writing. He had, to be sure, a mastery of expression which tempts forth such adjectives as felicitous, choice, sparkling, exquisite. Yet for all its excellence, this style availed him little except when he was exploiting the unique background of California in its golden era. His later eastern writings are flavorless, and when he tried to revive the western theme it was as though his perception of detail had been dulled.

Joaquin Miller likewise became a world celebrity through writing that was strictly western. He is accused, indeed, of playing up the outward manifestations of the West in a bid for attention, as when he paraded in London society attired in miner's boots and red flannel shirt. Yet the genuineness of his westernism is beyond dispute. He wrote with the fervor of sincerity. He did not desert California, and it was constantly recurrent as the theme of his poesy. If depth of inspiration were the only test, Miller would still rank as a major poet. Today, however, critics point out that he was guilty of slips in grammar, that his poorer poems detract from his best, and that his paean to the West is not distinctive. Nevertheless, he still stands head and shoulders above the other California poets of his day.

To single out Delano, Derby, Twain, Harte, and Miller may obscure the picture of the broader ranks of California writers. That these were numerous is an elementary fact. That they produced an astonishing quantity of creditable literature will also be admitted. An explanation must include comment on the caliber of the individuals brought to California in '49, allowance for the early material prosperity, recognition of the stimulation afforded by the majesty of Nature in the West, and allusion to the isolation which dictated western publishing instead of the mere purchase of eastern goods. These early Californians also had a high estimate of their own importance. They were the pioneers who had reached continent's end; they were erecting overnight a magnificent state; their gold was a decisive factor in preserving the Union. California writers, steeped in this feeling, were sure that they had something important to write about.

This confidence is of more fundamental significance than some of the more noticed characteristics—the fascination, for example, with California's novelty that elicited poems to "The Sequoias," "The Golden Gate," and "An Abalone Shell." The penchant for pen names is another superficiality in which the psychoanalyst might detect a hidden meaning. Besides being well-nigh universal, these pen names in a number of instances—to wit, Mark Twain and Joaquin Miller—succeeded in vanquishing the original names. Broad humor as a prominent feature of this writing has a more obvious significance, for the relish for laughter was a key trait among Californians of this generation. Impatience with artificial restraints, as when Bret Harte balked at censorship of "The Luck of Roaring Camp," is likewise important. It again illustrates the impulse toward realism, witnessed a little later by the coolness toward Bret Harte when it seemed that he had lost his grasp on the West as it actually was.

At bottom, the impulse toward realism doubtless rested on the assurance that the Californians had in the significance of their land, themselves, and their era. History, they were confident, was being made. For literature, therefore, what better function than to depict them and their achievements as they really were. The earnestness thus imparted to a generation of writers did not become sterile through deadly seriousness. Instead, it contributed a sense of high purpose, which proved an effective stimulant to noteworthy attainment. California writing was launched on a high plane, and an invigorating influence was imparted to the nation's literature.

23

STAGES AND STEAMERS

IN THE DROWSY CALM of the pastoral period California had made no transportation demands which could not be met by a saddled horse, an ox-drawn carreta, or the irregular sailings of the trading vessels. The Argonauts were not so easily content. Their restlessness led them to clamor for more convenient and more modern means of getting about, while their affluence enabled them to pay whatever was charged. The result was a revolution in communications within the state and a speedy provision of land and sea connections with other parts of the world, particularly with the eastern states.

Initial Steps

Local improvement began humbly in hit-or-miss fashion and by private initiative. For example, the first to give thought to the problem of mail delivery seems to have been a certain Alexander Todd, who came down from the diggings to the San Francisco post office, commissioned by a hundred-odd prospectors to carry up their letters. His rate was an ounce a letter, and his business acumen is further attested by his purchase of a skiff for $300 and his charge of $16 a head for the privilege of pulling an oar the hundred miles to Sacramento. Then came Bill Ballou, cutting the rate for letter delivery to a quarter-ounce and carrying a thimble as a measuring cup. With more competitors, the rate was slashed to a dollar and eventually to two bits.

These private mail carriers extended their operations throughout the diggings, supplementing the skeleton service which the national postal authorities, with only thirty-four post offices in the state by

June, 1851, were able to provide. By easy transition, letter carrying merged with gold delivery, and the two were often conducted in conjunction with pack-mule freighting. Banking was a more impressive outgrowth, and the national firms that opened California branches—such as Adams and Company in 1849, and Wells, Fargo and Company in 1852—reaped their largest income through commissions on remittances of gold. For many years, however, these larger concerns were supplemented throughout the interior by one-man express companies and middle-sized outfits carrying on where Alexander Todd and Bill Ballou had left off. Collectors of the franks of these lesser companies are able to list literally hundreds of outfits.

To provide for passenger conveyance was another golden opportunity. The first artery opened was the so-called river line to Sacramento. Sutter's launch had been an irregular forerunner, but Marshall's gold dictated more adequate appointments. At first all sorts of smaller craft were pressed into service. Ocean-going brigs and schooners could be worked up to Sacramento, and many were utilized thus. Competent pilots in the summer of '49 got $200 to $500 a trip and seemed worth it to those who essayed the voyage on their own. George F. Kent's journal, for example, has an exasperated entry about the grounding of the 123-ton *Rudolph* in the mud off what he called "Mosquito Creek," between Benicia and New York of the Pacific. The *Rudolph* stuck fast twice more before reaching Sacramento, but reconciled by this time to the uncertainties of California navigation, Kent was able to attain a more philosophic resignation.

Although the bay had boasted a tiny side-wheeler, brought from Sitka in 1847 and promptly wrecked, steam navigation really began in August and September of 1849, when several flat-bottomed side-wheelers and steam scows were put into commission. The *Washington,* launched at Benicia, seems to have been the first; it was followed by the *Edward Everett, Jr.,* which was assembled from parts brought out from New England, the *Sacramento,* and several others of clouded name and uncertain prowess. To judge from the record of wrecks, breakdowns, and short service, these pioneer vessels were poor makeshifts.

In October these experimental craft were eclipsed by the *Mint,* small and careening but fast, the 400-ton *McKim,* a propeller steamer, and the still larger *Senator.* Traffic was heavy and rates were high; in her first year of operation the *Senator* is said to have netted her owners $60,000 a month. By the end of 1850 there were fifty steamers, large and small, operating on the bay and the inland waterways. A notable addition to the fleet was the palatial *New World,* built in 1848 for excursion duty on the Hudson, boarded up and spirited away from the sheriff's attachment, so the story goes, and sailed around the Horn to far-off California. She was able to cut the *Senator's* time on the San Francisco-Sacramento run from ten hours to six.

Competitive rate wars, lowering the Sacramento fare from twenty-five or thirty dollars to one dollar, led to the organization in 1854 of the California Steam Navigation Company, capitalized at $2,500,-000. Stabilizing fares at ten dollars for cabin, seven dollars for deck passage, and six and eight dollars a ton for freight, the monopoly waxed fat. Would-be competition was forced out or bought out, and public protests against what were regarded as overcharges proved unavailing. Only the coming of the railroads caused the powerful company to unbend, and then, as far as the public was concerned, it amounted merely to the substitution of a new monopoly for the old. Besides dominating inland navigation the Steam Navigation Company acquired control of several coastal routes: to Humboldt Bay, to San Diego and way points, to the Columbia River, and finally, in 1867, to Alaska.

In the early years disasters were all too common. California waters had not been thoroughly charted; many of the vessels in use were outworn hulks; masters and crews were frequently lacking in skill and discretion; steamboat inspection was lax—in 1852 local inspectors still had to refer their reports to the New Orleans district office; and the passion for racing led to numerous boiler explosions. In the first half-dozen years the river boats had a score of accidents, with fatalities running as high as fifty persons. Still the Californians delighted in the luxury of steamboat rides, and the more steam was carried the better they liked it.

California Staging

Back in the autumn of '49, when the first paddle wheels churned the river waters to Sacramento and Stockton, the modernization of California land transport had begun. The pioneer seems to have been John Whistman, who, with an old French omnibus and a mixed team of mustangs and mules, offered an adventurous ride from San Francisco to San Jose. Passengers came forward at two ounces each and were elated at the nine-hour schedule. Winter rains curtailed the service to the eight miles between San Jose and Alviso, where steamers picked up passengers for San Francisco. The following spring a competing line was introduced by Ackley and Maurison, furnished, so it was advertised, "with the best stages and horses the country can produce." In the summer Whistman sold out to two experienced stage operators, Warren F. Hall and Jared B. Crandall, who reduced the fare to sixteen dollars, extended their line to Monterey, and a year later won a four-year contract to carry the mail to San Jose. In their lyric advertising, Hall and Crandall divided the emphasis between the safety of their stages, the beauty of the Santa Clara Valley, and the skill of their drivers. California afforded "no more charming drive," Hall and Crandall insisted, than on the line to San Jose, and they promised that passengers would find "pleasure united with business" as they were "whirled through the oak openings and across the level plains under the skillful driving of Professor Dillon or Crandall." Professor Crandall's most famous drive through the oak openings was in the fall of 1850, when with Governor Burnett on the box beside him he raced toward the state capital to beat the rival stage and to carry the news of California's admission to statehood.

Meanwhile, at Sacramento, in the fall of '49, young James Birch had appeared with an old ranch wagon and four fractious mustangs, offering a thirty-mile ride to Mormon Island at a fare of two ounces. The enthusiastic response to this initial service to the diggings attracted other men to the business, many of them like Birch experienced stage operators from New England or the Ohio Valley. Lines were multiplied and service extended to the major camps in the northern diggings, even as far as Shasta, 180 miles distant. By the fall of 1851 the San Francisco papers were ready to admit that Sacramento rather than the metropolis on the bay had become the hub of the stage lines. The *Alta's* Sacramento correspondent in November, 1851, listed the daily stages: six to Marysville, two to Coloma, and one each to Nevada City, Placerville, Auburn, Stockton, and Drytown-Jackson. Passengers, he added, were plentiful, the daily haul on the Sacramento-Marysville run averaging seventy each way and most of the other stages drawing a full complement. Fares had been reduced from the original dollar a mile, but they were still high enough to make the business very remunerative.

More striking than the spreading network of lines was the phenomenal improvement in equipment, both in horse flesh and rolling stock. The high prices current in California's flush times go far toward explaining this improvement, but it should be noted in addition that there was a healthy rivalry between the several proprietors and that these veterans of eastern staging took an intense pride in outfitting their lines with the very best. American horses soon replaced the native cow ponies. A few superior carriage horses had been brought out by the overland forty-niners; more were ordered from Ohio, Kentucky, Pennsylvania, and Virginia, and from $2,000 to $4,000 a span was not an unheard-of price for matched leaders, swing, or wheelers.

As to vehicles, the trend was toward the Concord type, manufactured by Abbott, Downing and Company of Concord, New Hampshire. The first such vehicle appeared at San Francisco on June 25, 1850, creating a sensation and inducing nostalgia on the part of the editor of the *Alta*. Additional Concord coaches were freighted round the Horn or caravaned overland until, by the midfifties, the California lines boasted newer and better equipment than was in use anywhere else.

The Concord was a work of art. Of its excellence the present generation, addicted to motorized transport and viewing only battered and patched museum specimens of the Concord, is naturally skeptical. In design the essentials were: a conventional running gear with a pair of "C"-shaped springs anchored to each axle, and stretching from these the thorough braces (manifold straps of stoutest leather), on which was cradled the egg-shaped body. Most significant was the thorough-brace suspension, which allowed the body to sway fore and aft. However much passengers might be inconvenienced by the constant pitching, the device was an effective shock absorber for the teams, especially on rough roads, and to spare the horses was a principal desideratum.

Abbott and Downing exploited this model to perfection. They chose materials most carefully: iron from Norway, well-seasoned ash and oak, and poplar for the body paneling. After some four decades of experience, workmanship had attained a high standard of skillfulness. Their coaches combined strength with lightness, and dependability when put to the most exacting use with beauty of line and ornamentation.

Nine or ten passengers could be squeezed into the standard stage with another dozen on top. Boots at front and back carried mail and baggage. The vehicle weighed only about 2,500 pounds, considerably less than our "light automobiles" today, and delivered in California it cost from $1,200 to $1,500. Though drawn at breakneck speed—ten, twelve, or even fifteen miles an hour—over roads of unconscionable roughness, these stages ran for years and years with almost no necessity for repairs. Over heavy grades or heavy roads the lighter and lower "mud wagons" were favored. The mud wagon seated about a dozen passengers in a more conventional wagon box, with or without an awning, but slung on thorough braces as in the standard coach.

The stage driver or "whip," as he preferred to be called, was one of the heroic figures of the old West. His wizardry in piloting a stage on a night run, his skill in careening down a mountain road, his prodigies in profanity, and later his exploits in foiling Indian attacks or attempted holdups surrounded him with the aura of a superman. And indeed, to manipulate whip and brake, to play upon the six reins so that each horse was individually controlled, and to be ready to act instantly in whatever emergency might arise called for a virtuoso.

The schedules maintained—sixty miles in six hours—and the record runs—160 miles at thirteen miles an hour—convey but inadequately the attainments of the California stage lines. By the mid-fifties service was unsurpassed, except perhaps by England's Royal Mail. And Englishmen who contrasted California's rough trails with England's macadamized post roads were astounded at such speed.

In 1854, year of the consolidation of the river boats, five sixths of the state's stage lines were amalgamated in the California Stage Company. Two New England whips headed the company, James Birch the pioneer and Frank Stevens, who until 1851 had operated a Sacramento tavern offering "Rest for the Weary and Storage for Trunks." Neither had passed twenty-five years of age, and most of their partners were likewise in the exuberant vigor of youth. The new company, capitalized at $1,000,000, advertised regular service on lines totaling 1,500 miles and "the most extensive and complete Line of stages in THE WORLD." Two years later, with 3,000 miles of stage lines in regular operation, not to mention the large fleet of steamboats plying the inland waters, the state could boast excellent facilities for handling intrastate passengers, mail, and express.

Panama Steamers

A companion problem was to break down California's isolation from the rest of the world. Under Spain and Mexico the greatest deterrent to development had been the remoteness of the province, and the authorities had never been able to overcome the obstacles symbolized by the Yuma Massacre, the inadequacy of San Blas, and the hazards of sailing up the coast. With the removal of the seat of government from Mexico City to Washington, the problem was altered without being perceptibly simplified. The overland routes from Missouri were as difficult as the Anza trail from Sonora, and despite improvement in ships, the round-the-Horn sailings or the broken voyage by Panama presented hardships comparable to those attending the earlier attempts to beat up the coast from Mexico.

At the very outset of the new regime, gold intensified the need for better contacts with California. The golden harvest must be channeled to the States and a California suddenly populous must be integrated with the rest of the nation. In the prevailing atmosphere of sectional distrust both these arguments had particular weight.

The most obvious answer to the problem seemed to be the development of the Panama route. Even before news of gold, Congress had undertaken to subsidize steamship lines by way of the isthmus to California and Oregon. The legislation was premised, not upon consideration for Pacific Coast settlements, but rather upon the supposition that commercial steamships could easily be transformed into auxiliary cruisers for the navy. Under terms of the first legislation in 1845 and 1847 the Post Office Department did not succeed in finding a contractor, even though the coöperation of naval officers was promised. Later in 1847, however, the Navy Department was authorized to act. It contracted with the United States Mail Steamship Company for semimonthly voyages from New York and New Orleans to Chagres and with the Pacific Mail Steamship Company for monthly voyages from Panama to Oregon. The annual subsidies were to be $290,000 and $199,000 respectively.

Service commenced just in time to catch the first flood of California-bound Argonauts. The rush of passengers brought others into the business, notably the mogul of Hudson River ferries and steamboats, "Commodore" Cornelius Vanderbilt, and the Atlantic and Gulf operator Charles W. Morgan. Utilizing the Nicaragua transit, these men offered sharp competition from 1851 to 1856. In the ensuing three years the Pacific Mail paid Vanderbilt $40,000 and then $56,000 a month to stay out of the business. In 1859 he got the mail contract. A sharp rate war was followed in 1860 by an agreement that Vanderbilt should have the Atlantic run and the Pacific Mail the Pacific run, and in 1865 the Pacific Mail purchased the Atlantic fleet.

For several seasons, despite the impressment of many smaller craft and a number of additions to the Panama fleet, accommodations were greatly overtaxed. The *California,* for example, though built for a maximum of 250, carried 365 on her maiden voyage, and a decade later the Vanderbilt line was accused of shipping 1,100 on a vessel licensed to carry but 750. Vanderbilt's steamers also had the name of being dirty and badly manned. Worse than the discomfort was the actual hazard to life. In the first half-dozen years of steamship operation to California, no less than a score of disasters occurred, several with appalling loss of life. The Pacific Mail had one loss, the $300,000 *Tennessee,* which went down off San Francisco in 1853; the Vanderbilt line lost five, and independent coastal and round-the-Horn shipping suffered the rest. In 1857 occurred the crowning disaster when, some 400 miles below Cape Hatteras, the palatial *Central America* spread her seams and foundered, carrying to a watery grave more than two million dollars worth of gold and 400 men.

Yet notwithstanding the risks which these wrecks symbolized, the Panama route came to be the favored path between California and the States. Completion of the Panama railroad reduced the transit schedule from three or four days to four hours. The larger steamers put into service also reduced the running time, especially on the Pacific, and by 1866 the schedule had been pared from thirty-three or thirty-four days to twenty-one. The fare fluctuated wildly, but in the later years it was usually less than half the original rate of $450 for first class and $225 for steerage. Government officials, politicians, businessmen, and men of means were almost unanimous in their choice of the Panama route. It was the choice also of the miners who, having struck it rich, wanted to return to their homes. Much California mail was carried by way of Panama, even after the opening of the overland stage line, and was delivered quite as expeditiously. Express was also carried, and the shipments of California gold, which in Civil War days assumed such significance, were all by way of Panama. Perhaps the best indication of the importance of the steamship line is that the surplus of westbound over eastbound passengers accounted for one fifth of California's population increase in the fifties and for one half in the next decade.

The Pacific Railroad Surveys

Yet the Panama steamers, especially in their early operations, did not impress as the ultimate solution of California's transportation problem. It was objected that they were too slow, too crowded, too roundabout. Also, there was the feeling that California, as a contiguous part of the United States, ought to have a direct connection rather than to be treated as an overseas possession, distant two ocean voyages and an isthmian transit through the territory of a foreign nation. Californians, not unmindful of their importance and aware of the shortcomings of the Panama service, loudly demanded an overland connection, arguing that it was the manifest duty of the federal government thus to provide for their convenience. In the East a number of men prominent in politics and journalism joined their voices to this chorus and urged upon the authorities the forging of a transcontinental link. The arguments they advanced were less those of constitutional obligation to the Californians and more those of national defense, national solidarity, and American opportunity on the Pacific.

The type of overland communication uppermost in the thoughts of most of these men was, strange to say, the railroad. It was only a score of years earlier that the first trains had begun operations near Baltimore. In those few years, however, the steam horse had proved a precocious upstart. By 1850 the section of the nation east of the Mississippi and north of the Ohio was crisscrossed by a maze of rail lines. The total mileage, some 9,818, was impressive, but practically all was accounted for by short lines of local inception and construction, built to handle a traffic already existent. To throw a line across 2,000 miles of unoccupied plains and mountains to the Pacific Coast was beyond the resources of any magnates then in the business, and with the small prospect for traffic it was not a proposition attractive to private enterprise. The advocates of a Pacific

railroad seem not to have grasped the fundamental distinction, just
as they underestimated the difficulties of actual construction. Besides, to any such practical objections there was a ready answer: the
federal government should see to the construction of the transcontinental.

That a road was not immediately authorized was largely due to the
sectional squabbling over location of its eastern terminus. True,
the Panama steamship companies lobbied against such bills, many
easterners were unconvinced that the federal government should embark on so grandiose an internal improvement, and the exact technique of federal aid was not immediately agreed upon. Nevertheless, had there been unanimity as to route it seems probable that
construction would have been begun in the early fifties. At any
rate, the federal government's first step toward establishing an overland connection with California was to appropriate $150,000 in
1853 for the survey of the several feasible Pacific railroad routes.

The surveys which the army thereupon conducted resulted in the
accumulation of a vast quantity of topographical, ethnological,
botanical, geological, zoölogical, and climatic information, impres-
sively stored up in the ponderous tomes of the *Reports*. The surveys
thus are of considerable geographic and academic interest, though
beyond the assertion that there were a half-dozen possible railroad
routes to the Pacific, their practical utility was slight. Sectional
bickerings prevented Congressional action until 1862, at which time
the politics of war determined the choice of route, and before actual
construction took place a more thorough plotting proved necessary.

The Overland Stage

In the meantime, Californians renewed their clamor for overland
communications and at the end of this decade were rewarded with
stage line, pony express, and telegraph. Although the telegraph
was something of permanent utility, overland mail and pony express
functioned but briefly. The latter did shorten the interval for communications between California and the States, though, as we have
seen, improvements on the Panama line soon reduced its schedule
to approximately the equivalent of the transcontinental stage. Toward the movement of passengers the pony express contributed nothing and the overland but a negligible amount. On the score of practical utility, then, they deserve but a fraction of the attention which

their spectacularity has won them in so many works of popular nature and sober history. Their true significance is that they gave practical demonstration of the possibility of through service on the overland routes, that by their very shortcomings they helped to evoke the railroad, and that by the boldness of their design they commanded attention to the problem of western communications. Incidentally, it is worth noting that it was precisely as an advertising medium that the pony express was started.

For the stage line there were antecedents in certain mail contracts, such as one in 1850 to a "camping-out" company which freighted the mail from Independence to Santa Fe and another in 1851 for a line from Independence to Salt Lake City. Birch's flourishing California Stage Company was much better supplied with the wherewithal to provide rapid through service.

Californians were giving much thought to the matter, but like their eastern brethren, they fell into the error of wasting most of their energy in bickering about the choice of route. Persuaded that Johnson's Pass was the best Sierra crossing, the state appropriated funds for road building, and in 1857 the intrepid Crandall inaugurated stage service across the Sierra from Placerville to Washoe. Meanwhile, some 75,000 California voters had memorialized Congress to construct a military wagon road to California by way of Salt Lake. This colossal petition, the largest thus far laid on the Congressional doorstep, led to an appropriation of $200,000 for roadwork along the southern route and one of $300,000 for the Salt Lake line, but with the western terminus fixed far to the north of Johnson's Pass. Thus was the confusion in California worse confounded.

Hot on the heels of this road appropriation came another measure most heartening to the advocates of the overland. The Postmaster-General was authorized to contract for six years at $600,000 a year for semiweekly service on a twenty-five-day schedule from the Mississippi to San Francisco. Ostensibly, the contractor would designate the route, but it was a foregone conclusion that Postmaster-General Aaron Brown of Tennessee would dictate the circuitous southern route. It was also freely predicted, despite the bid of an eastern coalition of seven men headed by John Butterfield, that the award would go to California's James Birch, hailed by the New York press as "a gentleman of large capital and much experience, and more competent, perhaps, than any other single man in the United States to execute this great mail contract."

Birch and Brown seemed to think so too, for as an apparent preliminary to the larger contract, the Postmaster-General awarded the Californian a $150,000 contract for monthly mail stages from San Antonio to San Diego. This line "from nowhere to nowhere," partly by relays and partly by camping out, and partly horse-drawn and partly mule-drawn (hence its nickname, "the Jackass"), defies explanation except as a subsidiary of the larger overland. It went into operation late in 1857 and gave Birch the honor of operating the first transcontinental stage line. By Presidential intervention, however, the greater opportunity was deflected from him into the hands of Butterfield and his associates. Birch had little time to ponder on the strange ways of statesmen, for that very fall, when still in his twenties, he perished at sea in the wreck of the *Central America*.

"The king is dead, long live the king!" To the fore now came the new ruler of the stages, John Butterfield. The task that confronted him called for all the experience that he had gained in midwestern freighting and staging, and for all the executive ability that he possessed. In twelve months, according to the terms of his contract, he must man, stock, and equip some 2,800 miles of stage line. For efficiency of administration he divided the line at El Paso into an eastern and a western section, each section consisting of four divisions 300 to 400 miles in length. West of El Paso the line was manned by Californians and stocked with California equipment.

By dint of hard work the preparations were completed on the appointed day, September 17, 1858, and stages set out simultaneously from Tipton, Missouri, the railhead west of St. Louis, and from San Francisco. Each completed the run with more than a day to spare, the eastbound coach to be greeted by a congratulatory telegram from President Buchanan and the westbound to encounter exuberant enthusiasm at San Francisco. As the *Bulletin* described the event:

At a quarter after four o'clock the coach turned from Market into Montgomery Street. The driver blew his horn and cracked his whip; at which the horses, four in number, almost seemed to partake of his enthusiasm, and dashed ahead at a clattering pace, and the dust flew from the glowing wheels. At the same time a shout was raised, that ran with the rapidity of an electric flash along Montgomery Street, which throughout its length was crowded by an excited populace. As the coach dashed along through the crowds, the hats of the spectators were whirled in the air and the hurrah was repeated from a thousand throats, responsive to which, the driver, the lion of the occasion, doffed his weather-beaten old slouch, and in uncovered dignity, like the victor of an old Olympic race, guided his foaming steeds toward the Post Office.

Diverse and contradictory are the descriptions of travel on Butterfield's Overland Mail. With no stopovers except to change horses, with no pretense at facilities for sleeping, and with not much preparation for meals en route, traveling the overland was hard work. For one passenger it induced insanity, and another pair got so on each other's nerves as to provoke a duel. Others, inured to western hardships, pronounced the ride a thrill and a pleasure. But with an eye to the mail rather than the passengers, the overland ran on, occasionally disturbed by floods or by Indian attacks on the stations and a few times requiring more than the allotted twenty-five days, though usually getting through with two or three days to spare.

Northern California never really warmed to the Butterfield line, principally because of the conviction that a faster schedule was easily possible on the central route. Crandall's stages were demonstrating the feasibility of the Sierra crossing. In 1858 Postmaster-General Brown loosed the federal purse strings slightly to contract with John M. Hockaday for weekly mail from Independence to Salt Lake City, and with George Chorpenning for carriage thence to Placerville. Commencing a few weeks prior to Butterfield's line, the central combination brought the mail through regularly, winter as well as summer, and often in less than the thirty-eight days which the schedule allowed; but the administration, so it seemed, was careful not to build this line up into a dangerous rival of the favored southern line. On one occasion the government's preference was brought into the open. This was in December, 1858, in connection with the President's annual message to Congress. Advance copies were promised to the Tehuantepec steamer, the Butterfield line, and the Hockaday line, but to the latter's dismay no copy was forthcoming for the Central Overland. Thus handicapped, the race went not to the swift but to the favorite. The week's head start enabled the Butterfield messenger to win, but Hockaday and Chorpenning's elapsed time of seventeen days and twelve hours was quicker by more than two days. Northern Californians, none too cordial toward Buchanan's southerners to start with, were all the more convinced of the superiority of the central route.

Postmaster-General Brown, though limiting the Central Overland to a niggardly $320,000 subvention, was ready to lay out funds for still other lines to California.   He let a contract for a monthly stage along the thirty-fifth parallel from Kansas City to Stockton, another for a stage from Neosho, Missouri, to Albuquerque, and a third for steamers from New Orleans to Tehuantepec and thence to San Francisco.   The San Antonio-San Diego, also established in 1858, was enlarged to a semimonthly line.   Brown's death early in the following spring brought in an economy-minded successor, who saved a million dollars a year by eliminating several of these lines and curtailing all the others, with the conspicuous exception of the Butterfield.

Deprived of their mail contracts, Hockaday and Chorpenning were reduced to sad straits.   The former was overshadowed and then bought out by the reigning entrepreneurs of Plains freighting, Russell, Majors, and Waddell.   Their stages, known as the Leavenworth and Pikes Peak Express, and then as the Central Overland California and Pike's Peak Express, did a good business to the Colorado mines and Salt Lake City, even though the cancellation of Chorpenning's contract left no through service to California.

The Pony Express and the Close of an Era

When a new menace appeared in the form of competitors on the Colorado run, William Russell resolved to gamble.   He announced to Senator Gwin that the C. O. C. and P. P. E. would establish a pony express on a ten-day schedule.   His partners were skeptical but considered their firm pledged to the venture, and on April 3, 1860, this most dramatic of transcontinental mails went into action.

Away across the endless dead level of prairie a black speck appears in the sky. . . . In a second or two it becomes a horse and rider, rising and falling, rising and falling—sweeping toward us nearer and nearer, and the flutter of hoofs comes faintly to the ear—another instant and a whoop and hurrah . *. . a wave of the rider's hand, but no reply, and a man and horse burst past our excited faces, and go sweeping away like a belated fragment of storm.

Mark Twain's magic pen has captured the contemporary and the permanent spell of this miracle of horseflesh and horsemanship. Practical details fade into insignificance, such as the half-ounce letters in oilskin pouches, the boy jockeys, unarmed and depending on their ponies' speed to escape the ambushes of designing savages, the seventy-five relays, the five-dollar postage, and the disappointingly small volume of westbound letters. As an advertisement of the central route, the Pony Express might or might not have been successful. Popular fancy was captivated, but before Congress attacked the problem of revamping the California mails, Lincoln had been elected, South Carolina had seceded, her sister states, Texas included, had followed, Fort Sumter had been fired upon, and the Civil War was under way. Willy-nilly, the Butterfield route was abandoned and its stock hustled northward to the Salt Lake line. Although the ponies ran a little longer, gladdening California with news little more than a week old, even that service was outmoded on October 26, 1861, by the completion of the Pacific telegraph. In actuality, the ponies' contribution was to expedite communications in the nineteen months immediately preceding the telegraph and, probably more important, to become the symbol of all the gallant efforts of the prerailroad era to provide the transcontinental link.

The day of the Concord was not over. Concentrating now on the central route, Congress on March 2, 1861, authorized a million-dollar subsidy for a daily stage. Arrangements were complicated by the necessity of compensating Butterfield for transferring northward and by the financial difficulties of the C. O. C. and P. P. E. due to the heavy drain of the Pony Express. Efficiency also demanded a route which would include on the main line both Denver, the metropolis of Colorado mining, and Salt Lake City, the Mormon metropolis. By July these problems were on the road toward solution. The first run was accomplished in seventeen days, and despite Indian hostility, the severe winter of 1861–1862, and floods in the following spring, the stages kept rolling.

Financially, however, Russell, Majors, and Waddell were at the end of their tether, and in March, 1862, they had to surrender to a new magnate, the expansive Ben Holladay. By those who did not like him, Holladay was accused of having all the vices of the unprincipled, domineering, coarse, and ruthless tycoons who were then riding the crest of big business' sudden rise. He had not imbibed of the traditions of staging as, for example, had Birch. He knew little of its niceties as a craft, he took no pride in the superlative qualities of Concords or of matched wheelers, and he was a demanding taskmaster rather than an inspiring leader for his employees.

On the other hand he had an astounding ability to get things done, he had at his command adequate finances, and he was adept in the financial legerdemain, shady and otherwise, practiced by so many of his contemporaries. In the four years of his control, western staging attained its largest scale. Holladay had some 3,300 miles of regular lines in operation and enjoyed a reputation, attested by Mark Twain, of getting the mail through. In 1866, on the eve of eclipse by the transcontinental railroad, Holladay gave further proof of his financial genius by selling out at a good price to Wells, Fargo and Company.

Most published accounts of prerailroad communication concentrate upon the more dramatic ventures, such as Butterfield's Overland Mail, Russell's Pony Express, the army's experiment in the fifties with a camel caravan, or John A. "Snowshoe" Thompson's ski trips across the Sierra with as much as 100 pounds of mail on his back. Some of the phases usually neglected seem to be of comparable or even greater significance, particularly the development of communications within the state by steamboat and stage, California's contribution to overland staging, the role of Crandall, Hockaday, and Chorpenning as pioneers on the central route, the culmination of the overland system under Holladay, and finally the continued dependence of Californians upon the Panama sailings of the Pacific Mail Steamship Company. Pony and stage sometimes outraced the steamer. They often monopolized public attention, but it took a doughtier foe to wrest away the bulk of the business in passengers, express, and even mail. Steamer patronage was well maintained, the peak being reached in 1868. The next year the joining of the rails at Promontory terminated a colorful and significant epoch and reduced both steamers and stages to roles subordinate to that of the new hero, the puffing locomotive.

24

BUILDING THE PACIFIC
RAILROAD

I N CALIFORNIA the first quarter-century of the American period abounded with epochal changes and remarkable achievements. They are encountered all along the line, in law and politics, in agriculture and industry, in literature, and in transportation. Most grandiose of all the projects attempted was one which loomed large on the national horizon as well as in California, namely, the building of the Pacific railroad.

From Asa Whitney to Theodore Judah

First proposed with any seriousness in 1845, it was for a number of years regarded as a most visionary scheme. Gradually its advocates gained a more sympathetic hearing. The gold rush added incentive, the surveys of 1853 to 1855 pronounced several routes feasible, overland stages and pony express popularized the idea, and the sectional crisis emphasized the necessity of binding the Far West to the nation. Notwithstanding the formidable and complex difficulties encountered, Asa Whitney's dream of 1845 was realized in 1869, just twenty-four years later. Much of the story obviously belongs to the nation and to the East, yet so much of the drama was enacted in California, and so pervasive and powerful has been the railroad's influence on the state, that local history must take notice.

Prior to the gold rush it was perfectly natural that planners of a Pacific railroad should look toward Oregon rather than California.

In the fifties, when the sights were shifted, it is understandable that hopes were pinned not merely on California but on the entire Pacific area which the railroad would unlock: Oregon and British Columbia, the Russian empire on the North Pacific, the islands of the South Seas, the Japan whose door Perry was even then opening, ancient China, and Columbus' India. The railroad, significantly, was always called the Pacific railroad.

Throughout the fifties the prospect for such a railroad was dimmed not only by calculations of probable cost and engineering difficulties but also by sectional jealousies which prevented agreement on any single route. Those interested in the existing transportation systems by stage and steamer exerted their influence against active federal support. Also, though the friends of the railroad were mostly individuals who were vaguely acquiescent in the notion that a railroad should be constructed, only a very few had any concrete ideas as to how to engineer or finance it, how much it would cost, how long it would take, how much private capital could be raised for the enterprise, or how much business the completed road might expect.

About the first to rescue the Pacific railroad from the limbo of hazy generalities and to discuss it in terms within the ken of engineers and bankers was a young construction engineer named Theodore D. Judah. Before 1854 he assisted in rebuilding the section of the Erie Canal between Jordan and Seneca and helped build the bridge at Vergennes, Vermont, and various New England and New York railroads, including the Niagara Gorge Railroad. Then, at the ripe age of twenty-eight, he was brought to California to build the Sacramento Valley Railroad to Folsom, twenty-two miles distant, and thence perhaps to Shasta or even to Oregon. To Folsom the rails were laid expeditiously, at a cost only slightly in excess of Judah's original estimate. Since it cut a day from the time required for freighting to the mines, the road became immediately profitable. Stage lines also transferred their depot to Folsom. This railroad was California's earliest. On a handcar over its first 400 feet of track, Judah himself enjoyed the first railroad ride in the state. Logically, other sections of track might have been added, but at this point Judah became disturbed by the company's heavy interest charges. He severed his connection with it, and track laying ceased.

Judah's miscellaneous employments in the next few years were overshadowed by his preoccupation with the idea of a Pacific railroad. When commissioned to chart a wagon route across the Sierra, he made his report primarily an argument for the railroad. With a one-horse wagon equipped with barometer, compass, and odometer, he made no less than twenty-two reconnaissances of Sierra passes and approaches, finally selecting the Dutch Flat route, which the Central Pacific eventually utilized. Selection of this route was one of Judah's major contributions to the ultimate railroad.

Meanwhile, he was still more active in advocating the idea. "Crazy Judah," people called him, because of his incessant harping on this theme. He is reminiscent of that earlier enthusiast for the Americanization of Oregon, the eccentric Hall J. Kelley. There was this difference, however; although Judah talked indefatigably about his obsession, his enthusiasm was buttressed by a seemingly inexhaustible store of facts and figures about the actual problems of construction. In other words, though he may have been infatuated with the idea, he was singularly well-informed, thoroughly practical, and unquestionably an expert.

Besides riding his hobby in California, where he gradually built up a following of more or less enthusiastic converts, Judah made several bids for support at Washington. He was there in 1856 and again in 1857, urging his favorite project upon Congressmen, Senators, and others influential in the government. The nature of his proposal is well summed up in a pamphlet that he had printed at Washington on the occasion of his second visit. It is entitled *A Practical Plan for Building the Pacific Railroad,* and it was just that. Judah began with a devastating criticism of the government surveys of 1853 to 1855, which the irrepressible John Phoenix was even then lampooning in the California press. Judah argued that most of the botanical and zoölogical information which the military surveys had amassed was irrelevant, and that prospective builders needed to know more about actual grades and alignments, about the requirements for tunnels, fills, and bridges, and about the availability of fuel, timber, and building stone. He urged Congress to appropriate $200,000 for such an "actual and reliable survey," which he represented as a necessary prerequisite if private capital was to be induced to take up the project. And he proposed that, as squatter sovereignty had taken the question of slavery extension out of the halls of Congress, so the choice of route could be removed from politics by leaving it to the capitalists. But sound though most of these arguments were, they were unavailing, and Congress in 1857 adopted none of the legislation proposed.

Two years later Judah had partial success in another quarter. The California legislature was persuaded to call a Pacific Railroad Convention, which met at San Francisco on September 20, 1859, with 100 delegates in attendance and John Bidwell presiding. The convention, of course, was an oratorical rather than a legislative body, yet it did achieve a unified statement of western recommendations regarding the transcontinental railroad. As its most active member, Judah was the natural choice to convey the convention's proposals to Congress. He sailed on October 20, in company with California's new Congressman, John C. Burch, who quickly became a convert to Judah's idea. Other California and Oregon representatives gave support, as did also Congressman John A. Logan of Illinois, who was able to procure a room in the Capitol for Judah's more effective lobbying. There the latter set up a Pacific Railroad Museum filled with maps, surveys, reports, and other materials calculated to sell the idea of the railroad. Yet despite the persuasiveness of his exhibit and his speeches the time was not yet ripe for federal action. When Judah sailed for the Pacific coast it was without having realized his hopes.

Organizing the Central Pacific

Back in California, Judah was off at once to the high Sierra to spend the entire summer in ceaseless search for the best route. By the time winter snows drove him down to the habited lowlands his fieldwork had removed from his mind any uncertainties about the feasibility of a trans-Sierra railroad. Encouraged by his close friend the Dutch Flat druggist, Dr. Daniel W. Strong, he drew up articles of association for a company to build such a railroad. Its name was to be the Central Pacific Railroad of California.

Before such a company could be incorporated, state law required that its stock be subscribed to the amount of $1,000 for each mile of trackage proposed, which in this instance meant $115,000. Judah, Strong, and a few Dutch Flat associates were good for $46,-500. It was with optimism, therefore, that Judah posted off to San Francisco to raise the remainder. For a time prospects seemed rosy, but in the end the metropolitan financiers proved too coldly calculating and the Central Pacific had to go begging to Sacramento. From the Wall Street of the West to the humble merchants of Sacramento was quite a comedown; it was the latter, however, whom Judah was finally able to wheedle into giving the necessary support.

The process of extracting this support was not without its drama. After sundry conferences and conversations, and after a first meeting had failed, a second meeting was called in a small room over the hardware store owned by Mark Hopkins and Collis P. Huntington. Those in attendance included Judah and Strong; James Bailey, jeweler; Cornelius Cole, lawyer; B. F. Leete, surveyor; the Robinson brothers; Lucius A. Booth; Leland Stanford, wholesale grocer; Charles Crocker, dry-goods merchant; and the hosts of the evening. Stanford was shortly to be the Republican candidate for governor and Cole later went to the United States Senate. At the time of the meeting, however, none of those present had a reputation more than local, none had previous experience in large-scale construction or financial enterprises, and their combined resources would not have paid for even as much of a railroad as the Sacramento Valley line to Folsom. This certainly was not the most promising personnel for the heroic venture of spanning the Sierra.

Yet Judah's persuasive powers were equal to the emergency. He adverted to the plan for a transcontinental railroad in which the Central Pacific was to be a unit, but he had the good judgment to build his plea on arguments which small-town merchants would be better able to comprehend. Eventually would come the railroad, but for the present all that was necessary was to charter the company and run the survey over the mountains to the state line. With this accomplished, the company would be in excellent position to get government subsidies, federal, state, and local. More to the point, it would control the lucrative traffic to and from Washoe. Even with a wagon road, Judah subtly pointed out to these Sacramento merchants, the Washoe market would be theirs. Thus persuaded, these tradesmen entered upon the speculation that was to bring four of their number fame and wealth beyond their wildest expectations.

It was conservatively that they ventured. At the meeting at which the minimum subscription for incorporation was reached, Huntington took no stock. Only after further appeal from Judah did he agree to lend a hand. He then promised to get six men to pay for the projected instrumental survey across the mountains, a valuable contribution to be sure, but one for which the six struck a hard bargain.   Judah put at the disposal of the company practically without compensation his fund of knowledge about railroad building, about the Dutch Flat route, and about lobbying at Washington.   Dr. Strong's early support was soon forgotten, but the six merchants— Stanford, Huntington, Bailey, Hopkins, Booth, and Crocker—who took only 800 of the original 85,000 shares, were rewarded with the positions respectively of president, vice-president, secretary, treasurer, and directors of the company.   There is a poetic injustice that control should have passed from the hands of Chief Engineer Judah to these men, but putting sentiment aside, the enlistment of these men into the enterprise was unquestionably one of Judah's major contributions to the Pacific railroad.

Work on the survey began forthwith.   Judah was greatly heartened to have at least a portion of the load lifted from his shoulders. The vast majority of Sacramentans, however, were most skeptical that the Central Pacific Company would surmount the Sierra by rail. Even with the $1,000-a-mile requirement railroad planning was a favorite California pastime, usually with abortive result.   Judah's project, more fantastic than the average, seemed most unlikely to eventuate, for as the survey progressed and demonstrated that a trans-Sierra railroad was an engineering possibility, the obstacles to be overcome were brought more clearly to view.   Never before had a railroad attempted to scale so formidable a barrier: an abrupt rise of 7,000 feet in twenty miles, with rugged mountainsides, deep canyons, dangerous slide areas, hard granite almost everywhere a cut or tunnel was indicated, and winter snowfalls of as much as thirty feet. Judah never minimized these difficulties, but in his reports he achieved an optimistic tone by harping on the magnitude of the Nevada traffic and the resources, such as timber, that the road would open up.

Next on Judah's program was another jaunt to Washington. Again he sailed in company with a Congressman-elect, Aaron Sargent, and again he was able to instill much of his enthusiasm into the representative.   Sargent not only agreed to sponsor the Pacific railroad bill, but also at the first opportunity spoke energetically for it, got a subcommittee appointed to take the measure in charge, and saw to it that Judah was named clerk of this subcommittee.   Judah was already secretary of the corresponding Senate committee, and soon acquired similar opportunity with the House's main committee on railroads, thus becoming a triply effective lobbyist. Even without his influence a Pacific railroad bill might have been enacted in 1862, because the secession of the southern states had removed opposition to a north-central route and because the Civil War set a special premium on California's gold and Nevada's silver. Yet the actual bill bears the unmistakable stamp of Judah's handiwork, particularly in the provision that the western unit, from Sacramento to the state line, should be built by the Central Pacific Company of California. Other provisions of the act were that the road should extend from the Missouri River to Sacramento and that, in addition to the 400-foot right-of-way, the companies should receive from the public domain the odd-numbered sections within ten miles of the line —that is, ten for each mile of track. Most important of all, the federal government agreed to advance, on thirty-year six per cent bonds for each mile of track laid, $16,000 to the mountains, $48,000 in the Rockies and the Sierra, and $32,000 on the intermountain section.

Returning to the coast, the master lobbyist found himself the hero of the hour, honored on all sides—except in his own company. Among the Central Pacific moguls the bone of contention was the perhaps inevitable one between builder and speculators. Judah envisioned the road as a link in the Pacific railroad, a permanent asset for future generations and something that should be built accordingly. The partners seemed to have designs merely on the Nevada business and the government subsidy, especially the latter. Track laying they regarded as a necessary evil, prerequisite though it was to collection of the subsidy. Survey beyond the mountains could also be postponed, and any other device that would cut expenses or expedite collection of the subsidy was sure to meet with their favor. The rift widened. Judah insisted that as chief engineer, indeed as the only competent engineer, he should have the final decision on construction matters. The partners responded by excluding him from any voice in company affairs. They called upon him to pay up the 10 per cent deposit on his stock, though his initial services to the company had been accepted as an in lieu payment. The last straw was his refusal to certify to the federal authorities that the line entered the mountains some twenty miles sooner than was actually the case. By enlisting the support of the state geologist,

Professor J. D. Whitney, the partners "moved the Sierra into the
middle of the valley" and profited thereby to the tune of some
$640,000, but Judah would not be a party to the deception.

The parting of the ways was now at hand. In October, 1863,
Judah sailed for New York. He had accepted $100,000 for his
interest in the Central Pacific and had taken options to buy out
Stanford, Huntington, Hopkins, and Crocker at $100,000 each. His
plan apparently was to persuade eastern capitalists, perhaps the
Vanderbilt interests, to buy out his shortsighted and unprincipled
antagonists. But the gods overruled. Contracting yellow fever at
Panama, Judah was brought ashore at New York a very sick man,
and on November 2, still four months short of his thirty-eighth birthday, he died. Thus for good or ill the Central Pacific Railroad was
left in the hands of the Californians who were soon to be ticketed
the Big Four. They exhibited a perfect willingness to allow Judah
to pass into oblivion. For a decade he had been the most active
proponent of the Pacific railroad. The Dutch Flat route, the Central Pacific Company, and the Pacific Railroad Act were monuments
to his competence as engineer, promoter, and lobbyist. His erstwhile
partners did not so much as name a whistle stop in his honor, nor
did they share any of the profits of the enterprise with his widow.

The Big Four at Work

The four men whose sway over the company was now complete
are among the most famous in California's annals. Making due
allowance for sporadic essays and for Oscar Lewis' successful venture
in group biography, these men still await full biographical treatment.
They and their relatives frowned on early proposals, while recent
scholars have not been attracted to the task, in realization, no doubt,
that many essential materials would not be available and that to do
the subject justice would call for the collaboration of a Horatio Alger,
an Ida Tarbell, and a Sinclair Lewis.

The four had much in common. Each had had a vigorous youth
in the East before coming to California in the gold rush. Each had
turned quickly from actual gold mining to the more profitable and
less speculative avenues of trade, demonstrating full capacity to look
out for his own interests. Hopkins was tall and spare, the other
three tall and robust; all were conspicuous by their abundance of
energy and their capacity for sustained effort. Huntington and

Wilmington in 1870

Los Angeles Title Insurance and Trust Company

Crocker, in particular, had given early indication of indomitable will. Crocker later indulged in periods of lethargy and Stanford was chided by Huntington for laziness, but through the sixties, at least, the four were unremitting drivers of themselves as well as of those who worked for them. Convinced by experience that the pursuit of wealth was man's highest calling, in common with their contemporaries in the mushrooming of American big business, the group which Matthew Josephson has labeled the "Robber Barons," they did not scruple about the methods to be employed in the accumulation of wealth and power. In all fairness, however, they should be measured not against an absolute standard but in the light of the thought patterns of their own generation.

Like-minded though these four individuals were, each was fitted for a special function, as a result of which a division of work was soon developed. Stanford became the titular head, the public-relations chief in California, and the spokesman of the company in seeking subventions from the state and the counties. Huntington stepped into Judah's place as contact man with the national government and became the chief money raiser in the East and the purchasing agent. Hopkins' role as office man was the least conspicuous, but as the balance wheel he restrained his rasher partners from steps that would have jeopardized the company. Crocker superintended actual construction, a task to which he was ideally suited and which later enabled him to discomfit Stanford and Huntington with the complacent assertion that, whatever the others had accomplished, he had built the road.

One of Judah's criticisms of his partners had been over the way in which construction contracts were handled. The first, to grade thirty-two miles of roadbed, was let at a handsome figure to the Charles Crocker Company, whose owners were the Big Four. With the chief critic silenced by death, this technique continued. Its effect is obvious. To the disadvantage of the numerous smaller stockholders in the railroad company, the executives voted themselves construction contracts that soon made them multimillionaires. Small wonder that the Charles Crocker Company was anathema to the unsuspecting purchasers of the Central Pacific stock and that the railroad acquired the sobriquet "the Dutch Flat swindle." The device was essentially the one made notorious by the Union Pacific and its dummy, the Crédit Mobilier.

Forty miles of track had to be laid before the federal subsidy was collectable. With materials at inflated prices because of the Civil War, with round-the-Horn shipping commanding emergency rates, and with the war and Nevada silver competing in the California labor mart, the Big Four found it very difficult to complete this first unit. Their own resources were inadequate, for they were still men of very moderate means, and investors were not expressing confidence by rushing forward to purchase stock. Early in 1863 Crocker was so discouraged by the outlook as to be willing to "take a clean shirt, and get out." It was Stanford who pulled a rabbit from the hat. The state government and several interested counties were induced to buy $1,500,000 worth of stock and to assume the interest payment on bonds to a like amount. Without this timely assistance the Central Pacific would have had difficulty building far enough to collect the initial federal subsidy.

On July 2, 1864, the company recorded another financial triumph when President Lincoln approved an amendment to the Pacific Railroad Act doubling the land grant, permitting advance payment of certain subsidies, and extending the time limit. Most important, the government agreed to reduce the security for its loans from a first to a second mortgage. Lobbyist Huntington had good reason to congratulate himself.

Brightening financial skies gave new zest for road building. Actual construction had gone forward haltingly, and two years after work had started there were only thirty-one miles in operation. The next six months witnessed better progress. By midsummer of 1865 trains were running fifty-six miles to Illinoistown, soon to be renamed in compliment to Vice-President Schuyler Colfax. Business was good too, and at ten cents a mile for passengers and fifteen cents a ton-mile for freight, operating revenue exceeded $1,000 a day. Central Pacific had surpassed the Union Pacific, which by the end of 1865 had only forty miles of track jutting westward over the open prairie from Omaha. Yet at the rate of construction thus far attained, and making no allowance for the greater difficulties ahead, it would have required forty years to join the rails.

Assurance of adequate financial support was one factor making possible a speeding up of construction. Another factor that seemed equally fundamental was the solution of the Central Pacific's labor problem. At first Crocker had relied upon California whites: Irish,

Americans, Germans, and other nationalities.   The wage scale had to be high and, worse yet, a majority of the recruits seemed to look upon railroad work as merely a convenient dodge for getting a free ride toward the Nevada mines.   In spite of all that could be done the labor turnover was excessive.   In desperation the Big Four considered heroic cures.   One proposal was to bring up several thousand Mexicans, a solution of the labor problem to which south-western railroads later turned for maintenance work and southern California agriculturists for crop harvesting.   But Mexicans did not build the Cental Pacific, nor did the 5,000 captured Confederate soldiers whom the federal government was requested to provide. The solution was found nearer at hand.

Crocker it was who had the inspiration to try the Chinese.   In the mines and in the northern towns the little yellow man was already a familiar figure.   Because of his small stature, most of Crocker's associates were skeptical that the Oriental would be equal to the heavy work required.   But the initial experiment with fifty Celestials proved that Oriental stamina was a more than adequate substitute for Occidental brawn.   Thereafter the Chinese contingent was steadily increased.   California supplied 2,000 in April, 1865, by the end of the season the number had increased to 6,000, and by 1869 a peak of 15,000 was reached.   The Chinese never threatened to strike as had the Irish-Americans.   They were tireless; pick, shovel and wheelbarrow were no mystery to them, and they soon became adept with drill, blasting powder, and the other fairly simple equipment with which the line across the Sierra was to be carved out.

At San Francisco, labor leaders frowned on the importation of shiploads of coolies.   In the sixties violence was threatened but not actually visited upon the hapless immigrants.   At the railhead, however, the expected opposition did not materialize.   The construction crew was being enlarged so rapidly that most of the whites could be promoted to "superior" work as teamsters, powdermen, or gang foreman, and there was little objection that the Chinese took over the back-breaking tasks.

Just beyond Colfax the railroad confronted a granite cliff, 1,000 feet high and practically vertical.   Cape Horn was its name, and rounding Cape Horn became the problem of the year.   Lowered by ropes from above, Chinese chiselers chipped out a narrow ledge, which after herculean effort was widened to accommodate the tracks.

A most spectacular achievement, it gave passengers the tingling sensation of being suspended in midair.

Cape Horn, for all its difficulty, was child's play compared with the difficulty of holing through the quarter-mile Summit Tunnel. The hard granite of the upper ridges defied the hand drills and black powder on which the tunnelers had relied. Crocker put crews of Chinese to work at both portals and sunk a shaft in the center so that they could peck away on four cutting surfaces. But drills and chisels dulled after a few blows and the powder charges fizzled out of the drill holes. Progress was counted by inches, and not until September, 1867, was the tunnel finished. In an endeavor to speed up the work Crocker began to use a new explosive, the dangerous and unpredictable nitroglycerin. He could not be persuaded, however, to experiment with the newly invented steam drill. Although his partners fumed and stormed, and Stanford sent one up to the railhead, Crocker stuck by his hand drills. A year or two later these were completely outmoded.

The Race with the Union Pacific

With a new construction engineer in charge, the Union Pacific was rapidly advancing its tracks across Nebraska. Grenville Dodge was a driver comparable to Crocker, and his Irish paddies were worthy rivals of "Crocker's Pets." In the race for track mileage, the open sesame to the government subsidy, the Central Pacific could not stand by to wait for Summit Tunnel to be holed through. Locomotives, flat cars, and rails were hauled on huge sledges across the divide, and grading and track laying were pushed down toward the Nevada line. These measures added two million dollars to expenses, but because of the prospect of the subsidy beyond the mountains it was counted good economy. The competitive urge for haste also dictated work right through the winter despite heavy snows and subzero temperatures, which cut efficiency to a fraction.

Clearing, grading, and track laying went forward at a snail's pace during the winter months, but over the higher portion of the completed line the tracks could not be kept open. Even five locomotives could not push a snowplow through the thirty-foot drifts above Cisco. In the interest of subsequent operations as well as of current construction, something had to be done. Snowsheds were the answer, and some thirty-seven miles of them were built at a cost of another two million dollars.

By June, 1868, the road was finally completed to the state line. Ahead lay the plums for which the Big Four had been straining: the open floor of the intermountain basin across which tracks could be laid for half the amount of the subsidy, and the traffic of the Mormons at Salt Lake. Authorized in 1866 to build beyond the state line, the Central Pacific girded itself for a final sprint. All was not smooth sailing. Prices of steel rails, locomotives, cars, and powder had not dropped as expected at the end of the Civil War. Freight rates round the Horn were still high and ships not always easy to charter. As the road pushed into Nevada, the cost of ties and timber, fuel and hay, once nominal, rocketed upward. And with every mile of track built, the railhead became that much more difficult and expensive of access. This latter difficulty came to bear even more heavily upon the Union Pacific as its single-track line stretched farther and farther westward.

Answering the demands for speed, both Dodge and Crocker whipped their construction crews into highly expert machines. Utilizing the factory method of division of labor, they perfected their techniques so that the rails went down at the rate of three, four, and five miles a day. In a final inspired burst of superefficiency, Crocker's Chinese laid ten miles in a single day.

As the two lines approached each other the nation suddenly realized that they might not meet. Why should they? As the law stood, each road might continue on across the continent with uninterrupted enjoyment of land grants and subsidies. An alarmed Congress intervened at the eleventh hour to designate Promontory, Utah, as the place where the rails should meet.

The conclusion of construction afforded an irresistible temptation for dramatics. The stage was set early in May. By Saturday, the eighth, Stanford had arrived by special train, ready for his histrionic role, but Vice-President Durant of the Union Pacific was delayed by washouts and by a strike occasioned by lack of money with which to pay off his workmen, and the celebration had to be postponed until Monday. On the afternoon of the tenth Durant's special finally arrived. With suitable flow of oratory, and to the tune of music from the Twenty-first Infantry band, the stage properties were brought forward: a laurel tie; the last rail; spikes of Comstock silver, of Arizona gold, iron, and silver, of Idaho and Montana gold and silver, and of California gold; and a silver sledgehammer from California. At last the final gold spike was ready to be driven home, with Stanford to have the honor of giving the coup de grâce. His blow was ill-directed. Durant's courtesy was equal to the occasion; he also scored a miss, and left the real driving for Dodge and the Central Pacific's construction engineer. Over the last rail two locomotives touched cowcatchers. Their engineers had the first drinks of champagne, and then the celebration became general.

The fashion often is to belittle this first Pacific railroad. Construction methods had been wasteful, and excessive haste had encouraged faulty construction. Much of the track was almost immediately in need of replacement and considerable portions were subsequently realigned. Both sections of the line had been built with a view to collecting the subsidies rather than to profiting through operations; witness the promptness with which the Union Pacific directors severed their connection with the company.

But though speculation may have overshadowed construction, the Pacific railroad remains one of the epochal developments in western history. Perhaps even more significantly than the discovery of gold, it marked the end of an old era and the opening of a new. For exactly a century, since the coming of Portolá and Serra in 1769, isolation had imposed a powerful restraint upon California's development. Now the barrier was broken through. Subsequent improvements were to batter it down still further, and what California was to lose in provincialism was to be more than compensated for in stimulus to new and greater attainments. The Pacific railroad heralded transformation of California and the West.

25

SOCIAL UNREST

CALIFORNIA'S INITIAL enthusiasm for the Pacific railroad soon gave way to an attitude of annoyance, distrust, and dislike. The change was an echo of the national conviction that the railroads were responsible for most of the country's economic ills, including the panic of 1873. California not only shared this opinion but also saw much local evidence that the railroad was to blame for the most pressing afflictions of the body politic, economic, and social. For all its promise of vitalizing the West, the railroad yielded a first crop of bitter fruit. Local shopkeepers found their business thrown into confusion by the stocks of new goods brought in by the iron horse; western publishers encountered unwonted competition in the deluge of printed matter flowing in from the East; and Sacramento, though it had taken the lead in building the Central Pacific, shortly found itself declining to a way station on the line to San Francisco. The railroad became a monster, or more concretely, the Octopus. It was the target for criticisms by all those whom the hard times of the seventies made discontented and bitter.

A Monopoly of California Rails

The railroad thus pilloried, though dominated by the same Big Four, was not just the transcontinental line so boldly, wastefully, and profitably constructed in the sixties. It had become much larger, much more complex, much more powerful; in the figure of speech of the period, the Octopus had thrown out additional tentacles.

Because of the meager documentation available concerning the early operation of the Big Four, it is not possible to speak with

absolute precision about the evolution of their plans.   There seems
to be no question, however, that their original purpose did not go
beyond the building of the transcontinental link, and that having
skimmed the cream of cash subsidies and land bounties they regarded
railroad operation as an unpromising business.   Their eastern con-
freres, the Union Pacific executives, being philosophers of the same
stamp, left that company promptly when the subsidies came to an
end.   But there was no one upon whom the Big Four could unload,
and so perforce they held on to the Central Pacific.

However reluctant they may have been to continue in railroading,
the Big Four were quick to see that their further success hinged
upon establishing a monopoly of California rails, particularly with
regard to San Francisco Bay.   To this end they moved rapidly.   The
Western Pacific Railroad Company, the Big Four under another alias,
was chartered to build from Sacramento to San Jose, and a branch
from Niles to Oakland gave virtual monopoly of the Oakland waterfront.   To control another approach they absorbed the California
Pacific which had a Sacramento-Vallejo franchise.   Its tracks were
carried to Benicia, a ferry crossed to Port Costa, and rails continued
to Oakland, completing the stranglehold on the East Bay.

Through grants from the state legislature the Big Four next sought
control of San Francisco's waterfront, but because of violent protests
from the press this grant was reduced to a mere sixty acres.   The
newspapers also foiled an attempt to get Congress to donate Goat
Island, which under its more limpid name Yerba Buena is now the
stepping stone for the Bay Bridge.   Undaunted, the Big Four purchased the San Francisco and San Jose, acquired two lesser lines
circling the southern arm of the bay, and effectively bottled up peninsular traffic.

In addition to the encirclement of San Francisco Bay, the railroad
magnates were taking steps toward dominating the rest of California.
As early as 1865 they had chartered the Southern Pacific, ostensibly
as a competitor, to build down the coast to San Diego.   They also
gobbled up an assortment of lines in the San Joaquin Valley, constructed occasional links, and extended through service to Goshen,
in Tulare County.   By 1871 their plans for the south came more
clearly into the open.   To the chagrin of the people of the southern
coastal counties it was announced that the Southern Pacific would
shift to the valley route.   Public interest would have been much

better served by a coast line, but along the latter were some 350 privately owned ranchos, whereas the inland route passed through government land from which the railroad's magnificent bounty could be carved. Also, the inland route was in easier striking distance of Needles and Yuma, gateways to the state which the Big Four wanted to control. Equally illuminating to the people of the state was the disclosure that the Southern Pacific was but another name for the Central Pacific. When its construction work was placed in the hands of Crocker's Contract and Finance Company, little doubt remained on that score.

Nor was public opinion reassured by the Southern Pacific's practice of holding up cities and towns for special subsidies on the threat of leaving them off the main line. This form of legalized blackmail was by no means confined to California and the Southern Pacific, but it was nonetheless galling. Los Angeles, for example, though the largest municipality in southern California, was threatened with a "run-around" if it did not hand over the Los Angeles and San Pedro Railroad, deed a sixty-acre depot site, and pay a bonus of $600,000. Spurning San Bernardino, the Southern Pacific built its own division point at Colton, three miles away.

Besides absorbing as many as possible of the local railroads in California, the Big Four took into account the menace of competing transcontinental lines. Many such lines had been projected, and several had advanced to the stage of more or less active construction. There was, for example, the Oregon Shortline, a northwestward extension of the Union Pacific to Portland. If it were completed, the Union Pacific would be in position to route California shipments over its own lines to Portland and thence by steamer to California, to the great discomfiture of the Central Pacific. To counterbalance such a potentiality (and also for the land grants that could thus be obtained) the Big Four bought the California and Oregon Railroad and began to build north from Sacramento, following closely the route outlined in the Williamson-Abbott survey of the fifties. In 1887 the tracks were joined at Ashland, staving off the competition not only of the Oregon Shortline but also of Henry Villard's Northern Pacific.

Meanwhile, the southern gateways to California were more seriously menaced, particularly by Thomas A. Scott's Texas and Pacific. Backed by the resources of the Pennsylvania Railroad, of which he was president, and extracting full benefit from the bestowal of passes, Scott was able to get Congress in 1871 to charter the Texas and Pacific to build from Texarkana and Marshall, Texas, along the thirty-second parallel to San Diego. Subsidies promised were calculated at $68,000,000. Huntington was no less active as a lobbyist. First he persuaded Congress to grant a comparable subsidy to the Southern Pacific to build from San Francisco to Yuma. Then he endeavored to get Congress to cancel the Texas Pacific franchise west of Yuma, where for many miles its tracks would have to parallel those of the Southern Pacific. From this beginning the contest between Scott and Huntington expanded into a battle royal. Huntington emerged with the spoils of victory, partly because he was able to enlist support from the territorial governments of Arizona and New Mexico and partly because the Southern Pacific set a more rapid pace in actual construction. For a time Yuma seemed to be the probable meeting place, then Tucson, then El Paso. With Scott's successor, Jay Gould, Huntington finally agreed on a junction at El Paso, with a traffic agreement, and with a transfer of the Texas Pacific land grant to the California company. Advantageous though this arrangement was, the Southern Pacific was ambitious for a line of its own to New Orleans; it built on eastward, local lines were bought up, and by the end of 1882 the goal was reached.

Although the Texas and Pacific was the first great rival in the south, there was also the Atlantic and Pacific casting a covetous eye westward along the thirty-fifth parallel toward the California entrance at Needles. Having crossed Tehachapi Pass on the way south toward Los Angeles, it was comparatively simple for the Big Four to build eastward from Mojave to Needles, a development designed, paradoxically enough, not to open that door but to close it against a competitive railroad. By the early eighties, therefore, the Big Four had made the monopoly of Caifornia rails well nigh complete. San Francisco Bay had been encircled. The coast line was not built, but spurs from Gilroy to Soledad and to Tres Pinos blocked the approach of any rival. The Central Valley was preempted, and Tehachapi Pass and San Gorgonio Pass grasped. Transcontinental rivals from the north or by way of Needles or Yuma seemed to be adequately guarded against. In 1884 nomenclature was simplified when this entire system was effectively coördinated in a new Southern Pacific Company, incorporated under the laws of Kentucky. To Californians, however, it was still the Octopus.

Rising Resentment against the Railroad

The paramount position of the railroad in the seventies is not easily comprehended by the present generation. Big business today is multiple; in modern California it is represented by the banks, the oil companies, the utilities, the moving picture studios, various manufacturers, chain stores, large department stores, metropolitan newspapers, and so forth. In the late nineteenth century all other enterprises were so overshadowed by the railroad as to be reduced to the stature of small business. The railroad was the biggest land-owner and the biggest employer of labor, its owners were the richest men in the state, its influence on government was supreme, and by arbitrary manipulation of freight rates it could make or break almost any merchant, industrialist, or agriculturist in the state.

Had this unusual power been used with generous and studious moderation it is possible that the monopoly would have had a high place in popular esteem, for its contribution to California development far surpassed that of any other man-made factor. But since its power was not exercised with such utopian beneficence, and no doubt in part because of its very magnitude, the railroad supplanted Joaquín Murieta as public enemy number one and, with or without cause, was blamed for everything that went wrong.

It was a period, furthermore, when a host of things seemed to be going wrong. California state government, never a glorious achievement of probity and efficiency, sank in the seventies to the nadir of disreputableness. San Francisco officials had reverted to the roguery of the early fifties, while at Sacramento the manifestations of corruption were equally prominent. No branch of government seemed to be exempt, neither the courts, the tax assessors, nor the executive officers; yet it was the legislature that seemed to be guilty of the most flagrant abuses. The scandalous laxity was in conformity with the mores of the day as represented by New York's Tweed Ring, Jay Gould's Black Friday, the Crédit Mobilier, the Star Route scandals, the Indian Frauds, and the Whisky Ring. It was also locally engendered through the proximity of frontier backgrounds, the precedents of vigilante days, the prevalence of speculative enterprise, the prominence of the nouveaux riches, and, Californians would have added, by the machinations of the railroad.

At the same time that the agencies of government were being perverted for the advantage of a few and to the disadvantage of the majority, Californians were becoming conscious of other economic abuses. One had to do with land monopoly, long to continue a burning issue. Many a writer since George has inveighed against the vast feudal estates of 400,000, 500,000 and even 1,000,000 acres held off the market and out of production for a speculative profit. Prospective farmers in the 1870's, as in the twentieth century, found that much of the best land was withheld from them, and it was the railroad's millions of acres that stood out most prominently. Water for irrigation was controlled to an even greater extent by the monopolists, thereby contributing to the building up of still larger holdings. Added to these factors were numerous instances when the railroads played fast and loose with prospective purchasers, raising the price after the settler had put in expensive improvements or proceeding with summary evictions. The dramatic climax for disputes of this sort was in the Mussel Slough tragedy in Tulare County in 1880, where an attempted eviction led to the killing of seven men. The railroad had the law on its side, and five settlers were sentenced to jail; but public opinion persisted that the railroad was in the wrong.

Overshadowing these complaints against the railroad was the more obvious one that its rate structure was unjust and antisocial. The railroad magnates replied that their rates were within or below the legal limit set in 1861 of ten cents a passenger-mile and fifteen cents a ton-mile and that railroad earnings were not excessive. The counterblast was that the Big Four had become very rich. Some of the practices criticized—for example, that of terminal rates to meet ship competition—have been upheld by the Interstate Commerce Commission and the courts. Others, such as the granting of rebates to favored shippers, have been outlawed. The fundamental contention of the critics, that transportation rates should be subject to government regulation, is taken for granted today, but in the California wonderland of the seventies it was inverted: state government was regulated by the railroad.

Given these conditions, it is natural that a popular hue and cry should have arisen for curbing the railroad. Yet with their characteristic faculty for obscuring the issue, the reform leaders gave first attention to another, only slightly related problem, namely, the Chinese.

The Anti-Chinese Movement

In gold rush days, when the first Celestials had appeared in California, they were given a cordial reception. Chinese had positions of honor at San Francisco's celebration of admission to statehood and again a few weeks later at the memorial services occasioned by Zachary Taylor's death. Never thereafter were they completely without friends in California, though some of their advocates distinguished sharply between houseboys, cooks, launderers, vegetable peddlers, and Chinatown merchants on the one hand and coolie laborers on the other. In the diggings, however, there was less of the race tolerance that often prevailed among the white-collar whites in cosmopolitan San Francisco. The hardy miners were convinced that Providence as well as the treaty negotiators at Guadalupe Hidalgo had made California a white man's country. Its mineral resources in particular were to be reserved for "Americans." Accordingly, they exerted pressure to get laws enacted, such as the Foreign Miners' License Law of 1850, which would discourage mining by non-Americans, and they took many forceful measures outside the law to make foreign miners uncomfortable. Objection was not raised to Englishmen, Germans, Scandinavians, or Irish, but with varying intensity was visited upon Frenchmen, Spanish Americans, Indians, Negroes, and especially upon the Chinese.

Conspicuously different in color, language, dress, and customs, the Chinese were looked upon as a race apart. By reason of the great dissimilarity of their culture and also by reason of their clannishness, they appeared destined to continue as such, while at the same time the easy accessibility of the teeming homeland held promise that their number would mount rapidly. The matter of numbers was certainly a fundamental cause for concern. By 1852 there were some 25,000 Chinese in California, making them the largest minority group. For the state at large one person out of ten was a Chinese, and in some of the mining counties the ratio was three out of ten. In the light of the prevailing American conviction regarding the superior privileges of the white race, it is not surprising that hostility toward the Orientals should have arisen.

The beginning was in local discriminatory measures, followed by the state tax on foreign miners. The first move on a state-wide basis to be directed expressly against the Chinese was the proposal of Senator George B. Tingley in 1852 that the state authorize and agree to supervise the contracting of Chinese labor on a ten-year basis. While admitting that California needed laborers as industrious and as orderly as the Chinese, the press remonstrated vigorously against Tingley's proposal. Speaking for the opposition, Senator Philip A. Roach asserted the doctrine that white labor should not be subjected to unfair competition with Orientals, who were content with an abnormally low standard of living. A modification of Tingley's bill had passed the Assembly, but public opinion welled up so vigorously that rejection by the Senate was by vote of eighteen to two.

On the heels of this action, Governor John Bigler addressed to the legislature a message urging the necessity of measures to check the tide of Asiatic immigration and to prevent the exportation of gold to China. Unquestionably this was a political maneuver in Bigler's campaign for reëlection. Whether it represented his studied conviction is a moot question, but the fact that he has the reputation of being an unprincipled and opportunist politician makes his use of this issue all the better index to the proclivities of the California voters.

Bigler's message did not lead to an exclusion act, but it did bring out into the open certain criticisms of the Chinese as transients, as morally depraved, and as a menace to the state's tranquillity. It stirred up a former missionary, the Reverend William Speer, to lecture on behalf of the Chinese, but on the other hand it encouraged a wave of anti-Chinese demonstrations and pogroms, especially in the mining counties. Presumably as a consequence, immigration slackened, and in 1853 the Chinese population had actually decreased by three or four thousand.

In April, 1855, hard times having called attention again to the straits of white labor, a law was enacted to impose a head tax of fifty dollars upon immigrants not eligible for citizenship. Though this was the device later to provide the most effective curb upon Asiatic immigration, the State Supreme Court ruled the act unconstitutional. Chinese continued to enter the state. Popular with capitalists, employers, and well-to-do householders, their entrenchment in certain occupations came to be relatively secure. Labor, however, had a constant tendency to regard them as unwelcome competitors, and whenever the demand for labor fell off, this intolerance was apt to manifest itself vociferously or even violently.

In the sixties the Civil War, Nevada silver, and the building of the Central Pacific improved the market for labor, and to that degree lessened the disposition to molest the Chinese. Because of the firm demand for white as well as yellow labor, Crocker's importation of thousands of coolies to man his construction crews did not lead to immediate trouble. But with the completion of the road and the laying off of entire gangs, labor's position became much less favorable, and, running true to form, labor leaders heaped most of the blame upon the hapless Chinese. The following biennium witnessed a new wave of repressive measures, most of them outside the law. There was mob violence at such widely separated places as Chico and San Diego, with houses and laundries burned, stores looted, and an occasional Chinese killed. The bloodiest pogrom was at Los Angeles, where resistance to a police raid on the Chinese quarter ignited the fuse. "The scum and dregs" of the city to the number of 1,000 —incidentally, a sizeable hoodlum element for a town of only 6,000 persons—descended furiously on Chinatown, laid it waste, and killed at least twenty-two Chinese. Local editors decried the violence and the notoriety, for this was the first time that Los Angeles had made the nation's headlines, but no serious attempt was made to mete out justice to the mob leaders.

Simple economic causation, as represented by hard times and unemployment, is not a sufficient explanation of this outburst of race hatred. Antipathy for the Chinese had been engendered over the years by charges that they were unsanitary and a disease menace; that they were addicted to strange vices; that most of their women were prostitutes; that their tong organization was un-American and subversive; that they spoke an outlandish jargon, subsisted upon peculiar food, and worshiped pagan gods; and that, as the first skirmishers for an army of 400,000,000 Celestials, they represented a towering Yellow Peril. On this wise was the California hysteria of 1871.

The hysteria was augmented, furthermore, by a feeling of frustration as a result of the failure of all previous attempts to regulate immigration. By 1871 the state and its subdivisions had enacted a whole series of regulatory measures, which had succeeded merely in harassing the Chinese without deterring them from coming or staying. In the state courts or the federal courts the more far-reaching of these measures had been declared void, as contraventions of the commerce clause in the national Constitution. In the immediate postwar years three further barriers to state action were erected: first, the Fourteenth Amendment, with its "due process" and "equal protection of the laws" clauses; second, the Burlingame Treaty of 1868, with its express guaranty of free migration; and third, the Civil Rights Act of 1870, with it prohibition of discrimination in the courts against any persons and of immigration taxes upon any particular group of foreigners. These several actions were decided upon with some cognizance of California problems, but by easterners who naturally did not have such acute awareness of the seriousness of the problem as did west coast residents.

As interpreted by the courts, this trilogy of amendment, treaty, and act seemed to close the door to state regulation. Justice Stephen J. Field of the United States Circuit Court, for example, passing on the state's attempt to require shipmasters and owners to give bond that persons brought into the state would not be likely to become public charges or prostitutes, ruled that the act for all its ingeniousness, was in conflict with the Fourteenth Amendment, the Burlingame Treaty, and the Civil Rights Act. A similar fate was in store for the Lodging House Law, imposing penalties for the renting of lodgings with less than 500 cubic feet of air space for each occupant, and for the reënacted Queue Ordinance, requiring that every prisoner committed to the county jail have his hair cut to within an inch of his scalp. By this time the legislature was convinced that the only hope lay in procuring national action. Consequently, it financed a lobby at Washington that procured the appointment of a Joint Congressional Committee of investigation, which came to San Francisco in October, 1876.

The Kearneyites

In California, meanwhile, the forces opposed to the Chinese, the railroad, the land monopoly, and the corrupt state government achieved a temporary fusion. Earlier organizations such as the Workingmen's Alliance, the Anti-Chinese Association, the Industrial Reformers, the People's Protective Alliance, and the Supreme Order of Caucasians had paved the way, while the Granger movement then sweeping the agrarian Midwest supplied inspiration and

example.   Newton Booth had won the governorship in 1871 on a
platform stressing Chinese exclusion and railroad regulation, but
it was not until six years later, when the full effects of the panic of
1873 were belatedly making themselves felt in California, that an
effective organization was achieved.

In July of that year, 1877, the discontented laborites of San
Francisco had displayed a tendency to get out of hand.   Their
demonstrations against the local Chinese and against the Pacific
Mail Steamship Company, the principal carrier of Chinese immigrants, were so alarming that the conservative element made haste
to organize a committee of safety.   William T. Coleman, of vigilante
fame, was placed in charge with a war chest of $100,000 and with
rifles and ammunition for 1,760 men.   He armed more than 1,000
men, most of them with pick handles, and undertook to patrol the
city.   There were several clashes, some damage to property, and
the loss of a few lives, but on the whole the rioting was less san-
guinary than in the similar and practically simultaneous labor riots
at Philadelphia.

By the fall of the year the San Francisco labor leaders had matured
a policy of political rather than direct action.   Their program may
be viewed in the platform of the Workingmen's party, organized on
October 5.   Included were demands for the eight-hour day, direct
election of United States Senators, compulsory education, a better
monetary system, abolition of contract labor on public works, abolition of the pardoning power of the executive, abolition of fee payments to public officials, state regulation of banks and industry (including railroads), and a more equitable taxation system.   Prosaic
as most of these planks, save perhaps the last, would sound today,
the platform was regarded in the seventies as alarmingly radical.

Still more alarming was the way in which the leaders of the Workingmen's party appealed for support and maintained their following.
Their method was to gather crowds at the sand lots across from the
city hall and, by inflammatory speeches, to rouse the passions of
their hearers.   Most popular among the speakers, and thereby ipso
facto head of the Workingmen's party, was a young Irishman, Denis
Kearney.   In his youth a seaman and more recently a San Francisco
drayman, Kearney had a close intellectual kinship with his audiences.
A born orator and a practical one, he delighted the sand-lotters with
fiery denunciations of the capitalists and the monopolists and their

hirelings, the corrupt politicians. His ungrammatical speeches bristled with such catch phrases as "The Chinese must go" and "Every workingman should get a musket." For the capitalists he recommended "a little judicious hanging," and if San Francisco did not accede to his demands he threatened it with "the fate of Moscow."

Such rabid incendiarism terrified the conservative element, especially when a mob of 2,000 was harangued in the very shadow of Crocker's mansion on exclusive Nob Hill. A few days later Kearney and five of his associates were arrested and sentenced to a fortnight in jail. Emerging from prison as a martyr, Kearney blithely resumed his habits of incendiary oratory. Nor was he quelled by a state law making it a felony to incite a riot or to advise and encourage criminal violence. He was lionized at a mammoth labor parade on Thanksgiving Day, 1877, and he dominated the first state convention of the Workingmen's party, which assembled at San Francisco the following January. In the literature of the day and in most historical writing, Kearney is depicted as a hotheaded anarchist who played upon the coarsest impulses of the rabble, yet in fairness it should be remembered that for all his vocal advocacy of terrorist measures he precipitated no riot and produced no actual violence; his incendiary talk was but a means of promoting political action.

In local elections in the bay region Kearney's Workingmen's party demonstrated such strength that it appeared altogether possible that the party could dominate the state constitutional convention, for which an election had been called for June 19. The campaign was well-contested. Democrats and Republicans, alarmed by the patent strength of the Kearneyites, sank their differences in most parts of the state and named nonpartisan candidates. Even so, the Workingmen's party might have seated a majority had it not been that dissension arose among its leaders, some of whom resented Kearney's extreme radicalism and others his personal ambitions. The final count indicated the election of fifty-one Workingmen, seventy-eight nonpartisans, eleven Republicans, ten Democrats, and two Independents. The Workingmen thus had a potent minority, especially since a number of delegates not of the party were committed to Granger ideals.

The New Constitution

The convention which assembled at Sacramento in September of that year is often compared with its predecessor at Monterey twenty-nine years earlier. With 152 delegates as contrasted to 48, it was obviously much more unwieldly. Its deliberations, or at least its debates, were likewise much longer, and the finished product which it presented to the state was a much more cumbersome, detailed, and complicated document. As to political sagacity, it would be rash indeed to argue that the men of '78 represented an improvement over the smaller group of '49. It was true, however, that the first constitution-makers had worked under a double disadvantage. In the first place, they had to draft a frame of government for a commonwealth whose future, however golden in prospect, was still inscrutable. In the second place, they had to keep a weather eye on national politics; while they were under some obligation to produce a constitution satisfactory to the Californians, it was imperative that the document be acceptable to the national authorities. The framers of the second constitution were not inhibited by fears of a federal veto; they were free to tackle the state's own problems. Also, they had the benefit of three decades of experience under the old constitution. California's problems had become well-defined actualities, and proposed solutions had been amply and repeatedly aired in electoral campaigns. Most noteworthy was the new consciousness of the social responsibilities of government. The convention in '49 had hardly considered social problems. It disposed of the whole matter of taxation, for example, in two sentences reputedly derived from Texas' first constitution. In a generation the pressing issues had come to be almost entirely social: the tax base; the regulation of banks, railroads, and big business; the land monopoly; and the Chinese.

Toward the solution of these problems the convention accomplished astonishingly little. It continued in session for almost half a year. Its thirty standing committees brought in wordy and conflicting reports. With its membership so evenly divided between liberals and conservatives, between Kearneyites and anti-Kearneyites, it was inevitable that the final product should be a "bundle of compromises."

The most prominent innovations included the following: To equalize tax valuations in the several counties and to assess intercounty railroad property a State Board of Equalization was created. To regulate a variety of railroad matters an elected Railroad Commission was provided. Another section increased the accountability of bank directors and stockholders, while still another specified the eight-hour day on public works. After bitter debate, a four-section anti-Chinese article was adopted, which (1) authorized the legislature to enact all measures necessary to protect the state from aliens who might prove "dangerous or detrimental"; (2) prohibited employment of Chinese by corporations; (3) prohibited such employment on public works; and, in an omnibus section, (4) outlawed Asiatic coolieism as slavery and authorized measures to prevent further immigration and to deal with those already in the state. Other measures for more stringent restrictions were argued down as certain to be declared in conflict with the national Constitution. Indeed, warnings were voiced that the sections adopted would not be upheld in the federal courts.

With the completion of the convention's labors, the arena of debate was transferred to the state at large. One hundred and twenty delegates approved the constitution, but when it was referred to the electorate, bitter opposition developed. The opposition of the railroad, the banks, and the Sacramento Board of Trade, an antecedent of the Chamber of Commerce, is readily understandable, if for no other reason than the radicalism of the Kearneyites. The Workingmen were equally dissatisfied, because the constitution did not go far enough in extending a protecting arm over labor. Party spokesmen attacked the constitution as vehemently as they had the capitalists, in consequence of which the parts of the state where the Workingmen's party was strongest voted against adoption. But the rural vote, swayed by Granger optimism concerning the Railroad Commission and the Board of Equalization, carried the constitution by a margin of less than 11,000 out of 145,000.

The outcome substantiated the fears of the liberal opposition. There were a few incidental improvements. The legislature was brought under more suitable restraint by a ban upon special legislation and upon appropriations of state funds to corporations or institutions not directly under state control. The governor's pardoning power was curbed, and the judiciary was remodeled for greater efficiency and expedition. But federal judges promptly invalidated the anti-Chinese sections and the legislation enacted to implement them. The Board of Equalization and the Railroad Commission fell far short of the expectation of the farmers; the latter came to be spoken of popularly as a state-financed publicity bureau for the railroad. To illustrate the abortive nature of the reforms one might mention a cartoon of 1881, in which a distraught farmer is depicted in the toils of a huge snake labeled "The New Constitution," or one might cite James Bryce's *American Commonwealth,* in which the California constitution is displayed as a "horrible example" of western democracy at work.

Chinese Exclusion

Frustrated though the California reformers had been, the dawn of the new decade brought one rift in the clouds. Effective restriction of Chinese immigration was soon a reality. California's efforts through local ordinance, state law, and constitutional provision had failed because they ran counter to the commerce clause, the Fourteenth Amendment, the Burlingame Treaty, and the Civil Rights Act. Repeated pleas for national action met opposition in the East, because most eastern Americans knew the Chinese only through the more favorable channels of missionary work or lucrative trade. Finally, the barrage of western protests, including a long memorial from the constitutional convention, broke down this eastern apathy. In 1878 Congress enacted the Fifteen Passengers Bill, which, as its name suggests, imposed a quantitative restriction on Chinese immigration. President Hayes vetoed the measure as a violation of the Burlingame Treaty, but in response to popular demand he sent a commission to China to negotiate a new treaty. The Chinese government agreed readily to permit the United States to "regulate, limit, or suspend" the entrance or residence of Chinese laborers, provided, however, that the action should be reasonable rather than absolute. Under the terms of this treaty in December, 1881, Congress voted a twenty-year exclusion bill, which President Arthur vetoed as unreasonable. A few months later he approved a ten-year exclusion bill.

Partial success seemed to fan the flames of anti-Chinese feeling in California. The drive was renewed to make the Celestials in the state uncomfortable and thus perhaps to force them out. At San Francisco, for example, there was a regulation concerning laundries which, by discriminatory enforcement, drove some 200 Chinese out of that business. There were also threats to move Chinatown to South San Francisco. On some of these local matters the courts came to the rescue of the persecuted yellow men. The Scott Act of 1888 forbidding reëntry of Chinese laborers and the Geary

Act of 1892 prohibiting Chinese immigration for another ten years were protested vigorously by China, but not until 1894 was she placated by the gesture of treaty revision. At long last, by treaty in 1901 and by legislation in 1902 and 1904, exclusion was put on a permanent basis and was made to apply to the insular as well as mainland possessions of the United States.

The other problems of the "discontented seventies" likewise proved too formidable for immediate and local settlement. The Octopus went on untrammeled, if not even abetted, by the Railroad Commission. The land monopoly had its wings but slightly clipped by the regulatory measures of the new constitution. Farmers discovered that the expected boon of lower taxes, lower rail rates, and lower interest rates had slipped from their grasp; nor was there immediate abatement of the nuisance of hydraulic mining. Most of these problems, the state and the nation were learning, were so large in scope that they could be met only by national regulation. In the eighties and the nineties California followed the nation-wide tendency to look to the central government for regulation of big business; and local attention, diverted by the upward trend in economic conditions, was concentrated upon the expansion of agriculture, the introduction of new crops and new farming methods, the stimulation of population growth, and the fascinating pastime of speculation in real estate.

Ineffectual and barren of result though it may appear to have been, the political ferment of the seventies is not without historical significance. In the hard times of that decade the common people of California, the urban laborers and the rural small farmers, saw themselves about to be crushed between the upper millstone of big business and the nether millstone of coolie labor. That they struck out somewhat blindly and with passion is not surprising; nor is it surprising that they accepted the leadership of a self-tutored, emotional, and irrational young Irishman. Yet the meagerness of immediate results was not entirely due to the local personnel. By the accident of our federal system, Chinese exclusion, though a matter of purely local importance, was the exclusive prerogative of the national authorities. Control of the Octopus, on the other hand, though constitutionally within the purview of state government, proved upon experience to be so herculean a task as to require national attack. In the last analysis, therefore, these Lochinvars of the West were merely expressing in higher dramatics the common national experience.

26

THE NEW SOUTH

THROUGHOUT THE FIRST DECADES of California's American period the changes that historians are fond of calling growth and development were largely confined to the northern part of the state. That was where the population growth had centered, where most of the city building, practically all the mining, the most rapid increase in grain production, the lion's share of industrialization, most of the banking and merchandizing, the main transportation improvements, the major innovations in politics and government, and the principal cultural advances had occurred. The southern counties, meanwhile, were undergoing a much more gradual transformation. Since the chief business of history is to record and analyze change in its myriad aspects, it is natural that for these years attention has been heavily weighted toward the north rather than toward the relatively "unhistorical" south. In the succeeding years, however, that section would register a phenomenal growth and become the cynosure of attention.

The Cow Counties in Transition

This late-century development rested on a real though unspectacular transition in the fifties, sixties, and seventies. While central and northern California mushroomed to half a million inhabitants, the counties south of the Tehachapi had a more modest but substantial increase from some 6,000 citizens in 1850 to about 26,000 in 1860, 39,000 in 1870, and an estimated 60,000 in 1875. Most of the newcomers were from the United States. In numbers they blanketed the natives of Spanish and Mexican extraction. Their culture was

more aggressive. Borne on the tide of mounting numbers, it over-
whelmed most of the habits of the old regime.

Nevertheless, the adaptation was mutual. Certain older elements
persisted, or gave way only gradually to the new. Through the
fifties, adobe continued to be the standard building material, though
bricks and boards began to enter competition. By the seventies new
construction was almost entirely in the form of frame buildings. To
the towns and irrigated fields of the early American years water was
brought, as in the past, by zanja. The cattle business, which boomed
and then declined with the droughts of the sixties, carried over the
essential methods, many appurtenances, and an extensive vocabulary
from the pastoral era of the Mexican period. The sheep industry,
boomed by the Civil War and curtailed by the droughts of the seventies, had a smaller but important Spanish content. The tillage
branch of agriculture, especially where it involved vineyards or irrigation, continued patterns that had prevailed at the missions. Into
it, however, many American and foreign elements were incorporated. By the seventies, for example, it was turning from Indian
labor to Chinese. Furthermore, the broad crop list tolerance of the
environment helped to give farming an exotic touch and helped it
toward a distinction that would be its own.

In transportation a more pronounced revolution came about.
Saddle horses, carretas, and the hide ships had been the carriers in
the Mexican period. Of these only the horses persisted, and their
relative importance went down as other facilities came into use. The
transit of American pioneers and gold seekers through the region
brought wagons, which soon supplanted the creaking carretas. A
more purposeful introduction of freighting equipment followed. At
an early date Alexander and Banning were freighting, virtually on a
public carrier basis, between Los Angeles and San Pedro. Wagons
such as these did the hauling to the ranchos, army posts, and Indian
reservations. In the fifties wagon freighters operated between Los
Angeles and Salt Lake City. In the seventies they gave the Cerro
Gordo mines of Inyo County their line of shipment and supply.

The stage was a more dashing symbol of the new era. In its
idealized form, a Concord coach drawn by six matched and blooded
horses, or in its lesser manifestations, with mud wagon and a pick-up
team, it seemed to be progress on wheels. Here also the earliest
line was between Los Angeles and San Pedro. Other lines, some on

intermittent schedule, were added before 1858, when the Butterfield line swept through from Tejon Pass to Yuma on its transcontinental way.

The rise of coastal shipping came about even more rapidly and meant considerably more to the region. Sailing ships and then steamers began where the hide ships left off. They quickly established themselves as the fundamental link for passengers and for freight between southern California and the affluence and splendor of San Francisco and the mines. Except as the jolting stage entered the picture, coastal shipping continued for a quarter century to be southern California's basic connection with the outer world. The region's economy was oriented coastward, and steamer day was the climax of the week.

The stage and freighting mogul Phineas Banning also brought southern California its first railroad. In 1863 he persuaded the legislature to authorize a bond issue by the city and county of Los Angeles for construction of a line connecting the pueblo and its port at San Pedro. The $150,000 bond issue was finally put to a vote in 1868, and late the next year this first railroad in the south began to operate. The next road, incorporated as the Los Angeles and Independence, was projected by a group of local citizens to link Los Angeles with the Cerro Gordo mines near the Nevada border. Taken over by Senator John P. Jones, the company went forward with elaborate plans for building over Cajon Pass and out onto the Mojave desert, but the only rails laid were between Los Angeles and Santa Monica. Late in 1875 Los Angeles thus acquired a second railroad to the sea.

From the fifties on, local editors and politicians had been clamoring for a transcontinental railroad to, or at least through, southern California. When at length the Southern Pacific came down the San Joaquin Valley pointing toward the gateway at Yuma or Needles, a civic crisis arose about how to persuade the Big Four to come through Los Angeles. By dint of the gift of a depot site, the Los Angeles and San Pedro, and $600,000 raised by a bond issue, the railroad builders were induced to put Los Angeles on their line instead of veering off from Tehachapi Pass to Antelope Valley. In 1876 when the Tehachapi was surmounted and the San Fernando tunnel holed through, Los Angeles could celebrate that the iron horse had really arrived.

The rise of newspapers, schools, and churches symbolized and assisted the transition from Mexican to American. Meanwhile, along with the north, the southern area had profited by the general untangling of the fetters that had restrained the state as a whole. With the outmoding of vigilante justice, the cessation of filibustering, the elimination of any menace of Indian attack, the fading of Civil War issues, the final adjudication of land titles, the achievement of Chinese exclusion, and the resolvement, at least temporarily, of the reform demands of the Grangers and Workingmen, southern California was ready to face a new day.

The Health Rush

At a very early date—as far back as Cabrillo, in fact—there was recognition of advantages in southern California's climate. At quite an early date there was thought of the climate as a health asset. One of the Mexican governors removed to the south for his health. The gold rush brought a liberal sprinkling of persons more intent on regaining health than on getting rich. Other health seekers came from time to time, a few by overland stage, more by ship or by covered wagon. As early as the forties, travel by prairie schooner was recommended as a sort of fresh air cure. In some instances it did cure, in others it proved too heroic a remedy.

For a while, southern California was too remote and too rough a frontier to have much appeal as a health resort. By the seventies, however, it was less beset by wild Indians, bandits, and desperadoes; it was outfitted with some improvements in transportation and accommodations; and it had developed a number of new pursuits in which invalids or their relatives might find opportunity or employment. Concurrently, the medical profession was entering a phase in which change of climate was a favorite prescription. This combination of circumstances touched off a rush of health seekers which proved to be the chief dynamic for southern California development in the seventies, eighties, and nineties.

Tuberculosis of the lungs, then usually called consumption, was the malady that did most to promote the health rush. Asthmatics and rheumatics were numerous also, and, indeed, there was hardly an illness known to man from which some sufferer did not seek relief, on doctor's orders or on his own initiative, by a removal to this region. At the outset the invalids usually went to the established towns, Los Angeles, San Diego, Santa Barbara, or San Bernardino. They found fewer conveniences than they would have liked and relatively few qualified physicians. In many instances, however, there was a quick recovery and as often a tendency to attribute it to the mild and equable temperature and the abundance of sunshine. To spread these tidings became a duty and a pleasure. The good news encouraged other afflicted ones to migrate to this health-giving land, crowding its housing to a still greater extent.

There were, of course, two obvious ways in which the housing shortage could be remedied: by building more hotels and houses in the old towns or by starting new towns in which such facilities might be made available. Both remedies were resorted to. The old towns were enlarged, particularly Los Angeles. A dozen or more new towns also took shape, including Pasadena, Riverside, Sierra Madre, Altadena, Santa Monica, Palm Springs, Ojai, and Nordhoff, many of them primarily health resorts.

In the course of this expansion a realization grew that, although there were underlying similarities, southern California did not have one climate spread indiscriminately over its entire area, but many variations. This gave basis for intercity rivalries in bidding for health seekers. Los Angeles and San Diego, for example, each claimed more equable temperatures and more sunny days. The fact of diversity led also to an assessment of local advantages in a great many places in southern California and to something approaching a medical climatology. Not all the claims made were valid, but some had general medical endorsement at the time; for example, that the seaside towns were advantageous for asthmatics and that the drier interior and foothill locations were to be preferred by consumptives. It was found also that the area abounded in thermal and mineral springs. To capitalize and encourage use of these waters, internally and externally, was the next step. Some developed into spas comparable to the famous watering places of Europe—the California Carlsbad, for example. A feature of this phase of health seeking in southern California was that use did not wait for analysis. Years later, when a state chemist was commissioned to run tests, it was revealed that some of the waters so freely drunk were harmful rather than beneficial. On the other hand, testimonials to the success of the water cure were not lacking.

The migration of thousands and then tens of thousands of invalids to southern California was accompanied by a migration of doctors, some of them health seekers themselves. Through their coming, and through the experience gained in local practice with this bonanza of patients, a medical advance took place. It was evidenced in part by the opening of rest homes, convalescent homes, hotel-hospitals, and eventually sanitaria and hospitals specializing in tuberculosis and other maladies. Through much of the period, however, it was a matter of putting up in an ordinary hotel room, finding a room or a house in town, or taking a small place in the country, and depending primarily on the health-giving environment for improvement.

Along with the medical advance it must be admitted that there was a great deal of quackery and a high susceptibility to cults and fads, some of which doubtless had validity. There were vegetarians and fruitarians, apostles of fresh air and those who stressed indirect ventilation, advocates of complete relaxation and others who were for hard work. One tubercular attributed his cure to clearing the brush and shouldering the stones from the field where he was setting out his vineyard.

Even with the rapid population growth southern California had a limited amount of so-called light work in which convalescents could engage. They flooded the white collar fields. A sizeable number, the majority of them townspeople rather than farmers in the East, turned to agriculture. In the fifties, when cattle raising was in the ascendant, they certainly could not have qualified as vaqueros. By the seventies, however, the region's agriculture had evolved to include many branches in which the physical demands were much lighter. Vines could be set out and brought to production without backbreaking labor. Oranges and other fruit trees could be grown with only intermittent attention. There were instances of women successfully embarking on this work. But perhaps the ideal agricultural opportunity that offered itself to the invalids was bee keeping. A few hives of Italian bees were brought to San Diego in 1857. In the seventies bee keeping spread rapidly, especially to the unoccupied interior of the southern counties. It was an agricultural frontier exceptional in several respects. It moved eastward, and advanced with minimal alteration of the landscape. In addition, its frontiersmen were mostly of urban backgrounds and recruited from the poor in health. By 1884 these apiarists achieved a production of 9,000,-

000 pounds. They went on to push California to first place among the states in honey production.

Important as they were in agriculture, the health seekers were perhaps even more significant in calling attention to southern California. Before their time, and after, the slogan "California for Wealth" drew people to the Golden State. Recognition of the region's potential as a place of retirement and as a vacation land remained in the future. Pilgrimage to Hollywood in hopes of getting into the movies also lay ahead. These and other practical talking points for boosting the region would prove effective. But they were worldly and even sordid as compared to the news of the healing climate. In time, promoters, realtors, and professional Californians would sound the region's praises; none, however, with so high a sense of calling as was felt by those who could hold out the promise of health.

The response was the first big rush to southern California, the health rush. Gaining momentum in the seventies, it was abetted by railroads and real estate speculation in the eighties. It continued in the nineties, and still goes on, though much less spectacularly, because at the turn of the century medicine found a new prescription for consumption and substituted institutional care instead of a better climate.

The census reports score the growth of southern California population to 76,000 in 1880, 221,000 in 1890, and 325,000 in 1900. They do not specify why these people came, but a conservative estimate is that at least a quarter of those present in 1900 had come as health seekers.

Advertising Railroad Lands

Rail connection with San Francisco, and with the East, by way of Sacramento, was achieved in 1876. It gave southern Californians an added sense of inclusion in the nation, then celebrating the centennial of its declared independence. With banquet, oratory, editorials, and parade the Angeleños hailed the coming of the railroad as the advent of a new era. To their chagrin they discovered that the immediate consequences of the entrance of the Southern Pacific, even with its additional lines to Needles and through Yuma to El Paso and New Orleans, were less overwhelming than had been expected. The major reason was probably that local economic productivity had not yet reached the point where it could take full advantage of the new facilities for rapid transit. Local citizens, however, were less aware of this condition than of another deterrent to utilization of the railroad, namely, the rate schedule, which was not only high but also discriminatory in favor of San Francisco. Nevertheless, the coming of the Southern Pacific was worth much. The sharpest contrast between the first and second quarter-centuries of American southern California was that the former was prerailroad and the latter a railroad era.

Although in the first decade after its entrance into the southern part of the state the Southern Pacific was not carrying a great many passengers or a great deal of freight, it was operating through another channel to foment the development of the region. For its construction activities the company had been rewarded with millions of acres of land—the company agent in 1882 set the figure at 10,445,-227 acres, most of it in the southern half of the state. The railroad moguls quickly saw that sales, especially to new farmers who would live on the land, would be doubly advantageous, for in addition to the purchase price the Southern Pacific would profit by the operating revenue which the new settlers would create. Animated thus the railroad embarked upon real estate promotion.

It set up a land office at Sacramento which professed to have a better listing of available land than had any of the government offices. Jerome Madden had charge of this office and of the publicity that issued from it. He arranged for special pictorial editions of various newspapers, such as the San Francisco *Spirit of the Times.* He ran advertisements in local newspapers and in eastern newspapers and periodicals. He prepared illustrated pamphlets, such as the *Southern Pacific Sketch Book,* of which 10,000 copies were printed in 1887, and these were distributed by ticket agents throughout the country. He was the author of another pamphlet directed more especially at prospective settlers, *The Lands of the Southern Pacific.* Numerous editions beginning in 1877 were distributed through these same channels. He also enlisted or appropriated the aid of several authors of established reputation and integrated their volumes of travel and description into the campaign to sell the railroad land. The stamp of railroad subsidy is unmistakable in Charles Nordhoff's *California for Health, Pleasure and Residence: A Book for Travellers and Settlers* (1874) and *A Guide to California the Golden State* (1883), and also in Ben C. Truman's *Homes and Happiness in the Golden State of California* (1883), I. N. Hoag's *California the Cornucopia of the World* (1884), and Madden's own *California: Its Attractions for the Invalid, Tourist, Capitalist, and Homeseeker* (1890). Equally effective, though apparently independent in origin, were such glowing descriptions as *Between the Gates,* by Benjamin F. Taylor (1878); *Old Mexico and Her Lost Provinces,* by W. H. Bishop (1883); *California of the South,* by Lindley and Widney (1888); and *Eine Blume aus dem goldenen Lande oder Los Angeles,* by Ludwig L. Salvator (1878). Since many of these books ran through several printings, the number of readers reached was considerable.

Another avenue for inexpensive advertising of the railroad lands was through coöperation with certain independent agencies for immigrant promotion. Such were the California Immigrant Union and the Pacific Coast Land Bureau. These organizations maintained representatives in the East and in Europe. Their publications, such as the Union's *All About California and the Inducements to Settle There* (1870) and the Bureau's *The California Guide Book,* made a particular point of stressing the advisability of buying railroad land in California. In addition, the railroad had its own agents, including I. N. Hoag, who conducted the California Immigration Commission at Chicago, E. Hawley at New York, a Mr. Schriever and a Mr. Meyer at New Orleans, and W. G. Kingsbury at London and on the continent.

California-bound emigrants were afforded several accommodations by the railroad. One was the emigrant car, in which, at no extra charge, sleeping and cooking facilities could be improvised. In Texas the railroad maintained emigrant houses where travelers might put up for a week without charge while seeking work or earning money to enable them to go on to California. The railroad ran an informal employment service; its agents would telegraph ahead to arrange for passengers to meet prospective employers, and for a fee, the European agents would locate young men as "farm pupils." Interpreters offered assistance to foreign-speaking immigrants. Fares to the West were made attractively low, and attached to the "land-seeker's ticket" was a nontransferrable voucher which could be applied at the full cost of the ticket on a purchase of railroad land. The land, furthermore, could be paid for on the installment plan.

Notwithstanding its patent efforts to develop the country the Southern Pacific was the target of much criticism and abuse. Its refusal of service or connections to towns which would not meet its demands for bonus and right-of-way, its arbitrary selection of certain sections to colonize and develop, while others were held off the market, and its high rates for freight and local fares were the principal causes for dissatisfaction. In the late seventies, as was related above, political reform and the creation of a state commission were counted upon to regulate the great monopoly. By the mideighties hopes were pinned upon the appearance of a competing railroad.

The Coming of the Santa Fe

Tom Scott's Texas and Pacific had promised to be the competitor but, thwarted by Huntington's implacable opposition, it had fallen by the wayside. Through Kansas a much less pretentious road was inching southwestward. This was the Atchison, Topeka and Santa Fe, chartered by Cyrus K. Holliday in 1859. Actual construction was not started until 1868, but within four years the rails stretched across Kansas to Dodge City, where an entirely unexpected business was encountered, namely, the hauling of Texas cattle to market. This operating revenue was a godsend to the Santa Fe, which, with a land grant of only 3,000,000 acres, had not appeared strong enough to build all the way to Santa Fe, much less to the Pacific. It did dispose of much of its Kansas land to good advantage, utilizing most of the promotional devices which the Southern Pacific was employing in California and also running excursion trains in June, when the prairie farms were looking their best.

From its limited scope as a cattle carrier through Kansas the Santa Fe was lifted by William B. Strong, who became general manager in 1877 and president in 1881. The franchise of the Atlantic and Pacific was purchased; tracks reached El Paso in 1881 and Guaymas, on the Gulf of California, in 1882, and another line of greater ultimate significance crossed Arizona toward Needles. Theoretically, the Southern Pacific had closed this gateway by building its Mojave-Needles line, but since the Santa Fe had reached Guaymas and could threaten competition by steamship to the California ports, Strong could demand concessions. First came a lease of the line to Mojave. Then by rapid strides the Santa Fe expanded its California facilities. Crossing Cajon Pass it reached San Bernardino in 1885. It pur-

Lordsburg College, earlier a Boom Hotel

chased the California Southern and got an outlet at San Diego. It
acquired rights to run over Southern Pacific tracks from Mojave to
San Francisco and from Colton to Los Angeles. Finally, in 1887, by
building from San Bernardino to Azusa and buying the Los Angeles
and San Gabriel, it got its own line into Los Angeles. Thus, some
eighteen years after the completion of the first transcontinental railroad, the Big Four's monopoly was finally challenged.

To the competition that ensued is due a large share of the credit
for California's, especially southern California's, subsequent development. More spectacular was the immediate influence in producing
the boom of 1887. Other conditions of course were favorable, what
with new vistas opening in agriculture, the Southern Pacific's advertising campaign in full swing, and the country in general enjoying
greater prosperity. Yet competitive rail rates touched off the charge.
Competition might have been minimized had the Southern Pacific
been willing to concede 50 per cent of the southern California business and 27 per cent of the northern. Refused this prorate, the
Santa Fe started a rate war that saw passenger fares from Kansas City
to Los Angeles brought down to five dollars and for a time even to
one dollar, and freight rates reduced almost in proportion. The
natural result was a stimulation of shipments and settlement and, for
the first time, a large stream of tourists to southern California.
Trains on both roads had to run in sections to accommodate all who
wanted to come.

The Boom Begins

The influx of so many visitors, their enthusiasm about southern
California as a place in which to live, to farm, and to do business,
and the concurrent arrival of numbers of new residents led to a
sudden awareness of glorious prospects. Astute real estate promoters, many of them experienced boomers from the Midwest, capitalized on this spirit of optimism. Few of the devices employed
were of local invention, but southern California proved a most congenial clime into which to transplant them. Flourishing vigorously,
they attained such proportions as to seem unquestionably Californian.

The first step was for an enterprising promoter to acquire title to
some tract of land on which his town or suburb could be plotted.
It seemed to matter little what sort of land was chosen. The site

of Ballona was swamp land; Chicago Park nestled in the rocky wash of the San Gabriel; Carlton perched precariously on a steep hillside east of Anaheim; Border City and Manchester were stranded on the far slope of the Sierra Madre, their only real asset a noble view of the Mojave Desert.   Elsewhere the subdivider ruthlessly hacked his way through orange groves.

The devastation thus wrought is often compared to the blight of the *Icerya purchasi*, or cottony cushion scale, which was introduced from Australia almost exactly at the time the boom began.   Seemingly immune to all varieties of chemical sprays, the scale wrought great havoc.   The Wolfskill grove was one of the first devastated, and the entire citrus industry seemed threatened with ruin.   To the rescue the Department of Agriculture summoned the Australian ladybug, which quickly exterminated the Icerya.   No comparable antidote, it has been remarked, was discovered to stay the hand of the subdivider.

Having plotted his tract, at least on paper, the real estate promoter embarked upon his sales campaign.   Choice of name was important.   The Gladstone promoters, for example, circulated the report that the British prime minister was coming to erect a winter home.   Lithographers and printers were called upon to produce brochures and pamphlets effulgent with roseate predictions.   Slogans such as "Buy Land in Los Angeles and Wear Diamonds" were blazoned across newspaper pages and flaunted on handbills.   Another standard device was to start the construction of some conspicuous building, usually a rambling frame hotel or sanatorium.   When the boom was over, these monstrosities and the white corner stakes were the only surviving landmarks for several of the towns so boldly conceived.

As contributory causes of the boom these untenanted buildings pale before some of the other antics of the boomers.   Sales depended less on the printed word and on buildings in construction than on ballyhoo of a more direct sort.   At barbecues and free lunches, with brass bands, processions, and free excursions, through the build-up of individual sales talks and the spellbinding of the auctioneer, they expatiated on the abundant prosperity that southern California was just about to grasp.   They specialized in overstatement, quoted one another's exaggerations, admitted that they exaggerated, but insisted that the truth would not fall far short.   Through such techniques were prices puffed up and excitement swelled.

The magnitude of the boom is indicated by several sorts of testimony. Real estate transfers brought to record in the county in 1887 totaled $98,084,162; and since many sales were on time contracts and since many of the contracts were reconveyed at a substantial advance, it is a conservative estimate that the year's sales surpassed $200,000,000. There are statistics likewise for the amount of subdividing that went on. Thus from January, 1887, to July, 1889, the records indicate some sixty new towns plotted, with a total acreage of 79,350. Or we may turn to the reminiscences of old timers who before the boom had known everyone in town and suddenly found Los Angeles filled with strange faces. This was literally true. The census-taker in 1880 had found only 11,183 Angeleños; in the summer of 1887 he would have found six or seven times as many.

Climax and Denouement

It was a boom replete with ridiculous features, many of which were recognized at the time. Editors in northern California held these excited southerners up to no end of ridicule even before the real estate market broke, and as early as 1890 T. S. Van Dyke lampooned them deliciously in his volume *Millionaires of a Day*. On the other hand, it is worth noting that outside the locality there was much trading in southern California futures. Simon Homberg, for example, the promotor of Border City and Manchester, marketed his lots solely in northern California, Oregon, and the East, and extracted from the gullible a cool $50,000.

Nevertheless, the boomers directed most of their fanfare toward swelling the local excitement. A measure of their success is that the record for real estate transfers in a single day rose to $664,000, to $730,000, and finally to $930,000. Those who had sold made every effort to buy in again. Men stood in line for hours to get choice lots in new subdivisions and refused as much as $500 for a place in the queue. The querulous few who questioned the soundness of the inflated values were silenced by pronouncements such as that of Philip D. Armour of the great packing company:

Boom—will it break soon? There is no boom to break! This is merely the preliminary to a boom which will so outclass the present activities that its sound will be as thunder to the cracking of a hickory nut!

This was in July. For a time it appeared that Armour was right. Early in 1888, however, purchasers began to be more wary; prices were reduced and still no takers appeared, and suddenly the whole top-heavy price structure came tumbling down. Expectations were rudely shattered. A host of purchasers on contract had no alternative but to forfeit the down payments they had made. Others who had stretched their credit to buy real estate were cleaned out. Among them were a number of long-time residents who had resisted the early excitement only to succumb in the end and plunge their all on the eve of the collapse. Departing trains now had the heavier business. Several of the communities for which the most roseate predictions had been made became deserted villages. Carlton, Nadeau, and Santiago were left without a single inhabitant; Chicago Park and Sunset had one resident each, the watchmen at the hotels with which the sucker list had been baited.

The setback was serious enough. A number of business houses were forced to the wall, local banks were hard put, and population and volume of business declined sharply. On the other hand, the catastrophe was not absolute. Even after the departure of thousands, 50,395 persons were present in Los Angeles at the time of the census of 1890, and twice that many were in the county. The banks were all able to weather the crisis, and the largest losses were in anticipated profits. As Van Dyke has one of his characters put it: "I had half a million dollars wiped out in the crash, and what's worse, $500 of it was cash." Indeed, the collapse of speculative real estate prices had its beneficial effects, for it terminated the complete infatuation of southern California with this artificial source of profits and redirected attention to the neglected opportunities for production of wealth through agriculture and industry.

The postboom years witnessed a back-to-the-farm movement. Groves that had been blighted by icerya or subdividers were restored to productivity, and thousands of acres of new lands were put to the plow and set out in vines or citrus. Not only did production mount, but with freight rates stabilized at a more reasonable level, the actual income for southern California was increased even further. In terms of percentages the nineties appear to have been a slack decade, yet the population increment for Los Angeles County was slightly larger than for the eighties (68,844 as against 68,073), and for Los Angeles City it was considerably larger (51,084 as against 39,212). The other southern counties made a more gradual recovery, but they likewise were soon participating in the general uptrend, and, as in Los Angeles, the emphasis came to be less upon the hollow pyramiding of real estate quotations and more upon a sounder expansion of agricultural and industrial production. It would be too much to say that the lesson had been learned with absolute perfection, yet never again was there so cavalier a disregard for the more fundamental elements of southern California economy.

27

BROADENING THE ECONOMIC BASE

CALIFORNIA'S ECONOMY had its first period of extraordinarily rapid change in the gold rush epoch, when development centered on gold and grain, lumber and beef, and was accompanied by a succession of transportation improvements culminating in the transcontinental railroad. The second fell in the years following the First World War. Its more conspicuous characteristics were large-scale production of petroleum, the moving picture industry, an augmented stream of tourists, and a number of grandiose engineering achievements. The attendant improvements in communication include the Panama Canal, the automobile and the network of automobile highways, airlines, and radio. Between these two peaks intervened a middle period, overlapping the last years of the nineteenth century and the first of the twentieth. Relatively quiet, this period was by no means devoid of advancements, and although the economic elements that were introduced between 1875 and 1914 were less spectacular than gold and the movies, several were of a very solid nature and have proved their permanent utility.

Selling California Oranges

One such element was the establishment of citrus raising as an industry. After secularization, the mission citrus trees were neglected. In the fifties, orange, lime, and lemon plantings were regenerated by seeds and seedlings from Hawaii and Central America, but the results were only mildly encouraging. By 1860 the state had only 4,000 bearing orange trees and 600 bearing lemon trees. Practically all were in southern California, and by all odds the largest concentration was in William Wolfskill's Los Angeles grove. A decade later the citrus trees in bearing numbered 45,000, including some extensive plantings as far north as Porterville and Oroville. The volume of production, however, was still small. In 1868 Los Angeles sent only 2,200 boxes of oranges to San Francisco, and there they had to compete with fruit from Hawaii and Sicily.

In the seventies and eighties, orange growing forged to the front. Two innovations share the credit. The first of these was the discovery of the agricultural possibilities of the uplands, such as those at Riverside, which opened new vistas. The Riverside tract had been poor grazing land; according to the current phrase, even the coyotes carried canteens. Louis Prévost's Silk Center had failed there, but when the colony led by J. W. North watered the land with a $50,000 canal and set out orange trees, several natural advantages came to light. The higher land proved less subject to frost than the lowlands, and there was no danger that tree roots would reach the water table and drown.

A more dramatic innovation was the introduction of the Washington navel orange. The Department of Agriculture at Washington, having received from a Presbyterian missionary at Bahia, in Brazil, a dozen budded trees of a seedless variety, sent two of the dozen to Mr. and Mrs. L. C. Tibbetts of Riverside. In the new environment these trees lived up to their Brazilian reputation, producing large, seedless oranges of excellent color and fine flavor. Budwood from these pioneer trees was transferred to thousands of specimens of the older stock. So great was the demand that the Tibbetts had to enclose the trees with an extra-high barbed-wire fence to discourage thievery. One of the parent trees still flourishes at Riverside, and the myriad progency of these trees, filling grove after grove, has been fundamental to the success of the California citrus industry.

In 1884 these oranges took practically all the prizes at the New Orleans exposition. Two years later shipments amounted to 2,250 carloads, and orange growing was southern California's most popular enterprise. In 1888 a blight on the grapevines led the Anaheim colonists to abandon viticulture in favor of oranges and English walnuts. There were other localities where vineyards gave way to tree planting. For the most part, however, the orange groves sprang up on lands hitherto unimproved, and largely on the highlands that had not been considered eligible for irrigation. Not all the skills of orange culture were acquired immediately, but the orange growers succeeded in getting good crops of good fruit.

Marketing was a harder nut to crack. By the close of the century there were not quite a million and a half potential orange consumers in California. If the industry was to flourish on a scale commensurate with the groves already set out, a much larger market outside the state had to be built up. The coming of the railroad and the invention of the refrigerator car opened the door for distant marketing. At the most, these were enabling acts and not the full explanation of the industry's rise. The early experience with shipments to the eastern states was not altogether encouraging. Freight charges, though moderated in the course of the rate war, were still pegged high. Delivery was not as rapid as it should have been for a somewhat perishable product. And worst of all, the growers were at the mercy of eastern commission houses and middlemen to whom the California fruit was but an incidental matter. They did little to push its sale, and the remittances they sent were often disappointingly small. There was need, it appeared, for more effective management of the distribution of orange shipments, for expediting of delivery, and for stimulation of demand. Eastern middlemen were not responsible for the fact that the orange was regarded as a luxury goods, as an ornament for the Thanksgiving Day table or the Christmas stocking, yet it was clear that they could not be counted on to elevate it from an exotic curiosity to a staple.

As the solution of these two problems of inefficient distribution and inadequate demand, the orange growers resorted to a coöperative association, the California Fruit Growers' Exchange. The association effected some improvements in production, for example, in pest control and frost prevention and in the substitution of clipper picking for hand pulling. It also standardized packing on a much higher level of efficiency and attractiveness. Early shipments had been too nearly orchard-run. The Exchange installed machinery for cleaning and grading the fruit and introduced techniques of wrapping, labeling, and packing, so that grocers could order California oranges with more precision as to size and quality than was true of most of the goods they handled in this prepackaged era.

All this had a bearing upon marketing, but the real work of the Exchange was to tackle the latter problem directly. The essential method was a simple one. Agents were stationed at the larger population centers in the East and kept close tab on the ratio of supply and demand in each locality. It was then a simple matter to reroute cars from an overstocked center to another that was running low. Thus the price structure was protected against breaks through the glutting of a particular market, and at the same time prospective purchasers seldom had to be turned away because a local supply had been exhausted.

The Exchange also set about systematically to whet the national appetite for California oranges. The devices it employed were legion. Special fruit trains were festooned with banners and became, in effect, moving billboards. The common billboard was also pressed into service, and newspaper advertisements throughout the land sang the praises of the California orange. "Oranges for Health —California for Wealth." A test campaign in Iowa in 1905 led to marked increase in sales and encouraged the Exchange to blanket the nation with the same sort of propaganda. The word "Sunkist" was thereupon forced into the national vocabulary. To stimulate consumption and to prevent the substitution of non-California and ipso facto inferior fruit, a silver orange spoon was offered for a dozen Sunkist wrappers and a dozen pennies. The Exchange followed up this offer by proffering other gadgets, notably the electric juice extractor, which by all that is reasonable would seem to have been a far more effective consumption stimulator than its antecedent.

At the head of the Exchange during its formative years was Francis Q. Storey, and to him is due much of the credit for the phenomenal rise of the association and the industry. In recent years the association has modernized its sales campaign. It has not neglected the golden opportunity afforded by the discovery of the vitamins and by the dictum of the pediatricians that every infant and youngster should have his daily ration of orange juice. Here verily was a greater godsend than a smudgeless orchard heater, another marketable by-product, or a new formula for profitable disposal of culls. The Exchange embraced the opportunity with appropriate zest, though at the same time it took whatever steps were necessary to consolidate its advantages. For example, when the sawmills which had been furnishing the boxes suddenly doubled their price, the Exchange bought itself a sawmill and a stand of timber and demonstrated its readiness to make its own boxes. In other directions the association has expanded, yet fundamentally it has adhered to its original principles.

One of the largest concerns in the state and a leading contributor to the material prosperity of southern California, the Exchange is a phenomenon of more than local interest. It ranks with the world's most successful coöperatives and has often elicited that sincerest flattery, imitation. In California, walnut growers and avocado growers have taken the same course. In New Zealand and Australia the citrus industry has followed the blueprint. In these instances success has been considerable, but not always are the results so happy. The method seems to have its best application in an association that can control the major fraction of production of some commodity for which the national market can be expanded. Some products, such as cotton, wheat, corn, hogs, and eggs, are raised by so many farmers that a coöperative to handle marketing would be extremely unwieldy. For other items, such as dates, domestic production is so small in comparison to imports that a coöperative association has uphill sledding. The California Fruit Growers' Exchange, in 1952 rechristened the Sunkist Fruit Growers' Exchange, remains a model coöperative and one that probably will not soon be surpassed.

George Chaffey, Irrigator

There is more to the record of agricultural expansion during this middle period. These were the years of peak production of wheat and barley, a holdover from the older economy. They witnessed also an expansion of grape and prune production, of dairying, and of wine making that would be interesting to explore, though less arresting than the record of orange growing and marketing. In the realm of agriculture, however, the second great advance was in irrigation. This was nothing new, for irrigation was an old California trait, one of the first that the Spaniards implanted in the province. It had declined with secularization but did not disappear, even though it had no part in the cattle raising of the pastoral days and little significance on the wheat and barley ranches of the early American period. Then, as California agriculture was broadened and particularly as the railroad era brought settlers into the San Joaquin Valley, irrigation increased. Some of the valley projects were coöperative ventures, laid out without much benefit of engineering and built by hand or by ordinary farm tools. Elsewhere in the valley the railroad controlled irrigation development, or some large company, such as Miller and Lux, took up the water rights and monopolized irrigation. Disputes over water rights were responsible for much of the resentment against the railroad in the valley. Yet here, as south of the Tehachapi, irrigation was requisite for all but a few crops.

By the eighties and nineties California irrigation was experiencing both expansion and refinement. Many individuals contributed, but the new developments are well typified and summarized in the work of an engineer from Canada, George Chaffey. When he arrived in southern California in 1880, the transforming power of irrigation was most strikingly apparent at Riverside, where the poorest grazing land of Rancho Jurupa had been made a show place of citrus culture. Brief residence at Riverside convinced Chaffey of the practicability of further development through irrigation. Late in 1881 he persuaded his brother to join with him in acquiring a tract of land, bringing water to it, and selling it as small farms and home sites.

On Thanksgiving Day of that year the brothers contracted for 1,000 acres of García's Rancho Cucamonga, with an accompanying water right in the adjacent mountains. Subsequently they added another 1,500 acres. After a famous Indian chief of Michigan and Ontario the colony was named Etiwanda. Construction of concrete pipe lines to deliver water to the upper corner of each ten-acre tract began forthwith, and before the end of 1882 some 1,400 acres had been sold. The features of particular significance were: the use of concrete pipes, which insured against water loss; the generation of electric power in conjunction with the delivery of the water; the adequacy of private capital for financing the development; and, most important, the attaching of perpetual water rights to ownership of each acre of land by means of a mutual water company. The problem of water law had been one of the thorniest faced by western jurisprudence. Chaffey's device of a mutual water company owning the water supply and the distributing system, and in turn owned by the landholders in the district, one share for each acre of land, proved a simple, sensible, and practical solution of a problem that had seemed insoluble.

From Etiwanda the Chaffeys went on to a larger project on the gently sloping plain at the mouth of San Antonio Canyon. The site for this colony, to be named Ontario, was acquired severally from

Rancho Cucamonga, the Kincaid ranch, the holdings of Henry Hancock, and by purchase of railroad and government lands. To the skeptical it seemed that San Antonio Canyon could not furnish enough water to supply so large a tract, especially since the town of Pomona was able to make good its claim to half the surface flow in the canyon. But Chaffey, acting upon the Spanish adage that "the rivers of California run bottom upward," drove a tunnel into the canyon bed. Penetrating some 2,850 feet, he struck a strong subterranean flow, which was conducted through a cement-lined ditch to a junction with the diverted surface flow. As an ocular demonstration of the abundance of water, he built a fountain near the Southern Pacific depot, which was turned on to spout water high in the air whenever a train came through.

Ontario and Pomona engaged in more or less good-natured rivalry throughout these early years. Ontarians delighted in the anecdote, good enough to be apocryphal, that a circus owner had refused to take his circus to Pomona because there was not enough water there to give his elephant a drink. Chaffey was responsible for a comparable quip on Ontario. Asked by the Baptists for a church site, he replied that he had it on good [Pomona Baptist] authority that there was not sufficient water in Ontario to meet the requirements of Baptist ritual. This byplay, however, should not obscure the fact that both communities flourished. Ontario had a special honor conferred on it when it was chosen in 1903 as the model irrigation colony and was played up as such at the St. Louis World's Fair in 1904. The tribute was not only to the efficient utilization of water in crop production but also to the high achievement in town planning, educational provisions, home beautification, and social benefits. Much of this Chaffey had planned.

In 1886, largely because of his success at Ontario, Chaffey was invited to undertake an even larger project in Australia. Mildura and Renmark were the results, both capably engineered but unprofitable because of political jealousies, inadequate transportation, and insufficient markets. When Chaffey returned to California in 1898, penniless and expecting to find himself discredited, he found on the contrary that Ontario very much wanted his services. Prolonged drought had reduced the water supply alarmingly. Put under contract of $500 a month to develop additional water, Chaffey resorted to portable pumps and artesian wells with tunneled outlets, thereby saving the colony from disaster. By bringing in artesian wells on an adjacent tract he was able also to recoup his personal fortune.

At this point Chaffey was drawn into a scheme to bring Colorado River water to the Colorado Desert, a proposal advanced intermittently since as early as 1853. The river had water in abundance. Aridity, it was already admitted, was a guaranty of fertility, but the general belief had been that a white population could not endure the heat of the Colorado Desert. Chaffey's Australian experience convinced him to the contrary, and when C. R. Rockwood's California Development Company approached him as the leading irrigation engineer of the Southwest and invited him to cut the Gordian knot of its difficulties, he responded with alacrity. A six-week reconnaissance of the region led to discovery of a canal route that could be developed for an estimated $100,000, a mere pittance compared to the vast acreage that could thus be brought under cultivation. Chaffey hastily contracted to do the work, and then discovered that the company did not have the promised option on the diversion point at Hanlon Heading, that it did not have the represented right-of-way through Mexico, that it was bankrupt and in jeopardy of losing its charter, and that it was obligated to accept some $350,000 worth of land scrip at par, which was about ten times the market value. His friends advised a break with this jumbled company, but he was determined to do the job. Within twelve months water was being delivered to Imperial Valley, its name another reminder of Chaffey's Canadian and Australian background. In modified form, his mutual water company device was also employed. By 1905 valley population had mounted to 14,000 and 120,000 acres were under cultivation. That same year, because of further difficulties with the California Development Company, Chaffey sold out his interests in the valley for $100,000 and retired as engineer of the water company.

The immediate sequel was a blunder by his successors. Troubled by silt at Hanlon Heading, these engineers opened a new and dangerous intake, and at the next high water the river broke through and began to pour all its water into the valley. Salton Sink changed into the Salton Sea, the railroad was forced to move its tracks, and Imperial Valley was threatened with complete inundation. The California Development Company's resources were entirely inadequately for damming a river 2,500 feet wide and thirty feet deep. In

June, 1905, it transferred its assets and the responsibility of stopping the flood to E. H. Harriman's Southern Pacific. The railroad engineers made two abortive attempts later in the summer and early in 1906 constructed a quarter-million-dollar dam, which was washed out by the first summer flood. Appeals to President Theodore Roosevelt were fruitless because the break was below the line in Mexico, so in the winter of 1906–1907 the railroad tried again. A heroic fifty-two-day drive, involving 6,000 carloads of rock and gravel and 1,200 piles and costing $1,600,000, finally closed the break and saved Imperial Valley. Yet the precarious position of the valley a couple of hundred feet below the level of the river denied the valley residents complete ease of mind until thirty years later, when Boulder Dam brought the river under final control.

Meanwhile, Chaffey had developed artesian water for another flourishing colony at Whittier and had laid plans for extending irrigation in Owens Valley in conjunction with hydroelectric development and an electric railway to Los Angeles. In this last project he was foiled by Los Angeles' own water and power designs, and his principal monuments remain Etiwanda, Whittier, Ontario, Imperial Valley, and, less ponderable but equally significant, the methods which he devised for California's material and social advancement. His irrigation projects, be it repeated, are but a generous sampling of the state-wide development from about 1880 to 1914.

Borax and Petroleum

Broadening agriculture was the keynote of the state's economic advance in this period, yet substantial expansion is to be noted also in industry. Meat packing, the canning and preserving of fruits and vegetables, and cement manufacture were prominent on the list, together with some holdovers from the earlier economy, such as flour milling, lumbering, and foundry work. Two new industries will serve as illustrations, borax and petroleum.

Though known to the ancients—Roman arenas were sometimes cleansed with it after gladiatorial combats—borax was not discovered in the New World until 1856. The first deposits were disappointingly small, but by 1880 Nevada prospectors were agog with hopes of finding a dry lake with a thick crust of the valuable chemical. In that year Aaron and Rosie Winters, marginal ranchers at Ash Meadows to the east of Death Valley, heard about the excitement in Nevada and picked up information as to the appearance and the simple flame test for the mineral. Applying the test on the salt marsh near Furnace Creek in Death Valley, they were rewarded with a green flame, indicative of the genuineness of the deposit. For $20,000 Winters sold out to William T. Coleman, former leader of the Second Vigilance Committtee and the Pick-handle Brigade, and F. M. (Borax) Smith of Nevada. These two men organized the Harmony Borax Company, later changed to the Pacific Coast Borax Company and in popular terminology to the Twenty Mule Team Company.

The difficulties confronted in the production of borax were severe and unusual. The deposit was located in a spot as forbidding as its name and generally believed to be uninhabitable for half the year. At best, work could proceed from October through May. The borax had to be extracted on the spot by boiling and crystallizing, and Death Valley had precious little fuel for such purposes. Greasewood, desert pine, and cedar were used; also loads of "desert hay," or sagebrush. A road had to be opened to the rails at Mojave, 165 miles distant. Most of the road was the tortuous, unimproved type customary in the mountain and desert West, but for an eight-mile stretch across the salt-encrusted floor of the valley it was an improved road—improved by sledge hammer—for the salt crust here was a tangle of peaks, ridges, and irregularities which was entirely impassable except in the six-foot swath that had been beaten down by sledge hammer.

Of the great wagons built at Mojave, with their five- and seven-foot wheels, their ten-ton capacity, and their fixed axles, so that turning was always by skidding, little need be said. Two such wagons and a water-tank trailer made a train, pulled by two wheel horses and eighteen mules, and conducted on a twenty-day schedule over the round trip by a driver and a swamper. The driver presided over whip and "jerk line," the single rein that stretched to the lead team. The swamper manned the brake on the second wagon, helped with the hitching and unhitching, the feeding, and the watering, and usually acted as cook. At this distance it all sounds very picturesque, but to the swampers and mule skinners of the eighties it was hard work and monotonous work, and not much enhanced by the imminence of disaster if wagons broke down or teams gave out, or if water tanks or supply stations were looted.

In the late eighties this spectacular phase of the borax industry was terminated by the discovery of colemanite, a lime and borax compound, first in the Calico Mountains near Daggett and shortly in the Funeral Mountains near Ryan. Railroad tracks penetrated to these mines, refining operations were transferred to San Francisco, and the twenty mule team rolled into the limbo of tradition, but leaving its reflection on the company's trademark and reëchoing a half-century later in a radio serial.

The petroleum industry may be introduced by a paraphrase of the preceding comments on borax. Though known to the California ancients, who used it medicinally and to caulk their cooking baskets, and though used by the Spaniards in roofing, petroleum was of no significance until the American period. In the fifties there were a few attempts to distill lamp oil from the seepages in Pico Canyon, at La Brea and Carpintería. It remained, however, for the Drake well in Pennsylvania in 1859 to show the way in well drilling. Under the stimulus of this example and encouraged by the numerous surface indications in California, wild-catting became a popular pastime in the sixties. Colonel R. S. Baker sunk some $65,000 on a tract not far from the present intersection of Wilshire and Hoover, in Los Angeles. Colonel Phineas T. Banning, B. D. Wilson, and others formed the Los Angeles Pioneer Oil Company and sank holes 75, 100, and even 200 feet deep at Wilmington, but their reward was more often water than oil. In Humboldt County a new town was optimistically named Petrolia. Santa Rosa, Santa Clara County, and the ocean front between Santa Barbara and Ventura had their wells, but the best early results were attained at Sulphur Mountain, back of Ventura, and by tunneling rather than by well drilling.

In the sixties, of course, the big oil industry in California was whaling. Shore stations operated at Monterey, Palos Verdes, and all along the coast from San Diego to Trinidad. In addition, large fleets were dispatched from San Francisco each summer to Arctic waters. The magnitude of this industry is indicated by some of the losses sustained. In 1871 an entire fleet of thirty-three vessels, carrying oil, bone, and ivory valued at $1,600,000, was lost in the ice field. In 1876 twelve vessels with cargo worth $2,500,000 were lost, and in 1890 six vessels out of a fleet of fifty-two. In view of the dimensions of this industry, both by shore stations and by the Arctic fleets from San Francisco, additional meaning attaches to the bold prediction of Geologist Benjamin Silliman in

1865 that California would be found to have more oil in its soil than all the whales in the Pacific Ocean. He ventured to suggest that this oil would eventually "lubricate the wheels of commerce and set a trade at work excelling in variety any that has thus far been known on this coast," a brash prediction, concerning which, said the San Francisco *Bulletin* on January 8, 1866, "We admit to being a little skeptical."

Almost a decade later J. DeBarth Shorb, a southern Californian who had dabbled in oil, concluded a ten-page review of the southern fields with this pronouncement:

> As a question of financial importance to the state at large, the petroleum interests of this State can never amount to anything. To obtain oil at all a large sum has to be expended; and when obtained nothing can be done with it that will give profit to the manufacturer.

His correspondent, the state geologist, incorporated this opinion in his article on California for the *Encyclopaedia Britannica*. And indeed, such pessimism seemed to be justified. The wells thus far, if not dug by pick and shovel, were drilled by spring pole. Transportation was in barrels on wagon, freight car, or ship. Tank cars and tankers were yet to come, and the first pipe line, a two-inch pipe from the Pico Canyon wells to the Newhall refinery, was not to be built until the next decade. Still farther off was the four-inch line from Pico Canyon to the sea at Ventura, completed in 1885. Nor was an adequate market immediately at hand. Kerosene had to compete with whale oil as well as candles, and, because the California oil had an asphaltum rather than a paraffin base, the derivation of lubricants was difficult. Consequently, the growth of the industry had to await the introduction of new uses and a broadening of demand as well as an increase in production.

The eighties saw new wells brought in and the opening of major fields in the Puente Hills, at Whittier, and at Summerland. Production reached a peak of 690,000 barrels in 1888. At Los Angeles, what was known as the Los Angeles-Salt Lake field was opened in 1893, this being the time and place of E. L. Doheny's entrance into the oil business. Though Doheny was to become Los Angeles' best-known oil man, his start was unpretentious enough. With pick and shovel and a hand windlass, he and his partner, C. A. Canfield, brought in a shallow well in the West Second Street district. The more important fields dating from the nineties were north of the

Tehachapi at Coalinga, McKittrick, Midway-Sunset, and Kern River. In the main they were responsible for the production increase to 4,000,000 barrels in 1900.

Small companies had predominated in the earlier oil production, but now larger companies began their domination of the field. The Harbison and Stewart Company became the Union Oil Company, the local Pacific Coast Oil Company was acquired by the Standard of New Jersey, and the Puente Oil Company enlarged into the California Petroleum Company, later to become a subsidiary of the Texas Company. Partly through these connections with the oil industry elsewhere, California came to share in the technological advances that were made in methods of locating fields, drilling, and refining. The relationship was by no means one-sided, for many engineering improvements originated in California and were copied where-ever oil was produced.

Even more noteworthy were the new uses discovered for California oil. An early use was to mix the nonvolatile residue with sand to make asphalt blocks for street paving, thus foreshadowing a large-scale use in highway construction. A far more important step is to be credited to E. L. Doheny. In the declining years of the century he persuaded the Santa Fe Railroad to experiment with crude oil as fuel for its locomotives. The experiment was a complete success, providing a cheaper, hotter, cleaner, and more convenient fuel; and oil-burning locomotives soon became the standard equipment throughout the Southwest, to the great relief of the passengers and the fireman's shovel. Success with oil-burning locomotives led to many other opportunities for fuel oil. In southern California, at least, it was the first source of industrial power made available in adequate quantity and at reasonable cost.

From 1900 to 1914 oil output mounted steadily and rapidly from 4,000,000 to 104,000,000 barrels, and not so much through new fields as by drilling more wells and deeper wells in the old fields. Oil consumption likewise was principally according to the developed pattern, the demand being for fuel oil, for oil to be used in paving, for illuminating oil, and for lubricants. A new consumer, destined to be the most voracious of all, was beginning to make its appearance, namely, the internal combustion engine. In these early years, however, the automobile was a luxury and not altogether reliable, the airplane was a curiosity, and the tractor an experiment. Horse and mule power were not yet bested on street, road, or furrow, though the handwriting was on the wall, with a promise for oil producers of a much greater demand to come.

No glance at the formative years of California's oil industry would be complete without some mention of speculation. Even today the increased expertness of oil geologists has not taken the gamble out of well drilling, and the stabilized market has not eliminated the hope of sudden wealth through a share in a new gusher. In this period chance was a more potent factor and investing in oil stocks a more reckless gesture. From the angle of promotion and stock trading, however, the California branch of the industry was part and parcel of the national phenomenon and little worse or better than other parts of the whole.

Here it is more to the point to notice the local effects of the industry: the development for the state of a new money crop worth annually an increasing number of millions of dollars; the growth of the industry with its steadily mounting payroll and capital investment in wells, refineries, tank farms, and pipe lines; and the provision for the first time of adequate power for the machinery of transportation and industry.

The Railroad Age

As to transportation, the turn-of-the-century generation was predominantly the railroad age. By 1880 mileage in the state amounted to 2,195. In the next decade, through the Santa Fe and Southern Pacific construction already described, it mounted to 4,356. Thereafter the rate of increase tapered off and popular fancy was less captivated by the achievements of railroad builders, yet for another quarter-century activity continued. In 1901 the Southern Pacific completed its Coast Line between San Francisco and Los Angeles. Four years later Senator William A. Clark brought southern California into closer connection with the Rocky Mountain states with his San Pedro, Los Angeles and Salt Lake Railroad, which in 1921 became a part of the Union Pacific system. A few years later the Western Pacific entered northern California by way of Feather River Canyon. These lines, together with a number of lesser projects, brought the total mileage at the outbreak of the First World War to approximately 8,000, at which figure it has remained almost constant ever since. Not only did this generation build California's railroads;

it used them to the practical exclusion of other avenues of transportation, such as waterways, highways, and air lanes.

Municipal Problems

Amplification of economic pursuits had as it corollary an increase in California population, in round numbers from 700,000 in 1875 to 3,000,000 in 1914, which in turn created certain municipal problems. San Diego faced several such problems, especially after the crash of the real estate boom in 1887. It came to have several prominent residents of wealth, energy, and vision, such as Edward W. Scripps, but the city's regeneration was largely the work of John D. Spreckels. Spreckels kept the Santa Fe's San Diego branch operating; he took over Coronado and built it up as a tourist attraction; organizing the Southern California Mountain Water Company, he assured the city an adequate water supply; several business blocks, the public library at Coronado, the city traction system, and the railroad to Yuma were among his contributions; and the Panama-California Exposition of 1915 was made possible chiefly through his generosity. Other cities which had no such godfather wrestled in these years with comparable problems and worked out, though not in unison, acceptable solutions.

At the turn of the century, through the practical genius of Henry E. Huntington the Los Angeles metropolitan area acquired a most excellent system of interurban and street railways, the Pacific Electric. It grew by absorption of older electric lines and by new construction, some of which was mainly for the purpose of opening new real estate subdivisions that Huntington wanted to promote. Despite these ulterior purposes, the network of lines interlocked in such a way as to make the whole area readily accessible. At the peak some six hundred cars were in operation on more than a thousand miles of track reaching out as far as Riverside and Santa Monica, San Fernando and Balboa. Schedules were fast and frequent and fares averaged less than three-fourths of a cent a mile. Besides the routine work of hauling passengers and freight throughout its empire, the Pacific Electric was a great recreational asset. It ran chartered excursions for Sunday School picnics and the like, and it featured day-long tours to the beaches, to Mission San Gabriel and the ostrich farm, to Long Beach, Balboa, and Santa Ana, and to the orange empire eastward from the city. Together with the inclined railway and trolley line up Mt. Lowe and the steamer excursion to Catalina, these tours for years channeled the tourist view of southern California and the inspection by most residents as well. Unfortunately for the popular repute of the Pacific Electric, its lines and equipment were continued without perceptible modification into the thirties, by which time the local transportation load was vastly greater, not to mention the snarls of automobile traffic. Eventually the cars gave way to buses, which have never remotely approached the satisfactoriness achieved for an earlier generation by the big red cars.

In the nineties the attraction of tourists and the promotion of trade were taken in hand by a Chamber of Commerce reorganized as an aftermath of the bursting of the boom, and its functioning has been a prominent feature ever since. In the nineties the city waged war with the Southern Pacific over the issue of a free harbor, while between 1905 and 1913 it achieved its first "final" solution of the problem of water supply.

A dry winter in 1904 put the city fathers into a receptive mood to listen to a proposition to bring in more water. An engineer and former mayor, Fred Eaton, had the matter under advisement and located a large supply of water in Owens Valley, together with an ancient river bed that would greatly simplify the problem of diverting this water to the parched city some 250 miles distant. Having acquired the necessary options, Eaton broached the matter to City Engineer William Mulholland, who endorsed it wholeheartedly to the city water board. That body acted at once. It acquired the site, approved Mulholland's plan for a $25,000,000 aqueduct, and broke the news by asking the voters of the city to authorize the necessary bond issue. As an engineering venture the aqueduct was a most creditable performance. Mulholland completed it within his estimate both as to time and money, and Los Angeles benefited not only by the 400 second-feet of water delivered but also by the provision of electric power at a very moderate cost.

In other respects the results were less happy. Owens Valley residents, who had success in their grasp in the reclamation of the valley, found their prospects dashed by the diversion of the water. Plenty of water for valley and city could have been impounded by a dam upstream from the cultivated area. Instead, the engineers proposed to follow the quicker and cheaper expedient of taking the water right out of the river. They were aided and abetted by the Secretary of the Interior, who stopped homesteading in the valley by declaring it forest land, and by President Roosevelt, who promptly endorsed a bill to give Los Angeles right of way for its aqueduct through Inyo, Kern, and Los Angeles counties. It was all done on the presumption that it would accomplish "the greatest good for the greatest number," yet the conviction has mounted that the planners of the aqueduct, besides devastating the valley, bilked the citizens of Los Angeles in order to reap swollen profits on San Fernando real estate irrigated with the first flow of water. When disgruntled ranchers resorted to dynamiting and other violent action, the city had excuse to proceed still more ruthlessly in forcing the settlers out of the valley. Vehement critics, including Walter Chalfant, Morrow Mayo, and Will Rogers, tilted a lance for the settlers and stirred the city's conscience to consider belated compensation, but this did not allay the desolation of the valley, or salve all the wounds, or undo the baleful publicity that redounded to the city because of the "rape of Owens Valley."

Meanwhile, San Francisco had endured its greatest ordeal. The earthquake of April 18, 1906, was followed by a fire which destroyed 28,000 buildings and devastated an area of four square miles, including most of the business district. Thousands of refugees were evacuated from the city; other thousands camped in Golden Gate Park. Predictions were hazarded that the city would not be rebuilt and certainly that Market Street would not come back, but almost before the ruins had ceased smouldering, the work of rebuilding began. Two men took the lead: General Hugh S. Johnson, better known to a subsequent generation for his place beside the blue eagle at the head of the N. I. R. A., who headed the relief work of the United States Army; and E. H. Harriman of the Southern Pacific, who put every resource of the railroad at the disposal of the emergency workers. Aided not a little by $300,000,000 in fire-insurance payments, San Franciscans built their city anew, finding in their adversity a determination and a sense of civic pride which even they had not known to exist. Yet the capacity for achievement thus dramatically demonstrated was basically the same as that which had given rise to the orange industry, the petroleum industry, and the several other elements of California's broadened economy.

28

THE SECOND GENERATION

For AMERICAN CALIFORNIA'S second generation, the key to the social and intellectual characteristics of the thirty-odd years prior to World War I is the recedence of frontier conditions. Improvements in communication broke down the barriers of isolation. Cumulative increase in population did away with much of the roughness that had characterized gold rush days. In the closing decades of the century California came closer to the national average in the ratio of the sexes in the population, in the proportions of the age groups, in occupations, and in habits of thought. Distinguishing qualities existed, but, to a far greater extent than before, descriptions of the life of the nation became applicable to California.

Viewed from a sufficient distance, this generation's outstanding intellectual experience was doubtless its exposure to the theory of evolution which Darwin had advanced in 1859. The protest of religion, especially Protestant theology, is often assumed to be the entire story, yet actually the impact was much broader. The postulate of evolution turned philosophers from transcendentalism to pragmatism. It fostered the concept of law as an organic growth changing with society rather than as a set of fundamental and immutable principles. It gave teachers an impetus to make education "functional," that is, articulated with social needs and ends. It stimulated the churches to socialize Christianity, as may be observed in such phenomena as medical missionaries, Christian Endeavor, Jane Addams' Hull House at Chicago, or Donaldina Cameron near San Francisco's Chinatown. Although Californians participated in this alteration of outlook, geographical remoteness from the centers of "culture" at Boston and New York and chronological proximity to frontier days seemed to ordain for them an inconspicuous place in American arts and letters. Nevertheless, in several fields of creative endeavor Californians of this generation achieved and deserved wide renown.

A Robust Victorianism

Socially speaking, the state was divided into two parts: rural California and San Francisco. Life in the smaller towns and in the country was the lot of four out of five in this generation, yet nowhere has it been adequately described. Whenever nonfictionists have considered this countryside they have been engrossed with the technological advances in railroad building, irrigation, new crops, and even real estate promotion, or they have centered on political issues to the neglect of sociological description. So with the novelists; when they depict these people, as did Frank Norris in *The Octopus,* it is primarily with a view to the problems of law and government and economics. Rural California before the First World War saw an agricultural expansion equaling that in the Plains region, yet no Willa Cather has risen to write an *O Pioneers,* much less an Ole Rölvaag to produce an epic *Giants in the Earth.*

The explanation is doubtless multiple. The rise of California farming had the characteristics of the growth of a great industry and seemed about as promising material for an absorbing human drama as the concurrent rise of the Standard Oil Company. Ownership tended toward capitalistic concentration. Labor ranks were manned largely by Orientals, first by Chinese coolies and later by Japanese. Expansion was achieved more by invoking machines and factory techniques or by scientific discoveries and inventions than by the sweat of pioneer homesteaders. The openness of the climate, the productiveness of the land, and the usually favorable market for California crops minimized the distress and the uncertainty that made the saga of the Prairie farmers so throbbing a narrative. It all simmers down, perhaps, to the fact that life in rural California, for all the expansion and the innovations, was no longer pioneering.

Furthermore, the hinterland was eclipsed by the metropolis. San Francisco in this second generation had manifold advantages. The fortunes of the railroad builders and the kings of the Comstock, added to the tribute paid by California gold, agriculture, and the commerce of the Pacific slope, made it a center of opulence.   Picturesqueness of setting and of history were additional assets.   Cosmopolitan population put San Francisco in a class with New Orleans for distinctiveness.   Unchallenged as yet by any other American port on the Pacific, it had the further advantage of being on the most favored route for travelers to and from the Orient or round the world. Thus, it was a mecca for globe-trotters, numbering among its more distinguished visitors former President Grant, Henry Ward Beecher, Adelina Patti, King Kalakaua, Rudyard Kipling, and Oscar Wilde. Still others who contributed to the tone of society were the officers of the United States Navy assigned to the San Francisco station and those of other navies who found frequent occasion to visit the bay.

The prevailing testimony of these visitors is that San Francisco was a fascinating place.   Physically, its charm sprang from the conjunction of bay and mountains and from the cool, gray briskness that is the standardized weather.

To this noble setting buildings contributed little.   Most business blocks were nondescript and unsubstantial.   Residences were unpretentious except for the ornate palaces of the plutocrats on Nob Hill, and these monstrosities, high-lighted by Charlie Crocker's thirty-foot spite fence and the brass fence that gave a man full-time employment as a polisher, were admired only as conspicuous proofs of great wealth.   The old Palace Hotel was a show place because of its very immensity.   Cliff House overlooking Seal Rocks was also on the itinerary of every visitor, and the underground passages in Chinatown had a reputation rivaling that of the sewers of Paris, but the two man-made features most often complimented were the generous width of Market Street and the cable cars.   In these the architects of the city had triumphed.

In more intimate details San Francisco made a better impression. The excellence of her restaurants was a tradition zealously upheld. Marchand's and the Poodle Dog offered a dollar dinner unsurpassed, while Louis' spread a four-course dinner that stirred Will Irwin to rhapsodies, and the price was fifteen cents with wine or twenty cents with coffee.   The French colony dating from the days of gold supplied the leading restaurateurs.   Home cooking by Chinese houseboys also attained a high standard of excellence.   The best foreign schools of cooking thus contributed to the California cuisine, where they were interlarded with sundry American dishes and recipes.   A further advantage was in the abundance of fresh vegetables which the gardens of the bay region provided so abundantly, in the many varieties of sea foods conveniently available, in the game that was readily obtained throughout this period, and in the fruits that were as luscious as they were cheap and abundant. Here was the wherewithal for epicurean feasts. And San Franciscans, it must be admitted, did their part nobly by supplying the restaurants an exacting but a large and appreciative patronage. If we are to believe the reminiscences of the period, gourmets and bon vivants constituted a large fraction of the population of the city. Good food and drink thus received the most appropriate encomium.

Preliminary to dining, San Franciscans of this generation were wont to stroll along the Cocktail Route. The cocktail, it was claimed, was a San Francisco invention; certainly it had a strong hold on these sturdy sons of the pioneers. From the Reception Saloon at Kearny and Sutter the route led to Haquette's Palace of Art, which was practically a museum; to the Cardinal; to the Occidental Bar; to the Bank Exchange, famous equally for its marble floors, its fine paintings, and its Pisco Punch; to another score or so of first-class saloons; and finally to Dunne Brothers, at Eddy and Market. Offering the most prodigal of free lunches, including such dishes as terrapin in a sauce of cream, butter, and sherry, and Virginia baked ham cooked in champagne, the Cocktail Route based its principal appeal on its provision for masculine conviviality. The habitués embraced, so it is claimed, every San Franciscan who mattered, and many sampled the food, the drinks, and the conversation at practically every station along the Route.

Since '49 the theater had been one of the more prominent embellishments of San Francisco. In the Champagne Days, which is Evelyn Wells' apt designation of the generation, San Franciscans could choose between Walter Morosco's Grand Opera House, which, under "the largest chandelier in America," specialized first in melodrama and then in opera; the Tivoli, with light and grand opera, and each seat equipped with a tray on which beer was served between acts; the Bella Union; the Alcazar, with its excellent stock company; the California, the Stockwell, the Columbia, sometimes with vaudeville, sometimes with concerts, sometimes with standard plays; the Baldwin Theater, admittedly the finest outside of New York; a Chinese theater in Chinatown; the Wigwam; and perhaps most distinctive, the Orpheum, where, for half a century after its founding in 1887, vaudeville reigned as a high art. A list of the artists who trod the boards in these always packed theaters would be a roll call of the generation's celebrities: Melba, Homer, Caruso, Alice Nielsen, Nat Goodwin, Lillian Russell, Julia Marlowe, Otis Skinner, De Wolf Hopper, Sarah Bernhardt, Weber and Fields. To enumerate the theaters, the players, and the plays gives but faint recognition to one of the most vital elements in old San Francisco.

Worth mentioning also were the city's clubs. Of these the most individualized was the Bohemian Club. Organized in 1871 by a group of newspaper men, of whom Henry George was one, this club was at first rigorously limited to actual writers, actors, musicians, painters, sculptors, and the like. Gradually the bars were lowered to admit prominent citizens who made no pretensions as creative artists. Membership advanced to 750, and the club treasurer ceased worrying about bills and deficits; nevertheless, the emphasis on things artistic persisted. The best exemplification of this was in the annual High Jinks, an elaborate and ambitious two-week toast to Nature, staged in a magnificent natural amphitheater in the redwoods, some fifty miles north of the city. The High Jinks represented amateur theatricals raised to the nth degree. It also displays San Franciscans' penchant for convivial communing with one another and for giving generous attention to the amenities of life.

The pictures usually offered of San Francisco society before the fire stagger the imagination. It may be well to recall that some business was transacted in between visits to the Cocktail Route, the restaurants, the theaters, and the clubs. When the earthquake and fire wiped out so many of the material elements of these Champagne Days, the effect was to give free rein to the imagination in reminiscences about "the city that was." But after allowing all the bubbles to rise, there is left a heady drink that suggests a gay, volatile, open-handed society in which Victorianism was well ventilated by gusts of robust westernism.

The Arts

In the actual practice of the arts Californians of the second generation seem to have been practically sterile in certain fields, such as architecture and sculpture, and to have achieved moderately in others, such as painting and writing. After a beginning of some promise in the religious art of the missions, painting broke off to start anew with the coming of crude limners in the late Mexican period, though the best "California art" of the era was in the form of portraits and landscapes to illustrate the accounts of foreign visitors to the province. The Mexican War brought other artists who recorded their impressions with pencil or brush and the gold rush brought still more. Charles Nahl, with his numerous genre pictures of California life, was the most famous of these, but there were many others: R. J. Holt, Thomas F. Ayres, W. S. Jewett, S. W. Shaw, S. S. Osgood, Thomas S. Officer, F. A. Butman, Thomas Hill, and Albert Bierstadt. Jewett not only brought the California landscape into its own but was commissioned to do a portrait of John A. Sutter for the State Capitol at a fee of $5,000. Ayres is noteworthy as the artist-discoverer of Yosemite Valley. A large pastel of his, when redrawn on stone by Nahl, became a most popular lithograph print. Tom Hill and Bierstadt worked the Yosemite vein even more assiduously.

The California nature theme, particularly Yosemite, came to be such a standard motif as to occasion complaint from one critic in 1875 against these "hackneyed landscapes," which he said were repainted year after year with only "a new rock and a cow or two introduced to give an air of originality." The theme and several of the artists continued, though the most prolific and popular painter at the end of the century, William Keith, turned from the grand view to more poetic studies in lighting effects and to intimate glimpses of the university campus at Berkeley. The missions were another favorite subject. Edward Vischer's etchings, which survive now only in the form of lithograph prints, formed the first complete series; but Keith painted them all in 1880, and his example was followed by artist after artist.

Douglas Tilden, who did the Donohue Fountain in San Francisco, the gigantic lever-punch operated by five muscular mechanics, is reckoned the leading sculptor. Southern California had its painters, including Gutzon Borglum, William L. Judson, Elmer Wachtel, and William Wendt. The last-named artist devoted himself especially to realistic portrayal of the brilliantly lighted southland. Many other artists could be mentioned, but it is doubtless more to the point to record the organization of the San Francisco Art Association in 1871 with Virgil Williams as its leading spirit, of Judson's Arroyo Guild at Pasadena in the nineties, and of the California Art Club at Los Angeles with Wendt as its most active member. These organizations not only propagated painting but also widened the circle of appreciation of art and enlarged the clientele for the purchase of canvases. Throughout the generation there was much talk about California as a future center of art. It was a goal, however, very much for the future, and apart from a bolder use of color California painting was dominated by the precepts laid down at Düsseldorf, Barbizon, and Paris.

Poets and Novelists

In writing, a more promising tradition had been shaped by the gold rush generation, a tradition so closely interwoven with the conditions of that earlier day that their successors were unable to uphold it. No humorist attained the dimensions of Derby; no California stories could compete with Mark Twain's "Jumping Frog" or Bret Harte's "Outcasts of Poker Flat," and, except for Gelett Burgess' "Purple Cow," no bit of doggerel had the vogue of Bret Harte's "Heathen Chinee." Nor was there any literary journal so distinctively and meritoriously western as the old *Overland Monthly.*

Poets in goodly numbers were still prompted by the muse, but the verse they produced was, with very few exceptions, not of superior quality. Joaquin Miller and Ina Coolbrith continued to write, and Miss Coolbrith was belatedly chosen poet laureate of the state, but the most famous poem of the generation was Edwin Markham's mawkish "The Man with the Hoe."

Quantity of output in novels, meanwhile, exceeded even that in verse. In the front rank marched an oddly assorted quartet: Gertrude Atherton, Helen Hunt Jackson, Frank Norris, and Jack London. After them trooped a legion of lesser writers who occasionally came forth with an important book, such as Charles Tenney Jackson's *The Day of Souls,* a poignant drama of San Francisco before the Fire, or Mary Austin's *Isidro.* The characteristics of this group are sufficiently exemplified by its leaders.

Gertrude Atherton displayed a curious ability to set her stories against backgrounds as diverse as Periclean Athens, modern Austria, colonial Jamaica, and pastoral California, and to suffuse them with the flavor of reality. Her novels, of which there are two score or more, gained a following in England and on the Continent as well as in the United States. Locally, she is of most interest when interpreting early California in *Rezanov,* in *The Splendid Idle Forties,* or in her *Intimate History.* In these works her imaginative reconstruction of bygone scenes was assisted by traditive materials from her people, her husband's people, and their friends in old San Francisco. Helen Hunt Jackson came to California only belatedly. She had served a long apprenticeship in New England and the East writing children's stories, romantic verse, and sentimental novels. In 1872 a transcontinental trip to view Yosemite introduced her to California. Nine years later, when she first came to southern California, she was a much-changed person. Marriage to William S. Jackson of Colorado Springs had given her a broader outlook and a more mature attitude. She had also become vitally interested in the problem of Indian rights and that very year she was bringing together her philippics against the United States Indian policies under the title *A Century of Dishonor.* Although this treatise led to her appointment with Abbot Kinney, founder of the California replica of Venice, to make a report on the conditions and needs of the Mission Indians, published at Washington in 1883, Mrs. Jackson felt that thus far she had not sufficiently stirred the nation's conscience. She turned, therefore, to the medium of the novel and strove through *Ramona* (1884) to obtain effective reforms. Although *Ramona* did not achieve all that its author had hoped, it swept the nation. After many years it is still read, besides being dramatized annually at Hemet in the Ramona country and periodically on the screen. Strictly speaking, Helen Hunt Jackson was not a Californian, but it was here that she found her noblest theme.

Frank Norris was an author wholly Californian. His first published works revealed him as a romantic. By some, this is regarded merely as a passing phase from which he soon turned to naturalism; others aver that it was his device to build up a popular following for the more solid works to come. At any rate, with *McTeague* in 1899, though he retained certain romantic devices, Norris became the first thoroughgoing disciple in America of the naturalism which Zola had popularized in France. Written with power and with insight into Mac's brutal sadism that would do credit to a trained psychologist, *McTeague* is a study in character disintegration induced by economic pressure. After another exercise on the debasement of an individual through the play of inexorable circumstances, in the unfinished work, "Vandover and the Brute," Norris turned from the psychological to the sociological. His final works, *The Octopus* (1901) and *The Pit* (1903), hinge again on economic determinism, but this time it was a whole farming population caught in the arms of a man-made machine. They have an epic sweep that is in keeping with the broad valley in which *The Octopus* is set. Rich in action and peopled with a large cast of characters whose metamorphosis by the wheat is magnificently portrayed, *The Octopus* would have gone far, just as a novel. But in it Norris deserted the amoral attitude of naturalism to pass judgment and to cry out for social reforms. Whatever this may have done to the book as literature, it gave it additional significance historically by linking it directly with the reform movement which culminated in the election of 1910 and the legislature of 1911.

Many readers of Jack London have reckoned him merely a master storyteller, vivid in his landscapes, authentic in his settings, apt in characterization, and attaining high velocity of action. *The Call of the Wild* (1903), *The Sea Wolf* (1904), and most of his later popular writings were of this stamp. Betimes, however, London was a Marxian Socialist and revolutionist, as *The Iron Heel* (1908) and *The Revolution* (1910) clearly show, and elsewhere in his publications one runs across other preachments of the struggle of the classes. More restraint and polish would have put him in Norris' "respectable" bracket, but probably at the expense of the spontaneity and forthrightness of style which won him so many readers. Even more than Norris, London represents the bitter reaction against capitalism on the part of a small but vocal minority in his generation. *Martin Eden* (1909), one of two excursions into autobiography, offers an unusual perspective of Jack's unorthordox student days.

Reminiscence Glorifies the Past

Not far removed from the novelists were those who committed their reminiscences to print. The principal works of this nature, by Horace Bell, William Heath Davis, and Harris Newmark, are improperly weighted with two for the south and one for the north, though by including Frémont's memoirs and more recently published reminiscences by Cornelius Cole, Frank A. Leach, Sarah Bixby Smith, J. A. Graves, Amelia R. Neville, Boyle Workman, and William T. Ellis, the balance is readjusted. Bell's *Reminiscences of a Ranger,* published in 1881, has a certain claim to fame as an early Los Angeles imprint. Bell's primary consideration, and to a degree this is true of Davis also, seems to have been not to let his story lose anything in the telling. He mixed legend and rumor with sober fact and made no pretense of following a chronological outline. With his memory jogged by a searching of the old newspaper files, Newmark was far more literal and much more cyclopedic, yet he had one thing in common with Bell and Davis, and for that matter with practically all those who indulge in reminiscences: he pushed the horizon back as far as possible.

Davis was largely concerned with the processes leading up to American acquisition of California. Bell's chief interest was in Los Angeles of the fifties and of the Civil War period. Newmark, though continuing toward 1913, gave three fourths of his space to the fifties, sixties, and seventies. Cole in 1908 was content to carry his memoirs up to about 1875, and Mrs. Neville saved but one chapter for the gay nineties. Even Leach, who as Director of the United States Mint at San Francisco in 1906 had had an exciting and important role in the weeks following the earthquake and fire, could not resist dallying for half his volume with the fabulous fifties and sixties. So it went for most of those who reminisced, including the scores of personages who were waited upon, notebook in hand, by Bancroft's secretaries. The result is that the American conquest, the gold rush, and the Civil War period are better covered in reminiscences than is the subsequent epoch. On the other hand the publication of the first of these memoirs in the eighties indicates that Californians were ready to take an active interest in the history of their state.

In southern California reminiscence was carried a step farther by the dynamic Charles F. Lummis. Lummis had walked out from Cincinnati, with a stopover in New Mexico's Indian country. He engaged in some orthodox journalism as city editor of the Los Angeles *Times,* but soon gave himself over completely to his enthusiasms: the Indians, the Spanish pioneers, and the wonders of the Southwest. Practically all he did can be related to one or more of these causes. The monthly that he created, *Land of Sunshine,* later renamed *Out West,* boosted California and the Southwest with eulogies of the climate and resources and with descriptions of expanding agriculture and industry. It was also the organ for the

Bean Field,
Orange County

Edward Weston

Sequoia League, a Lummis society dedicated to the rehabilitation of the first Americans, and for the Landmarks Society, whose name is self-explanatory. It was Lummis' habit in his journal to run translations of basic documents relating to the Spanish pioneers, for example, Benavides' *Memorial on New Mexico*. Still another monument to him is the Southwest Museum, an endowed institution which has done more than any other one factor to put Los Angeles on the anthropological map.

Constitutionally a rebel against the dictates of convention, Lummis preferred the company of kindred spirits. His house, which was of his own devising and making, was a constant resort for ambitious artists and writers, of whom Mary Austin was perhaps the most gifted. A bohemian salon it was, but at the same time his hospitality was in the old California tradition. Lummis also incorporated his ideas in books. *The Spanish Pioneers and the California Missions* proclaimed his admiration for Spanish achievement and argued its significance to the people of the United States. His *Land of Poco Tiempo* is a New Mexican travel book by one most simpático, while his *Little Flowers of Our Lost Romance* is a delightful excursion into the epoch of the Spanish borderlands.

The Great Bancroft and Lesser Historians

Meanwhile, California's past was attracting the attention of several local historians. As such it is hardly fair to include Josiah Royce, because by this time he was a Harvard professor, he wrote his *California* by request rather than in response to an irresistible inner urge, and the suggestion had arisen because Houghton Mifflin Company was embracing all the states in the American Commonwealths Series. But the multivolume histories of Bancroft, Hittell, and Eldredge issued unmistakably from the California environment; they were fruits of second-generation scholarship, and at this writing they are still the best of the large and comprehensive histories of the state.

Hubert Howe Bancroft was a historian the like of whom has very seldom if ever been produced. He came into the profession by what would now be termed the commercial entrance, for he was first of all a San Francisco book dealer and publisher. Having one day in 1859 ranged on a shelf some fifty or seventy-five works on California that happened to be in his stock, he got into the habit of adding

other volumes to this collection.   The habit grew, and from sporadic
forays in other book shops in San Francisco he soon went on to systematic purchases in the East.   Personally, and through agents, he
searched through catalogs and stocks in London and Paris, in Spain
and Italy, and throughout the Continent, meanwhile broadening his
interest to take in the entire Pacific slope of North America.   On the
cogent theory that completeness of the collection was the greatest
desideratum and that even the most insignificant item might have real
value when placed in such company, he made it his policy to buy
every book or pamphlet that had any material whatsoever on the
history of this area.   Under this impetus his collection mounted
rapidly.   At first the fifty volumes had seemed a creditable showing.
Within three years the total reached 1,000 titles, shortly thereafter
5,000, and by 1868, 10,000.

At this point Bancroft recites that he was ready to rest on his
oars, when there came to him an announcement of an auction sale
of some 7,000 volumes of Mexicana, the library of José María
Andrade, former intimate of Maximilian and now a refugee from the
republicans.   The catalog opened to Bancroft a new vista for the
rounding out of his collection.   It had not occurred to him that
Mexico, with a history of publishing reaching back a full century
earlier than Massachusetts, had untold riches for the collector of
Pacific Coast materials.   Equally patent was the fact that a collection
such as the Andrade would not come on the market again in Bancroft's day, if ever.   There was not time to check the catalog against
his own holdings; nor could he attend the auction at Leipzig.   All
he could do was authorize his London agent to expend $5,000 on
his behalf.   The result was an addition of 3,000 volumes, printed
and manuscript.   Very few were duplicates of Bancroft's earlier
purchases, and these were more than offset by works of the greatest
importance.   Other auctions and special sales found Bancroft a discriminating but liberal bidder, notably at the dispersals of the E. G.
Squier collection of Central American materials, of the Caleb Cush-
ing library, and of the collection of José Fernando Ramírez, another
Maximilian exile.   At this latter auction in 1880 prices of Mexicana had advanced so sharply that Bancroft's bill for a much smaller
lot than he had taken of the Andrade collection amounted to almost
$30,000.   In terms of that valuation he calculated his whole library as
worth a million dollars.

The total number of titles eventually ran to some 60,000, and besides the books and pamphlets, two other classes of materials were collected. One was newspapers, of which Bancroft acquired runs totaling something like 500 years, or the approximate equivalent of 5,000 volumes. The other was manuscripts. Some of the highest prices that he paid were for transcripts from the official archives of church and state or for original documents. In the seventies he encouraged many old-timers to record their experiences and recollections, and these statements, together with many documents, family and otherwise, which were turned over to him, constituted a most valuable branch of his collection.

Had Bancroft been content with collecting, his name would still be first in the roster of contributors to California historiography. The Bancroft Library, while in his possession and later as the property of the University of California, became the focal point, the foundation, and the inspiration for most of the subsequent exploration of this field. But though he began as a collector, Bancroft soon conceived a much more gargantuan task, that of sifting, correlating, and evaluating all the material he had collected and of writing from it a complete history of the Pacific slope. Needless to say, no human being could have done all this alone. Bancroft made no pretense of doing so. He employed numerous assistants, some of whom, such as Henry Oak, Thomas Savage, and Frances Fuller Victor, were historians in their own right. By trial and error a technique developed. At first Bancroft set men to work making literal extracts from the sources. These proving too cumbersome and less satisfactory than the originals in their context, he turned to an elaborate index, which likewise proved too complex. The next resort was a simple subject index on three by five slips, which were organized on a topical basis and then subdivided locationally and chronologically. This master index to his library was years in the making and cost an estimated $35,000, yet Bancroft considered that a bargain price for a key that would unlock the knowledge stored up in his vast collection. It was an Aladdin's lamp, as he worded it, enabling a man to "seat himself at a bare table and say to a boy, Bring me all that is known about the conquest of Darien, the mines of Nevada, . . . [or] the town of Querétaro . . . and straightway, as at the call of a magician, such knowledge is spread before him, with the volumes opened at the page."

With the aid of the index, then, Bancroft and his staff went through the subject matter of Pacific slope history item by item, viewing the evidence, weighing it, comparing, and interpreting. The facts as they saw them were written up in the text proper, while divergent or variant testimony fell into the footnotes in company with verbatim quotations from many supporting witnesses. Thus the work proceeded, with the mark of the index in evidence in such matters as the general organization, in which chronological arrangement was made subordinate to the geographical divisions. The end result was thirty-nine fat volumes, uneven in quality, but cyclopedic in detail and crammed with citations of every conceivable authority. Well-digested history it doubtless is not, but a more comprehensive compilation of sources would be difficult to imagine.

The historical profession, mayhap in outstripped jealousy, for many years looked askance at Bancroft, ridiculing his coöperative technique, scoffing at his "factory" methods, and denying him the recognition of authorship. The latter criticism has a measure of justification, for Bancroft wrote far less than half of the actual text; yet the criticism might come with better grace if research assistants and secretaries were unknown in the profession. The defects in the Bancroft *Histories,* however, are traceable to human frailities, to occasional intemperateness of expression, and to the nonexistence of any considerable number of preceding monographic studies to chart the way for his general account, rather than to flaws in the system itself. In history proper the method has not been reapplied except perhaps in the Federal Writers' Project and the Historical Records Survey and some of the works on the military services in World War II, but the employment of a staff under sentence of anonymity by the editors of *Time* and of *Fortune* and by the Walt Disney Productions is a modern recrudescence of Bancroft's literary workshop.

Concurrently with the great Bancroft, Theodore H. Hittell was turning aside from his law practice to undertake a history of California. Hittell worked alone; he utilized just such materials as did Bancroft, though of necessity on a selective rather than on an all-inclusive basis; he was accorded many facilities at the Bancroft Library; his legal background made him particularly well qualified to deal with certain phases of California history, and he was gifted in literary style. Consequently, his four-volume work, published in

1885 and 1897, is a notable milestone in local historical publication, still reckoned second only to Bancroft's.

Whereas other historians were overshadowed by these two, their activity in the pursuit of local historical studies is symptomatic of the outlook of the generation. Mention should be made of George Davidson, Nestor of California geographers and author of half a dozen important works on California's Age of Discovery. At the Santa Babara Mission, meanwhile, Father Zephyrin Engelhardt was devoting himself to a study of the missions of Baja and Alta California. Like Bancroft a devotee of compendiousness rather than discrimination, Engelhardt suffused with his own religious ardor the record of Jesuit and Franciscan labors in the Californias.

The third of the larger state histories was a by-product of the Panama-Pacific Exposition of 1915. Sailing under the name of its editor, Zoeth Skinner Eldredge, the first three and a half volumes were actually written by Clinton A. Snowden and the fifth volume consists of articles by selected specialists. Eldredge, however, deserves recognition for the general planning of the work and also for a two-volume study of the beginnings of San Francisco, which he had published three years earlier.

Henry George and Ambrose Bierce

In the field of political economy California was producing an even greater luminary, Henry George. George has been called, and rightly, America's most original economist; in the vigor of his thinking he need share the laurels only with Thorstein Veblen. The young George showed few signs of oncoming greatness. Leaving school at fourteen, he sailed before the mast from Philadelphia to Australia, came on to Salem, Oregon, where he worked in a print shop, and at length to San Francisco, where he held divers positions with print shops and newspapers, his chief reward being in the experience gained.

A Jeffersonian and a Democrat, George found in California as well as in his own experiences much food for thought on the injustices of the economic order. For California in the sixties, though endowed with abundant resources that should have made it a land of almost limitless opportunities, was rapidly falling into the hands of land monopolists. The swollen fortunes of the railroad builders, the tremendous land grants with which the United States subsidized them, the scandals current in connection with swamplands and fraudulent grants, the speculative profits at Oakland when it was made the terminus of the transcontinental railroad, the opulence of the Comstock fortunes—of such was the atmosphere of San Francisco in the formative years of George's thinking. Here certainly was basis for placing the blame on land monopoly and for seeking to eliminate private enjoyment of unearned increment. True enough, the same general conditions were observable elsewhere. On a visit to New York, George was struck by the juxtaposition of a most flourishing, profitable commerce with slums in which thousands lived in direst poverty. Throughout American history the thread of land speculation had been present, from the Ohio Valley before the Revolution to the Oakland water front after the railroad and from the Yazoo frauds to the California swamplands.

The economic philosophy that George worked out owed little to academic economists, for whom, by the way, he had the utmost contempt. He was a free-lance thinker, a seeker after origins, thinking, as Tom Paine had recommended, "as if he were the first man who ever thought." His cardinal principles were the inequity and iniquity of land monopoly, the viciousness of unearned increment, the conception of the landlord as a parasite, the assertion of the right of every human being to himself and to the use of his rightful share of the free gifts of nature, and the advocacy of a tax on land—that is, on rent, which he identified with unearned increment—as the panacea for the ills of society. An interesting corollary was to the effect that capital and labor were linked hand in hand, that interest and wages would rise and fall together, and that what was good for one would be beneficial to the other.

Nowadays George is charged with oversimplification, both in his analysis and in the remedy proposed. Not all unearned increment, to cite one example, is to be classified as rent. Nor is reason alone an adequate agent for the achievement of social reform. He was an archidealist, a quixotic "knight-errant from out of the newest West." Yet despite the correctness of these suggestions and notwithstanding that the single tax has not been adopted, Henry George has been the most influential American economist. A pioneer in analyzing exploitative capital, he attempted to bring the science of economics out of its ivory tower and make it face the problems of the common man. In this his success, of course, was only relative, yet he more than any other humanized and democratized the science of economics.

Measuring in terms of the total circulation of his writings, no other California writer compares with George. Heading the list is his magnum opus, *Progress and Poverty,* which was rejected by all the eastern publishers. George's printer friends in San Francisco had more confidence in him; they helped him set up the type, make the plates, and run off an edition of 500 copies. With the chief expense of publication thus covered, D. Appleton and Company agreed to take over the book, but the firm's lack of confidence in it is apparent in their refusal to take out an English copyright. Certain San Francisco reviewers derided the book, but the American press was warmer, and British critics on such journals as the *Times* and the *Edinburgh Review* hailed it with the greatest enthusiasm. George also made a triumphant tour de force of England and Scotland on the lecture platform. Thereafter he continued to be doubly successful as lecturer and writer, though not as the Socialist candidate for Mayor of New York. Of *Progress and Poverty* a conservative estimate is that two million copies were printed in the twenty-five years subsequent to 1879, while in the same period there circulated at least three million copies of his other writings, notably *Protection and Free Trade.* More years have elapsed and still George is read wholesale. Though his books would not have died, their vigor is additionally sustained by his ardent disciples, who still spread the gospel according to George.

George the mild-mannered, the self-effacing, was not the only prodigy supplied to letters by San Francisco journalism. The hallmark of genius was equally unmistakable in caustic, perverse Ambrose Bierce. His road to writing was also an indirect one. After a boyhood of poverty and deprivation in Ohio and Indiana, he enlisted in the northern army, saw active service in the Civil War, during which he was brevetted major, and came in 1866 to San Francisco, where he was soon ensconced as a watchman at the Mint. The San Francisco press at this time was filled with boisterous comments on the passing scene from such writers as Mark Twain and Dan De Quille. Bierce was moved to try his pen at this sort of writing, first as a side line and then in lieu of his work as watchman. He became "Town Crier" for the *News Letter* and, beginning in 1868, doubled as editor as well as columnist.

For the next three decades, with only an occasional interlude, Bierce regaled San Franciscans with a regular column in which he impaled whatever or whoever incurred his displeasure.   First it was as "Town Crier" for the *News Letter,* then as "Prattle" for the *Wasp,* and then as "Prattle" for Hearst's *Examiner.*   Much that he wrote was drivel, but Homer having nodded, a columnist must certainly have that privilege.   By their hide-bound conservatism and by their negative character the ideals Bierce stood for do not stir the imagination.   The people, in his estimation, "were a great beast," and democracy he decried as a prelude to anarchy.   For the *Argonaut* he turned loose his siege guns on Denis Kearney and the Sand-Lotters, and he had equal contempt for social reformers like Henry George who used an intellectual approach.   His early writing, too, was monotonously devoted to bludgeoning invective suffused with venom, and many of his most acerbic attacks were upon innocent young authors whose only offense was in publishing an imperfect book or one which violated a Biercian canon.

By the eighties, when he carried his "Prattle" to Hearst's paper, Bierce was still the implacable critic, but he had acquired a more appropriate adversary in the Southern Pacific and had exchanged his sledgehammer for a rapier.   These should have been his pleasantest years, if the word may be applied to one whose business was insult and abuse.   Certainly they were his most productive, for in addition to his regular column he wrote much else.   It was then that he wrote and published most of his Civil War stories, which, together with his horror stories, are the basis for much of his reputation as a writer. It was also under Hearst that Bierce achieved his greatest journalistic triumph.   When the Southern Pacific in the nineties brought up the Funding Bill, which would have postponed for ninety-nine years its reckoning with the federal treasury, the young publisher sent the old misanthrope, admittedly his ace writer, to do battle for the people against the great corporation.   Victory was his, and Bierce could exult that the pen was mightier than the pocketbook.

Subsequent years added little to Bierce's literary stature.   He continued for a time in California and then transferred his residence to the East.   Finally in 1913, old and ill and embittered, he crossed over into Mexico, making a dramatic departure from the ken of history but a glamorous entrance into the realm of fantastic legend. Most astounding rumors filtered back about his mythical deeds, none of which, however, has been corroborated under scrutiny. This mysterious denouement, along with Bierce's virtuosity as a gadfly, has deprived him of full consideration as a literary figure. The man has eclipsed the writer. His war stories, to be sure, have been praised as among the best short stories of all time, precision-built and forceful. His horror stories, though less famous than Poe's, attain comparable effects without the necessity of invoking the supernatural or the abnormal.

Bierce's greatest genius, and that for which he may eventually be recognized, was not in the short story or even in the retort discourteous. Rather it was in phrasing pithy, catchy statements of truths eternal. In verse, in doggerel, in simple phrases and sentences, or in the form of short fables, he turned out these aphorisms by the hundreds. For the production of inevitable sayings such as these Bierce had the necessary attributes. He was, as all who knew him would admit, sufficiently cynical, competent to see beneath the surface to the essential realities, and blessed with a superiority complex that encouraged him to pass judgment. In addition, he had developed an exquisite style, perfect in structure and unerring in word choice.

Such a genius, one might say, must be independent of time and place. Bierce might just as well have written proverbs for Confucius or King Solomon as for San Francisco's champagne generation. Yet it is easy to see that Bierce was encouraged by his environment. California writers of the gold rush era had established a tradition of outspokenness bordering on impertinence, and Bierce's position on Hearst's yellowing journal provided the ideal sounding board plus the necessary incentive for the grinding out of these immortal pungencies that best establish his genius. By no means a normal specimen of the second generation, he was, nonetheless, a product of it.

Colleges and Universities

Another tangible expression of the cultural interests of this generation was its development of institutions of higher learning. The state's population growth, coupled with the national tendency to put more emphasis on going to college, set the stage for such expansion.

The transcontinental railroads made it convenient for young people to go east for their schooling, and many did. Notwithstanding these "exports," from the eighties to the teens California far exceeded the rate of the nation in expanding and improving her colleges and universities.

Carried over from the gold rush epoch, there were a number of colleges and universities, so-called, among them the state university, the College of the Pacific, several Catholic schools, a state normal school established at San Francisco in 1862, and another at San Jose dating from 1871. In the ensuing years, a dozen or more sister institutions were added, the majority under denominational auspices. With a donated site in the southwestern part of Los Angeles, the University of Southern California was founded in 1879 by the Methodists. Three years later Los Angeles qualified for a branch of the San Jose state normal school, the cell from which the University of California at Los Angeles would eventually develop. In Oakland, Mills Seminary, which had been functioning for a number of years, was reinstituted as Mills College in 1885. A charter was obtained in 1887 for the Occidental Presbyterian University of Los Angeles, later simplified to Occidental College. A few months later the Congregationalists chartered Pomona College. In September, 1888, these institutions enrolled their first students. At the Quaker colony of Whittier there was talk of a college almost from the beginning. It materialized in 1901. In 1891 the Church of the Brethren launched Lordsburg College, later named LaVerne, and in 1909 the University of Redlands opened classes in the First Baptist Church.

Most of the schools founded in this period had the primary aim of providing a general education in the liberal arts tradition and of supplementing this program with teacher training. One exception was Amos G. Throop's school at Pasadena. It went through a succession of name changes from Throop University, to Throop Polytechnic Institute, to Throop College of Technology, to California Polytechnic Institute, to California Institute of Technology, meanwhile evolving into an institution with primary stress on engineering and the physical sciences. In all these institutions the achievement of true collegiate status came only gradually. For example, the University of Southern California in 1891 had 192 students enrolled in the preparatory department and only 25 in the collegiate department. Furthermore, each college started on the most meager of financing, a few acres of ground, perhaps a hotel building in which classes could meet, some town lots that could be leased or bought, and seldom more than a few thousand dollars in pledges and cash.

This being the setting, the announcement of the Leland Stanfords late in 1885 that, as a memorial to their son, they would bestow the bulk of their fortune upon a university was electrifying news. The initial conveyance was of properties appraised at six million dollars, with another million and a quarter for buildings. The Stanfords promised additional gifts and bequests, which were expected to bring the total to about thirty million. At the time, Columbia's productive capital was $4,680,590, Harvard's was $4,511,862, and Johns Hopkins' was $3,000,000. Thus the prospect was that Stanford would start as the richest of all universities.

Even this largess did not dispel skepticism that a first-rate university could be achieved. Since the peak enrollment at the University of California was only 332, experts wondered whether there would be any students at Stanford. The difficulties in getting good men to come to Berkeley, or to stay there, made others doubt that a competent faculty could be assembled at the new university. There was some awareness, too, that the strength of a university is in large degree a matter of spirit and tradition and not to be acquired overnight. The founders, however, had an inspiring model in mind— Cornell University, a happy combination of the applied sciences of engineering and agriculture and the humanistic studies. They were even more fortunate in the selection of the first president, David Starr Jordan, an icthyologist of the first water, a man of vision and initiative, forceful and compelling in expression both in writing and in speaking, at heart a poet, and an inspiring leader.

With its wealth, its dynamic head, and its fresh purpose, Stanford University was likened to a giant meteor flashing across the western firmament. Lack of students was never a problem; the 1891 registration was a surprising 490, and three years later 1,100 were enrolled and growth continued. Despite its incomparable riches, Stanford did not immediately outshine all other American universities; the law of momentum, to which universities are particularly subject, would have precluded any such result. Furthermore, with the hard times following the Panic of 1893, it looked as though the university's wealth would evaporate. Mrs. Stanford came to the rescue, drawing on the estate left by her husband to round out the now meager income from the properties previously assigned to the university. In the intellectual life of the West, Stanford quickly became an active factor. Life and study in the environment that it offered could be ennobling as well as quickening to the mind. President Jordan and members of the faculty took leading roles in public affairs. And the existence of Stanford University prompted those controlling the destinies of other California schools to hasten the improvement of their institutions.

The prime example of this type of response was in the revitalizing of the University of California during the presidency of Benjamin Ide Wheeler, 1899–1919. Aware that personal interferences by members of the board of regents had been a handicap to the institution, he conditioned his acceptance of the presidency on the board's adoption of a set of rules that he held to be "absolutely essential to the existence of anything like a proper university spirit, indeed, of a university." These were: that the president should be the sole organ of communication between faculty and regents; that the president should have sole initiative in appointments, removals, and matters of salary; and that, however divided in discussions during meetings, the board as a unit should support the president. The balancing factor did not have to be stated—that should the board lose confidence in the president, it could have his resignation.

As the real leader of the university, Wheeler built soundly. The school of commerce and the summer session were early additions. Through an open contest the university had previously gained a comprehensive building plan, the work of M. Bernard of Paris. Though never to be realized in its entirety, this plan, and the rapid increases in enrollment, inspired active building. California Hall, Boalt Hall, the Hearst Mining Building, the Agriculture Building, the Doe Memorial Library, and Wheeler Hall all rose during Wheeler's presidency. Mausoleum-like in white stone, they seemed somewhat alien to the land, especially in contrast to the warmth of tile and terracotta in the Stanford quadrangle.

In addition to his talent for rallying support for the university, Wheeler offered it his personal philosophy. The phrase in which he summed it up was "the abundant life." He wanted the students, while they were at the university, not to be superficial, and not to narrow themselves to a single specialization, but to live abundantly. He wanted them also to prepare for, and to get into the proper frame of mind for, a lifetime characterized by this same breadth and depth. In his day the University of California faculty made advances in research and taught a great many practical and useful subjects. To Wheeler, the things of greater importance were the kind of experience the students could be led to have and the outlook and inspiration that they could carry away. Therein, he was in step with Jordan and the more thoughtful heads of other California schools of his day.

In another generation, the fields of honor in a university would be the recondite and deadly sciences and the practical professions, such as medicine and engineering. Of the California faculty in Wheeler's day, it is revealing that the brightest luminaries included, and perhaps were, a professor of English and a professor of history. Charles Mills Gayley had a long and fruitful career in research and writing. His popular lectures to the public and to undergraduates were his chief glory. He developed a course on great books long before their Chicago discovery, and it soon filled the largest hall and became a campus institution. Its only rival in popularity was H. Morse Stephens' survey of the history of the Western world. Both men mingled freely with the students; Stephens, as a bachelor living at the Faculty Club on the campus, had an advantage here. He was seldom mistaken for a profound scholar, but he had a great hold on the students which persisted with the alumni. When he died, the legislature adjourned out of respect to his memory; the Student Union building is named in his honor. Gayley and Stephens arrived independently at the pattern which they gave their careers. Nonetheless, both were exemplars of the abundant life that Wheeler stressed.

29

POLITICAL REFORM

STATE POLITICS, as we took leave of it a few chapters ago, was at one of those peaks of exaltation with all problems seemingly solved. The new constitution, elaborated by the convention in 1879, contained, if not the summation of all human knowledge, at least a working compromise on the issues that had been central in the unrest of the seventies. Kearneyites and Grangers found satisfaction in the provisions for a state railroad commission and a board for tax equalization and in the prospect of Chinese exclusion. Conservatives were relieved that the whole program of the malcontents had not been carried into effect. The air having been cleared, interest in state government flagged.

Other factors prompted the disregard of state politics. For one thing, California found itself on an economic upturn. The pinch of hard times, which had contributed to urban and rural discontent in the preceding decade, was largely forgotten in the more prosperous eighties. For another, national issues absorbed much attention, what with Garfield's assassination; Arthur's Civil Service reforms; the "rum, Romanism, and rebellion" campaign, in which Cleveland squeezed in ahead of the "plumed knight," Blaine; much talk about tariffs, silver purchase, interstate commerce regulation, and trust-baiting; and international incidents concerning Venezuela, Samoa, and Hawaii.

State elections, meanwhile, seemed a subordinate branch of politics. Democrats and Republicans were alternately in office, but the margin of victory was usually slight and the distinction of party objectives not much greater. Few individuals were of sufficient importance that their names need intrude upon a general history. Washington Bartlett, who was inaugurated governor in 1887 with popularity unsurpassed, died in office just a few months later. His successor built up an unenviable reputation as the "Great Pardoner." The election of 1890 was supposed to hinge on the question of state division, but, although the southern California candidate was elected, no steps were taken toward division. Four years later James H. Budd won the governorship by emphasizing that he was young, that he was a graduate of the state university, and that he traveled by buckboard rather than railroad.

Combating the Southern Pacific

Gradually, local issues recaptured attention. As early as 1880 the settlers at Mussel Slough, near modern Hanford in Tulare County, were disillusioned concerning the effectiveness of the new constitution as a check upon the Southern Pacific. They had occupied and improved the land under what they thought were bona fide offers. On various pretexts the railroad delayed conveying title and finally quoted a price far in excess of that originally contemplated. The settlers demurred and began to organize for more effective protest. When the railroad attempted to get evictions in favor of two hired purchasers, Walter J. Crow and M. J. Hart, a clash ensued. In a few moments of gunplay Hart and five of the settlers were killed outright or given mortal wounds. Crow slipped away and hid in a wheatfield, but when he tried to climb the fence and get away he was picked off by an unidentified settler. Under indictment for resisting a United States officer, seven of the settlers were taken to San Francisco for trial. Five of them were convicted and sentenced to eight months in the San Jose jail. In the climate of opinion that prevailed, they, rather than the railroad, emerged as heroic. Several crusading novels, including Josiah Royce's *The Feud of Oakfield Creek* and Frank Norris' *The Octopus,* seized on the Mussel Slough incident as a dramatization of the burning resentment against the railroad's heartless domination.

To what extent the railroad was guilty of the many malpractices charged is difficult to say. Denunciation of big business was then the national pastime, and since the railroad was by all odds the biggest of California's corporations, it stood out as the natural target. On the other hand there was hardly an office, from the seats in the

United States Senate down through the governorship and the courts to the most inconsiderable town office, in which the right man could not do the railroad a service. Suspecting the worst, critics charged freely and proved occasionally that California was governed by the Southern Pacific machine. The railroad became the stalking horse of the demagogue and attack on it the touchstone of California politics.

Thrice in the eighties and nineties the railroad's willingness to influence government was exposed with unmistakable candor: in the publication of the Colton Letters, in Los Angeles' fight for a free harbor, and in the defeat of the Funding Bill. In the seventies David D. Colton had annexed himself to the Southern Pacific to the extent that its moguls were often referred to as the Big Four and a Half. As the phrase suggests, Colton never quite attained a parity with Stanford, Huntington, Crocker, and Hopkins; but he did enjoy Huntington's confidence, and the latter wrote to him freely and candidly about his experiences as a lobbyist at Washington. The partners went so far as to define the conditions under which Colton might join the inner circle, but at the time of his death in 1878 they were busily engaged in squeezing him out. His widow at first accepted a modest settlement, but when she saw that identical securities in the Hopkins estate were valued at a much higher figure, she charged that she had been defrauded and brought suit to recover. Mrs. Colton's lawyers got little satisfaction for their client, but they contributed much to the entertainment of the railroad baiters and to the enlightenment of historians by reading into the record letter after letter in which Huntington had described with utter frankness his methods as a lobbyist. Some 600 of these letters were spread upon the court record, ostensibly to demonstrate that Colton had been a key man in railroad councils. To the public, however, they were a devastating indictment of the railroad's chicanery.

The Free Harbor Fight

The free harbor fight is a longer story. Since Spanish days the inadequacy of the natural harbor at San Pedro had been recognized as a serious barrier to the development of Los Angeles. In the Mexican period hide and tallow traders did their largest business with the cattlemen of the district and imposed no price differential because of the atrocious harbor, but as an American city Los Angeles obviously could not go far without better port facilities. For many years

Phineas Banning was the leading advocate and almost the only advocate of action. To him are to be credited most of the federal appropriations from 1869 to 1892. Aggregating more than $500,000, they were expended upon deepening, widening, and improving the entrance to Wilmington Estuary so that vessels of eighteen-foot draft could be accommodated.

As larger ships came into service on the Pacific more heroic steps seemed to be indicated, and as early as 1881 there was a concerted demand for a large breakwater which would provide a deep-water harbor. The Chamber of Commerce endorsed the idea and the several newspapers also took up cudgels in its behalf. Whenever an influential person visited southern California the Chamber of Commerce would take him in tow and seek to impress upon him the merits of the harbor project. Senator William P. Frye of Maine, chairman of the Senate's Committee on Commerce, was such a visitor in 1889. To the discomfiture of the local boosters the Senator was not favorably impressed. He made embarrassing remarks, such as: "Where are all the ships?" "You propose to ask the Government to create a harbor for you, almost out of whole cloth!" and "It will cost four or five millions to build you say. Well, is your whole country worth that much?" As crowning insult he suggested a removal of Los Angeles to San Diego's excellent harbor. After this contretemps the harbor advocates were greatly heartened by an appropriation of $5,000 the next year to finance an investigation of possible sites for Los Angeles' deep-water harbor.

Three sites came under consideration. One was Santa Monica, which a Comstock mine superintendent and Nevada Senator, John P. Jones, had fostered as the seaport for what he thought would prove another Comstock Lode in southwestern Nevada. The ore output was not up to his expectations, and Jones was glad to sell the railroad line from Los Angeles to Santa Monica and the wharf jutting out into the ocean to the Southern Pacific. Redondo, a few miles to the south, was a parallel case. The monotony of its open beach was broken by a wharf constructed by John C. Ainsworth of Portland, and threading inland to Los Angeles was a narrow-gauge railroad. The other possibility, of course, was San Pedro. There nature had not been much more generous than at Santa Monica or Redondo, but the deep water, which a breakwater would make calm, was at least adjacent to the already improved Wilmington Estuary, and San Pedro was reached not only by the Southern Pacific but also by the Terminal Railroad, which would assure access for all competing lines.   The commission reported in favor of San Pedro and estimated the cost of the proposed breakwater at $4,000,000.

Thus far the problem of the harbor advocates had seemed to be merely that of extracting an appropriation from Congress, and in view of the pork-barrel character of the biennial Rivers and Harbors Bill this did not promise to be a hopeless task.   In 1892, however, Collis P. Huntington jolted Los Angeles from its complacency by announcing to a Senate committee that, since piles could not be driven into the rocky bottom at San Pedro, the Southern Pacific was abandoning that port in favor of Santa Monica.   Army engineers were again dispatched to examine the sites and again reported in favor of San Pedro, but the Southern Pacific continued work on its million-dollar wharf at Santa Monica.   The real explanation obviously was not any difference in ocean bottoms but that, owning all the ocean frontage below the Palisades at Santa Monica, the Southern Pacific had a sure monopoly there.

From this beginning the harbor fight widened and deepened. Huntington advised the Chamber of Commerce to abandon its "hopeless" advocacy of San Pedro, urged the Chamber to join forces with him to get an appropriation for Santa Monica, and reminded that he had "some little influence at Washington—as much as some other people, perhaps."   He revealed that eighty-three members of the Chamber had signed an endorsement of Santa Monica, whereupon a poll of the members was ordered, the result being 328 to 131 in favor of San Pedro.   Organizing the Free Harbor League, Angeleños sent a barrage of letters to quondam neighbors and friends who were now representing eastern states and districts in the national Congress.   With its population so largely and recently recruited from the East, Los Angeles was in better position to exert such pressure than almost any other city in the nation.   The Santa Fe Railroad was also a potent advocate of San Pedro.   Its $500,000,000 investment, it represented to Congress, would be jeopardized if public funds were appropriated for the improvement of Huntington's private harbor at Santa Monica.   Los Angeles newspapers, notably the *Times,* were actively engaged.   Several eastern journals were equally outspoken; the New York *World,* for example, pointedly inquired whether this was "a government for the people, or a government by Mr. Huntington, for Mr. Huntington."

The Congress of 1896 being economy-minded, a $390,000 request for inner harbor improvements at San Pedro was judged all that it was politic to ask. When the Rivers and Harbors Bill came out of committee, however, it surprisingly contained a $2,900,000 item for a deep-water breakwater at Santa Monica. In view of Huntington's well-nurtured prowess as a lobbyist this development was perhaps not so surprising after all, but it threw consternation into the San Pedro camp. The brunt of the battle was borne by Senator Stephen M. White, whose statue in consequence has long embellished the Los Angeles Civic Center. Before the Senate he berated government by special interest, debating the issue vigorously with Senator Frye, who had cast so many aspersions on Los Angeles' seagoing aspirations. The $2,900,000 was voted, but still another commission was delegated to decide whether it should be spent at Santa Monica or San Pedro. The decision again favored San Pedro, and so, with irony that was not lost on the Angeleños, the money that Huntington had extracted from a parsimonious Congress became available for the harbor he opposed.

This was the real turning point in the fight, but Huntington had not exhausted his stock of obstructionist tactics. He got the Secretary of War, Russel A. Algers, who was soon to acquire notoriety in connection with "embalmed beef," to delay the start on one pretext and then another: alleged sunken rocks at the harbor entrance, no money to call for bids, and so on ad infinitum. A Senate resolution failed to produce results, and not until President McKinley prodded him did he act. In the House in 1898 there was one more protest against the expenditure of public funds for a harbor when the Southern Pacific stood ready to build one free of charge at Santa Monica, but this suggestion was excoriated by Representative Harry A. Cooper of Wisconsin, and San Pedro was saved again. Finally, in 1899 the President touched a button that was supposed to dump the first load of rock for the breakwater. The transcontinental hookup was faulty and the rock had to be dumped by hand, but the work at last had started. San Pedro had prevailed over Santa Monica and, more important, Los Angeles' deep-water harbor was to be its own rather than enmeshed by the Southern Pacific.

In comparison with later expenditures on harbor improvement this initial appropriation was small. By 1950 the federal government had put some $36,500,000 into breakwaters and dredging and some $74,000,000 into developing Terminal Island Naval Base. The Los Angeles Harbor Commission and private interests meanwhile had invested some $66,000,000 and the City of Long Beach more than $100,000,000. Yet the beginnings and especially the manner of the start were fundamental. Establishment of a "free" harbor was an indispensable basis for the growth that has ensued.

To the railroad, the Funding Bill considerably overshadowed the harbor fight. It proposed that the thirty-year six-per-cent bonds which had secured the government's original subsidy be replaced both for principal and interest by ninety-nine year bonds at one half of one per cent. This, of course, would have been almost tantamount to cancellation, yet except for three or four impediments Huntington would probably have succeeded in putting the scheme over. One obstacle was the determined opposition of Adolph Sutro, Mayor of San Francisco. Sutro had become incensed because the street railway company of San Francisco, a Southern Pacific subsidiary, would not concede a five-cent fare to the gardens which he proposed to give to the city. More specifically against the Funding Bill, young William Randolph Hearst arrayed the power of his press. To Washington he sent acerbic Ambrose Bierce to train his brilliant and caustic pen upon Huntington and his Funding Bill. With Bierce was an expert cartoonist, Homer Davenport, who turned out a daily representation of Huntington in the act of despoiling the nation. Bierce is credited with defeating the Funding Bill, yet assists should be scored for the Colton Letters and the Los Angeles free harbor fight. The Colton Letters, likewise front-page copy, had been read into the record in various Congressional hearings. They fixed for Huntington a reputation as an unscrupulous and predatory figure. The harbor fight was a more recent illustration of the manner in which Huntington's railroad put its selfish interests above the general weal. Against such a background the Funding Bill had too rough a course to run.

At the close of the century Californians, in common with other Americans, had their attention diverted from local problems by Bryan's Cross of Gold speech, the blowing up of the *Maine,* Dewey at Manila Bay, Hobson at Santiago, and Roosevelt's Rough Riders at

San Juan Hill. Not till 1901 did the Southern Pacific become news again. By that time Huntington, last of the Big Four, had passed on to his reward, and the Southern Pacific properties were gathered up by Edward H. Harriman and merged with the Union Pacific system, which the latter had just resuscitated. This concentration of more than 15,000 miles of track under one management paralleled the rise of other gigantic trusts, the United States Steel Corporation and the Northern Securities Company, against which Theodore Roosevelt's spectacular trust-busting campaign was launched. Repercussions reached California, but meanwhile, San Francisco's municipal problems held the center of the stage.

San Francisco Prosecutes Graft

In 1901, after bitter turmoil between organized labor and the Employers' Association, a certain Eugene E. Schmitz was elected Mayor of San Francisco as the standard-bearer of a newly organized Union Labor party. Schmitz' qualifications for office were not impressive —his previous occupation being that of theater musician—but he was reëlected in 1903 and again in 1905. The admitted power behind the throne was a member of the San Francisco bar, Abe Ruef, and the Union Labor label, though still good for many votes, was something of a misnomer. Prior to the election of 1905 it was a recognized fact that the Schmitz government, or rather the Ruef machine, was in unseemly intimacy with established vice and that it was guilty of corrupt practices. Yet the would-be reformers in 1905 conducted so ineffective a campaign that Ruef not only reëlected his mayor but also carried into office for the first time his full slate of supervisors.

Throughout this half-decade San Francisco had been growing even more rapidly than California as a whole. The rate of increase was approximately 10 per cent a year. Such growth naturally meant that public utilities would expand and that in the course of this expansion they would have to make franchise and other arrangements with the city government. Ruef's machine exacted tribute from saloons, gambling houses, houses of prostitution, French restaurants, prize fights, and the like, but its more ambitious levies were upon telephone, gas, water, and streetcar companies. Ruef's hand in demanding a payoff was oftentimes strengthened by an aroused public opinion as to what sort of expansion would be best. Thus, in the case of the United Railroads Company, its proposal of an overhead trolley system was violently opposed by Rudolph Spreckels, James D. Phelan, and other leaders in wealth and civic pride, who insisted that for beauty and for fire protection their city should have the underground conduit system along with Washington and New York.

The earthquake and fire of April, 1906, reversed the population trend in San Francisco, but the rebuilding that was necessitated presented even greater opportunities for the Ruef machine. In the alleged closing of the cable slots, the United Railroads found excuse to substitute trolley lines on Market Street. Notwithstanding a wave of protest, the city fathers granted the company on May 21 a blanket franchise to install trolley lines throughout its system. This affront to the popular will, together with a sharp lapse in police efficiency and lavish expenditures on the part of Mayor Schmitz and the $100-a-month supervisors, led to a mass meeting at which the Ruef machine was denounced and then to an announcement by District Attorney William H. Langdon that charges of graft and malfeasance in office would be laid before the Grand Jury. Langdon revealed that Francis J. Heney, who had made a reputation by exposing timber frauds in Oregon, had been taken in as a special deputy to direct the graft prosecution, that William J. Burns had been retained as investigator, and that Rudolph Spreckels had agreed to underwrite the necessary expenses.

The battle royal that followed had all the elements of drama. The machine struck the first blow by having Acting Mayor Gallagher remove Langdon as District Attorney and name Ruef in his place. Langdon, however, refused to vacate the office, and Heney would not be dismissed as deputy. At the impaneling of the Grand Jury the presiding judge recognized the right of Langdon and Heney to proceed, and in another court they got an injunction against Ruef's attempt to take over the office of District Attorney.

The Grand Jury was not long in bringing in five indictments each against Ruef and Schmitz for practicing extortion against the French restaurants. Trial should have proceeded at once, but Ruef's lawyers, availing themselves of every possible stratagem, were able to delay it some three months. Meanwhile, the prosecution got proof that Ruef's henchmen, the supervisors, had taken bribes from several public-service corporations. Seventeen of the eighteen signed detailed affidavits to this effect and repeated their stories before the Grand Jury, explaining how some $200,000 in bribe money had come to them: $9,000 from the prize-fight trust, $13,350 from the Pacific Gas and Electric Company, $62,000 from the Home Telephone Company, $85,000 from the United Railroads, and the balance from the Pacific States Telephone Company and the Parkside Transit Company. Thereupon the Grand Jury returned an additional sixty-five indictments against Ruef and a lesser number against various persons for giving these bribes. On the extortion charge Ruef pleaded guilty, and Schmitz was convicted on the jury's first ballot.

Langdon and Heney next sought convictions of the bribe-givers. They were not surprised that these men brought to court an even larger battery of legal talent than had represented Ruef and Schmitz or that these lawyers again raised all possible objections to the Grand Jury that had returned the indictments. These attacks were fought down successfully in court, but not so the out-of-court campaign waged against the prosecution. Small newspapers in San Francisco and elsewhere in the state were subsidized to attack the prosecution. The San Francisco *Chronicle* came out with all manner of criticism, Hearst's *Examiner* systematically pilloried Langdon and Heney, Burns, Spreckels, and Phelan, and the Los Angeles *Times* savagely attacked Heney and his associates. Social distinctions were thrust upon the defendants—Patrick Calhoun of the United Railroads Company, for example, was inducted into the Olympic Club—and discrimination both social and economic was made operative against the prosecution.

Although the prosecution secured a conviction against Louis Glass of the Pacific Gas and Electric Company in the first bribe-giving case brought to trial, the tide turned rapidly. Tirey Ford, chief counsel for the United Railroads, was tried three times on three separate counts. The first jury divided; the other two returned verdicts of not guilty. That was about as close as the prosecution came again to getting a conviction for bribe-giving. At several elections the people of San Francisco recorded a vote of confidence in the prosecution—Langdon was reëlected district attorney in 1907; Judge Frank H. Dunne was reëlected to his office in 1909 and Judge William P. Lawlor in 1912—but the main objective of Prosecutor Heney, that of procuring punishment for the men of wealth who had done the bribing, could not be attained. Spreckels' expectation that the trail would lead to William F. Herrin, attorney for the Southern Pacific and boss of its political machine, was likewise not attained. On appeal, even the conviction of Louis Glass was reversed.

For a time it appeared that Ruef would also go scot free. The higher state courts, in decisions that must be reckoned very bad law, reversed the findings of the Grand Jury and the trial court and released both Schmitz and Ruef. The latter was immediately brought to trial on one of the bribery charges, and, when the jury divided, the process was repeated on another bribery charge. Midway in this trial Prosecutor Heney was shot down in open court by a juror whom he had challenged. In jail, this assailant was silenced by what may have been murder or suicide. With Heney unable to continue, Hiram Johnson and Matt Sullivan stepped into the breach and won a conviction. Ruef was sentenced to fourteen years in San Quentin.

Meanwhile, the prosecution was proceeding as best it could with the trial of Patrick Calhoun, President of the United Railroads. Calhoun's legal staff was even larger and more brilliant than that which Ruef had employed. To secure a jury 2,370 veniremen had to be called and 922 examined, a process that took three full months. The trial itself consumed five months and eight days, after which the jury failed to agree. The prosecution began a second trial, but before half a jury was impaneled, the election of 1909 intervened. Langdon declined to run again, and it was Heney against Charles M. Fickert for district attorney. Fickert's election was perhaps not a valid index to San Francisco's attitude toward the graft prosecution and defense, but it was so interpreted, and thereafter no serious effort was made to secure convictions of any of the defendants. Over the protests of Judge Lawlor the second Calhoun trial was terminated and the remaining indictments were dismissed.

In some respects the most striking features of the four-year program of graft prosecution had been the kidnaping of Fremont Older, outspoken partisan of the prosecution and editor of the *Bulletin;* the bombing of the house of Supervisor Gallagher, a key witness; and the courtroom shooting of Prosecutor Heney. This violence, whether or not directly instigated by the graft defendants, hampered the prosecution, even though it also enhanced it somewhat in popularity. With regard to the legal procedures themselves, a more prominent feature was the hamstringing of the prosecution by the refusal of many witnesses to testify, by the departure of witness after witness from the state, by the secreting or removal of much documentary evidence—for example, the cash book of the United Railroads—by the subornation of witnesses, and by the fixing of juries.

Yet all this pales into insignificance in comparison with the propagandist methods whereby public opinion in San Francisco was converted to sympathy for the defendants. In less than five years the determination to call to an accounting all those who had prostituted the city's government had softened into an attitude that it would be "best for business" to forget about it all. Any animosity that was left was directed against the prosecutors; they were held up to scorn as the vicious monsters. The tactics in the courtroom, in the press, in politics, in business, and in society whereby this was accomplished have been suggested. No better illustration could be asked than Fremont Older's sudden compassion for Abe Ruef and his agitation for a pardon after the latter had languished in San Quentin for twelve months. Historians also, though admitting that more penitentiary sentences would have been in order, have usually been content to gloss the conclusion over with such innocuous platitudes as the assertion that "the political atmosphere of the city was cleansed" or that there was "a renaissance of idealism." The plain fact seems to be that the political atmosphere of San Francisco remained foggy, and so important a step as the cleaning up of the Barbary Coast was left for a subsequent administration.

The Good Government Movement

Partly out of the San Francisco example and partly by independent origin, a movement for reform in municipal government cropped up in other parts of the state. In Los Angeles the spearhead was Dr. John R. Haynes. Some years earlier he had turned from medicine to real estate with substantial profit. He also had become an ardent enthusiast for direct legislation. Almost single-handedly he saw to it that Los Angeles' new city charter, adopted in 1902, incorporated provision for the initiative, referendum, and recall. The first use of the recall seemed proper enough: to remove a councilman who had voted to award the city's legal advertising to the Los Angeles *Times* even though there was another bid $15,000 lower. Nevertheless, there were staid citizens who looked upon the experiment in thoroughgoing democracy as revolutionary and dangerous.

Direct legislation was merely one facet of the push for better government in Los Angeles, and many others in addition to Haynes took part in the work.   Some of the interest in reform was traceable to the shortcomings of local officials, some to the disclosures in the muckraking literature then so popular, but much of it was in direct protest against the undisguised political control of southern California by Walter Parker of the Southern Pacific machine.   A Good Government League was organized to work for a clean-up.   In 1906 a slate of reform candidates was entered in the city election.   On 17 of 23 positions the reformers were successful, though they did not beat the machine candidate for mayor, A. C. Harper.

A year later, however, Harper was found vulnerable.   The *Herald* began an onslaught on his administration.   Editor T. E. Gibbon ran front-page editorials boxed in red, asking "Is Vice Protected in Los Angeles?"   He printed open letters to the chief of police, with diagrams to illustrate, pointing out places that ought to be raided.   The staff cartoonist did his part.   Vice, it was revealed, had been buying engraved protection certificates which purported to be stock certificates in the Pacific Sugar Corporation, the Pacific Sugar Company, the Pacific Securities Company, and the equally nebulous though less saccharine Utah-Los Angeles Oil Company.   Reinforced by the *Evening Express,* the Municipal League, and the District Attorney, Gibbon set the stage for a recall election with "Uncle" George Alexander of the city council as the reform candidate.   Two weeks before election day Harper decided that discretion was the better part of valor.   He withdrew from the race, leaving Alexander to win by a landslide, and the bottom dropped out of the market for stock of the Pacific Sugar Corporation and its peers.

Other cities indulged in lesser reforms.   Sacramento voted itself a new charter and employed the initiative to grant a franchise to the Western Pacific Railroad.   Santa Barbara and Palo Alto adopted new charters; San Francisco adopted the recall in 1907; and in several other municipalities the trilogy of initiative, referendum, and recall was made available.

The Lincoln-Roosevelt League

With so much of reform in the air locally and with Theodore Roosevelt chanting the same refrain nationally, it was natural that similar proposals should be made concerning the state government.

Provocation was not lacking. James H. Budd had given the state
a notably economical administration from 1895 to 1899, and George
C. Pardee proved his integrity and his independence of machine politics and of the great corporations during his term of office from 1903
to 1907. On the whole, however, its state government was something in which California could not take pride. The legislature pro-
gressively and inexcusably padded its payroll. Legislative elections
of United States Senators were handled on a frankly partisan basis
with every indication of venality. Machine control of nominating
conventions was particularly galling, notably at Santa Cruz in 1906,
when the Republicans summarily shelved Pardee in favor of a more
compliant tool. At this convention the most powerful boss was none
other than Abe Ruef. Additional cause for dissatisfaction was provided aplenty by the legislature of 1907, which set a new record for
wastefulness, unscrupulousness, and subservience to the machine.
Herein lay the immediate suggestion of the reform movement which
culminated in 1910, but of course the legislature of 1907, the Santa
Cruz convention of 1906, and the Senatorial deadlock of 1899 were
only surface symptoms. Underneath ran a deeper current of resentment that the state was in the grasp of the machine which the Southern Pacific had set up.

Sundry reform efforts were made in the nineties and in the following decade. Public ownership of railroads and utilities was one solution suggested, and at Fresno early in 1906 a Public Ownership
Party was launched. It proved no more successful than the Iroquois
Clubs, organized in the Democratic party and designed to coerce that
party into more progressive action. Another group of Democrats
organized the Independence League and boomed Langdon for governor in 1906, but without avail.

The next year the Lincoln-Roosevelt League took shape. Plans
were first discussed at Los Angeles by a small group assembled by
Chester A. Rowell of the Fresno *Republican* and Edward A. Dickson
of the Los Angeles *Express*. Formal organization, with Frank R.
Devlin as president, was achieved at Oakland in August, 1907.
The platform, in brief, called for: (1) "the emancipation of the Re-
publican party in California from domination by . . . the Southern
Pacific Railroad Company and allied interests"; (2) "the selection of
delegates to the next Republican national convention pledged to . . .
Roosevelt's policies"; (3) "the election of a free, honest, and capable

legislature"; (4) "the pledging of all delegates to conventions against the iniquitous practice of 'trading' "; (5) direct election of United States Senators; and (6) direct primaries for the nomination of candidates for all state and local offices.

To rouse support for this program the League depended primarily upon volunteer and personal work. Half a dozen newspapers, influential but not the largest in the state, supported the League from its inception. Besides Rowell's and Dickson's papers these included the Oakland *Tribune,* the Sacramento *Bee,* and Older's San Francisco *Bulletin.* Many smaller papers joined in, and an official organ, the *California Weekly,* was launched. Even a few Democratic papers, such as the Los Angeles *Herald,* were cordial. Reform advocates organized clubs in almost every part of the state, and speakers headed by Chester Rowell carried the campaign from one end of the state to the other.

As a first major objective the League's executive committee focused on the election of 1908 and determined to win enough seats in the legislature so that a direct primary law could be enacted. In the meantime, a few trial balloons were sent up in the shape of candidates in municipal elections, and as early as September of 1907 the first of these came in a winner: Clinton L. White, who was elected Mayor of Sacramento. The League got some valuable publicity at the special session of the legislature called in November of 1907, and the work of organizing and agitating went steadily forward.

In May of the following year the League sought to win control of the state convention to elect delegates to the Republican national convention. Since only a minority of the members of this convention were to be elected and the rest named by county conventions, the League was at a considerable disadvantage, and did well to gain something like 44 per cent of the seats in the convention. This was not enough to enable it to name the state chairman or to control the state central committee or its executive committee, but at least the League members were encouraged to continue their war against special privilege.

Seeing the handwriting on the wall, the old political bosses had allowed the legislature of 1907 to propose to the people at the election in November, 1908, a constitutional amendment authorizing enactment of a direct primary law. Heartily advocated by the Lincoln-Roosevelt forces, this amendment carried by a large majority.

The new legislature also was sufficiently Lincoln-Roosevelt that a comprehensive measure on the subject was enacted early in 1909. Since the direct primary had been regarded as the means for gaining all other reforms, there was some talk of disbanding the League. The vast majority, however, believed that the League faced an equally important task in the election of 1910.

For that campaign Hiram W. Johnson was prevailed upon to be the Lincoln-Roosevelt candidate for governor. He had built up a most successful legal practice and had greatly enhanced his personal popularity by volunteering to assist in the San Francisco graft prosecution after the shooting of Heney. He put on a whirlwind campaign for the Republican nomination, traveling some 20,000 miles by automobile, and this in a day when such travel was far more arduous than today. Everywhere he went Johnson reiterated his promise to "kick the Southern Pacific Railroad out of the Republican Party and out of the state government." He won the nomination hands down and carried with him the League candidates for almost every nomination.

Although the Democrats had elected but one governor in the preceding twenty years, they managed to make the campaign of 1910 an interesting one. The liberal faction controlled the Democratic convention and against Johnson put up Theodore A. Bell, who had been the party's national chairman two years earlier. Bell and the Democrats could insist with a measure of accuracy that they were even more progressive than Johnson and the Lincoln-Roosevelt Republicans. History, as represented in previous platforms, corroborated Bell's claim; and current intentions, as represented by the platforms of 1910, were also not unfavorable to the Democrats. There were in fact some fourteen major points on which the two parties made equally radical demands. These included: the initiative, referendum, and recall; regulation of public utilities; a nonpartisan judiciary; the Australian ballot; conservation of natural resources; segregation of first offenders in a reformatory; direct election of United States Senators; Asiatic exclusion; simplification and tightening of the administration of justice in criminal cases; government support for a Panama steamship line; government appropriations for roads, rivers, and harbors; votes for women; an income tax; and elimination of corrupt control, a euphemism for Southern Pacific machine control, of politics. With the voters it was not so much a question as to which group was sincere but as to which group would best be able to carry out the platform promises. By a margin of 177,191 to 154,835 the task was entrusted to Hiram Johnson and his Lincoln-Roosevelt cohorts.

Reforms Accomplished

To expedite the enactment of the many reform measures contemplated, the triumphant Republicans assembled immediately after the election at Santa Barbara and then adjourned to San Francisco, where a dozen committees were appointed to draft bills and constitutional amendments. Some legislators disapproved of this procedure, though a number of Democrats joined in. It served, at any rate, to give the legislature of 1911 a running start, and it went far toward enabling that body to enact, in the words of Theodore Roosevelt, "the most comprehensive program of constructive legislation ever passed at a single session of an American legislature." Even the opposition gave grudging recognition. The San Francisco *Call* continued to refer to the "Legislature of a Thousand Freaks," but the San Francisco *Chronicle* conceded that it was the most industrious legislature in the state's history and that most of the laws enacted were excellent.

Johnson deserves much of the credit. His inaugural address was a clarion call to progressives in both parties to fulfill the promises they had made. He injected a controversial note by urging that the state ballot be shortened and responsibility concentrated by instituting the appointive cabinet system for most of the state offices, and his advocacy of making the recall applicable to the governor and to all judges was also regarded as ultraradical. Under his dynamic leadership, however, the legislators set aside party jealousies. In so far as they were constitutionally empowered they enacted laws to carry into effect the Lincoln-Roosevelt program. To cover other points they initiated twenty-three constitutional amendments, on which the people voted on October 11. A short session gave effect to the amendments thus adopted.

Some of these measures, such as the workmen's compensation act and the law for the regulation of weights and measures, aimed at social betterment. Most were designed, however, to insure to the voters effective control of the government and thereby to make impossible machine-controlled corruption such as had prevailed. The creation of a new railroad commission was in some respects the most direct blow against the old regime, yet it was but one element in a much more comprehensive attack. The Southern Pacific, incidentally, made public announcement of its retirement from the political arena.

The Lincoln-Roosevelt or Johnsonian progressives continued in the ascendant for some years. In Johnson and his handpicked successor, William D. Stephens, they held the governorship for a dozen years, and throughout most of this period they had effective control in the legislature. Nevertheless, they were unable to maintain the pace set in 1911. Some legislation of importance was enacted at the next session, but thereafter the Johnson and Stephens administrations were relatively unproductive.

The main reason for this slowing down was that the Lincoln-Roosevelts had run out of ideas. By 1914 they had achieved practically complete success in translating their platform into law. Some of them envisioned other vital steps that might be taken—some, for example, were hard at work for public ownership of utilities—but the group was not agreed on a program for further action. Nor was public opinion prepared for it. Even with the most dynamic and purposeful leadership, a few years would properly have gone to consolidating the gains already made.

On top of this factor there were great distractions. In 1912 the patron saint of the League, Theodore Roosevelt, broke with the Republicans and rallied his forces as the Progressive party. Most of the California progressives went along with him. In recognition of the strength of progressivism in California, Johnson was nominated as Roosevelt's running mate on the Bull Moose ticket. Because they still had control of the Republican party organization in California, the Johnson forces were able to keep Taft off the California ballot. As a write-in candidate he ran far behind. Roosevelt and Johnson carried eleven of the state's electoral votes and Wilson picked up the other two.

Four years later, when in theory, at least, the Republican party was reunited, Johnson won the senatorship by almost 300,000 votes, but the presidential nominee, Charles Evans Hughes, ran far behind and by 3,773 votes lost the state and the presidency to Wilson. Though an eminent figure, Hughes was a man of a good deal of reserve, coldness, and conservatism. He had shown no sympathy with labor and no appreciation of the achievements of the California progres-sives.   Furthermore, when he made a campaign visit to California in August, he allowed himself to be taken completely in tow by William H. Crocker and Francis V. Keesling, Old Guard Republicans. On the train from Oregon he slighted Chester Rowell; in San Fran-cisco he ignored Mayor James Rolph; and in Long Beach, though under the same hotel roof with Governor Johnson, he did not see to it that a meeting was arranged.   The Long Beach affront no doubt was unintentional, but Hughes' complete neglect of the Johnson wing of the party was so consistent that it inevitably gave the impression of being calculated.   After the votes had been counted, the Old Guard Republicans threw the entire blame on Johnson, charging that out of vindictiveness he had not given Hughes' candidacy genuine support.   Johnson angrily retorted that the Old Guard had so mis-used Hughes and his California visit that the injury could not be undone.   Most of the contemporary and later discussion of this elec-tion concerns what might have been.   The fact most clearly estab-lished is that the Old Guard alone could not carry California.   Even with the advantage of the Republican label and of Johnson on the same ticket, Hughes needed to give more convincing demonstration of agreement with Lincoln-Roosevelt Johnsonian progressivism.

The 1916 campaign had another aftermath that illustrates a weak-ness among the California progressives.   As a political move to appeal to the southern California voters, William D. Stephens had been persuaded to run for lieutenant-governor rather than for re-election to Congress.   The understanding was that if elected to the Senate, Johnson would resign the governorship to Stephens.   John-son, however, made no move to do so in November or December. In January, when the legislature assembled, he continued as gov-ernor.   When some of Stephens' friends protested and intimated court action, it merely threw Johnson into choleric fury.   He delayed his resignation until March, when a special session of Congress was called and no alternative was left.   This was one among a number of occasions when deep rifts developed among the Lincoln-Roosevelt group.   Many, perhaps most, of these men were strong-minded indi-viduals.   Common cause had held them together for awhile.   But this was not an amalgam that would endure the fire of Johnsonian rage and vindictiveness.

For Johnson, the Lincoln-Roosevelt League was a springboard to

Governor's Mansion, Sacramento

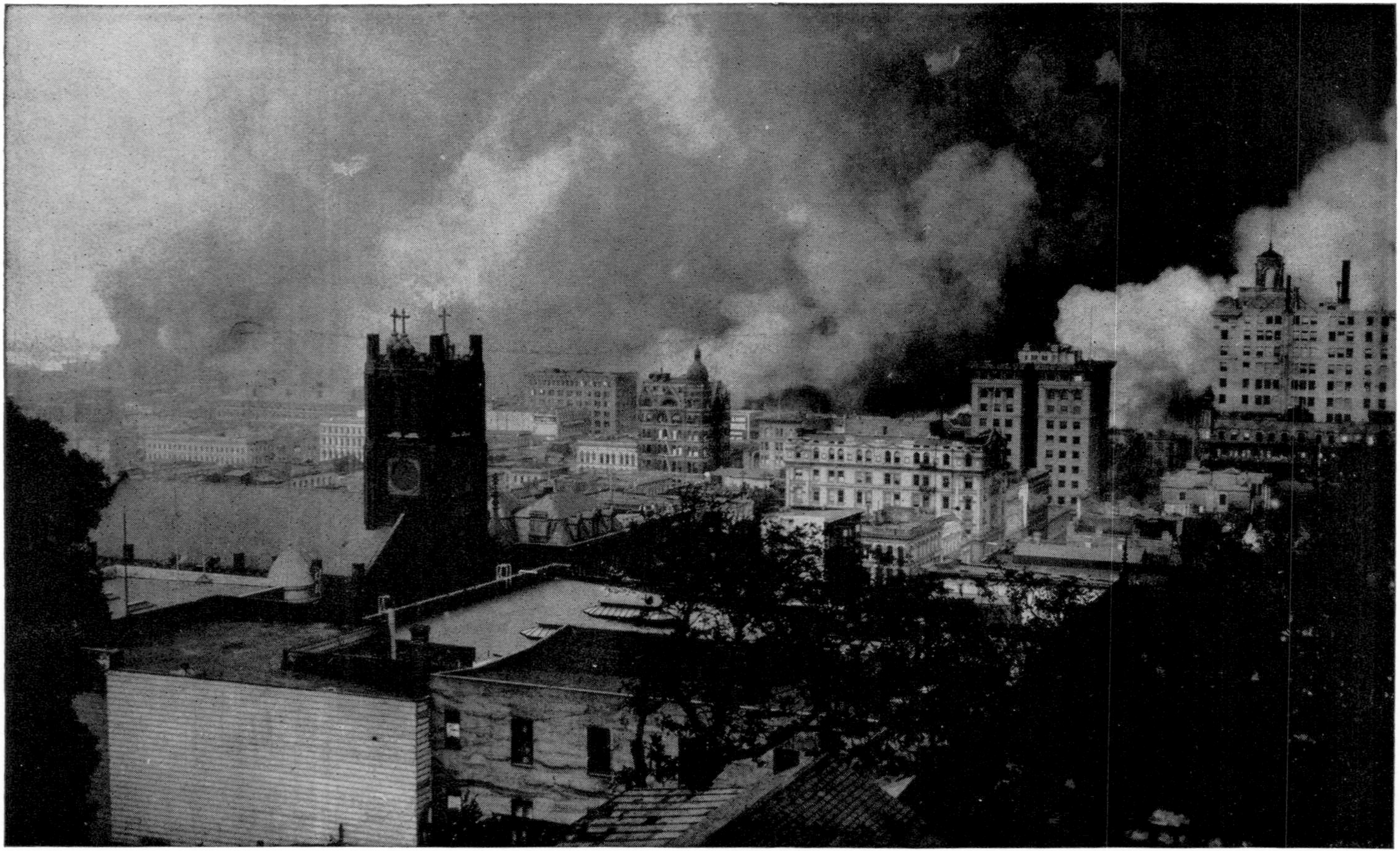

Los Angeles Title Insurance and Trust Company

the United States Senate. On the whole, however, the leaders in the League did not move on to public office. Roused to political action by the manifest abuses in California government, they organized, campaigned, and captured the Republican party, and through it the state government. With systematic determination in the legislature of 1911, they enacted their program. Incidental additions were made in the years that followed, and by momentum the group retained control of the state government throughout the decade, gradually relinquishing leadership to regular Republicans who were less or not at all progressive. Lack of a program for continuing reform, the distractions of national politics and the First World War, and a series of personal quarrels within their ranks weakened the movement, but not before it had given the state a decade of remarkably high-minded and uncorrupted government.

Lincoln-Rooseveltianism was a reform movement that captured the popular fancy with unprecedented rapidity. Here were reformers who translated their theories into practice with unusual thoroughness and efficiency. They were most astute politicians. Californians rightly took great pride in this demonstration of political acumen and statesmanship, and the nation gave it an attention not completely distracted by the fiasco of Rooseveltian progressivism or by the First World War. It stands as the high-water mark in California's record of political achievement.

30

CLASS CONFLICT

IN THE PERIOD SPANNING the turn of the century California experienced a gratifying development along almost every line. Improved transportation, expanded agriculture, and increased activity in commerce and industry yielded a substantial economic growth. The traditional bulwarks of society—the home, the church, and the school—registered noteworthy gains during this period. On the political front, too, it was an epoch of truly remarkable achievement. In the light of all these advances it is surprising and regrettable that these years are equally characterized by bitter class conflict. Some of it was racist; the greater part was in the area of labor relations and had as its crux the question "Should labor be permitted to organize?"

The Anti-Japanese Movement

One feature of this social conflict was a rising clamor for Japanese exclusion. Until the nineties very few Japanese had come to California. In that decade immigration was at the nominal rate of about 1,000 a year, but in 1900 entrants numbered 12,626, while the 1910 census showed a total of 41,356 in the state and the 1920 census a total of 71,952. Representing but 2 per cent of the total population, this racial minority may seem too trivial to have caused much concern, yet Californians worked themselves up to a high pitch of excitement; a state historian in 1922, disturbed by the influx of Japanese and other foreigners, opined that it was altogether likely that California's most difficult task would be to remain American. The state still harbored a remembrance of the long and bitter contest for Chinese exclusion, and many of the arguments that had been employed against the Celestials seemed equally applicable against the Nipponese. Peculiar and distinguishable by pigment, stature, conformity, language, and customs, they were regarded as not likely to prove completely assimilable. Furthermore, having congregated in certain localities, the Japanese were much more conspicuous than their actual numbers would have predicated.

As early as 1886, when there were only 400 in the state, the slogan "The Japs Must Go" was first voiced. In 1900 San Francisco was the scene of a mass meeting for a similar purpose. Five years later trade-union men there organized the Asiatic Exclusion League, and the *Chronicle* ran a series of articles advocating exclusion. Then, in 1906, the San Francisco school board precipitated an international incident by announcing that Oriental students, numbering then about ninety, would be segregated. President Roosevelt intervened, and the objectionable order was rescinded only to be reissued later in the year. The United States Attorney General thereupon brought action against the mayor and the school board. There was a conference at Washington, attended by Mayor Schmitz, who hoped thus to refurbish his reputation tarnished by the graft prosecution, and a compromise was effected whereby the board's order was modified.

The federal authorities, meanwhile, undertook to limit the immigration of Japanese laborers. Early in 1907 Congress legislated against the admission of Japanese from Canada, Mexico, or the United States' Pacific islands. Shortly thereafter Elihu Root and Ambassador Takahira drafted the Gentlemen's Agreement, whereby Japan promised to grant passports to nonlaborers only, or to laborers who were going to join a parent, wife, or child, resume a domicile in the United States, or take possession of a previously acquired farm. So far as California was concerned, this was a palliative rather than a solution. Smuggling across the Mexican border proceeded apace, and the agreement itself contained loopholes for further immigration. Most colorful of these was the permission for Japanese to come to the United States to join their spouses. Under this authorization picture brides by the thousand entered California. Sociologically there was much to be said for the coming of these women, for otherwise the Japanese in the state would have been virtually under sentence of involuntary bacherlorhood. On the other hand Californians denounced it as a subterfuge, stood aghast at the high birth rate among the Japanese, and protested also that the picture bride was usually another field laborer.

Much of the talk about the menace of Japanese laborers was merely window dressing. Throughout the nineties and the following decade, when they were functioning primarily as agricultural laborers, the Japanese were accepted with a minimum of distrust. They did work that white workers did not want to do and were not generally regarded as competitors. Even the San Francisco school incident was very much magnified by the supersensitiveness of Japan and did not signify a unanimous stand against the Japanese.

At the beginning of the modern period, however, the crusade against the Japanese mounted in intensity. By organizing and demanding higher pay they incurred the displeasure of their employers. At the same time they evinced an increasing tendency to switch from farm labor to farming. In the rice districts of Glenn, Colusa, and Butte counties, in the Delta area, in vineyards and orchards around Fresno and Tulare, in Los Angeles and Orange County vegetable and berry gardens, and in Imperial Valley, Japanese growers became more and more numerous. By 1920 the farmland that they owned or leased was set at 535,000 acres, much of it the most productive land in the state. This advance of the Japanese into the entrepreneur class put them into competition with established producers, and although in the agitation that followed appeal was made to the old shibboleths against coolie labor, the drive was more against the Japanese as capitalists than as laborers.

The first major salvo of the campaign was the Alien Land Law, the Webb Act of 1913. The burden of this measure was that aliens who were not eligible to citizenship would not be permitted to acquire farmland or to lease parcels of agricultural land for more than three years. Ostensibly it applied to all Orientals and to other aliens who could not or would not seek United States citizenship; practically its application was to the Japanese alone. The national authorities, as repeatedly before, became alarmed that the measure would jeopardize cordial relations with Japan. President Wilson sent telegrams to Governor Johnson and, while the bill was still before the legislature, dispatched Secretary of State Bryan to Sacramento to lobby for its defeat or modification. Despite this pressure, the legislature passed the bill and the governor promptly signed it.

Had the spirit of the act been enforced, Japanese agriculturists would soon have been squeezed out. It developed, however, that there were many ways to escape its full rigors, through indirect leasing, through the device of incorporation, and through vesting ownership in California Japanese who had already acquired citizenship. By the end of the decade the Japanese, still constituting only 2 per cent of the population, controlled more than 11 per cent of the state's agricultural land. California thereupon resolved to try again. The legislature in 1919 had before it a more stringent land law, which failed of passage only because Secretary of State Lansing represented that to offend Japan would endanger the peace negotiations at Paris. Deference to the makers of the Versailles Treaty was only a temporary staying of California action. The following year the State Board of Control published an elaborate and highly partisan report entitled *California and the Oriental,* which the governor prefaced with a fervid justification of the California attitude. Later in 1920 an initiative measure, approved by a majority vote in every county, tightened the restrictions. In 1952 the State Supreme Court belatedly ruled the Webb Act unconstitutional.

Regulation of immigration, of course, was a prerogative of the central government. Californians were not reticent about proposing national legislation, and beginning in 1911 various measures designed to achieve exclusion had been introduced in Congress. None succeeded until 1924, when Congress had under consideration a general curb on immigration. Californians, in what must be regarded as an excess of zeal, had written into this bill a provision forbidding the entrance of immigrants not eligible to citizenship. Translated into practical diction this meant no Japanese. Secretary of State Hughes urged the more diplomatic procedure of applying the same quota arrangement that was being set up for European nations, which would have worked out to admit only 246 Japanese a year. This counsel of tact, however, was set aside. Ambassador Hanihara protested that the measure would have "grave consequences." Congress took umbrage at this "veiled threat" and passed the bill promptly, and President Coolidge, though regretting the anti-Japanese clause, approved the bill as a whole. Needless to say, the Japanese entrants after 1924 were few and were considerably exceeded by the number departing. The California Japanese, however, went on increasing in number; in 1930 there were 97,456, and in 1940 there were close to 120,000.   They continued prominent in the agricultural areas mentioned above, in the operation of vegetable markets, as residential gardeners, and in the fishing industry, especially at San Pedro.

The California campaign for Japanese exclusion generated more international friction than had the earlier move against the Chinese, but it was not accompanied by so much violence.   It produced quicker action than had the anti-Chinese drive, mainly because the United States was concerned about Japanese immigration to Hawaii and the Philippines.   Most Californians in 1940 were probably content that Japanese immigration had ceased.   The more reflective, however, could not take pride in the methods whereby that end was achieved, nor did they subscribe to the alarmist arguments of the Anglo-American nativists of the teens and twenties.   As for assimilation, the nativists certainly had been in error.   True enough, Japanese blood was not disappearing in the general stream, but the more important process of cultural assimilation was running a rapid course.   By 1940 almost two thirds of the Japanese were second generation Californians and therefore citizens, Americans in fact as well as in technicality.

Other Labor Recruits

With Japanese immigration forbidden and with most of the Japanese in California preferring to work for themselves, the state's agriculturists stood in need of a new supply of cheap labor.   In the Filipinos they found such a supply providentially available, for raising the American flag over the islands had made the inhabitants nationals, if not citizens.   In 1923 some 2,426 Filipinos were brought in, and for the rest of the decade the number mounted until the total stood at about 35,000.   At first the Filipinos were regarded as very good and docile workers.   Within a few years, however, the pendulum of employer opinion swung against them.   The accumulated criticism of earlier Orientals was heaped on their heads, a few knifing affrays were magnified, and their association with white dance-hall girls was adjudged a scandal.   Violence was visited upon them, notably at Watsonville in 1930 and in the Salinas lettuce fields four years later. There was also a proposal for their exclusion, which in 1935 was achieved by indirection through a "free transportation" measure specifying that no Filipino who accepted free passage home could return to continental United States. Pursuant to this law thousands were deported.

The attitude toward the Mexicans went through a similar pattern of change. Until the late teens Mexicans were not of much significance in farm labor except in Imperial Valley, but as the older sources of labor supply were cut off or proved inadequate, an increasing dependence was placed upon Mexicans. The year 1920 is referred to as a Mexican harvest, and throughout the twenties Mexicans were the most numerous element in California fieldwork. In the late twenties, however, Congress had under consideration bills to put the Mexicans on the quota basis. With the depression, also, the cities began to object more and more to maintaining aliens on relief through the winter so that they could work on the farms for low wages during the harvest season. With federal authorities exercising a more careful supervision at the border, the number of Mexican entrants fell to a fraction of its former figure, while tens of thousands of others were repatriated—that is to say, deported.

The last group given a twirl on the vicious circle of recruitment, low wages, hard working conditions, and talk of ejection and exclusion were the Dust Bowl refugees from the Midwest. These Okies and Arkies were not Orientals, but the cycle of changing attitude toward them was almost precisely the one previously enacted with the Chinese, the Japanese, the Hindus, and the Filipinos.

While other western states, from British Columbia and Idaho to Arizona and Sonora, have felt the urge for Oriental exclusion, the experience has not been nation-wide, nor has it anywhere been so pronounced as in California. Other local issues have corresponded more closely to those of the nation, notably the one that has been the key social problem of the modern era, the relationship of capital and labor.

Labor versus Capital

Beginning with a printers' union in 1850, San Francisco added many labor organizations in the years that followed. These trade unions did much to stabilize wages and control working conditions, and they also brought to pass several items of labor legislation, including a mechanics' lien law and an eight-hour day in government work. In the troubled seventies labor's aims were unfortunately diverted to the crusade against the Chinese, but in the following decades, largely under the leadership of Frank B. Roney, attention was turned to more fundamental problems. Roney centered his efforts on the waterfront, notorious for shanghaiing and other abuses.

After a waterfront strike and a brewery strike in 1886, and one by the metal workers in 1890, Roney led in the formation of the Coast Seamen's Union in 1891. Its distinguishing features were that from its San Francisco headquarters it embraced the entire Pacific Coast, that in effect it tied together a group of unions, and that it had stability. That same year San Francisco employers organized a Board of Manufacturers and Employers as a counterpoise to unified labor. The showdown between these two groups came in a waterfront strike in 1893. Labor might have won, but the public was antagonized by a Christmas Day bomb explosion at a non-union boarding house, killing eight and injuring several others.

When the Spanish-American War and the gold rush to the Klondike gave a new basis for prosperity, labor made another effort to strengthen its position. Again the employers were equally alert. The waterfront and seagoing workers joined in the City Front Federation, which soon was countered by the Employers Council. On July 30, 1901, the Federation called a waterfront strike, and a large number of sympathetic strikes soon followed. The employers, with a war chest of $250,000, fought back. Altogether there were some three hundred assaults reported and five men were killed. After three months the strike ended in a stalemate. The net effect, however, was advantageous to labor because of the continuing strength of the unions. San Francisco became, in effect, a closed-shop city, the first in the nation. At the polls, too, the Union Labor party prevailed and held control of the city government for a decade.

Meanwhile, the scene of sharpest controversy had shifted to Los Angeles. The contest began in 1890 with a walkout of typographers on four newspapers which had threatened a 20 per cent wage cut. Three of the papers settled quickly, but the *Times,* commanded by the militant Harrison Gray Otis, would have nothing more to do with union printers. Nonunion men were imported, with the natural consequence of altercations both verbal and physical. Other unions expressed sympathy, and Otis expanded his diatribes to include not only union printers but everything that smacked of unionism. The unions attempted a boycott of the *Times* and of merchants advertising in it. Their campaign was more ingenious than effective, but against a less resourceful fighter than Otis and in a city more stable than Los Angeles it probably would have succeeded. Los Angeles was growing so rapidly that new subscribers and purchasers were constantly entering to take the place of those participating in the boycott, and the farming folk who comprised a good fraction of the increase were little disposed toward regimentation in the cause of unionism.

Taking advantage of the railroad strikes of 1893–1894, which interfered seriously with the marketing of southern California fruit crops, Otis berated the unions for their "robber rule" and "organized despotism." He did not hesitate to vilify merchants who stopped advertising in his paper, and with others of like sentiment he organized an aggressive employers' union, the Merchants and Manufacturers Association, which soon had 6,000 dues-paying members. The M. and M. had other pretexts for existence, but its primary function was to combat unionism. In this battle it obviously had extraordinary powers of coercion, particularly upon businessmen who, forgetful of their class obligations, showed a disposition to truckle to labor. Bank loans could be withheld, settlement of accounts could be delayed, orders could be diverted to other firms, and a blacklist could be employed. The structural resemblance to labor's boycott is striking, but the effectiveness was considerably greater. The M. and M., in fact, was one of the biggest guns in Otis' artillery.

Otis' pugnacious attitude was instrumental in making the Los Angeles controversy a national issue between capital and labor. There were other factors, of course, such as the wage differential as compared to San Francisco, which made Bay City employers and labor leaders desirous of seeing Los Angeles unionized, but it was largely because of the truculence of the *Times* that Los Angeles became the battle front for the nation's forces for closed shop and open shop.

Sundry strikes took place with their full complement of violence, and always with the *Times* a willing participant against the strikers. Then, in the summer of 1910 matters came to a climax with a strike of the Structural Iron Workers, in which the local union was aided and abetted by a contingent from San Francisco. Strikers and strikebreakers slugged and blackjacked each other, and when the city council passed an antipicketing ordinance and the Superior Court granted injunctions against the strikers, the police entered the fray.

Hundreds of pickets were arrested and sentenced to a fifty-dollar fine or fifty days in jail. When jury trials were demanded, however, most of the strikers were acquitted, which encouraged the unions to believe that public opinion after all was on their side. The atmosphere, meanwhile, continued tense. Otis mounted a small cannon on his automobile, and the *Times* surpassed itself in derogation of the unions. Fomenting the excitement still further, the police reported discovery of unexploded bombs planted at the Hall of Records and the Alexandria Hotel.

In this atmosphere of hate and recrimination surcharged with hysteria Los Angeles was aroused just after one o'clock on the morning of October 1 by a series of explosions, their roar audible for ten miles. The scene of disaster, it was soon discovered, was the Times Building. The explosions immediately turned the building into an inferno in which twenty men were killed and seventeen injured.

From an auxiliary plant a few blocks away the survivors got out a morning edition in which the blame for the disaster was placed squarely upon unionist bombs. Police and grand-jury investigations, as well as special reports by investigators for the mayor and the city council, supported the opinion that the building had been dynamited. Labor retorted that the basement showed no effect of dynamite's downward action, that broken windows were conspicuously absent, that escaping gas had overcome several persons in the building during the day, and that because of his "criminal negligence" in maintaining a "gas-polluted fire-trap" Otis should be tried for manslaughter. People in Los Angeles and over the country knew not what to think, whether the cause had been dynamite or gas, and the majority answered the riddle according to their previous predilections for the *Times* and the open shop, or for unionism and the closed shop.

Almost seven months later the *Times* blazoned forth with headlines announcing that the dynamiters had been caught and were en route to Los Angeles in custody of William J. Burns private detectives. Still more sensational was the identity of the men seized: Ortie McManigal and J. B. McNamara, apprehended in Detroit, and J. J. McNamara of Indianapolis. McManigal and J. B. McNamara were well-known union men, while J. J. McNamara was secretary of the Structural Iron Workers' Union. The *Times* did not play up the method of the seizure of the first two in Detroit, their conveyance to Chicago, and irregular extradition from Illinois, or the irregularities surrounding the extradition of J. J. McNamara from Indiana. Union

sympathizers over the nation, however, well remembered the kidnaping of three other labor leaders in 1907 and their arraignment
for a dynamite murder in Idaho. Prosecuted by William E. Borah
and defended by Clarence Darrow, these men had been acquitted
after a sensational trial. The secret arrest of the McNamaras had all
the earmarks of another "capitalist conspiracy" and was denounced
as such by Samuel Gompers of the American Federation of Labor,
by Eugene V. Debs of the Socialist party, and by numerous other
national figures.

Needless to say, the ensuing trial was much more than a personal
and local issue. The American Federation of Labor retained Darrow to conduct the defense, and by appropriation and private dona-
tion union labor and its adherents supplied him with a quarter of a
million dollars. The prosecution, similarly, had ample financial
support from such organizations as the National Manufacturers'
Association as well as from local interested parties. In addition,
the trial had a political hookup. Job Harriman, attorney for the
local labor council and an associate in the McNamaras' defense, was
running for mayor of Los Angeles on the Socialist ticket. His
candidacy was inextricably bound up with the insistence that the
McNamaras were victims of an iniquitous conspiracy. Furthermore,
victory in Los Angeles would be of inestimable value as a stimulant
for the rising trend toward Socialism then sweeping the country.

In October, 1911, the trial of J. B. McNamara at last got under
way. Neither side seemed anxious to hasten its course. Darrow,
according to the statement subsequently recorded in his autobiography, was convinced before the trial had started that his clients could
not be saved. Delay, however, would enhance the Socialist-Labor
chances in the election, while the prospect of Darrow's cross-exami-
nation of Otis and others was by no means reassuring to the prosecution. Consequently, though there was nothing on the surface to
indicate it, settlement out of court seemed the best solution for both
sides. Through the mediation of Lincoln Steffens a bargain was
struck, and on December 1, to the stupefaction of all who were not
in on the secret, the McNamara brothers appeared in court and
changed their pleas to guilty. On the third they were sentenced,
J. B. to life imprisonment and J. J. to fifteen years.

Just why the defense took this course is not entirely clear. For
Socialism and for organized labor it was a most bitter blow. Instead
of being swept into office as he confidently expected, Job Harriman

was hopelessly snowed under in the Los Angeles election. Socialist candidates elsewhere were adversely affected, and the Socialist party has never regained the strength or promise that it enjoyed prior to the McNamara confession. For the next twenty or twenty-five years the same can almost be said of the American Federation of Labor. For Socialism and for the union, conviction without confession would have been a more satisfactory outcome, for then many would have believed that the brothers were really innocent. Darrow doubtless realized all this, but he may have believed it the only way to save his clients from the gallows. The McNamaras may have thought so too, for some most sinister rumors were being circulated—as of a Burns dictaphone installed in Darrow's office—and to this day it has not been revealed how conclusive was the proof which the prosecution had amassed.

The McNamara case still has many mysterious angles. It is impossible, for example, to reconcile the statements in the McNamara confession with the description of the planting of the bomb as elaborated in the *Times* or with the version vouchsafed to the *Saturday Evening Post* twenty years later. The participants in the deal that led up to the confession, though voluble on some points, have been close-mouthed about the most essential features and to a considerable extent have carried the secret with them to their graves.

The evidence is clear, at any rate, that the bargain turned out to be more one-sided than had been expected. The prosecution made no recommendation of leniency; the judge, who had been a party to the bargain and whom Steffens had advised to speak to the defendants "as one criminal to another," instead denounced them bitterly and sentenced J. J. to fifteen years instead of the expected ten. Los Angeles capitalists, furthermore, did not take the steps of which Steffens had been so confident toward establishing a peaceful understanding with labor. With the wind taken out of the sails of the labor movement, the employers pushed their advantage and were able to keep Los Angeles for some years longer the stronghold of the open shop.

The I. W. W. and Mooney

Even before the McNamara case monopolized the headlines the Industrial Workers of the World had invaded California. Ridiculed as the "wobblies" and attributed the slogan "I Won't Work," the

I. W. W. was well fitted to implant ideas of labor organization in fields that the trade unions had thus far neglected. Organizers, drifting south from the lumber camps in the Northwest, found willing listeners in California mine and lumber crews and in the agricultural labor gangs. Most of the workers involved were relatively unskilled, which placed them outside the preferred province of the American Federation of Labor and made a union's effectiveness uncertain, but the wobblies were not daunted.

In 1910 their local at Fresno took umbrage at interference with I. W. W. meetings and launched a fight for free speech. The technique was simple. The wobblies got themselves arrested singly and in groups until the jail could hold no more. Wobbly endurance and willingness to absorb punishment were pitted against the capacity of the law enforcement agencies and the patience of the community. Capacity and patience were exhausted first. Anti-wobbly demonstrators burned the I. W. W. headquarters, and the police, exasperated by the wobbly ritual of singing in jail, tried to silence it with a fire hose. After months of strife, Fresno made partial concessions.

Two years later the I. W. W. mobilized for a similar campaign against San Diego. There were very few wobblies in the vicinity and only a few thousand in the entire state, but, summoned by grapevine and moving in by boxcar, they rapidly converged on the city to reenact the Fresno routine of getting arrested and going to jail. The San Diego police meted out rough treatment; one of the jailed wobblies was kicked to death. With police encouragement a vigilante group rounded up several hundred wobblies, ran them through a gauntlet, and drove them away. Governor Johnson then sent an investigator to the scene, and after a time the state lent its support to the principle of free speech. These free speech fights demonstrated the fanatical devotion of the wobblies to their cause. This fanaticism in turn gave them influence, especially among unskilled labor, out of all proportion to their numbers.

A case in point was the Wheatland riot in August, 1913. On the Durst hop ranch near Wheatland some 2,800 workers were camped in unspeakable filth and discomfort. They had been recruited by advertisements for twice as many pickers as were needed, were paid wages that fluctuated between seventy-eight cents and a dollar a day, were gouged by a company store, and were detained in the camp by a 10 per cent holdback on their wages. At that, conditions were not unlike those that had prevailed for years in California farm labor camps. In this camp an I. W. W. local was formed by some thirty men. On August 3 they called a meeting for the purpose of demanding better living conditions. As the meeting closed, a sheriff's posse, accompanied by the district attorney, arrived on the scene and attempted to arrest Blackie Ford, the I. W. W. leader and spokesman. A shot in the air, fired "to sober the mob," started a riot in which the sheriff, the district attorney, and two workers were killed and many others injured. Most of the workers fled the camp. The National Guard was ordered out and patrolled Wheatland for a week, while the Burns operatives combed the state for wobblies. How many were arrested no one has been able to compute because many were jailed without proper booking or were held privately by the Burns detectives. Herman Suhr, an associate of Ford's who had left the camp before the riot, was seized in Arizona, popped into a box car, and without formality of extradition was shipped back to California. Eight months later Ford and Suhr were convicted on charge of murder and sentenced to life imprisonment. Though less famous, they are more genuine martyrs to labor's cause than the McNamara brothers could have been.

The Wheatland tragedy did call attention to the dire plight of California's agricultural laborers. The state government was stimulated to begin regulation of labor camps. A Commission on Immigration and Housing was created with Simon J. Lubin as chairman, and working and living conditions were somewhat ameliorated. Another episode conducive to greater public attention to the problems of the unskilled and seasonally unemployed workers was the march of Kelley's Army on Sacramento. Modeled on Coxey's Army, Kelley's 1,500 encamped at Sacramento to demand "charitable assistance." They were greeted instead by a pick-handle brigade, were driven across the river, had their blankets burned, and were denied further access to the city.

The First World War, meanwhile, was exerting new influences on labor-capital relations. In all quarters the tendency was to identify strikes with breach of patriotism. In Los Angeles, however, the war years witnessed a strengthening of unions, perhaps because business leaders were more interested for the nonce in reaping profits than in keeping labor in check. In the north the war years were chosen as the time for a new campaign for the open shop, this time in the guise of a preparedness measure. This, in brief, was the psychological setting for San Francisco's Preparedness Day bombing on July 22, 1916, with its toll of ten lives.

The arrest and conviction of Tom Mooney and Warren K. Billings are in the category of common knowledge, and still more so is the twenty-two year struggle to obtain Mooney's release, for this has been the ranking labor cause célèbre of the nation. For Mooney the death penalty was fixed, but under a deluge of protests, including a strong suggestion from President Wilson, Governor Stephens commuted the sentence to life imprisonment. Labor partisans had little doubt that the case had been a frame-up, and as defense attorneys proved that prosecution witnesses had been guilty of perjury, an increasing number of persons became convinced of Mooney's innocence. Although the majority of the prosecution staff recommended pardon and the trial judge and jury publicly retracted their decision, every effort of the defense attorneys to get a reversal or a new trial met with failure. California governors also refused pardon until Culbert L. Olson took office in January, 1939. Then, at last, Mooney won an unconditional pardon. Billings presumably was no more guilty than Mooney, but as a "second offender" he was not eligible for pardon. Nine months later by commutation of sentence he also was released.

Anent Mooney, the hard-hearted have insisted that he was worth more to the labor cause in San Quentin than out. Be that as it may, his detention there long after it was clear that he had been convicted on perjured testimony was certainly not advantageous to the anti-union cause; the gentlemen of this persuasion might better have exerted their influence for his release.

Criminal Syndicalism and the Decline of the Unions

Immediately after the First World War the American people entered a period of particular hysteria. The tensions of the war were partly responsible. Resort to dynamiting as a means of persuasion toward unionism was another factor, as was the I. W. W.'s practice of sabotage, and by easy extension all Socialists were assumed to be anarchists and nihilists. With the Russian Revolution of 1917 engineered by men presumed to be of the same stripe, social conflict in America acquired an international overtone which suggested that world upheaval was the menace to be feared. The infamous Palmer raids and the unseating of the Socialist members of the New York legislature are two well-known consequences. California fell in with the hysteria with her accustomed vigor and, as might have been predicted in terms of prior episodes of social conflict, aimed retaliation primarily against unionism.

As modus operandi, the state legislature in 1919 enacted a criminal syndicalism law similar to the one with which Idaho had led the way two years earlier. The act defined criminal syndicalism in dragnet fashion as "any doctrine or precept advocating, teaching or aiding and abetting the commission of crime, sabotage . . . , or unlawful acts of force or violence or unlawful methods of terrorism as a means of accomplishing a change in industrial ownership or control, or effecting any political change." In terms of the act, guilt attached equally to doing the deed, advocating it, or belonging to an organization that advocated it. Penalty was set at imprisonment for one to fourteen years. The California act bore general resemblance to those legislated by some twenty-one states, mostly western, and by Alaska and Hawaii. Elsewhere the acts soon became dead letters, but in California there was rigorous enforcement. In the first five years 531 persons were arrested, 264 were brought to trial, and 164 were convicted.

The most widely noted criminal syndicalism prosecution was of a respected philanthropist, Anita Whitney. In 1919, when her Socialist party local broke off and joined the Communist Labor party, she went as a delegate to a state convention in Oakland. At the convention, which was open to reporters and the public, she took a strong stand against revolutionary unionism and in favor of working for reform through the ballot. The state convention, however, voted a preference for the other method. It also gave pro forma approval to the national convention's program, which in passing included endorsement of the I. W. W. Three weeks later Miss Whitney was arrested for violation of the criminal syndicalism law.

In the protracted trial the bulk of the evidence adduced concerned alleged atrocities committed by the I. W. W. On the basis of her attendance at the state convention of the Communist Labor party, which approved the national convention's program and thereby endorsed the I. W. W., she was convicted of the felony of association with a group which advocated, taught, or aided and abetted criminal syndicalism. Appeals kept this case in court until 1927, when the

United States Supreme Court by a split decision upheld the conviction. More impressed by the dissenting opinion of Justice Brandeis, and convinced that Miss Whitney, "lifelong friend of the unfortunate," was "not in any true sense a criminal," Governor C. C. Young decided that "to condemn her to a felon's cell" was "absolutely unthinkable." Instead, he issued a pardon.

Practicing idealists from the upper strata could be caught in the toils of the criminal syndicalism act. Members of various unions as well as of left-wing political groups were in jeopardy of it. Its most frequent targets, however, were the I. W. W. members. They comprised the bulk of the persons arrested, tried, and convicted. In the free speech fights, on charges of sabotage, and on other charges, the wobblies had seen a good deal of the courts prior to the enactment of this particular law and on the whole had little confidence in them. They seldom carried their disdain so far as the fifty-three "Silent Defendants," indicted earlier in 1919 for mass trial at Sacramento, who declined to attempt any defense. Many a wobbly, however, pleaded his own case, and, even when there was counsel, the main batteries of legal talent were always with the prosecution. In these trials it became almost impossible to present defense witnesses, whereas the prosecution again and again relied on Elbert Coutts, W. E. Townsend, and John Dymond, professional witnesses. Furthermore, in the temper of the times mere membership in the I. W. W. or association with it was regarded as felonious. Ease of obtaining convictions undoubtedly explains the frequency with which this particular charge was brought.

In 1923, when the I. W. W. called a waterfront strike at San Pedro, the immediate response was to invoke the criminal syndicalism law against the strike leaders. Attempts to suppress the strike by direct action followed. There were wholesale arrests—one haul was variously estimated at 700 to 1,200 men taken off to stockades in Griffith Park. When Upton Sinclair came to a strike meeting and started to read the Constitution of the United States, he was arrested and held in jail for twenty-four hours. Within a month the strike was called off.

Resentment against the I. W. W. continued; in fact, mounted. In March, 1924, the Ku Klux Klan demonstrated against it. Other incidents followed, including a sacking of the I. W. W. headquarters, a vigilante assault on a benefit party, in which a number of children

were beaten and tortured, and a tarring and feathering of several of
the leaders.   After 1924, the I. W. W. ceased to be a power at San
Pedro, though its influence lived on in other waterfront and maritime
unions.   Its hold on farm and forest laborers also declined rapidly,
partly because of pressures from without and partly because of dissensions within.

At about the same time, public opinion took a turn against the
criminal syndicalism statute.   J. W. S. Butler, president of the State
Bar Association, David Starr Jordan, Max Radin of the University
of California Law School, and other responsible citizens urged its
repeal.   It was not removed from the statute books, but, after 1924,
actions under it ceased for the time being.   The major reason may
well have been that the I. W. W. was no longer the threat it once had
seemed to be.

Throughout the twenties the general tenor of labor-capital relations was one of greatly diminished strength for unionism.   Following the defeat of a waterfront strike in 1919 and a building trades
strike in 1921, San Francisco was more open shop than closed.   In
Los Angeles, unionism declined at about the same rate, and some of
the concomitant features eclipsed the plain fact.   The meretricious
label "American plan" supplanted the term "open shop," the menace
of Red Russia was taken very seriously, property rights were exalted
as the citadel of patriotism, and organizations such as the Better
America Federation made anti-liberalism and anti-unionism the prime
virtues.   The decade ended with unionism and liberalism at low ebb.

31

PROSPERITY

SINCE THE GOLD DISCOVERY gave its fillip, California has
enjoyed a practically uninterrupted growth. There have been intervals of hard times, such as in the nineties, but every successive census
has shown a population increase and the other indexes have moved
constantly upward. More dramatically, the steady climb has been
punctuated by spurts of very rapid growth. One such was touched
off by gold; another came with the boom of the eighties; still another
arrived in the aftermath of the First World War and was most pronounced in the twenties.

In 1914 the state's population stood at less than three million.
By 1930 it was five and two thirds million, by 1940 just short of seven
million. The statistics on bank clearings, postal receipts, freight shipments, property assessments and tax receipts, building permits, crop
harvests, and industrial production advanced even more. This rapid
growth, furthermore, involved a wholesale transformation. By 1940
the majority of Californians lived in dwellings constructed within the
quarter century, did business in buildings equally recent, and moved
about on a network of paved streets and highways that had not existed
in 1914. For a few commodities like gold, wheat, and beef, the
aggregate totals for pre-1914 production were not matched in the
span between 1914 and 1940. For other old stand-bys, including
oranges, walnuts, wines, and deciduous fruits, the output of this
quarter century surpassed that of all the preceding years. For another long list, including cotton, moving pictures, head lettuce, airplanes, and raisins, the years this side of 1914 are the only ones of

importance.   These new products suggest that the economic development of this more recent period was not a mere automatic outgrowth
of the processes initiated by the historic heroes from Serra and Anza
to Stanford and Huntington.   The new era gave promise of earning
eventual recognition as the most significant thus far in the pageant of
local history.

The Automobile Age

The new day is perhaps best characterized as the automobile age.
The preceding years, it will be recalled, had belonged to the railroad; now the motor car was in the ascendant.   In car manufacture
California lagged far behind Michigan and its neighboring states and
consequently did not generate any great corporation of its own comparable to the Central Pacific-Southern Pacific Railroad.   Through
local emphasis on designing and building racing cars it did contribute
to the evolution of the automobile.   In the matter of using the new
machines, furthermore, Californians yielded to none.   Here the contributions are even more notable, including the center line that bisects
highways the world over and the automatic traffic signal that also has
become universal in distribution.

As the most avid of car users, Californians geared their culture to
the machine in a degree unexceeded.   Los Angeles citizens, to cite
one example, became more dependent upon their private automobiles to get to their work and their play than the inhabitants of any
other city, while the University of California at Los Angeles earned
the doubtful distinction that a larger fraction of its faculty and students
drove daily to and from its campus than was the case with any other
reputable university.   In 1936 California exceeded even New York in
the number of fatalities charged to the automobile.   Pleasanter clues
may be mentioned.   Radio came to the state virtually as an automobile accessory, with the first large stations controlled by the Packard and Cadillac distributors, while an automobile club organ, *Westways,* took rank as the best California monthly.

This enthusiastic reception came in spite of the fact that acquisition and operation of automobiles was not entirely easy.   California
car registrations were surprisingly large in view of the price differential of $150 to $300 maintained against western purchasers under
the guise of rail freight charges from Detroit.   Even after assembling
plants were put in operation at Oakland, Long Beach, and Los An-

geles this charge was maintained. California's urban parking facilities were by no means ideal, her streets were originally laid out for horse and buggy traffic, the San Francisco Bay barrier to vehicular circulation was conquered only in part by ferries and bridges, and after a quarter century of construction the state's network of paved highways was still less extensive than those of several more compact states, New York, Illinois, Pennsylvania, and Ohio.

Offsetting these disadvantages were numerous favorable conditions, in particular the benign climate, which imposes no closed season for automobile use. Large-scale production of petroleum made for a reasonable gasoline price. A most conservative height limit for office buildings and the preference for individual houses rather than apartments promoted in Los Angeles a tendency to spread out. In this city and elsewhere throughout the state, population grew more rapidly than existing systems of public transportation could be expanded to meet the demand, and dependence on private automobiles seemed a simpler solution. The automobile, at any rate, became an integral element, if not the dominant note, in the California scene.

Many of the consequences seem to have been inevitable, or were so much a part of the national experience that they need not be voiced. Every American soon took it for granted that a large fraction of any city's police force would be assigned to traffic duty, that state troopers, officers, or rangers would patrol the highways by motorcycle, that state and local governments would spend more for highway construction and maintenance than for any other function except public education and perhaps relief, and that there would be a garage with every house and a filling station at every other corner. California lived up to this standard, if not beyond it, and when a historian or sociologist finally arises to assess the role of the automobile in American civilization, this state should provide many of the more striking illustrations.

Passing notice should be accorded several industries subsidiary to the automobile. Such a one is the manufacture of Portland cement. This product, of course, has a variety of other uses. It goes into sidewalks and foundations, by the carload into steel-skeletoned business blocks and factories, and by the trainload into such structures as Boulder Dam. Nevertheless, it was the demand for paving material that maintained California cement manufactures a comfortable second to Pennsylvania's, with annual production at times mounting as high as 13,000,000 barrels.

Advertising California

Advertising of the booster sort, often branded as ballyhoo, was another prominent characteristic of the interbella period. Earlier enthusiasts, newspaper editors, railroad land agents, and chambers of commerce had established a tradition of proclaiming California's advantages. Such organizations as Californians, Inc., and the All-Year Club expanded this art and got city, county, and state funds allotted to finance such promotion efforts. Whereas the stress was once upon getting agriculturists to move to California, the emphasis now shifted to persauding industries to locate new plants on the west coast, opening new markets for California products in the East or abroad, bringing conventions to California cities, and promoting tourist travel into the state. The time-honored devices of illustrated brochures, special editions of newspapers, and dissemination of booster literature continued, and in the moving pictures those who would make California appear at her most glamorous found an invaluable ally.

Two other advertising mediums proved effective. One was through annual celebrations such as Santa Barbara's summer fiesta, the Salinas rodeo, and the San Bernardino Orange Show. Most famous and most successful of these were Pasadena's Tournament of Roses and the Rose Bowl game, the latter flattered by imitation all across the continent. Special celebrations, though less numerous, were even more pretentious. In beautiful Balboa Park, San Diego staged the Panama-California Exposition in 1915. San Francisco concurrently celebrated the completion of the canal with an even larger display, the Panama-Pacific Exposition. In 1932 Los Angeles was host to the Olympic Games, and in 1939 and in 1940, on an island created for the purpose in the bay just north of Yerba Buena, San Francisco signalized the completion of her great bridges with the Golden Gate International Exposition. How many visitors were brought to the state by these special attractions would be difficult to measure, for the standard inducements such as Yosemite and the big trees, Death Valley, Catalina, San Francisco, and Hollywood drew large numbers even in exposition years.

In the longer view, the fairs and the parades were but surface waves on a much deeper current. They were for the most part merely excuses to visit California, and probably second in frequency of effectiveness to something much more prosaic, the excuse of visiting friends or relatives. With California's population drawn so largely from outside its borders, the number of persons who could avail themselves of this excuse was legion. For some, doubtless, it was the real reason for a trip to California; for a larger number, however, the impulse was more profound. The majority set out not merely to see Treasure Island or Uncle Henry but for a look at Hollywood and Yosemite, for a taste of the California sunshine, a glimpse of orange trees in blossom and in fruit, and for a sample of the life abundant for which California had become a synonym. Thus did advertising bear fruit, or, if you please, the truth come into its own. For a quarter century, at any rate, one of the steadiest and most profitable California crops was the tourist crop. As in the preceding generation, those who visited were very apt to want to stay, and tourists thus were important not only for the money that they spent and for the business that they created, but also for their contribution to the increasing permanent population.

These elements were among the more conspicuous characteristics. It may be objected that they are unsubstantial, that the state was not assured of prospering just because hordes of persons came flocking in, because the whole population was seized with a frenzy for gadding about in motor cars, because advertising budgets reached new highs, or because the state's recreational opportunities gained wider recognition. As a matter of fact, these elements form a sounder economic base than might be assumed. Although Californians could hardly make a living by washing one another's cars, with so large a population it was natural that hundreds of thousands should be engaged in the service occupations as grocers and haberdashers, as druggists and bankers, as salesmen and clerks, as lawyers, teachers, physicians, dentists, and barbers. Thanks to the funds of the tourists and to a considerable income from investments outside the state, California could afford a larger budget for "non-productive" service and distribution than the average commonwealth. Enterprises unquestionably "productive" more than kept pace.

First Place in Agriculture

Among these the advance of agriculture is noteworthy. In 1909, a representative year toward the close of the second generation, the total value of California field crops was calculated at $95,757,000 and of fruit crops at $48,718,000. By 1937 the total figure had advanced to $648,200,000, which put California first among the forty-eight states. This phenomenal advance was achieved through far-reaching alteration of the crop list and by innovations of method in several of the older branches of agriculture. Certain crops, such as the grains, shared in this advance hardly at all. Others, like potatoes, sugar beets, and alfalfa, advanced as much as 150 per cent in the three decades, but without keeping pace with the industry as a whole. Most of the increase is accounted for by expansion of orange raising and wine production and by several crops that had been insignificant prior to 1914.

The California orange since the seventies had been the winter-ripening navel, but early in the new century growers began to set out Valencias. The new variety possessed several points of superiority, not least of which was that it ripened in the summer when the nation's appetite for cool drinks was at its best. The two varieties made available a year-round supply of California oranges, which fell in line admirably with the marketing program of the Fruit Growers' Exchange. By the early twenties the Valencia had caught up with the navel and thereafter the gain continued steadily until in 1936 the acreages were 143,000 and 88,000, respectively. In 1909 the value of the orange crop was put at $12,000,000. In the thirties, despite adverse prices, there were several $100,000,000 years, and acreage and total production still increased.

Most of the expansion of orange plantings was predicated on uninterrupted prosperity. When the depression of the thirties slashed prices 60 per cent or more, the growers faced serious difficulty. A satisfactory remedy was not easy to find. Production costs, including irrigation, fertilizing, spraying, and orchard heating, were more or less fixed, and production itself was not subject to annual control by such devices as plowing under every fourth row. The Exchange continued its efforts to expand the market, but the main reliance was upon the prorate, a device to regulate the quantity of fruit offered for sale. By this method, which entailed destroying quantities of good fruit, the industry bolstered its price structure, though according to the growers' definition, prices were still too low. It is a narrow and artificial view, however, to judge an industry solely in terms of the money value of its product. The more significant criterion for the orange business is its phenomenal increase in acreage, production, and consumption, not only in the prosperous twenties but also in the hard times of the thirties.

On a smaller scale the walnut growers enacted the same drama. From very modest beginnings in the pre-war era they expanded their plantings so that the annual crop approached 100,000,000 pounds. This, they found, was somewhat more than could be marketed, and through their Exchange they, too, attempted to set up a prorate to peg the price above the cost of production. In size, the walnut industry compares with the orange industry approximately as does a walnut with an orange. The walnut, however, is not to be despised; 100,000,000 pounds of walnuts is a considerable quantity, surpassing in value the total crop production of New Hampshire, Vermont, Rhode Island, Delaware, Nevada, or Wyoming.

Viticulture ranked as the second branch of California agriculture. Building upon the Spanish foundation and benefiting from the new varieties imported by Agoston Haraszthy in the fifties and from the experience gained by the pioneer vineyardists in succeeding decades, the industry became one of California's most distinctive and at the same time most successful. At the outset of the modern period the Eighteenth Amendment threatened the vineyardists with ruin, for up to that time by far the largest fraction of California grapes had gone into wine. Long before repeal the wine market was recaptured through the sale of "grape concentrate" and "wine bricks" from which wine of a sort could be concocted in the home.

Meanwhile, the vineyardists set out to sell their produce in two other guises, as table grapes and as raisins. The former had long been esteemed in the local markets; now refrigeration and rapid transit made it possible to whisk them across the continent to eastern markets. Raisins, on the other hand, had been so indifferent in quality that they were practically unmarketable. Dried grapes was their unappetizing name. A modern triumph of the industry was in the introduction of better methods of manufacture, and in stimulation of sales under the Sunmaid label and organization. Science was enlisted to assist other branches of viticulture, particularly for the improvement of wine-making processes, and the gains were less spectacular, chiefly because the start was not from zero as with raisins. By the late thirties, wine grapes, table grapes, and raisins brought

California vineyardists an annual income of approximately $50,000,-000. In 1937 the state produced almost two and a half million tons, or 90 per cent of the nation's total.

The list of crops in which California by that time led the nation is by no means ended. In fruits for canning and drying she was easily first. The peach crop exceeded the total for the next ten states on the list, and domination in apricot production was still more pronounced. The pear crop was a trifle larger than the Oregon-Washington total and almost as large as the total for the other forty-five states. The prune, once regarded as being as plebeian as the dried apple, was another California specialty. Production mounted steadily throughout the thirties as well as the twenties until the annual output reached half a billion pounds. At the same time, improved techniques in drying made the prune a much more delectable morsel and removed much of the stigma that used to be attached to it.

Although they doubtless will never rise to first place in national production, California apples moved into the ten million dollar class in the twenties. The potentialities appeared greater for certain subtropical fruits. Figs had been raised for many years. The date palm was introduced by the Spanish missionaries as a decorative tree, but commercial plantings were of little significance until this century. The avocado, a still more recent importation from Mexico, gained popularity rapidly. Miscellaneous groves of olives, almonds, cherries, and the like aggregated still another ten million dollars annually. The grand total was a diversified yet specialized fruit industry comprising almost half of the state's agriculture.

In the production of field crops, likewise, phenomenal expansion characterized the period. Truck gardening, which had flourished earlier for the supply of the local market, led in the expansion. The state's increased population and the trend toward a larger per capita consumption of vegetables would have permitted a trebling of production. That the increase was much greater was because a nation-wide market was opened by the twin devices of canning and refrigeration. Canneries operated before 1914, but with disturbing uncertainty as to the quality of output. Only more recently were processes perfected to insure standardized and palatable products. Refrigerated cars to make possible Atlantic seaboard delivery of Salinas Valley lettuce, Imperial Valley cantaloupes, or Tagus Ranch pears were a new facility. On this multiple basis California advanced to first place in production of tomatoes and lettuce, asparagus and artichokes, cantaloupes, carrots, cauliflower, celery, peas and garlic. Truck farmers were assisted no little, it must be admitted, by California's long season which makes possible several harvests, by the early season which gives her first call on the eastern markets, and by the boon of irrigation which accounts for much of the uniformity in size and the attractive appearance of California vegetables.

In the Sacramento Valley, Japanese introduced the cultivation of rice. The acreage was smaller than in Louisiana, Texas, or Arkansas, but the yield per acre was the highest in the United States and placed California third in production. In 1937 the harvest exceeded 10,000,000 bushels. The reclaimed swamp land on which the rice plantations were located soon ranked with the most valuable farm land in the state.

Another lusty upstart was cotton. Experiments had been made in the sixties and seventies but with disappointing result. In 1910 a fresh attempt was made with a new variety, the Acala. Results were more encouraging, and when World War I boomed the market, plantings were greatly increased in Imperial Valley, in Riverside County, and in the southern part of the San Joaquin Valley. Largely because the plantings throughout were restricted to the single variety, thereby avoiding mongrelization through cross pollenizing, the yield per acre was more than twice the national average, and, because of longer staple, the price was better, too. Cotton became a $40,000,000 crop, which put California ahead of Oklahoma, Missouri, Tennessee, Virginia, and Florida, and within challenging distance of such cotton kingdom strongholds as the Carolinas, Georgia, Alabama, and Louisiana.

The remaining third of California agriculture centered on livestock and poultry. Dairying headed this division, consuming the larger share of the state's $50,000,000 alfalfa crop, and producing enough milk and cream, butter and cheese, ice cream and condensed milk to meet the major requirements of the state's population. As a dairy producer California by 1940 was surpassed only by some eight states clustered around Wisconsin. Meat production was second to dairying on California stock farms. Although the state lagged far behind Texas in cattle and Iowa in hogs, and though East Los Angeles and South San Francisco did not rank with South Chicago or Kansas City in meat packing, California had more cattle than any state in the old South and than any state west of Kansas. In wool production its rank was third. Poultry raising was much emphasized, with many turkey ranches in the semi-arid south and with myriad chicken ranches all over the state. Petaluma and San Fernando were the egg centers par excellence, but the standardized and streamlined versions of the old-fashioned hen-roost were encountered almost everywhere. In 1929 the egg count was 159,000,000 dozen.

In butter and eggs, meat and potatoes, cabbages, onions, and numerous incidental crops, modern California had, so to speak, lifted herself by her own bootstraps. Increased local demand required something like a three-fold increase in production. These lines were important, but not the essence of the state's agriculture, for which the distinctive note was provided rather by production for the national and to some extent the world market. This production spread over a long list of commodities, from exotic dates and avocadoes to things as common as carrots, yet in each instance California climatic and soil conditions afforded either a monopoly of opportunity or at least a very great advantage over the less fortunately situated portions of the United States. Availing themselves of these opportunities and contributing no little ingenuity, California agriculturists forged into first place.

A prevailing characteristic of this agricultural development was its industrial technique and method. Profiting by the findings of agricultural research, tooling for assembly-line operations, and incorporating on the scale of big business, the typical farms became, in actuality, factories in the fields. A correlative fact was the presence of an exploitative attitude toward farm labor. From Indians to tramps, to Chinese, to Japanese, to Filipinos, to Hindus, to Mexicans, the farm labor force had been in a position of inferiority. This inherited pattern and the nationwide practice in the twenties go far to explain the attitude that was prevalent.

Black Gold and Other Minerals

In mineral production California rose to third from the top, with Texas and Pennsylvania in the van. The calculation of annual value of output ran beyond $440,000,000, most of it accounted for by the yearly outflow of more than 200,000,000 barrels of oil. Even without petroleum, California would have been an important mining state. The annual gold output exceeded a million ounces, now priced at $35.02 an ounce. Other metals were of less significance, but the list of nonmetallic minerals was long and imposing, some fifty different minerals being produced in San Bernardino County alone. The cement industry, with a yearly production in excess of 10,000,000 barrels has already been mentioned. Sand and crushed rock were used in proportion, and clay products, from rough tile and brick to glazed tile and tableware, were an embellishment and a continuation of one of the old mission industries.

A narrative of the beginnings of the petroleum industry was offered in an earlier chapter. In review it may be cited that production, after advancing gradually to 4,000,000 barrels in 1900, had shot up to 77,000,000 in 1910 and to 104,000,000 in 1914. Meanwhile, new uses were discovered supplementing the original employment in kerosene lamps and lanterns, and oil was furnishing fuel for locomotives, heating furnaces, and orchard heaters, was finding favor in paving operations, and was gaining an even larger market as gasoline for automobile consumption. There was technological progress also, especially in the latter portion of the period, and this included improved methods of drilling and refining, the construction of pipelines, tank cars and tankers, and the solidification of financial control in the hands of a few large companies.

From 1914 to 1920 production ranged between 89,000,000 and 105,000,000 barrels, with no new fields of importance being opened. Whatever excitement was missing in these years was more than atoned for in the ensuing decade when one fabulous strike followed hot upon another. First came the Huntington Beach field in 1920 and the next year Santa Fe Springs and Signal Hill. By 1923 these three fields, all in the Los Angeles area, were producing respectively 113,-000, 332,000, and 244,000 barrels a day, carrying the state's total for the year to 264,000,000 barrels. In such an outpouring the existing facilities for storage and refining were completely engulfed. The oil companies escaped inundation by putting their tankers on a rapid shuttle service through the Panama Canal to refineries on the Atlantic seaboard. There were in 1924 some 1,704 transits by tankers, the best business the canal had enjoyed up to that time, and good business for the oil companies too, since this was a cheaper method of delivering oil than to ship it from the midcontinent fields.

Canal shipments of oil soon fell off about a third, partly because of the availability of Mexican and South American oil and the opening of the tremendously productive Midcontinent field in Texas and Oklahoma. California production, however, declined but slightly. In the late twenties it maintained an average of 241,000,000 barrels, in the early thirties was off to 184,000,000, but then mounted again to more than 200,000,000 barrels. The same major fields were still heavy producers, in some instances from deeper sands, and in 1928 Kettleman Hills near Coalinga came in as another bonanza.

New wells, however were a less striking feature than some of the other changes in the industry.   One development was the expansion of storage facilities with huge tank farms at Richmond, Bakersfield, Coalinga, El Segundo, and Long Beach so that almost two years' production could be held in storage.   Refineries also expanded and turned out three and a third billion gallons of gasoline annually and other products in proportion.   Significant also was the expansion of the local market.   The state's automobiles, airplanes, trucks, buses, and tractors consumed annually a quantity of gasoline exceeded only in New York, and the demand for fuel oil grew correspondingly, thanks to diesel motors and engines, the augmented number of orchard heaters, and the expansion of California industry. Only an eighth of the electricity consumed was generated in steam plants such as the huge installation of the Southern California Edison Company at Long Beach, but the cost of this oil-generated current was the yardstick for determining the price of hydroelectric power from Boulder Dam.

After 1920 the production and consumption of natural gas also increased tremendously.   For domestic uses, including home heating, it became the favored fuel and had industrial significance as well. Over a sixteen-year period the increase in billions of cubic feet consumed was from 66 to 320, while other large quantities were converted into casinghead gasoline or reintroduced into the oil sands to rejuvenate faltering wells.

Industry

Local industries in the twenties and thirties were those catering primarily or exclusively to California consumers and those aimed at larger markets.   The first group included certain lines of manufacturing that are of necessity conducted near the point of consumption; for example, baking, printing, the operation of foundries and

machine shops, the manufacture of concrete products, and the operation of planing mills.   These were generously represented in the
state, and in the latter two, because of the demands of irrigation and
flood control projects and because of the great activity in the building
trades, California rose to first rank.   The presence by 1940 of almost
seven million persons and the remoteness from eastern industrial
centers ordained a considerable development of industry.

In addition to these lines where the initial impetus was to meet
the demands of the local market, California plants supplied outlying
areas as well.   This was true, for example, in the manufacture of
drilling and refining equipment for the petroleum industry, in the
production of mining machinery, in the making of furniture, and in
the manufacture of automobile tires and tubes.

In the last analysis, however, it was manufactures only incidentally
for the local market which made California an industrial center
surpassed by only some seven states in the Middle Atlantic and
Great Lakes area.   These more ambitious branches included oil
refining, the canning and preserving of fruits, vegetables, and fish,
wine making, the manufacture of clothing, especially for women, and,
by no means least, motion picture production.   In few of these lines
was output large prior to 1914.

Some years prior to that date the movies were transferred from
Edison's laboratory to a set of unpretentious studios in Brooklyn and
began to be an industry.   There it was that the earliest masterpieces
such as *The Great Train Robbery* were filmed, and until 1910 no
films were even shown in Hollywood, the city fathers looking askance
at recreational establishments of dubious morality.   In 1910, however, the Horsley brothers, tiring of the handicap of Brooklyn's
gloomy skies, transferred their business to a Hollywood barn.   Other
companies followed suit, and Hollywood soon came to be the industry's recognized capital.   Early arrivals included the Bison Company
and Biograph, David Wark Griffith, Mack Sennett, Owen Moore and
Mary Pickford, Jesse L. Lasky, Cecil B. DeMille, William Farnum,
and Charlie Chaplin.   For some years the industry coasted along
on its curiosity value, namely, of showing pictures that moved.
Modern critics are most disdainful of early filmdom, charging that
from the beginning it "was almost exclusively in the hands of the
lowest type of business men, the lowest type of actors, and the lowest
type of writers; to wit, honky-tonk impresarios, hams and hacks."

By 1915 the movies could demand at least quantitative respect; Mary Pickford was on salary at $1,000 a week and Griffith's *The Birth of a Nation,* having cost a million dollars to produce and destined to gross fifteen times that sum, was by any definition colossal. With this epic the movie magnates entered into direct competition with the olive bottlers for a lien on the adjectives of magnitude. Since then they have employed them indiscriminately, though justifiably in such instances as *The Four Horsemen of the Apocalypse, Ben Hur, The Big Parade,* and *Snow White and the Seven Dwarfs.*

The passing years have brought, naturally enough, a number of changes and some improvements. A wave of scandals in the early twenties—the Arbuckle incident, Wallace Reid's death, and the Taylor murder—led the magnates to cast their problems in the lap of Will H. Hays, who left Harding's cabinet to become czar of the movies' public relations. Introduction of sound and color wrought further alteration. By running up the cost of shooting they set a penalty on interminable retakes and a premium on workmanlike performances. The talkies, furthermore, made demands on the players almost comparable to those of the stage. They led, in fact, to a great influx of experienced actors and thus contributed to the artistic refinement of the movies. Doubtless the number of true artists who have found expression in moving pictures is larger, but the critics are agreed on two in particular, Chaplin and Walt Disney. Though readily distinguishable from each other they had this much in common: they both recognized that a picture is not merely a transplanted stage play, that its strongest point is action and its most powerful expression is through pantomime.

To revert to things material, which is the burden of this chapter, the moving picture industry plotted itself a most astounding graph. Particularly spectacular was the up-curve for exhibitions. The beginnings had been very humble—Los Angeles' first projection parlor was operated in connection with a peep-show and was arranged accordingly; through holes in a partition seven patrons could peek into the darkened room at the screen. By 1910, however, the number of theaters equipped to show movies had grown enormously, and throughout the next two decades the trend continued.

Even at nominal admission charges—a nickel was for some years the standard price—the revenue to the producers became fabulous. Money poured in so rapidly that the movie people literally did not

Golden Gate Bridge

know what to do with it.   The players offered to take a share, and
salaries of the stars were boosted to five, ten, or twenty thousand
dollars a week.   Writers, directors, producers, and technicians shared
in the bonanza.   There were expenses, of course, for film, costumes,
sets, transportation, and so forth, but the principal loot was still in
the hands of the magnates.   Some of it went into publicity, many
of the fabulous salaries of the stars being chargeable thus.   Other
millions were plowed back into new productions or into equipment.
Lesser sums went into what might be called research, though most
of the improvements in film, cameras, sound-recording machines,
color processes, and the like, were made by the supply houses rather
than the producing companies.   After all these deductions a tidy
sum remained, and this along with much of the income of the
players, directors, and writers was poured out lavishly in conspicuous expenditure.

Hollywood's nouveaux riches have been held up to greater ridicule
than perhaps any suddenly wealthy group since the dawn of history.
In large degree the lampooning was based on fact, for the atrocities
committed at their behest by architects, interior decorators, automobile salesmen, caterers, and entertainers have been wonderful and
fearful to behold.   The social impact upon the community through
premieres and previews, night life and progressive marriage, has also
been a source of much concern to the guardians of southern California
taste and morals.   Gossip-mongering reporters broadcast these details to the world at large, with nothing lost in the telling, but often
with special impingement upon the Los Angeles area.

Passing by these sociological conundrums one notes that the moving picture industry released in southern California a very considerable purchasing power, esteemed alike by builders, tradesmen, salesmen, domestics, and members of the professions.   Quantitative statement is not easy because not even the stars spent all their income
locally, and, since the industry put its financial center in New York,
some of the profits were diverted from the state.   Nevertheless, the
residuum was large.   In 1935, salaries and wages totaled $98,000,-
000 and cost of production stood at $165,000,000.   How far income
exceeded cost was not revealed, but even these figures establish the
industry as a California asset comparable to the orange.

The movies in addition had a publicity value almost impossible
to exaggerate.   What suburb the world over has been so widely

heralded as Hollywood? The films have acted as a lodestone draw-ing countless tourists to the state, tourists who are said to have spent $200,000,000 in southern California in 1938. Hollywood's con-tribution to certain allied industries must be mentioned too. The studios created a style center for women's apparel rivaled only by Paris, and California clothing manufacturers capitalized on this advantage. In radio, the congregation of talent near the movie lots led the nation's broadcasting systems to establish studios in Holly-wood secondary only to New York's Radio Center.

Public Improvements

In this era of prosperity the engineers were busy on a variety of projects, and planning others still more ambitious. One important set had to do with highways. In the fifties and sixties stage lines had spread to the far corners of the state over unimproved roads. With the coming of the railroads, wagon roads fell back into strictly local use, from which the automobile elevated them only gradually. In the wagon and buggy era there was some agitation for good roads, even for paved roads. In 1909 the legislature ordered a sur-vey for a state highway system, and this action was followed by bond issues in 1910, 1915, and 1918, for eighteen, fifteen, and forty mil-lion dollars, respectively.

As was the case elsewhere, the first so-called highways were not much more than surfaced wagon roads, not engineered specifically as a runway for motor-driven vehicles. By the twenties, however, rapid progress had been made. One main artery followed the ap-proximate route of El Camino Real, through the Santa Clara, Salinas, and Santa Maria valleys from San Francisco to Santa Barbara, and thence by the inland route to San Fernando and Los Angeles, and on by the coast to San Diego. The other main artery reached south from Oregon, took advantage of the open expanse of the great Central Valley, and crossed Tejon Pass to Los Angeles. Laterals attached most of the centers of population with these main arteries, and highways reached eastward to the Colorado crossings at Yuma and Needles and to the trans-Sierra gateway at Reno. Extension of the Redwood Highway northward along the coast came more slowly, but by mid-decade it was surfaced and open all the way to Oregon.

Since many of the property lines in California antedated the quadrangular surveys typical of the United States as a whole, roads and highways were less rigidly held to the straight lines and square corners of the section lines. The terrain set up many difficult problems. One, on the coast route, was to negotiate the transfers from valley to valley, as at Cuesta grade near San Luis Obispo. Another was to cope with the constantly shifting sands near Yuma. Several miles of movable plank road were the initial solution to this problem. Still another difficulty was how to surmount the mountain barrier between Bakersfield and Los Angeles. The twisting, switchbacking old ridge route was a devious answer to that problem, achieved in the pattern of the period with as little earth moving as possible, and with no compunction about the number or sharpness of the turns. It was an adventurous ride, blamed for much carsickness, and calling for prodigious exercise of the steering wheel.

The arms of San Francisco Bay, such a boon to water transportation, were an equivalent obstacle to automobile traffic. An obvious palliative was to add automobile ferries to those already serving railroad passengers and commuters. In the twenties this service was available from San Francico to Sausalito, Oakland, and Berkeley, from Richmond to San Rafael, and across Carquinez Straits at Vallejo and Benicia. Bridges, it was suggested, would speed up this traffic. Several such were built—at Antioch, Crockett, Dumbarton, and San Mateo. They did help, but in each instance they merely cut off the end of an arm of the bay. A bolder remedy in the form of bridges direct from San Francisco to Oakland and to Marin County advanced to the planning stage, but in the twenties neither got beyond paper.

The problems of water and power were recognized as even more vital. In earlier days the water resources most conveniently available for irrigation and for municipal supply had been developed. In the time of George Chaffey several more dramatic steps had been taken, most rewardingly in the diversion of Colorado River water into Imperial Valley, and most flamboyantly in the siphoning of the Owens River to Los Angeles. In many instances hydroelectric energy had been generated as a sort of by-product of the water supplying. In the teens and twenties still other power plants were installed along Sierra streams. Just prior to the completion of the big dams at Boulder, Shasta, and Friant the aggregate of this hydroelectric output was almost a fifth of the national total.

Through the twenties the Owens Valley Aqueduct was much in the news. In 1923, following a succession of dry years, Los Angeles began to buy up additional farms in the valley and to transfer their water to the aqueduct. The remaining residents of the valley, especially the townspeople, were incensed at this blighting of their homeland. The Owens Valley champions protested vocally and editorially, then by placing a token charge of dynamite alongside the aqueduct, then by seizing a spillway in the Alabama Hills and turning the flow of water out upon the desert, and finally by more damaging sabotage of wells, pump, and aqueduct sections. The city put detectives to work, but never brought any of the dynamiters to trial. The protesters took it the more amiss because much of their water was not piped to Angeleños' homes, but used instead to irrigate the San Fernando Valley. A syndicate dominated by the Otis-Chandler interests had bought 47,000 acres in this valley in 1910. The aqueduct water increased its value as much as a hundred fold.

More serious violence seemed to impend, but on August 4, 1927, Owens Valley had a great setback. The principal bank of the county closed its doors. Its president, N. N. Watterson, and cashier, M. G. Watterson, who had symbolized the cause of the settlers against the city, had misapplied the bank's funds to the tune of some two million dollars. The settlers, many of them bankrupt through this peculation, had no alternative but to give in.

The following March 12, a 180-foot dam that Mulholland had built in San Francisquito Canyon suddenly gave way, sending a monstrous wall of water cascading down the narrow valley of the Santa Clara. When it struck Santa Paula, fifty miles away, the crest was still twenty-five feet high. The toll of lives was 385, the property damage millions of dollars. An appraisal committee assessed the property losses and the city promptly met these claims. Remembering the dynamite blasts along the aqueduct, there was an impulse to blame the disaster on sabotage, but inspection revealed that the dam was built on and anchored to a weak and faulted rock formation. Capable geological advice would have prevented this catastrophe.

Concurrently, San Francisco was solving its water problem. Initially it had depended on local wells. By 1901, however, when it was apparent that a supplement was needed, Mayor James D. Phelan filed an application for water from the Tuolumne River just north of Yosemite. Nature lovers protested and nothing was accomplished until 1913 when Congress authorized the diversion and confirmed San Francisco's title to water rights in the amount of 420,000 acre feet a year. Legal, financial, and physical difficulties, together with the opposition of the Pacific Gas and Electric and the Spring Valley Water Company, delayed the work. Finally, in 1931, after an expenditure of $121,000,000, the Hetch Hetchy Dam, the transmission lines, and the 186-mile aqueduct were realities, and San Francisco had all the water it would need in the foreseeable future.

Meanwhile, in the southern part of the state, Imperial Valley was haunted by fear of a repetition of its 1905 deluge, and burgeoning Los Angeles faced the necessity of arranging for more water than the Owens Valley Aqueduct could deliver. A flood control and water diversion project on the Colorado was a possible answer. The planning passed the desultory stage in 1921, but an entire decade was required to get the consent of Mexico, and of the other states which share the river, and to get authorization from the federal government. Actual construction did not begin until 1931.

On the basis of surveys and calculations by the Bureau of Reclamation, a bill was introduced in Congress in 1921 calling for construction of a dam in Boulder Canyon. The states of the upper basin showed a reluctance, though their basic demand for an assignment of half the total flow of the river was met in the compact signed in 1922 by representatives of all the states except Arizona. Secretary of Commerce Herbert Hoover had a large hand in bringing about this agreement. Interstate jealousies and reluctance to permit public power development caused further delay. Finally, in 1928 the Swing-Johnson Act provided for the authorization of Boulder Dam. The measure specified a strictly limited federal support. The United States would advance the necessary funds, ultimately $160,-000,000, but only if there were firm contracts for the purchase of the generated power sufficient to repay the construction costs, plus interest, within fifty years. California communities and utility companies signed such contracts and thus made possible the actual construction of the dam.

Both the water and the power were to be available on the basis of F. O. B. the dam. It was up to purchasers to arrange for conveyance and delivery. In Imperial and Coachella valleys plans went forward for the $78,000,000 All-American Canal and distribution facilities, its cost to be repaid in full by the people of the district.

The southern California contractors for hydroelectric power from the dam planned and prepared to finance $56,000,000 worth of transmission lines. Los Angeles and forty-four neighboring communities joined in the Metropolitan Water District and prepared to invest $200,000,000 building Parker Dam, the Metropolitan Aqueduct, its branches, pumping plants, storage reservoirs, and treating plants, through which Colorado River water would be delivered at the rate of a billion gallons a day. There was much effort and attention toward deciding on and perfecting these plans in the twenties. Less decisively, the people of the Sacramento-San Joaquin Valley were facing up to their water problem, though the solution was not effectively outlined until the thirties.

The Speculative Urge

For the United States as a whole the postwar twenties were a sort of binge, with prohibition, bootleggers, and speakeasies, with a runaway stock market, an increasing degree of corporate concentration as exemplified in chain stores, and a resurgence of hyperpatriotism and nativism as expressed in isolationism, the Ku Klux Klan, and the Scopes and Sacco-Vanzetti trials. California shared in these aberrations, and with some distinctiveness.

Through mergers and consolidations, locally-owned and directed banks gave place to the branches of a few mammoth organizations, chief of which was Gianinni's Bank of Italy. By removing much of the personal equation from their lending and collecting, these banks improved soundness and security, at the same time concentrating power to an alarming degree. They also had a hand in broadening interest in investment, some of it highly speculative. A host of persons who had never previously paid attention to stock quotations bought shares in Transamerica and other such issues and hung on the rise and fall of the market.

The speculative urge was more purely evident in the uncritical support given to real estate schemes such as were promoted at Atascadero, and in the rage, especially in Los Angeles, for oil stocks. The particular darling of the Los Angeles public was C. C. Julian, an ornate showman and a master of breezy, folksy, spellbinding appeal. In the chatty monologue of his newspaper ads he invited the folks to take shares in the bonanza of Santa Fe Springs' gushing wells. Julian Petroleum stock sold rapidly and paid handsome dividends.

From 1922 to 1925 his ventures spiralled upward, but at that point the major interests protested his stock issues, pressured the newspapers to refuse his advertising, and persuaded the refineries to quit handling his oil. In the crisis that ensued, Julian lost control of his company.

His successors, S. C. Lewis and Jacob Berman, had to borrow money extravagantly to keep the company afloat. A favorite speculation, participated in by a bankers' pool from the most respected element in the community, a Jewish pool made up of affluent merchants and bankers, and the Tia Juana pool, composed of gamblers and race-track habitués, was in lending money, at exorbitant interest and bonuses, to Julian Petroleum. As security for these loans, Lewis and Berman resorted to counterfeiting stock, eventually in the amount of 3,000,015 shares. On May 7, 1927, this bubble burst and $150,000,000 in supposed worth vanished from the grasp of 40,000 eager investors. Julian perhaps had set the stage for such a disaster, but there is no evidence that he was culpable for what others did to Julian "Pete."

This spectacular failure was followed by the receivership of the Richfield Oil Company in 1931, with revelation of unconscionable extravagances by its officials and an operating loss of $56,000,000. Embezzlement and fraud and poor judgment brought many other companies to bankruptcy, including the Guarantee Building and Loan Association and the American Mortgage Company. Indeed, in bankruptcies for fraud, Los Angeles led the nation at the end of the twenties.

Slightly translated, the speculative urge of southern Californians in the twenties was expressed also in attention to new cults of philosophy and religion. The region abounded in health faddists; in naturopaths and other exponents of medical unorthodoxy; in apostles of new thought, variously defined; and in indigenous sects. The latter may be illustrated by a funerary establishment designed to banish all that is somber and depressing. The dramatic evangelism of Aimee Semple McPherson was even more innate to the twenties. Sister Aimee began to preach the Four Square Gospel in Los Angeles in 1922. Within a very short time she had a devoted following of thousands, which built the huge Angelus Temple, with an auditorium to seat 5,000. In 1926 Aimee disappeared. Last seen on the beach near Ocean Park, she was presumed to have drowned.

Eight days later, however, she reappeared at Agua Prieta, Sonora, returned to a triumphal reception at Los Angeles, and gave out a story that she had been kidnapped. When reporters exposed this story as a hoax, she was arrested on the charge of falsifying and thereby interfering with the orderly processes of the law. The charge later was dropped. Her followers continued loyal to the time of her death in 1945, never, however, exceeding in numbers or vigor the peak attained in the twenties. Because of her penchant for showmanship, the Los Angeles press and the more sophisticated element in the community dealt lampooningly with Aimee. Thereby they obscured the substantial amount of real good that she did in helping the sick and needy, cheering the unhappy, providing social opportunity for the lonely, and uplifting her followers.

Politics as Usual

Prosperity tends to promote complacency. The American people exhibited this attitude toward their national government during the twenties, and Californians did the same, both with regard to business and to state and local government. In William D. Stephens, Friend W. Richardson, and C. C. Young there was a succession of Republican governors spanning the decade. Legislatures met with calendrical regularity but enacted few measures of much moment. In fact, they sedulously avoided one issue that many of their constituents regarded as imperative, that of reapportionment.

The unequal growth of the state, with the center of gravity shifting more and more southward, lent increasing unreality to the representational system. In the normal course of events each decennial census should be followed by a revision of electoral districts for the House of Representatives and for the state legislature, provided, of course, that there has been a sufficient population shift or increase. The federal constitution strongly implies this by providing that representation be apportioned among the several states according to population, and the state constitution is even more mandatory in its requirement. Such an apportionment had been made by Congress in 1911, with California assigned eleven representatives, and the legislature had supplemented it with an appropriate local measure. When the census of 1920 established the increase in California population at 44.1 per cent, the natural expectation was that the state would be allotted three or four additional Congressmen and that in local reapportionment Los Angeles and southern California would be the chief gainers. Successive Congresses, however, neglected to act, and their remissness gave the legislature excuse not to reapportion its own districts.

For five years this condition prevailed. In the state, meanwhile, several alignments were discernible: Republicans versus Democrats, the north versus the south, San Francisco versus Los Angeles, and the rural districts versus the urban centers. Some had little to do with reapportionment. The Republican party, for example, was so preponderant that no conceivable redistricting could do it much harm or good. The north-south rivalry, though frequently a rallying cry in the controversy to follow, seems to have been invoked primarily out of deference to tradition. Certainly in its more extreme form, the threat of state division, it was able to gather only the most limited support. The rivalry of the two cities had more of reality, and the issue between city and country was sharply drawn.

In 1926, the legislature having indicated clearly that it would not act, two contradictory initiative amendments were laid before the electorate. One, ineptly called the Los Angeles plan, called for reapportionment according to population for both houses of the legislature, delegated power to act to a commission of ex officio members if the legislature failed to act, and also made available judicial remedy. The other plan was advanced by various farm groups, the Farm Bureau Federation, the State Grange, the Farmer's Union, and the Agricultural Legislative Committee, and also by the San Francisco Chamber of Commerce. Labeled the Federal plan, it apportioned seats in the lower house according to population and in the upper house according to the counties at the rate of not more than one to a county and not more than three counties to a district. Most of the arguments advanced for this plan do not stand up under examination. The analogy to the national practice was erroneous and misleading. Distribution would not have been on anything like an equal-area basis; nor did the plan assure a well-balanced legislature in which neither the cities nor the farm areas would predominate. More realistic and more effective was the unvoiced argument that by its rotten-borough system the plan would perpetuate the countryside in its control of the senate, while rural assemblymen would often hold the balance of power between the Los Angeles and San Francisco representatives.

The voters in their wisdom chose the Federal rather than the Los Angeles plan, only the latter county expressing a preference for representation on a straight population basis, and the legislature in 1927 marked out the districts. Opponents of the plan staged a forlorn protest by invoking the referendum against this act in 1928, but interest was apathetic. Half a million persons who participated in the presidential vote did not bother to cast their votes on the referendum,· and though San Francisco joined Los Angeles on this vote, the referendum lost.

This action, however, laid reapportionment to rest only temporarily. In 1929 Congress at last decreed reapportionment of representation in its own lower house, the same to be computed on the basis of the forthcoming census of 1930. So rapid had been the state's increase that this worked out to enlarge California's representation from eleven to twenty. By reason of this law, together with the initiative amendment of 1926, the legislature in 1931 had the double duty of relocating assembly and Congressional districts.

The whole story cannot be related here; nor have all the facts been brought to light. The contest began even before the legislature convened, with drives for the speakership by Edgar C. Levey of San Francisco and Walter J. Little of Santa Monica. Both professed to favor reapportionment on the basis of population, but it was generally understood that Little's program would be more in accord with the census figures and hence more favorable to Los Angeles and southern California. Levey won the speakership, forty-one to thirty-nine. The committee he appointed drafted bills assigning ten Congressmen to each section and dividing the assembly seats almost evenly between north and south. A senate committee countered with a proposal to allot the Congressmen nine and eleven and the assemblymen thirty-eight and forty-two, north and south. After a bitter fight, in which all manner of pressure was exerted to influence the votes of assemblymen, the San Joaquin Valley delegation cast the balance in favor of the senate's bill, the McKinley-Little program.

Los Angeles and the south reckoned it a great victory for justice and for themselves. It marked, so they felt, the attainment of political maturity and would put an end, so they hoped, to the political domination which San Francisco and the north had been able to prolong for some years after the center of population had shifted southward. In practice it became clear that San Francisco's voice in state government was still large, and clearer still that the Federal system gave rural California relatively the greatest representation in the legislature. Hearst and others agitated against the Federal system and proposed divers remedies, from the mild device of making the rotten boroughs slightly less rotten by permitting the lumping of five counties in a senatorial district, to the more drastic step of adopting the unicameral legislature. With the urban centers leaning toward Democratic liberalism and the farm provinces a stronghold of Republican conservatism, the question acquired a partisan flavor hitherto lacking. None of the schemes for revision, however, came anywhere near acceptance.

Reapportionment was followed shortly by a revision of the taxation system which amounted, in effect, to reassessment. The change was a complicated one but necessary, it was pleaded, to keep the schools functioning in the districts that had been hardest hit by the depression. Several steps were involved. One was to make state funds available to local public schools up to and including junior colleges in proportion to daily attendance. To get the necessary funds into the state treasury, the property of public-service corporations was to be transferred from local assessment rolls and placed under state taxation, and two new taxes were to be instituted, a retail sales tax and an income tax.

Largely on the argument of saving the schools, the program was put over. Two important details, however, did not work out according to the blueprint. The transfer of a large part of the school burden afforded only slight and temporary relief to local taxpayers, because removal of the corporations from the assessment rolls narrowed the tax base while other branches of local government immediately raised their demands. Local property owners, accordingly, paid practically as much as before. The other slip was that the sales tax, which everyone recognized would bear more heavily on the poor, was not balanced by an income tax. Governor James M. Rolph found excuse to veto the latter measure. A fair interpretation, it may be said, was that those who paid the sales tax had the privilege of saving the schools, while taxable incomes went unscathed and the corporations had their tax burdens lightened.

32

DEPRESSION

VIEWED WITH HINDSIGHT—one of the more casual synonyms for history—imperfections show up in the American prosperity of the twenties, some of which were suspected at the time. The boom in business was highly selective; automobiles and radios sold as never before, but such key industries as soft coal mining, textiles, and agriculture were not prospering. Labor-saving machinery gave production a tremendous boost, but no means had been devised to give a similar lift to consumer purchasing power. Installment buying was the closest approach, but at most it was a palliative, a method of putting a mortgage on future orders. The unevenness of prosperity showed in the 312 per cent increase in speculative gains, 1923 to 1928, while wages crept up only 12 per cent. In the midst of the prosperity, too, there was an alarming amount of poverty; unemployment, to cite one example, went up from 1,500,000 in 1926 to 1,800,000 in 1929.

The speculative superstructure toppled first. To many Americans it seemed a matter of comparative indifference that the paper profits of the market players were swept away. Soon, however, the paralysis spread through the whole economy. Wages, salaries, and dividends were slashed; national income dropped from 81 billion in 1929 to 41 billion in 1932; stores and factories closed, Hoovervilles and apple-selling came into being; and the roster of unemployed mounted to 10 million in 1931, and to 14 or 15 million the next year.

Earlier drops in the business cycle, such as the panics of 1857, 1873, and 1893, had had only a delayed reaction in California. By 1929 the state was closely enmeshed with the nation. Furthermore, much that it had to offer in the national market was of the sort that would be particularly sensitive to recession. Its fruits were only partially regarded as staples. Its moving pictures were somewhat less than absolute necessities. Its vacation opportunities would go begging in a period of austerity. This time, California felt the impact as abruptly as any part of the country, save perhaps Wall Street itself. Before the depression was over, some of its consequences would be brought home in aggravated form. For example, California became a special asylum for the unemployed. They were attracted by the mildness of the climate, which made it seem a better place in which to endure privation, and they were lured by the state's traditional aura as a land of promise and opportunity.

In the state as in the nation, the very volume of distress among the impoverished and the unemployed called aloud for action. The Hoover administration sought to cope with the depression by pronouncements of confidence in America. Later, through the Reconstruction Finance Corporation, it gave aid to major industries. Its philosophy, however, was that relief to individuals should come from private sources or local governments, and only with reluctance did it move on at length to federal contributions for such purposes. The California state government was equally hesitant. The first major decision in coping with the depression was in the election of James (Sunny Jim) Rolph as governor in November, 1930.

In his long tenure as mayor of San Francisco, the major qualifications Rolph had evinced were as official greeter, hand shaker, and parade reviewer. Unfortunately, in his term at Sacramento there was not much to be sunny about. It was not in the cards that he would mobilize the state government to meet the emergency. With the accession of Franklin Delano Roosevelt as President in 1933, the national government launched the New Deal as an effort to achieve relief, recovery, and reform. Many phases of the New Deal had impact on California. Its state government, however, declined to get in step and continued, insofar as possible, to practice the philosophy of Coolidge and Hoover Republicanism.

The Restiveness of Labor

One predictable and pronounced feature of the depression period was the restiveness of labor. With prices cascading, employers sought to protect their interests by slashing wages, and workers often felt that this tendency was carried too far. The feature of greatest novelty was the attempt to organize farm labor and to stage a series of great agricultural strikes.

Prior to 1929 there had been some gestures toward organizing agricultural workers in the state, by the American Federation of Labor among the cannery workers, by racial associations among the Japanese and the Mexicans, and by the I. W. W. in its peculiar and impractical program among the casual laborers. None of these efforts had appreciable effect on the status of farm labor.

Early in 1930 two spontaneous strikes occurred in Imperial Valley protesting lowered wages in the fields and the packing sheds. After the strikes failed, the heads of the Trade Union Unity League called a conference of worker delegates from the entire valley. This move provoked arrest of some 100 workers, trial of a number of the leaders for violation of the criminal syndicalism statute, and conviction of eight of them.

Capitalizing on the resentment that this repression produced, the Communist party began a drive to organize the farm workers. The strategy was to take advantage of every labor dispute and every strike that developed spontaneously, and to try to build these pieces into a cohesive statewide movement. This foreign label, added to the rise of unionism where it had never existed before, roused bitter resistance. At Vacaville, late in 1932, a masked mob answered a fruit workers strike by seizing six of the leaders, flogging them, shearing their heads, and annointing them with red enamel. Strikes followed among the pea pickers at Decoto, the cherry pickers at Mountain View and Sunnyvale, the peach gatherers at Merced and elsewhere, among the grape workers at Lodi and Fresno, in the pear harvest in the Santa Clara Valley, and in the general fruit gathering on the Tagus Ranch.

Though not always initiated by Communist organizers, these strikes were incorporated into the program of the Cannery and Agricultural Workers' Industrial Union. It went on in the fall of 1933 to organize a cotton pickers strike that boycotted the fields throughout the San Joaquin Valley, maintained a headquarters camp of some 5,000 persons near Corcoran, and withheld 18,000 workers from the fields. This was followed by an Imperial Valley strike in the winter of 1933–1934, and another wave of walkouts in the northern fruit districts in 1934.

Opposition to these strikes took the form of bitter denunciation in the press, vigilante violence aimed primarily at the leadership, and use of local police, sheriffs' deputies, and state police to break up strike meetings and disperse their camps. As in the routing of the T. U. U. L., the criminal syndicalism law was invoked against the C. A. W. I. U. After its second state convention in 1934, all its leaders who had not previously been taken care of were brought to trial and convicted under this act. In this fashion the union was broken, despite its record of winning 21 strikes out of 24 and advancing the prevailing wage from 15 cents an hour to 25.

Paralleling this effort to unionize the farm labor force there was an effort to rebuild unionism in San Francisco. From 1921 to 1933 the city's unions were at minimum strength and the port was on what amounted to an open shop basis. During these years, notwithstanding its natural advantages, San Francisco by no means kept pace with other Pacific Coast ports. Its share of tonnage decreased from 36 to 21 per cent and other indexes went down in proportion. The open shop was not to blame, but it did not prevent this decline. In the company-controlled hiring, grave abuses developed, and these were aggravated by the depression. When Section 7A of the National Recovery Act outlined a procedure whereby labor could choose its bargaining agency, the waterfront workers, with little delay, made choice of the International Longshoremen's Association. In May, 1934, this organization felt strong enough to make a series of demands: for a minimum wage of a dollar an hour, a six-hour day and a thirty-hour week so as to spread the work among a number of men, union control of the hiring halls, and various lesser concessions.

The operators rejected all these demands and countered with the charge that the I. L. A. was Communist and radical. President Roosevelt, Senator Robert Wagner, and members of the national and regional boards tried to bring about a settlement, but failed, and on May 9 the strike began, tying up all the ports on the coast. Almost immediately it erupted into violence at San Francisco. A climax came on July 5, when strike-breakers under police escort tried to move cargo. The strikers resisted, overturned trucks and burned them, dumped goods into the streets, and answered tear gas and pistol fire with cobblestones and brickbats. Two of the strikers were killed and more than a hundred seriously injured. A funeral procession 10,000 strong marched up Market Street and created a profound

impression on the entire community. Governor Merriam deployed
the National Guard, and as a protest against the partisanship of the
forces of government the labor leaders decided to invoke a general
strike. It took place from July 16 to 19. Except for a few authorized necessities, nothing was sold or delivered. The more conservative union leaders were not willing to see it through to a conclusion.
In effect they sabotaged the strike. The "sympathetic strikers," including even the teamsters, went back to work. By the end of July
the longshoremen were back on the job also. By arbitration award
in October, control of the hiring halls was assigned to the union.
With Joseph G. Ryan having to yield to Harry Bridges in the I. L. A.,
and with the organization of the Maritime Federation of the Pacific,
the strike marked a long step in the direction of industrial unionism,
a trend represented on the national scene by John L. Lewis and the
C. I. O. defection from the A. F. of L.

There was, however, a division of opinion. Bridges and the
longshoremen went with the C. I. O.; Harry Lundeberg and the
sailors union stayed with the A. F. of L. Out of this schizophrenia
of labor arose a bewildering array of petty strikes and work stoppages
—561 between October, 1934, and November, 1936—crippling to
operators and shippers, a nuisance to the public, and extremely damaging to the goodwill that union labor might otherwise have deserved.
At the time, these jurisdictional disputes were more damaging to
labor's reputation than the recurrent charge that the unions were
Communist dominated.

Despite the drawbacks, the maritime unions continued in strength
throughout the thirties. Unionism in general likewise made great
strides, first under the temporary benediction of the Blue Eagle of
the N. I. R. A., and later under the National Labor Relations Board.
By 1940 San Francisco and the Bay region had more union members
than ever before, including even newsboys and bootblacks. Although Los Angeles still purported to be open shop, it had a nucleus
of solid unionization in the harbor district; the more concentrated
industries, such as airplane building, automobile assembly, tire manufacture, and oil production and refining were thoroughly organized;
the motion picture industry was practically solid; and organizers had
made some progress in other lines, such as the building trades and
truck driving. Between 1933 and 1940 union membership advanced
from 33,000 to 200,000.

As to rural labor, however, after the liquidation of the C. A. W. I. U. in 1934 there was no revival of effective unionism.   On the contrary, the larger agriculturists formed a union of employers, the Associated Farmers, and whenever labor troubles occurred, they supplanted or subordinated the regular peace officers, armed enough men with guns, pick handles, and tear gas, and resorted to enough violence to crush the strike.   Farm fascism or, in other parlance, vigilanteism seemed to have an effective check on the movement to unionize farm labor.   The most hopeful sign was at the close of the decade when Carey McWilliams' *Factories in the Fields* and John Steinbeck's *The Grapes of Wrath* called attention to the plight of the migratory workers in clarion voice and stirred the public conscience.

Technocracy and Utopia

In the prosperous twenties Californians had evinced a remarkable waywardness in philosophy and religion.   In the depression decade the state spawned equally fantastic schemes for economic legerdemain.   Since the state had contributed Henry George and the Single Tax, and had harbored communitarian ventures at Kaweah, Delhi, Llano, and elsewhere, perhaps this susceptibility should not surprise.   The degree with which visionary and unscientific programs took hold was, nevertheless, amazing.

The first of any consequence was Technocracy.   Technocracy had honorable origin at Columbia University as a study of energy as the foundation of civilization.   Howard Scott brought it to California as a crusade encrusted with an impressive pseudo-scientific vocabulary.   He quickly recruited a large number of adherents, who, as a group, made up in enthusiasm for whatever they lacked in understanding.   The most notable of the new disciples was Manchester Boddy, owner and editor of the Los Angeles *Daily News*.   He used its columns to spread the new gospel and did so with such effectiveness that Technocracy swept the state.   Twenty years later a few clubs devoted to economic salvation through the proper utilization of modern science were still meeting.

In July, 1933, a competitor arose in the Utopian Society.   An "educational" society, utilizing initiation ceremonies, secret rituals, and pageantry borrowed from the old morality plays, it claimed to be the answer to the ills of society.   From modest beginnings with initiation cycles performed in private homes, it gained adherents so rapidly that the largest auditoriums in Los Angeles were filled. At the peak, a half million Utopians was the estimate, practically all of them in southern California. The doctrine of Utopia was, in essence, that private ownership and the profit system were to blame for all evil. With modern machines and proper management, three hours work a day by those between twenty-five and forty-five years of age would produce all that was needed by the entire population. Education until twenty-five and pensions after forty-five was the motto. The truth probably was that the social and inspirational qualities of the meetings had more to do with the popularity of the society than did its teachings. After about two years the movement faded away, almost as rapidly as it had arisen. It was part of the ferment out of which arose Epic.

The Epic Crusade

The Epic movement obviously was nurtured on the distress of the depression. Obviously it was encouraged by the New Deal, by Roosevelt's remarks about the forgotten man, and by the nation-wide fervor that was engendered when the N. I. R. A. was introduced to the country. Some months before the primary a group of liberal Democrats and Socialists persuaded Upton Sinclair to register as a Democrat and seek that party's nomination for governor. A lifelong Socialist, a writer rather than a speaker, an idealist rather than a practical politician, Sinclair was in some respects as unpromising a candidate as could have been found. On the other hand he had boldness of imagination, determination, an incorruptible character, and unexpected powers of dynamic leadership. Already the author of some forty-eight books, plays, and pamphlets, Sinclair adopted the novel expedient of building his campaign around a book. Formulating the program he wanted to carry into effect, Sinclair envisioned the obstacles that would confront him, the way they would be overcome, and the eventual triumph of his plan. All this he wrote up in a booklet entitled *I, Governor of California, and How I Ended Poverty: A True Story of the Future.* The campaign was then simply an endeavor to make this book come true.

Sinclair's plan had twelve points, chief of which were the proposals for state land colonies where the unemployed might farm under the guidance of experts, similar operation of idle factories, and a state distribution system for the exchange of these several products—all to be financed by state-issued scrip.   It proposed repeal of the sales tax, enactment of a steeply graduated income tax, and increases in inheritance and public utility corporation taxes.   It contained a proposal for tax exemption on homes occupied by the owners and on ranches cultivated by the owners, provided the assessed value did not exceed $3,000.   There was a Georgian proposal for a 10 per cent tax on unimproved building lots and on agricultural land not under cultivation.   Finally, there was provision for fifty-dollar-a-month pensions to the aged needy, to the physically incapacitated, and to widows with dependent children.

How the plan would have worked can be answered only on the basis of theory.   It had elements that were most attractive to the unemployed, the poor, and the left wing.   Those same elements antagonized and alarmed the propertied classes.   The campaign was waged, therefore, with reforming fervor and hope arrayed against distrust and resistance to change.   The Epics had only a minimum of financial support, not enough to buy much radio time or to make available the other channels of campaigning usually employed.   Sinclair's supporters had to depend instead upon volunteer workers, rallies, and clubs, upon their candidate's pamphlets, which, after all, were better than his radio performances, and upon the mistakes of the opposition.

Although handicapped with the colorless Frank Merriam as a candidate, the opposition had a wealth of political experience and an unlimited war chest.   Practically all the newspapers were against Sinclair.   The radio beat out heated warnings against giving him office, billboards carried the same message, and the voters were deluged with handbills, pamphlets, and letters urging them to "save the state" with Merriam.   Sinclair was maligned as "an Anarchist, a free-lover, an agent of Moscow, a Communist, an anti-Christ."   Just before the election the motion picture industry released what purported to be newsreels introducing the tramps who would allegedly descend upon California if Epic were adopted.   A Literary Digest poll, perhaps in honest error, found 62 per cent of the voters for Merriam, though in the election he got only 49 per cent.

On top of all this, Sinclair was opposed by many Socialists and Democrats.   Norman Thomas and other Socialists complained that he had deserted true socialism.   Conservative Democrats announced for Merriam, and many liberal Democrats threw their votes to Raymond Haight, the Progressive candidate. George Creel, a leading Democrat, denounced Sinclair, and President Roosevelt withheld his support. In the end it was virtually Sinclair and the Epics against the world.

In retrospect it is difficult to recapture the feeling of bitter partisanship that suffused the state. Part of it was due, no doubt, to the threat to entrenched privilege which Sinclair's plan obviously contained. Others were sure that his real intentions were to go far beyond the announced plan and that the latter was merely an entering wedge for a program of socialization which would exceed anything Russia had seen. Many conservatives were also habituated to the thought that the Soviets were behind every movement in America bearing the reform label. The combination of fear and hate, of concern for the preservation of property rights and national institutions, and of political experience and financial resources was more than the Epics could overcome. The Epics won Sinclair the nomination and elected a number of assemblymen, state senators, and Congressmen, but they fell short in the final vote for governor. It was 1,138,620 for Merriam, 879,557 for Sinclair, and 302,519 for Haight. The state was saved from however much of his platform Sinclair might have tried to carry into effect, and had instead a continuation of the cautiousness and the laissez faire with which Merriam had been facing the depression crisis.

The Townsend Plan

In its timing, Epic encroached on its precursors, Technocracy and Utopianism. In like fashion, it had to compete with a counter-attraction, the Townsend Plan. The inspiration for this panacea came to a retired physician of Long Beach, Dr. Francis E. Townsend, at about the time that Epic was taking shape. He proposed to cure the depression by the simple device of giving every person over sixty $200 a month, with the provisio that each installment be spent within the month, the funds to be raised by a 2 per cent transactions tax. Notwithstanding the obvious fallacies involved, the package of old-age pensions and limited inflation had instantaneous appeal. Townsend clubs sprang up as if by chain reaction, contributions from hopeful oldsters poured in to the "national headquarters," and the publications that Townsend set up sold in great quantity.

Though not launched until a few months before the 1934 election, the Townsend Plan was a factor in its outcome. Sinclair denounced the plan as economic heresy. Merriam endorsed it, and there can be no doubt that it helped elect him. At the 1935 legislature, too, an early order of business was to consider a memorial to Congress in favor of enactment of the Townsend Plan. Republican votes put it over, and the Townsendites in appreciation began to boom Merriam for President. That the Republicans, who had been so righteous about saving the state from Sinclair's experiments, should plump for the folly of Townsendism is only explainable as politics—or as confidence that the federal government would not be stampeded.

The Townsend idea had a lively persistence. It moved out into the national arena and got support from candidates in many states. As a matter of fact, its original intention was that the federal government should be the agency to give it effect. At the state level it also continued to exert pressure. Exactly how much influence can be attributed to it is hard to measure, but certainly it is to be credited with accelerating the increase in California old-age pensions and the adoption of the national security program.

In California, derivative programs threw other scares into the camp of economic stability. In 1938 a certain Robert Noble conjured up a plan for rewarding everyone over fifty with $25 every Tuesday in state warrants redeemable at the end of the year, provided that a weekly stamp tax of 2 per cent was affixed. Since its money-making apparatus was self-contained, the economic fallacy should have been apparent even to the most unwary, but such was not the reception. Taken in hand by an astute promoter, Willis Allen, the scheme came close to adoption. By advancing the amount and the day, Allen achieved an alliterative title, Thirty Dollars Every Thursday. In the course of the campaign the nonsensical nickname Ham and Eggs was added, and for a while this seemed to help in the promotion. With relative ease Allen got 700,000 signatures, far more than were needed to qualify his proposed constitutional amendment for the November ballot. He took a leaf out of Townsend's method in appealing to the old folks for contributions for the drive to get them something for nothing, and at the same time stimulate recovery from the depression. Backed by these contributions and by the advertising revenue of the pension paper that he published, Allen staged a vigorous campaign. It made use of the radio, but depended largely on mass meetings and volunteer solicitation of votes. Certain candidates for office, among them Culbert Olson and Sheridan Downey, Democratic aspirants for governor and United States Senate, made a bid for the pensioner vote by endorsing Ham and Eggs, but the sober element in the state was solid against it. There was something of a counter campaign, but the general attitude was that a proposal so fantastic really had no chance of adoption. It was a shock, therefore, when the count showed more than a million votes cast in its favor and that a shift of a few hundred thousand more would have enacted it.

A greater shock came in Allen's announcement that the Retirement Life Payments proposal would immediately be requalified for the ballot, this time with a million signatures. The petition went into circulation, the radio and the newssheet were kept going, and the campaign of soliciting dollars from the aged was intensified. The Chamber of Commerce and its business cohorts perforce continued and stepped up their opposition. The million signatures were achieved, were publicly delivered to Governor Olson on May 18, 1939, and he was put on the spot to call a special election. The Ham and Eggers hoped for an August date, but Olson set November 7, and by that time the fervor had waned to the extent that the proposition got only 993,000 out of 2,975,000 votes. That was not the end of pension schemes, but it was the last of Ham and Eggs.

Except for the scene-stealing Epic campaign, Californians throughout the thirties were more absorbed in national issues than in those of the state and more attentive to national politics. The recovery and reform efforts of the New Deal, the reciprocal trade agreements, labor relations as provided for in Section 7A, agricultural benefits, devaluation of the dollar, the threat to pack the Supreme Court, and the third term issue—questions such as these got attention almost to the exclusion of matters concerned merely with the state. California voting behavior was equivocal and contained a paradox easier to describe than to explain. At each opportunity the state went for Roosevelt, and as regularly it returned its old hero, Hiram Johnson, to the Senate. It elected a fair number of New Dealers to Congress, but not until 1938 did it choose a Democratic Senator, governor, or legislature. Throughout most of the decade, in fact, the state government was so out of sympathy with the New Deal program that it held coöperation to a minimum. For example, not until the very end of the Public Works program were the regents of the University of California willing to accept federal money for much-needed university buildings.

In national politics, bitterness intensified as it became apparent that Roosevelt would seek a third and a fourth election. As for California politics, however, the reactionary and radical factions of 1934 moved toward each other, and by 1938 were merely conservative and liberal. Another four years of depression made almost everyone accept the procedure of government relief as a matter of course. In 1938 the Democrats offered a more conventional candidate for governor, the politically experienced Culbert L. Olson, and elected him without much difficulty. A former Epic, Olson was committed to modest reforms, which incorporated a few of the Sinclair planks; for example, relief through production for use. He entered office handicapped by ill health; his friends in the assembly were a majority, but proved disunited and inept; and the unrepresentative senate was still dominated by the conservatives. It was Olson who pardoned Mooney, and he took a few other steps that might be adjudged liberal. He appointed Democrats to office, and among his selections were some that were egregiously bad. At the time, however, Hitler and Mussolini were plunging toward war. The war came in the ninth month of his governorship, and thereafter the thoughts of Californians ran far more to national and world problems than to what might be done at Sacramento.

In retrospect, the most notable fact about the Olson administration was a facing up at last to the problems of the migratory laborers in California agriculture. By the thirties the pattern was well established that a great part of the state's agriculture, including practically all the larger operations, depended seasonally on a large force of casual laborers. Employer interest seemed to be in having the labor force amply large and unorganized, and in having wage ceilings set, and held to, throughout the season and throughout the state. Local associations in effect set these ceilings, and after 1920 there was statewide coordination through the Agriculture Committee of the State Chamber of Commerce. Following the strikes and attempts at unionizing in the early thirties, still another agency was created, the Associated Farmers, its prime function being to break strikes and to keep the casual labor force fluid and unorganized. Until the thirties, the laborers engaged had been tramp or foreign and thus had an inferiority handicap. In the thirties, the general depression and the local distress in the Dust Bowl sent some 300,000 old-line Americans, the so-called Oakies, to California, most of them intending to do farm work. The distress and degradation that these people encountered, and the application of force to keep them tractable, have been brought into the realm of general knowledge.

The problems admittedly were complicated and difficult. How to assure a living wage and yet keep costs within bounds, how to provide adequate housing and yet keep this labor mobile, how to have labor available at the right season and not swamp the relief rolls in the intervening months—these were some of the difficulties innate to the set-up. Some of them still plague California.

Under Olson, the state government, in coöperation with federal agencies, moved toward ameliorating the conditions. One line of action was to enforce minimum sanitary requirements at the labor camps and to set up government camps where at least a part of this working force could be accommodated. Another line of action was to try to regulate the calls for labor in particular harvests so that they would not exceed the actual needs. Still another was to try to restrict the police to police activity rather than have them act as auxiliaries to strike-breaking. A contributory factor of great importance in this approach to the farm labor problem was the detailed investigation carried out by the LaFollette Committee. Before major corrective legislation could be achieved at the state or national level, however, the labor requirements of defense preparations and then of the war effort siphoned off the labor surplus and decidedly altered the problems. The working out of durable and mutually satisfactory farm labor relations consequently was deferred to a later day. Meanwhile, the Oakies and the Arkies, who for a time were regarded as such a problem group, were quickly assimilated into California's already heterogeneous population.

Public Works

In a planned economy, which of course California has not had, a depression would be the time for public works. One such enterprise of major proportions was ready for action early in the thirties, the project of damming the Colorado. In accordance with the Boulder Canyon Act, and with the underwriting power contracts in hand from southern California, the Secretary of the Interior took bids, and, in February, 1931, directed that construction should begin.

Because the great dam, 1,282 feet in length, 727 feet high, 661 feet thick at the base and 45 at the top, was a bigger job and risk than any one company was prepared to handle, the contract was taken by a combine known as the Six Companies. Under the driving direction of Frank Crowe, the task, including preliminary diversion of the river, the building of a railway spur to the site, and the creation of Boulder City to house the workmen, was completed by March, 1936. The dam freed Imperial Valley of flood danger. It created a lake that would store 32,000,000 acre feet of water, and its generators would produce power at the rate of more than 1,000,000 kilowatts.

While the dam was rising, work got under way on the delivery adjuncts, the transmission lines, the All-American Canal, and the Metropolitan Aqueduct, which in sum cost more than twice as much as the dam itself. By 1941 all three were in operation. They, too, were products of the depression decade.

In this decade California finally decided to come to grips with the water problem of the Sacramento-San Joaquin Valley. The basic idea was to divert surplus water from the northern half of the valley to the southern, thereby minimizing flood danger in the north and alleviating aridity in the south. Supplementary aims were to develop hydroelectric power, improve navigability of the Sacramento, prevent saline intrusion in the Delta area, and furnish water to several towns and cities along the straits.

As early as 1874, B. S. Alexander had proposed such a project. In 1919 Robert Bradford Marshall adopted it and began to popularize it as the Marshall Plan. Some of his details were unduly simplified; he made drawings of canals, wide enough for sailboats, leading down both sides of the great valley. In 1921 the legislature appropriated $200,000 for a scientific study of the plan, but voted down a Water and Power Bill which would have supported the project. In 1922, 1924, and 1926 William Kent, John R. Haynes, James D. Phelan, and Rudolph Spreckels saw to it that the proposal was on the ballot as an initiative measure. Each time the Pacific Gas and Electric Company vigorously opposed it and the measure did not pass.

In 1933, however, the legislature, conservative though it was, passed the Central Valley Project Act, authorizing a bond issue of $170,000,000 to cover construction costs. The private utility companies forced a referendum, in which the measure was upheld by 459,712 to 426,109. Instead of trying to find takers for the bond issue, the state government pinned its hopes on getting the federal government to adopt the project and succeeded in 1935 to the extent of a $12,000,000 initial appropriation. Two years later, Congress officially declared it a federal reclamation project. The engineering plans, meanwhile, were carried forward, and by the end of the decade work was launched on the two major dams, Shasta and Friant. The role of Shasta Dam is to impound some 4,500,000 acre feet of water on the upper Sacramento, regulate the flow, and generate electric power, some of which is budgeted to pump to the canal that carries water a hundred miles up the San Joaquin Valley. Friant Dam, near Fresno, is for impounding the San Joaquin River, and the 160-mile Friant-Kern Canal has the function of diverting this water southward to the driest part of the Central Valley.

Most of the work on these key units was to fall in the following decade, and other amplifications of the project were reserved for the more distant future. Decision was deferred also on many knotty problems of administration and control. Should the Reclamation Bureau, the Army Engineers, or the state exercise control? Should publicly-owned distributors have preference in sales of power? Should the Reclamation Bureau's customary 160-acre limitation on water sales be enforced? These and other fundamental questions were left to be answered later. Because the project lay entirely within the state, some of the patterns in other river developments were not entirely applicable. Since, if fully developed its potentialities so far exceeded others, such as the Tennessee Valley Authority, the ultimate arrangement would be a matter of very great moment. With the advocates of effective public control on the one hand and private interests, as represented by the Pacific Gas and Electric and the great landowners on the other, an epic tug of war was in the making. The depression-ridden thirties left these matters unresolved but did posterity the inestimable service of crystallizing the plans and launching this most ambitious project.

In the never-ending task of modernizing the state highway system, and in a public building program involving schools, libraries, courthouses, and government office buildings, much of it federally-financed, California advanced during the thirties. It was a period during which private enterprise was less venturesome, though, with the Federal Housing Authority as angel, a fair amount of residential construction did take place. The railroads also began to re-equip with

diesels and streamliners.   In agriculture, cotton raising and dairying
expanded rapidly, as did the commercial fishing based at California
ports.   Several branches of industry gained, notably cement making,
but the most striking innovation was the rise of airplane building.

Until the midthirties California's best known contribution to aviation was that Lindbergh's *Spirit of St. Louis* had been assembled
and conditioned at San Diego.   Shortly thereafter, the plants of
Douglas, Lockheed, and North American at Santa Monica, El Segundo, Inglewood, and Burbank gave the state high rank in plane
manufacture.   The availability of electric power was a factor, as was
the reservoir of skilled labor.   The climate of southern California
was congenial to the sprawling plants and afforded open weather for
test flights the year around.   By the end of the decade this industry
accounted for more than 10 per cent of industrial employment in
the state.

In a way, the inescapably dominant note of the thirties was the
reality of the depression, its body blows to the economy, and its dis-
jointing of society.   A feature of almost comparable significance was
the tendency to look to the federal government to provide a remedy.
It was a time when the graphs and the indexes were down.   Nevertheless, in addition to construction on the Colorado and planning in
the Central Valley, California made substantial progress during this
troubled decade.   The annual totals in many lines of production advanced, including cotton, fruits, milk, canned goods, oil refining,
moving pictures, airplanes, and paved highways.   Though not so
spectacularly as in better times, the state continued its population
climb, moving from 5,677,251 in 1930 to 6,907,387 in 1940, thereby
acquiring a larger increment than any other state.   All told, there was
solid achievement despite adversity.

33

THINGS CULTURAL

INVISIBLE THOUGH THEY ARE, the bonds of social convention are tenacious. The men of the gold rush era, though engaged in work that was often peculiar, did their utmost to reproduce the pattern of living they had known back home. Likewise, the people of the second generation, though operating an economy that was distinctive, felt a compunction to conform to the national standard in things cultural. California women, to the best of their ability, dressed exactly like their sisters in the East, and male attire ran to the conventional somber colors, hard collars and cuffs, high shoes, and no laying aside of vests or hats. In architecture the fearsome ornateness and eclecticism of the period had full force locally as well as in the East.

Upon the next generation, bounded roughly by the two World Wars, national urges in things social continued to have great effect. The people of the state were first of all Americans and Californians secondly. They went hand in hand with the rest of the country in discarding chewing tobacco and taking up the cigarette, in accepting women at the polls and in employment, in filling the home with gadgets and machines, in going along with the trend toward chain stores and packaged goods, in moving about with increased ease, and in recognizing that many of the problems of the time were beyond solution by local authority or by private initiative. In some respects the Californians of these interbella years went beyond the national average; for example, in gearing themselves to the automobile, in shifting to suburban residence, and in adapting their dress and dwellings to the climate. In these and in other perhaps more significant particulars they moved toward a cultural pattern that would be distinctively Californian.

The Environment Rediscovered

Not least among the factors promoting this modification was what might be called a rediscovery of the environment. The wonders of the Yosemite, it is true, had been extolled for a generation, and the High Sierra had its devotees. The health rush had involved climatological appraisal, and the state's agriculture, by trial and science, had achieved an adjustment to the environmental facts. Yet overall appreciation of what Nature offered waited almost perforce until the twentieth century when the automobile made the remote parts of the state accessible.

With literally thousands and tens of thousands turning out where only dozens had gone before, problems arose of how to accommodate such crowds and how to preserve the beauties and wonders of Nature against such an onslaught. The answer, now commonplace, was through the National Parks Service and the taking charge of parks, monuments, forests, beaches, and historic sites by federal or state custodians.

As long ago as 1864 Yosemite Valley was designated a state park. In 1890, alerted by the intrusions of cattlemen and sheepherders, the federal government set aside about a thousand square miles adjoining this valley as Yosemite National Park. At the same time, stirred by the Kaweah communitarians and their project for lumbering in the vicinity of the big trees, Congress also created Sequoia and General Grant National Parks, embracing about 250 square miles. In most cases the military was put in charge, which usually meant control without specialized personnel. This was one reason for the friction with the civilians whom the state had placed in charge at Yosemite Valley. In 1906 Yosemite was unified through reconveyance of title to the federal government, but not until 1916, with the creation of the National Parks Service, was the care put on a really satisfactory basis. At Sequoia, civilian control began in 1914. The modern program has this degree of recency.

Also in the more recent period, substantial additions were made to the areas protected by park control. In 1926 about 350 square miles in the Mt. Whitney-Kern River district were added to the Sequoia. In 1933 Death Valley and its environs, almost 3,000 square miles of exposed geology and unbelievable color effects, became a national monument. In 1940 the Kings Canyon area immediately north of Sequoia, some 700 square miles in extent, was made a national park. Mt. Lassen, the Lava Beds, the Pinnacles, the Devil's Post Pile, and Muir Woods are other national parks or monuments.

The state too has taken jurisdiction over a number of sites, some of them historic, such as the Mother Lode town of Columbia and the Marshall monument at Coloma. But most of them were at favored and threatened beach frontages or at the most spectacular of the redwood groves from Del Norte County south as far as the Big Sur. A few of these sites, such as Santa Cruz Big Trees, were subject to earlier pilgrimage by rail, but practically all came to be of major interest only in the automobile era. Thus, the state park system, like the national, assumed its real proportions and importance in the period after the First World War.

In 1915 San Francisco celebrated the completion of the Panama Canal with the Panama-Pacific Exposition on the flats to leeward of the Golden Gate. Notable for its encouragement of arts and letters, for its exhibits and lighting effects, this fair was of less enduring influence than the concurrent Panama-California Exposition at San Diego. The directors of the San Diego fair dramatized the regional culture of the Southwest, presenting a review of the patterns of living from prehistoric times to the twentieth century, with stress on the blossoming of the desert and the semi-arid land whenever irrigation was applied, and displayed an architecture skillfully attuned to the land and climate. Some of the buildings were permanent structures for Balboa Park, but the architectural influence was even more pervasive. Asked to utilize Pan American relationships, Bertram Goodhue drew on the elements of the Spanish Renaissance and the Spanish colonial. Working primarily in bright tones of tile and stucco, with towers, domes, and arcades, he achieved variety, sparkle, and brilliance. Enthusiastically received by visitors to the fair, this theme infected the architectural trends of the time, especially in southern California.

In the realm of residential design, Richard Neutra, Frank Lloyd Wright, and others began to use the functional approach and took into account the opportunities of the locale. Once it was conceded that a California house did not have to look like a Spanish castle, a Cape Cod cottage, or a midwestern farmhouse, it was possible to open

it so that the patio or garden became an integral part of the living area
and to make other innovations to fit the surroundings. A great deal
of construction was as conservative as ever, but the leaven of seizing
upon the local advantages was increasingly present. The Los Angeles Union Station is an example of this adaption of architecture
to its environment.

In dress, likewise, this generation of Californians came to be less
formal and less confined. The escape from corsets, collars, and
excess layers of cloth was, to be sure, not confined to California, but
the benign climate, the prevalence of vacationers, and the boldness
of the state's own clothing designers made this unconventionality
more tempting.

In addition to the day-to-day enjoyment of the outdoors and the
daily adjustments to it, Californians devised a number of ways of
capitalizing upon it. One was through the staging of special events
such as the expositions of 1915, the Los Angeles performance of the
Olympic Games in 1932, another fair at San Diego in 1935, and the
Golden Gate International Exposition at Treasure Island in 1938.
Other activities were annual performances such as the Salinas Rodeo,
the Santa Barbara Fiesta, and the Pasadena Tournament of Roses
and Rose Bowl game. Still another salute to the climate was in
carrying the theater and the concert outdoors. Here again something of the sort is done at Tanglewood, by the Potomac, and elsewhere. The beginning may have been the High Jinks of the Bohemian Club of San Francisco. Then came outdoor theater and
pageantry in Marin County and in the Greek Theater in Berkeley.
John McGroarty's Mission Play ran for many years at San Gabriel,
and Ramona has had even longer popularity at Hemet. Hollywood's
Pilgrimage Play is another hardy perennial.

At the turn of the century the Point Loma Colony had an amphitheater in which Greek plays and classical music were performed.
Open-air concerts at the Ford Bowl in Balboa Park were a feature
of the 1915 exposition. At Ojai some years later an annual music
festival was initiated. Most ambitious of all were the Symphonies
Under the Stars in Hollywood Bowl, begun in 1921 and continued in
spite of the competition of radio and television and the handicaps
of traffic congestion and airplane interference.

Besides these al fresco concerts, Los Angeles had opportunity to
hear its Philharmonic Orchestra, established in 1919 through the

philanthropy of W. A. Clark, Jr. The San Francisco Symphony Orchestra dated back even farther. San Francisco also supported its own opera company, and in 1932 outfitted it with a home in the Civic Center, the first municipal opera house in the United States. No less significant as an institution in this epoch, and reaching a much larger audience, was the Standard Hour, a weekly radio program in which the San Francisco and Los Angeles orchestras were the most frequent performers.

The Creative Mind

Since the time of the first railroad and Comstock fortunes, the number of privately owned masterpieces of art in California has constantly mounted. Hung side by side these would make something less than a Louvre, but a very creditable, instructive, and inspiring display. Although many of these canvases remained in sterile seclusion, there was most encouraging progress in making them available to the public. Old museums, such as the M. H. DeYoung in Golden Gate Park, were enlarged and enriched, and new galleries of even greater size and distinction were opened. These include the Palace of the Legion of Honor in San Francisco, the Los Angeles Museum of History, Science and Art, the Fine Arts Gallery in San Diego's Balboa Park, the Louis Terah Haggin Memorial Galleries at Stockton, and the Henry E. Huntington Art Gallery at San Marino. Thus it had come about that Californians had access to a superior array of fine works of art.

Several of these galleries served as focal points for contemporary art work. The Carmel and Laguna Beach art colonies attracted large contingents of painters, poets, composers, and kindred spirits. Many another creative artist rose above outward circumstance and served his muse to the best of his ability, though dwelling in an orthodox bungalow hard by a bustling boulevard or in the lee of a movie lot.

Of the notable artists of the period, three men working in diverse media illustrate a tendency that was growing. One was Edward Borein of Santa Barbara, who used his exceptional talent in printmaking to revitalize on copper the life of the western range. Another, already mentioned, was architect Richard Neutra, who by a combination of sanity and imagination helped to keep the modern trend in architecture from degenerating into mere convention. The

Colorado River Association

Hoover Dam

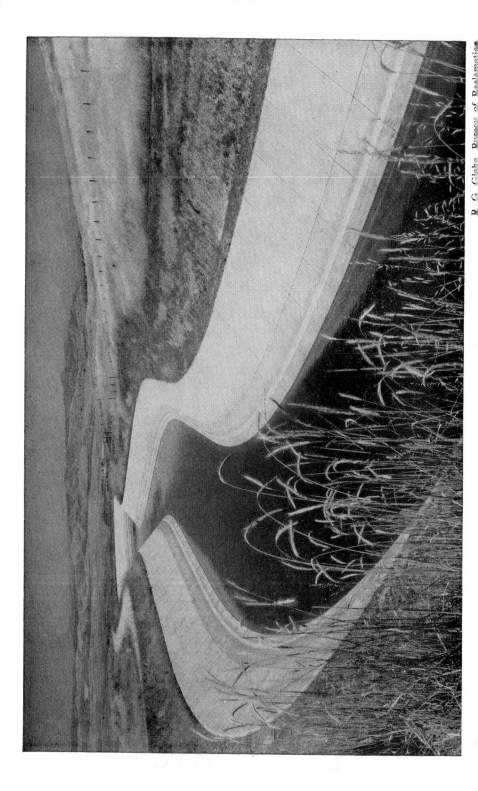

third, Edward Weston, used camera and tripod rather than easel or drafting board and found beauty lurking not only at California's showplaces but also in her most casual scenes. Borein represents the possibility of finding artistic values in the state's past; Neutra and Weston, a sharper discernment of the artistic implications of this land and climate, and a readiness to utilize new approaches in capitalizing upon them. The eventual California art will embody this awareness of local history and of the local setting or it will not deserve the adjective.

The patronage of music brought a goodly number of performers to California. Other artists were attracted by the no longer silent films, and still others by the climatic advantages of life in California. A few, such as Lawrence Tibbett and Luisa Tetrazzini, are listed as California contributions to music, but to what extent the state can lay claim to Charles Wakefield Cadman or Carrie Jacobs Bond, or to the recent German exiles Arnold Schoenberg and Otto Klemperer, is a debatable point. The important thing is that there was mustered in the state a generous allotment of the world's most talented musicians.

In the realm of letters the historian encounters a similar problem. If every modern writer who ever set foot on California soil were to be included, from native son Robert Frost, who has completely naturalized himself as a New Englander, to Theodore Dreiser, who sojourned briefly in Hollywood on salary from the moving pictures, the group would be misleadingly large and distinguished. As a matter of fact, genuine California writers were not quite so numerous, partly because the concentration of American publishers in and around New York City made it highly advisable for certain classes of writers to congregate there. On the other hand, California's tradition of literary excellence is stronger than for any other of the arts, and modern exemplars of this tradition have given the state a creditable position.

In one branch of literature, which, to be sure, is not yet recognized and indeed has seldom been proposed as such, California obviously excelled. This is the scenario. Those not written in Hollywood were rewritten there. The moving picture companies retained writers on the lavish scale characteristic of their other operations. It is often asserted that these subventions are no real service to letters, that when writers come to Hollywood their tendency is to "go Hollywood" with stultifying effects upon their true genius. In part this is incident to the endeavor of novelists and short-story writers to adapt themselves to the peculiar techniques of scenario writing. No insurmountable barrier would seem to stand in the way of maintenance or even improvement in quality of output by members of the moving picture writing corps. The humorous philosophers, such as Will Rogers and Irvin S. Cobb, have had the best success so far in grafting moving picture work upon a career already flourishing without sacrificing the original. Others doubtless will discover the secret.

In this epoch California had a broad phalanx of novelists and story writers who achieved popularity with their readers but whom the critics classify as competent rather than great. Willard Huntington Wright, better known as S. S. Van Dine, the mystery writer, belongs in this category. Other examples are the journalist-novelists Max Miller and Lee Shippey, and Rupert Hughes, who in his more serious vein was a Washington biographer. Many would deposit Upton Sinclair in this same group. By their very number, however, his works required a shelf of their own. From *The Jungle,* a pre-California book in 1906, on through *The Brass Check, The Goose-Step, The Goslings, Mammonart, Money Writes!, Oil, Boston,* and two score others, his books are distinguished by a sharp disapproval of feature after feature of our political, social, and economic system and by an emphatic demand for reform.

With the short story as their favorite medium, two younger writers showed great promise. With a technique reminiscent of Browning's *The Ring and the Book,* Edwin Corle, in *Mojave* (1934) and *Fig Tree John* (1938), made himself at home among the Indians, prospectors, hitchhikers, and laborers of the California deserts. Swinging to fame with the title *The Daring Young Man on the Flying Trapeze* (1934), William Saroyan became even more widely noticed for his unorthodox, meandering stories, some of them tragic, others mirthful, and all of them built around characterization more than plot.

In the same decade another young writer, John Steinbeck, began to publish short stories about the paisanos of Monterey County. *The Pastures of Heaven* (1932) and *To a God Unknown* (1933) were loose groupings of such stories. *Tortilla Flat* (1935), though similarly formed, has sufficient unity to pass as a novel. In these early works Steinbeck revealed powers of acute observation, a sense of sympathetic amusement over the foibles of the paisanos, and a capacity for most felicitous expression. With *In Dubious Battle* (1936) and *Of Mice and Men* (1937) he took up the cudgels more vigorously for the downtrodden laborers in California agriculture. Then in 1939 he capped this arch with a novel of epic theme and proportions, *The Grapes of Wrath,* which depicts the hegira of Dust Bowl refugees to California and their grievous mistreatment and suffering as migratory farm laborers. As a novel of protest it dwarfs the best previous California efforts, Helen Hunt Jackson's *Ramona* and Frank Norris' *The Octopus.*

Through the quarter century the chief writers of verse in California were the minor and very minor poets. At the opening of the period two disciples of Ambrose Bierce, George Sterling and Herman Scheffauer, loomed above this average of mediocrity, but in 1927 both cut short their careers by suicide. Two years earlier Robinson Jeffers had made his first bid for fame with the publication of *Roan Stallion.* Half a dozen other volumes followed, all set against the background of the Carmel region and the rugged Big Sur country. Jeffers' poetry shows a marked influence of place. He acknowledges a large debt to "the magnificent unspoiled scenery" of the Monterey peninsula, to "the introverted and storm-twisted beauty of Point Lobos," to the bold headlands jutting out into fog and ocean, and to "the savage beauty of canyon and sea-cliff." The pounding of the ocean, the waves and spray, the gulls, the hawks, the tortured cypress, the towering redwoods—these and a thousand other elements of the "Jeffers country" are the recurrent materials of his writing. Without them it would lose much of its strength and character.

Universals are his chosen subject matter, particularly love and hate, revenge, remorse, and expiation. His longer narratives relentlessly pursue these themes, and even in his shorter poems, less morbid with suffering and violence, a steady seriousness dominates. Much that man has done Jeffers thoroughly disapproves. His respect is for Nature realistically appraised, rather than for man, and consequently, despite the haunting beauty of much that he has written, he is not and will not be the people's poet. Yet he is the one Californian thus far who may be ranked as a major poet.

Schools and Libraries

In facilities for the spread, care, and increase of knowledge California registered a substantial advance in the interval between the two World Wars. For the dissemination of knowledge the dependence was chiefly on institutions established much earlier, but modified by more modern theories and conditions. In large degree the reliance was on the public school system. At the elementary and secondary levels these schools were organized in districts and were locally controlled, subject, however, to certain standards enforced by the state superintendent. The certification of teachers, for example, was set up as a state function, part of the requirement being graduation from college in order to qualify for elementary teaching and a year of advanced work in order to qualify for high school teaching. The state specified minimum salaries, and in order to eliminate the extreme differences in tax burden it adopted the practice of making sizeable remittances to each district proportionate to the average daily attendance.

As the richest state in the West, California could afford to appropriate generously for the school program. As of 1940 the per capita expenditure was exceeded only in New York. The problem, however, was rendered difficult by the extremely rapid increase in school population, which more than doubled between 1914 and 1940. The school districts had to race to catch up with the needs for buildings, equipment, and staff.

In this epoch the California schools showed a moderate willingness to experiment. Architecturally, and most markedly at the college level, they stuck pretty closely to the stereotyped imitations of midwestern business blocks and medieval castles. At intervals, however, a school board authorized a functional structure designed to take full advantage of the sunlight and the fresh air that are California's priceless heritage. By the end of the period this type of school architecture was in the ascendant. As for teaching methods, a restrained experimentalism was also afoot. One trend was toward the project method in the grades in place of formal drill. An early example of change was in the introduction of laboratory science in the high schools. A subsequent example was the fusion course.

Other innovations that developed were in the degree to which bus transportation made possible the consolidation of small schools, in the toning up of standards in the high schools through the state university's system of entrance requirements and accrediting, in the generous provision for vocational and adult education, and in the popularity of the junior college. The latter type of school had a shadowy beginning in 1907, when high schools were authorized to offer postgraduate work. A decade later junior colleges were made an integral part of the state school system. By 1939, with 49 institutions of this rank, 42 of them public, California was far and away the leading utilizer of the junior college. By 1951 the number had grown to 75, with total enrollment at 302,130, which was more than in all the rest of the nation.

The higher echelon of the state's educational system included seven or eight state normal schools, a larger number of privately controlled colleges and universities, and the state university. In the course of these years the normal schools broadened their programs and became state colleges, though still putting much emphasis on teacher training. The private schools, headed in enrollment by the University of Southern California and Stanford, in most instances rested on foundations laid in the preceding generation. The state university was in the midst of a rapid expansion, in 1919 annexing the Los Angeles State Normal School as a seventh campus, and throughout the twenties and thirties gaining in enrollment at an unprecedented rate. By 1940 its student body was larger than any other university's anywhere. More significant, its Berkeley faculty, according to the findings of a Carnegie Institution survey, was surpassed in "distinction" only by the faculty of Harvard and that but slightly.

In library building, California had done well also. No library in the state in 1940 was on a par with the British Museum, the Bibliotèque Nationale, the Library of Congress, the Harvard Library, or a dozen others in the older parts of the nation and world. By their essentially accumulative nature, libraries are the product of time, and in California time had been short. The oldest of its major collections was the State Library, in its early years a victim of mismanagement, but later vastly improved. The most notable general collection was that of the University of California; in seventy years it had carried its accessions well beyond the million mark. Less venerable and less extensive holdings included those of Los Angeles Public, Stanford University, the University of Southern California, Claremont Colleges, and the University of California at Los Angeles. Special mention should be made of the device of branch libraries and interlibrary loans whereby the state, county, and city libraries conspired to make books readily available at a multitude of stations. Without such machinery the Los Angeles Public would not have achieved the largest circulation among American libraries.

By a liberal outlay of funds, a tireless zest in pursuit of materials, or a combination of the two, several world-famous special collections had been assembled. The Bancroft Library of Pacific States materials has been described. Stanford University boasted the Hoover Library of War, Revolution, and Peace, unsurpassed on certain phases of the First World War, the Russian Revolution, and the relief efforts. At San Marino the Henry E. Huntington Library and Art Gallery was opened to visitors and researchers. Its rich store of English paintings, English history and literature, and Californiana represented lavish expenditure of the Huntington millions. As for California materials, it had become a good second to the Bancroft. In this field, too, research was greatly assisted by the special collections of the California Historical Society and the Southwest Museum, the Cowan collection at the University of California at Los Angeles, the assemblage started by Lummis at the Los Angeles Public, the Mason collection at Pomona, and the Layne collection at the University of Southern California. Other collections, such as the Clark in Los Angeles and the Sutro in San Francisco, had special resources in other fields.

In sum, these aids and materials for research in the humanities make a respectable total. Yet it would have been quite out of step with modern times if they had been as impressive or represented a tithe of the investment in facilities for research in the sciences. Needless to say, they did not. In research laboratories maintained by many of the industries, such as the oil and the airplane companies, and in laboratories at the major universities, special provisions were made for a great variety of scientific research. Some of it was intended to be immediately practical. On the whole, this was the case in the industrial research centers. The university's researchers in agricultural science were also, in effect, on call to try to solve any problem that might arise in crop production. Hopes of allaying suffering and improving health underlay the researches in medicine.

The practical utility of the study carried on, however, was not always expected to be direct. Into this category of basic research some of the largest investments went, particularly into the "unapplied" branches of astronomy, chemistry, and physics. Private, state, and federal funds were drawn upon, in varying proportion and fashion, to underwrite these research preparations. The astronomical record will serve as an example.

In 1874 an eccentric millionaire, James Lick, donated $700,000 to the University of California with which to build an observatory. His first thought was to put it at Fourth and Market in San Francisco, then he veered to the idea of a mountaintop and settled on Mt. Hamilton, south of San Jose, partly because it overlooked the site of a flour mill of his. Thus was initiated the scientifically advantageous device of perching a telescope in the clear atmosphere of the mountains. With a 35-inch refracting telescope, for many years the second most powerful in existence, the Lick Observatory was a focal point for astronomical research.

Thaddeus S. C. Lowe, Lewis Spence, and other promoters and popular scientists were inspired by the Lick Observatory and longed for something like it, only larger, in southern California. Their notion was taken up at the turn of the century by a trained astronomer, George Ellery Hale, who raised support for a scientific search for an ideal observatory site. The specifications included such factors as latitude 30 to 35 north, moderate but not excessive altitude, equable temperature, stability of weather, a minimum of clouds and overcast, no undue turbulence of air currents, and accessibility to an inhabited center where machine shops, supplies, and accommodations for visitors could be had. Mt. Wilson met the specifications. Hale then went to work on acquaintances of means, many of whom had retired to Pasadena's millionaire's row. By 1917 he had a 100-inch telescope ready to operate—for the next twenty years the world's largest—together with the other appurtenances for effective study and research.

As the work at Mt. Wilson progressed, Hale raised his sights to a still more ambitious project. In 1928 he persuaded the Rockefeller Foundation to commission a still larger telescope and to budget $6,000,000 for the purpose. The sea of lights that had developed on the plains below Mt. Wilson ruled it out as the location. While the 200-inch refractor was being ground, southern California was combed for the most eligible site, the choice falling on Mt. Palomar in San Diego County. The partly ground glass arrived in Pasadena in 1936; another twelve years of painstaking work were necessary before the telescope was completed and installed, ready to reach out to the very boundaries of the universe.

Meanwhile, other arsenals for scientific research were being prepared. At Pasadena, as a sort of adjunct to his observatory, Hale envisioned a scientific institute. He was able to interest a number of wealthy Pasadenans to finance the idea. In 1917 Robert A. Millikan joined forces with Hale. He was as adept as Hale in enlisting benefactors of great wealth and he had a remarkable gift for selecting areas of research in which the prospect for significant findings was at a maximum. Within a very few years the California Institute won recognition as one of the most effective agencies of its kind in the country. The assembled staff and faculty deserved much of the credit, enabled, however, by the material equipment supplied by Hale, Millikan, and the donors.

In quantity and caliber of research facilities the institute was surpassed by the university at Berkeley. There a noteworthy improvement likewise took place in the interval between the two wars. It was catholic, embracing practically all the branches of science, but its most arresting feature was the Radiation Laboratory at work on the then mystical experiment in atomic fission. Perhaps the most surprising thing was that a state as new as California, only recently graduated from frontier status, should be almost without peer in its marshalling of forces for exploration of the frontiers of scientific knowledge.

Historical Scholarship

So far as appreciation of scholarship was concerned, it was the scientists of this epoch who collected the major plaudits. Astronomers such as Hale and Edwin Hubble certainly deserved them. Berkeley had an active coterie of anthropologists of great reputation. Its department of physics and its school of chemistry had equal distinction, and the college of agriculture, though somewhat narrowed to California's peculiar problems, ranked with the best. These examples could be extended. Scholarly attainment, however, was not confined to the sciences. It occurred also in the humanities, for which the field of history may be taken as an example.

First of all, the between-the-wars period witnessed improvement of facilities for historical study and research. The older libraries at Berkeley, Stanford, Sacramento, and Los Angeles constantly expanded their resources. To them were added certain new collections, notably the Hoover and the Huntington, veritable arsenals for the researcher in history. Monographs published under the auspices of the Hoover Library by 1940 were into their second dozen, which indicates but inadequately the extent to which this collection had been utilized. Although at the Huntington the casual observer saw first of all the crowds pressing in to view the book exhibits, the paintings, and the gardens, behind the scenes a constantly mounting group of "readers" was hard at work on problems of English literature and history, and of California history. Certain new techniques, notably the perfection of the photofilm method of copying books and manuscripts and interlibrary loan service, opened unexpected doors to California historians. Among the results thus made possible were California books on such outlandish subjects as the modern French Empire in Africa and the Orient, the Spanish Floridas, and the dissolution of the Carolingian fisc.

California history, meanwhile, was brought under scrutiny by a number of very competent amateurs, that is, historians in the business for the fun of it rather than because of any economic urge. Many of the best results in this quarter century were achieved by historians of this group. Their works are cited by the score in the bibliography subjoined, but too much emphasis cannot be laid on the great service to local historiography rendered by these men in the pursuit of their avocation. At the head of the lists in their respective divisions stand the bibliographies of Wagner and Cowan, Hanna's chronological commentary, Wagner's analyses of cartography and explorations, the biographies by Harding, Lyman, Watson, and Dana, and the miscellaneous writings of a host of others, among them Layne, Wheat, Wells, Dobie, Chalfant, Glasscock, and McWilliams. California is doubly fortunate to have had its past explored by so doughty a band. In this connection it is significant that the California Historical Society, the Historical Society of Southern California, and numerous local societies actively meeting, collecting, and publishing have been maintained by energetic groups of nonprofessional enthusiasts.

Yet the normal thing in the modern era of specialization is that historical research should be primarily the work of professionals. In Bancroft's day California history was not written thus, and as recently as 1907, when the Native Sons of the Golden West proposed to endow a chair of California history, the president of the University of California demurred, in chagrin we hope, because there was no scholar at the university or elsewhere competent to fill such a chair. To the credit of the university it must be admitted that, assisted by the Native Sons, it set out at once to remedy that defect.

In 1906 the university had acquired the Bancroft Library, consisting of some 60,000 volumes of books, manuscripts, and newspapers. Then in 1910 H. Morse Stephens, head of the history department, persuaded the Native Sons to advance funds sufficient for two annual traveling fellowships. The following year Herbert E. Bolton was brought to the department expressly for the purpose of directing and leading the utilization of the resources of the Bancroft Library in graduate work and research. These elements, the Bancroft materials, the fellowships, Morse Stephens and Bolton, explain much of the renown earned by the Berkeley history department. Recognition is also due the department for its all-round strength. A few years earlier the department had been said to consist of a sham giant surrounded by real pygmies, but the addition of Americanists Priestley, McCormac, and Chapman, and of a group of specialists in the European field headed by Morris, Paetow, Palm, and Kerner gave the university a distinguished staff unequaled within a radius of half the breadth of the continent. Later this brilliance was further enhanced by the provision of two endowed chairs, to which were called James Westfall Thompson, the celebrated medievalist, and Frederic L. Paxson, outstanding authority on the American frontier and the recent history of the United States.

There were, however, two particular concepts that were fundamental to the flourishing of the Berkeley graduate work in history. One was the realization that the archives of Spain and Mexico contained a marvelous wealth of materials for the history of California and of every other part of the New World in which Spain had once been interested. Bancroft had had only a slight awareness of the existence of these materials; Stephens got a notion of the extent of the Spanish archives when he made a preliminary survey in 1910; Bolton was already conversant with Mexico's archival riches, for he had examined them with care and had prepared a guide to their resources for United States history. For the other fundamental, Bolton was primarily responsible. It was a simple idea, yet revolutionary, namely, that American history is best studied not within state or national confines but on a continental or, better still, on a hemispheric basis. Thoughtful analysis of California's history would seem to point inevitably to this deduction, but if Bancroft grasped it, the only evidence is that he decided to broaden his project to take in the entire Pacific slope, and other historians had been content to stay within the United States, or even within a portion of it.

Catalyzed by this vision of broader horizons, nurtured on the riches that Bancroft had stored up, vitalized by the magnificent documentation preserved in the Spanish and Mexican archives, stimulated and assisted by the Native Sons Fellowships, and inspired by the leadership of Stephens and Bolton, the Berkeley graduate group in American history made itself one of the most dynamic, prolific, and significant in the country. Its doctors of philosophy predominated in the field of Hispanic American history, they became major workers in the field of the Spanish borderlands, prominent in the field of the American westward movement and the American West, including Hawaii, and the leading exponents of the study of the history of the Americas, the Western Hemisphere in its entirety. Concerning this group the term "California school" gained currency, and more legitimately than if it were applied to any set of the state's poets, novelists, painters, or sculptors.

Many of these historians have engaged in studies that relate distantly or not at all to California. Others have turned their attention to local problems with such commendable result that of the references, other than first-hand accounts, tabulated in the accompanying bibliography more than half are to be credited to this California school. Outstanding among these are Bolton's works on Kino, Anza, Crespi, and Paloú; Charles E. Chapman's *Catalogue;* his volume on the founding; the Chapman-Cleland *History;* Owen Coy's work on the gold rush era; Cardinal Goodwin's studies of the establishment of state government and of Frémont; and Joseph Ellison's account of early federal relations. Thus the list begins; it goes on to include published items running the whole gamut of the state's history, not to mention scores of manuscript theses deposited in the university library. These works naturally are as variegated as the men who produced them, yet practically all exemplify these characteristics: they are based to a very large degree on sources and on fresh sources, and they treat of California as an element in continental and world relationships rather than as a state poised in a vacuum. Much was accomplished; much remained to be done. Every indication was that this phase of California historiography was still an open chapter.

34

WARTIME GROWTH

IN 1939, though the decade just closing had been one of travail, California could look back on an epoch of lusty growth. In the comparatively short span of ninety years as an American state she had come from nowhere to be fifth among the states in population, fifth in taxable income, near the top in agricultural production, and perhaps over the top in attention claimed. No other state had matched this increase; sober opinion doubted that even California could maintain the pace.

In September, 1939, however, Hitler sent his Panzers into Poland, and overnight Europe was caught up in a war that soon had world dimensions. For a time the United States remained neutral, though this was a war about which it was impossible to remain dispassionate and from which it was most difficult to remain detached. The fact of world war, even though the United States was not a belligerent, radically changed the outlook for California. Then, on December 7, 1941, by attack without warning on Pearl Harbor, Japan snatched away America's neutrality and plunged the nation into the vortex of the European as well as the Pacific war. This development was a stimulant to the economy such as the state had never experienced. It involved a degree of planned and coordinated effort that had not been present before, and it provided a special patriotic incentive that was entirely new. Thus mobilized, California achieved material gains that surpassed even the greatest of her earlier attainments.

Plant and Potential

When the war started, California's economy was set up and adjusted to the needs and opportunities of peacetime. Annual income as of 1939–1940 stood as approximately five billion dollars.   Primary production in fisheries, forests, mines, farms, and factories accounted for about half of the total.   Fisheries yielded some $20,000,000; forests $87,000,000; mines about $400,000,000, the greater part in petroleum; agriculture $625,000,000; construction $417,000,000; and manufacturing, on goods with a market value of $2,798,000,000, was credited with addition of $1,135,000,000 through processing. The other half of the annual income came from values added through distribution and services, a broad category including everything from wholesale and retail trade, to utilities and transportation, to hotels, laundries, and theaters, to personal service and the professions.   Part of this income was derived from investments outside the state and from expenditures by tourists and other visitors.

A peculiarity of the economy was that, whereas the nation as a whole had an almost equal number engaged in primary production industries and in the distribution and service trades, in California the division was more nearly on a one-third, two-thirds basis.   Clerks, salesmen, businessmen, service station operators, teachers, money lenders, lawyers, and the like outnumbered mill hands, farmers, construction workers, and miners two to one.   For the waging of old-fashioned war, this personnel factor would not have been a good omen.

Several lines of production also seemed unwarlike.   An early move was to shut down the $50,000,000 a year gold mining industry in an effort to shift its skilled labor to producing more critical minerals. In the nineteenth century the fruits and nuts that constituted about 30 per cent of the agricultural output and the vegetables that ran to another 18 per cent would not have been counted sinews of war. Of the 381,000 persons engaged in manufacturing it appeared that the 71,700 engaged in food and beverage production, the 31,100 moving picture makers, the 22,400 apparel workers, and the 13,200 furniture makers, to cite just a few examples, were hardly in position directly to win the war.   Iron and steel workers in 1939 numbered only 26,900, and aircraft and ship builders only 22,600.   The war, of course, was waged in a more modern fashion, utilizing a new assortment of skills and materiel.   Even so, to meet the requirements of the war, many Californians would have to shift to entirely different work.

The other side of the picture was that by 1939 California had in production a number of the requisites for up-to-date warfare.   Since this war would not be fought on hardtack and embalmed beef, the state's agriculture did not have to be completely revamped. In gasoline and fuel oil the petroleum industry was producing two prime essentials. In machine shops, automobile assembly plants, tire factories, electrical equipment plants, and precision instrument shops the state had nuclei for military production. Furthermore, it was off to a good start in plane building and possessed certain natural advantages for shipbuilding.

In the face of Japanese aggression against China and the rise of militarism in Europe, the United States began to step up its preparedness for war. Before Pearl Harbor there were several dividends for California. The most spectacular was in the awarding of contracts for training and combat planes and for ships, mostly Liberty and Victory type freighters and transports. With federal funds made available to cover part of the cost of airplane factory expansion and to cover almost the entire outlay for shipbuilding facilities, a rapid build-up of plants occurred. Employment rolls in these industries mushroomed by 1941 to some 5½ times what they had been in 1939, and production advanced from $106,000,000 to $708,000,000—all this before the United States became a belligerent.

Capitalizing on the mildness of the climate and the open spaces available, the federal authorities also turned to California for troop training sites. Held over from earlier wars and alarms were a number of installations, including Mare Island Navy Yard, lesser facilities for the Navy at San Francisco and San Diego, Army headquarters for the Ninth Corps Area at the Presidio in San Francisco, subordinate centers at Fort Ord and Fort McArthur, and air bases at March Field and Hamilton Field. The Navy was at work on an airfield at Alameda and had plans for Treasure Island when the exposition closed. As the prewar draft put more and more men into uniform California began to blossom with an array of mammoth training stations.

Yet the defense contracts and the involuntary visitors in uniform hardly balanced the specter of disruption of the economy. Pessimists wondered what would happen to the state's more frivolous enterprises, such as the production of fruits, wine, off-season vegetables, moving pictures, and sports apparel, if the nation had to buckle down to an all-out war effort, which in turn would exercise first claim on transportation facilities. When the emergency actually came, the dislocation was as serious as had been forecast, but not in the exact pattern predicted.

A more realistic expectation would have been that in a mechanized, aerial, and global war California's size, position, wealth, agriculture, oil, minerals, manufacturing, and science presaged for her a most active part.

War Industries

In the twenty-seven months following Hitler's invasion of Poland the United States moved closer and closer to war. In so far as possible it solidified its position with the Latin American nations. A perimeter was marked off in hopes of sealing the Western Hemisphere against aggression. American forces undertook patrols and convoying half way across the Atlantic, and firing on submarines was authorized. Generous credits were arranged for Britain and her allies, and in the destroyers-for-bases deal the United States strained neutrality still further. Throughout this period there was attention to the menace of Japanese aggression, but the primary concern of the American government was obviously to fend against the danger represented by totalitarianism in Europe. With Pearl Harbor the tempo changed, but not the emphasis. Confronted with the problem of waging war on two fronts, American strategists determined to be content with holding tactics in the Pacific until the Germans were coped with. Meanwhile, the problem was to build up military strength. It was a setting in which the munitions maker was a heroic figure.

Toward aircraft production in California a good beginning had been made. This program was now stepped up to an all-out effort. The national government put up $150,000,000 for plant expansion, to which was added $79,000,000 in private capital. Vast, sprawling plants soon took shape at Burbank, Santa Monica, El Segundo, Inglewood, Long Beach, and San Diego, camouflaged in imitation of residential subdivisions. A rumor circulated that the Ocean Park pier, which drew a bead on the Douglas plant, was to be re-aligned to set up the U. C. L. A. campus as a decoy. To Douglas, Lockheed, North American, Vultee, Hughes, and a host of subsidiary parts suppliers, the contracts poured out. By June, 1945, they totalled $2,136,119,000 in San Diego County and $7,093,837,000 in Los Angeles County.

From considerably fewer than 20,000 employees on the job in 1939 these plants built up their working force to a peak of 243,000 in August, 1943. A fraction of these workers came to the job sufficiently skilled. A larger number had to be trained as riveters, welders, machinists, and the like. The saving factor was that a division of labor approximating the assembly line was possible, and narrowly specialized skills sufficed.

The shipbuilding story is strikingly similar. From a mere 4,000 men on the job in 1939 there was an upsurge to a peak of 282,000 in August, 1943. Contracts for wartime shipbuilding amounted to $5,155,516,000. The greater part, some $3,053,119,000, went to yards at Richmond, Sausalito, South San Francisco, and elsewhere in the Bay region. Los Angeles trailed with $1,709,974,000 in contracts. The plants were financed almost entirely by the federal government, which posted $409,000,000 to go with $29,000,000 in private capital. Several companies engaged in the work, but the one enterpriser who emerged as a public figure was Henry J. Kaiser. His fame derived in part from his other interests, which included cement, aluminum, and steel, a tank factory at Willow Run, and plans for automobile manufacture, but for a time he was thought of primarily as Kaiser the shipbuilder. His approach to the problem was not unlike that applied in the great construction projects at Boulder, Friant, or Shasta. Here were plans and blueprints to be transformed into reality. The methods of organization and procedure, and some of the key personnel that had been used in such projects, could be readily applied to the new assignment.

Although by 1939 California had some 675 plants producing and fabricating iron and steel, the majority were relatively small, supplied only a small fraction of the western market, and were at the fabricating level. A regional deficiency long recognized was the slight development of basic production of iron and steel. As of 1939 the available capacity was no more than a million tons of ingots a year. Wartime concern about decentralizing industry, about lessening the load on the railroads, and about insuring a supply of material to the western warplants led to a sudden expansion of plant. At Geneva, Utah, the federal government built a $200,000,000 steel mill rated at 1,280,000 tons capacity. Through government loans it assisted in the enlargement of the United States Steel, Bethlehem Steel, and independent mills at San Francisco and Los Angeles. Also, with a loan from the Reconstruction Finance Corporation, Kaiser built at Fontana an integrated blast furnace and rolling mill of 700,000 tons capacity. Some 50 miles east of Los Angeles, dependent on coal from Utah 500 miles away, on iron ore from Eagle Mountain 150 miles away, and on rail freight for the delivery of its products, it was expected to be at a disadvantage in competition with tidewater-located mills. Nevertheless, the mill prospered sufficiently to justify a postwar enlargement of its capacity. Percentagewise, the California steel industry seemed an almost infinitesimal part of the national total. By 1945, after all this expansion, the state accounted for only 1.5 per cent of the nation's pig iron. The wartime increase, however, was a tonic to the West and a harbinger of a better rounded and possibly unmonopolized set-up of basic industry.

After aircraft, ships, and steel, the next most conspicuous industrial change of the war years was in the oil industry. With the particular assignment of fueling the war in the Pacific, the California oil companies stepped up their production of crude oil, added to their refineries, and increased the output of gasoline and fuel oil by more than 50 per cent between 1939 and 1945. New cracking equipment enabled them to distill a considerably higher proportion of high test aviation gasoline. Alongside the refineries arose another series of plants dedicated to the transmutation of crude oil into rubber. To begin with, the process was fantastically expensive and noisome in odor, but as Japanese conquests in Malaya and the Dutch East Indies cut off access to natural rubber, it was a war necessity. The end result was a synthetic with certain marked superiorities over natural rubber, and therefore of continuing importance beyond the war years. Eventually, too, the cost of production was brought down.

Many other industries were also boosted by the war effort. In some instances it was a matter of an older factory being converted; for example, from the making of furniture to plywood boats, or from radios to sonar equipment. In more instances, entirely new factories were improvised to produce airplane parts, shell casings, landing field lights, electronic equipment, and other such war supplies. The largest expansion in this miscellaneous industrial activity was in machinery, electrical equipment, rubber goods, sheet metal, and light metals products. Other lines, such as chemicals and clay and sand products, advanced more gradually. Even with certain industries, such as automobile manufacture, artificially restrained, the overall picture was one of tremendous growth. Factory output rose from $2,798,180,000 in 1939 to a resounding $10,141,496,000 in 1944.

Theoretically, there might have been advantages in a dispersal of this manufacturing as widely as possible over the state. In practice there were reasons of convenience which tended to cluster most of it in the localities where industrial beginnings had already been made. The Los Angeles area, the San Francisco Bay region, including the East Bay, and the San Diego area were the most favored centers. Los Angeles had the largest population increase during the war year— —better than 300,000—but more startling gains included San Diego's spurt from 203,000 to 362,000; Richmond's from 23,000 to 93,000; and Alameda's from 36,000 to 90,000.

Agriculture at War

The offhand prediction about California agriculture at the outset of the war was that, because of its emphasis on luxury and semi-luxury items, it would have to undergo major revision. Certain incidental lines, such as flower growing, were candidates for curtailment, and by plan or otherwise there was a reduction in the acreage planted to strawberries and sugarbeets. Of the fifty crops on the Department of Agriculture's list, all the others held their own or showed an increase. The handicaps of competition for labor supply and transport to market were offset by the nationwide prosperity, the enlarged number of potential customers in California, and the government purchases for servicemen in training in the state and for provisioning the armed forces in the Pacific theater.

In actual distribution through the branches of agriculture, the increase was without great distinction as to crop. From 1940 to 1944, for example, the income from dairying advanced from $91,000,000 to $192,000,000, that from beef cattle, hogs, and lambs rose from $88,000,000 to $175,000,000, that from poultry went up from $45,000,000 to $119,000,000, with the total for livestock and livestock products going from $232,000,000 to $500,000,000.

Cotton, meanwhile, advanced from $25,000,000 to $51,000,000, other field crops from $74,000,000 to $161,000,000, and vegetables from $123,000,000 to $284,000,000. In this general category, as in livestock raising, farm income more than doubled during the war.

Fruits and nuts showed an even more striking upsurge. Citrus went from $91,000,000 to $262,000,000, grapes from $35,000,000 to $184,000,000, the deciduous fruit crop from $57,000,000 to $217,000,000, and nuts from $14,000,000 to $39,000,000. Overall, this meant three and a half times as much income.

These figures are a reminder that California agriculture is responsive to the state of the market and that even the tree-borne part of its output can be stepped up by more intensive cultivation, the application of more water and plant food, and more thorough harvesting. The total realized, $1,744,000,000 in 1944 as against $625,000,000 in 1939, was almost a three-fold increase and only less startling than the strides being made in industry. Furthermore, while California had climbed only to eighth or ninth among the states in manufacturing, in agriculture she was in first place.

The Manhattan Project

With far less fanfare California scientists applied their talents to the problems of the war. At Stanford, Berkeley, and Los Angeles, area training programs were started for those who might be assigned responsibilities of military government in occupied countries. At the Institute of Technology and at the University of California at Los Angeles there were elaborate programs of training in meteorology. A variety of other specialized training programs was conducted at the colleges and universities. Conventional civilian instruction continued alongside these programs, except at the Davis campus of the university, which was turned over to the Air Force for the duration.

Capitalizing on the reservoir of researchers assembled in the state, the national authorities turned to them for a variety of services. Some went into the field with the armed forces, as for example a geologist, who advised on problems of terrain that would be encountered in the island-to-island progression in the Pacific. Others were asked to participate in research studies at laboratories set up by the armed forces, such as the sonar laboratory on Point Loma or the Naval Research Center at Inyokern. Still others, with contracted support from federal funds, were encouraged to stay on in their laboratories and work on a specified problem critical in the war effort. The emphasis was upon science that could be applied, as in the search for a better drug to cope with malaria. Some scientists expressed concern that there would be an exhaustion of the pure or theoretical science waiting application. Yet the range of assignments was broad and quite a bit of basic research was involved. The dimensions of this activity are suggested by the total of $57,000,000 in research contracts entered into by the University of California. Other institutions in the state had proportionate share.

The most spectacular of these projects was in atomic research. At the Radiation Laboratory in Berkeley, Dr. E. O. Lawrence had built the first cyclotron and thus paved the way for the production of U-235 and the atomic bomb. The discovery of two other elements, neptunium and plutonium, took place at the Radiation Laboratory. Under the Manhattan Project, the University of California accepted responsibility for setting up the establishment at Los Alamos in New Mexico, where further atomic research was conducted and the first atomic bombs were actually produced. Like many of the other wartime projects, this one was shrouded in as much secrecy as possible, and many facts about it were held in confidence after the war. Selection of the University of California to conduct the enterprise was a tribute to the state's high attainment in scientific study and in managerial skill.

Troop Training and Staging Area

It is notorious and, at least to a degree, understandable that wars are fought without any sparing of the cost. Except that a strong effort was made to curb inflation, the United States made no pretense of economizing on the Second World War. There were times, however, when factors quite extraneous led to provident decisions. One was the selection of California as a major area for troop training. Continuing the process begun before American involvement as a belligerent, the Army developed huge training camps near Monterey, Paso Robles, San Luis Obispo, and Santa Maria. The Marines opened a West Coast Quantico near Oceanside, the Navy built up its facilities at San Diego, and the Air Force added major training fields near Victorville, Merced, and Santa Ana. All told, these training centers amounted to more than 10 per cent of the national total. Much of the construction was routine; barracks, for example, were said to be built according to blueprints left over from the First World War. Yet there was some accommodation to the environment and some use of its particular features. At Oceanside, for example, the Marines had an ideal setting for practice landings, and on the desert beyond Palm Springs General Patton's Third Army found plenty of heat and sand in which to make preparation for the African campaign.

In addition to housing this many-sided training program, California was the principal staging area for the Pacific War. For its part in this work, the Navy enlarged and improved its facilities at Mare Island, San Francisco, and San Diego. It also took over Treasure Island and converted it into a naval station, acquired Terminal Island in Los Angeles harbor, and, at a cost of $78,000,000, converted it into a base, and by comparable work developed Port Hueneme as an efficient working port. Most of the troops sent out into the Pacific embarked at San Francisco or Los Angeles. In cargo loading for the Pacific convoys Port Hueneme had a substantial share.

Relocation of the Japanese

Californians in 1941 had not entirely escaped from the heritage of anti-Japanese sentiment built up earlier in the century. The Japanese seemed inscrutable. Many had not sufficiently Americanized themselves in language and looks. In several lines of business they were formidable competitors. Their imperial homeland, too, had roused general apprehensions by its aggressions in China.

In this setting it was perhaps natural that a species of horror-fiction anecdotes circulated widely about what the Japanese Americans would do if war came. This fisherman, it was said, would put on his uniform as an officer of the Imperial Navy and lead the Japanese fleet into Los Angeles Harbor. That gardener would signal in a landing party. Another was to dynamite the Los Angeles Aqueduct, others would demolish the San Francisco bridges, while the maid in the Beverly Hills mansion was to assassinate her mistress. Those who retailed these stories did not really believe them; nevertheless, there was at least a suspicion that some of these scare stories might come true.

Against this background, the news from Pearl Harbor had particular impact. The losses officially admitted were heavy enough; rumor multiplied them, and the popular supposition was that, with the Pacific fleet and the Hawaiian bastion knocked out, the west coast was wide open to attack. Except through limited submarine action, the sinking of a tanker off Crescent City, and the lobbing of a few shells into the Goleta oil fields, the attack did not come. The general belief, however, was that it could have happened.

On December 7 the Department of Justice took prompt action to restrain enemy aliens. It imposed contraband rules, travel restrictions, and inspections, and it moved in quickly to arrest aliens known or suspected to be dangerous to the public safety. On December 7 some 736 Japanese aliens were arrested; by February more than 2,000 were being detained. This work seemed thoroughly efficacious. A difference of opinion developed, however, between the Department of Justice and General John L. DeWitt, head of the Western Defense Command, about what further steps should be taken. At his urging, the Department stepped up its rules and raids; but without more specific evidence than he presented, it was unwilling to go as far as he wanted. By mid-February an impasse had developed between the General and the Department. In part, and perhaps in very large part, the General's demands for more drastic measures were the outgrowth of heavy pressures exerted by west coast civilians.

The first loud voice in this campaign was that of radio commentator John B. Hughes, who on January 5 took up the theme that all the Japanese ought to be removed. His cry got an immediate echo from groups habitually anti-Japanese, including the California Joint Immigration Committee, the Native Sons, and the American Legion. Agricultural and marketing organizations and certain labor unions joined the chorus, and practically all the newspapers agreed that "the Japs must go." Public officials and politicians were equally clamorous. The west coast delegations in Congress were unanimous on the issue, while on the scene the most active official spokesmen were State Attorney General Earl Warren and Mayor Fletcher Bowron of Los Angeles. In speaking to the district attorneys and sheriffs of the state, Warren interpreted the total absence of fifth column and sabotage activity as "a studied effort" on the part of the Japanese to hold any such action until the zero hour. Bowron got all Japanese removed from city jobs, pressed the issue in Washington, and declaimed over the radio that the Japanese in California were "a hotbed and a nerve center for spying and sabotage." Both Warren and Bowron carried their urgings direct to DeWitt.

From early January to February 5 DeWitt's requests to the Justice Department were solely for more vigorous controls on enemy aliens. On February 5 his office gave out a statement that "military judgment" called for the removal of all Japanese. Subsequently this demand was laid more categorically before the Department of Jus-

tice. That Department pleaded lack of authority to carry out such
a removal, lack of facilities for any such undertaking, and lack of
evidence submitted to demonstrate that removal was called for. It
was not in a position to deny the military necessity alleged by DeWitt.
Higher authority would have to decide.

On February 19, President Roosevelt took the fateful step of transferring control of enemy aliens to the War Department. Through a
series of public proclamations General DeWitt then ordered "volun-
tary" departure of Japanese from designated coastal areas, an 8:00
P.M. to 6:00 A.M. curfew, other restrictions, and, on March 27,
evacution of all Japanese, citizens and aliens alike. Some 110,000
persons were subject to this order; two-thirds of them American citizens. The Japanese Americans of western Washington and Oregon
and southern Arizona were included, but the main body to be evacuated was from California.

In an age when almost that many persons turned out for a football
game and several times as many flocked to the beaches on a holiday
or to the Tournament of Roses parade, it might seem that the removal
could have been accomplished overnight. Actually it took from
April to August. Assembly centers were improvised at race tracks
and fair grounds. Summoned to register and then to report on specified dates, the Japanese were taken to these centers. At best there
was little time to wind up business affairs, dispose of property, and
get ready to leave. From these makeshift camps the evacuees were
transferred to more distant relocation centers, two of them on the
eastern margin of California, the other eight scattered as far east as
Arkansas.

Although the terminology was polite—these were called relocation rather than concentration camps—barbed wire fences and armed
guards gave the opposite impression. Without the goodwill of the
administrators headed by Dillon Myer, the lot of the evacuees would
have been much worse. Even so, the uprooting and the detention
were enough to impose a severe psychological strain. To the more
sensitive the inescapable imputation of disloyalty and inferiority before the law was the hardest cross to bear. All felt the stigma of
being sentenced to sit out the war idle and unproductive. In time,
to be sure, some of them were released from the centers. Through
enlistment or the draft many of the young men went off to the battle-
fields in Europe and later in the Pacific, where they performed with

extraordinary valor. A few were released to go to guaranteed jobs outside General DeWitt's proscribed area. Late in the war, a few were permitted to come back into California. Most were kept in camp until after V-J Day and the centers were not closed until January 1, 1946.

The wherefore of this wholesale removal cannot in its entirety be weighed in the balance. Since, fortunately, there was no Japanese assault on the mainland, the question of military necessity was not tested. Several of the arguments for relocation—for example, the citing of sabotage in Hawaii—have been shown up as altogether false. In marshalling arguments DeWitt showed great indebtedness to the civilian agitators for removal and an equal degree of dominance by these pressure groups. Some of the pressure groups, in turn, made no bones about their ulterior motives. The fundamental force thus can be clearly identified as lying in these elements in the California population, as nurtured on the accumulated spirit of opposition to Orientals, and as quickened by considerations of economic or political advantage. The clamor and the hysteria were none the less genuine. There was a measure of accuracy in the claim that relocation was to protect the evacuees from mob violence—certainly no compliment to the law-abiding quality of the Caucasian Californians.

In passing, it should be remarked that a few Californians questioned the propriety of the action and worked for good treatment of the evacuees and for provision for their ultimate return. The Fair Play Committee, headed by Galen M. Fisher and including a select group of prominent businessmen and educators in its number, was most active along this line, though not in position at the outset to challenge the military necessity for removal.

That justification, on the other hand, was rendered suspect by the contrast of Hawaii. There, a larger number of Japanese, less Americanized than those on the mainland, were not removed. The area was at least as critical as the west coast; but the general in charge was quite a different man from DeWitt, and the community was far less prone to racist extravagance.

In California the Japanese were sorely missed. The decline in the quality of fruits and vegetables in the local market was a token of the loss sustained. At a time when production for the war effort was at a premium the retirement of these thousands of competent enterprisers and workers was economically unsound. To the Japanese it meant a more direct loss, which by one calculation amounted to $365,000,000. What scars it would leave on their regard for America could not be forecast.

There was an inescapable consequence, too, for the constitutional system of the United States. Except for the weaker parallel of Indian removal in Jackson's day, there was no precedent in American annals for a mass internment of aliens and citizens alike, without evidence of disloyalty, and with race as the sole basis of determining who should be interned. Prior to 1942 most Americans assumed that the Constitution was a safeguard against such arbitrary treatment. Belatedly, the issue was taken to court and, about the time the war ended, there were rulings that the color of military necessity had been sufficient, but that the federal government had a limited liability for damages. Yet a precedent of group proscription had been set, which would stand as a legacy of the hysteria which led to the expulsion of the Japanese Americans.

The Population Spiral

War is a habitual disturber of the population patterns. In addition to the shifting of the Japanese, the Second World War transferred more than 700,000 Californians into the armed services. It also brought about major changes in employment and a flood tide of migration to the state that exceeded the rate ever previously attained. The population movements in the gold rush and the boom of the eighties were small by comparison. That in the booming twenties was more grandiose, but the war years' increase, 1,916,000 between 1940 and 1945, was almost as large as that for the entire decade of the twenties, 2,251,000.

An inevitable concomitant of the spiraling of industrial activity was expansion of the industrial labor force. In 1939 there had been 381,000 thus employed. In 1943 almost three times as many, 1,121,200, were at work. Over the same four years, the personnel employed in agriculture increased by 31,000, that in utilities and transportation by 58,000, that in trade by 54,000, and that in government by 188,000. Thus, the aircraft and shipbuilding plants, which boosted their labor force by 462,000, were not the only elements active in increasing employment.

In many instances the workers moving into these expanding fields of employment came by shift-over from other going elements in the state's economy. Bakers became riveters, gas station attendants turned welders, clerks took hold of factory tools, and so on down the line. In the overall picture, the statistics show clearly where the extra workers did and did not come from. The service trades released a net total of 55,000; mining, 15,000; construction, 8,000; printing, 1,400; and automobile making, 1,300. Those were the only lines of employment where there was a net decrease, and with a million new jobs to fill and half that many servicemen and Japanese to replace, these transfers left about 95 per cent of the new jobs unfilled.

The new recruits included some young people going to work a year or two earlier than they normally would have. They included thousands of women who in peacetime would have stayed at home. They included a few men who had other work but took on a war job in addition. A much larger number were new arrivals pulled in from all the outlying states by the war's requirements and the good wages that prevailed. Some Mexican nationals joined the trek. The vast majority, however, were from other parts of the Union. They were a reasonably accurate cross section of America, drawn, however, more from the South and West than from the industrialized Northeast, much more concentrated in the working-age bracket than had been true in the eighties or the twenties, and including more Negroes than had been observed in California generally.

Even without the complications of war, such an influx of new inhabitants would have created a serious housing problem. True enough, the curtailment of nonessential construction released certain materials. Highway building, for example, was practically called off for the duration. On the other hand, the priorities exercised by the military and the defense plants hampered the building program. The most effective solution in meeting the immediate emergency was the company construction of temporary housing units as an adjunct to the war plants. On the hills above Vallejo and Marin City, on the flats at Richmond, and at various locations in southern California, seried ranks of these structures took shape. Built without much benefit of architecture, intended to provide only minimum shelter, and that only for the duration, these buildings did not adorn the landscape or provide for California living at its best. A limited amount of private dwelling construction went on, most of it held to unpretentious small homes, and some of it even starker prefabricated houses. Many of the newcomers substituted a trailer for a home.   Trailer camps blossomed as a new variety of real estate subdivision.

The added throng strained other facilities.   The utility agencies— water, electricity, gas, telephone, and sewer—were hard put to achieve the sudden expansion that was necessary.   The same was true of the public transportation companies, streetcar and bus.   School districts in the vicinity of the war plants were confronted with a sudden enrollment jump far above previous expectations, and the problem of what to do about it was complicated by the thought that at war's end the workers might all depart and the school population revert to what had been normal.   The state program of equalizing school costs helped greatly, though the system of allotment on the basis of average daily attendance in the preceding year did not fit the emergency.   The answer on the school problem in some instances was to erect and staff a new school.   Often it was to crowd more pupils into the existing buildings and often to make these schools and teachers do double duty through half-day sessions.

The problem of accommodating the newcomers was broader than housing, utilities, transportation, and schools.   Involved also were all the matters of governmental service, such as police and fire protection, garbage collection, and public health; all the matters of shopping centers and the supply of groceries, drugs, clothing, and furniture; all the matters of social provision, churches, theaters, public parks, and the like.   In earlier stages of growth such elements had tagged along or had seemed to come automatically as population grew.   The war did not repeal the natural impulses to try to fill these needs, but shortages and priorities made it difficult, if not impossible, to do so.   These difficulties were not peculiar to California, but they were present only in other suddenly congested areas.   A fixed impression of the period is one of standing in line to board a crowded bus, standing in line to buy vegetables, taking a number and waiting one's turn at the meat counter, queueing up at Christmas time to buy a box of candy.   A penalty for California's very rapid growth was that shortages were more acute, the ration point system therefore subjected to more strain, and its abuses more of a temptation than in more normal parts of the country.   The temptation being greater, it may well be that black market and under-the-counter transactions were worse.

One element of shortage and rationing certainly came home to

California with special force. In the more compact eastern communities, where public transportation was convenient and cheap, and the private automobile something of a luxury, gasoline rationing was just an incident. The average Californian, however, was as dedependent on his car as an Eskimo on his snowshoes, the full gasoline tank was a more compelling symbol than the full dinner pail had ever been, and to qualify for a B ration book was an achievement supreme. Streets and parking lots had good business-hour patronage, but the open highways were strangely deserted. The fact was that pleasure driving all but disappeared. To avoid being grounded most people had to confine their driving to business and shopping.

Another respect in which California was unusual was in its presumed exposure to attack. At continent's end, and with its population massed near the coast, it was in position to catch the first blows of a Japanese assault on the mainland. Furthermore, its war plants and military installations seemed to set it up as a target worth striking. Accordingly, there was concern about this exposure. Some individuals were fatalists enough to take the hazard lightly; others built private bomb shelters and kept their cars stocked for a flight to the desert. Also, it was a flourishing area for civilian defense. Householders were encouraged to lay in a supply of primitive fire-fighting equipment—ladders, rope, axes, and sand. Enrolled as air raid wardens, they were issued stirrup pumps, helmets, armbands, and stickers for their cars. They took first aid courses and learned to apply traction splints. To fire and temblor drills the schools added air raid exercises. Neighborhoods organized telephone chains to spread warnings quickly, and wardens stood watches at the communications centers. Perhaps more usefully, many citizens worked as airplane spotters. In prospect of air raids, the defense authorities designated bomb shelters, decreed blackout preparations, and followed with several alerts.

Barrage balloons, radar emplacements, searchlights, and antiaircraft batteries provided the similitude of war. On one occasion, which went down in history as "the battle of Los Angeles," the guns were actually unlimbered. Whether the target was a cloud, an escaped balloon, the successive shell bursts, a strayed plane, or enemy aircraft was not vouchsafed. Rumors quickly encompassed all conceivable explanations, and the authorities did not bother to clear up the mystery. Seemingly, the "battle" involved much warlike exercise and no casualties.

In retrospect, the activity of civilian defense seems to have been mostly waste motion, though perhaps worthwhile as a morale builder. It did knit communities together to a degree seldom achieved before or since. As in other parts of the nation, Californians quickened their patriotism by inserting the national anthem in theater programs and church services. They expressed their loyalty, too, as was done throughout the country, by giving blood to the Red Cross, buying defense bonds, and working with the U.S.O. The Hollywood professionals made special contributions to morale building and entertainment of troops at home and abroad.

Yet the more solid achievement of California's war effort was in its men who entered the services, the troop training program centered in the state, and in producing the sinews of war. In these accomplishments California could take real pride. In them, too, her people reaped very substantial profits. During the war years their annual income advanced from a gross of just over $5,000,000,000 to almost $13,000,000,000, while the holdings in liquid assets increased from $4,500,000, to $15,250,000,000. Even with allowance for inflation estimated at 30 per cent, this was a remarkable prospering. Although proprietors and labor each had about a three-fold increase in cash income, it was not shared absolutely evenly. White collar workers lagged behind, farmers ran ahead of everyone else in the gains in cash income, and many industrialists had capital gains not yet converted into cash, yet the most striking features were the general sharing in the gains and the fact that California had built a complex and high-powered economic machine. In time of war it could produce at a prodigious rate. Just how useful and profitable it would turn out to be in time of peace was left for the postwar era to find out.

35

PEACE AND ITS PROBLEMS

THE SECOND WORLD WAR was unique in the amount of talk that went on about the problems that peace would bring. In every earlier war Americans had taken it for granted that it would be good to demobilize and get back to normal living. Throughout the period of this war they were equally intent on ending the carnage and the suffering, but they were beset by a haunting concern that peace might plunge the world into a depression like that of 1929 and the thirties. Even if the world and the nation managed to escape that catastrophe, there was fear that California, having gone to extremes in girding for war production, would have special difficulty in readjusting to the pursuits of peacetime. California, it was reasoned, might be in for a depression all its own.

Planning for Peace

On the one hand, this worry made management hesitant about plant expansion that might be idle after the war. It was reminiscent of the gold rush period, when clouded land titles and the belief that prosperity would not outlast the placer deposits encouraged a fly-by-night attitude toward California business and industry. Twentieth century investors entertained a somewhat similar pessimism concerning the war prosperity. Therein lay a practical justification for the almost complete federal underwriting of the shipbuilding yards.

As of the 1940's, on the other hand, economic planning, at least to the extent of assessing future prospects, had become commonplace. Business concerns attempted it for their own particular fields and moved toward a broader perspective on the problem through the Taxpayers Association and the State Chamber of Commerce. It was taken for granted that government agencies should work along this line.

Through boards, bureaus, commissions, departments, and divisions, the state took cognizance of natural resources, industrial relations, employment, public works, agriculture, and many other factors basic to the economic welfare of its people. For years a State Planning Board undertook to coordinate the future books of the several state agencies. Then in 1943 the legislature created the State Reconstruction and Reemployment Commission, to work with the legislative committees on postwar construction and rehabilitation, and to draft a master plan for the expected emergency. The adage now ran "In time of war, prepare for peace." The federal government was concerned also about successful execution of the peaceward maneuver. The armed services hoped to avoid the confusion that had beset demobilization in 1918; the Air Force, for example, planned to convert the Santa Ana camp into an indoctrination center, indoctrinating for civilian life.

At the state level, perhaps the most practical step taken was to stockpile plans and funds for highway construction, school buildings, state office buildings, and other public works not mandatory for the war effort but vital for the long term needs of the state. As an element in this preparation, $170,000,000 was laid aside for the delayed building program of the University of California. With the postwar necessities in mind, Governor Earl Warren resisted proposals for tax cutting and at the same time imposed a reasonable degree of economy in the state's operations. The result was that at the end of the war, the state was not only out of the red, but had a reserve built up with which to meet the postwar requirements.

Demobilization

Because the human mind has a preference for neatness, there is a temptation to think of a war as starting abruptly, like sprinters getting away from their marks, and as stopping with equal suddenness, like the morning paper caromed against the front door. In actuality, even after the formal declaration, the effort of waging modern war takes time to build up, and, more surprising, a tapering off period is apt to start even before the end of hostilities. So it was with the Second World War. Months before the actual downfall of Hitler it became obvious that the amassing of troops and materiel for the European theater had been carried far enough. With the victories in Sicily and Italy, the Normandy landings, and the break-through to Berlin, that part of the war receded into history. The European war machine was too cumbersome to turn around and bring to bear against Japan, but some of its parts could be diverted, and were, thereby reducing the pressure on the California training centers and war industries.

Demobilization, therefore, began long before the news of the fall of Berlin and the Japanese surrender. California's two foremost war industries strikingly illustrate this fact. Both in shipbuilding and in aircraft construction employment came to its peak in August, 1943, two years before the end of the fighting. By V-J Day the shipbuilders were down from their 282,000 maximum to 128,500, and in another six months had cut to 34,400. The aircrafters were also at maximum in August, 1943, with 243,000 employed. By V-J Day their rolls had been reduced to 111,200, and in another six months fell to 52,700. In various other fields the reconversion began before the war was over.

As demobilization occurred, some of the released war workers contributed toward relieving the tension by packing up and going back home to Texas or Georgia or wherever they had come from. This exodus, however, did not live up to expectations. Despite the wartime crowding and the presumed end of bonanza employment, many of these Californians-come-lately had developed a real taste for life in this part of the West. The same feeling infected a good fraction of the servicemen who had trained in California, not to mention their relatives who had come to the state as camp followers. Many of these determined to take up permanent residence in the state, and by the end of 1945, when release from the services was by no means finished, some 186,000 veterans had executed the transfer. Here was a potent addition to the working force, because these were young people in the full vigor of their productive capacity. Their coming also meant that in California veterans would be proportionately stronger than in the nation as a whole.

New Construction

The clearest sign that peace was abroad in the land was the revival of nonmilitary construction. Work on state highways, quiescent

Ansel Adams

El Capitan, Yosemite Valley

Diesel and Cab-ahead Locomotive on the Tehachapi Grade

for the duration, began again. There was a backlog of repair work to bring existing roads into good condition. Then new construction was carried out to enable motorists to by-pass towns and cities. The viaduct for Highway 101 through San Rafael, the highway skirting San Jose, and the express routings past Fresno and Bakersfield are examples. For the larger centers such as Los Angeles, San Francisco, and San Diego it was more difficult to score a complete miss, but with diversionary systems such as the Nineteenth Avenue route, the Sepulveda by-pass, and Mission Valley Road, some of the traffic was removed from the central business districts.

Another focus of special attention was on highway widening at points of greatest congestion and danger. Wherever traffic jams threatened, special remedies were sought. Thus, section after section of the main-traveled roads came in for widening and often for dividing. The work was scattered in purposeful fashion throughout the state, with special attention directed to the approaches to towns and cities and to the grades and tortuous curves where traffic was slowed. Consequently, some of the widening and dividing had to be done where the terrain made it most difficult—as in Gaviota Canyon, Grapevine Canyon, and in the roughest part of the Ridge Route. By 1952 this kind of face lifting had been given to the crucial parts of 101 from Petaluma to San Diego. On 99, from Oakland and Sacramento to Los Angeles, the average number of lanes was even higher, with the entire distance from Bakersfield to Los Angeles four or more lanes in width and most of it divided.

At long last this program of eliminating grade intersections was carried into the cities. The San Francisco bridge approaches and the Pasadena Freeway were prewar examples. After the war, work commenced on the Hollywood and Harbor freeways through Los Angeles and on other similar projects for expediting and safening city traffic.

The relaxing of wartime restrictions likewise unleashed a new tide of business construction. Some of it was industrial, such as the $65,000,000 addition to the Kaiser steel mill at Fontana, undertaken in 1952. Some of it was commercial, such as the Crenshaw and Westchester shopping centers in Los Angeles, the Prudential Life building on Wilshire, and the Statler Hotel at Wilshire and Figueroa. Some of it was directed toward the housing problem, as in the battery of ten-story apartments in Park La Brea in Los Angeles, the rows of apartments farther out Wilshire, the phalanxes of apartments and multiple dwellings in southwestern San Francisco, and the rows of new single dwellings in Marin County, San Fernando Valley, Westchester. and elsewhere. There was a revival too of building individual residences. Indicative of the volume of residential expansion is the figure of 500,000 new residential units, house and apartment, constructed in Los Angeles County in the first seven postwar years—more than the grand total of residential units new and old in Boston and Pittsburgh.

Along with a great deal that was purely conventional, the modern architecture of the prewar period was picked up and extended. Use of plastics and light metals was more extensive than it had been, and floor plans and exposures were influenced by a re-appraisal of the functions that a California dwelling would be called upon to serve. Architecturally, however, there was more to be said for the light, clean lines achieved in large-building construction, as in the Permanente Hospital in Oakland or the Prudential building, than for the improvements in residential design. Indeed, the more striking feature of the postwar residential building surge was not strictly architectural. Instead it involved unified tract development, whereby the subdividing, the laying of streets and utilities, the building, and the landscaping were combined in one mass production operation. The residential growth of towns and cities came to be increasingly in this pattern. In some instances, architectural monotony was blatant; in others, integrated efficiency and park-like spaciousness were achieved.

With the cooperation of the federal government, California cities also embarked upon public housing. Encouraged by the good results attained at Aliso Village, Bell Gardens, and Banning Park, Los Angeles contracted in 1949 for slum clearance and erection of some 11,000 residence units at a cost of $110,000,000. Three years later strident opposition developed, in part, at least, from private building interests, and the program was interrupted. By that time, through purchase and condemnation, the tangle of private property titles in ten tracts had been changed to public ownership and most of the slum-like structures had been cleared away. It was, however, still unresolved whether low-cost public housing would be erected on these sites. The other possibility was that the cleared tracts might pass into private hands for any sort of construction that promised highest profits.

Industrial Expansion

In many lines of commercial and industrial activity, postwar changes occurred which were akin to new construction. Often these changes took place behind plant or factory walls and were not visible to the passer-by. In the aircraft plants, for example, the wartime models rapidly became obsolete and there was a shift to jet propulsion and other radical innovations in mechanics and design. To a considerable extent these advances necessitated retooling—an internal variety of new construction.

On the railroads the re-equipping of the postwar era was easier to see. In the thirties the Southern Pacific had used articulated, lightweight streamliners—the Daylight and the Lark—between San Francisco and Los Angeles; the Santa Fe had a streamliner on the San Joaquin Valley run and the Chief and El Capitan from Los Angeles to Chicago; the Union Pacific was pioneering even more venturesomely with the diesel-powered City of San Francisco and City of Los Angeles on the Chicago runs. By the time of the war, all the railroads were turning gradually to diesels for heavy freighting and for switching. In the postwar era the trend toward diesels and streamliners went into high gear. The Santa Fe added a Super Chief to Chicago and motor cars to San Diego and converted practically all its operations to streamliners and diesels. The Union Pacific moved in the same direction. The Southern Pacific put new Daylights on the San Joaquin and Cascade runs and shiny new streamliners on the Golden State route to Chicago and the Sunset route to New Orleans. The Western Pacific, in coöperation with eastern affiliates, launched the California Zephyr on the Feather River-Moffat Tunnel route to Chicago. Even the most casual observer could see that California railroading had entered a new day.

The change was signalized also by a railroad-sponsored amendment to the state constitution to permit the operation of longer freights with fewer brakemen. The proposal was in step with the realities of diesel power. The campaign, however, was pitched on the level of labor baiting and the slogan employed was "Get rid of featherbedding."

Other California businesses were on the upgrade. Automobile assembly plants resumed full operation and were enlarged. For them a large backlog of demand had accumulated. The same was true for tire manufacturers, and in almost the same degree for the apparel manufacturers. Furniture was wanted for all the new dwellings and as replacements in older residences. Some of it was imported from Grand Rapids, but much of it was produced in local plants in styles that ran the gamut from the traditional to the most modern. For ingredient parts the automobile and aircraft assemblers turned increasingly to local plants. Factories were erected to supply goods that had not been in significant demand before the war. Television sets headed the list, but a new or rapidly expanding market was recognized for many other items, including deep freeze lockers and garbage disposal units. More than in the prewar period, the industrial expansion was in the form of branch plants for eastern industry, as in the Budweiser brewery in San Fernando Valley. Local enterprise was represented, however, both in large installations such as the Permanente plant at Moss Landing and in many a smaller establishment.

Agriculture, meanwhile, enjoyed a continuing prosperity. It was achieved without spectacular addition to the crop list. The staples, in fact, continued to be almost the same as before, though a few crops, such as cotton, gained in acreage. Quick freezing opened new markets for fruits and vegetables and, most strikingly, for dressed poultry. Some good land went out of production, especially in Los Angeles County, where the spread of industry and residence encroached on the agricultural domain. Nevertheless, agricultural production and income held up.

In trades and services there was a continuing expansion. Assisted by the benefits made available to veterans whose education had been interrupted by the war, the colleges and universities ran to near capacity enrollments. The public schools faced new crises with an influx of youngsters, especially in the larger cities, and had to accelerate their building programs. Los Angeles voted $75,000,000 in bonds in 1948 to end half-day sessions, and had to do it again in 1952 to the tune of $140,000,000 to combat this same plague. Expansion of shopping facilities through new supermarkets, new outlets for eastern firms such as Ohrbach's, new branches for local firms as in Bullock's Pasadena, and Robinson's Beverly Hills, and entire new shopping centers, such as at Crenshaw and Westchester, set the pace in the march of commerce.

Basis of Growth

The explanation for this general postwar development in industry, agriculture, and trade was multiple. In large degree it was due to the continuation of the emergency and of militarism. Since at the close of the war Russia immediately loomed as a menace to the free world hardly less fearsome than the combination of Germany, Italy, and Japan, warlike expenditures were renewed almost as soon as they had been cut back. Through the Marshall Plan and subsequent programs of strengthening the allies against Russia, the United States continued to boom the market for many of the things that California could produce. In the summer of 1950 the outbreak of war in Korea still further stimulated the military build-up and the emergency orders to California plants. The plain fact was that the postwar period turned out not to be postwar in reality, but a time of continued tension, emergency requirements, and deficit spending. In it, too, the controls that had held inflation to a minimum during the war were rapidly breached. Runaway prices, along with new spending for war, gave the economy an artificial stimulation.

In state and nation, nevertheless, there were elements also of a healthier prospering. Because the national market was good, buoyed up by the new wave of warlike spending, California products were in excellent demand. On the local scene, too, the postwar prosperity had solid basis. One of the solid factors showed in the continued population growth. The wartime pace, with almost two million added in the first half of the decade, was not maintained, but the increase in the next five years was well above a million, so that the census takers in 1950 found some 10,586,223 Californians, a 53.3 per cent increase over 1940. So far as numerical growth was concerned, the forties thus were far and away the prize of all decades. In fact, the gold rush, the boom of the eighties, and the greater boom of the twenties, all put together did not add so many new residents as came in the wartime and postwar forties. Nor did the trend cease. By 1952 the state's population had passed 11,000,000.

Politics

Throughout the forties and into the fifties the problems of war and of troubled peace kept attention focused on national and international politics and government. The same tendency, perhaps not quite so strong, had operated throughout the preceding epoch of the depression. State and local issues occasionally rose to the forefront, but the general pattern was that they received only secondary notice.

By the forties California had evolved a system of state government that was peculiar, if not unique.   Its 1879 constitution, too long and too legislative to start with, invited constant amendment.   The procedure of amendment was simple; the legislature, by majority vote, could submit proposed amendments, and the electorate, by a majority vote, could adopt them.   In the period of Lincoln-Roosevelt progressivism another door was opened.   If voters in the number of 8 per cent of the votes cast in the last gubernatorial election petitioned, a proposed amendment could qualify for the ballot.   Between 1879 and 1950 the legislature laid some 477 amendments before the voters, 248 of which were adopted.   By initiative between 1911 and 1950 another 73 amendments qualified for the ballot, of which 21 were adopted.   The 1951 legislature considered 96 proposed amendments and approved 14 for the 1952 ballot.   The consequences of this mass exercise of the amending power have been to lengthen the ballot beyond the limen of wise discrimination for practically all the voters, to make the constitution into a patchwork miscellany, and to write into it a multitude of special interest provisions.

By direct legislation through the initiative and referendum, also available since 1911, and through ordinary legislative enactment, much else was added that defined the governmental processes in the state.   At least in terms of political theory, several of the key features militated against responsible government.   One of these was the authorization in 1913 for candidates to file for nomination by more than one party.   Conceived in admiration for the good points of nonpartisanship, cross filing in time practically destroyed party responsibility and denied the voters at the final elections a real choice between parties.   Through the rotten borough system for representation in the state senate, adopted in 1926 and upheld by the electorate in 1948, the upper house of the legislature was deliberately made unrepresentative of the people, and to that degree, irresponsible.

In actual practice, there are things to be said for the state government's record through the forties and into the fifties.   At the outset Culbert L. Olson was governor.   Handicapped by ill health and by dissension in the Democratic ranks, Olson was largely ineffectual. In 1942 Earl Warren handily won the governorship.   In 1946 he gained the Democratic as well as the Republican nomination, and in 1950 he defeated James Roosevelt for another four-year term.   In 1948 his party made him the vice-presidential nominee, and in 1952 he won out over a reactionary group that bitterly contested his choice as the state's favorite son as candidate for President.

Under Warren the state has moved ahead with an impressive program of public improvements in highways, freeways, and state and institutional buildings. Helped of course by the uninterrupted prosperity, it has operated with a balanced budget. Furthermore, Warren's appointments have been well chosen and the entire executive and administrative branch of the state government has functioned without indications of corruption or venality. Through repeated advocacy of a compulsory health program, Warren roused enthusiasm among liberals while inviting the wrath of reactionaries and the American Medical Association. The legislature being what it was, this proposal had no likelihood of enactment. As a man of rectitude and goodwill, not extremist enough to satisfy either the ultra-conservatives or the ultra-liberals, Warren gained the consistent support of the broad ranks of the political middle roaders, including many registered Democrats. Enjoying far longer tenure of office than any of his predecessors, he has been honored by a widespread opinion that the state has not had a better head.

For the legislature, however, no such compliments were current or in order. The weakness of party controls was partly to blame. The constant influx of new, unattached, and unoriented voters also militated against the maintenance of proper checks upon representatives. Prosperity and preoccupation with larger matters made the voters inattentive, while the devices for direct legislation gave assemblymen and senators a convenient means of shunting embarrassing issues to the electorate. These several factors debilitating to the legislature played into the hands of what was sometimes called the "third house," the professional lobbyists.

The Lobbyists

Lobbying is not quite the oldest profession. In California it did not appear in the constitutional convention in 1849, and in the first legislature it was present only in the mild form of Senator Green's private bar and his ready motion to adjourn and drink. By 1907 it was in full flower, though with the peculiarity that the control was frankly in the hands of a machine run by the one business that was big, the Southern Pacific Railroad. The Lincoln-Roosevelters broke this machine. They were accused of substituting a machine of their own, but it was one of politics and patronage. By the twenties, however, conditions were ripe for lobbyists to rise again. The unrepresentative character of the legislature, especially after 1926, made that body particularly susceptible. The torrent of migration delivered a voting majority with no knowledge of the old machine and the fight against it. The overnight growth of many corporations and combines as formidable as the Octopus of old, and each with a special interest to be served, gave incentive for a rebirth of lobbying.

In the thirties, in particular, with the return of legalized liquor, racing, and gambling, the new style of lobbying forged ahead. In 1939 some of its details were itemized in detective H. R. Philbrick's report to the Sacramento grand jury. This report spelled out in detail how influence had been brought to bear on certain legislators by retainers, donations, and campaign contributions, and how large a part of this influence was funneled and directed by professional lobbyists. Through the accounts of one such man, Arthur H. Samish, Philbrick had traced $496,138.62 in 1935–1938, all provided by individuals and organizations with a direct interest in legislation.

The Philbrick report created little stir at the time, although some of the legislators named failed of re-election. Any general concern about "government by lobbyists" was postponed until after the war. It was not aroused until 1949, when Carey McWilliams, in the *Nation* of July 9, and Lester Velie, in the August 13 and 20 issues of *Collier's,* offered candid exposé of Samish and his methods. He freely admitted that the legislature did his bidding. A posed photograph with a puppet "Mr. Legislature" held on his knee did not exaggerate. The beauty of his system was that it was within the law, and part of it through the law. As public relations counsellor for the brewers, the liquor wholesalers, the motor carriers, and other clients, Samish worked through front organizations which carried on public relations drives, donated to campaigns, entertained influential persons, and retained a surprising number of lawyers, especially legislator-lawyers. The reciprocal favors asked were limited. Usually they seemed to concern mere details in the grand total of legislation and in many instances details remote from the interests of a particular legislator's constituents.

On the state as a whole, the weight of lobbyist control was most felt through the welter of "fair trade and practices" codes of the sort popularized under the N.I.R.A. of the early New Deal. These codes enlisted the police power of the state to curb competition and, by corollary, to award special privilege to established elements in business and the professions. The Alcoholic Beverage Control Act of 1934, for example, was deliberately made so complicated that it was almost impossible for a retailer to avoid violating it. The kind of violation most rigorously policed became that having to do with price cutting. In many other lines state law moved in to prevent competition. It became a crime, for example, to sell milk below the fixed price or above a specified cream content. In a price regulating system of all floor and no ceiling, the consumer would seem to be the forgotten man. There was a gimmick, however, that ensured that the lobbyist would not be forgotten by his clients. Even after a law to the advantage of such a client was passed and in force, it was comparatively simple to point to agitation against it or to a proposed amending act and thus to get a continuing retainer for "the man who gets things done."

For his bragging, Samish was barred from the floor of the 1949 legislature. Other more general measures aimed at lobbyist control were enacted, but with only limited effect. Three years later lobbyists still outnumbered legislators three to one and there had been no significant reduction in the laws subserving special interests.

Throughout the Samish era the prevalence of direct legislation called for another breed of lobbyists to work upon the electorate. The first to gain any wide notice were advertisers temporarily on leave. In 1936, for example, Don Francisco added to his luster as a public relations expert by masterminding the campaign to defeat the initiative for a graduated chain store tax. The methods used were akin to those of advertising, since they consisted of ad writing, slogan devising, testimonials, and display through billboards, leaflets, planted stories, sky writing, and radio messages. The art, however, is somewhat distinct, and specialists appeared, notably Clem Whitaker of Campaigns, Inc. On a fee basis, this concern handled some sixty-five campaigns in a fifteen-year period, twice defeating health insurance proposals, and in 1948 carrying the "anti-featherbedding" initiative and defeating reapportionment.

By midcentury there had developed a rather general awareness of Samish and his power and much more limited knowledge of the work of agencies such as Campaigns, Inc. Curiously, though it was known that this kind of string pulling went on, almost no one asked for whom the strings were pulled.   It was as though in the heyday of the Southern Pacific machine popular thought had been only about Herrin and Parker.   Actually, those who had favors to ask of the legislature or of the voters were many and varied.   They included the state employees, labor, the aged, the school teachers, the banks, the railroads, the utilities, the big newspapers, the great landowners, the oil companies, the agriculturists, and all sorts of industrial and business groups.   Some depended on reason and numbers to persuade.   Others, serving more narrow interests, had greater need of the wiles of the professional intermediaries.   The people at large, however, seldom looked beyond the agents.

A marked peculiarity in political behavior in California was the disparity between the registration and the election results.   With the advent of the New Deal, Democratic registration caught and passed the Republican.   By 1940 the margin was over 900,000, and by 1950 the figures were 3,062,205 to 1,944,812.   In the presidential elections from 1932 through 1948 the state regularly went Democratic, though only in 1936 by any great margin.   In almost every other respect the Republicans prevailed.   Warren was consistently re-elected, Knowland and Nixon were sent to the Senate, Republicans were as numerous as Democrats in the congressional delegation, and the state legislature was regularly in Republican hands.   Malapportionment and gerrymandering could have had something to do with this.   The New Deal was to some extent compartmentalized as a national functioning, and the tradition of local Republicanism ran strong.   Clearly the strange current of local nonpartisanship operated to the advantage of the Republicans.   To judge by the quantity of billboards, campaign literature, and radio time, the Republican chests were better filled, and certainly it was true that the Republicans were far superior in composing internal differences at election time.   Through more astute campaigning they succeeded time and again in persuading a sufficient number of the electors to go against the predilection they had expressed when they registered Democratic.

In the arena of local government, the postwar years were measurably uneventful, especially in the cities which enjoyed the council-manager form of government.   In San Francisco they were enlivened by a dispute over municipal advertising, resolved by Mayor Roger Lapham's triumph over an attempted recall, and by a series of sentimental moves to save the cable cars. In Los Angeles Mayor Bowron survived an attempted recall, but in 1953, the forces intent on breaking the public housing contract defeated him at the polls. Meanwhile, the 1950 Grand Jury and the *Daily News* had exposed gross abuses on the part of the school board. One by one, the board members departed the scene, two by failing of re-election, and five by resignation or court order. One by one, however, the remaining board members filled the vacancies, and public voice on representation thus was postponed for two to four years.

The Tidelands and Fallbrook

In 1945 the state authorities were startled to receive from the federal government a summons to vacate the three-mile belt of territorial waters and specifically to cease collecting royalties on oil extracted from this strip. The state constitution of 1849, formally approved by act of Congress in 1850, defined the western boundary of the state as three miles out in the Pacific, following the general direction of the coast, and including islands, bays, and harbors. The practice from that date forward had been that the state controlled and possessed property rights in this offshore belt. On occasion the federal government had come to the state for lease or title to particular areas within this belt. Consenting to a suit before the United States Supreme Court, California met with an adverse decision in 1947 which set aside almost a century of practice and ruled that, by law, the United States had always had "paramount rights" in this band of territorial waters.

Rallying support from other states, particularly Texas and Louisiana, which also were deriving revenues from offshore oil deposits, California sought legislation by Congress which would quitclaim these subsoil rights to the adjacent states. In 1952 a measure passed Congress, only to be vetoed. To carry through with such a quitclaim was a featured Republican campaign promise in the fall of that year, and in May, 1953, a bill to this effect was enacted.

Meanwhile, the problem at law was to determine the exact location of the territorial belt. The Supreme Court appointed a special master to take testimony, hear argument, and recommend a decision. Pending that outcome, the state continued to administer the old leases and to impound the millions that were involved. The federal position was that the Department of State could set the territorial belt where it pleased, and that it was pleased to set it as far inshore as possible, with its landward margin at the low tide mark, except where deeply-indented, narrow-mouthed bays existed. The line proposed did not recognize any bays at Santa Monica or Monterey and cut across San Pedro Bay inside the breakwater, thus classifying most of the port's anchorage area as open sea. The state countered with the contention that the court was not bound by the State Department ruling, that the waters along specified segments of the coast were in fact sheltered and protected, that some of them had been used as ports and roadsteads since the earliest recorded days or even from time immemorial, and that, historically, certain of these bodies of water qualified as bays and harbors. A case was made that the expanse of water out to the southern California islands was protected and therefore inland.

A peculiarity of the litigation was that the quiet voices of the witnesses and the attorneys were frequently drowned by the trumpetings of Secretary Harold Ickes, in whose office the federal claim was born, by the anti-federal blasts of the states-rights press, and by the strident demands of Texas politicians for promises of the tidelands as the price for the state's electoral votes. In the controversy, the points really at issue were almost completely obscured from the public.

The same sort of thing happened even more glaringly in the Fallbrook contest. In 1942, when the Navy Department bought Rancho Santa Margarita for development as a Marine base, it also acquired the water rights that went with the land. Challenged in 1946 by water claims filed by the Santa Margarita Mutual Water Company and the Fallbrook Public Utility District, the Navy brought suit to get court determination of all water rights in the Santa Margarita watershed. Clamorous objections were raised immediately, with the Los Angeles *Times* spearheading the opposition. In a barrage of special articles the *Times* branded the action a water grab, shed copious tears over the 14,000 to 16,000 citizens whose water might be shut off, though actually only about 2,300 were involved, and falsely charged that uniformed Marines had been deployed as process servers. The clamor was carried to Washington, where Senator Knowland and Congressman Jackson got a rider attached to an appropriation bill forbidding Justice Department participation in the suit. *The Fallbrook Story* was recorded on film to carry the charges of federal mendacity to women's clubs, luncheon clubs, and any others interested. On September 12, 13, and 15, 1952, the Los Angeles *Daily News* exposed the more glaring inaccuracies and misrepresentations in the *Times* coverage, but the rank and file of southern Californians, having heard and read so much more on the other side, still found it hard to understand why Judge Yankwich ruled that the case was in order and that the trial must go on. As of late 1952, the federal investment of $130,000,000 and the whole operation of Camp Pendleton stood in jeopardy.

The Drive for Conformity

Throughout the nation in general, and in California in particular, the postwar years were characterized by fear of Russia and by hatred of Communism and by a series of repressive measures touched off by this fear and hatred. Soviet obstructionist tactics in the United Nations, Stalin's aggressions in Europe and Asia, the war in Korea, and the disclosures of atomic spy work justified most serious concern. On the national plane the expression of this concern was set against the background of politics-serving hyperbole as practiced by Dies, McCarthy, and their company. The full story of this activity, of the writing and speaking that accompanied it, the loyalty board procedures set up by the President's order, the Smith and McCarran Acts, and the various trials, is national history rather than local.

There were ramifications, however, with special impact on California. One in 1952 concerned the trial and conviction of fourteen officers in the Communist party on charges of conspiring to teach and advocate the overthrow of the government by force and violence. Another was in the attention of the House Un-American Activities Committee to suspected Communists in the movie industry, radio, television, journalism, medicine, law, education, and the ministry. While theoretically engaged in ferreting out information on which it could recommend legislation, the committee called on witness after witness to testify as to his own past or present membership in the Communist party and allegedly associated bodies and to name other participants. Depending on how it was invoked, the Fifth Amendment might or might not protect a witness who declined to answer. If it did not protect, he was subject to conviction for contempt of Congress, as the Hollywood Ten found out. If it did protect, or if he answered all questions, the witness was still almost certain to lose

his job.   In most of the fields involved, a mere summons by the committee was enough for blacklisting.   No one has maintained that
all those caught in this purge were Communists.   Some were staunch
exponents of the traditional American respect for the right to dissent and the right of privacy of opinion.

The nationwide exercise about Reds also came home to California
through the Tenney Committee, created by the legislature in the
image of the Dies Committee.   From 1941, when it was organized,
until 1949, it was headed and dominated by Senator Jack B. Tenney.
Committee hearings seldom had the calm or the safeguards of judicial
proceedings.   At the outset the committee, in theory at least, was
gathering facts as a prelude to lawmaking.   It soon shifted to the
business of exposing suspects, and its hearings took on more and
more the aspect of the hippodrome.   Nor was the committee's touch
discriminating.   On the basis of evidence far less than conclusive it
branded certain organizations as Communist or Communist front.
If members in these organizations cropped up in others, they too were
pronounced Communist fronts and, by circular reasoning, whoever
was in them was a Communist sympathizer.   Thus, the committee
netted a long list of organizations and a longer list of individuals
whom it proceeded to denounce.

In 1949, when several bills that he had introduced were summarily rejected, Tenney, laying the blame on Samish, stepped down
from his committee post.   The press, in taking stock of the work
of his committee, noted no apparent harm done to Communism (an
evaluation endorsed by the chief historian of the committee's work)
but severe damage to liberalism.   The Los Angeles *Daily News*
attributed in part to Tenney the fact that every "organized movement
. . . for progressive improvement of conditions is howled down or
smeared as 'Red!' "   The Sacramento *Bee* urged the new chairman,
Senator Hugh M. Burns, to "follow a course of sober investigation,"
and the San Francisco *Chronicle* warned against continued rambling
"into fields of character assassination and guilt by association which
had nothing to do with overt subversiveness."   Burns did not offer
that much reassurance, but he did announce that the work of the
committee would be primarily educative.

The Dies and Tenney committees were part of a larger antagonism, some of which they had helped to create.   Nominally aimed
at Reds and Communism, the animus actually was far broader than

these two words could cover, and at its extreme was opposed to every advocacy of change. The postwar years witnessed many expressions of this antagonism. Censorship was one. In 1948 the Supervisors of Los Angeles County voted to set up a board of censors to screen the books in the County Library for Communist subversiveness, though later they reconsidered. There was clamor in Burbank to have Communist books branded as such, and in Los Angeles, in 1952, the school board was induced to dismantle its program for study of the United Nations and UNESCO. A few years earlier, the unconventional but hardly unpatriotic *Building America* series had been banned from the state's approved list.

Required oaths of denial became even more epidemic. They varied in wording and specificity and they came with and without lists of suspect organizations in which membership had to be confessed. They cropped up in private employment, as when the head of radio station KFI required of his 200 employees a denial of Communist party affiliation. Mostly they were levied on public employees, beginning with Los Angeles County in 1947, Los Angeles City in 1948, the University of California in 1949, all state employees and all civilian defense workers in 1950, and the school teachers of Los Angeles in 1952. By that seventh postwar year literally millions of such oaths had been sworn, ostensibly with a view to containing a Communist population which the F.B.I. placed at well below five thousand souls.

The test oath program was protested as a violation of the spirit, if not the letter, of the national and state constitutions and as hostile to the respect for minority and dissenting opinion which is necessary to the safe functioning of American democracy. The conformity and complete orthodoxy toward which it aimed were criticized as dangerous to the well-being of American society, and the silencing of criticism was deplored as a disservice to the sovereign people who need to hear a rounded discussion of vital issues. As applied to school and university personnel, these oaths of conformity were criticized as a blow to academic freedom, an interference with the objective pursuit of truth, and a constraint upon the opportunity to learn. This reasoning is brilliantly set forth in the briefs of Stanley A. Weigel in the Tolman case. The Third District Court ruled in April, 1951, in an eloquent opinion by Justice Paul Peek, that the university oath was a violation of tenure, destructive of true scholarship, and unconstitutional. This decision, however, along with questions on the validity of several other oath requirements, passed under the scrutiny of the State Supreme Court, and meanwhile the various elements of the test oath program had full effect. The twenty-six professors dismissed from the university, allegedly for insubordination, still were kept out, even though the university's special "loyalty" test was abolished six months after the District Court decision.

Another year later, in October, 1952, on the ground that the legislature previously had fully occupied the field of spelling out "loyalty" requirements, the Supreme Court ruled the university's special "loyalty" rules invalid. It ordered that the men dismissed be restored to their regular posts in the faculty. The university complied to the extent of offering new appointments for the spring semester of 1953, but left the matter of the intervening two and a half years to further litigation. On the basis of this limited restoration, half a dozen of those dismissed resumed teaching in February, 1953.

On the same day in October, with Justice Jesse W. Carter in vigorous dissent, the Supreme Court upheld the test oath enacted by the legislature in 1950 for all state servants and employees. This oath of denial, the court ruled, was identical to the affirmative pledge of loyalty that had been in the constitution since 1849, and therefore it was in order for the legislature to set it up as an additional requirement. A fortnight later, the electorate clinched the matter by approving an amendment whereby the test oath phraseology of the 1950 enactment was written into the constitution, along with the affirmation that always had been required.

That these various test oath programs were always genuinely and solely anti-Communist was suspect. The authors and advocates of several of them claimed to be out to get fellow travelers, socialists, leftists, radicals, and other such persons—a whole segment of the political spectrum, and not just one color. In fact, the test oath proved such a scattergun that principled conservatives were not uncommonly its victims. In consequence, the impact upon the community was to intimidate nonconformity of all sorts, including speaking out on controversial issues and joining or supporting any group that was at all unpopular and might therefore be stigmatized as Communist.

Facing the Unpredictable

Although the hysteria-stimulated drive for conformity was one of the most pronounced features of the postwar era, it was not the only element of concern about the future. The inhabitants of this area had the discomfort in many other matters of facing the unpredictable. In international relations the hostility of Russia had not been abated. The search for allies, as plied through the Marshall Plan and its sequels, had not yielded complete assurance. The United Nations had succeeded far better than the earlier League of Nations, yet many Americans were grudging supporters and many were outright opponents. Guided missiles, snorkel submarines, and, above all, the existence of atomic bombs cancelled out most of the old bases for security and seemed to leave even the strongest nation a pawn of fate.

The woes of inflation, which were allowed to accelerate in the postwar years, also contributed to the feeling of instability. National income, it is true, rose as rapidly as the cost of living, which doubled in the thirteen years between 1939 and 1952, primarily in the last of those years. As always with such shifts, the change was not uniform throughout the economy. The real worth of savings and insurance benefits declined, and although wages moved up in fairly close pursuit of the advancing prices, white collar salaries and incomes lagged behind. Thus, many persons were by-passed in the flush of prosperity. Such persons, even though the national debt was altogether domestic, saw good reason to worry about the strain on the nation's credit and about the depletion of natural resources.

In their own back yard Californians had further excuse for a feeling of instability. The state government, it was true, had a negligible indebtedness, but state and local taxes stood at an all-time high, and, as of 1950, the state budget was the largest in the nation. With automobile registrations past the four million mark, California was not only in first place, but had almost a tenth of the total in the nation. A consequence was that, despite the highway and freeway improvements, many residents found the traffic competition worse than ever, and accident and insurance rates continued to mount. In the mountain-girt Los Angeles basin the price of industrialization had been smog, and neither regulation nor science nor magic had been able to exorcise it. In the need for more housing, more schools, and expanded utilities, the state was continuing to feel all the customary growing pains.

A more fundamentally disturbing thought was the question whether the state's resources were adequate for the future. The petroleum supply obviously was exhaustible; already gas and oil were being piped in from midcontinent fields. The water problem was recognized as more crucial. A succession of dry years in the late forties reminded that California was living close to its water limit and indeed in some localities had gone beyond the limit by dangerous lowering of the water table.

The Central Valley project, if extended according to the more elaborate blueprints, could develop much more power and some additional water. Actual construction was moving ahead. Yet an undercurrent of scheming to end federal control set up the hazard that concern for the general welfare might cease to be paramount in the administration of the project. The state's apportionment of water from the Colorado had been limited by earlier agreements. In 1945, over California's most strenuous objections, the United States entered into a treaty which allotted Mexico 1,500,000 acre-feet a year from the Colorado in return for 350,000 acre-feet for the lower Rio Grande. This allotment precluded any further siphoning from the Colorado and made it doubtful that the Metropolitan Aqueduct and the All-American Canal could always run at full capacity. An Arizona proposal of a fantastically expensive project to pump water to the Salt River Valley loomed as a further threat.

The places where California might seek further replenishment were discouragingly remote—geographically as far away as the Columbia River; scientifically as far away as an economical method of softening the ocean. Rather than by running out of room, climate, materials, or ideas, California, it appeared, might find its growth leveled off in the not too distant future when the last acre-foot had been tapped. Worry on this score, it must be admitted, was left largely to the professionals. The data were not challenged, but perhaps in remembrance of Chaffey, Mulholland, Hetch Hetchy, and Hoover, there was a tendency to hope that another miracle could be worked.

The more characteristic human behavior, of course, is to live in the present, reckoning as sufficient to the day the problems thereof. At midcentury, the problems that pressed were to readjust the economy, to push forward construction to make up for the wartime lag and to accommodate the continuing population growth, to work through the nation and the United Nations for genuine peace, and somehow to keep up with inflation. In things material, at least, Californians were succeeding more than tolerably well in coping with these immediate problems.

36

THE SCENE AT MIDCENTURY

CALIFORNIANS ARRIVED at mid-twentieth century in a mood to take stock of themselves and their state. One reason, of course, was that the world had just emerged from the greatest of all wars thus far and the problems of readjustment were complicated by the obvious possibility of another similar catastrophe. Another reason was that California had reached a time of centennial, or rather of centennials. The half decade from 1946 to 1950 held the hundredth anniversaries of American conquest, the gold discovery and rush, the first constitution, and admission to statehood. Interspersed were the century markers of many other historic events— the Bear Flag revolt, the rebellion and reconquest of southern California, the first newspaper, the first American-type school, the first steamer, the first legislature, and so on. There was such a crowding of these events that the periodical *Westways* could observe them almost month by month through this period with a page devoted to the stirring episodes of a hundred years ago to the day.

Celebrating the Centennials

Always ready to capitalize on historic windfalls, the state made the most of the opportunity. It established a commission to cooperate with the chambers of commerce, the Native Sons and Daughters, the Pioneer Society, and the various historical societies to see to it that the centennials were properly observed, albeit with some hazard of antiquarianism. Celebrations involving pageantry as well as oratory were scheduled for the climactic points in this season of historical review. On July 7, 1946, the flag raising at

Monterey was re-enacted. Celebrants gathered at Colton Hall in the fall of '49 to honor the work of the founding fathers. The largest and most enthusiastic conclave was at Coloma on January 24, 1948. That placid hamlet was aswarm for a day with an estimated 40,000 persons, a goodly number of them rigged out in approximation of what the original Argonauts might have worn. The brethren of E Clampus Vitus lent their dignity to the occasion. The governor and other notables spoke on a nationwide hook-up, and the only fly in the ointment was that the sheriff of Los Angeles County proclaimed that this celebration was all very well, but the first gold discovery had been in his county six years before Marshall's find on the South Fork of the American.

Across the continent at Washington, the Library of Congress assembled a rich exhibit of books, manuscripts, and pictures recalling the days of the conquest and the gold rush. In coöperation with the state, these materials were shown at the State Capitol and elsewhere, and, at San Diego in the summer of 1950, were joined with an exhibit of newspapers covering California's 105 years of journalism. Possibly more effective than any such displays was a mobile museum, patterned after the Freedom Train, but fitted into two buses which went on tour to practically every school district in the state. Along with select books and manuscripts, the display featured historic memorabilia ranging from the Drake Plate and the Golden Spike to the doll that Patty Reed had clung to through the entire Donner Party ordeal.

No one composed an ode in honor of the centennials, but novelists, radio writers, and movie makers took up the theme with gusto. Research likewise was stimulated. At Monterey, for example, preparatory to the flag raising ceremony, a team of archeologists probed the soil near the customhouse, located the spot where the Stars and Stripes had been raised a century earlier, and *in situ* there found the butt end of the original pole. This fragment was reverently extracted, a new pole was stepped in, and with complete veracity as to locus, the ceremony could be re-enacted. A like investigation at Coloma, combining field work with research in the historical literature, authenticated the location of the mill, the race, and the approximate spot of the gold discovery.

In expectation of the centennials, the University of California launched an ambitious series of popular monographs intended to present the entire sweep of California history.   Other writers and publishers also responded to the centennial theme; in fact, for a time there was a flood of books issuing from the presses.   The range was from novels, anthologies, and picture books, to solid research studies and hitherto unpublished original documents.   Alongside these new books came an equal number of reprints of classics of the conquest and gold rush epoch, many of them enriched by scholarly annotations and more of them sumptuously printed. Joseph A. Sullivan of Oakland took the lead in the reprint field.   By 1952 his series had run to more than thirty titles.   Other publishers such as Dawson, Delkin, Knopf, Kovach, Grabhorn, Stanford, and the University of California, had busied themselves in this field too, with the result that several score important works of California's Golden Age were once more available in print.

The surface effect of all this celebrating was to glorify the past, especially that vibrant segment removed a round hundred years. The centennials prompted reminiscence and review of pioneer achievements, no doubt with emphasis on the robust and adventurous. Curiously, and perhaps inevitably, the acclaim was not pure ancestor worship.   In fact, the predominant theme of many of the speeches was the backwardness of the ancients and the glorious achievements of the moderns.   The temptation to this sort of lese majeste was great—in the hundred years from the first census to 1950, Californians had increased in number more than ten thousand per cent, and in many other respects the advances had been incalculable. Much of the oratory was devoted to this marvelous growth, and with historical soundness too, for merit of foundation-laying is best demonstrated by the structures built upon them.

Problems and Attitudes

Entering upon her second American century, California was bolstered by an unparalleled prosperity.   Population, production, wealth, and income, even with allowance for inflation, stood at levels never before attained.   This material well-being, furthermore, was weathering the changeover from the war-oriented set-up and registering continued gains.

There were reminders, nevertheless, of problems still to be solved. The population contained many disparate groups—a Mexican contingent including a large number of immigrants recently arrived; a

Negro population suddenly swelled by the wartime influx; fifty thousand or more Japanese Americans back from the relocation camps; a sprinkling of displaced persons from Europe; and literally millions of new residents lately arrived from the other forty-seven states. What with the actual differences, the crowding, and the background of race prejudice intermittently at fever heat, it was inevitable that social tension should arise. A number of factors worked toward reducing the friction. The courts invalidated restrictive covenants in residential areas and diminished, without entirely destroying, other discriminatory practices. The two major parties made an earnest effort to embrace all creeds and races. Unions operated on a non-discriminatory basis, as did the public schools. Churches were much slower in discarding segregation, but in athletics full participation was taken for granted. Ralph Bunche and Jackie Robinson were reckoned among California's most illustrious sons. Yet there were still allegations that the police enforced one law for minority group members and another for other citizens, and there were occasional incidents, such as a bombing in the West Adams district, which indicated that all was not serene. The larger truth was that the state was making good strides in social assimilation and, on practically all the newcomers, was working the old familiar magic which in a short span would transform them into dyed-in-the-wool Californians.

The capital-labor front was another place where tension was present. The federal offices of conciliation and mediation succeeded in averting strikes in most instances, and most persons were prepared to admit that unions were here to stay. The phrase, "American plan," had dropped out of the vocabulary and eulogies of the open shop were seldom heard. On the other hand, the union bosses were scathingly denounced, and whenever a dereliction was pinned on any union leader, as the courts did on Harry Bridges, the papers with an anti-union tradition heaped steady abuse upon him. On the whole, however, labor and management were much less at loggerheads than in earlier times. A question remained whether the public interest was being served well. Reciprocal increases in prices and wages drove a good many purchasers out of the market—out of the barber shops, for example—and thus were not an unmixed contribution to the general welfare.

The combination of war, prosperity, and anti-Communist concentration distracted attention from the problem of achieving better government. Nor was there any organization as vigorous as the Lincoln-Roosevelt League or Dr. Haynes' Good Government group crusading in its favor. There was, however, some awareness that eternal vigilance is necessary to keep government good as well as to make it so in the first place, and forces, some of them little organized, were pressing in that direction. Presumably with a view to nourishing civic responsibility, the legislature had made instruction in American history and political institutions compulsory at the college level. In these classrooms, in occasional editorials, and in public discussions, the record of actual performance in local and state government was held up against the yardstick of the ideal. Occasionally the discrepancy was so marked as to bring forth a protest from a grand jury or from the populace. On the whole, however, Californians were satisfied with the performance of their public servants; so well satisfied, in fact, that they hesitated even to vote for more representative apportionment.

A reduction in localism and isolationism was one of the most visible characteristics of the time. The shrinking world, the tremendous accelerations of communications and transportation, and the entwining of interests on a nationwide and worldwide basis practically forced an abandonment of isolation. By some, to be sure, it was given up in fact more than in spirit; the state had its share of reluctant internationalists. Yet the force of circumstances compelled attention to international and national problems, which by their gravity were more demanding than any state issues. Perhaps it was a logical corollary that localism should also subside. As recently as the thirties southern California had been restive. In the fifties the state still taxed in this region somewhat more heavily than it appropriated or served, but the cry for state division was no longer raised. The intangibles of history, of course, were all against division, and the traditions of being Californian were worth the slight additional outlay to the tax collector. Provincialism within the state, and within the nation and the world, had become less marked.

Cultural Lag

Notwithstanding the broadened outlook, the fattened purses, and the far more productive economy, midcentury found California in a cultural recession. The premiums put on war, science, and material gains perhaps necessarily implied a neglect of things cultural. That there was such a decline was commonly remarked. The fact may seem conjectural, though in part it is substantiated by details that can be measured. Hollywood Bowl, to take one example, fell on evil days of declining attendance, experimented with lighter programs, had to suspend operations at the outset of the 1951 season, and was resuscitated with difficulty.

In the field of creative writing, the evidence of a falling off is almost as concrete. The Steinbeck and Jeffers record is not the whole story, but it will illustrate.

From the heights of *The Grapes of Wrath*, Steinbeck stepped down to a propagandist piece, *The Moon Is Down*, and to lighter works such as *Cannery Row* and *The Wayward Bus*. These were close in setting and in theme to his accustomed vein, but neither was notable for theme or power. In 1952 he was ready with a more ambitious novel, *East of Eden*, a three-generation story, again in the Salinas Valley setting. The critics gave it close attention, recognized masterly deftness in narration and description, were not altogether persauded by the theme or its exposition, and objected that the book as a whole was loose and amorphous, complaints that had not been made against *In Dubious Battle* or *The Grapes of Wrath*.

From 1924 to 1938 Jeffers maintained a pace of almost a book a year. Thereafter he became an infrequent voice. Besides a poetic translation of Euripedes' *Medea*, in 1946, there were only two slender volumes, *Be Angry at the Sun*, in 1941, and *The Double Axe*, in 1948. For Jeffers, the times were very much out of joint. All along he had had distinct reservations about the nobility of man; his credo, often expressed, was that only Nature is significant and worthy of being eternal. The coming of the Second World War and what seemed to him the United States' prompt and willful intervention in it were to him intolerable. Seeing the world bent on self-destruction, he was impelled to take his stand for complete political isolationism. His publisher, in turn, felt impelled to dull or sharpen *The Double Axe* by inserting a note disavowing this political view. Some logicians retorted that the publisher thereby gave full endorsement to every other unconventional view that the poet had expressed.

But isolationism aside, the poetry in these later volumes hardly measured up to Jeffers' earlier writing and certainly did not add to his stature.   As before, there were hauntingly beautiful tributes to the sea-girt shore and to the ocean that Jeffers had made his own, and again there were passages that brought home a discerning judgment with fiery sharpness.   Yet these are not the sustained qualities of these volumes.   So far as current appeal was concerned, they had two great drawbacks.   To many potential readers the preachment of isolation was altogether unacceptable, while the ingredient parts, the subordinate themes in particular, continued to repel.   Except as Judith Anderson made his *Medea* a resoundingly successful vehicle, Jeffers reached even less of a public in the war and postwar years than he had in times past.

Other poets and novelists, it is true, wrote on.   Some of them, like Idwal Jones, carried over from the prewar era; others, such as Budd Schulberg, were new figures.   There were writers who reached the multitudes, as did Kathleen Windsor with *Forever Amber,* or Frederick Faust as the most prolific author of westerns.   Raymond Chandler and Erle Stanley Gardner ranked high in the mystery field, and Joseph Henry Jackson was widely read as book reviewer and anthologist.   Evelyn Waugh, in his burlesque of Forest Lawn, and Aldous Huxley, in his intrusion on the aged Hearst, underscored certain passing thoughts on the current scene.   But no poet or novelist scaled the heights where Steinbeck and Jeffers once had stood. Therein is the evidence of cultural lag.

In reportorial writing there were gains.   *Fortnight* set out to be a west coast *Time,* and *Frontier* became a monthly analysis of western problems.   Both these journals, but the latter in particular, attracted writers of discernment.   Meanwhile, on a more academic level Stanford University, aided by the Rockefeller Foundation, launched *The Pacific Spectator,* a journal of literary criticism and opinion.   At book length, too, a number of writers were engaged in extended commentary on modern California and its background. Noteworthy titles included *From Wilderness to Empire* and *California in Our Time* by Robert G. Cleland, *A Mirror for Californians* by Oliver Carlson, and a spate of volumes by Carey McWilliams, notably *Southern California Country* and *California, The Great Exception.* With fact and interpretation books such as these dealt with many vital issues, sometimes more frankly than suited the popular taste.

By midcentury California journalism had fallen into step with the national pattern.   It had registered important technical gains, as through the use of wirephoto. In contrast to a century earlier, when papers had been highly individualized and competitive, the trend had shifted toward a one-party press, one-paper towns, and heavy dependence on syndicated features and news. As papers grew into giants or spread into chains, the weight of publisher policy became increasingly evident and editors and columnists often seemed hardly more than mouthpieces. Such a paper might prosper mightily; it could be a real power; it might pocket a mayor or a city council; yet sheets of lesser magnitude were more apt to attract a let-the-chips-fall-where-they-may newspaperman such as Leslie Claypool.

Radio and televison, when they came on the scene, gave promise of presenting the news more impartially and offering a better fare of unbiased and intelligent discussion. They have provided such a forum—for example, through the interviewing programs—but more adequately on national than on local issues. There are a few outspoken commentators such as Chet Huntley, but a tendency to avoid controversial issues, particularly their less popular side, is more characteristic. In journalistic and editorial content, thus, the programs seen and heard in California bear close resemblance to those reaching the rest of the nation, and the affinity to what the newspapers carry is also close.

The theater and concert stage persisted into this modern era but, per capita at least, on a less flourishing scale. Radio, television, and moving pictures were more characteristic, and for all three California had become an important producing center. With frequency modulation, the coaxial cable, drive-in theaters, and popcorn machines, they scored technical advances. In content and artistry they may have improved too, yet as media for creative work they had limitations. In all three, production costs ran high and could be recouped only at the box office or through the indirect box office of advertising revenue. Regimentation to popular taste thus was inevitable, not to mention a further rigidity of political orthodoxy imposed through the policing activity of external forces. Creative achievement was still possible, but the conditions for it were not most propitious.

In the realm of historical scholarship, in which Californians had performed so well in the twenties and thirties, the subsequent record was mixed. With some change in personnel, the amateur contributors kept up their good work. Carl Wheat and Neal Harlow in the field of cartography, Irene Paden on the prairie schooner trails and detours, Oscar Lewis and William Camp on San Francisco and vicinity, W. W. Robinson and Remi Nadeau in the field of the local history of southern California, and Carey McWilliams in his volumes of social analysis are worthy representatives of the volunteer workers in the state's historical vineyard. Through a massive presentation of the gold rush diaries of J. Goldsborough Bruff, Georgia Willis Read and Ruth Gaines were out-of-state, in fact, across-the-continent participants in this sort of work. Professional historians, outfitted with the Ph.D., and institutionalized within the state, also came forth with an impressive array of studies. These ranged from works on maritime commerce by Adele Ogden, John H. Kemble, and Raymond Rydell, through southern California studies by Robert G. Cleland, William B. Rice, Glenn S. Dumke, and Franklin Walker, to analysis of gold mining by Rodman W. Paul, and studies in political history by William H. Ellison, Walton Bean, and George E. Mowry.

There were respects, however, in which professional scholarship was less fruitful than it had been. After successive reductions in the amount of support, the Native Sons of the Golden West terminated their fellowship program in Pacific Coast history in 1950. Meanwhile, through changes in personnel and emphasis, the history department at Berkeley lost much of its distinctiveness. Historical studies, it is true, were on the increase at other centers throughout the state, but the influence was not as marked as in the days when "the California school" of historians was readily identifiable. The best compensatory factor was the development of a new focal point for regional studies at the Huntington Library. The Huntington collections and a supporting grant from the Rockefeller Foundation provided the sinews, and the example and guidance of Robert G. Cleland provided the leadership.

Another new development which augured well for the future was the choice of Pasadena as headquarters for the fabulously rich Ford Foundation. The world was to be its province, as grants to universities in Germany and Pakistan soon attested, but it seemed logical that some of the cultural advantages would rub off on nearer neighbors. In 1953, however, after the resignation of Paul Hoffman as its president, the Foundation decamped to New York.

Past, Present, and Future

A little over a hundred years ago, Alfred Robinson, under the title *Life in California,* described the conditions and customs of the people he had come to know so well in the course of the hide trade. In the 1930's, guidebooks like those of Aubrey Drury and the Federal Writers' Project took inventory of the state. They found many of the Robinson place names and some of the scenery intact, but a society so different that it hardly seemed possible that it was the same land. Since then further drastic changes have taken place, and were a modern Robinson to attempt to bring this book up to date and offer a description of life in contemporary California, the revision would have to be almost absolute.

The fact of the matter is that California has risen to high estate. Numerous in population, rich in industrial as well as agricultural and mineral production, and equipped with many facilities for gracious living, the state has come a long way. Indeed, there are indexes of growth that indicate that the advance has been unparalleled in any other state. There are other satisfactions about being a Californian which are not so susceptible of exact measurement. Some are tangible enough, even sensory, like the boon of the open climate, sometimes quoted as adding a thousand dollars, after taxes, to any stated income. Others are less ponderable, yet real enough, as the satisfaction of being part of a growing and improving community.

The time was when Californians were readily distinguishable by their unquenchable booster spirit. That time perhaps still is, though in large degree this incessant bragging has retreated into anecdote. Pride in the state and its achievements is still very much present. Whatever tempering there has been of the puffing and boasting may be merely to let the state's advantages, its prodigious growth, and its prospects speak for themselves.

An explanation sometimes offered for the stupendousness of California attainment is that its people are a special variant of Americans. The outstanding performances of California athletes at tennis and in the Olympic Games could be cited as evidence. Nor can there be any gainsaying that the successive migrations that built up this population were selective processes. At various times, however, they seem to have brought the devout and the ungodly, the propertied and the unpropertied, the radicals and the conservatives, the robust and the sickly, the adventurous and the timorous, prospective heroines for the movies and practiced eastern gangsters, so that in the end these selective forces nearly cancel each other out. Certain statistics suggest that the state's residents are near the national average, others that they are somewhat apart from it, yet the deviaion is not enough to explain the state's peculiarities or its special achievements.

Geographical determinism is another possible explanation of how the state came to be what it is. Present-day California is closely integrated with its environment. Its current pursuits are grounded on the complex of natural resources—oil and other minerals, forests, fisheries, fertile soils, harnessable water power, unlimited sunshine, and water not quite so abundant. Contemporary life is adjusted to these environmental facts in many ways; for example, in the addiction to suburban residence, and in the modification of clothing and housing in grateful tribute to the duly heralded climate. Without the natural advantages, today's agriculture, industry, and much else could not flourish. No one would pretend that the orange groves, truck gardens, motion picture industry, residential forms, or recreational patterns could be transplanted bodily to Iowa or Maine. Yet the backwardness of the Indian period forcibly reminds that geography alone was not sufficient to bring forth the flowering that we now behold.

Whether for the society on the Stanislaus that Bret Harte immortalized or for the society of all California today, still another determinant must be taken into account, and that is history. In ordinary lands, where change is slow and migration incidental, the vast majority are born into a historical as well as a physical environment, grow up in it, and, try as they may, cannot be altogether ignorant of it. Half or more of contemporary Californians do not have this grounding, because they have arrived recently in a strange land and an unfamiliar stream of history. They become, nevertheless, beneficiaries or creatures of this heritage. They find themselves in a setting more prosperous because gold was discovered, in an agriculture of large units partly due to the early development of such holdings, in a politics made confusing by the early excesses of nonpartisanship and direct legislation, and in a journalism still expressing the rancor against labor that was instilled several decades ago.

To round out the awareness of the past is an uphill pull. As various passages in this record have indicated, such study and notice are gradually advancing. With emphasis on the remote, the bizarre, and the dramatic, this recognition often lacks in discrimination. The first Spanish explorer is mentioned more often than the builder of the first cement plant. The Franciscan fathers are much better known than the fathers of irrigation, the citrus industry, or refrigeration and canning. The leaders of the Bear Flag revolt are more famous than the founders of the state university or the builders of the bay bridges. In time, the perspective will be corrected. Already it is being improved through increasing attention to the recent past.

As this historical background becomes more familiar, there should be better grasp of the opportunities and the limitations which California presents, better understanding of the problems that have been recurrent, the solutions attempted, and how they turned out, some recognition of the hazards that lie ahead, and some comprehension of the means of coping with them.

Perhaps the dominant realization that a full view of this history will yield is that it has not ended. The book is not closed, as on the Roman Empire, but remains open. Nor has the point been reached, as with Eskimo attunement to the Arctic, where any further developments are rendered unnecessary. The essence of California history has been change upon change. The legacy which past generations hand on to those of the present and the future is not a matter of a perfected solution to all possible problems. Rather, it is a record of persistent development, of techniques that have worked and that, with alert attention, may keep on working. Beyond that it is a challenge to pick up where the past has left off and build a still better California, perhaps improved in things material, and certainly made more satisfying to the mind and the spirit.

Kaiser Steel Corporation

Steel Mill at Fontana

A COMMENTARY ON
CALIFORNIANA

LITERATURE ON CALIFORNIA HISTORY is so rich and varied that a complete bibliography would fill many volumes. This discussion has a more modest purpose. First, its aim is to give at least an impression of the nature and quality of the materials available. Second, it is intended as a guide for further reading. Practically every reference cited deals in graphic detail with some phase of the state's history. Most are firsthand accounts or are based directly on the sources. Many show analytical power and skill in presentation.

Manuscripts and Bibliographies

Part of the manuscripts basic to California's history are scattered in private hands or forgotten in trunks, attics, and business files. Others are assembled in the official archives of towns, counties, and the state. The United States government, and Mexico and Spain, which earlier controlled the province, also have archives rich in materials for this history. Other important collections, more expressly for use by historians, are to be found at the Bancroft Library, the Huntington Library, the State Library, the Library of Congress, and other such places in and out of the state.

The first serious attempt to tabulate references on California history was in the *Works* (39 v., San Francisco, 1882–91) of Hubert Howe Bancroft. His lists, however, are sketchy, and the evaluation of items is scattered through thousands of footnotes. A more convenient tool, annotated, but not always in terms of value for history, is Robert E. Cowan's *A Bibliography of the History of California and the Pacific West, 1510–1906* (San Francisco, 1914). A second edition (3 v., San Francisco, 1933) increases the entries from about 850 to almost 5,000, but reduces the comment. Useful specialized bibliographies include *California Local History, A Centennial Bibliography* (Stanford, 1950), edited by Ethel Blumann and Mabel W. Thomas; Henry R. Wagner, *The Spanish Southwest, 1542–1794* (Berkeley, 1924; rev. ed., Albuquerque, 1937) and *The Plains and the Rockies* (San Francisco, 1920; rev. ed., San Francisco, 1937); and Oscar O. Winther, *The Trans-Mississippi West, A Guide to Its Periodical Literature, 1811–1938* (Bloomington, Indiana, 1942). See also Phil T. Hanna, *Libros Californianos* (Los Angeles, 1931); *The Zamorano Eighty* (Los Angeles, 1945); and two cumulative dealers' catalogues by Glen Dawson, *California* and *West and Pacific* (Los Angeles, 1943 and 1947). Bibliographical information in varying amount is to be found in the general histories and in the journals, particularly the book review sections of the *Pacific Historical Review* and the Historical Society of Southern California *Quarterly*, and in the lists in the California Historical Society *Quarterly*.

General Histories

First in dimensions and in significance among the general histories stand the publications of Hubert Howe Bancroft. He and his employees amassed and organized a tremendous body of material on the history of the western half of North America and presented their findings in thirty-nine volumes which have been called, on the one hand, "an immense drifting miscellany," and, on the other, "American historiography's greatest single achievement." Practically every volume of the *Works* contains some important information on California, and the seven labeled *History of California* (San Francisco, 1884–90) are the foundation for most subsequent work in the field. Theodore H. Hittell, *History of California* (4 v., San Francisco, 1885–97) is a substantial work, especially valuable on the early American period. The *History of California* (5 v., New York, 1915), edited by Zoeth S. Eldredge, is a fluent retelling of the story; the essays of the specialists, comprising the fifth volume, have scholarly merit. In 1929–31 the Powell Publishing Company issued a nine-volume set entitled *California,* individual volumes of which are cited below.

The first authoritative survey in shorter compass was in the companion volumes by Charles E. Chapman, *A History of California, The Spanish Period* (New York, 1921), the first general work utilizing the results of research in the archives of Spain and Mexico, and by Robert G. Cleland, *A History of California, The American Period* (New York, 1922), strongest on the processes leading up to acquisition by the United States. Cleland's *From Wilderness to Empire, A History of California, 1542–1900* (New York, 1944) and *California in Our Time, 1900–1940* (New York, 1947) revise and extend this account. There are single-volume treatments by A. A. Gray (Boston, 1934) and by Rockwell D. Hunt and Nellie V. Sánchez (New York, 1929). Gertrude Atherton, *California, An Intimate History* (New York, 1914) and John Steven McGroarty,

California, Its History and Romance (Los Angeles, 1911) have had wide appeal, but the one dwells on nineteenth century San Francisco and the other is carried away by the romantic mission period.

Much of California history is presented in works of lesser scope such as James M. Guinn, *Los Angeles and Environs* (3 v., Los Angeles, 1915) and Irving B. Richman, *California under Spain and Mexico* (Boston, 1911), a competent account of the pre-American period, with valuable notes by Herbert E. Bolton. California in its broader setting is presented in works such as John W. Caughey, *History of the Pacific Coast* (Los Angeles, 1933).

Attention is called also to the regular appearance of articles pertaining to California in the *Pacific Historical Review* (hereafter cited as *PHR*), the California Historical Society *Quarterly* (CHSQ), and the Historical Society of Southern California *Publications* and *Quarterly* (HSSCQ), and to occasional articles in other periodicals, such as the *Hispanic American Historical Review,* the *Southwestern Historical Quarterly,* the *Oregon Historical Quarterly,* the *Huntington Library Quarterly,* the *Grizzly Bear,* and *Westways.*

1. The Land and Its Influence

Although the best introduction to California geography is to make a leisurely tour of the state, the armchair approach can be a partial substitute. A statewide panorama is offered in Aubrey Drury, *California, An Intimate Guide* (New York, 1935); more elaborately in Federal Writers' Project, *California, A Guide to the Golden State* (New York, 1939); and, in a different vein, by H. E. Rensch, E. G. Rensch, and Mildred Brooke Hoover, *Historic Spots in California* (3 v., Stanford, 1932–37). Howard C. Fairbanks, *California* (San Francisco, 1920) and H. E. Floercky, *Visual Geography of California* (Sacramento, 1933) are elementary geographies. Fairbanks, *A Topographic, Climatic and Regional Study of California* (Chicago, 1938) is a succinct analysis, and Peveril Meigs, 3rd, *Climates of California* (Sacramento, 1938) is more comprehensive than its title suggests, but there is no adequate geography designed for mature readers.

Piecemeal descriptions abound, in topical studies such as William L. Dawson, *The Birds of California* (4 v., Los Angeles, 1921); Willis L. Jepson, *The Trees of California* (San Francisco, 1909); Jepson, *A Manual of the Flowering Plants of California* (Berkeley, 1925); Howard E. McMinn, *An Illustrated Manual of California Shrubs* (New York, 1939); Edith S. Clements, *Flowers of Coast and Sierra* (New York, 1928); and François E. Matthes, *Geologic History of the Yosemite Valley* (Washington, 1930), *The Incomparable Valley, A Geologic Interpretation of the Yosemite* (Berkeley, 1950), and *Sequoia National Park, A Geological Album* (Berkeley, 1950). Other descriptions are regional, as Godfrey Sykes, *The Colorado Delta* (Washington, 1937); E. C. Jaeger, *The California Deserts* (Stanford, 1933); George Wharton James, *The*

Wonders of the Colorado Desert (Boston, 1906); Mary Austin, *The Land of Little Rain* (Boston, 1903); and John Muir, *The Mountains of California* (New York, 1894) and *The Yosemite* (New York, 1912). Each generation has produced rhapsodic descriptions of the state. Thomas J. Farnham's *Travels in California* (New York, 1844) was surpassed by Charles Nordhoff, *California for Health, Pleasure and Residence* (New York, 1872), which gave way to Sutton Palmer and Mary Austin, *California, The Land of the Sun* (New York, 1914) and George Wharton James, *California, Romantic and Beautiful* (Boston, 1914), and they in turn to Evelyn Neuenburg, *California Lure, The Golden State in Pictures* (Pasadena, 1946). This list could be much extended, especially by including localized descriptions. There are travel accounts that are particularly vivid in description; for example, John C. Frémont, *Report of the Exploring Expedition . . . in the Year 1842, and . . . in the Years 1843–'44* (Washington, 1845) and William H. Brewer, *Up and Down California in 1860–1864* (New Haven, 1930). In recent years California has had representation in the several series devoted to mountains, rivers, lakes, and regions. Titles include Roderick Peattie, *The Pacific Coast Ranges* (New York, 1946) and *The Sierra Nevada* (New York, 1947); Anne B. Fisher, *The Salinas, Upside-down River* (New York, 1945); George and Bliss Hinkle, *Sierra-Nevada Lakes* (Indianapolis, 1949); Edwin Corle, *Desert Country* (New York, 1941); and Carey McWilliams, *Southern California Country* (New York, 1946).

2. The Indians

The recording of data on the California Indians began with the early Spaniards, the most illuminating being Father Gerónimo Boscana's "Chinigchinich" on the Juaneño and Gabrielino. Alfred Robinson included an English translation with his *Life in California* (New York, 1846). It was reprinted in 1860 in the *California Farmer* and again, with valuable notes by John P. Harrington, at Santa Ana in 1933. Hugo Reid's notes on the Gabrielino, written for the Los Angeles *Star* in 1852, were reprinted as *The Indians of Los Angeles County* (Los Angeles, 1926). In like manner *The Indians of Southern California in 1852* (San Marino, 1952), edited by John W. Caughey, makes available the B. D. Wilson report, serialized in the Los Angeles *Star* in 1868. To the *California Farmer* in many installments, 1860–1863, Alexander S. Taylor contributed "Indianology of California," a vast miscellany on all aspects of Indian history, some of it otherwise lost to memory. These efforts were surpassed by Stephen Powers, *Tribes of California* (Washington, 1877). His keenness in observation and his grasp of Indian mentality make up in large part for the inexpertness of his ethnology. Concurrently, Bancroft and his staff were at work compiling *The Native Races* (5 v., New York, 1874–75), which took stock of pre-Columbian culture in western America from Panama to Alaska.

Scientific study of the Indians came later. Its results are set forth in many formidable monographs, particularly in the University of California Publications in Archaeology and Ethnology. For the Californians and their neighbors, data such as these are catalogued in the *Handbook of the American Indians North of Mexico* (2 v., Washington, 1907–10), edited by F. W. Hodge, and are drawn on in more summary fashion in Clark Wissler, *The American Indian* (New York, 1922) and Caughey, *History of the Pacific Coast.* On the Californians, the standard authority is A. L. Kroeber, *Handbook of the Indians of California* (Washington, 1925), a veritable mine of information, and most readable. For a quick view, see Kroeber's chapter in Eldredge, *History of California*, V, 117–138 and R. M. Underhill, *Red Man's America* (Chicago, 1953), 270–291.

David P. Barrows, *The Ethno-Botany of the Coahuilla Indians of Southern California* (Chicago, 1900) is an excellent introduction to the culture of the southern California interior. R. F. Heizer and J. E. Mills, *The Four Ages of Tsurai* (Berkeley, 1952) starts at 1775 and recounts the known facts about an Indian village on Trinidad Bay. George Wharton James, *Indian Basketry* (New York, 1904) deals with one culture trait; examples of another, the Indians' traditive literature, are collected in E. W. Gifford and G. H. Block, *California Indian Nights Entertainment* (Glendale, 1930). Such materials are also used in Jaime DeAngulo, *Indian Tales* (New York, 1953), a simply worded introduction to the Chemehuevi of northern California. R. F. Heizer and M. A. Whipple, *The California Indians, A Source Book* (Berkeley, 1951) anthologizes essays as well as original materials to give a rounded survey of what is known about the original Californians.

3. Spanish Foundations

Excellent brief narratives of the first Spanish activities in America are Irving B. Richman, *The Spanish Conquerors* (New Haven, 1919) and Carlos Navarro y Lamarca, *Compendia de la historia general de América* (2 v., Buenos Aires, 1910–13). For more extended accounts, see Arthur Helps, *The Spanish Conquest in America* (4 v., London, 1855–61); John Fiske, *The Discovery of America* (2 v., New York, 1892), not always satisfactorily critical; a curiously organized but penetrating work by E. J. Payne, *The History of the New World Called America* (2 v., Oxford, 1892–99), and H. H. Bancroft, *History of Central America, I.*

On the conquest of the Aztecs, the classics are *The Conquest of Mexico* (3 v., New York, 1843), by William H. Prescott, one of the first great American historians, and *Historia verdadera de la conquista de la Nueva España,* a stirring account by the observant Bernal Díaz del Castillo, one of Cortés' soldiers. The latter is available in several translations, notably A. P. Maudslay's (5 v., London, 1908–16), and a poetic paraphrase by Archibald MacLeish, *Conquistador* (Boston, 1932). Another main source is *Letters of Cortés* (2 v., New York, 1908), edited by F. A. MacNutt. There are biographies of Cortés by F. A. MacNutt (New York, 1909) and Salvador de Madariaga (New York, 1941).

bilization is discussed in Arthur S. Aiton, *Antonio de ?iceroy of New Spain* (Durham, 1927) and C. Pérez *Antonio de Mendoza* (Santiago, 1928). The mining ed in J. Lloyd Mecham, *Francisco de Ibarra and ....urham*, 1927) and Philip W. Powell, *Soldiers, Indians ....er: The Northward Advance of New Spain, 1550–1600* (Berkeley, 1952).

Institutional development is well summarized in Wilhelm Roscher, *The Spanish Colonial System* (translated by E. G. Bourne; New York, 1904) and is treated more at length in Clarence H. Haring, *The Spanish Empire in America* (New York, 1947); Herbert I. Priestley, *The Coming of the White Man* (New York, 1929); and Bailey W. Diffie, *Latin American Civilization* (Harrisburg, Pennsylvania, 1945). The contrasts of early and late colonial method are discussed in Herbert E. Bolton, *Wider Horizons of American History* (New York, 1939).

4. Discovery of California

The basic works on the discovery and the coastal exploration that followed are Henry R. Wagner, *Spanish Voyages to the Northwest Coast of America in the Sixteenth Century* (San Francisco, 1929) and *Cartography of the Northwest Coast of America to the Year 1800* (2 v., Berkeley, 1937). The first reproduces many important source materials and the second is generously illustrated with facsimiles of early maps. See also Wagner, *Juan Rodríguez Cabrillo, Discoverer of the Coast of California* (San Francisco, 1941).

On exploration by land in the thirties and forties, the literature is much more abundant. Original narratives include F. W. Hodge, ed., *Spanish Explorers in the Southern United States* (New York, 1907); H. E. Bolton, *Spanish Exploration in the Southwest, 1542–1706* (New York, 1916); Fanny R. Bandelier, *The Journey of Alvar Núñez Cabeza de Vaca* (New York, 1905); G. P. Winship, ed., *The Coronado Expedition* (Washington, 1896); and George P. Hammond and Agapito Rey, eds., *Narratives of the Coronado Expedition* (Albuquerque, 1940). Among the more important secondary works are Morris Bishop, *The Odyssey of Cabeza de Vaca* (New York, 1933); Haniel Long, *The Power within Us* (New York, 1944); Cleve Hallenbeck, *Alvar Núñez Cabeza de Vaca* (Glendale, 1939); Carl Saur, *The Road to Cíbola* (Berkeley, 1932); Cleve Hallenbeck, *The Journey of Fray Marcos de Niza* (Dallas, 1949); A. Grove Day, *Coronado's Quest* (Berkeley, 1940); and Herbert E. Bolton, *Coronado on the Turquoise Trail* (Albuquerque, 1949). The whole sweep of northward exploration is covered in Bolton, *The Spanish Borderlands* (New Haven, 1921). On the derivation of California's name, see Ruth Putnam, *California, the Name* (Berkeley, 1917).

5. Exploration Renewed

Frontier advance into the Chichimeco country is the theme of Powell, *Soldiers, Indians and Silver;* Mecham, *Francisco de Ibarra;* and Vito

Alessio Robles, *Francisco de Urdiñola y el norte de la Nueva España* (Mexico, 1931). The Crónica of Baltasar de Obregón, one of Ibarra's men, is a more picturesque narrative. It is available in Spanish, edited by Mariano Cuevas (Mexico, 1924), and in English translation by George P. Hammond and Agapito Rey (Los Angeles, 1928). Charles W. Hackett, ed., *Historical Documents Relating to New Mexico, Nueva Vizcaya, and Approaches Thereto, to 1773* (3 v., Washington, 1923–37) is a source book on the subsequent frontier advance. Other original narratives available include Hammond and Rey, eds., *The Gallegos Relation of the Rodríguez Expedition to New Mexico* (Santa Fe, 1927) and *Expedition into New Mexico Made by Antonio de Espejo, 1582–1583, as Revealed in the Journal of Diego Pérez de Luxán* (Los Angeles, 1929). One of Oñate's men, Gaspar Pérez de Villagrá, wrote a metrical history of the conquest, published at Alcalá in 1610. An excellent translation was made by Gilberto Espinosa, *History of New Mexico* (Los Angeles, 1933).

The sea explorers are most effectively treated in Henry R. Wagner, *Spanish Voyages to the Northwest Coast* and *Cartography of the Northwest Coast*. For a brief discussion see Chapman, *History of California*, 84–142. William L. Schurz, *The Manila Galleon* (New York, 1939) is the first complete volume on the Philippine-Mexican trade. An often-quoted description of a passage on the galleon is "A Voyage Round the World by Dr. John Francis Gemelli Careri," in A. and J. Churchill, *A Collection of Voyages and Travels*, IV (London, 1752), 453–473. Other source materials are presented in G. B. Griffin, ed., "Documents from the Sutro Collection," HSSC *Publications*, II (1891). Of the many works on Drake, the two which lay most stress on his California ventures are H. R. Wagner, *Sir Francis Drake's Voyage around the World, Its Aims and Achievements* (San Francisco, 1926) and the California Historical Society's *Drake's Plate of Brass, Evidence of His Visit to California in 1579* (San Francisco, 1937).

6. The Jesuit Missions

The Jesuits were indefatigable chroniclers as well as frontiersmen. In consequence, government and church archives are rich in manuscript materials, part of which has been exploited by historical researchers. For the work on the northwest frontier, two essays by Herbert E. Bolton are an admirable introduction, "The Mission as a Frontier Institution in the Spanish American Colonies" and "The Black Robes of New Spain," both reprinted in his *Wider Horizons in American History* (New York, 1939). Other general accounts are Francisco Javier Alegre, *Historia de la Companía de Jesús en Nueva-España* (3 v., Mexico, 1841–42) and Mariano Cuevas, *Historia de la iglesia en México* (4 v., Mexico, 1928).

Peter M. Dunne is the principal historian of the missionary advance into Sinaloa and beyond. See his *Pioneer Black Robes on the West Coast* (Berkeley, 1940); *Pioneer Jesuits in Northern Mexico* (Berkeley,

1944); and *Early Jesuit Missions in Tarahumara* (Berkeley, 1948). Earlier Jesuit labors are described in Michael Kenny, *The Romance of the Floridas* (New York, 1934) and Jerome V. Jacobsen, *Educational Foundations of the Jesuits in Sixteenth-Century New Spain* (Berkeley, 1938). William E. Shiels, *Gonzalo de Tapia, 1561–1594* (New York, 1934) is a biography of the earliest Jesuit missionary on the Pacific slope. Subsequent steps are recorded in Andrés Pérez de Ribas, *Historia de los triumphos de Nuestra Santa Fee* (Madrid, 1645). H. H. Bancroft, *History of the North Mexican States* is worth consulting also.

The literature on Kino is abundant and excellent. The basic item is the padre's own "Celestial favors," translated by Herbert E. Bolton under the title *Kino's Historical Memoir of Pimería Alta* (2 v., Cleveland, 1919). Bolton, *The Padre on Horseback* (San Francisco, 1932) is an admiring sketch of Kino's career. R. K. Wyllys, *Pioneer Padre* (Dallas, 1935) tells the story in much more detail, but in turn is far surpassed by Bolton, *The Rim of Christendom* (New York, 1936), a full-length, life-like portrait of this most remarkable man. Frank C. Lockwood touches the subject in *Pioneer Days in Arizona* (New York, 1932), *Story of the Spanish Missions of the Middle Southwest* (Santa Ana, 1934), and *With Padre Kino on the Trail* (Tucson, 1934). On the later status of this frontier, see George P. Hammond, "Pimería Alta after Kino's Time," *New Mexico Historical Review*, IV (1929), 220–238; R. K. Wyllys, "Padre Luís Velarde's Relación of Pimería Alta," *ibid.*, VI (1931), 111–157; and Theodore E. Treutlein, ed., *Pfefferkorn's Description of Sonora* (Albuquerque, 1949). Carl Lumholtz set down a most graphic description of Pimería in *New Trails in Mexico* (New York, 1912).

7. Baja California

The cornerstone of the collector's library of Californiana has long been the *Noticia de la California* of Miguel Venegas (3 v., Madrid, 1757). Actually written by another Jesuit, Andrés Marcos Burriel, from materials gathered by Venegas, it is the standard record of the peninsula missions. Other general accounts of this mission field are Francisco Javier Clavigero, *Storia della Callifornia* (Venice, 1789), available in translation by Sara E. Lake and A. A. Gray as *The History of [Lower] California* (Stanford, 1937), and Constantino Bayle, *Historia de los descubrimientos y colonización de los padres de la Companía de Jesús en la Baja California* (Madrid, 1933). On the earlier pearl fishing, see Sanford Mosk, "The Cardona Company and the Pearl Fisheries of Lower California," *PHR*, III (1934), 50–61, and various documents in Pacheco y Cárdenas, *Colección de documentos inéditos* (34 v., Madrid, 1864–81).

A section of Bolton, *Rim of Christendom*, pp. 87–228, is devoted to Kino's work in Baja California. Charles N. Rudkin, *Father Kino at La Paz* (Los Angeles, 1952) translates a report dated April, 1683. Numerous other works describe the heroic labors of particular missionaries. Miguel Venegas' laudatory biography of the founder of the first missions,

Juan María de Salvatierra (Mexico, 1754), has been translated by Marguerite Eyer Wilbur (Cleveland, 1929). Juan José Villavicencio, *Vida y virtudes de el venerable y apostólico padre Juan de Ugarte* (Mexico, 1852) is another Jesuit eulogy. Francisco María Picolo, *Informe del estado de la nueva christiandad de California* (Mexico, 1702) is a report on the first five years of missionary endeavor. The turbulent thirties are the subject of Sigismundo Taraval, *The Indian Uprising of Lower California, 1734–1737*, translated by Marguerite Eyer Wilbur (Los Angeles, 1931). The closing years of the Jesuit period are best described in Jacob Baegert, *Nachrichten von der amerikanischen Halbinsel californien* (Mannheim, 1772). A Spanish translation by Pedro R. Hendrichs, with ethnological introduction by Paul Kirchhoff was published in Mexico in 1942. M. M. Brandenburg and Carl L. Baumann, *Observations in Lower California* (Berkeley, 1952) is an English translation. The melancholy story of declining Indian population is told in S. F. Cook, *The Extent and Significance of Disease among the Indians of Baja California, 1697–1773* (Berkeley, 1937). The findings of scholarship on the Jesuit era in the peninsula are well expressed in Peter M. Dunne, *Black Robes in Lower California* (Berkeley, 1952).

Dominican labors in the peninsula are represented in a slender sheaf of reports by Luis Sales, *Noticias de la provincia de California* (Valencia, 1794) and in an anthropogeographic study by Peveril Meigs, 3rd, *The Dominican Mission Frontier of Lower California* (Berkeley, 1935).

J. Ross Browne, *Sketch of the Settlement and Exploration of Lower California* (San Francisco, 1869); Albert W. North, *The Mother of California* (San Francisco, 1908) and *Camp and Camino in Lower California* (New York, 1910) are popular expositions giving much attention to description. A still more vivid picture of life in the peninsula after the mission period is Antonio de Fierro Blanco, *The Journey of the Flame* (Boston, 1933), which purports to be a reminiscence but actually makes use of the findings of recent research. A fascinating tale, this book has been called the best on Baja California. Later manipulations of the Pious Fund are traced in William E. McDonald, "The Pious Fund of the Californias," *Catholic Historical Review*, XIX (1934), 427–436.

8. Planting the Colony

The political and personal factors that provided the immediate background for the occupation of Alta California are effectively delineated in Herbert I. Priestley, *José de Gálvez, Visitador-General of New Spain* (Berkeley, 1916). Charles E. Chapman, *The Founding of Spanish California* (New York, 1916) goes back to Kino's time for a running start and focuses attention more directly upon the problems encountered in advancing the frontier northwestward. These two volumes were pioneers in drawing upon the resources of the Spanish archives. Original narratives of 1769–1770 written by Portolá, Costansó, Vila, and Fages appear in translation in the *Publications* of the Academy of Pacific Coast History,

I–II (Berkeley, 1910–11). H. E. Bolton, *Fray Juan Crespi, Missionary Explorer* (Berkeley, 1927) is largely documentary. So, also, is Douglas E. Watson, *The Spanish Occupation of California* (San Francisco, 1934). The major compendium of primary material on the first dozen years of Spanish occupancy of California is Francisco Palóu, *Noticias de la Nueva California,* completed in 1783, published in Spanish in 1857 and again in 1874, and in translation by Herbert E. Bolton as *Historical Memoirs of New California* (4 v., Berkeley, 1926). Palóu's, *Junípero Serra* (Mexico, 1787; translation by C. S. Williams, Pasadena, 1913) enjoys the double distinction of being the earliest California biography and the best biography of California's most renowned character. It is virtually a history of the province to 1784. The story of Serra's life has been capably sketched on smaller canvas in Abigail H. Fitch, *Junípero Serra* (Chicago, 1914) and with more admiration than accuracy in Agnes Repplier, *Junípero Serra, Pioneer Colonist of California* (New York, 1933). See also Charles J. G. Maximin Piette, *Evocation de Junípero Serra, fondateur de la Californie* (Washington, 1946) and *Le Secret de Junípero Serra, fondateur de la Californie-Nouvelle* (2 v., Washington, 1949). On the mission beginnings, and indeed on every phase of their history, a necessary citation is Zephyrin Engelhardt, *The Missions and Missionaries of California* (4 v., San Francisco, 1908–15). Engelhardt also wrote separate volumes on most of the individual missions.

9. The Formative Years

Several of the works cited in the preceding section, but particularly Palóu's *Noticias* and his *Junípero Serra,* are rich in materials for these years. For a good statement of Bucareli's contributions, see Chapman, *The Founding of Spanish California,* his *History of California,* and Richman, *California under Spain and Mexico.* Herbert E. Bolton, *Anza's California Expeditions* (5 v., Berkeley, 1930) is the complete record of the opening and use of the trail from Sonora. The first volume, reprinted as *Outpost of Empire* (New York, 1931), is a clear narrative of the two expeditions and the founding of San Francisco. The others contain annotated translations of trail diaries and correspondence pertaining to the expeditions. Font's complete diary of the second expedition, which comprises the fourth volume, is the peer of any American travel book. This work corrects and largely supersedes Z. S. Eldredge, *The Beginnings of San Francisco* (2 v., San Francisco, 1912). It also makes better known Father Francisco Garcés, the central figure in Elliott Coues, *On the Trail of a Spanish Pioneer* (2 v., New York, 1900). Anza's later career in New Mexico is described in Alfred B. Thomas, *Forgotten Frontiers* (Norman, 1932).

Herbert I. Priestley, *A Historical, Political and Natural Description of California by Pedro Fages* (Berkeley, 1937) is an official report on the province as of 1775. Bolton's works on Palóu, Crespi, and Anza contain information on the voyages to the North Pacific. See also Benito de la Sierra, "The Hezeta Expedition to the Northwest Coast in 1775," *CHSQ*, IX (1930), 201–242, and the account of the second pilot of the Bodega voyage, Francisco Antonio Maurelle, *Journal of a Voyage in 1775, to Explore the Coast of America, Northward of California* (London, 1781). The causes of the Yuma Massacre are illuminated in HSSC *Publications*, 1931, and in Alfred B. Thomas, *Teodoro de Croix* (Norman, 1941). On the aftermath, Herbert I. Priestley has translated a diary of Pedro Fages, "The Colorado River Campaign, 1781–1782," *Publications* of the Academy of Pacific Coast History, III (1913).

10. Local Annals

Bancroft deals generously with these latter years of Spanish control, devoting to them half of the first volume and the entire second volume of his *California*, in all, a full thousand pages. Engelhardt's account in *The Missions and Missionaries of California* is almost as voluminous. Satisfactory short narratives are available in Chapman, *History of California* and Richman, *California under Spain and Mexico*. Hubert Howe Bancroft, *California Pastoral* (San Francisco, 1888) plays up the romance of the period, as do Nellie V. Sánchez, *Spanish Arcadia* (Los Angeles, 1929) and Alberta Johnson Denis, *Spanish Alta California* (New York, 1927). Of dozens of rhapsodic tributes to the missions it will suffice to mention George Wharton James, *In and Out of the Old Missions of California* (Boston, 1916); Charles Francis Saunders and J. Smeaton Chase, *The California Padres and Their Missions* (Boston, 1915); John A. Berger, *The Franciscan Missions of California* (New York, 1948); and Will Connell, *The Missions of California* (New York, 1941), a book of photographs.

At the sesquicentennial of the founding of the pueblo of Los Angeles, the Historical Society of Southern California devoted its annual *Publication* (1931) to that theme. Activities to the north are related in Henry R. Wagner, *Spanish Explorations in Juan de Fuca Strait* (Santa Ana, 1933) and W. R. Manning, *The Nootka Sound Controversy* (Washington, 1905). Two original narratives of the first Russian contact with California have been edited by T. C. Russell, *The Rezanov Voyage to Nueva California in 1806* (San Francisco, 1926) and *Langsdorff's Narrative of the Rezanov Voyage to Nueva California in 1806* (San Francisco, 1927). The same story is dramatized in Gertrude Atherton, *Rezanov* (New York, 1906) and Hector Chevigny, *Lost Empire, The Life and Adventures of Nikolai Petrovich Rezanov* (New York, 1937). Various aspects of the Russian experiment in California are discussed in the *CHSQ* for September, 1933. In the *Publications* of the Academy of Pacific Coast History, II (1911), 329–350, appears Fray Narciso Durán's diary of an expedition on the Sacramento and San Joaquin Rivers in 1817.

Descriptions by visitors to the province are to be found in Jean François Galaup de la Pérouse, *Voyage de la Pérouse autour du monde*

(4 v., Paris, 1797); Edith C. Galbraith, "Malaspina's Voyage Around the
World," CHSQ, III (1924), 215–237; Lesley B. Simpson, *California in
1792, The Expedition of José Longinos Martínez* (San Marino, 1938);
George Vancouver, *A Voyage of Discovery to the North Pacific Ocean*
(3 v., London, 1798); and Louis Choris, *Voyage pittoresque autour du
monde* (Paris, 1822), translated with some additions in August C. Mahr,
The Visit of the "Rurik" to San Francisco in 1816 (Stanford, 1932).

11. A Mexican Province

The works of Bancroft, Sánchez, Denis, Richman, and Chapman cited
in the preceding section pertain equally to the Mexican regime. To
them should be added Alexander Forbes, *California, A History of Upper
and Lower California* (London, 1839), the first book on California written in English; also several descriptions by foreign traders who came in
the twenties and thirties. Among the latter are the famous *Two Years
Before the Mast,* by Richard Henry Dana, Jr. (New York, 1840), and
Alfred Robinson's graphic *Life in California* (New York, 1846). William Heath Davis, *Sixty Years in California* (San Francisco, 1889; and,
with fifteen years added to the title but not to the content, San Francisco, 1929) harks back to this same epoch. The most thorough exposition is an unpublished doctoral dissertation by George Tays, "Revolutionary California: The Political History of California during the Mexican
Period, 1822–1844" (Berkeley, 1932). The social and economic scene
in southern California is best described in Robert G. Cleland, *The Cattle
on a Thousand Hills* (San Marino, 1941).

On the Bouchard episode, Peter Corney, *Voyages in the Northern
Pacific* (Honolulu, 1896), though by a participant, is not altogether
accurate. Recent researchers have reconstructed the story with greater
reliability and in more circumstantial detail; see Ricardo Caillet-Bois,
Nuestros corsarios: Brown y Bouchard en el Pacifico, 1815–1816 (Buenos
Aires, 1930) and Lewis Bealer, "Bouchard in the Islands of the Pacific," *PHR*, IV (1935), 328–342. Gerald J. Geary, *The Secularization
of the California Missions* (Washington, 1934), though partisan, is a
convenient record of an unfortunate process. This and other phases of
the Mexican regime are dealt with in J. J. Hill, *History of Warner's
Ranch and Its Environs* (Los Angeles, 1927); George Tays, "Mariano
Guadalupe Vallejo and Sonoma—A Biography and a History," *CHSQ*,
XVI–XVII (1937–38); Marion Lydia Lothrop, "The Indian Campaigns
of General M. G. Vallejo," *Quarterly* of the Society of California
Pioneers, IX (1932), 161–205; Myrtle Mason McKittrick, *Vallejo, Son
of California* (Portland, 1944); and George L. Harding, *Don Agustín V.
Zamorano, Statesman, Soldier, Craftsman, and California's First Printer*
(Los Angeles, 1934).

For this quarter century also, travelers' descriptions are particularly
illuminating. These include A. Duhaut-Cilly, *Voyage autour du monde*
(2 v., Paris, 1834–35), its California portion translated by Charles F.

Carter, CHSQ, VIII–IX (1929–30); Frederick W. Beechey, N(
a Voyage to the Pacific (2 v., London, 1831); George Simpso
tive of a Journey Round the World (2 v., London, 1847); Charle
Narrative of the United States Exploring Expedition (5 v., Phil;
1844); Hall J. Kelley, Narrative of Events and Difficulties in the
zation of Oregon (Boston, 1852); Eugene Duflot de Mofras, Expι∪ιαιιοη
du territoire de l'Orégon, des Californies, et de la Mer Vermeille (2 v.,
Paris, 1844), translated by Marguerite Eyer Wilbur (2 v., Santa Ana,
1938); and G. M. Waseurtz af Sandels, "The King's Orphan's Manuscript," Quarterly of the Society of California Pioneers, III (1926), 58–
98. Much illuminating detail on life in Mexican California is contained
in George P. Hammond, ed., The Larkin Papers (10 v., Berkeley,
1951–).

12. The Coming of the Traders

On the fur trading operations along the Pacific Coast, much of which
lay north of California, the references are many and diffuse. An introduction is offered in Caughey, History of the Pacific Coast and Bancroft, History of the Northwest Coast. California otter hunting and
trade are described by two participants: Richard J. Cleveland, Narrative
of Voyages and Commercial Enterprises (Cambridge, 1842) and William
Shaler, "Journal of a Voyage from China to the Northwestern Coast of
America Made in 1804," American Register, III (1808), 136–175, reprinted in part in Cleland, History of California, and in its entirety, with
introduction by Lindley Bynum (Claremont, 1935). The prime reference on this commerce is Adele Ogden, The California Sea Otter Trade,
1784–1848 (Berkeley, 1941). On this and subsequent maritime contacts, see also Raymond A. Rydell, Cape Horn to the Pacific (Berkeley,
1952) and Samuel E. Morison, The Maritime History of Massachusetts,
1783–1860 (Boston, 1921).

For the hide trade, the classics are Dana, Two Years Before the Mast
and Robinson, Life in California. With these should be mentioned
W. D. Phelps, Fore and Aft, or Leaves from the Life of an Old Sailor
(Boston, 1871); D. Mackenzie Brown, ed., China Trade Days in Cali-
fornia, Selected Letters from the Thompson Papers, 1832–1863 (Berkeley,
1947); and Susanna B. Dakin, The Lives of William Hartnell (Stanford,
1949). Brief but revealing comments by Californians are José Arnaz,
"Memoirs of a Merchant," translated in Touring Topics, September and
October, 1928, and Prudencia Higuera, "Trading with the Americans,"
Century, XLI (1890), 192–193. See also Adele Ogden, "Hides and
Tallow: McCulloch, Hartnell and Company, 1822–1828," CHSQ, VI
(1927), 254–264; "Boston Hide Droghers along the California Shores,"
ibid., VIII (1929), 289–305; "Alfred Robinson, New England Merchant
in Mexican California," ibid., XXIII (1944), 193–218; and "Business
Letters of Alfred Robinson," ibid., 301–334.

On the trade with New Mexico, consult Eleanor Lawrence, "Mexican

Trade between Santa Fe and Los Angeles, 1830–1848," *ibid.*, X (1931), 27–39; J. J. Hill, "The Old Spanish Trail," *Hispanic American Historical Review*, IV (1921), 444–473; and B. D. Wilson, "Observations on Early Days in California and New Mexico," HSSC *Publications*, XVI (1934), 74–150.

13. Mountain Men

The standard work on the western fur trade is Hiram M. Chittenden, *The American Fur Trade of the Far West* (3 v., New York, 1902). Robert G. Cleland, *This Reckless Breed of Men* (New York, 1950) is an important supplement for the Southwest. Descriptions of the fur trapper at work appear in George F. Ruxton, *Life in the Far West* (New York, 1859); Lewis H. Garrard, *Wah-To-Yah and the Taos Trail* (Cincinnati, 1850); Warren A. Ferris, *Life in the Rocky Mountains* (various editions); Stanley Vestal, *Mountain Men* (Boston, 1937); and A. B. Guthrie, *The Big Sky* (New York, 1947).

A fair wealth of original narratives is available by men who penetrated to California. For Smith's exploits, the documentation includes H. C. Dale, *The Ashley-Smith Explorations and the Discovery of a Central Route to the Pacific, 1822–1829* (Cleveland, 1918) and Maurice S. Sullivan, *The Travels of Jedediah Smith* (Santa Ana, 1934). *The Personal Narrative of James O. Pattie* (Cincinnati, 1831) is a vivid adventure tale, not always to be taken literally. Charles L. Camp, "The Chronicles of George C. Yount," CHSQ, II (1923), 3–66, describes a subsequent entry from New Mexico. Two members of the Walker party left accounts: *Narrative of the Adventures of Zenas Leonard* (Clearfield, Pa., 1839) and *The Life and Adventures of George Nidever*, edited by William H. Ellison (Berkeley, 1937). Blanche C. Grant has edited *Kit Carson's Own Story of His Life* (Taos, 1926), and DeWitt C. Peters, *Life and Adventures of Kit Carson* (New York, 1859) is in part Carson's own account.

Biographies are still more numerous: Maurice S. Sullivan, *The Life of Jedediah Smith* (New York, 1936); Edwin L. Sabin, *Kit Carson Days, 1809–1868* (2 v., New York, 1914); Stanley Vestal, *Kit Carson: The Happy Warrior of the Old West* (Boston, 1928); LeRoy R. Hafen and W. J. Ghent, *Broken Hand, The Life Story of Thomas Fitzpatrick* (New York, 1931); Douglas S. Watson, *West Wind, The Life Story of Joseph Reddeford Walker* (Los Angeles, 1934); T. D. Bonner, *The Life and Adventures of James P. Beckwourth* (New York, 1856); Charles Kelly, *Old Greenwood, The Story of Caleb Greenwood* (Salt Lake City, 1936); Alpheus H. Favour, *Old Bill Williams, Mountain Man* (Chapel Hill, 1936); C. P. Williams, *Lone Elk* [Bill Williams] (Denver, 1935); and Joseph J. Hill, "Ewing Young in the Fur Trade of the American Southwest," *Oregon Historical Quarterly*, XXIV (1923), 1–35. Francis P. Farquhar, "Exploration of the Sierra Nevada," CHSQ, IV (1925), 3–58, traces the Sierra crossings. Alice B. Maloney, ed., *Fur Brigade to the*

Bonaventura (San Francisco, 1945) concerns Hudson's Bay Company participation in the California fur trade.

14. Pioneers

Hubert Howe Bancroft's "Pioneer Register," inserted as an appendix in his *History of California,* is a Who's Who of Californians to 1848. On the men who came to trade, there is a fair-sized literature, the biggest item being Hammond, *The Larkin Papers.* The biography of Larkin by Reuben L. Underhill, *From Cowhides to Golden Fleece* (Stanford, 1939) was intended for the general reader; that by Robert J. Parker, *Chapters in the Early Life of Thomas Oliver Larkin* (San Francisco, 1939) is fragmentary. In addition to her biography of Hartnell, Susanna B. Dakin has a book on one of the early southern residents, *A Scotch Paisano, Hugo Reid's Life in California, 1832–1852* (Berkeley, 1939). Abel Stearns deserves full treatment. At present the nearest approaches are Pearl P. Stamps, "Abel Stearns, California Pioneer," *Grizzly Bear,* May–August, 1926, and Cleland, *The Cattle on a Thousand Hills.* George D. Lyman, *John Marsh, Pioneer* (New York, 1930) is the best rounded of all these biographies. The most popular subject, however, has been John A. Sutter. Douglas S. Watson edited his *Diary* (San Francisco, 1932); Edwin G. Gudde edited his Bancroft dictation as *Sutter's Own Story* (New York, 1936); Julian Dana wrote somewhat journalistically in *Sutter of California* (New York, 1936); and James P. Zollinger, in *Sutter, The Man and His Empire* (New York, 1939) excelled on the European preliminaries. Robinson's *Life in California* and Davis' reminiscences are pertinent.

On the overland pioneers, there is general coverage in William J. Ghent, *The Road to Oregon* (New York, 1929); Owen C. Coy, *The Great Trek* (Los Angeles, 1931); and special detail on tracing the routes in Irene D. Paden, *In the Wake of the Prairie Schooner* (New York, 1943) and *Prairie Schooner Detours* (New York, 1949). John Bidwell, *A Journey to California in 1841* (Liberty, Mo., 1842) is supplemented for the Bartleson-Bidwell party by Nicholas "Cheyenne" Dawson, *California in '41, Texas in '51* (Austin, 1894) and for the Workman-Rowland party by Wilson's "Observations." Charles L. Camp, ed., *James Clyman, American Frontiersman, 1792–1881* (San Francisco, 1928) tells, among other things, of his overland trip to Oregon and thence to California. Lansford W. Hastings, *The Emigrant's Guide to Oregon and California* (Cincinnati, 1845) and Thomas J. Farnham, *Travels in California and Scenes in the Pacific Ocean* (New York, 1844) are examples of the promotional literature. Rockwell D. Hunt, *John Bidwell, Prince of California Pioneers* (Caldwell, Idaho, 1942) is scholarly and laudatory. See also Ruby J. Swartzlow, "Peter Lassen, Northern California's Trail-blazer," *CHSQ,* XVIII (1939), 291–314, and John W. Caughey, "Don Benito Wilson, An Average Southern Californian," *Huntington Library Quarterly,* II (1939), 285–300.

The stark tragedy of the Donner party inevitably attracted special attention. Over the years the most widely read account has been Charles F. McGlashan, *History of the Donner Party* (Truckee, 1879), a product of careful investigation and familiarity with the environment. Eliza P. Houghton, *The Expedition of the Donner Party and Its Tragic Fate* (Chicago, 1911) is by one of the Donner children who, as a four-year-old, survived the ordeal. It is based on traditive material more than on her own recollections. Of recent treatments, the most satisfactory are George R. Stewart, Jr., *Ordeal by Hunger, The Story of the Donner Party* (New York, 1936) and the passages in Bernard De Voto, *The Year of Decision, 1846* (Boston, 1943). Original testimony includes "Diary of Patrick Breen," *Publications* of the Academy of Pacific Coast History, I (1910), 269–284, and *Thrilling and Tragic Journal Written by George McKinstry, Jr.* (West Hoboken, N. J., 1917). The general historians, Bancroft in particular, have gone into the matter with thoroughness. The more successful emigrants of 1846 are well represented by Edwin Bryant, *What I Saw in California* (New York, 1848) and J. Q. Thornton, *Oregon and California* (2 v., New York, 1849). Thornton was at some pains to set down all the information he could gather about the Donners. For the migration of the following year, see Douglas C. McMurtrie, ed., *Overland to California in 1847, Letters . . . by Chester Ingersoll* (Chicago, 1937) and Charles L. Camp, "William Alexander Trubody and the Overland Pioneers of 1847," *CHSQ*, XVI (1937), 122–143.

15. American Acquisition

Development of official interest is most thoroughly explored in Robert G. Cleland, "The Early Sentiment for the Annexation of California," *Southwestern Historical Quarterly*, VIII (1915). Rival aspirations are treated in E. D. Adams, "British Interest in California," *American Historical Review*, XIV (1919), 744–763; A. P. Nasatir, "The French Consulate in California," *CHSQ*, XI–XIII (1932–34); and Rufus K. Wyllys, "French Imperialists in California," *ibid.*, VIII (1929), 116–130. Polk's California policy is described in E. I. McCormac, *James K. Polk, A Political Biography* (Berkeley, 1922) and in somewhat harsher terms by Richard R. Stenberg, "Polk and Frémont, 1845–1846," *PHR*, VII (1938), 211–227.

Frémont's role in California affairs has been the subject of perennial debate ever since John S. Hittell had the temerity to berate him in *A History of the City of San Francisco and Incidentally of the State of California* (San Francisco, 1878). The debate was joined by John Bidwell, Willard B. Farwell, Josiah Royce, and William Carey Jones, writing in national and local periodicals; by Bancroft, Theodore H. Hittell, and subsequent historians of the state; by Josiah Royce in his philosophical *California, from the Conquest in 1846 to the Second Vigilance Committee* (Boston, 1886); and by the Frémonts, both man and wife. Frémont's

Memoirs of My Life (New York, 1887) proved less ambitious than its title, but covered the California episodes. See also Jessie Benton Frémont, *Souvenirs of My Time* (Boston, 1887) and *Far West Sketches* (Boston, 1890); Catherine Coffin Phillips, *Jessie Benton Frémont, A Woman Who Made History* (San Francisco, 1935); and Irving Stone, *Immortal Wife* (New York, 1944).

In 1856, when Frémont was candidate for President, biographers Smucker, Upham, and Bigelow severally bestowed unstinted praise on their hero. In *A Man Unafraid* (n. p., 1927) Herbert Bashford and Harr Wagner were equally fulsome. In *Frémont, The West's Greatest Adventurer* (2 v., New York, 1928) Allan Nevins resorted also to numerous superlatives, some of which were eliminated in his *Frémont, Pathmarker of the West* (New York, 1939). Cardinal L. Goodwin, *John Charles Frémont, An Explanation of His Career* (Stanford, 1930) is decidedly less laudatory. On the travels, Frederic S. Dellenbaugh, *Frémont and '49* (New York, 1914) is particularly competent. The Carson literature has additional information on Frémont's expeditions, as do Charles H. Carey, ed., *The Journals of Theodore Talbot* (Portland, 1931) and S. N. Carvalho, *Incidents of Travel and Adventure in the Far West* (New York, 1857).

On the Bear Flag movement, supplementary sources are William B. Ide, *Who Conquered California?* (Claremont, N. H., 1880); W. F. Swasey, *The Early Days and Men of California* (San Francisco, 1891); Fred B. Rogers, *Bear Flag Lieutenant, The Life Story of Henry L. Ford* (San Francisco, 1951); and intermittent contributions to the CHSQ by John A. Hussey. Archibald Gillespie's letters to the Secretary of the Navy were published in CHSQ, XVII–XVIII (1938–39). Assemblages of documents on "The Bear Flag Movement" are in *ibid.*, I and III (1922 and 1924), and on "The Frémont Episode," *ibid.*, III–IX (1924–30). See also Oscar Lewis, ed., *California in 1846* (San Francisco, 1934).

On the War with Mexico, there is general coverage in Justin H. Smith, *The War with Mexico* (2 v., New York, 1919). The California operations are more specifically described in several of the works cited above and in a group of articles by James M. Guinn in HSSC *Publications*. For the Navy's part, see Edwin A. Sherman, *The Life of . . . John Drake Sloat* (Oakland, 1902); Samuel J. Bayard, *A Sketch of the Life of Com. Robert F. Stockton* (New York, 1856); extracts from the log which Robert Carson Duvall kept on the *Savannah*, CHSQ, III (1924), 105–124; Lieutenant Tunis A. M. Craven's journal on the *Dale*, published in part in *ibid.*, XX (1941), 193–234; and Thomas C. Lancey, "The Cruise of the *Dale*," published serially in the San Jose *Pioneer*, 1879–81. *Naval Sketches of the War in California* (New York, 1939) reproduces twenty-eight drawings made by William H. Meyers, gunner on the *Dale*.

William H. Emory, *Notes of a Military Reconnoissance from Fort Leavenworth, in Missouri, to San Diego, in California* (Washington,

1848) and George W. Ames, Jr., ed., *A Doctor Comes to California, The Diary of John S. Griffin* (San Francisco, 1943) are the principal narratives of the Army of the West. See also James M. Cutts, *The Conquest of California and New Mexico* (Philadelphia, 1847) and Arthur Woodward, *Lances at San Pascual* (San Francisco, 1948), a painstaking rehearsal of the battle. Daniel Tyler, *A Concise History of the Mormon Battalion* (Salt Lake City, 1881); Henry Standage, *The March of the Mormon Battalion* (New York, 1928); and Philip St. George Cooke, *The Conquest of New Mexico and California* (New York, 1878) bring the Mormon contingent across the continent. Francis D. Clark, *The First Regiment of New York Volunteers* (New York, 1882) and the John McHenry Hollingsworth journal, CHSQ, I (1922), 207–270, concern Sevenson's Regiment. On the peninsular phase, see Peter Gerhard, "Baja California in the Mexican War, 1846–1848," *PHR,* XV (1946), 418–424.

16. Gold

Materials on the gold rush are abundant. The most comprehensive view is in John W. Caughey, *Gold Is the Cornerstone* (Berkeley, 1948). Valeska Bari, ed., *The Course of Empire* (New York, 1931) is a balanced offering of excerpts from firsthand accounts. Joseph Henry Jackson, *Gold Rush Album* (New York, 1949) is a picture book viewing the subject in the round. Hubert Howe Bancroft, *California Inter Pocula* (San Francisco, 1888), inspired in title, deals with most phases, as do Stewart Edward White, *The Forty-niners* (New Haven, 1918) and John W. Caughey, ed., *Rushing for Gold* (Berkeley, 1949). Elizabeth L. Egenhoff, *The Elephant as They Saw It* (San Francisco, 1949) features contemporary pictures and statements on California gold mining.

California Gold Discovery, Centennial Papers on the Time, the Site, and Artifacts, a special publication of the California Historical Society (San Francisco, 1947), is the most useful on its particular topics. E. Gould Buffum, *Six Months in the Gold Mines* (Philadelphia, 1850); James H. Carson, *Early Recollections of the Mines* (Stockton, 1852); and William R. Ryan, *Personal Adventures in Upper and Lower California, in 1848–49* (2 v., London, 1851) chronicle experiences in 1848.

Octavius T. Howe, *Argonauts of '49* (Cambridge, 1923), though limited to companies from Massachusetts, is the nearest approach to a monograph on the Cape Horn Argonauts. For briefer treatment, see Oscar Lewis, *Sea Routes to the Gold Fields* (New York, 1949) and the appropriate chapter in Rydell, *Cape Horn to the Pacific.* Carolyn Hale Ross, ed., *The Log of a Forty-niner* (Boston, 1923); Franklin A. Buck, *A Yankee Trader in the Gold Rush* (Boston, 1930); and Enos Christman, *One Man's Gold* (New York, 1930) are representative accounts. On the Panama route, see Bayard Taylor, *Eldorado, or Adventures in the Path of Empire* (2 v., New York, 1850); Carl Meyer, *Nach dem Sacramento* (Aarau, 1855; translated by Ruth Frey Axe, Claremont, 1938);

Charles A. Barker, ed., *Memoirs of Elisha Oscar Crosby* (San Marino, 1945); and John W. Caughey, ed., *Seeing the Elephant, Letters of R. R. Taylor, Forty-niner* (Los Angeles, 1951).

The saga of the overland march of the gold seekers is best read in some of their journals, notably Alonzo Delano, *Life on the Plains and among the Diggings* (Auburn, N. Y., 1854); Georgia Willis Read and Ruth Gaines, eds., *Gold Rush: The Journals, Drawings, and Other Papers of J. Goldsborough Bruff* (2 v., New York, 1944); David M. Potter, ed., *Trail to California: The Overland Journal of Vincent Geiger and Wakeman Bryarly* (New Haven, 1945); *Autobiography of Isaac J. Wistar* (2 v., Philadelphia, 1914); Sarah Royce, *A Frontier Lady* (New Haven, 1932); and for 1850, Eleazer S. Ingalls, *Across the Plains in 1850* (Chicago, 1930); Georgia Willis Read, ed., *A Pioneer of 1850* (Boston, 1927); and Leander V. Loomis, *A Journal of the Birmingham Emigrating Company* (Salt Lake City, 1928). Walker D. Wyman, *California Emigrant Letters* (New York, 1952) is a gathering of letters written home by forty-niners en route and in California. Of the guidebooks available in 1849, the most helpful was Joseph E. Ware, *The Emigrants' Guide to California* (St. Louis, 1849), reprinted with introduction and notes by John W. Caughey (Princeton, 1932). Excellent recent studies are Paden, *The Wake of the Prairie Schooner;* Coy, *The Great Trek;* and, with exaggerated drama, Archer B. Hulbert, *Forty-niners* (Boston, 1931).

Southwestern offshoots from the main trail are described in W. L. Manly, *Death Valley in '49* (San Jose, 1894); John W. Caughey, "Southwest from Salt Lake in 1849," *PHR,* VI (1937), 143–181; John G. Ellenbecker, *The Jayhawkers of Death Valley* (Marysville, Kansas, 1938); and Carl I. Wheat, "Trailing the Forty-niners through Death Valley," *Sierra Club Bulletin,* XXIV (1939) 74–108. Still more southerly routes are described in Ralph P. Bieber, *Southern Trails to California in 1849* (Glendale, 1937); Grant Foreman, *Marcy and the Gold Seekers* (Norman, 1939); H. M. T. Powell, *The Santa Fe Trail to California* (San Francisco, 1931); Charles Pancoast, *A Quaker Forty-niner* (Philadelphia, 1930); John W. Audubon, *Audubon's Western Journal* (Cleveland, 1906); and George W. B. Evans, *Mexican Gold Trail* (San Marino, 1945).

Rodman W. Paul, *California Gold* (Cambridge, 1947) is a detailed analysis of the miner at work. Chauncey L. Canfield, *The Diary of a Forty-niner* (New York, 1906), though fictional in plot, is graphic on mining methods. "How We Get Gold in California," *Harper's Magazine,* XX (1860), 598–616, is by a veteran of '49. See also Buffum, *Six Months in the Gold Fields;* J. D. Borthwick, *Three Years in California* (Edinburgh, 1857); Vicente Pérez de Rosales, *Recuerdos del pasado* (Santiago, 1890), translated by Edwin S. Morby as *California Adventure* (San Francisco, 1947). The classic description of life in the diggings is in the "Shirley Letters," contributed to the *Pioneer* in

1854 and reissued in book form in 1922, 1933, and 1949. Other sensitive descriptions occur in Royce, *A Frontier Lady;* Delano, *Life on the Plains and among the Diggings;* Pérez Rosales, *Recuerdos del pasado;* Friederich Gerstäcker, *Californische Skizzen* (Leipzig, 1856), translated by George Cosgrove as *Scenes of Life in California* (San Francisco, 1942); John Steele, *In Camp and Cabin* (Chicago, 1928); Frank Marryat, *Mountains and Molehills* (London, 1855); and John W. Caughey, ed., "Life in California in 1849, as Described in the Journal of George F. Kent," CHS*Q,* XX (1941), 26–46.

Charles H. Shinn, *Mining Camps* (New York, 1885) emphasizes the development of law and government. Olaf P. Jenkins, *Geologic Guidebook along Highway 49* (San Francisco, 1948) and Joseph H. Jackson, *Anybody's Gold* (New York, 1941) are aids for revisiting the Mother Lode. For additional references, see Caughey, *Gold Is the Cornerstone.*

17. A New Economy

The first half-dozen chapters of the final volume of Bancroft's *History of California* pertain to this economic transformation. See also Robert G. Cleland and Osgood Hardy, *March of Industry* (Los Angeles, 1929), which is the nearest approach to an economic history of the state. Many references of the early American period shed light on the rise of agriculture, industry, and commerce; for example, Harris Newmark, *Sixty Years in Southern California, 1853–1913* (New York, 1916); B. E. Lloyd, *Lights and Shades in San Francisco* (San Francisco, 1876); W. F. Swasey, *Early Days and Men of California* (Oakland, 1891); and Frank Soulé, John H. Gihon, and James Nisbet, *The Annals of San Francisco* (New York, 1855).

Of the volumes compiled expressly for the purpose of describing California's economy, the most successful was John S. Hittell, *The Resources of California* (San Francisco, 1863), which ran through seven editions. Hittell also assembled a handbook on *Mining in the Pacific States of North America* (San Francisco, 1882). Titus Fey Cronise, *The Natural Wealth of California* (San Francisco, 1868), even bulkier than Hittell's *Resources,* rivaled it in popularity, while on the West in general, J. Ross Browne, *Resources of the Pacific Slope* (San Francisco, 1869) was an alternative choice.

On the agricultural development in the first American decades, see the chapter by Frank Adams in Claude B. Hutchison, ed., *California Agriculture* (Berkeley, 1946); E. T. Treadwell's rather superficial biography of Henry Miller, *The Cattle King* (New York, 1931); Vincent P. Carosso, *The California Wine Industry, 1830–1895* (Berkeley, 1951); and Walton Bean, "James Warren and the Beginnings of Agricultural Institutions in California," *PHR,* XIII (1944), 361–375; and, for southern California, Cleland, *The Cattle on a Thousand Hills* and Caughey, "Don Benito Wilson." Owen C. Coy, *The Humboldt Bay Region, 1850–1875* (Los Angeles, 1929) and George W. and Helen P. Beattie, *Heritage of the Valley* [San Bernardino] (Pasadena, 1939) are important local histories.

The state's banking history is detailed in Ira B. Cross, *Financing an Empire* (4 v., Chicago, 1927), while biographies of William Ralston by Cecil J. Tilton (Boston, 1935), Julian Dana (New York, 1936), and George D. Lyman (New York, 1937) summarize the problems and progress of San Francisco. On Los Angeles for the same period, there is information in Newmark, *Sixty Years in Southern California;* Benjamin Hayes, *Pioneer Notes* (Los Angeles, 1922); Horace Bell, *Reminiscences of a Ranger* (Los Angeles, 1881) and *On the Old West Coast* (New York, 1930); and particularly in William B. Rice, *The Los Angeles Star, 1851–1864* (Berkeley, 1947). See also Benjamin S. Harrisou, *Fortune Favors the Brave: The Life and Times of Horace Bell, Pioneer Californian* (Los Angeles, 1953).

The glories of the Comstock were recorded not only by Mark Twain in *Roughing It* (Hartford, 1872), but also by his crony William Wright, who wrote under the pen name Dan DeQuille. The latter's *The Big Bonanza* (Hartford, 1876) and *A History of the Comstock Mines* (Virginia, Nevada, 1889) are masterpieces. Another volume, sometimes designated the best on the Comstock, is Charles H. Shinn, *The Story of the Mine* (New York, 1896). A recent recrudescence of interest in the Comstock is evidenced in Swift Paine, *Eilley Orrum—Queen of Comstock* (Indianapolis, 1929); C. B. Glasscock, *The Big Bonanza* (Indianapolis, 1931); George D. Lyman, *The Saga of the Comstock* (New York, 1934); Wells Drury, *An Editor on the Comstock Lode* (New York, 1936); Harry M. Gorham, *My Memories of the Comstock* (Los Angeles, 1939); Duncan Emrich, ed., *Comstock Bonanza* (New York, 1950); and Lucius Beebe and Charles Clegg, *Legends of the Comstock Lode* (Oakland, 1950).

18. Political Experiment

The road to statehood is the theme of Cardinal L. Goodwin, *The Establishment of State Government in California, 1846–1850* (New York, 1914) and Joseph Ellison, "The Struggle for Civil Government in California, 1846–1850," CHSQ, X (1931), 3–26, 129–164, 220–244. Walter Colton, *Three Years in California* (New York, 1850) and Samuel H. Willey's reminiscent account, *The Transition Period of California* (San Francisco, 1901), describe the period of military government. J. Ross Browne's official *Record of the Debates in the Convention of California, on the Formation of the State Constitution* (Washington, 1850) is supplemented by Barker, *Memoirs of Elisha Oscar Crosby*. See also Rockwell D. Hunt, *The Genesis of California's First Constitution* (Baltimore, 1895); Bayrd Still, "California's First Constitution, A Reflection of the Political Philosophy of the Frontier," *PHR*, IV (1935), 221–234; and Grace E. Tower, "Sentiment in California for Admission into the Union," HSSC *Publications*, XIII (1925), 149–227.

William H. Ellison, *A Self-governing Dominion: California, 1849–1860* (Berkeley, 1950) analyzes the issues of 1849 and the fifties. Joseph Ellison, *California and the Nation, 1850–1869* (Berkeley, 1927) follows federal relations to the end of the next decade. William H. Ellison, ed., "Memoirs of Hon. William M. Gwin," CHSQ, XIX (1940), 1–26, 157–184, 256–277, 344–367, is an important source. See also Hallie Mae McPherson, "William McKendree Gwin, Expansionist" (manuscript thesis, Berkeley, 1931); James O'Meara, *Broderick and Gwin* (San Francisco, 1881); Jeremiah Lynch, *A Senator of the Fifties, David C. Broderick of California* (San Francisco, 1911); A. E. Wagstaff, *Life of David S. Terry* (San Francisco, 1892); Peyton Hurt, *The Know Nothing Party in California* (San Francisco, 1930); and William H. Ellison, "The Movement for State Division in California, 1849–1860," *Texas State Historical Quarterly*, XVII (1914), 101–139. Royce, *California*, the Bancroft and Hittell histories, and James A. B. Scherer, *Thirty-first Star* (New York, 1942) also dwell on these matters.

Civil War issues loom large in Ellison, *California and the Nation* and Milton H. Shutes, *Lincoln and California* (Stanford, 1943). John J. Earle, "Sentiment of the People of California with Respect to the Civil War," American Historical Association *Publications,* 1907, is primarily an analysis of public opinion. Subordinate episodes are discussed in Percival J. Cooney, "Southern California in Civil War Days," HSSC *Publications,* XIII (1924), 54–68; Horace Davis, "The Home Guard of 1861," *The Pacific Ocean in History* (New York, 1917), 363–372; and C. J. Stillé, *History of the United States Sanitary Commission* (Philadelphia, 1866). W. D. Simonds, *Starr King in California* (San Francisco, 1917) and Charles W. Wendte, *Thomas Starr King, Patriot and Preacher* (Boston, 1921) eulogize one orator; E. R. Kennedy, *The Contest for California in 1861* (Boston, 1912) and Milton H. Shutes, "Colonel E. D. Baker," CHSQ, XVII (1938), 303–324, award the palm to another. G. T. Clark, *Leland Stanford* (Stanford, 1931) is not always adequately critical. Cornelius Cole, *Memoirs* (New York, 1908) and Stephen J. Field, *Personal Reminiscences of Early Days in California* (n. p., 1880) refer largely to these years.

19. Vigilantes and Filibusters

Hubert Howe Bancroft, *Popular Tribunals* (2 v., San Francisco, 1887) has a wealth of detail on California vigilance, both urban and rural. Most of the available literature, for example, James A. B. Scherer, *The Lion of the Vigilantes: William T. Coleman and the Life of Old San Francisco* (Indianapolis, 1939) centers on San Francisco. Mary Floyd Williams, *Papers of the San Francisco Committee of Vigilance of 1851* (Berkeley, 1919) and *History of the San Francisco Committee of Vigilance of 1851* (Berkeley, 1921) are authoritative on this first committee. The case for the second committee is stated in moderation by one of its number in Frank M. Smith, *The San Francisco Vigilance Committee of*

1856 (San Francisco, 1883), with less restraint in Stanton A. Coblentz, *Villains and Vigilantes: The Story of James King of William and Pioneer Justice in California* (New York, 1936), and sympathetically in Scherer's life of Coleman. The Law and Order viewpoint is reflected in James O'Meara, *The Vigilance Committee of 1856* (San Francisco, 1887); William Tecumseh Sherman, *Memoirs* (2 v., New York, 1875); in Sherman's article in *Century Magazine* in 1891; in "The Law and Order View of the San Francisco Vigilance Committee of 1856," arranged from the correspondence of J. Neely Johnson by Herbert G. Florcken, CHSQ, XIV–XV (1935–36), and with some asperity in I. J. Wistar's *Autobiography*. A forthcoming biography of David S. Terry by Russell Buchanan should also be noted. Most historians have sided with the vigilantes, as did the major California newspapers of the fifties.

On filibustering, the prime authority is Rufus K. Wyllys, *The French in Sonora, 1850–1854* (Berkeley, 1932). William O. Scroggs, *Filibusters and Financiers* (New York, 1916) centers on William Walker's activities, primarily in Nicaragua, on which see also William V. Wells, *Walker's Expedition to Nicaragua* (New York, 1856) and William Walker, *The War in Nicaragua* (Mobile, Alabama, 1860). Another phase of his work is covered in R. K. Wyllys, "The Republic of Lower California, 1853–1854," *PHR*, II (1933), 194–213. For the last episode, see Wyllys, "Henry A. Crabb, A Tragedy of the Sonora Frontier," *ibid.*, IX (1940), 183–194. See also B. S. Harrison, *Fortune Favors the Brave*.

20. Land Titles

In their histories Bancroft and Hittell devote long chapters to the question of Mexican land titles; both are harshly critical of the course followed by the national authorities. W. W. Robinson, *Land in California* (Berkeley, 1948) takes a more tolerant view of the federal procedures. Treatments of particular phases include John Curry, "Treaty of Guadalupe Hidalgo and Private Land Claims," in Oscar T. Shuck, *History of the Bench and Bar in California* (Los Angeles, 1901); Josiah Royce, "The Squatter Riot of '50 in Sacramento," *Overland Monthly*, n. s. VI (1885), 225–246; William W. Morrow, *Spanish and Mexican Private Land Grants* (San Francisco, 1923); and Henry George, *Our Land Policy, National and State* (San Francisco, 1874). Alston G. Field, "Attorney-General Black and the California Land Claims," *PHR*, IV (1935), 235–245, supports the thesis that Black rendered a great service in fighting fraudulent claims. W. W. Robinson, *Ranchos Become Cities* (Pasadena, 1939), and E. Palmer Conner, *The Romance of the Ranchos* (Los Angeles, n. d.) trace ownership transfers of certain southern ranchos.

Numerous contemporary pamphlets are worth noting: Henry W. Halleck, *Report on Land Titles in California* (Washington, 1850); William Carey Jones, *Land Titles in California* (Washington, 1850); William M. Gwin, *Speeches . . . on Private Land Titles* (Washington, 1851); Albert

Wheeler, *Land Titles in San Francisco* (San Francisco, 1852); *Report of the Attorney-General* . . . *on the Resolutions of the Legislature of California* (Washington, 1860); and *Letters of William Carey Jones in Review of Attorney-General Black's Report* (San Francisco, 1860). Ogden Hoffman, *Report of Land Cases Determined in the United States District Court for the Northern District of California* (San Francisco, 1862) covers cases tried between June, 1853, and June, 1858. Later records of federal and state courts contain much scattered material on the subject. On mining titles, the principal reference is Gregory Yale, *Legal Titles to Mining Claims and Water Rights in California* (San Francisco, 1867).

21. Liquidating the Indians

Bancroft has a forthright discussion of the treatment of the Indians in his *History of California* and in *California Inter Pocula*. William H. Ellison, "The Federal Indian Policy in California, 1846–1860," *Mississippi Valley Historical Review*, IX (1922), 37–67, is to the point. See also his "The California Indian Frontier," *Grizzly Bear*, March, 1922, and "Rejection of California Indian Treaties—A Study of Local Influence on National Policy," *ibid.*, May–July, 1925. A more general work noting the spread of the reservation system is Alban W. Hoopes, *Indian Affairs and Their Administration, with Special Reference to the Far West, 1849–1860* (Philadelphia, 1932). Edward E. Dale, *The Indians of the Southwest* (Norman, 1949) gives still broader coverage. See also Charles C. Royce, *Indian Land Cessions in the United States* (Washington, 1899) and Stephen Bonsal, *Edward Fitzgerald Beale, A Pioneer in the Path of Empire, 1822–1903* (New York, 1912), a biography of the originator of the reservation system.

Contemporary comments include B. D. Wilson's report, in John W. Caughey, ed., *The Indians of Southern California in 1852* (San Marino, 1952); a caustic appraisal by J. Ross Browne, "The Indian Reservations in California," *Harper's Magazine*, August, 1861; Stephen Powers, *The Indian Tribes;* Lafayette H. Bunnell, *The Discovery of the Yosemite and the Indian War of 1851* (New York, 1880); and William R. Benson, "The Stone and Kelsey 'Massacre' on the Shores of Clear Lake in 1849—The Indian Viewpoint," CHSQ, XI (1932), 266–273. Sherbourne F. Cook, *The Conflict between the California Indians ana White Civilization* (Berkeley, 1943) charts and analyzes the decline in numbers.

Narratives of several officers who participated in the Modoc War are available in C. T. Brady, *Northwestern Fights and Fighters* (New York, 1907). For more detailed accounts consult the official reports: LaFayette Grover, *Modoc War: Report of Governor Grover* . . . *and the Reports from the Field of Maj. Gen. John F. Miller and Gen. John E. Ross* (Salem, 1874) and Alvan Gillem, *Final Report of the Operations of the Troops in the Modoc Country* (Washington, 1877). Indian agent A. B. Meacham leans toward the melodramatic in his *Wigwam and War-path, or The Royal Chief in Chains* (Boston, 1875). In *The Indian History of the Modoc War*, by Jeff C. Riddle (n. p., 1914), the adjective in the title is at least partly justified.

The pleas for a just and more generous treatment voiced by Helen Hunt Jackson in *A Century of Dishonor* (New York, 1881) and *Ramona* (Boston, 1884) and, with the collaboration of Abbot Kinney, in *Report on the Conditions and Needs of the Mission Indians* (Washington, 1883) were continued and reinvigorated by Charles F. Lummis in the columns of *Land of Sunshine* and *Out West*. Of Helen Hunt Jackson's life, there is a thorough study by Ruth Odell (New York, 1939).

22. Cultural Awakening

Pauline Jacobsen, *City of the Golden 'Fifties* (Berkeley, 1941) pictures the life of San Francisco and, to a degree, that of the state. Other works, such as T. A. Barry and B. A. Patten, *Men and Memories of San Francisco* (San Francisco, 1873); Idwal Jones, *Ark of Empire, San Francisco's Montgomery Block* (New York, 1951); and Robert E. Cowan, *Forgotten Characters of Old San Francisco* (Los Angeles, 1938) support this description.

William W. Ferrier, *Ninety Years of Education in California* (Berkeley, 1937) is the basic reference on educational beginnings. See also his *Origin and Development of the University of California* (Berkeley, 1930); John Swett, *History of the Public School System of California* (San Francisco, 1876); William G. Carr, *John Swett, The Biography of an Educational Pioneer* (Santa Ana, 1933); and William W. Ferrier, *Henry Durant, First President of the University of California* (Berkeley, 1942). On the pioneer theater, G. R. MacMinn, *The Theater of the Golden Era* (Caldwell, 1941) and Constance Rourke, *Troupers of the Gold Coast* (New York, 1928) are supplemented by a series of articles by Lois Foster Rodecape in the CHSQ. Early journalism is described in E. C. Kemble, *A History of California Newspapers* (New York, 1927; first published in the Sacramento *Union* in 1857); John P. Young, *Journalism in California* (San Francisco, 1915); John Bruce, *Gaudy Century, The Story of San Francisco's Hundred Years of Robust Journalism* (New York, 1948); and Carl I. Wheat, *The Pioneer Press of California* (Oakland, 1948). On individual papers, see William B. Rice, *The Los Angeles Star, 1851–1864* (Berkeley, 1947) and John D. Carter, "The San Francisco Bulletin, 1855–1865" (manuscript thesis, Berkeley, 1941). Harrison, *Fortune Favors the Brave* (Los Angeles, 1953) describes Horace Bell's editorship of the *Porcupine*.

Franklin Walker, *San Francisco's Literary Frontier* (New York, 1939) is a sheaf of biographical sketches of early California writers with much sage comment on their works and on the society in which they moved. His *A Literary History of Southern California* (Berkeley, 1950) has longer timespan but is likewise a social as well as a literary history. For all its superlatives, Ella Sterling Cummins [Mighels], *The Story of the*

Files (San Francisco, 1893) is a useful general survey. Hubert Howe Bancroft has a long chapter on the subject in *Essays and Miscellany* (San Francisco, 1890).

Much of the actual writing of the period is available in the collected works of Mark Twain and Bret Harte, and in the volumes of Delano, Derby, Stoddard, Miller, and others. Reprintings and new editions have been numerous. Anthologies include May Wentworth, *Poets of the Pacific* (San Francisco, 1865); *Outcroppings* (San Francisco, 1866); Oscar T. Shuck, *California Anthology* (San Francisco, 1880); and Edwin Markham, *Songs and Stories* (Los Angeles, 1931). Among biographies, mention should be made of George R. Stewart, Jr., *John Phoenix, Esq., the Veritable Squibob* (New York, 1937); Stewart, *Bret Harte, Argonaut and Exile* (Boston, 1931); Bernard De Voto, *Mark Twain's America* (Boston, 1932); Ivan Benson, *Mark Twain's Western Years* (Stanford, 1938); Francis J. Rock, *J. Ross Browne* (Washington, 1929); and Martin S. Peterson, *Joaquin Miller, Literary Frontiersman* (Stanford, 1937).

23. Stages and Steamers

Six Horses, by William and George Hugh Banning (New York, 1930) graphically describes western stages, with special reference to James Birch and the California developments. The beginnings are described in Ernest A. Wiltsee, *The Pioneer Miner and the Pack Mule Express* (San Francisco, 1931) and Oscar O. Winther, *Express and Stagecoach Days in California* (Stanford, 1936). On transcontinental staging, the standard authority is LeRoy R. Hafen, *The Overland Mail, 1849–1869* (Cleveland, 1926). Roscoe P. and Margaret B. Conkling, *The Butterfield Overland Mail, 1857–1869* (3 v., Glendale, 1948) offers voluminous detail on the Butterfield stations and route. There are popular histories of Wells Fargo by Neill C. Wilson (New York, 1936), Edward Hungerland (New York, 1949), and Lucius Beebe and Charles Clegg (New York, 1949), the last largely in pictures. Glenn D. Bradley, *The Story of the Pony Express* (Chicago, 1913); Arthur Chapman, *The Pony Express* (New York, 1932); and William L. Visscher, *A Thrilling and Truthful History of the Pony Express* (Chicago, 1908) pay tribute to a romantic interlude, as do Lewis B. Lesley, *Uncle Sam's Camels* (Cambridge, 1929) and Harlan D. Fowler, *Camels to California* (Stanford, 1950) to one more ridiculous. W. Turrentine Jackson, *Wagon Roads West* (Berkeley, 1952) treats the western demands and the federal activity in the exploration and improvement of western roads.

Vivid narratives of the transcontinental journey by stage are numerous. Waterman L. Ormsby's account as the only through passenger on the first westbound stage is presented in Lyle H. Wright and Josephine M. Bynum, eds., *The Butterfield Overland Mail* (San Marino, 1942) and in Walter B. Lang, ed., *The First Overland Mail* (2 v., Washington, 1940, 1945). An eastbound report with expressive subtitle is William B. Tallack, *The California Overland Express, the Longest Stage Ride in the World* (reprinted, Los Angeles, 1935). "Parson's Progress to California," HSSCQ, XXI (1939), 45–78, is the account of a trip from Texas in 1859. The central route is represented by Horace Greeley, *An Overland Journey* (New York, 1860); Samuel Bowles, *Across the Continent, A Summer's Journey* (Springfield, Mass., 1865); Demas Barnes, *From the Atlantic to the Pacific, Overland* (New York, 1866); Albert D. Richardson, *Beyond the Mississippi* (Hartford, 1867); and Mark Twain, *Roughing It* (Hartford, 1872).

Jerry MacMullen, *Paddlewheel Days in California* (Stanford, 1944) tells the story of the ships on San Francisco Bay and its tributaries. Jack McNairn and Jerry MacMullen, *Ships of the Redwood Coast* (Stanford, 1945) does the same for the coasting trade north of San Francisco. A. H. Clark, *The Clipper Ship Era, 1843–1869* (New York, 1910) relates largely to California voyages. There are chapters on the subject in Morison, *The Maritime History of Massachusetts;* Rydell, *Cape Horn to the Pacific;* and Robert G. Albion, *The Rise of the Port of New York, 1815–1860* (New York, 1939). John H. Kemble, *The Panama Route, 1848–1869* (Berkeley, 1943) covers the Panama steamer lines. Victor M. Berthold, *The Pioneer Steamer "California," 1848–1849* (Boston, 1932) is a biography of the first steamer on the Panama run. On the isthmian link see F. N. Otis, *Illustrated History of the Panama Railroad* (New York, 1861). Much of the maritime history of California for this period is covered in Felix Riesenberg, Jr., *Golden Gate, The Story of San Francisco Harbor* (New York, 1940) and William M. Camp, *San Francisco, Port of Gold* (New York, 1947).

24. Building the Pacific Railroad

The *Pacific Railroad Reports,* thirteen quarto volumes with numerous maps, plates, and colored plates (Washington, 1855), were of little practical assistance to the actual builders, but they are a formidable representation of active governmental interest. George L. Albright attempted, without entire success, to reduce the meat of these reports to one slender narrative, *Official Explorations for Pacific Railroads, 1853–1855* (Berkeley, 1921). Grant Foreman, *A Pathfinder in the Southwest* (Norman, 1941) reproduces Whipple's report of the survey along the thirty-fifth parallel.

E. L. Sabin, *Building the Pacific Railway* (Philadelphia, 1919); Robert L. Fulton, *Epic of the Overland* (San Francisco, 1924); and John D. Galloway, *The First Transcontinental Railroad* (New York, 1950) describe the construction of the Union Pacific-Central Pacific line, Galloway with the most technical detail. Briefer presentations are in Robert E. Riegel, *The Story of the Western Railroads* (New York, 1926); John Moody, *The Railroad Builders* (New Haven, 1921); and Glenn C. Quiett, *They Built the West* (New York, 1934). Chief engineer Grenville M. Dodge committed to print his memoirs on *How We Built the Union Pacific Railway* (Omaha, 1903). This narrative is expanded and regularized in a splendid book by J. R. Perkins, *Trails, Rails and War* (Indianapolis, 1929).

On the building of the Central Pacific, the fundamental item is Carl I. Wheat, "A Sketch of the Life of Theodore D. Judah," *CHSQ,* IV (1925), 219–271. See also Judah's pamphlet, *A Practical Plan for Building the Pacific Railroad* (Washington, 1857). Except for George T. Clark, *Leland Stanford,* the heads of the Central Pacific have not figured in full-length biographies. Oscar Lewis, *The Big Four* (New York, 1938) mingles praise for their achievement with denunciation for undue acquisitiveness. Hubert Howe Bancroft, *Chronicles of the Builders* (8 v., San Francisco, 1891–1892) pays special attention to the railroad men.

For vivacious descriptions of travel on the first trains, one may turn to Samuel Bowles, *Our New West* (Hartford, 1869) and Robert Louis Stevenson, *Across the Plains* (London, 1892). A trip on a Southern Pacific emigrant train is described with graphic detail in "California in the Eighties, as Pictured in the Letters of Anna Seward," *CHSQ,* XVI (1937), 291–303.

25. Social Unrest

Doris M. Wright, "The Making of Cosmopolitan California," *CHSQ,* XIX (1940), 323–343, XX (1941), 65–79, is a stock-taking on the elements that had gone into the California population by 1870. On rural population and problems, see Paul S. Taylor, "Foundations of California Rural Society," *CHSQ,* XXIV (1945), 139–161, and Ezra S. Carr, *The Patrons of Husbandry on the Pacific Coast* (San Francisco, 1875).

The rising resentment against the railroad is described in several of the titles in the section above, particularly in the latter part of Lewis, *The Big Four.* See also Stuart Daggett, *Chapters on the History of the Southern Pacific* (New York, 1922) and, as sidelights on the corporation's unpopularity, C. B. Glasscock, *Bandits and the Southern Pacific* (New York, 1929) and Wallace Smith, *Prodigal Sons, The Adventures of Christopher Evans and John Sontag* (Boston, 1951).

Mary R. Coolidge, *Chinese Immigration* (New York, 1909) is a standard authority on California's first Oriental problem. On special phases, consult Rodman W. Paul, "The Origin of the Chinese Issue in California," *Mississippi Valley Historical Review,* XXV (1938), 181–196, and Elmer C. Sandmeyer, *The Anti-Chinese Movement in California* (Urbana, Illinois, 1939).

Henry George contributed an article on "The Kearney Agitation in California" to the *Popular Science Monthly,* XVII (1880), 433–453, and James Bryce devoted a chapter to "Kearneyism in California," in his *The American Commonwealth* (3 v., New York, 1888). See also Ira B. Cross, *A History of the Labor Movement in California* (Berkeley, 1935) and *Frank B. Roney, Irish Rebel and California Labor Leader: An Autobiography* (Berkeley, 1931). On the constitutional convention, consult Winfield J. Davis, *History of Political Conventions in California* (Sacramento, 1893) and Carl Brent Swisher, *Motivation and Political Technique in the California Constitutional Convention, 1878–1879* (Claremont, 1930).

26. The New South

On the health rush, the chief authority is John E. Baur, "The Health Rush to Southern California" (manuscript dissertation, U.C.L.A., 1951); published samples are "The Health Seekers and Early Southern California Agriculture," *PHR*, XX (1951), 347–363, and "Los Angeles County in the Health Rush," *CHSQ*, XXXI (1952), 13–31. The general setting is charted in J. J. Warner, Benjamin Hayes, and J. P. Widney, *An Historical Sketch of Los Angeles County* (Los Angeles, 1876) and Ludwig L. Salvator, *Eine Blume aus dem goldenen Lande oder Los Angeles* (Prag, 1878), translated by Marguerite Eyer Wilbur as *Los Angeles in the Sunny Seventies* (Los Angeles, 1929).

Railroad building in the region in the seventies and eighties is the special theme of Remi A. Nadeau, *City-makers, The Men Who Transformed Los Angeles from Village to Metropolis . . . , 1868–1876* (New York, 1948) and Franklyn Hoyt, "Railroad Building in Southern California" (manuscript dissertation, U.S.C., 1951), parts of which have appeared in the *PHR* and the *HSSCQ*. See also "Building the Railroad down the San Joaquin in 1871," *CHSQ*, XVIII (1939), 22–31, and Gilbert H. Kneiss, *Bonanza Railroads* (Stanford, 1941). For more general treatment of railroad development, consult Quiett, *They Built the West*; Daggett, *Chapters in the History of the Southern Pacific*; Neill C. Wilson and Frank J. Taylor, *Southern Pacific, The Roaring Story of a Fighting Railroad* (New York, 1952); Glenn D. Bradley, *Story of the Santa Fe* (Boston, 1920); James Marshall, *Santa Fe, The Railroad That Built an Empire* (New York, 1949); and L. L. Waters, *Steel Trails to Santa Fe* (Lawrence, Kansas, 1950).

The promotional literature that contributed to the boom may be sampled in California Immigrant Union, *All about California and the Inducements to Settle There* (San Francisco, 1870); Charles Nordhoff, *California for Health, Pleasure, and Residence* (New York, 1872); Jerome Madden, *The Lands of the Southern Pacific Railroad Company of California* (San Francisco, 1876); Benjamin F. Taylor, *Between the Gates* (Chicago, 1878); William H. Bishop, *Old Mexico and Her Lost Provinces* (New York, 1883); Ben C. Truman, *Homes and Happiness in the Golden State of California* (San Francisco, 1883); T. S. Van Dyke, *Southern California* (New York, 1886); and Walter Lindley and J. P. Widney, *California of the South* (New York, 1888). Further information is afforded by Newmark, *Sixty Years in Southern California;* Guinn, *Los Angeles and Its Environs;* Charles Dudley Warner, *Our Italy* (New York, 1891); and with a profusion of illustrations in Laurance L. Hill,

La Reina, Los Angeles in Three Centuries (Los Angeles, 1929) and W.
W. Robinson, *Panorama: A Picture-History of Southern California* (Los
Angeles, 1953). Edna M. Parker, "The Southern Pacific Railroad and
Settlement in Southern California," *PHR*, VI (1937), 103–119, deals
with one aspect of the promotion. For the boom as a whole, the one full
treatment is Glenn S. Dumke, *The Boom of the Eighties in Southern
California* (San Marino, 1944). T. S. Van Dyke, *Millionaires of a Day*
(New York, 1890) is a hilarious lampoon that should be required reading
for every California realtor. Walker, *A Literary History of Southern
California* takes stock of the cultural consequences. See also Oscar O.
Winther, "The Use of Climate in Promoting Southern California," *Mississippi
Valley Historical Review*, XXXIII (1946), 411–424, and "The
Rise of Metropolitan Los Angeles, 1870–1900," *Huntington Library
Quarterly*, X (1947), 391–405.

27. Broadening the Economic Base

Cleland and Hardy, *March of Industry* charts the economic development
through these decades. The more spectacular phases are played
up in Quiett, *They Built the West*. On agriculture, there is general
coverage in Hutchison, *California Agriculture*. Works such as E. J.
Wickson, *California Fruits* (Los Angeles, 1910), Wallace Smith, *Garden
of the Sun* (Los Angeles, 1939), and scattered papers such as F. A.
Magnuson, "History of the Beet Sugar Industry in California," *HSSC
Publications*, XI (1918), 68–79, deal with limited phases, but much more
monographic work is needed. R. M. McCurdy, *The History of the California
Fruit Growers Exchange* (Los Angeles, 1925); Kelsey B. Gardner
and A. W. McKay, *The California Fruit Growers Exchange System*
(Washington, 1950); William W. Cumberland, *Cooperative Marketing,
Its Advantages as Exemplified in the California Fruit Growers Exchange*
(Princeton, 1917); and Charles C. Teague, *Fifty Years a Rancher* (Los
Angeles, 1944) cover a development of major importance. E. Kraemer
and H. E. Erdman follow the cooperative method into another branch
in their *History of Cooperation in Marketing California Fresh Deciduous
Fruits* (Berkeley, 1933). Luther Burbank's autobiography, *The Harvest
of the Years* (Boston, 1927), chronicles another set of contributions to
California's rapidly evolving agriculture.

On irrigation, the most convenient volume is J. A. Alexander, *The
Life of George Chaffey* (Melbourne, 1928). Elwood Mead, *Irrigation
Institutions* (New York, 1903) has a chapter on California. Samuel C.
Weyl, *Water Rights in the Western States* (San Francisco, 1905) is, of
necessity, technical, while W. E. Smythe, *The Conquest of Arid America*
(London, 1905) and William H. Hall, *Irrigation in California* (Sacramento,
1888) are heavy tomes but not insufferably dry. Among the
Imperial Valley descriptions are H. T. Cory, *The Imperial Valley and
the Salton Sea* (San Francisco, 1915); E. F. Howe and W. J. Hall, *The
Story of the First Decade in Imperial Valley* (Imperial, 1910); George

Kennan, *The Salton Sea: An Account of Harriman's Fight with the Colorado River* (New York, 1917); and Otis B. Tout, *The First Thirty Years, 1901–1931* (San Diego, n. d.).

John R. Spears, *Illustrated Sketches of Death Valley* (Chicago, 1892) affords a glimpse of the borax industry. It is dealt with in more detail in Ruth C. Woodman, *The Story of the Pacific Coast Borax Company* (Los Angeles, 1951). For further data, consult W. A. Chalfant, *Death Valley, The Facts* (Stanford, 1930); Scherer, *The Lion of the Vigilantes;* and Federal Writers' Project, *Death Valley, A Guide* (Boston, 1939). Phases of the rise of the oil industry are covered in Frank Latta, *Black Gold in the Joaquin* (Caldwell, Idaho, 1949) and Frank J. Taylor and Earl M. Welty, *Black Bonanza: How an Oil Hunt Grew into the Union Oil Company of California* (New York, 1950). The flowering of other industries is touched upon in certain biographies, such as C. B. Glasscock, *Lucky Baldwin* (New York, 1935); H. Austin Adams, *John D. Spreckels* (San Diego, 1924); Gilson Gardner, *Lusty Scripps* (New York, 1932); William H. B. Kilner, *Arthur Letts, 1862–1923* (Los Angeles, 1927); and Robert O. Schad, "Henry E. Huntington," *Huntington Library Bulletin*, I (1931), 3–32.

On Owens Valley, Mary Austin, *The Land of Little Rain* (New York, 1903) is a picture before Los Angeles took a hand. *Report of the Aqueduct Investigating Board* (Los Angeles, 1912) tells of the inception of the project; *Final Report of Construction of the Los Angeles Aqueduct* (Los Angeles, 1916) describes the actual building. W. A. Chalfant, *The Story of Inyo* (Chicago, 1922); Morrow Mayo, *Los Angeles* (New York, 1933); and Carey McWilliams, *Southern California Country* (New York, 1946) comment scathingly on the methods of getting the water. The best overall narrative is Remi A. Nadeau, *The Water Seekers* (New York, 1950).

On the San Francisco disaster of 1906, most of the literature is sensational or highly technical. Trumbull White, *Complete Story of the San Francisco Horror* (n. p., 1906) and the anonymous *San Francisco Earthquake Horror* (Chicago, 1906) fall in the first category; in the second are Adolphus W. Greely, *The Earthquake in California* (Washington, 1906); David Starr Jordan, *The California Earthquake of 1906* (San Francisco, 1907); and A. C. Lawson, *The California Earthquake of April 18, 1906* (Washington, 1908).

28. The Second Generation

Reminiscences of San Francisco "before the Fire" are both numerous and glowing. The tone is set by Will Irwin's nostalgic essay, *The City That Was* (New York, 1906). Evelyn Wells, *Champagne Days of San Francisco* (New York, 1939) is an effective dramatization incorporating a multitude of authentic details. Oscar Lewis and Carroll D. Hall, *Bonanza Inn, America's First Luxury Hotel* (New York, 1939) throws a similar halo around the city's chief show place, Ralston's Palace. Charles

C. Dobie, *San Francisco's Chinatown* (New York, 1936) is a tribute to a most picturesque quarter; other writers have dwelt on the less distinctive but more notorious Barbary Coast, while more genteel memoirs are embodied in Amelia R. Neville, *The Fantastic City* (Boston, 1932). Other sidelights are Irving McKee, "The Shooting of Charles DeYoung," *PHR*, XVI (1937), 271–284, and M. M. Marberry, *The Golden Voice, A Biography of Isaac Kalloch* (New York, 1947). See also Edgar M. Kahn, *Cable Car Days in San Francisco* (Stanford, 1940); Frank Parker, *Anatomy of the San Francisco Cable Car* (Stanford, 1946); and Lucius Beebe and Charles Clegg, *Cable Car Carnival* (Oakland, 1951).

Arthur Millier, "Growth of Art in California," in Frank J. Taylor, *Land of Homes* (Los Angeles, 1929), 311–341, is an introduction to a neglected topic. Eugen Neuhaus, *William Keith, The Man and the Artist* (Berkeley, 1938) is a sketch of the best-known painter of the generation.

Literature on the writing folk is more plentiful and, in addition, direct appraisal through study of their works is entirely feasible. Outstanding among critical analyses are Walker, *San Francisco's Literary Frontier,* which contains appraisals of Coolbrith, Bancroft, George, and Bierce, in addition to the earlier writers; Walker, *A Literary History of Southern California;* John W. Caughey, "Headlands in California Writing" in Roderick Peattie, *The Coast Ranges* (New York, 1946), 165–185; and the final and uncompleted volume of Vernon L. Parrington, *Main Currents in American Thought* (3 v., New York, 1927–30), in which there are generous fragments on Norris, London, and George.

On individual authors, the following are noted: Gertrude Atherton, *Adventures of a Novelist* (New York, 1932); Ruth Odell, *Helen Hunt Jackson* (New York, 1939); Franklin Walker, *Frank Norris* (Garden City, 1932); Irving Stone, *Sailor on Horseback, The Biography of Jack London* (Cambridge, 1938); and Joan London, *Jack London and His Times* (New York, 1939). For perspective on Robert Louis Stevenson's California experiences, see J. C. Furnas, *Journey to Windward* (New York, 1951). On the local events, see Henry M. Bland, *Stevenson's California* (San Jose, 1924); Anne Roller Issler, *Stevenson at Silverado* (Caldwell, Idaho, 1939) and *Our Mountain Heritage, Silverado and Robert Louis Stevenson* (Stanford, 1950); and Anne Fisher, *No More a Stranger* (Stanford, 1946). The writings of Charles F. Lummis, though not autobiographical in title, are self-revealing. In *Earth Horizon* (New York, 1932) Mary Austin has much to say of her literary associates as well as of herself.

John W. Caughey, *Hubert Howe Bancroft, Historian of the West* (Berkeley, 1946) is a full-length study of an unusual man. On his technique of production, see also Bancroft's *Literary Industries* (San Francisco, 1890) and William A. Morris, "The Origin and Authorship of the Bancroft Pacific States Publications," *Oregon Historical Quarterly,* IV (1903), 287–364. Of the myriad works on George, the biography by Henry George, Jr. (2 v., New York, 1911) is basic. George R.

Geiger, *The Philosophy of Henry George* (New York, 1933) is a cogent explanation. Arthur N. Young, *The Single Tax Movement in the United States* (Princeton, 1916) carries on with the Georgian disciples. Ambrose Bierce is on display in his *Collected Works* (12 v., New York, 1909–12), a badly-planned and poorly-edited set. There are numerous short appraisals, such as Wilson Follett, "Ambrose, Son of Marcus Aurelius," *Atlantic Monthly*, CLX (July, 1937), 32–42. Of the biographies, that by Carey McWilliams (New York, 1929) is somewhat more satisfactory than those by Vincent Starrett (Chicago, 1920), Adolphe D. De Castro (New York, 1929), Walter Neale (New York, 1929), and Paul Fatout (Norman, 1951). See also John Tebbel, *The Life and Good Times of William Randolph Hearst* (New York, 1952).

On collegiate developments in this generation there is material in Ferrier, *Ninety Years of Education in California* and *Origin and Development of the University of California*. For southern California, Laurance L. Hill, *Six Collegiate Decades* (Los Angeles, 1929) is introductory. David Starr Jordan's educational theories are set forth in his voluminous writings, for example, *The Voice of the Scholar* (San Francisco, 1903) and *The Days of a Man* (2 v., New York, 1922), and obliquely in such works as R. L. Duffus, *The Innocents at Cedro* (New York, 1944). See also Edward M. Burns, *David Starr Jordan, Prophet of Freedom* (Stanford, 1953). For further data on the University of California, see Benjamin Ide Wheeler, *The Abundant Life* (Berkeley, 1926) and Benjamin P. Kurtz, *Charles Mills Gayley* (Berkeley, 1943).

29. Political Reform

Except for scattered articles, little has been written on state politics in the eighties and nineties. Edith Dobie, *Political Career of Stephen M. White* (Stanford, 1927) does justice to a minor figure. Charles D. Willard, *The Free Harbor Contest at Los Angeles* (Los Angeles, 1899) is a forceful account. See also Ella A. Ludwig, *History of the Harbor District of Los Angeles* (Los Angeles, 1928); Charles H. Matson, *The Story of Los Angeles Harbor* (Los Angeles, 1935); and divers brochures issued by the Harbor Commissioners.

Franklin Hichborn, *"The System," as Uncovered by the San Francisco Graft Prosecution* (San Francisco, 1915) is a classic on the fight to break the Ruef-Schmitz ring. Fremont Older, *My Own Story* (San Francisco, 1919) is largely concerned with the same subject. See also Evelyn Wells, *Fremont Older* (New York, 1936); Samuel P. Orth, *The Boss and the Machine* (New Haven, 1919); and J. Lincoln Steffens, *Autobiography* (2 v., New York, 1931). A more recent and extended treatment is Walton Bean, *Boss Ruef's San Francisco* (Berkeley, 1952).

For the Lincoln-Roosevelt League and the Johnson reforms there is basic material in Franklin Hichborn, *Story of the Session of the California Legislature of 1909, 1911, and 1913* (San Francisco, 1909, 1911, and 1913). Files of the League's organs, *The California Weekly*, 1908–1910, and *The California Outlook: A Progressive Weekly*, 1911–

1912, reveal much of the technique employed, as well as a more elaborated statement of the objectives. National periodicals also carried a great deal of contemporary comment. J. Gregg Layne, *The Lincoln-Roosevelt League, Its Origin and Accomplishments* (Los Angeles, 1943) is a summary statement, important chiefly for documents quoted. Alice Rose, "The Rise of California Insurgency" (manuscript dissertation, Stanford, 1942) is a much more fundamental work. George E. Mowry, *The California Progressives* (Berkeley, 1951) is both thorough and analytical.

30. Class Conflict

California and the Oriental, the report of the State Board of Control (Sacramento, 1920), elaborates the slogan "The Japs Must Go." Several authors demolish the major arguments advanced against the Japanese, notably T. Iyenaga and Kenoske Sato, *Japan and the California Problem* (New York, 1921) and K. K. Kawakami, *The Real Japanese Question* (New York, 1921). These works, together with H. A. Millis, *The Japanese Problem in the United States* (New York, 1915); Yamato Ichihashi, *Japanese in the United States* (Stanford, 1932); Thomas A. Bailey, *Theodore Roosevelt and the Japanese-American Crisis* (Stanford, 1934); and Carey McWilliams, *Prejudice: Japanese-Americans, Symbol of Racial Intolerance* (Boston, 1945) explain how the movement gained such momentum. The periodical literature is also extensive; for example, Raymond L. Buell, "The Development of the Anti-Japanese Agitation in the United States," *Political Science Quarterly,* XXXVII (1922), 605–638, and Thomas A. Bailey, "California, Japan, and the Alien Land Legislation of 1913," *PHR,* I (1932), 36–59.

The experiences of other minority groups are related in *Facts about Filipino Immigration into California* and *Mexicans in California,* issued by the Department of Industrial Relations (Sacramento, 1930); Bruno Lasker, *Filipino Immigration to Continental United States and Hawaii* (Chicago, 1931); Dhan Gopal Mukerji, *Caste and Outcast* (New York, 1923); Rajani Kanta Das, *Hindustani Workers on the Pacific Coast* (Berlin, 1923); Paul S. Taylor, *Mexican Labor in the United States* (Berkeley, 1929); and Carey McWilliams, *North from Mexico* (Boston, 1949) and *Factories in the Field* (Boston, 1939).

California labor relations are seen in the large in Cross, *History of the Labor Movement in California* and, more rapidly, in Carey McWilliams, *California, The Great Exception* (New York, 1949). On more restricted phases, see Lucille Eaves, *History of California Labor Legislation* (Berkeley, 1910) and Frederick L. Ryan, *Industrial Relations in the San Francisco Building Trades* (Norman, 1936). Louis Adamic, *Dynamite* (New York, 1929) discusses the labor war in Los Angeles without sparing the capitalists. To balance, one may refer to "The Forty Years War," a supplement issued by the Los Angeles *Times* on October 1, 1929, on the anniversary of the disaster at its plant. Comment on the McNamara case is to be found in William J. Burns, *The Masked War* (New York, 1913); Ortie McManigal, *The National Dynamite Plot* (Los Angeles, 1913); *The Autobiography of Lincoln Steffens;* and Clarence Darrow, *The Story of My Life* (New York, 1932).

Carleton Parker's analysis of the I.W.W. and the reasons for its rise introduces a much misunderstood subject. See his "The I.W.W.," *Atlantic Monthly,* CXX (1917), 651–662; his *The Casual Laborer and Other Essays* (New York, 1920); and Cornelia S. Parker, *An American Idyll, Carleton H. Parker* (Boston, 1919). Paul F. Brissenden, *The I.W.W., a Study of American Syndicalism* (New York, 1920) surveys the movement as a whole. For the state, the most thorough analysis is Hyman Weintraub, "The I.W.W. in California, 1905–1931" (manuscript thesis, U.C.L.A., 1947). Thinly disguised as fiction, part of the story appears in Wallace Stegner, *The Preacher and the Slave* (Boston, 1950). On Mooney and Billings, consult Ernest J. Hopkins, *What Happened in the Mooney Case* (New York, 1932).

Eldredge F. Dowell, *A History of Criminal Syndicalism Legislation in the United States* (Baltimore, 1939) trains the spotlight on one of the darkest blots on California's escutcheon. See also Franklin Hichborn, *The Case of Charlotte Anita Whitney* (San Francisco, 1920); Woodrow C. Whitten, "Trial of Charlotte Anita Whitney," *PHR,* XV (1946), 286–294; and his manuscript dissertation, "Criminal Syndicalism and the Law, California, 1919–1927" (Berkeley, 1941).

31. Prosperity

In a forthcoming volume, Glenn S. Dumke takes stock of the state in the prosperous twenties. Cleland and Hardy, *March of Industry* reaches into the decade. Its tables and maps are a valuable adjunct. Highly useful also are the reports of the Bureau of the Census and certain state issues such as *California Crop Reports, Economic Resources and Extractive Industries of California,* and the annual bulletins of the California State Mining Bureau, *California Mineral Production.* Anton Wagner, *Los Angeles: Werden, Leben und Gestalt der Zweimillionenstadt in Südkalifornien* (Leipzig, 1935) is a geographer's analysis of the factors that contributed to the rise of the state's largest city. Similar studies of other parts of California would help toward a better understanding of this epoch of rapid development.

The growing addiction to the automobile can be followed in *Touring Topics* and its successor *Westways,* particularly in the December, 1950, issue, marking the fiftieth anniversary of the Automobile Club of Southern California. On the oil industry, see Latta, *Black Gold in the Joaquin* and Taylor and Welty, *Black Bonanza.* Lewis Jacobs, *The Rise of the American Film, A Critical History* (New York, 1939) analyzes economic growth, artistic development, and social impact.

Much that has been written on, as well as for, the movies is superficial. Charily, one may recommend John Drinkwater, *The Life and Adventures of Carl Laemmle* (New York, 1931); Gene Fowler, *Father Goose* [Mack Sennett] (New York, 1934); Charlie Chaplin, *My Trip Abroad* (New York, 1922); William S. Hart, *My Life East and West* (Boston, 1929); *Upton Sinclair Presents William Fox* (Los Angeles, 1933); and Harold Stearns, *The Stage and the Movies in America, A Reappraisal* (London, 1937). Possibly more to the point are such books as Budd Schulberg, *What Makes Sammy Run?* (New York, 1941); his *The Disenchanted* (New York, 1950); and Arthur Mizener, *The Far Side of Paradise* (Boston, 1951).

David O. Woodbury, *The Colorado Conquest* (Indianapolis, 1941) and the latter half of Remi A. Nadeau, *The Water Seekers* (New York, 1950) follow the Colorado River project from idea to reality. Lewis R. Freeman, *The Colorado River* (New York, 1923) is the saga of the undammed river. G. Bailey, *Water Resources of California* (Sacramento, 1927) and Ernest L. Bogart, *The Water Problem of Southern California* (Urbana, Illinois, 1934) survey needs and resources. In the guise of an uncolored report of impartial fact-finding, the Los Angeles Department of Water and Power in 1928 issued an effective argument, *Data on Available Water Supply and Future Requirements of Los Angeles and the Metropolitan Area.* Reuel Olson, *The Colorado River Compact* (Los Angeles, 1926) follows the early proposals and negotiations. F. E. Weymouth, *Summary of Metropolitan Aqueduct Situation* (Los Angeles, 1931) is a report by the engineer principally responsible for the creation of the Metropolitan Water District. Ralph B. Simmons, *Boulder Dam and the Great Southwest* (Los Angeles, 1936) presents good photographs but an unduly effusive text; Abe Burrows' *Boulder Dam* is a proper antidote. On the growth of the principal privately owned utility company see Charles Coleman, *Pacific Gas and Electric of California* (New York, 1952).

C. C. Julian and Aimee Semple McPherson are viewed as sociological phenomena in McWilliams, *Southern California Country.* Nancy Barr Mavity, *Sister Aimee* (New York, 1931) does justice to the most widely heralded southern Californian of the twenties. On the political front, a key issue is discussed in Thomas S. Barclay, "Reapportionment in California," *PHR,* V (1936), 93–129. See also Winston W. Crouch and Dean E. McHenry, *California Government, Politics and Administration* (revised edition, Berkeley, 1949).

32. Depression

Dixon Wecter, *The Age of the Great Depression* (New York, 1948) portrays the nationwide impact of hard times after 1929. There is no comparable study for California, though Paul N. Woolf, *Economic Trends in California, 1929–1934* (Sacramento, 1935); Leigh Athearn, *A Study of . . . the California State Relief Administration from 1935–*

1939 (Los Angeles, 1939); and California State Chamber of Commerce, *Economic Survey of California and Its Counties, 1942* (San Francisco, 1943) inform on certain aspects.

The labor problems of this decade are discussed in Camp, *San Francisco, Port of Gold* and McWilliams, *California, The Great Exception.* On the San Francisco general strike, see Paul Eliel, *The Waterfront and General Strikes, San Francisco, 1934* (San Francisco, 1934) and Mike Quin, *The Big Strike* (Olema, Calif., 1949). On the plight of the migratory farm workers, Carey McWilliams, *Factories in the Field* (Boston, 1939) is supplemented by Carleton Beals, *American Earth, The Biography of a Nation* (Philadephia, 1939) and by several of John Steinbeck's novels, particularly *In Dubious Battle* (New York, 1936) and *The Grapes of Wrath* (New York, 1939). For a contemporary evaluation, see John W. Caughey, "Current Discussion of California's Migrant Labor Problem," *PHR,* VIII (1939), 347–354. For a much broader view, see Clarke A. Chambers, *California Farm Organizations . . . , 1929–1941* (Berkeley, 1952).

Technocracy, Utopia, and the other cults and isms are admirably handled in McWilliams, *Southern California Country* and Cleland, *California in Our Time.* On Epic, the documentation begins with Upton Sinclair, *I, Governor of California* (Los Angeles, 1933) and *I, Candidate for Governor, and How I Got Licked* (New York, 1934). The papers and periodicals of the day gave much attention. Important, too, is the Sinclair Democrat organ, the *Epic News,* files of which suddenly became a rarity. There are good appraisals of Epic and of the Townsend movement in the McWilliams and Cleland volumes cited above and in Oliver Carlson, *A Mirror for Californians* (Indianapolis, 1941). John Phillips, *Inside California* (Los Angeles, 1939) berates the Olson administration. A less partisan appraisal is in a forthcoming study by Robert Burke.

On actual construction in the Boulder Canyon project, see Ray L. Wilbur and Elwood Mead, *Construction of Hoover Dam* (Washington, 1935); George A. Pettitt, *So Boulder Dam Was Built* (Berkeley, 1935); and Metropolitan Water District bulletins, such as *The Colorado Aqueduct* (Los Angeles, 1939) and *The Great Aqueduct* (Los Angeles, 1941). An early analysis of the Central Valley project is Peveril Meigs, 3rd, "Water Planning in the Great Central Valley, California," *Geographical Review,* XXIX (1939), 252–273. Robert De Roos, *The Thirsty Land, The Story of the Central Valley Project* (Stanford, 1948) is a popular, somewhat partisan analysis; Walter E. Packard, *The Economic Implications of the Central Valley Project* (Los Angeles, 1942) is more technical. On various phases and implications of the project, there are studies such as Marion Clawson, *Acreage Limitation in the Central Valley* (Berkeley, 1944), *The Effect of the Central Valley Project on the Agricultural and Industrial Economy and on the Social Character of California* (Berkeley, 1945), and *History of Legislation and Policy Formation of the Central Valley Project* (Berkeley, 1946).

33. Things Cultural

Rediscovery of the environment is represented in guidebooks such as those by Aubrey Drury and the Federal Writers' Project, in the publications of the automobile clubs, in photographic albums such as Edward Weston, *California and the West* (New York, 1940), and Ansel Adams, *The Sierra Nevada* (Berkeley, 1938) and *My Camera in Yosemite Valley* (Boston, 1949), and in a new round of nature writing in the series devoted respectively to regions, rivers, mountains, and lakes. Edwin Corle, *Desert Country* (New York, 1941); Carey McWilliams, *Southern California Country* (New York, 1946); Anne B. Fisher, *The Salinas, Upside-down River* (New York, 1945); Roderick Peattie, *The Pacific Coast Ranges* (New York, 1946) and *The Sierra Nevada* (New York, 1947); and George and Bliss Hinkle, *Sierra-Nevada Lakes* (Indianapolis, 1949) are examples.

The literature on the national parks and monuments is extensive. François E. Matthes, *Geologic History of the Yosemite Valley* (Washington, 1930), *The Incomparable Valley, A Geologic Interpretation of the Yosemite* (Berkeley, 1950), and *Sequoia National Park, A Geological Album* (Berkeley, 1950) carry the horizon back to the ultimate beginnings. Carl P. Russell, *One Hundred Years in Yosemite* (Stanford, 1931; and Berkeley, 1947) recites the human history. Books such as Federal Writers' Project, *Death Valley, A Guide* (Boston, 1939); Katherine Ames Taylor, *Yosemite Trails and Tales* (Stanford, 1948); and John R. White and Samuel J. Pusateri, *Sequoia and Kings Canyon National Parks* (Stanford, 1949) are designed for current visitors.

Harry T. Moore, *The Novels of John Steinbeck* (Chicago, 1939) and Lawrence C. Powell, *An Introduction to Robinson Jeffers* (Dijon, France, 1932; revised and enlarged, Pasadena, 1940) are preliminary appraisals of the foremost novelist and poet of this period. The better wisdom is to turn to the actual creative writings as they exist in the whole or as sampled in George Sterling, ed., *Continent's End, An Anthology of Contemporary California Poets* (San Francisco, 1925); Joseph Henry Jackson, ed., *Continent's End, A Collection of California Writing* (New York, 1944); and Jackson, ed., *The Western Gate, A San Francisco Reader* (New York, 1952).

The astronomy story is detailed in G. Edward Pendray, *Men, Mirrors, and Stars* (New York, 1935) and David O. Woodbury, *The Glass Giant of Palomar* (Indianapolis, 1946). It, and the other phases of scientific advancement, are noted in McWilliams, *California, The Great Exception*. On the directions in historical scholarship, there are data and suggestions in *New Spain and the Anglo-American West* (2 v., Los Angeles, 1932) and *Greater America: Essays in Honor of Herbert Eugene Bolton* (Berkeley, 1945). See also George P. Hammond, "In Memoriam: Herbert Eugene Bolton," *The Americas*, IX (1953), 391–398, and John W. Caughey, "Herbert Eugene Bolton," *PHR*, XXII (1953), 109–112.

34. Wartime Growth

McWilliams, *California, The Great Exception,* though broader in scope, is the closest approach to a survey of California during the war years. The reports of the Bureau of the Census and of various state agencies provide a wealth of statistics, which the period's newspapers and magazines help to round out to a meaningful description. Particularly useful is the California State Chamber of Commerce, "Economic Survey of California and Its Counties," *California Blue Book, 1946* (Sacramento, 1946), 409–772. Davis McEntire, *The Population of California* (San Francisco, 1946) and Marion Clawson, "What It Means To Be a Californian," CHSQ, XXIV (1945), 139–161, deal with characteristics as well as numbers.

On the relocation of the Japanese, there is a fair amount of material. Morton Grodzins, *Americans Betrayed* (Chicago, 1949) is a scientific analysis of the motivation. Western Defense Command and Fourth Army, *Japanese Evacuation from the West Coast, 1942* (Washington, 1943) is General De Witt's official apologia. Carey McWilliams, *Prejudice: Japanese-Americans, Symbols of Racial Intolerance* (Boston, 1944) and Bradford Smith, *Americans from Japan* (Philadelphia, 1948) are sharply critical. Miné Okubo, *Citizen 13660* (New York, 1946) is a restrained account by one of the evacuees. The formal report of the administrators is War Relocation Authority, *A Story of Human Conservation* (Washington, 1946). The sociological consequences are meticulously reported in Dorothy S. Thomas and Richard S. Nishomoto, *The Spoilage* (Berkeley, 1946); Leonard Bloom and Ruth Riemer, *Removal and Return, The Socio-economic Effects of the War on Japanese Americans* (Berkeley, 1949); and Dorothy S. Thomas, *The Salvage* (Berkeley, 1952).

35. Peace and Its Problems

For the postwar years, the statistical data of the reports of the Bureau of the Census and of the various state agencies, and the day-to-day chronicle in the newspapers are supplemented by two periodicals, *Fortnight,* launched in 1946, and *Frontier,* begun in 1949. McWilliams, *California, The Great Exception* has continuing usefulness. H. R. Philbrick, *Legislative Investigative Report* (Sacramento, 1939) gives background data on lobbying. David Farrelly and Ivan Hinderacker, *The Politics of California* (New York, 1951), and Winston W. Crouch, Dean E. McHenry, John C. Bollens, and Stanley Scott, *State and Local Government in California* (Berkeley, 1952) make constant reference to recent political history. Local manifestations of the drive for conformity are dealt with in Edward L. Barrett, Jr., *The Tenney Committee* (Ithaca, New York, 1951), George R. Stewart, *The Year of the Oath* (New York, 1950), John W. Caughey, "A University in Jeopardy," *Harper's Magazine,* November, 1950, pp. 68–75, and David

Hulburd, *This Happened in Pasadena* (New York, 1951). One aspect of the centennial celebration is covered in Glenn S. Dumke, "Books of the California Centennial," *PHR*, XXI (1952), 145–158.

ADDITIONAL REFERENCES

Charles A. Barker, *Henry George* (New York, 1955).

John E. Baur, *The California Health-Seekers* (San Marino, 1959).

Edwin R. Bingham, *Charles F. Lummis, Editor of the Southwest* (San Marino, 1955).

William Bronson, *The Earth Shook, the Sky Burned* [the San Francisco Earthquake and Fire] (Garden City, 1959).

A. Russell Buchanan, *David S. Terry of California, Dueling Judge* (San Marino, 1956).

Robert E. Burke, *Olson's New Deal for California* (Berkeley, 1953).

Robert S. Fletcher, *Eureka: From Cleveland by Ship to California, 1849–1850* (Durham, N. C., 1959).

Maynard J. Geiger, ed. and tr., *Palou's Life of Fray Junípero Serra* (Washington, 1955).

Harold Gilliam, *San Francisco Bay* (Garden City, 1957).

Emmett A. Greenwalt, *Point Loma Community in California* (Berkeley, 1955).

Robert V. Hine, *California's Utopian Colonies* (San Marino, 1953).

John H. Kemble, *San Francisco Bay: A Pictorial Maritime History* (Cambridge, Md., 1957).

Theodora Kroeber, *The Inland Whale* [Indian stories] (Bloomington, Ind., 1959).

Howard Lamar, ed., *The Cruise of the Portsmouth, 1845–1847,* by Joseph T. Downey (New Haven, 1958).

Dale L. Morgan, *Jedediah Smith and the Opening of the West* (Indianapolis, 1953).

_____, ed., *The Overland Diary of James A. Pritchard* (Denver, 1959).

Ruth Waldo Newhall, *The Newhall Ranch* (San Marino, 1958).

John E. Pomfret, ed., *California Gold Rush Voyages* (San Marino, 1954).

Charles Preuss, *Exploring with Frémont* (Norman, 1958).

Fred B. Rogers, *Filings from an Old Saw* [Joseph T. Downey] (San Francisco, 1956).

_____, *Montgomery and the Portsmouth* (San Francisco, 1958).

_____, *A Navy Surgeon in California, 1846–1847* [Marius Duvall] (San Francisco, 1957).

A. R. Rojas, *Lore of the California Vaquero* (Fresno, 1958).

Andrew F. Rolle, *An American in California: The Biography of William Heath Davis* (San Marino, 1956).

Tracy I. Storer and Lloyd P. Tevis, Jr., *California Grizzly* (Berkeley, 1955).

Hyman G. Weintraub, *Andrew Furuseth, Emancipator of the Seaman* (Berkeley, 1959).

Thurman Wilkins, *Clarence King* (New York, 1958).

INDEX